TRAVEL

WHERE TO GO WHEN

TRAVEL
WHERE TO GO WHEN

CRAIG DOYLE

CONSULTANT EDITOR

LONDON, NEW YORK, MELBOURNE,
MUNICH AND DELHI

MANAGING EDITORS Vivien Antwi
& Christine Stroyan
SENIOR EDITOR Hugh Thompson
PROJECT EDITOR Ellie Smith
EDITOR Emma Gibbs

DESIGN MANAGERS Mabel Chan & Sunita Gahir
ART EDITOR Shahid Mahmood
DESIGNERS Marisa Renzullo
& Paul Jackson
DTP DESIGNERS Natasha Lu & Jenn Hadley

PICTURE RESEARCHER Sarah Smithies
CARTOGRAPHERS Casper Morris
Dominic Beddow from Draughtsman Ltd
& Ed Merritt from Merrit Cartographic
PRODUCTION CONTROLLER Shane Higgins

PUBLISHER Douglas Amrine

Reproduced by Media Development Printing
Printed and bound in Singapore by Star Standard

First Published in Great Britain in 2007
by Dorling Kindersley Limited
80 Strand, London WC2R 0RL
Reprinted with revisions 2009

This edition published 2009 for Index Books Ltd

Copyright © 2007, 2009 Dorling Kindersley Limited,
London

Foreword copyright © Craig Doyle 2009

www.traveldk.com

Every effort has been made to ensure that this book is as up-to-date as
possible at the time of going to press. Some details, however, such as
telephone numbers, opening hours, prices, and travel information are liable
to change. The publishers cannot accept responsibility for any consequences
arising from the use of this book, nor for any material on third-party websites,
and cannot guarantee that any website address in this book will be a suitable
source of travel information. We value the views and suggestions of our
readers very highly. Please write to: Publisher, DK Travel Guides,
Dorling Kindersley, 80 Strand, London, WC2R 0RL, Great Britain.

COVER IMAGE: Camel train walking through the Yamuna River,
behind the Taj Mahal, Agra, India
TITLE PAGE IMAGE: Woman in carnival costume, Mexico
HALF TITLE IMAGE: Beach on the Canary Islands
FOREWORD IMAGE: Montreal at night

CONTENTS

FOREWORD

Being involved in this fabulous book has given me a chance to reflect on the hundreds of trips I made as a presenter for the BBC Holiday programme and relive some of the great times with my suitcase. I'd also like to confess to a couple of minor crimes against friends, family and people I have met along the way; every time I said travel reporting was just like any other job, with long hours and irritations that made it very hard work, I was lying. I did it to stop the outbursts from friends about how lucky I was to have the best job in the world! Truthfully, it was usually a joy and rarely a chore. Secondly, when asked about my favourite destination, I also lied. It's an impossible question to answer. Moods change, places change, needs change, and with them the places you aspire to visit change. One true favourite? Forget about it. The world has too much diversity and beauty to pick just one.

Faced with so much choice, how do you decide where to go on holiday? I am regularly asked by friends and family to choose holidays for them; I always refuse. The research that goes into the decision, the discussions, the rows, the excitement and anticipation, and even the sulking when you don't get your own way are all part of the

process. Real travel does require a little bit of work, if you are to get the most out of those precious weeks away, but it is well worth it. I find the thought of exploring a new city, mountain range or jungle makes me tingle before I even leave the house. What will I discover, taste or meet this time? Of course the planning stage can be confusing and stressful, so this book is designed to give you a guiding hand and get you tingling too. There's no easy answer to where *you* should go, but this book will certainly help.

Unlike most travel books which are designed to act as a map and directory, the purpose of this one is to inspire. Torn between an exotic journey and a ski trip? This book opens up the wonders of Rajasthan in November and Whistler's glistening slopes in March. Everybody's heard of Sydney's New Year celebrations and New York's great museums but what about where to get the best views of the fireworks and the best way to see what the Big Apple has to offer? And what can you do in the lesser-known parts of the world? Just flick though and let your imagination run wild, from insider tips on cruising around the Galápagos Islands to a romantic stay in the tropical Perhentian Islands. This is not a hotel guide, it's an experience guide. So free your mind, clear your diary and get ready to travel, even if it's only from your armchair!

CRAIG DOYLE

JANUARY

Where to Go: January

January opens with a bang for much of the world and the excitement of New Year helps soften the fact that much of the northern hemisphere is shrouded in cold, damp cloud. New Year's resolutions to keep fit can be kick-started with calorie-busting ski trips to Europe or North America; while southern Europe's temperate climate is also ideal for tennis or a few gentle rounds of golf. The natural world is also sensitive to the seasons, whether cold – as in the forests of Poland – or warm, as in the waters around Indonesia. Don't overlook fiery Viking celebrations in Shetland or the more child-friendly fireworks as China celebrates New Year at the end of the month. Below you'll find all the destinations in this chapter as well as some extra suggestions to provide inspiration.

FESTIVALS AND CULTURE

LALIBELA Colourful religious procession

UNFORGETTABLE JOURNEYS

PATAGONIA Dramatic icy scenery in the Beagle Channel

NATURAL WONDERS

COSTA RICA Poison-dart tree frog

LALIBELA
ETHIOPIA, AFRICA

Amazing churches hewn directly into solid rock

See the wonders of the man-made castles of Gondar, the natural beauty of the Simien Mts, and the spiritual faith that built the rock-cut churches.
See pp14–15

SHETLAND ISLES
SCOTLAND, EUROPE

Up Helly Aa is a fiery and spectacular extravaganza

Midwinter at Lerwick sees torch-lit processions and a Viking ship being burned in this lively festival in the usually peaceful Scottish isles.
www.shetlandtourism.com

PATAGONIAN CRUISE
ARGENTINA, SOUTH AMERICA

Take a voyage of discovery at the "end of the world"

Follow legendary seafarers through the Magellan Strait and Beagle Channel to see whales, elephant seals, icebergs and mighty glaciers.
See pp28–9

SIWA OASIS
EGYPT, AFRICA

Camels, dates and mirages on a tour of the western oases

Take a historical journey through the heart of the north African desert, amid sand dunes and plateaus, home to Bedouin tribes.
www.touregypt.net

"Scarlet macaws screech overhead; howler monkeys play in the forest canopy; crocodiles thrash around in the mud."

COSTA RICA
CENTRAL AMERICA

An exquisite pocket of natural beauty and coastal rainforest

Manuel Antonio National Park combines palm-fringed beaches with mangrove swamps and a forest ecosystem full of wildlife.
See pp30–31

BANGKOK
THAILAND, ASIA

Frenetic and busy city dotted with beautiful temples

Marvel at the huge golden buddhas, bustling colourful floating market and the splendid Grand Palace – Wat Phra Keow.
See pp22–3

"Once the visitor can look beyond the obvious distractions, Bangkok has an astonishing beauty and grace."

THE GHAN RAILWAY
AUSTRALIA, AUSTRALASIA

From the top of the country to the bottom by rail

Crossing a continent as large as Australia is not to be taken lightly. The Ghan is the ultimate railway journey from Darwin to Adelaide.
www.railaustralia.com.au

BUNAKEN MARINE PK
INDONESIA, ASIA

Unspoilt reefs iridescent with vivid corals and gleaming fish

With excellent visibility and great variety in fish and corals – soft and hard, this underwater park is one of the best for seeing marine life.
www.sulawesi-info.com

MONTE CARLO
MONACO, EUROPE

See the famous car rally or try your luck at the casino

Elegant riviera destination with a year-round mild climate. If you're not a petrolhead, enjoy the opera, ballet, or simply go for the roulette.
www.monte-carlo.mc

AVIEMORE
SCOTLAND, EUROPE

Not quite the Iditarod, but it's the place to dogsled in the UK

The UK dog-sled rally lasts a week and you can intersperse the dog fun with some wild trekking or highland dancing for Burns' Night.
www.visitaviemore.com

GAMBIA RIVER
GAMBIA, AFRICA

Be at one with nature in a tranquil riverside eco-lodge

Witness real Gambian culture first-hand while staying in a stilt lodge surrounded by animal-rich river and swamp environments.
www.responsibletravel.com

ROMINCKA FOREST
POLAND, EUROPE

A medieval forest where bison, wolves, and wild boar abound

Visit these ancient forests, little-touched by man, and one of the last bastions for the large and magnificent mammals in Europe.
www.naturetrek.co.uk

ST PETERSBURG
RUSSIAN FEDERATION, EUROPE

Imperial city of the Tsars, filled with great art and architecture

St Petersburg, set on a network of pretty canals, is one of the world's most cultured cities, and home to the peerless Hermitage Museum.
See pp20–21

DAKAR RALLY
SENEGAL, AFRICA

One of the legendary journeys from Europe to West Africa

You may not want to compete in the race itself, but you can catch some of the excitement in Dakar – and enjoy golden sandy beaches.
www.dakar.com

TROMSØ
NORWAY, EUROPE

Probably the best place to see the Northern Lights

It will be cold, snowy and beautiful by day and night. This month also sees international film and music festivals come to town.
www.destinasjontromso.no

Previous page: Ornate interior of Saint Isaac's Cathedral in St Petersburg

Weather Watch

❶ While much of the USA shivers in the grip of winter, the Caribbean is warm and sunny. Jamaica is cooled a little by air from over the sea and US mainland, and it is also the driest time of year.

❷ Costa Rica's dry season is Dec–Apr, and this is the best time to visit. It's windy on the central plateau but much hotter at lower altitudes.

❸ Scandinavia usually has deep snow at this time of year – the severe climate is similar to Alaska's. St Petersburg is pretty in the snow but also very cold.

❹ Tanzania's position close to the Equator means that the temperature doesn't vary much seasonally. On the high mountain plateau it won't get too hot and it should be dry – but it can snow at any time.

❺ Hong Kong has a wet tropical climate, but January is the driest and coolest time of year. The average daytime temperature is comfortable and there shouldn't be any rain to spoil the fireworks.

❻ The interior of Australia can be very hot and dry. If the winds blow out from the interior then the coast can suffer from very high temperatures too.

LUXURY AND ROMANCE

JUKKASJÄRVI Fire blazing in the icy fireplace of the Icehotel's lobby

ACTIVE ADVENTURES

KILIMANJARO Masai crossing the plains in front of Kilimanjaro

FAMILY GETAWAYS

HONG KONG Child enjoying the New Year decorations

MERIDA
VENEZUELA, SOUTH AMERICA

This wonderful city is flanked by two vast mountain ranges

Stay in romantic posadas outside the city, explore the Sierra Nevada by day and relax in a luxurious spa before dinner.
www.steppestravel.co.uk

JUKKASJÄRVI
SWEDEN, EUROPE

Enjoy a magical stay in a hotel built almost entirely of ice

Snuggle up together to view the spectacular Northern Lights from your bed, while spending the days exploring a winter wonderland.
See pp18–19

JAMAICA
CARIBBEAN

Savour the heady rum aromas and the hot rhythm of reggae

But there's more than just parties – try snorkelling, or hiking in the Blue Mountains before soaking up the sun on a fabulous beach.
See pp24–5

MALDIVES
INDIAN OCEAN

Over a thousand sunny islands lapped by turquoise waters

Cruise the quiet atolls in a luxury sailboat, snorkel through crystal waters over sparkling coral reefs and wind down at a relaxing spa.
See pp16–17

CRANS MONTANA
SWITZERLAND, EUROPE

Float gracefully over a perfect Swiss pastoral scene

The swish Swiss resort is awash with colour for its annual balloon festival – a great sight whether you're in the basket or skiing on the slopes.
www.myswitzerland.com

"White-hot blazing beaches dissolving into bathtub-warm waters of greens and blues."

KILIMANJARO
TANZANIA, AFRICA

A majestic adventure that can be enjoyed at all ages

Watching the sunrise from the top of the iconic Mt Kilimanjaro is something to tell the grandchildren. Needs fitness, but no climbing skills.
See pp26–7

BANSKO
BULGARIA, EUROPE

Charming (and economical) skiing in a beautiful location

Relatively undeveloped, Bansko's quaint streets, wooden taverns and friendly people will delight all – and the skiing's pretty good too.
www.bulgariaski.com

JACKSON HOLE
USA, NORTH AMERICA

This is big thrill territory for skilful skiers

Top skiing opportunities with huge descents – and a small, friendly and uncrowded town inhabited by real cowboys.
See pp12–13

ALGARVE
PORTUGAL, EUROPE

Improve your tennis or golf swing (or both)

Sunny all the year round but cool enough for energetic sports, the Algarve is perfect for both tennis and golf with plenty of facilities.
www.algarve-information.com

CAIRO TO CAPE TOWN
AFRICA

Epic bike ride that will work off any Christmas excesses

You may not want to do all 12,000 km (7,500 miles) – it takes just over three months – so you can select one or more stages.
www.tourdafrique.com

"The wafting, smoky smell of incense accompanies the larger-than-life lions and dragons dancing playfully through the streets."

CENTER PARCS
ENGLAND, EUROPE

Hundreds of activities for children (and adults)

Under the all-weather dome your children can splash to their heart's content (and well-being) – and there is so much more to do.
www.centerparcs.co.uk

KIAWAH ISLAND
USA, NORTH AMERICA

A delightful island resort that is relatively quiet in winter

The water is too cold to swim but the open spaces of the beach provide plenty of activities for the kids and adults alike.
www.kiawahisland.org

HONG KONG
CHINA, ASIA

See Chinese New Year arrive with spectacular fireworks

Hong Kong is a fantastical mix of tradition and modernity – visit incense-wreathed temples and cloud-bursting skyscrapers.
See pp32–3

MIAMI
USA, NORTH AMERICA

There's a lot going on in this funky, vibrant city

There's the beach, great shopping, Seaquarium, Art Deco architecture, and trips to the Everglades and Kennedy Space Center.
www.miamigov.com

GRAN CANARIA
SPAIN, EUROPE

Year-round mild weather and plenty of facilities for families

Swimming, surfing, cycling and just exploring the island should provide enough activity to keep everyone busy and happy.
www.grancanaria.com

GETTING THERE
The town of Jackson in northwest Wyoming is well-served by airlines, with connecting flights from Chicago, Dallas, Salt Lake City and Denver, among others. The airport is 10 minutes from the town centre.

GETTING AROUND
There are regular shuttle buses between the town and ski resort.

WEATHER
January temperatures rarely climb above 0°C. The weather can be capricious – blue skies or monumental snowfall.

ACCOMMODATION
Alpine House Inn is a B&B owned by two former Olympians; doubles from £60; www.alpinehouse.com

Teton Village Resort has self-catering apartments; one-bedroom apartments from £85; www.teton-village.com

Four Seasons, luxury hotel at the Jackson Hole resort with ski in/ski out access; from £180; www.fourseasons.com

EATING OUT
Whatever your taste and budget, you'll find it here, from traditional barbecue to sushi and, of course, thick slabs of beef. A local favourite is Bubba's BBQ, from around £8.

PRICE FOR TWO
£200 per day including accommodation, food, ski passes, trips, transportation and admissions.

FURTHER INFORMATION
www.jacksonhole.com

Fur-Trapping Country
Jackson Hole got its name from the fur trappers who used to enter the valley by descending from the steep-sloped mountains that surround it, thus giving the impression that they were entering a hole. One of these mountains is the iconic Grand Teton, a craggy slab that dominates the town and its surroundings. The "Jackson" comes from one of the beaver trappers, David Edward Jackson, who used to hunt for the valuable skins here in the early 19th century – he was also one of the pioneers of the Oregon Trail.

Above (left to right): Skiing at the Teton Village Resort in Jackson Hole; cowboy skier; Teton National Park
Main: Snowboarder soars over the wide open pistes of Jackson Hole

DEEP-POWDER SNOWFIELDS

AMONG SKIERS, JACKSON HOLE IS LEGENDARY for its steep and challenging terrain, including Corbett's Couloir, a narrow plunge only for the foolhardy or Olympic contender. For the rest of us mere mortals, there are groomed pistes – called "trails" in the USA – for effortless cruising, and deep-powder snowfields that leave skiers and snowboarders desperate to get back to them. Situated in the heart of the dramatic Tetons, Jackson Hole Mountain Resort is made up of two distinct mountains – Rendezvous and Apres Vous – which offer snow-seekers plentiful and varied opportunities.

Because of its relative isolation in the northwestern corner of Wyoming, the slopes here are rarely crowded, allowing skiers and boarders to feel as though they alone own the mountains. One of the most ethereal moments occurs during a temperature inversion, when the valley is shrouded in fog but skiers above bask in blue skies, and the sensation is of skiing off the mountain into the clouds. Away from the resort, the town of Jackson is still very much a place of cowboys, who work on the surrounding cattle ranches. Country music rings out from "honky tonk" bars, wooden pavements clunk under the footfalls of cowboy boots, and the tradition of Western friendliness lives on – passers-by tip their cowboy hats and greet you with a "howdy".

Beyond the groomed snowfields, residents and visitors alike continue to be enchanted by Yellowstone National Park, which lies on the town's doorstep. With its amazing concentration of geological and biological riches – 200 active geysers, at least 100 known waterfalls, 1,050 species of plants, and endangered species such as the grey wolf, grizzly bear, bald eagle and lynx – it is no surprise that the park is crowded with visitors in warm-weather months. But it is in winter, when Yellowstone is a serene landscape of white, dotted by animals grazing in spots where geysers have melted the snow, that visitors are offered a memorable glimpse of a once wild land.

…the valley is shrouded in fog but skiers above bask in blue skies, and the sensation is of skiing off the mountain into the clouds…

Inset: Cable car to the summit of Rendezvous Mountain
Below (left and right): Antler Arch in the town square; the Playhouse, Jackson

SKIER'S DIARY

January is a great time to visit Jackson Hole – both for the snow and for its scenic beauty. The weather is generally clear and sunny, but there can be periods of very heavy snowfall – average snowfall each year is around 1,166 cm (459 inches). The slopes here are ideal for all levels of skier and snowboarder.

A Week on the Slopes

Head to the slopes as soon as possible to make the most of the powder – advanced skiers and snowboarders will enjoy the exciting, steep terrain of Rendezvous Mountain and for beginners there are gentle slopes at the base of Apres Vous Mountain. In the evenings, learn to two-step at the Million Dollar Cowboy Bar or catch a show at the Playhouse.

JAN

DAYS 1–2

To get a glimpse of the area's wildlife visit Yellowstone National Park, where you will pass herds of buffalo and trumpeter swans. If you're lucky, you'll even see wolves. Watch the regular eruption of Old Faithful Geyser, which spouts steamy water some 30 m (100 ft) into the air several times an hour. Take a tour, drive the northern part of the park, or even cross-country ski your way around. Alternatively, take a dogsled tour through serene valley trails dotted with towering pines.

DAY 3

Continue skiing and/or boarding on the many pistes or take a guided heli-ski trip. For a little culture, visit the National Museum of Wildlife Art for stunning paintings, sculptures and photographs. A horse-drawn sleigh ride is a great way to see the National Elk Refuge, the winter home of 8,000 of these stately creatures, who disappear back into the mountains when the snow melts.

DAYS 4–5

For a change of scenery, head to the other side of the Teton Pass for a day at Grand Targhee. If you are a better-than-average skier or boarder, take advantage of snowcat skiing or boarding on untracked powder which is not accessible by chairlift or hiking. Strap on a pair of snowshoes and take a walk in Grand Teton National Park, guided by a trained naturalist.

DAYS 6–7

Dos and Don'ts

✓ Join the locals on Sunday evenings at The Stagecoach, a diner that turns into a "honky tonk" one night a week.

✗ Don't pack formal clothes, since this is a casual place more orientated to sports and leisure.

✓ Look at the arches anchoring each of the four corners of the town square, formed by thousands of intertwined elk antlers, all shed by the protected herd living just outside town.

✓ Shop for Native American jewellery, crafted by local tribal members using turquoise- and lapis-coloured oyster shells.

FEB
MAR
APR
MAY
JUN
JUL
AUG
SEP
OCT
NOV
DEC

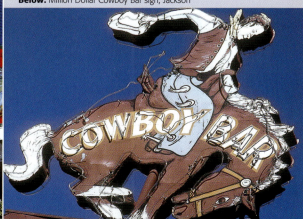

Below: Million Dollar Cowboy Bar sign, Jackson

GETTING THERE
Lalibela lies in northern Ethiopia, in East Africa. International flights arrive into Addis Ababa, 640 km (400 miles) away, from where you can catch a domestic flight on to Lalibela.

GETTING AROUND
Internal flights are cheap, around £60 per flight. Car hire is expensive; expect to pay from around £25/50 per day for a car/4WD with a driver.

WEATHER
Addis Ababa has an average temperature of 24°C but Lalibela's altitude keeps the heat down at around 16°C. Night temperatures drop to just above freezing.

ACCOMMODATION
Ghion Hotel Group have a number of hotels on the Historic Route, including Hotel Roha in Lalibela, Tana Hotel in Bahir Dar, Goha Hotel in Gonder, and the National in Addis Ababa; doubles from £25; www.ghionhotel.com.et

In Addis Ababa, the Hilton has a central location and good facilities; doubles from £70; www.hilton.com

EATING OUT
Try *doro wat*, a spicy chicken stew served on top of *injera* – a large, grey, pancake. Ethiopian cuisine is delicious and very cheap, but it can take a little getting used to.

PRICE FOR TWO
£100–120 per day including accommodation, food, local flights and car hire.

FURTHER INFORMATION
www.tourismethiopia.org

Who Built the Churches?
According to some scholars, a workforce of 40,000 would have been required to build the churches, althought the locals claim celestial assistance. Apparently toiling all the hours of daylight, the earthly labourers were replaced by heavenly ones who toiled at night. In this way, the churches were built at a miraculous speed. But foreign intervention, whether celestial or mortal, can almost certainly be ruled out – Lalibela represents the pinnacle of an ancient Ethiopian building tradition.

Main: Christian Ethiopians in a procession during *Leddet* (Christmas) in Lalibela

AFRICAN PILGRIMAGE

DUBBED "AFRICA'S PETRA", Lalibela ranks among the greatest religio-historical sites on the African continent – perhaps even in the Christian world. Though travellers have for centuries returned with tales of the fabulous and enigmatic rock-hewn churches, the site still remains little known and little developed.

Lying high in the wild and rugged Lasta Mountains, Lalibela remains a very isolated place. Today, the journey overland is still quite a long and arduous one – the sense of arrival at the little town is palpable, rather like that felt at the end of a great pilgrimage. In fact, Lalibela *is* a centre of pilgrimage.

The churches sit in carved recesses in the rock, their roofs at ground level, making this a most unusual and remarkable holy site. The 11 medieval churches give the impression of a place that has not changed for centuries – robed priests still float among the dimly-lit passageways and tunnels, and from hidden crypts and grottoes you can

Top: A religious procession in Lalibela

Above: Interior of Beta Ghiorghis church in Lalibela

Below: Dramatic Blue Nile Falls, the second largest waterfall in Africa

Bottom: A child in a papyrus canoe paddles past pelicans on Lake Tana

FESTIVAL DIARY

Ethiopian Christmas, *Leddet*, takes place from 6 to 7 January each year and is a particularly good time to visit Lalibela. *Timkat* (Epiphany) on 19 January is another colourful occasion. Three days suffice to see the churches in Lalibela – many travellers visit as part of the "Historic Route" of northern Ethiopia.

Two Weeks on the Historic Route

JAN

From Addis Ababa, fly straight on to Lalibela, set high among the Lasta Mountains. Watch the amazing procession between the rock-hewn churches to celebrate Christmas.

4th – 7th

Spend some days exploring outside the town, where churches are hidden like jewels among the stark Ethiopian landscape.

Return to Addis Ababa and tour the amazing *Merkato*, one of the largest outdoor markets in Africa, where you can buy anything from precious metals to camels.

8th – 10th

Visit the town's museums – the National Museum is particularly important as it has the fossils of what is thought to be our earliest human ancestor. Head for a *tej beat* – a kind of Ethiopian pub – or take in a show of traditional Ethiopian dancing over a meal of local dishes.

Make a boat trip to the isolated island monasteries of Lake Tana at Bahir Dar and visit the spectacular Blue Nile Falls.

11th – 13th

Fly to Gondar, known as Ethiopia's Camelot for its series of castles and former days of courtly conspiracy, pageantry and intrigue. Take a drive to the beautiful Simien Mountains, where you can walk, trek, picnic and nature watch.

14th – 15th

Continue by air to Aksum, the site of a powerful 3rd-century kingdom, and explore the remains of the princely tombs and palaces.

16th – 17th

Dos and Don'ts

✓ If you want to visit during a festival, be sure to make travel arrangements well in advance – at least several months.

✓ Taste the local tipple, *tej*, a potent honey wine once deemed fit for Ethiopian kings; Lalibela is famous for it.

✗ Don't wear shorts and t-shirts when visiting churches – long sleeves and trousers are more appropriate.

✓ Engage a qualified guide. You'll gain more from your visit and it will temper the touts.

FEB
MAR
APR
MAY
JUN
JUL
AUG
SEP
OCT
NOV
DEC

Below: Castles dot the Ethiopian landscape at Gondar

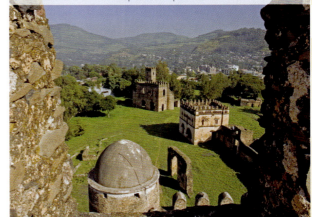

hear the sound of their chanting. In the deep, cool recesses of the interior of the rock, the smell of incense and beeswax candles – an exotic and alluring fragrance – still pervades, while hermits, silent in the study of the scriptures, occupy tiny, rudely hewn holes. From miles around comes a steady trickle of pilgrims praying for health, wealth and good fortune.

At festival time, the trickle turns almost torrential, with pilgrims travelling for days and even weeks to reach the little town. Processions, chanting, singing and dancing ring out from all corners and the town is coloured by the bright and beautiful textiles worn by the participants. To visitors, it feels as though they've travelled six or seven centuries back in time. And in a way they have. Biblical it seems and biblical it is; as the second country in the world to adopt Christianity (around AD 350), Ethiopia's connection with the religion is long and strong.

Not merely carved into the rock, but freed wholly from it, Lalibela's churches are undeniably awe-inspiring. Francisco Alvares, a Portuguese priest who visited in the 16th century, described them as "edifices, the likes of which – and so many – cannot be found anywhere else in the world".

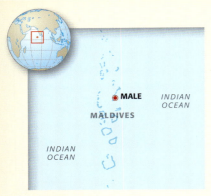

GARLAND OF GLISTENING GEMS

T HE ONLY WAY TO DESCRIBE THIS GROUP of lush and tropical remote islands, each one with its own coral reefs and shallow turquoise lagoons, floating in the idyllic Indian Ocean is to call it "heaven on earth". On land, there are masses of coconut palms and fruit trees and the white sand beaches that ring each island are scattered with beautiful shells of all shapes and description. Underwater, there are magical gardens, home to an astounding wealth of marine life.

It is warm and humid here with the cool sea breeze breaking the languorous monotony of the heat. From December to March, during the dry season, the gentle northeast monsoon hits these equatorial islands, but the skies stay blue and the water remains calm. It is a drier monsoon when compared to the southwest monsoon that arrives in April and stays till October.

GETTING THERE
The island nation lies 340 km (211 miles) southwest of India. The international airport is in Malé, the capital. Trivandrum in Kerala is a 40-minute flight away. There is a ferry service from the airport island just off Malé.

GETTING AROUND
Dhonis (wooden boats) are the most popular way of getting around. Malé and some larger islands offer taxis, but most islands are small enough to cover on foot.

WEATHER
January has warm days cooled by sea breezes and average high temperatures of 30°C.

ACCOMMODATION
The Nasandhura Palace Hotel in Malé is a good budget option; doubles from £115; www.nasandhurapalace.com

On the private island of Lankanfushi is the exclusive Soneva Gili Resort and Spa; doubles from £650; www.six-senses.com

A traditional *dhoni* at Dhoni Mighili, North Ari Atoll. Each *dhoni* goes with a beach house; doubles from £1,190; www.dhonimighili.com

EATING OUT
Maldivian food is spicy, but milder than that found in neighbouring countries. Seafood predominates; try local fare such as *garudhiya*, fish soup with lemon and onions.

PRICE FOR TWO
£340–360 per day including accommodation, food and a dive.

FURTHER INFORMATION
www.visitmaldives.com

Ancient Maldives

Lying at the crossroads of ancient sea routes, the Maldives assimilated various cultural and religious influences. Archeological remains indicate that there was a prolonged Buddhist period in the Maldives reaching its apex between the 9th and 12th centuries AD. With the spread of Islam to west Asia, the Arabs extended their maritime trade links to south Asia. This Arabian influence culminated in the ruling monarch converting to Islam in the 12th century. The small National Museum on Malé displays a range of Buddhist and Islamic artifacts.

Main: Dreamy hotel setting of thatched huts, palms and the open waters of the Indian Ocean

Left: Colourful grouper swims by a coral reef

Right (left to right): Snorkeller investigates the coral reef offshore; Dhigufinolhu atoll ringed by pristine white sandy beaches; pet cockatoo and macaw on Maga Island

Right panel (top to bottom): Sunset over the calm waters surrounding the islands; typical thatched resort cabins; bathroom of a Maldive resort hotel

However, in every season, the Maldives is paradise. Time spent relaxing here transports you far away from the mundane realities of urban living. Every activity is geared toward making you relax and unravelling the tension and stress of modern life. Your body clock gets back into step with the simple rhythms of nature governed by the rising and setting of the sun; only primitive needs – eating and sleeping – exist and are easily appeased. The body is toned by diving, surfing, swimming and sun bathing; the spirit is revived by watching the spectacular sunsets; and the mind is rested.

If some mental stimulation is required, you'll find the Maldives is also surprisingly rich in culture. Over the centuries, Arab and Chinese seafarers passed through these islands as did Vasco da Gama, the French brothers Parmentier, Ibn Batuta and other famous explorers. Islam arrived in the 12th century and the Maldives is still a predominantly Sunni Islamic state. But ruins tell of past Buddhist and Hindu influence as well as a matriarchal dynasty that may have ruled for 300 years.

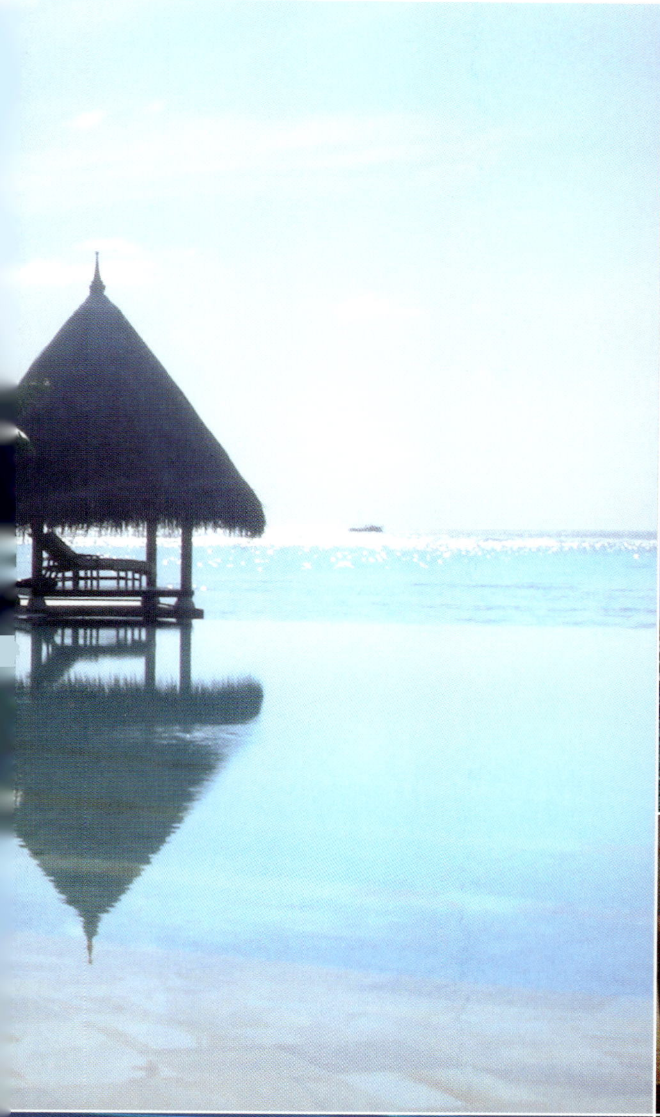

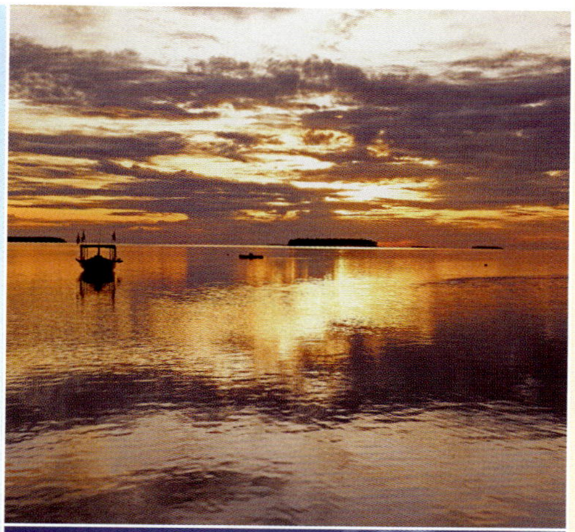

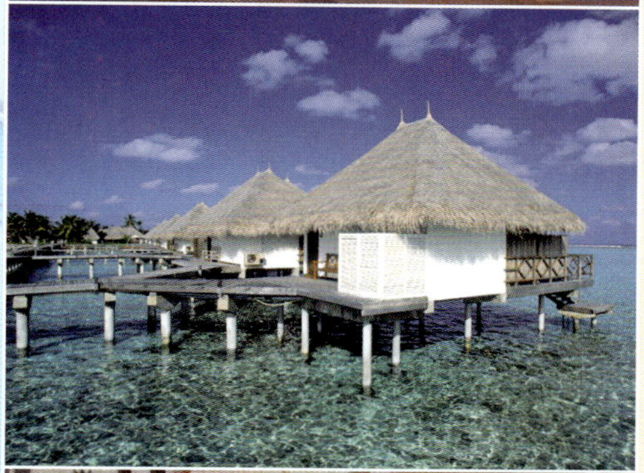

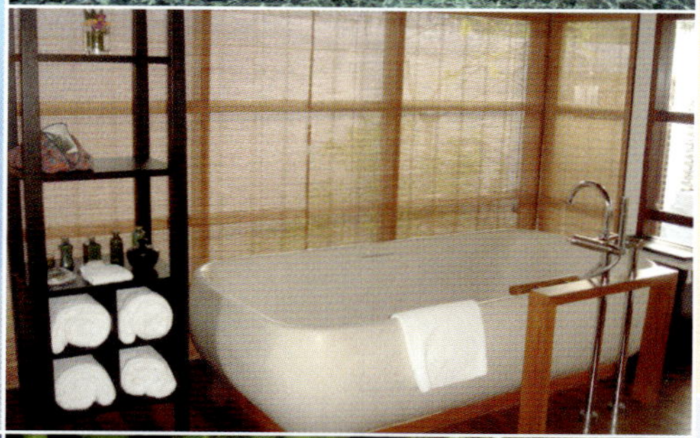

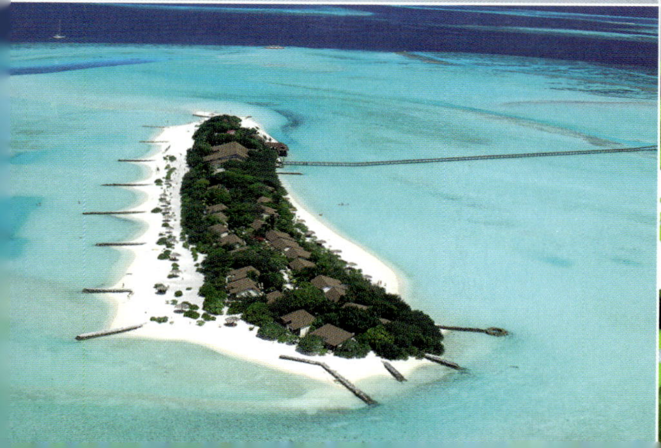

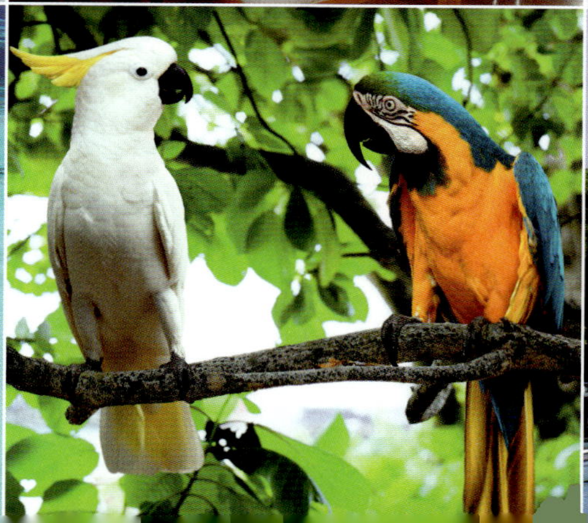

ATOLL DIARY

The Maldives is famed for its exquisitely clear waters, coral gardens, and tropical fish. Average underwater visibility is 30 m (98 ft), with water temperatures remaining quite warm through the year. All resorts in the Maldives have dive schools with instructors, and many resorts have access to excellent reefs.

Six Days Island Hopping

JAN

DAY 1 Fly into Malé International Airport, transfer to a *dhoni* or an air taxi, and head to your resort. After a lazy lunch under the palms, spend the rest of the afternoon relaxing on the beach or kayaking in the clear shallows.

DAY 2 Go island hopping. Stop off at uninhabited islands that are not only great for lounging, but are also perfect for diving (with a partner). The reefs and atolls are home to about 700 varieties of fish. Sharks, whales, and manta rays can be spotted in the open ocean.

DAY 3 Take an excursion to Malé and spend a leisurely day exploring the capital on foot. Visit the National Museum, housed in the former Presidential Palace, and the Grand Mosque, whose golden dome and slender minaret dominate the Malé cityscape. Walk along the seafront, which is busy with fishermen's boats, *dhonis*, and ferries. Head back to your resort to gear up for a night fishing excursion.

DAY 4 Dedicate the day to well-being. Head off to the resort spa to be pampered with a wide range of treatments then unwind as you watch the sun set.

DAY 5 Wake up early to experience the quiet beauty of the dawn on the beach then spend the morning snorkelling. Most resort islands have their own coral reefs just a few strokes away from the beach. Join an afternoon excursion to view the acrobatic spinner dolphins.

DAY 6 To properly explore the ocean, join an early morning diving trip – they'll know where to take you to see some truly amazing underwater fish and corals. Return to the resort before heading home.

Dos and Don'ts

- ✓ Negotiate with the owner of the *dhoni* or speedboat before hiring one. Repeated use of the same boat will get cheaper rates and better service.
- ✗ Don't walk on, or touch, the coral. Not only is this bad for the coral, but it could also be bad for you – coral is sharp and can also be poisonous.
- ✓ Pack lots of light cotton and linen clothes as the country is hot almost all year; nude bathing is strictly prohibited.

Below: Golden dome of the Grand Mosque in Malé

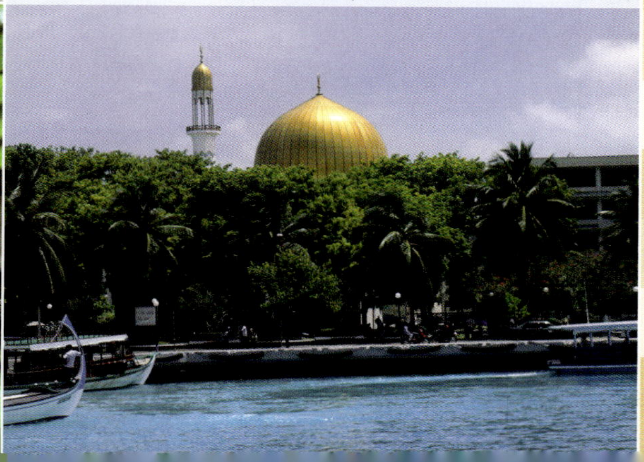

GETTING THERE
Jukkasjärvi is in northern Sweden, 200 km (125 miles) north of the Arctic Circle. The nearest airport is in Kiruna, 12 km (7½ miles) away, reached by a 90-minute flight from Stockholm.

GETTING AROUND
Local buses connect the Icehotel to Kiruna airport on weekdays. Transfers by taxi (£8) and dogsled (£95) can also be arranged.

WEATHER
The average temperature in January is -12°C and the ground is snow-covered.

ACCOMMODATION
Typically, one night is spent in an ice room and two in heated Nordic or Aurora chalets, or the resort's Kaamos Hotel; www.icehotel.com

Aurora chalets have large skylights for viewing the Northern Lights; doubles from £230.

In the ice rooms, guests sleep in sleeping bags, on top of an ice block that is covered by a thick mattress and reindeer skins; doubles from £250.

EATING OUT
Local specialities such as Arctic char, bleak roe, reindeer venison, ptarmigan, forest mushrooms and berries are all are served stylishly at the Icehotel (mains from £22) and buffet-style in the resort's Old Homestead Restaurant (mains from £13). Lapplandia, a nearby restaurant, serves award-winning cuisine (mains from £22).

PRICE FOR TWO
£320–500 per day including accommodation, food, excursions and local travel.

FURTHER INFORMATION
www.visitsweden.com

The Saami People

The brightly embroidered clothing of the Saami people lends a colourful accent to the white landscape of a Lapland winter. These nomadic people still follow their reindeer herds, living in *lavvu* (tents), which are made of wooden poles covered with hides. Inside, central fires create warmth, over which meals are cooked. Visitors to Jukkasjärvi can meet the Saami and learn about their lifestyle in a number of excursions, some include riding on a reindeer sled and feasting on traditional foods cooked over a *lavvu* fire.

Above (left to right): Huskies from a dogsled pack; gathered around the fire in a Saami hut; dogsledding as the sun goes down

NORTHERN EXPOSURE

Enter a frozen world, where the land lies under a blanket of white and your hotel is built of ice. Inside its crystal-clear walls – water from northern Sweden's river Torne has no air bubbles to cloud its ice – the world takes on a blue glow, as though you are living inside a glacier. This is the Arctic world of Jukkasjärvi, Sweden, just 120 km (75 miles) from the North Pole.

Every December, an entirely new Icehotel is constructed here, its architecture unlike any Icehotel before it. Rooms and suites are individually designed by leading artists from all over the world, creating a collection of ultimate one-of-a-kind hotel rooms. Even the chandelier that lights the dramatic pillared ice foyer is made of shimmering ice.

Nowhere can the celestial light of the Icehotel be more appreciated than in the Ice Church, built from scratch each year on the Torne River. Here, lit by the soft glow of candles, couples can enjoy a most memorable wedding, before spending the night in one of the hotel's honeymoon suites, where even the bed is a work of art.

> At night, the sky seems alive, swept by the billowing coloured curtains of the Northern Lights.

In the Absolut Ice Bar, guests relax on ice blocks covered with reindeer hides, drinking cocktails of bright Arctic berry juices and vodka. You can be sure these are well chilled – they are served in glasses made of ice.

Wintery activities fill the short days here, allowing guests to explore the magical surroundings; from exciting dog and reindeer sled rides through the snow-blanketed forests to snowshoe hikes, snowmobile exploration and moose-watching safaris. Those inspired by the magical surroundings can take ice sculpture lessons to learn how to craft the beautiful Torne ice. At night, the sky seems alive, swept by the billowing coloured curtains of the Northern Lights; after a unique night in an ice room, spend the night in a cosy Aurora chalet, where skylights let you gaze up at this other-worldly spectacle.

Main: Main lobby of the Icehotel with its ice chandelier
Inset: The Northern Lights flash across the forested horizon
Below (left and right): Aurora chalet, a cosier alternative to the main Icehotel rooms; bed glows invitingly in one of the Icehotel's suites

LAPLAND DIARY

The crisp January days of northern Sweden are short, and the star-filled nights are long, but this is the best time to see the luminous colours of the legendary Aurora Borealis. A three-night stay allows time to ride a dogsled, try your hand at ice-sculpting or snowshoeing, and to relax in a sauna under the stars.

Four Days of Arctic Snow

On arrival, transfer to the Icehotel by a husky-pulled sled for a thrilling introduction to the frozen landscape.

Take a guided tour of the hotel, which gives you the opportunity to see the uniquely designed suites. Enjoy a chilled drink in the Icebar to get you into the mood for a night in an ice room.

Spend the day on one of the hotel's organized excursions: join a local Saami guide to visit a homestead at Sautosjohkka, where you can experience the traditional culture, including lunch cooked over a campfire and reindeer sleigh rides; or take a snowmobile excursion to the winter grazing land of the moose.

In the evening, dine on local specialities in the Icehotel's upmarket restaurant (eating off plates made of river ice), before spending the night in an Aurora chalet to watch the Northern Lights from your bed.

Spend the morning creating your own ice sculpture, under the expert guidance of an ice artist. In the afternoon, step into snowshoes and go for a guided walk through the snow-covered forest to a lookout point above the hotel and town. Enjoy local cakes and a hot drink before the walk back – or be adventurous and try lowering yourself down the cliff face on ropes.

For a memorable final evening, join the Northern Lights Safari for a guided snowmobile excursion to experience this magical phenomenon. Alternatively, relax in an outdoor hot tub under the stars.

Take a final tour of the hotel for photos, before a hearty buffet lunch at the Old Homestead.

Dos and Don'ts

✓ Make sure that you book well in advance, especially over holiday periods as rooms book up very quickly.

✗ Don't forget to bring suitable clothes, it is essential to enjoy the experience fully – layering is key. Thermal underwear is especially recommended.

✗ Don't take cotton clothes as the material can chill rather than warm you.

✓ Remember to use daylight hours to the full, as they are short-lived in the Scandinavian winter.

Below: Fire blazing in the icy fireplace of the Icehotel's lobby

| JAN |
| DAY 1 |
| DAY 2 |
| DAY 3 |
| DAY 4 |
| FEB |
| MAR |
| APR |
| MAY |
| JUN |
| JUL |
| AUG |
| SEP |
| OCT |
| NOV |
| DEC |

SPLENDOUR IN THE SNOW

THE ETERNAL ENIGMA THAT IS RUSSIA comes closest to the West, literally and figuratively, in the city of St Petersburg, glittering beside the River Neva just off the Baltic Sea. Founded three centuries ago by the larger-than-life, modernizing Tsar Peter the Great, St Petersburg was conceived as, and remains today, Russia's "window on the west".

Peter created his new capital on a marshy site that had to be drained by the canals that now add so much to its beauty. St Petersburg's lovely, sweeping waterways provoke comparisons with Venice and Amsterdam, and the splendour of its broad, planned avenues, monumental Rococo and Classical buildings and lovely parks certainly has a European orderliness and pomp – but all with an unmistakable Russian twist. The result is a visual grandeur that takes the breath away – most sharply around the

GETTING THERE
St Petersburg is 400 km (250 miles) northwest of Russia's capital, Moscow. Its airport has direct flights from many European capitals.

GETTING AROUND
St Petersburg's large, efficient metro is the best way to get around. Suburban trains, buses, trams, trolleybuses and *marshrutky* (minibuses) fill out the network.

WEATHER
Daytime temperatures hover around a bracing -10°C, dropping further at night, but it's worth braving the cold as the city is at its most beautiful under a blanket of snow.

ACCOMMODATION
Brothers Karamazov, a tasteful, well-run hotel, has doubles from £95; www.karamazovhotel.ru

Nevsky Association Hotels has six stylish, central mini-hotels; doubles from £140; www.hon.ru

Grand Hotel Europe offers extreme elegance in an opulent 1870s monument; doubles from £250; www.grand-hotel-europe.com

EATING OUT
Mechta Molokhovets on ulitsa Radisheva 10 serves classic Russian dishes, specializing in *kulebyaka*, a pie with a variety of fillings including fish and meat, in a romantic setting (main dishes around £15).

PRICE FOR TWO
£250–275 per day including accommodation, food, local travel and entrance charges.

FURTHER INFORMATION
www.saint-petersburg.com

Rasputin

Rasputin (1869–1916) experienced a vision as a young man that persuaded him that sinning, and then repenting, could bring people closer to God. Combined with his magnetic personality, his beliefs gained considerable appeal among the aristocracy of St Petersburg. Having cured the Tsarina's son of haemophilia, Rasputin developed an unhealthy influence over the royal family ultimately leading to his death at the hands of Prince Felix Yusupov.

Main: Snowfall at the Winter Palace

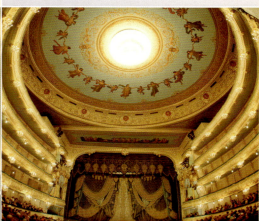

Left: Ornate dome in the Mariinsky Theatre

Right (left and right): Soviet memorabilia at a souvenir market; ballerina prepares backstage for her performance at the Rimsky-Korsakov Conservatory

Tsars' stunning gold, mint green and white Winter Palace, overlooking the broad Neva, and along the straight-as-a-die main artery, the Nevsky Prospekt.

The Winter Palace is today the centrepiece of the State Hermitage Museum, one of the world's great art collections and the flagship of many fascinating museums and galleries in a city that has always been a cultural capital. Russian ballet was born in St Petersburg and its streets are still stalked by the ghosts of Tchaikovsky, Dostoevsky, Rimsky-Korsakov, Nijinsky and Pushkin, who all played out long passages of their often tragic lives here.

Much refurbished for its tricentenary in 2003, today St Petersburg is making the most of the interest and investment directed towards it by the West. With an excitingly creative entertainment and nightlife scene, irresistible shopping and mouth-watering restaurants, it is undoubtedly the most chic city in eastern Europe.

Above: Studying the portraiture in the State Hermitage Museum in the Winter Palace

Below: Decorated ceiling in the Church of Our Saviour on Spilled Blood

CULTURAL DIARY

January is in the thick of the Russian winter, when all those dreams of golden domes above snow-covered roofs, frozen rivers, hearty food and drink, and *troikas* (horse-drawn carriages) trotting along the icy streets, come true. Russia is fully adapted to its climate and life goes merrily on through the snow.

A Week in the Tsar's City

Take a walk around the historic State Hermitage area on the south bank of the Neva, then along part of Nevsky Prospekt, great for shopping, monumental architecture, entertainment and atmosphere.

The State Hermitage is one of the world's greatest art museums, set in the stunning Winter Palace and a highlight of any visit to the city. Sample the nightlife at JFC Jazz Club, DJ bar Dacha or dance club Second Floor.

Explore the lavish imperial palaces and parks at Petrodvorets, the "Russian Versailles". Later, see the famous Kirov Ballet at the Mariinsky Theatre.

The area around western Nevsky Prospekt is rich with sights, including the lavish St Isaac's and Kazan cathedrals, the onion-domed Church of Our Saviour on Spilled Blood, and the Russian, Pushkin and Vodka museums.

To continue sightseeing, cross to the north bank of the Neva to see the Peter & Paul Fortress (St Petersburg's oldest building). Alternatively, carve some ice at the SKA Sports Palace, with indoor and outdoor skating rinks.

For a day in the country, take a trip out to the great imperial estate Tsarskoe Selo, with its Baroque Catherine Palace and park. Back in town, go to the avant-garde music bar Fish Fabrique.

The graves of Tchaikovsky and Dostoevsky can be found in the Alexander Nevsky Monastery – pay your respects here before finishing your trip with the contemporary galleries of the Free Arts Foundation.

Dos and Don'ts

- ☑ Dress in easily removable layers, as you'll be moving in and out between centrally heated buildings and the below-zero temperatures outside.
- ☒ Don't drink the water! St Petersburg's tap water is notorious for harbouring the nasty parasite *Giardia lamblia*.
- ☑ Watch out for pickpockets, especially around the meeting of Nevsky Prospekt and the Griboedova Canal.
- ☑ In working churches, men should bare their heads and women should generally cover theirs.

Below: The Winter Canal in the evening sun

JAN

DAY 1

DAY 2

DAY 3

DAY 4

DAY 5

DAY 6

DAY 7

FEB

MAR

APR

MAY

JUN

JUL

AUG

SEP

OCT

NOV

DEC

GETTING THERE
Bangkok is the capital of Thailand, in Southeast Asia. Suvarnabhumi International Airport is around 45 minutes by taxi from the downtown areas.

GETTING AROUND
The Skytrain is the fastest way to get around but it doesn't serve all areas, so combine it with boats, taxis or tuk-tuks (although always agree a price first).

WEATHER
In January, the weather in Bangkok is sunny and hot, averaging around 28°C.

ACCOMMODATION
Majestic Grande Hotel is conveniently located near the shopping district; doubles from £50; www.majesticgrande.com

Marriott Resort & Spa has a riverside setting; doubles from £80; www.marriott.com

The Oriental, a legendary 19th-century landmark, offers complete luxury; doubles from £175; www.mandarinoriental.com

EATING OUT
Thai food is characterized by the use of coconut milk, chillies, *nam plah* (fish sauce) and lemongrass. Street stalls offer cheap, good local food like *satay* (skewered meat) – choose the busiest stalls as food is more likely to be freshly cooked.

PRICE FOR TWO
£100–150 per day including accommodation, food, trips and sightseeing.

FURTHER INFORMATION
www.bangkok.com

Thai Massage

A real full-body Thai massage is one of the greatest physical experiences you can possibly enjoy – or endure. Over 3,000 years, the technique has evolved into a heavenly perfection. Originally developed in India, it was learned and practised by Thai monks who wanted to aid physical and mental relaxation, clearness of mind and health. Therapists use their hands, elbows, thumbs and even feet in the massage, making it a particularly intense, but memorable, experience.

Main: Traders in their boats at a floating market, Bangkok
Above (left to right): The Grand Palace illuminated at night; incense burning at a shrine; novice monk praying at Wat In

UNDER GOLDEN ROOFS

At first sight, Bangkok is an incomprehensible, sprawling megalopolis of some eight million, a chaotic capital of dust, smog, dirt and tuk-tuk driven traffic made for daredevils. However, once you look beyond the obvious distractions, Bangkok has an astonishing beauty and grace: in the early morning, see the wet and humid mist lift from the Chao Phraya river, revealing the golden spiralling towers of the Grand Palace and the many temples glistening in the distance. Look close to hand and you will see the little details that present life here with an almost spiritual significance: the shopkeepers who put lit incense sticks and food oblations in front of their shops' little statue of Buddha; the craftsmen working on the roadsides, carving intricate figurines and accessories; diligent vendors in the markets; the immensely agile street cooks preparing satays; and monks carefully preparing the temples for the day.

Bangkok was built in 1872 and was destined to be even grander and exuberant than the old capital it replaced, Ayutthaya. Since then, the city has seen major development and has lost its old Asian Venice-style look – most of the canals (*khlongs*) were transformed into streets during the mid-20th century. But the river still sets the pace of the city; a tour on a hired longtail boat splashing through the water is often the fastest way to move around. A sense of the city's past can still be experienced in Thon Buri, where the narrow canals form an impervious maze of sounds and sights. Walk across one of the markets such as the Chatuchak Weekend Market, or even venture out of the city to the floating market at Damnoen Saduak, south of the city – it's overly popular with tourists but you will at least see the joy and zeal of Thais buying and selling. But even these secular activities are embedded in a deeply peaceful and spiritual texture of life, permeating everyone in the country, where harmony and balance still rule the day.

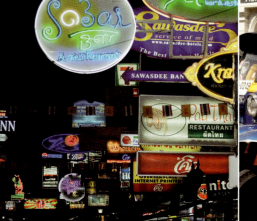

> See the wet and humid mist lift from the Chao Phraya river, revealing the golden spiralling towers of the Grand Palace.

Inset: Ornate detail on a *wat* (temple)
Below (left and right): Khao San Road at night; brightly coloured tuk-tuks

TEMPLE CITY DIARY

While the temples, sights, markets and palaces of Bangkok offer enough thrills to fill a whole week, it is possible to squeeze most of the highlights into three days and enjoy some extraordinary sights outside the city on the fourth. To extend your trip, consider heading south to Ang Thong National Park (*see pp50–51*).

Four Days in the Chaotic Capital

JAN

Start your visit with a tour of Rattanakosin, the historic royal city quarter, home to the Grand Palace (former royal residence) and Wat Phra Kaeo, the Temple of the Emerald Buddha, one of the world's greatest temples. Finally, for a great view of the city, climb up the 320 steps to the Golden Mount. In the evening, have a streetside dinner near the Khao San Road – a backpacker enclave that has become a dining destination for young Thais. Afterwards, watch a traditional Thai dance show at the National Theatre.

DAY 1

For more temples, hire a longtail boat up the river to Banglamphu to see the Temple of the Standing Buddha, Wat In. From here, it is a short walk to Thon Buri, where you can take a boat through the canals and experience more traditional Bangkok life. After lunch, head to the markets in Little India and Chinatown, for authentic foods and spice shopping.

DAY 2

Bangkok is famous for its shopping – if it's a weekend, make sure you don't miss Chatuchak Weekend Market, which is huge and sells absolutely everything. Have lunch here, then move onto the glossy shopping malls around Siam Square – MBK in particular has a very southeast Asian feel about it and a great food court.

DAY 3

Finally, head out of town for some fresh air. Visit the floating market at Damnoen Saduak, about two hours out of the city – or for an even longer trip, see the infamous bridge on the River Kwai near Kanchanaburi. The walk along the (modern) railway tracks where Allied POWs once laboured is a sobering experience.

DAY 4

Dos and Don'ts

- ✓ Travel by boat where possible – it's cheap and a great way to see the city, away from the smog-filled streets.

- ✗ Don't be fooled by people who stop in the street to ask where you are going and then tell you that it is closed – this is usually a ruse to take you to a shop elsewhere so they can get a commission for your custom.

- ✓ Show respect for the king and his family in a conversation, and also for images of the king. If, for example, a bank note falls onto the ground, do not step on it – that is considered extremely disrespectful.

FEB

MAR

APR

MAY

JUN

JUL

AUG

SEP

OCT

NOV

DEC

Below: Traditional dancers performing at the National Theatre

GETTING THERE
Jamaica is an island in the western Caribbean. It has two international airports – Montego Bay and Kingston.

GETTING AROUND
Kingston has public buses. Elsewhere local minibuses connect towns, but are not for the faint of heart. Charter flights serve regional airports. Rent a car or use taxis for local journeys and trips into the countryside.

WEATHER
Clear and balmy with average January temperatures of about 25°C, with the odd cloudy day and occasional cool spells.

ACCOMMODATION
Time N Place, Falmouth, with a private white sandy beach; doubles from £40; www.mytimenplace.com

Hibiscus Lodge, Ocho Rios, is a favourite; doubles from £65; tel. (876) 974 2676.

The Caves, Negril, is the ultimate in relaxation; doubles from £270; www.islandoutpost.com

EATING OUT
Jamaica has its own cuisine, from codfish breakfasts to pepperpot stew, curried goat and mouth-searing jerk. You can fill up at streetside stalls for £2.50 or spend £25 for gourmet fare at a fancy hotel.

PRICE FOR TWO
£115–130 per day including accommodation, food and car hire.

FURTHER INFORMATION
www.visitjamaica.com

Rastafarians

Jamaica's homegrown religious adherents are recognizable by their dreadlocks. Evolving in the early 20th-century from the "back to Africa" movement, the faith deifies Ethiopian Emperor Haile Selassie. Appropriating biblical passages to justify use of marijuana, smoked for enlightenment, believers adopt an Old Testament lifestyle, are vegetarians, and shun Western consumerism.

RUM, REGGAE AND RELAXATION

JAMAICA, ONE OF THE MOST EXCITING AND DIVERSE ISLANDS in the Caribbean, has lost none of the appeal that lured the likes of Sir Noel Coward, who built a home called Firefly, and Ian Fleming, who penned his James Bond novels close by at his home near Ocho Rios. White-hot blazing beaches dissolving into bathtub-warm waters of greens and blues; sparkling waterfalls tumbling through emerald forests; tree-covered mountains soaring to 2,196 m (7,200 ft); these elements define Jamaica's beauty, but there is also the surprising contrast with the semi-arid, cactus-studded southwest.

From the tropical lassitude of laid-back Treasure Beach to the hedonistic idyll of Negril, each resort area has its own distinct flavour. Where you stay can define your experience. Fortunately,

Left (left and right): Luxurious white house on Millionaires' Row; bottles lit up at a beach bar

Right: Refreshingly cool and lush Blue Mountains

Main: Waves lapping gently onto Long Bay, Port Antonio, one of the many picturesque beaches on the island

Jamaica is renowned both for its pampering historic hotels serving traditional English afternoon teas, and for hip boutique hotels infused with romantic ambience and contemporary décor. Many travellers prefer large-scale all-inclusive resorts while others opt for private villas tucked into coves as serene as their innermost thoughts.

Away from the hotels, clamber up Dunn's River Falls, where waters cascade down a limestone staircase to the beach. Sailing down the Martha Brae River on a bamboo raft is another quintessential Jamaican experience. Practise your golf swing on fairways that look over teal-blue seas or seek out crocodiles and manatees in the swampy wetlands of the Black Morass and snorkel and scuba dive amid coral reefs teeming with tropical fish. Drift along the coast on a sailboat for a rum-infused cruise, while at night you can dance to the infectious rhythms of home-grown reggae. As the day draws to a close, head to the Negril cliffs of West End to catch a live concert and watch the sun slide from view below a molten sky turned to flaming orange and plum purple.

CARIBBEAN DIARY

Jamaica is the Caribbean's most exciting island, with a unique culture and cuisine, rich history, dramatic scenery, lovely beaches, and superb accommodation exuding an air of romance. You'll need a minimum of one week to sample the highlights, shown at their best in January's perfect, balmy temperatures.

A Week in a Romantic Idyll

JAN

DAY 1
Montego Bay has plenty of attractions, but depending on the time of your arrival, head to Negril, where the island's loveliest, and most popular, beach awaits.

DAY 2
Relax on the beach and enjoy snorkelling or diving in the crystal-clear waters. After a sunset cruise with cocktails, take in an open-air reggae concert.

DAY 3
Take a boat trip up the Black River to spot crocodiles and tropical birds. Treasure Beach is nearby and this fishing community is a calming place to rest.

DAY 4
Cross the crisp and scenic Dry Harbour Mountains via Nine Miles, where Bob Marley was born and is buried. Arrive in Ocho Rios after a full day touring, relax with a sundowner on your veranda or hotel beach.

DAY 5
Clamber up the tiered cascades of Dunn's River Falls and, later, swim with dolphins at nearby Dolphin Cove. This afternoon, drive to Firefly, former home of playwright Sir Noel Coward.

DAY 6
Head to Chukka Cove for horse riding in the hills. After exploring Cranbrook Botanical Garden, go west to spend the night near the Georgian town of Falmouth.

DAY 7
Take a bamboo raft trip on the Martha Brae River before transferring to Montego Bay for your homebound flight.

Dos and Don'ts

✓ Pass on trying the local and ubiquitous *ganja* (marijuana)! Drug possession is illegal and foreigners receive no special favours in court.

✗ Don't make the popular all-inclusive resorts the centre of a holiday. You can't discover the island from inside a hotel.

✓ Dress appropriately away from the beach. Jamaica is a conservative society and locals in rural areas are easily offended by tourists wearing skimpy clothing.

FEB

MAR

APR

MAY

JUN

JUL

AUG

SEP

OCT

NOV

DEC

Below: Cascading Dunn's River Falls

GETTING THERE
Tanzania lies in East Africa between Kenya and Mozambique. International airports are at Dar es Salaam, Kilimanjaro and Zanzibar.

GETTING AROUND
Various local airlines and bus companies connect Tanzania's main attractions at reasonable prices. Car rental costs from £30 per day (4WD from £75).

WEATHER
Tanzania's weather varies dramatically. The coastal strip is hot and humid, but the altitude of the highlands tempers an otherwise tropical climate. January falls during the warmest period.

ACCOMMODATION
The Royal Palm is perfectly located in Dar es Salaam's city centre; doubles from £115; www.moevenpick-hotels.com

Near Moshi, the Lutheran Uhuru Hostel has doubles from £20; www.transkibo.com

In Arusha, the Outpost has dorm beds from £15; www.outposttanzania.com

In Zanzibar Town, Shangani Hotel is comfortable; doubles from £45; www.shanganihotel.com

EATING OUT
Look out for a local favourite, *nyama choma*, barbecued meat. On the coast and in Zanzibar, don't miss the seafood.

PRICE FOR TWO
£75–105 per day including accommodation, food, local travel and Kilimanjaro trek.

FURTHER INFORMATION
www.tanzania.go.tz

The Masai

The Masai are a tribe of nomad pastoralists indigenous to northern Tanzania and Kenya. The Masai's ability to maintain their traditional lifestyle has been challenged to a large degree by their former grazing lands being turned into game reserves, notably the Masai Mara and the Serengeti. The cattle, which the tribesmen believe have been given solely to their people by their rain god, play an integral role in Masai life both for building (using the dried dung) and nourishment purposes.

Main: Summit of Mount Kilimanjaro rises dramatically out of the clouds with its crater well defined in the glacial ice

CONQUERING KILIMANJARO

THE PATCHWORK OF DUSTY BROWNS dotted with the occasional giraffe, gazelle or zebra that you see from your plane as you fly in to Dar es Salaam signals a gentle and graceful start to your adventure in Tanzania. But don't get too comfortable – you are about to climb the highest mountain in Africa. As your trek up Kilimanjaro progresses, the landscape alters constantly. First comes the lush tropical forest that resounds with the peeps and whistles of bird song. Strange smells hang heavy, dank and unfamiliar on the thick forest air. Occasionally, through a gap in the trees, you can glimpse a spectacular view of the plains, a prelude to what's to come.

Before long, the going suddenly seems easier, and the forest gives way to heathland. Giant groundsel and huge, spiny-looking lobelias, colonize this corner, while birds and animals seem spookily absent. Then the heathland gives way to desert, and things just seem to get tougher. Altitude has kicked in and is declaring itself to the

Top: Thousands of flamingos in the Ngorongoro Crater at Ngorongoro National Park

Above: Getting close to the wildlife on safari

Below: Trekking through the wilderness of Kilimanjaro National Park

ADVENTURE DIARY

In January, you'll avoid the rains (mid-March to May and November to December). Three weeks allow enough time to go on safari, climb Kilimanjaro and relax in Zanzibar, but two are enough for the classic "bush and beach" itinerary – a week on the safari circuit or climbing, followed by a week on the island sands.

Three Weeks in Africa's East

JAN

DAY 1

After touchdown in Dar es Salaam, spend a day visiting the old colonial buildings, museums and seaport, followed by a visit to the colourful markets.

DAYS 2–8

Next head north to Arusha, the safari capital of Tanzania, and spend at least a week on the safari circuit, starting with the small Arusha National Park.

Head next for the Ngorongoro Conservation Area with its extraordinary centrepiece, the Crater, home to almost every species of African plains mammal.

At Selous Game Reserve, one of the largest in the world, take a boat tour up the Rufiji River.

Don't miss Serengeti National Park, arguably Africa's finest, known for its mass of mammals.

DAYS 9–14

After your week of safari, consider a crack at Mount Kilimanjaro. Spend five days and four nights on a guided trek slowly scaling the highest peak in Africa. At 5,892 m (19,326 ft), views are guaranteed, and previous climbing experience is not required.

DAYS 15–21

Spend the third week in Zanzibar relaxing on postcard-perfect beaches and gorging on superb seafood.

Lose yourself exploring Stone Town. Take a tour of the old slave markets, forts and palaces. Travel the island on a spice tour, search for dolphins in sapphire seas, or colobus monkeys in shaded forests.

Finally, check out Tanzania's underwater sights by snorkelling or diving off stunning coral reefs.

Dos and Don'ts

☑ Shake hands with locals and spend time on pleasantries. Tanzanians ask after one another's family and friends.

☒ Don't accept food or drink from strangers when you are on public transport.

☑ Treat locals with respect. Politeness, respect and modesty are highly valued in traditional Tanzanian society.

☑ Be wary of street and safari touts. A calm, but firm decline of their services is best if you don't want to engage them.

FEB

MAR

APR

MAY

JUN

JUL

AUG

SEP

OCT

NOV

DEC

trekkers by way of a thumping headache and seemingly unquenchable thirst. Soon tundra alters the environs again and you can sense the end is in sight.

On summit day, it's an early start at 1am. Before long, the tundra turns to dry, frozen scree making the journey tough and a little treacherous. "*Poli, poli*" – "slowly, slowly" – comes the almost mesmerizing mantra of the guides. Meanwhile, a bitter wind occasionally blasts across the mountainside. The temperature has just dropped to -10°C.

At 4am, however, temperatures – in tandem with the sun – at last begin to rise. Like a stage curtain suddenly lifted to reveal a beautiful backdrop, Africa's plains appear. Stretching for hundreds of miles below, the views seem truly ethereal. Meanwhile, burnished by the sun, the glaciers have turned copper and gold. Past Gillman's Point on the lip of the crater, then descending, apparently endlessly, into the crater itself, it's a slippery final furlong back up to the summit. But standing at last astride one of the Seven Summits of the seven continents in the thin, silvery light of the morning, it is easy to understand the lure of this great African mountain.

Below: Relaxing at a beach hut bar in Zanzibar

GETTING THERE
International flights land at Santiago, the capital of Chile. From here, a 5-hour flight will take you on to Punta Arenas, 2,140 km (1,330 miles) south of Santiago and the starting point of the cruise.

GETTING AROUND
There are frequent port stops on the cruise, which allow passengers to explore on foot.

WEATHER
In January you can expect temperatures of 5–15°C, with occasional rain, although Santiago is sunny and pleasant.

ACCOMMODATION
In Santiago, try the luxurious Park Plaza; doubles from £65; www.parkplaza.cl

Las Hayas Resort Hotel, Ushuaia is around 3 km (1½ miles) out of town, by the bay; doubles from £150; www.lashayashotel.com

A four-night cruise aboard the Mare Australis costs from £1,300 for a double cabin and includes full board; www.australis.com

EATING OUT
In both Santiago and Ushuaia seafood is a speciality and crab, mussels and other fresh catch are delicious. Meals on board include both regional and international cuisine.

PRICE FOR TWO
Around £150 per day on land, including accommodation, food and local transport. The cruise costs around £370 per day and includes full board and excursions.

FURTHER INFORMATION
www.patagonia-travel.com

AT THE WORLD'S END

AS DAWN BREAKS ON THE BEAGLE CHANNEL, the early morning light gradually illuminates the electric blue ice of the floating glaciers that surround your ship, and the intense, wintry silence is broken by an occasional thunderous crack as huge chunks of ice detach themselves and fall into the ocean. This is southern Patagonia: a land of tremendous glaciers, dense native forest and incredible wildlife.

A cruise through this astonishing landscape slowly reveals these sights to the traveller as the ship sails through the legendary Strait of Magellan from Punta Arenas in Chile to Ushuaia in Argentina – the world's southernmost city. Weaving through a sinuous network of fjords, channels and islands, the boat affords you a taste of this extreme land, from the vivid greens and varied fauna of the National Parks to the biting winds that howl against the blue-white glaciers.

Main: Sunrise over the Beagle Channel

Tierra del Fuego Park

The Tierra del Fuego National Park was set up in 1960 and covers 630 sq km (245 sq miles) of the southwest corner of Tierra del Fuego. The park is home to a wide range of southern Patagonian flora and fauna – such as the cute-looking and endangered Patagonian hare *(above)*. In the windswept coastal region of the park, albatrosses, oystercatchers and upland geese can be spotted. Further inland, in the forests of ñire, lenga and coihue trees, beavers and foxes make their homes.

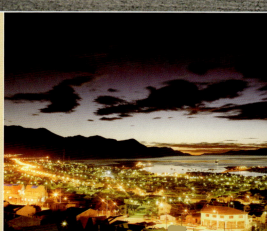

Left: Patagonian cowboy or *gaucho* wearing the striking local textiles

Right (left to right): Looking over the port in Ushuaia at dusk; llama near Punta Arenas; the "Train at the End of the World" winds through the Tierra del Fuego National Park; dramatic icy scenery in the Beagle Channel

Zodiac and walking excursions ensure that there are ample opportunities to explore this fascinating land and its outstanding flora and fauna. Over 60,000 penguins crowd the tiny landmass of Magdalena Island, their little black and white figures an irresistible spectacle as they waddle on the shore. From the look-out at Pia Fjord, you can see the entire Pia Glacier, nestled between mountains as it edges towards the sea, and at Tucker Islet, playful southern dolphins escort your ship into the bay and sea lions lumber along a rocky promontory.

Looking out over Cape Horn and beyond, where Atlantic and Pacific Oceans collide, the sensation is one of utter remoteness. Tiny ice flecks pepper the powerful sea and fierce winds that once thwarted so many expeditions blow persistently here, at the final stop before Antarctica and the end of the earth. This extraordinary journey to the southernmost confines of the continent reveals a landscape that is beautiful, desolate and absolutely unforgettable.

PATAGONIAN DIARY

This unique journey takes you from Punta Arenas in Chile, through the Strait of Magellan to Ushuaia in Argentina. The cruise lasts for four days but add on a day or so in Santiago to explore Chile's vibrant capital, and enjoy the sunny January weather before heading into the cold and icy south.

A Week Cruising the South

JAN

Spend the day exploring Santiago – take the funicular up to Cerro San Cristóbal before a seafood lunch in the bustling central market. Afterwards, visit the Museo Chileno de Arte Precolombino for fascinating artifacts.

DAY 1

Fly south to the town of Punta Arenas, the starting point for the cruise. The ship sets sail around 6pm, but you will need to check in at the port mid-afternoon.

DAY 2

Disembark at Marinelli Glacier in Ainsworth Bay and hike through the forest to Brookes Glacier, a jaw-dropping experience and home to a vast colony of elephant seals. Alternatively, take the trip out to Magdalena Island to see the thousands of penguins. Later, you may catch a glimpse of dolphins as the boat moves through Tucker Islet.

After navigating through the main part of the Beagle Channel, you will disembark at the Pia Glacier. A walk up to the look-out point allows you to trace the flow of ice from the Darwin Mountains to the sea. Afterwards, the ship continues through the Beagle Channel to the spectacular "Glacier Avenue".

DAYS 3–4

The cruise continues to stunning Cape Horn, where the Atlantic and Pacific Oceans meet. In the afternoon, visit Puerto Williams, home to just 2,000 inhabitants.

DAY 5

This morning you arrive at Ushuaia. From here you can take the "Train at the End of the World" through the Tierra del Fuego. Enjoy the fantastic fresh fish for dinner.

DAY 6

Return to Santiago and pick up some South American souvenirs, before heading home.

DAY 7

FEB

MAR

APR

MAY

JUN

JUL

AUG

SEP

OCT

NOV

DEC

Dos and Don'ts

☑ Try the local beer in Punta Arenas – Austral, made in the southernmost brewery in the world – the best in Chile.

☒ Don't underestimate the cold. Temperatures are consistently low, and it can get pretty cold on board – take plenty of layers.

☑ Be prepared for seasickness – the Beagle Channel can be very rough.

☑ Look out for *centolla* – king crab – while in Ushuaia, a speciality of the region.

Below: Ushuaia lighthouse

GETTING THERE
Costa Rica is in Central America. The capital is
San José, which has an international airport.

GETTING AROUND
All of the country can be reached by bus or
small aeroplane. However, it is far better to
explore Costa Rica by 4WD vehicle.

WEATHER
January is in the dry season and temperatures
in San José average between 14–24°C. In
the lowlands it gets much hotter.

ACCOMMODATION
Arenal Observatory Lodge, Arenal National
Park, most with volcano views; doubles from
£30; www.arenal.net/observatory-lodge

Hotel Grano de Oro, San José, is a luxurious
hotel in an old Victorian mansion; doubles
from £55; www.hotelgranodeoro.com

Capitán Suizo, Tamarindo, is set in colourful
tropical gardens; doubles from £100;
www.hotelcapitansuizo.com

EATING OUT
You can eat well for less than £5. The
national dish, *gallo pinto*, is a mix of rice and
beans and is often served at breakfast with
scrambled eggs and a drink of *agua dulce* –
pure sugar cane diluted in hot water.

PRICE FOR TWO
£80–90 per day including accommodation,
food, car hire and internal flights.

FURTHER INFORMATION
www.visitcostarica.com

Poison-Dart Frogs

As if enamelled with the gaudy colours that
advertize their toxicity, poison-dart frogs are easily
spotted hopping about the floor of moist forests.
Barely bigger than a thumbnail, they pack a deadly
punch. Their skins exude among the most lethal
toxins known to man. Indigenous communities
have traditionally used the frog's toxins to tip their
hunting darts – hence their name.

JEWEL-COLOURED JUNGLE

SCARLET MACAWS SCREECH OVERHEAD; howler monkeys play in the dense forest canopy; crocodiles thrash around in the mud. Costa Rica is one great menagerie where the wildlife loves to put on a song and dance. Seeing the abundance of colourful animals and birds is thrilling, and a major draw of any visit to this tiny Central American country, home to an astonishing 5 percent of the world's identified living species. Cloaked in a thousand shades of green, the nation boasts dozens of national parks and wildlife reserves spanning a spectrum of diverse terrains and 12 different life zones. Mountaintop cloud forests of Monteverde, ethereally smothered in mists, are a world apart from the tropical dry forest of the Pacific

> Scarlet macaws screech overhead; howler monkeys play in the forest canopy; crocodiles thrash around in the mud.

northwest, the mangroves of Terraba-Sierpe, or the lowland rainforests of Corcovado and Tortuguero – the latter a watery world cut through by canals tailor-made for wildlife viewing.

The primary forests spill onto long swathes of lonesome white, brown or black sand where marine turtles deposit their precious eggs and paw-prints might betray the passing of a jaguar or any of the nation's five other species of wild cat.

The sheer ruggedness of the coasts and the mountainous interior is part of the appeal. Volcanoes stud the mountain spine; Arenal spews out lava almost daily, you can drive to the summit of Poás and Irazú to peer into their lake-filled craters, and much of the non-volcanic Talamanca range is an unexplored realm of hulking grandeur. Here Cerro Chirripó, Costa Rica's highest mountain, tempts hikers to ascend through cloud forest and *páramo* – a high plateau – for all-round views from the summit. Stitching the varied ecosystems together into a seamless vacation is easy given the country's small size and splendid transport facilities. Many visitors prefer adrenaline-charged adventures as a way to immerse themselves in nature: quad-biking adventures, horse riding, exhilarating zipline rides through the forest canopy, or whitewater rafting on the Pacuare or Reventazón rivers. Whichever way you choose to explore the country, Costa Rica will inspire you.

Main: Green violetear feeding at a colourful bromeliad
Below (left and right): Beach on Tortuga Island; scarlet macaw
Inset: Crater lake on Poás volcano

TROPICAL DIARY

With so many ecosystems and terrains, parks and wildlife reserves, Costa Rica is the perfect place to experience the diversity of the American tropics. By way of contrast, the capital San José has some excellent architecture and museums and can be explored in one or two days or used as a base for forays.

Ten Days in the Rainforests

JAN

Explore San José's Pre-Columbian Gold Museum for a sense of the country's ancient past.

Later, visit the National Theatre to marvel at Costa Rica's premier architectural treasure.

DAY 1

Book an overnight excursion with early morning flight to Tortuguero National Park. A guided boat trip guarantees fabulous wildlife sightings including caymans, howler monkeys and great green macaws then transfer by boat and bus to San José.

DAY 2

Rent a car and drive to La Fortuna, a small township at the base of the Arenal volcano. You can also try rafting and canopy ziplining.

DAY 3

Cross the Cordillera Central to arrive at Monteverde, famous for its cloud forest reserve.

In the afternoon, visit Selvatura to view the spectacular Whitten Collection of insects.

DAY 4

Hire a local guide to accompany you while hiking the cloud forest reserve. There are also opportunities to go horseback riding and visit a serpentarium.

DAY 5

Back down the mountain. Call in at the indigenous pottery-making village of Guaitíl. Arrive in Tamarindo for some riding and fishing.

DAYS 6–8

Return to San José and charter a flight to Corcovado National Park for wildlife viewing in the rainforest.

DAYS 9–10

Dos and Don'ts

✓ When hiking keep your eyes on the trail – you don't want to step on a snake.

✗ Don't miss out on spotting the wildlife – hire a professional guide or join a tour. Local guides can spot far more birds and animals than you could ever wish to see, while also teaching you about their ecology.

✓ Use mosquito repellent in the southern lowland zones, where malaria is present. Long sleeves and trousers are also a wise idea to help keep bugs at bay.

FEB

MAR

APR

MAY

JUN

JUL

AUG

SEP

OCT

NOV

DEC

Below: National Theatre, San José

GETTING THERE
Hong Kong consists of Hong Kong Island in the south, the peninsula of Kowloon and the New Territories in the north, and numerous other islands. This area lies on the southeastern tip of the Chinese mainland. It is served by Hong Kong International Airport, 25 minutes from the centre by Airport Express train.

GETTING AROUND
Hong Kong is best explored by foot or by using the excellent public transport system, consisting of the Mass Transit Railway (the city's metro), buses, trams and taxis.

WEATHER
In January the temperature averages 13–18°C and is generally dry.

ACCOMMODATION
A cheap option is the Chungking House; suites from £45; www.chungkinghouse.com

An affordable luxury option is the Harbour Plaza hotel in Kowloon; two doubles from £190; www.harbour-plaza.com

Pride of place goes to the 1928 Peninsula; two doubles from £500; www.peninsula.com

EATING OUT
One of the best Cantonese restaurants is One Harbour Road (Grand Hyatt, Wan Chai). The cheapest options are the many delicious dim sum restaurants and snack stands.

PRICE FOR A FAMILY OF FOUR
£230–280 per day including accommodation, food and a one-day pass for Disneyland.

FURTHER INFORMATION
www.discoverhongkong.com

Hong Kong Disneyland
A recent addition to the Disneyland empire, Hong Kong's version has all the traditional Disney characters that you would expect to keep children (and big kids) entertained. In a bizarre contrast to Chinese Kowloon, walk down Main Street USA and take a step back in time to America of yesteryear, jump on a spaceship in Tomorrowland and finish with a spin around the park on the back of a large plastic elephant. All are as chaotic as the Hong Kong that you left behind at those magical gates.

Main: As part of the Chinese New Year celebrations, a dragon winds its way through the streets of Hong Kong
Above (top to bottom): Food market; view of Hong Kong from the Peak; busy Kowloon at night; Chinese junk in the harbour

CHINESE NEW YEAR

Firecrackers explode on the streets, their echoes thrown back from the tiny shop fronts, their metallic booms and bangs travelling up the skyscraper façades into the skies amid blazes of thick smoke. The sounds of drums, gongs and cymbals – played almost feverishly by young men, flexing their muscles to get as much noise out of their instruments as possible – and the wafting, smoky smell of burning incense accompany the larger-than-life lions and dragons dancing playfully through the streets. It's Chinese New Year, possibly the most joyous and social annual celebration on earth, celebrated in Hong Kong with the same superstitious rituals, joy and fun with which it has been staged for centuries. Bright yellow and red colours, along with the outfits of the paper lions that look kitschy to the untrained Western eye, transform the glitzy Asian metropolis into a Mardi Gras-like party. Whoever is visited by the lion-dancers – businesses, hotels and families alike – can feel lucky, as the lions and their noises are

Top: Child looking up at the colourful windmills that are bought to bring good fortune

Above: Chinese New Year ornament hangs from a branch

Below: Thousands of worshippers pray for good fortune at the Wong Tai Sin Temple

ORIENTAL DIARY

Hong Kong is a compact place, with two main urban areas; Kowloon in the north, and Hong Kong Island in the south. They are interconnected by ferry and rail. Outlying areas such as the Chinese islands and the historic ex-Portuguese colony of Macau are fascinating too. For exact dates of Chinese New Year see p327.

Ten Days in Colourful China

JAN

Head directly into the city and spend your first two days in chaotic and colourful Kowloon, the most Chinese part of town. Shop on Nathan Road, and wander through exquisite markets like the Jade Market on Kansu Street. In the evenings, visit the Temple Street Night Market and sample the dim sum.

DAYS 1–2

Cruise the harbour by setting off on one of the Star Ferries to the Downtown area of Central. Once there, start at the Statue Square with its historic buildings and awe-inspiring modern architecture. Later, stroll along Hollywood Road and visit the mystical Man Mo Temple. Finally, ride the Peak Railway to Victoria Peak to see the famous view of Hong Kong twinkling below.

DAY 3

Leave the city and visit two islands nearby. First, board the ferry to Cheung Chau Island, a beautiful, quaint fishing community with shipyards, harbours and temples. Then move on to Lantau Island and visit the Big Buddha and Po Lin Monastery. Spend the evenings exploring the waterfront back in Kowloon.

DAYS 4–6

Have a day in Hong Kong Disneyland enjoying the much-loved Disney attractions like Adventureland, Fantasyland and Tomorrowland, slowing down the pace with a picnic in the charming Arboretum.

DAY 7

As a grand finale to your Hong Kong experience, spend your last few days absorbing the customs and traditions of the New Year celebrations. Watch the incredible fireworks by the harbour, join in the lively street parades and shop at the fantastic markets.

DAYS 8–10

Dos and Don'ts

✗ Don't even think of renting a car for exploring downtown Hong Kong or when visiting the surrounding countryside. Public transport and taxis are easily available.

✓ Many travel guides recommend avoiding Central on Sundays, when Philippine women spend their only free day picnicking and chatting on the pavements and at bus stations. Do go and watch one of the city's most fascinating social events unfolding in front of your eyes.

✗ Avoid going up to the Peak on weekends, on Sundays in particular, as throngs of tourists block the view.

FEB
MAR
APR
MAY
JUN
JUL
AUG
SEP
OCT
NOV
DEC

chasing off not only the previous year, but also bad luck for the coming year and evil spirits. The Lion Dances are held on the days after the New Year has begun but preparations for the festivities start days before, when everyone cleans their houses and offices to wipe off the last year; many paint or decorate their windows and doors in red and with paper cut-outs showing symbols for wealth, joy, longevity and a marriage blessed with children. On New Year's Eve, families feast on a sumptuous meal of many courses, open their doors and windows to let in good luck and the New Year, and at midnight welcome it with fireworks and firecrackers. Hong Kong offers the most spectacular firework shows of all Chinese cities, when hundreds of thousands of spectators watch the sky as the fantastical sparkling display illuminates the skyline and the mountains.

The next day, as festivities continue, walk around the city, visit the flower markets, where the Chinese buy their "lucky" blossoms to decorate homes, and tour the temples, where locals pray for good luck and prosperity. As always in Chinese life, the mundane joins the spiritual, so whatever you do, you will feel as if you are immersed in this special event.

Below: Looking towards Hong Kong Island from Kowloon

FEBRUARY

Where to Go: **February**

In the northern hemisphere, although the cloud cover is starting to thin, thick snow is possible on the eastern seaboard of the USA and across northern Europe. Heading towards the Equator, the Caribbean and Central America should be quite welcoming, and even further south, Brazil's Bahia state is hot and steamy – as is its Carnival. Much of the world also puts on a Carnival – an over-the-top celebration before the Lent fast. North and southern Africa are also sunny and worth considering – but keep to the coast. India and Thailand will see plenty of sun but, on the other side of the Himalayas, China's weather varies from frozen in the north to cloudy in the south. Below you'll find all the destinations in this chapter as well as some extra suggestions to provide a little inspiration.

FESTIVALS AND CULTURE

HAVANA Musicians playing in the streets

UNFORGETTABLE JOURNEYS

NILE CRUISE Exploring the Great Pyramids of Giza

NATURAL WONDERS

ANTARCTICA Penguins resting on a sculpted iceberg

HAVANA
CUBA, CARIBBEAN

A city that throbs day and night with rhythm and music

The best cigars in the world, crisp refreshing *mojitos* and an Afro-Latin beat that makes your feet move – an unbeatable combination for fun.
See pp46–7

BINCHE
BELGIUM, EUROPE

Travel back in time to the 15th century in this beautiful town

See how Belgium celebrates Carnival – with colourful parades and spectacular outfits that haven't changed for hundreds of years.
www.visitbelgium.com

NILE CRUISE
EGYPT, AFRICA

Take a leisurely cruise 5,000 years back in time

Cruise the Nile between Cairo, with its minarets and mighty pyramids, and ancient Thebes with its myriad beautiful tombs and temples.
See pp42–3

BLUE TRAIN
SOUTH AFRICA, AFRICA

Enjoy a moving 5-star hotel through this beautiful country

From Pretoria to Cape Town with a side trip to Johannesburg; riding the luxurious train is definitely a once in a lifetime experience.
www.bluetrain.co.za

"Days are spent cruising waters where…icebergs the size of ships drift by in the deep blue seas."

ANTARCTIC PENINSULA
ANTARCTICA

A setting of incomparable beauty and savage wilderness

See whales breach, penguins march, and seals recline; and all the while, the icebergs beautiful and menacing, drift slowly by.
See pp38–9

ANGKOR
CAMBODIA, ASIA

Ancient capital cloaked in the jungle, home to a vast temple

Set deep in a lush environment, the mystical temples of Angkor are carved with exquisite tableaux that come to life in the rising sun.
See pp40–41

"See the exquisitely carved *apsaras*, the celestial dancers, almost naked and voluptuously beautiful."

COTE D'AZUR
FRANCE, EUROPE

Drive along the French Riviera free from the summer crowds

Hire a car for a leisurely journey along the coast – enjoy the mild winter weather, charming towns and fantastic food.
www.guideriviera.com

KANHA NATIONAL PK
INDIA, ASIA

A huge wildlife sanctuary that harbours the magnificent tiger

And tigers are not the only animal to see; there's porcupines, gaur, nilgai, antelope, mongoose, and over 175 species of birds.
www.kanhanationalpark.com

DEVON
ENGLAND, EUROPE

Stay on a cottage in the pretty south Devon "Riviera"

It's milder than you'd think and there's plenty of nature – try pony trekking, bird watching and filling up on delicious cream teas.
www.discoverdevon.com

AGRIGENTO
ITALY, EUROPE

Enjoy the ancient ruins and simple life of sunny Sicily

A remarkable collection of ancient Greek sites in excellent condition, as well as a pretty medieval town and beautiful Sicilian countryside.
www.travelplan.it

COPPER CANYON
MEXICO, NORTH AMERICA

Hike, bike or take the train through these great canyons

A connected run of six canyons each one bigger than the Grand Canyon is the setting for this extraordinary journey.
www.great-adventures.com

SEA OF CORTEZ
MEXICO, NORTH AMERICA

Swim with sealions and manta rays from your beachside hut

Go sea kayaking in the incredibly rich wildlife environment of this scenic gulf coast and islands – see whales, dolphins and sea birds.
www.loretobay.com

SALVADOR
BRAZIL, SOUTH AMERICA

Salvador's "carnaval" is a joyous bacchanalian revel

This is a carnival where you take part in the parades instead of watching – and the music and partying is second to none.
See pp58–9

TIKAL & AITITLAN
GUATEMALA, CENTRAL AMERICA

See the astonishing ruins of the once mighty Mayan nation

Do your own version of the "Ruta Maya" to see the ancient pyramids and temples and the spectacularly pretty lake Aititlan.
www.larutamayaonline.com

BWINDI NATIONAL PK
UGANDA & RWANDA, AFRICA

Few experiences match seeing a silverback gorilla up close

Trek through the impenetrable jungle to see firsthand the awesome power, and humanity, of these magnificent creatures.
www.uwa.or.ug/bwindi.html

Previous page: Holy bathing in the Yamuna River near the Taj Mahal

Weather Watch

❶ Snow depth reaches its seasonal maximum in Canada – good for skiers and the Winterlude festival in Ottawa, but icy winds off the Great Lakes can sometimes cause severe blizzards.

❷ Brazilian coastal towns have a wet tropical climate and Salvador is fairly hot and humid now – but that's not going to spoil the Carnival.

❸ Zermatt sits high up on a mountain ridge and the chill weather brings good snow; further south in Europe, Sicily is much lower and winter is milder.

❹ The Nile in Egypt has an average rainfall of zero every month, but February is one of the coolest months of the year – even as far south as Aswan.

❺ India and Cambodia are in the Asian monsoon region (see p329) and this month is a good time to visit before it gets unbearably hot and humid.

❻ New Zealand has a very variable climate – it can rain, snow and be sunny in the space of a few hours. February is the last month of summer, the sea is nice and warm and there's plenty of sun.

LUXURY AND ROMANCE

AGRA The stunning symmetry of the Taj Mahal

ACTIVE ADVENTURES

ZERMATT Skiing on the smooth Alpine slopes

FAMILY GETAWAYS

OTTAWA A glittering and elaborate ice sculpture

AGRA
INDIA, ASIA

Agra and Jaipur – the most romantic places in the world?

Watch as the Taj Mahal, romance set in stone, adopts the changing hues of the sky and explore the elegant "pink city" of Jaipur.
See pp52–3

MOMBASA
KENYA, AFRICA

Stay in a luxury treehouse hotel on a forested cove beach

Enjoy a romantically isolated hotel with all the luxuries you could ask for – spa therapies, private deck for sea views or star gazing and more.
www.kenya-safari-africa.com

ANG THONG NATIONAL PK
THAILAND, ASIA

Deserted, sandy and unspoiled

This delightful chain of 40 islands has plenty of space for Robinson Crusoe-type daydreams set to a soundtrack of exotic bird calls.
See pp50–51

DUBAI
UAE, MIDDLE EAST

Super-luxurious but actually great value for money

Shopping is so big here – the malls are like palaces and they have a festival for it! You can also enjoy boat trips and the beaches.
www.dubai.com

ALENTEJO PLAINS
PORTUGAL, EUROPE

Stay at a romantic fortified pousada overlooking the plains

The area is scattered with old villages, untouched by tourism, where busy markets sell olives, cheeses and local pottery.
www.pousadasofportugal.com

> "Rocky outcrops, covered with deep green, lush vegetation, interspersed with hidden coves and sandy, dreamy beaches."

ZERMATT
SWITZERLAND, EUROPE

Relax in some peace and quiet under the Matterhorn

Cars have been banned from the town so it's quiet and peaceful, with great skiing and other snow sports for every age and ability.
See pp48–9

LAKE BAIKAL
RUSSIA, ASIA

Make like a cold sturgeon and dive under the thick ice

Not for the faint-hearted – this ice safari will introduce you to seals and the amazing underwater scenery in the crystalline water.
en.baikaldiving.ru

GOLDEN TRIANGLE
THAILAND, ASIA

Go trekking in Chiang Rai and learn how to drive an elephant

Try the Camp Experience to go on jungle treks through hill tribe villages, trips on the Mekong and to an elephant training school.
fourseasons.com/goldentriangle

THE LAKE DISTRICT
CHILE, SOUTH AMERICA

A delightful mix of "Swiss" scenery, exercise and luxury

Trek round turquoise lakes, through deep emerald forests, up snow-capped volcanoes and relax in a luxury thermal spa hotel.
www.baileyrobinson.com

CAPE VERDE ISLES
CAPE VERDE, AFRICA

A hot destination for surfers, windsurfers and kitesurfers

Always known as a windsurfing destination, winter swells also bring top quality waves to these islands. Enjoy the music too.
www.club-mistral.com

FLORIDA KEYS
USA, NORTH AMERICA

The Overseas Highway leads to a beautiful and magical world

The strip of islands, improbably joined by the highway, allows for watersports galore, fine weather and an interesting counter culture.
See pp54–5

YORK
ENGLAND, EUROPE

Enjoy a traditional Viking festival at the Jorvik Centre

Viking street performers, colourful processions, and clanging weapon displays aim to ban the winter blues at the Jolablot festival.
www.jorvik-viking-centre.co.uk

AGADIR
MOROCCO, AFRICA

Sun, sea and a modern city makes life a breeze in Agadir

Agadir offers good value for families, if little genuine North African culture. Wide open spaces and plenty of water sports.
www.agadir-tourism.com

> "The road is one-of-a-kind, connecting the curved line of lush, green islands like a string of tropical pearls."

OTTAWA
CANADA, NORTH AMERICA

Go a little crazy in the snow in this massive winter festival

The canal becomes a skaters' superhighway, there's ice and snow sculptures, a winter slide park and the ice-hogs too.
See pp44–5

NORTH ISLAND
NEW ZEALAND, AUSTRALASIA

Superb destination for little hobbits to scamper around in

You'll find plenty of open space in this Middle Earth – walking, beaches, barbecues, water sports, and interesting Maori culture too.
See pp56–7

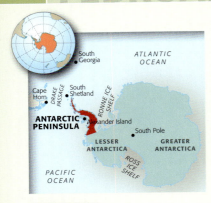

GETTING THERE
Antarctica, an island continent, is the world's southernmost destination. Ships to Antarctica sail from the town of Ushuaia, on the southern tip of Argentina. Flights to Ushuaia depart from Buenos Aires, Argentina or from Santiago, Chile.

GETTING AROUND
Cruise ships enter the glacial bays and Zodiacs (inflatable boats) are used to land on the ice. Specialist cruises may provide kayaks.

WEATHER
February is nearing the end of summer in Antarctica. Temperatures in coastal regions average between 5°C and -5°C.

ACCOMMODATION
There is no accommodation on land. Ships sailing to Antarctica may be expeditions with 50 to 100 passengers from lines such as Lindblad (www.lindbladexpeditions.com), Quark (www.quarkexpeditions.com) and Clipper (www.clippercruise.com) or may be large cruise ships such as the Explorer II (www.antarcticabound.com) or the Discovery (www.discoveryworldcruises.com), with up to 400 on board. Smaller ships offer more landings and more time on shore; cruise ships provide more amenities on board and more stability in rough waters.

EATING OUT
All meals are aboard ship.

PRICE FOR CRUISE
Voyages to the Antarctic Peninsula, 7 to 11 days, begin at £2,200 per person for larger ships, £4,000 for smaller vessels.

FURTHER INFORMATION
www.iaato.org

Who Rules Over Antarctica?
Signed on 1 December 1959, the Antarctic Treaty established a legal structure for the management of Antarctica whereby all decisions are reached by consensus. By 2005, there were 45 members, including the seven nations that claim sections of Antarctica as national territory. These are: Argentina, Australia, Chile, France, New Zealand, Norway and the UK. The USA and Russia have reserved the right to make claims with the USA refusing to recognize the claims of other countries.

Above (left to right): Humpback whale tail crashing through the icy Antarctic waters; adult emperor penguin feeds its hungry chick, Atka Bay, Weddell Sea; Weddell seal, King George Island
Main: Ice cave in a glacier, Paradise Bay

FROZEN WILDERNESS

A SETTING OF INCOMPARABLE BEAUTY, Antarctica is an unforgettable travel adventure and one of the few untouched expanses left in the world. Days are spent cruising waters where breaching whales are often spotted and icebergs the size of ships drift by in the deep blue seas. Sometimes lounging fur seals can be seen taking a ride on top of a floating berg. As there are no piers or docks, sturdy rubber Zodiac boats are boarded for landing, giving you your first thrilling chance to walk among the penguins and admire the stunning icy vistas. In the evenings, Zodiacs often go out for a sail offering the chance to get close-up views of the scenery with giant icebergs looming in the ghostly dusk of the Antarctic summer.

Expert scientists onboard enrich the voyage with illustrated talks about the intrepid early explorers to Antarctica and the unique geology and wildlife that are found there. To preserve the unspoiled nature of this icy continent, regulations limit the number of passengers allowed ashore at any one time, resulting in a truly intimate experience with the landscape and wildlife.

Most fascinating of all are the penguins, found in their thousands – including seven varieties peculiar to the south-polar region. The birds lay their eggs in December so by February visitors can see fat, fluffy chicks being cared for in their pebble-nests. Gentoo, adelie and chinstrap are the most common varieties seen on the shorter cruises. Longer itineraries add the South Shetland Islands and South Georgia, home to the large and colourful king penguins that strut territorially around the shore. Visitors are kept at a safe distance from nesting penguins, but many birds seem oblivious and often waddle right up to the odd visiting creatures and their madly clicking cameras who are likely to be rewarded with an unforgettable image.

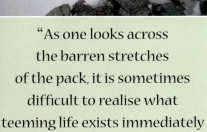

> "As one looks across the barren stretches of the pack, it is sometimes difficult to realise what teeming life exists immediately beneath its surface."
>
> Robert F. Scott

Below (left to right): Chinstrap and gentoo penguins rest on a sculpted iceberg of old compressed ice; signpost outside the Halley Research Station; paddling in double kayaks amongst the icebergs
Inset: Mawson's Hut at Cape Dennison on Commonwealth Bay

WILDLIFE DIARY

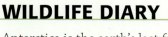

Antarctica is the earth's last frontier, a pristine paradise of majestic mountains, gigantic icebergs and vast expanses of polar ice, a beautiful sight against the blue ocean. Cruises arrive during the summer (November to March), when waters are navigable and temperatures, although cold, allow exploration on land.

Eight Days Among the 'Bergs

Arrive in Ushuaia and settle into your ship's cabin. Later, take a walk through town and a brief half-day tour to Tierra del Fuego National Park.

DAY 1

Sail through the notorious Drake Passage, hoping for calm waters. Watch the petrels, gulls and perhaps an albatross follow in the wake of the boat.

Listen to talks on board about the unique geography and wildlife of Antarctica.

DAY 2

Go ashore to meet the penguins. Exact stops are determined by weather and sea conditions. Usual landings include Deception and Cuverville Islands and Port Lockroy, populated with gentoo penguins. Also, Half Moon Island, with its rocky volcanic landscape.

Get the camera ready for the spectacular Lemaire Channel, a narrow strait bordered by sheer cliffs. Then on to the aptly named Paradise Bay, ringed by ice cliffs. Stop by the Chilean research base here and pick up some information sheets.

DAYS 3–6

Back to open sea for the return cruise around Cape Horn, where the Atlantic and Pacific oceans meet, and through the Drake Passage. On board, listen to tales of legendary Antarctic adventurers like Ernest Shackleton.

DAY 7

Disembark in Ushuaia for some last-minute souvenir buying before flying back to Buenos Aires or Santiago.

DAY 8

Dos and Don'ts

✓ Plan your expedition ahead – almost every cruise line offers discounts for early reservations.

✗ Don't pack heavy parkas until you check your cruise details – most cruise lines give passengers insulated parkas as a gift.

✓ Pack clothing that can be layered. The changeable weather can be unseasonably warm or windy and cold. Remember too it will be midsummer in stopovers such as Buenos Aires or Santiago.

✗ Don't forget to bring seasickness pills. The notorious Drake Passage can be as smooth as a pond or may serve up storms with 10 m (30 ft) waves; it is best to be prepared.

JAN
FEB
MAR
APR
MAY
JUN
JUL
AUG
SEP
OCT
NOV
DEC

GETTING THERE
Angkor is in Cambodia. International flights arrive at Siem Reap, 6 km (4 miles) away. Internal flights connect Phnom Penh, the capital, with Siem Reap. Buses and shared taxis go from Phnom Penh and the Thai border to Siem Reap.

GETTING AROUND
Individually, hire a taxi with a guide or hire a bicycle. Or flag down a *moto*, a moped with a driver who will take you round all the temples for around £2.50–5 a day.

WEATHER
Cambodia is tropical and hot, with average daytime temperatures of 30°C. February is one of the best months, dry and bright.

ACCOMMODATION
Angkor Village Hotel looks over lush gardens; doubles from £50; www.angkorvillage.com

Grand Hotel d'Angkor is very luxurious; doubles from £140; www.siemreap.raffles.com

La Residence d'Angkor, a Pansea-Orient Express hotel built in local wood with a swimming pool; doubles from £155; www.pansea.com

EATING OUT
Delicious local specialities are usually served with a soup accompaniment. Try the *omlar machou banle* (sour fish soup). The Foreign Correspondents Club is great for elegant dining.

PRICE FOR TWO
£85–110 per day including accommodation, food, temple pass (£20 for 3 days and £30 for 1 week) and local travel.

FURTHER INFORMATION
www.tourismcambodia.com

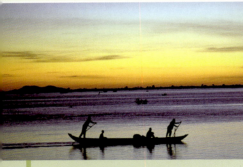

The Tonlé Sap

Angkor is strategically close to the Tonlé Sap lake in the centre of Cambodia. During the annual monsoon rains, the Mekong River reverses its flow, backing up into the lake which swells to six times its normal size, flooding the surrounding forests and rice paddies. The Khmers built reservoirs to harness the water. Measuring 25,000 sq km (9,650 sq miles), the lake contains 300 species of fish and attracts 105 bird species. The teeming lake means that 40,000 fishing families earn their livelihood from the waters.

Main: Buddhist monks sit in contemplation at the Banteay Srei Temple

JUNGLE-COVERED RUINS

AT DAWN, AS IF ON CUE, THE SILENCE AT ANGKOR WAT IS SUDDENLY BROKEN by the piercing trill of cicadas. Simultaneously, the first rays of the sun appear behind the darkened silhouette of the temple, slowly rising over the five lotus-bud-shaped towers, and illuminating the long causeway. It is a magical moment in a mystical place that has witnessed each new day since the 12th century. Aligned with the sun and the moon, Angkor Wat, with its towers, galleries, courtyards and moat, is the biggest religious monument in the world, a recreation of the Hindu cosmos, built by the Khmer king Suryavarman II as his mausoleum.

Yet it is alive with vivid sculptures and the morning light is perfect for looking at bas-reliefs of mythical battles that look more like ballets, and scenes from the Hindu epics, the *Mahabharata* and the *Ramayana*. As you climb towards the central sanctuary, marvel at the detail of the exquisitely carved *apsaras*, the celestial dancers.

Left (left to right): Aerial view of Angkor Wat with its surrounding moat in the foreground; Temple of Pre Rup; detail from Banteay Srei Temple; waterlily at Angkor Wat; detail of dancing nymphs at Angkor Wat

Below: Working in the paddy fields at Banteay Srei Temple

Inset: Carving from the Bayon, in Angkor

The first rays of the sun appear behind the darkened silhouette of the temple, slowly rising over the five lotus-bud-shaped towers…It is a magical moment.

TEMPLE DIARY

Before the humidity and heat of the approaching rainy season, February skies are brilliant blue and cloudless. Every detail of every monument is picked out with sparkling clarity. Walking on the forest paths around the temples is a delight – dry underfoot and perfect if you decide to bicycle.

Five Days Exploring the Temples

Visit the oldest temples, 12 km (7½ miles) from Siem Reap, known as the Roluos group – Preah Ko, Bakong and Lolei – which date from the 9th century.

Later, visit Ta Prohm, Jayavarman VII's temple consumed by jungle. As a World Heritage Site, Angkor's forest setting is protected as well as the temples.

Spend a morning at Angkor Wat, examining the structure, with five majestic towers symbolizing Mount Meru, and magnificent carvings.

Then travel through the South Gate, stopping to look at the gods and demons, *devas* and *asuras*, and go into city of Angkor Thom. At its centre is the vast temple of the Bayon. See the Terrace of the Elephants, carved with elephants, horses and polo players, and the Terrace of the Leper King, with its depictions of spirits.

Head to Siem Reap for a lake trip on the Tonlé Sap and some wildlife spotting. You will also see the locals fishing for their daily catch. In the evening, enjoy a traditional dance show as you sample the regional fare.

Start early and visit Banteay Samre, with its fine bas-reliefs and stone-vaulted galleries, and continue to Banteay Srei, a 10th-century temple in the jungle. It is the most ornately and exquisitely carved of all.

Venture further afield to the jungle-covered temple of Beng Melea, 40 km (25 miles) east of the Bayon. Return to Angkor Wat for sunset and a tour of the 800-m (2,625-ft) bas-relief surrounding the temple depicting the Churning of the Ocean of Milk.

Dos and Don'ts

✓ Do smile and greet people with the words "Sok Sabay".

✗ Don't take a photograph of someone without asking.

✓ Do smile a lot when you are bargaining and remember it's fun and a great way of making contact with local people.

✗ There are still some landmines around Beng Melea and in other remote areas; don't stray from marked paths here.

✓ Do perform a traditional *wai*, bowing with hands joined together. Sadly, this gracious greeting, filled with significance, is being replaced by the Western handshake.

JAN

FEB

DAY 1

DAY 2

DAY 3

DAY 4

DAY 5

MAR

APR

MAY

JUN

JUL

AUG

SEP

OCT

NOV

DEC

Below: Ancient Ta Prohm Temple

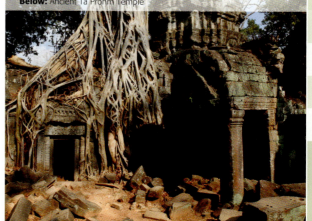

More than 1,850 of them bring the temple to life, framed in floral decoration, with their voluptuous figures, towering head-dresses, ornate jewellery and enigmatic smiles.

After such grandeur, head for smaller temples, like Ta Prohm. When you get to the temple, still covered in jungle, its collapsing galleries swathed in huge silk cotton trees which prise apart the stones, it's like finding a lost city in the forest. Imagine then what it must have been like in the 19th century to have rediscovered the ruins of Angkor, which had slumbered in oblivion for over 400 years after the Khmer Empire's decline. Deeper in the forest lies an even older temple, Banteay Srei, a miniature, fairytale temple in red sandstone, covered with perfectly preserved 10th-century carvings. At sunset, climb Phnom Bakheng, the temple mountain where, in the distance, you can see the five towers of Angkor Wat turn to gold in the fading light. If you are lucky you'll witness the flight of the bats as they emerge from the nooks and crannies to feed, before everything slowly disappears into the shadows and darkness descends.

GETTING THERE
Egypt is in northeast Africa. International flights arrive into the capital Cairo; some go to Luxor.

GETTING AROUND
Within Cairo, use taxis or the metro. The best way to see the temples is to travel by boat down the Nile between Luxor and Aswan.

WEATHER
February is warm and pleasant, with temperatures ranging from 12–24°C and low humidity.

ACCOMMODATION
In Cairo, historic Mena House Oberoi is situated right by the pyramids; doubles from £155; www.oberoimenahouse.com

Sofitel Old Cataract Hotel, Aswan, was the inspiration for Agatha Christie's novel *Death on the Nile*. Closed due to restoration, it will reopen in May 2010. The Mövenpick Resort, Aswan, is an excellent alternative; doubles from £100; www.movenpick-hotels.com

A number of tour operators offer Nile cruise packages. A typical 7- to 11-day cruise should cost around £599 per person, including flights (from Europe), but shop around carefully.

EATING OUT
Boats have at least one restaurant. If your cruise includes time in Cairo, try Egyptian staples like *fuul* (black-eyed beans, garlic and olive oil).

PRICE FOR TWO
To organize the whole trip yourself expect to pay about £140–180 per day for accommodation, food, entrance fees and transport within Egypt.

FURTHER INFORMATION
www.touregypt.net

Early Nile Travellers
A trip to Egypt was one of the most exciting activities available to the 19th-century traveller. The pace up the Nile was languid; a steamer took three weeks to reach Aswan; under sail, it could take up to twelve. Slow days on deck alternated with treks across the sands to marvel at the latest discoveries – new finds were being made almost monthly during this grand age of exploration. It was not unknown for tourists themselves to discover ancient tombs.

LAND OF THE PHARAOHS

To celebrate their victory in the Alexandrian War, Cleopatra and her consort Julius Caesar enjoyed a leisurely two-month cruise down the Nile. Sadly, that is no longer an option, as the longest Nile cruise these days lasts no more than 12 days, but it remains a spectacular and enchanting voyage nonetheless, with as much to see – if not more – than in the days of the fabled queen of Egypt. Most cruises sail between Luxor, which as Thebes was the almighty capital of the pharaohs at the peak of ancient Egypt's power, and Aswan, a small desert market town beside the First Cataract, where the Nile crashes over boulders and rocky islets, making it impossible for river traffic to continue on south. Between these two points are languorous passages of lush palm groves and the fields of crops to which the waters of the river give life, punctuated by a succession of small riverside

Main: Feluccas sailing near Elephantine Island

Above (top to bottom): The terrace of the Old Cataract Hotel in Aswan; a Nile cruiser in front of Kom Ombo temple; watching the sunset from the *SS Abu*

Bottom (left to right): Painted limestone decoration of Anubis in the Valley of the Kings; the four mammoth statues of Rameses II at Abu Simbel; walking through the Hypostyle Hall in Karnak Temple; the Temple of Horus at Edfu

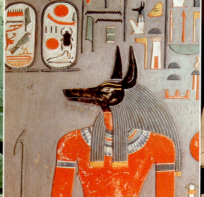

towns centred on ancient temples raised by the Ptolemaic dynasty. The temple at Edfu, built over 2,000 years ago in honour of the falcon-headed god Horus, is the best preserved in Egypt, while Kom Ombo is dedicated to Sobek the crocodile god, with a pool in which live reptiles were once kept. Separate cruises now sail from just south of Aswan to the massive rock temple of Abu Simbel, fronted by four colossal statues of a seated Rameses II. To approach this temple by water today is to understand the state of awe that it was intended to produce in Egypt's enemies, should they have approached the pharaohs' domain by river from the south.

The scenery, too, is timeless, often little changed from the time when the temples were built – fields of rice, cotton and sugar cane, collections of mud-brick huts, and reed-fringed riverbanks. And on the boat, sun decks are lined with phalanxes of wicker chairs patrolled by stately staff in flowing white robes, ever ready with ice-clinking drinks. Fantasies of *Death on the Nile*-style high adventure are easily indulged along this ancient river.

RIVER DIARY

February is an ideal time for a Nile cruise as the river is at its fullest. It is possible to travel between Luxor and Aswan in just two or three days, but most cruises stretch to at least seven by bookending the time spent on the water with a stay in Cairo and extended time in Luxor and/or Aswan.

A Week in Ancient Egypt

DAY 1 Arrive in Cairo and visit the Egyptian Museum for a crash course in Egyptian history. See the treasures of Tutankhamun and get an idea of the Pharaonic timeline.

DAY 2 Hire a car and driver and see the pyramids. Not just the big three – get your driver to go on to Saqqara for some early pyramid designs. Then visit Khan al-Khalili – yes it is a tourist trap, but it is surrounded by beautiful, crumbly mosques, caravanserais and palaces.

DAYS 3–6 Take the short 1-hour flight to Luxor where you join your boat. Enjoy a drink on the deck as night falls.

Still in Luxor, make an early morning expedition to the West Bank of the Nile to see the sights, including the beautiful painted tombs in the Valley of the Kings and majestic temples, then return to the boat.

Wake up at Edfu and disembark after breakfast on board to visit the Temple of Horus. After lunch, the boat sets sail for Aswan where it moors for the night.

A day spent exploring Aswan, a sleepy Nile-side town. The river here is wide and picturesque, dotted with islands, which can be visited by felucca, the small triangular-sailed boat that is characteristic of Egypt.

Make the trip to Abu Simbel before reboarding in the afternoon and sailing back to dock at Kom Ombo.

Most of the last day is spent sailing, reaching Luxor late afternoon, where you can stroll through the streets and browse the shops for locally made jewellery and trinkets.

DAY 7 A last day in Luxor with a visit to the absolutely enormous Karnak Temple. Fly home via Cairo.

Dos and Don'ts

✓ Do a little background reading beforehand otherwise all those pharaohs' names can get awfully confusing.

✗ Don't expect a leisurely week – most cruise programmes are so packed that they leave little time for indolence.

✓ Take the chance to visit Karnak or Luxor Temple by night when the mysticism and magnetism of these ancient sights is eerily enhanced by moonlight.

✗ Don't miss the optional excursion to Abu Simbel – for many this is the highlight of the entire trip.

JAN FEB MAR APR MAY JUN JUL AUG SEP OCT NOV DEC

Below: Exploring the Great Pyramids of Giza by camel

GETTING THERE
Ottawa is in Ontario province, Canada, about 450 km (280 miles) northeast of Toronto. The city is well served by international flights and the airport is 20 minutes from the centre. There are also air, bus and train links to other Canadian cities.

GETTING AROUND
Ottawa is easily explored on foot. The small O-Train line is convenient and easy to use, and buses also serve the city centre and outskirts.

WEATHER
In February, the average daytime temperature is -9°C. Night-time can be considerably colder.

ACCOMMODATION
The Gasthaus Switzerland Inn has a relaxed European atmosphere; rooms from £70; www.gasthausswitzerlandinn.com

Cardinal Suites has spacious two room apartments from £90; www.cardinalsuites.com

Fairmont Château Laurier, the "grande dame" of Ottawa's hotels, has family rooms from £115; www.fairmont.com/laurier

EATING OUT
Try *poutine*, a popular snack of French fries, cheese curds and gravy. A decent three-course meal costs about £15 per person. Sophisticated fare is served at Signatures, a Cordon Bleu cooking school (£40 for four-course set menu).

PRICE FOR A FAMILY OF FOUR
About £210 per day including accommodation, food, entry to museums and local travel.

FURTHER INFORMATION
www.ottawatourism.ca

Pride and Peace
In 1841 Lower and Upper Canada joined together to form one province – with an alternating capital. In 1857, Ottawa was chosen to be the new fixed capital and a set of Parliament buildings was proudly erected. Fire destroyed these in 1916 and they were immediately rebuilt in the same style as the originals – Gothic Revival. As they were being built World War I ended, and the 92-m (300-ft) high Peace Tower was added to commemorate this. There are excellent views from the observation deck.

Main: People of all ages skating on the iced-over Rideau Canal.

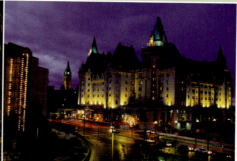

Above (left to right): Visitor mesmerized by a painting in the National Gallery of Canada; the extravagant nave of Notre-Dame Basilica, the oldest surviving church in Ottawa; the imposing exterior of the Fairmont Château Laurier Hotel

WINTER PLAYGROUND

I T MAY HAVE BEEN YEARS since you strapped on a pair of ice skates, but the rhythm comes back to you – it's as easy as falling off a log; and fall you will. After bruising your dignity (and other parts) a few times, you're soon sliding and gliding along the glassy ice surface of Ottawa's Rideau Canal, past elegant embassies and under arched bridges. The hiss of steel on ice announces that someone is passing you. A man old enough to be your grandfather effortlessly and gracefully swooshes past followed by young couples pushing well-wrapped toddlers on sleds.

Ottawa is blessed (or cursed) with some of the coldest winters of any national capital. In a city where the snow often starts to fall in November and hangs around until March, people have two choices: huddle indoors or make the best of it. Many Ottawans disregard the thermometer and spend the season enjoying all the sports, shopping and museums this national capital has to offer. During Winterlude, a three-week festival each February, the parks resound with the buzz of chain saws and the tap of chisels as sculptors create beautiful gleaming fancies from ice and snow, and kids shriek on dogsled rides or have their chilly faces painted. The snow and ice turn the whole city into a huge winter playground. But despite their miraculous internal heating, even kids get cold. To warm up, families can visit the antique steam locomotives at the Canada Science and Technology Museum and the reconstructed dinosaur skeletons at the Canadian Museum of Nature.

As dusk steals over this rugged city, the temperature drops even further, fresh snow squeaks satisfyingly underfoot and visitors are drawn to the warm, inviting lights of cafés and bars. On weekend nights during Winterlude, music-lovers wrap mittened hands around steaming cups of hot chocolate and huddle shoulder to shoulder to watch an eclectic array of bands play outdoor concerts under a glittering canopy of stars.

Sculptors create beautiful gleaming fancies from ice, and kids shriek on dogsled rides... turning the whole city into a winter playground.

Inset: Detail from a Nuuchahnulth totem pole in the Museum of Civilization
Below (left to right): Children racing down snow slides; cross-country ski races in Gatineau Park; a glittering and elaborate ice sculpture

WINTERLUDE DIARY

Winterlude officially lasts for three weeks in February, but almost all of the concerts, races and other activities take place on the weekends. It's best therefore to come for a four-day weekend, from Friday to Monday, in order to enjoy the best of the festival as well as the rest of the city's highlights.

A Weekend on Ice

Start your day by visiting the National Gallery of Canada. Don't miss the wilderness paintings of the Post-Impressionist Group of Seven, who blazed a trail for other Canadian artists in the early 20th century. Go window-shopping in the nearby Byward Market, where you can choose from dozens of restaurants for lunch. Rent ice skates for everyone and spend the afternoon on the Rideau Canal.

Kids love the Jacques Cartier Park, where they can careen down snow slides and check out the snow sculpture competition. Learn about totem poles, watch an IMAX movie and explore a reconstructed 19th-century Canadian street at the Canadian Museum of Civilization. Outdoor concerts are held at several venues around town in the evenings – be sure to don your warmest clothes.

Relax over Sunday brunch at a downtown hotel, watch ice sculptors at work at Confederation Park, check out beautiful 19th-century Notre-Dame Basilica or tour the Neo-Gothic Parliament Buildings, where highlights include the vaulted Library of Parliament with its statue of Queen Victoria. In the evening, catch a performance at the National Arts Centre – a play, ballet or concert.

For some fresh air away from the city, head to Gatineau Park for a morning of snowshoeing or cross-country skiing. Return to Ottawa and explore the trendy boutiques and restaurants of the Glebe.

Dos and Don'ts

✓ Learn the lingo for Canada's currency. The 1-dollar coin, with its engraved loon, is a "loonie". The newer 2-dollar coin is, naturally enough, a "toonie".

✗ Don't rent a car. Ottawa's system of one-way streets can be difficult to navigate, especially at night, and February weather can make roads slippery and dangerous.

✓ Before a performance at the National Arts Centre, sample Canadian fare in the centre's restaurant overlooking the canal.

✗ Don't go to the canal on mild weekend afternoons, when crowds reduce the ice surface to mush.

✓ Warm up by snacking on a local speciality, a deep-fried pastry called a BeaverTail – you need calories in the cold.

JAN
FEB
FRI
SAT
SUN
MON
MAR
APR
MAY
JUN
JUL
AUG
SEP
OCT
NOV
DEC

Left (left and right): Taking a re...
on a doorstep in the old area of
Havana; relaxing at the beautiful
Playa del Este, one of Cuba's mo...
beautiful beaches

GETTING THERE
Havana fronts onto the Florida Straits on the northwest coast of Cuba, 150 km (94 miles) south of the tip of the Florida Keys. The main airport is José Martí, where all of the many international airlines serving Cuba today have to land. It is 18 km (12 miles) to central Havana.

GETTING AROUND
The cheapest and easiest ways around Havana are taxis, cycle-rickshaws and by foot.

WEATHER
February is the driest, least humid month, when the average daytime temperature is a sunny 22°C, cooled by the northerly trade winds which blow over the island.

ACCOMMODATION
Hostal Valencia is tastefully furnished and central; doubles from £40; tel. (0053) 767 1037.

Hotel Nacional de Cuba is a 1930s classic with gardens overlooking the seafront; doubles from £90; www.hotelnacionaldecuba.com

Hotel Parque Central, has a stunning view over Havana from its 9th floor; doubles from £100; www.hotelparquecentral.com

EATING OUT
Bakeries are great for finger foods, such as *pastelitos* (small flaky turnovers filled with meat, cheese or guava). Try Los Nardos in the Old Town for Cuban fare; tel. (7) 863 2985.

PRICE FOR TWO
£125–150 per day including accommodation, food and car hire for one day.

FURTHER INFORMATION
www.cubaweb.cu

Cuban Cigars
The cigar is an inextricable part of Cuba's culture and history, and is – for some – its essence. After Columbus' voyage, tobacco was imported to Spain. However, the first smokers were imprisoned because people believed that cigar smoke produced diabolical effects. Even so, tobacco grew in popularity and was exported, with government agencies set up to maintain a monopoly. After the Cuban revolution, the US embargo had a serious effect on cigar sales, but the recent fashion for cigar smoking has reversed the trend.

Main: A 1950s Chrysler parked in front of a crumbling old building in Havana

HAVANA NIGHTS

Havana is the world capital of Afro-Latin music and dance, and for over 50 years the Tropicana has been at its epicentre. It all took off in 1939 when a brilliant idea was conceived in a suburban villa with a vast, sprawling tropical garden: rig an open-air stage through this jungle setting and fill the walkways with hundreds of performers, in thrall to a loud Afro-Latin beat, costumed lavishly and choreographed lasciviously enough to waft any audience away into an exotic wonderland. Stars like Nat King Cole sang to Hollywood actors, American gangsters, international jet-setters, charter-flown tourists and Batista's political elite. The Tropicana, which came to typify the pre-revolutionary decadence of Batista's Cuba, survived the revolution and February is the perfect time to visit. With very little rainfall – if any – the show is highly unlikely to be moved indoors and revellers can spend a night in the balmy outdoors as the show continues on into the early hours.

Left (left and right): Ornate Hall of the Lost Steps in the Capitolo; elderly musicians playing their instruments on the streets of Havana

Below: Bartender lines up a row of the infamous Cuban *mojitos*

Inset: Detail of a brightly glazed tile panel in Havana

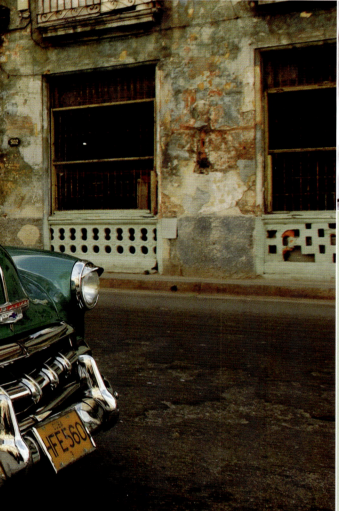

Havana is the world capital of Afro-Latin music and dance and, for over 50 years, the Tropicana has been at its epicentre.

TROPICANA DIARY

Havana is perfect for visiting in February. The weather is sunny and dry during the day and great for exploring this historic city and venturing to the beautiful sandy beaches nearby. In the evenings, dress in your finery and let your hair down dancing on stage at the famously colourful Tropicana nightclub.

Five Days in the Cuban Capital

Take a tour of Havana in a 1950s American classic car with a driver and guide. Sip a *mojito* (rum, lime, sugar and mint) on the terrace of the Hotel Inglaterra, the best place in town to people-watch.

Stroll the streets of Old Havana, a UNESCO World Heritage Site since 1982, finishing up at the Floridita, Hemingway's old haunt, for the perfect daiquiri.

Visit the Museum of the Revolution, the Capitol and the Vintage Car Museum, with a relaxing long lunch with the locals at Los Nardos in the Old Town.

Tour the Partagas Cigar Factory to hear about the Cuban tobacco industry and experience the sight of Cuban communism in the workplace. Then head along to the Cuban Museum of Contemporary Art.

In the evening, take your seat at a ballet in the National Theatre to see why Cubans, in whatever style, are deemed the world's best dancers.

Hire a car for the day to explore Havana's environs. Make for Hemingway's fascinating rural retreat, the Finca, then head down to the Playa del Este for an afternoon at Havana's best beach.

Later, celebrate your last evening in Havana with drinks and show at the world-famous Tropicana.

Buy last-minute souvenirs from the Feria, Old Havana's largest street market, before heading home. Alternatively, extend your time in Cuba with a second week of sand and relaxation at one of the beaches.

Dos and Don'ts

✓ Travel with pounds sterling, dollars or euros, in perfect-condition cash notes, to convert into Cuban pesos, CUCS, pegged at parity with the euro. Be aware of the 11% tax added to all credit card use.

✗ Never buy cigars from a street vendor, only from government shops, and keep the receipt for airport customs – "Black economy" cigars are confiscated.

✓ Always cross-check your bill with the price-list or fall prey to endless "mistakes".

✓ Only buy Chilean wines of the latest vintage possible. Anything else is more than likely to be oxidized.

JAN
FEB
DAY 1
DAY 2
DAY 3
DAY 4
DAY 5
MAR
APR
MAY
JUN
JUL
AUG
SEP
OCT
NOV
DEC

Below: Dancers performing an elaborate routine at the Tropicana

Havana too, like the Tropicana, is full of rhythmic sounds, and throbs with music from midday every day with a distinct air of the 1950s. Poignancy pervades the city: patched-up dinosaurs of cars belch and clatter past crumbling mansions, barely lit by the street lamps. In the Old Town, Habana Vieja, the grand Baroque buildings of Catedral de San Cristóbal and Palacio de los Capitanes Generales stand out with their rich marbles and undulating lines, hinting at a refined and wealthy past that touchingly contrasts with the impoverished, unemployed young couples who go down to the Malecon at sunset, and sit and kiss on the sea-wall. In Centro Habana, admire the Capitolo, one of the symbols of the city and a loose copy of the Washington DC Capitol. Inside you can take a walk through the sumptuous "Hall of the Lost Steps" with the strange acoustics that give it its name. Later, visit Cuba's colonial past with a perfectly mixed *mojito* in the rooftop bar of Hotel Inglaterra and watch the stylish Cubans at play. Always present is an underlying sense that Havana stopped in 1960, making it one of the most intriguing and haunting cities on earth.

GETTING THERE
Zermatt is accessible via the famously reliable Swiss train system from any of the country's three international airports – Zurich, Geneva, Basel – and also from Milan in Italy.

GETTING AROUND
The village is car-free and entirely walkable. Or, hop aboard a solar-powered bus, take a horse-drawn sleigh, or hire Zermatt's version of a taxi, a four-seat electric golf cart.

WEATHER
February temperatures are generally -7 to 7°C with brilliant sunshine. The valley village is protected from strong winds, but the summits are very exposed.

ACCOMMODATION
Hotel Jaegerhof is a traditional pine chalet-style hotel in the village centre; doubles from £85; www.hoteljaegerhofzermatt.ch

Schweizerhof Hotel on Bahnhofstrasse has an indoor pool; doubles from £220; www.seilerhotels.ch

Riffelberg has amazing mid-mountain views; doubles from £200; www.matterhorn-group.ch

EATING OUT
Walliserstube specializes in fondue and is moderately-priced. Le Mazot, in a charming old farmhouse, is known for its grilled lamb and excellent service; expect to pay from £25.

PRICE FOR TWO
£200–260 per day including accommodation, food and a three-day ski-pass.

FURTHER INFORMATION
www.zermatt.ch

The Iconic Mountain

Zermatt's blend of traditional Alpine village and sophisticated holiday resort is dominated by the Matterhorn (4,478 m/14,693 ft), a hooked pyramid ever-changing as shadow and light dance across its instantly recognizable face. There's year-round skiing on the glacier and a strong tradition of respect for the mountain that claims many lives every year. Yet mountaineers continue to climb and conquer – but never tame the Matterhorn.

Above (left to right): Gornergrat train station in the Alps; ice climbing above Zermatt; skiing on the smooth slopes
Main: The Matterhorn in the morning mist with the village of Zermatt below

SKI THE MATTERHORN

In THIS QUINTESSENTIAL SWISS VILLAGE, picturesque chalets dot the hillsides and horse-drawn sleighs ply the main street, where cars are forbidden, all under the watchful gaze of the most famous landmark in Switzerland, the mighty Matterhorn mountain. Even residents must leave their vehicles at the base of the valley, at Taesch, and take the short train ride to Zermatt.

The friendly atmosphere on the main street during the day, as skiers with gear over their shoulders pass *hausfrauen* (housewives) with grocery bags over their arms, turns positively festive after dark. Bahnhofstrasse morphs into a street fair, as groups of friends wander towards a favourite restaurant or club, stopping en route to window shop at the elegant boutiques along the way.

Nearly half of Europe's 76 peaks that are over 4,000 m (13,125 ft) are in the area around Zermatt. The vista from the top of the mountains is staggering. So is the view while you ski and snowboard, with the striking, severe Matterhorn facing you most of the time. Choosing a gentle, groomed piste is a great way to let your equipment think for itself so that you can admire the surroundings.

It is possible to cover 12,500 m (41,000 ft) of height difference in one day in this vast terrain without ever using the same piste, lift or cableway twice. Enthusiasts can participate in the ski safari which is made up of three connected peaks in the surrounding mountains, the Rothorn, with its steep funicular, the Gornegrat, accessed by a picturesque red train, and Klein Matterhorn, via cable car. Skiers with deeper pockets can take a helicopter from the village to the top.

Many extended families have lived here for 300 years or more, and their surnames repeat themselves in the signs around town as mountain guides, restaurateurs and hoteliers. For all its sophistication and world fame, Zermatt remains a small town and has managed to retain its quaint charm.

> In this quintessential Swiss village, picturesque chalets dot the hillsides and horse-drawn sleighs ply the main street.

Inset: Fluhalp refuge in Zermatt
Below (left and right): Busy Bahnhofstrasse; aerial view of Zermatt

MOUNTAIN DIARY

In February, the village of Zermatt, below the Matterhorn, is the perfect place for a snow-filled activity holiday. The village itself is a great centre for nightlife and shopping and there are plenty of alternatives to skiing. Extend the trip by visiting Lucerne (see pp200–1).

Five Days in the Peaks

Zermatt is dominated by the formidable view and the expansive selection of pistes on the Matterhorn. Learn a bit about the mountain with a visit to the Matterhorn Museum, dedicated to the mountaineers and guides who have conquered it, or died trying, and the geology of the Alps.

Take a mountain-climbing lesson indoors, or an ice-climbing lesson outdoors. Go under the glacier at the mountaintop Glacier Palace, highest of its kind in the world, with ice sculptures, wine tasting and real crevasses to explore.

In the morning, ski over to Italy, on the other side of the Matterhorn, for a welcome lunch. It's best to do this only in clear weather, to prevent being stranded in Cervinia if the lift closes.

Take the Gornergrat railway towards the highest igloo village and spend a night in the snow in an igloo. Choose between a romantic suite for two or a group igloo for up to six people (www.iglu-dorf.com).

On your final day, strap on a pair of ice skates and glide around Zermatt's beautiful ice rink taking in the village life as it buzzes around you.

Dos and Don'ts

✓ Hire a guide to take you to more remote areas for untracked snow and unforgettable views.

✗ Don't miss out by spending all of your time in one place, split your visit and spend some of the time at a hotel in the village, and some in a mountaintop hotel, where breakfast is served with a panoramic sunrise.

✓ Be prepared to stop to allow a herd of black-nosed sheep to cross the piste, herded by a shepherd.

JAN
FEB
DAY 1
DAY 2
DAY 3
DAY 4
DAY 5
MAR
APR
MAY
JUN
JUL
AUG
SEP
OCT
NOV
DEC

Below: View from the panorama wagon of the Glacier Express

LAOS
Chiang Mai
THAILAND
Bangkok
ANDAMAN SEA
CAMBODIA
VIETNAM
ANG THONG NATIONAL PARK
Phuket
GULF OF THAILAND
MALAYSIA

GETTING THERE
Ang Thong National Park consists of 42 islands off the east coast of southern Thailand. International flights arrive into Bangkok, from where you can catch a domestic flight to Koh Samui.

GETTING AROUND
Get around Koh Samui by taxi, or hire a car or motorcycle. To reach the marine park, take a boat tour or hire a local fishing boat. Koh Tao and Koh Pha Ngan can be reached by ferry.

WEATHER
In February the weather is dry with an average temperature of around 30°C.

ACCOMMODATION
Laem Set Inn has a friendly ambience and a secluded position on the south coast; doubles from £20; www.laemset.com

Chaba Cabana Beach Resort, traditionally decorated room, situated on Chaweng Beach; doubles from £100; www.chabanet.com

Tongsai Bay is a rustic yet luxurious resort; doubles from £175; www.tongsaibay.co.th

EATING OUT
Many of the hotels offer excellent Thai food, but for a special treat visit the many tiny, authentic seafood restaurants in the northern fishing town of Bophut, where historic houses cling to the narrow beach road and offer great sea views.

PRICE FOR TWO
£110–140 per day including accommodation, food, local transport and sightseeing trips.

FURTHER INFORMATION
www.kohsamui.com

The Perfect Beach
When Alex Garland wrote his backpacker's nightmare book *The Beach*, he chose the mystical Ang Thong National Park as a backdrop. But the real "Beach" feeling can only be experienced by camping on one of its islands. Obtain a permit from the Park Rangers (Park Office, 26/1 Mu 5 Talad Land Rd, Surat Thani; tel. (077) 283 025), and choose your perfect beach. For the ultimate beach party, visit Koh Pha Ngan at full moon when thousands of backpackers congregate to party.

EMERALD ARCHIPELAGO

WHETHER BY SPEEDBOAT, longtail boat, sailing catamaran or kayak, the first approach to the 42 islands of Ang Thong National Marine Park is always stunning. Rocky outcrops, covered with deep green vegetation, interspersed with hidden coves and dreamy sandy beaches, appear one by one from the glistening turquoise sea. As you draw closer to the islands, the sea shines with an almost mystical glow, a sight that never fails to entrance even the most world-weary traveller. Situated off the southeastern coast of Thailand, the protected status of these emerald islands has ensured that they have remained unspoiled by tourism. Their strange shapes have inspired appropriately bizarre names such as Tree Sorrow, Sleeping Cow and Rhinoceros Island, which add to their mystical attractions.

The islands of Hin Nippon and Koh Wao have two of the park's top snorkelling spots. Although the marine life may be more abundant in other areas, the huge, brain-like corals found in these waters are truly spectacular. Continue on to Koh Wua Talab, a coconut-covered island with probably the most

Below (top to bottom): Tranquil Lamai Beach; Thai dancer on Koh Samui; view of Ang Thong National Marine Park.

beautiful beach in the park. Talk to the park rangers to learn more about the diverse marine life and climb to the top of the 120-m (400-ft) peak for a magnificent view of the surrounding islands, scattered across the vivid turquoise sea, which is especially striking at sunset.

But the true highlight of any tour is a visit to beautiful Koh Mae Ko, where a mountain hike will lead you to a lookout over Thale Noi. This hidden turquoise saltwater lake is bordered by sheer cliffs, and it is from this that the islands take their name – Ang Thong means "golden basin". From here, you can also look out across the whole archipelago, as well as the two larger neighbouring islands that sit outside the marine park, Koh Tao and Koh Pha Ngan. Both of these islands, but Koh Tao in particular, have fantastic snorkelling and dive spots, rivalling even those in the marine park. Explore the calm clear waters around Koh Tao, where spots like beautiful Ao Leuk boast some of the best marine life that Thailand has to offer. Or, seek out one of the many island beaches where, protected by dramatic limestone cliffs, you can find your own secluded hideaway to soak up the lush, vivid beauty that surrounds you.

BEACH DIARY

February is a great time to visit Ang Thong National Marine Park as the weather is warm and the seas are calm. Accommodation in the park is restricted to camping – it's easier to base yourself on Koh Samui (just outside the park) and take day trips from there. Extend your trip with a visit to Bangkok (see pp22–3).

A Week of Island-Hopping

Spend your first few days relaxing on Koh Samui, the gateway to Ang Thong National Marine Park. Take your pick from the beaches – busy but beautiful Chaweng, pretty Lamai, Maenam with its lovely views of Koh Pha Ngan, or one of the more secluded beaches on the south and west coasts. Enjoy a Thai massage on the beach or water sports in the clear, warm waters.

Get up early to join a chartered boat tour into the marine park. If you are a novice snorkeller, choose one of the mainstream tour packages; for an extra thrill, you might want to consider going there on a sailing catamaran, perhaps to Han Nippon or Koh Wao. If you are a veteran snorkeller or experienced diver, hire a local fisherman to take you out in his longtail boat. Make sure that your visit includes time on the islands so that you can enjoy the beautiful beaches, such as on Koh Wua Talab, where you can also hike through the lush interior to enjoy beautiful views of the archipelago.

Take a boat to Koh Tao or Koh Pha Ngan. For diving and snorkelling, head to the fish-filled waters off Ao Leuk on Koh Tao, but if you just want to relax then enjoy the quietness of Koh Pha Ngan.

Head back into the marine park to visit Koh Mae Ko to see Thale Noi, a beautiful saltwater lake in an amazing setting surrounded by limestone mountains, and enjoy the wonderful views.

Spend the day back on Koh Samui, where you can trek around the island on elephant-back, visit Big Buddha or do little more than laze on the beach.

Dos and Don'ts

✗ If you need to complain, remain friendly but be firm in your wishes. Don't raise your voice – this would not only dishonour you but also the person you are addressing.

✓ Take care not to touch or remove any corals or fish. Human contact like this will eventually destroy the coral, which has devastating effects on the area's fragile ecosystem and its inhabitants.

✗ Don't snorkel or dive alone. The waters are generally calm but sudden current and weather changes can take you by surprise.

Main: The Big Buddha statue on Koh Samui

Above (top to bottom): Beautiful pink lotus flower on Koh Samui; simple beach huts on Chaweng Beach

Below: Vibrant traditional decorations on a local fishing boat

Below: The beautiful turquoise waters of Thale Noi Lake

JAN

FEB

DAYS 1–3

DAY 4

DAY 5

DAY 6

DAY 7

MAR

APR

MAY

JUN

JUL

AUG

SEP

OCT

NOV

DEC

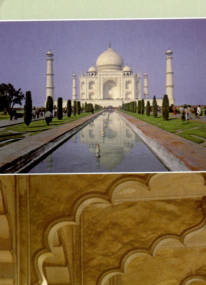

GETTING THERE
Agra is 200 km (125 miles) from New Delhi. There are daily 30-minute flights between Delhi and Kheria airport, less than 10 km (6 miles) from Agra. By car the journey takes 3–4 hours.

GETTING AROUND
Choose from auto-rickshaws, *tongas* (horse-drawn carriages), cycle-rickshaws and taxis.

WEATHER
February is an ideal time to visit as the weather is extremely pleasant with an average maximum temperature of about 26°C.

ACCOMMODATION
The Hotel Mansingh Palace has good-value doubles from £50; www.mansinghhotels.com

The Hotel Taj View also has stunning vistas of the Taj Mahal; doubles from £175; www.tajhotels.com

Enjoy fabulous views from the Oberoi Amarvilas; doubles from £350; www.oberoiamarvilas.com

EATING OUT
Agra is renowned for its rich Mughlai cuisine which typically uses a clay oven *tandoor*. But look out too for *korma* (slow-braised meat, yoghurt and spices) and *biryani* (rice cooked with meat korma and saffron). Try the North Indian fare at the pricey but excellent Esphahan at the Oberoi Amarvilas – with live music.

PRICE FOR TWO
£125–150 per day including accommodation, food, entrance charges and local travel.

FURTHER INFORMATION
www.agratourism.org
www.up-tourism.com/destination/agra/agra.htm

Legends of the Taj

There's a myriad legends about the Taj Mahal. Some say that it took 20,000 craftsmen and 1,000 elephants 22 years to build the building and then decorate it with calligraphy and over 20 different semi-precious stones. Another story has it that Shah Jahan planned to construct a tomb for himself on the opposite side of the Jamuna River in black marble. Finally, a grim legend is that, once finished, Shah Jahan had the hands of all the craftsmen cut off so that another Taj could never be built.

Above (top to bottom): Symmetry of the Taj Mahal; ornate arches in the Red Fort; view across to the Jewel House, Fatehpur Sikri; trimming the Taj Mahal's lawns with an ox-drawn mower

THE ARCHITECTURE OF LOVE

AS YOU WANDER AROUND THE WELL-PRESERVED TOMBS, palaces and forts of Mughal India, it is easy to imagine yourself transported back in time. Fatehpur Sikri, the elegant capital Emperor Akbar built out of red sandstone in 1585, is in immaculate condition, as though awaiting the return of the imperial court. Walking from courtyard to courtyard, you can almost hear Sufi music coming from a nearby shrine, played for the graceful dancers performing on the giant chessboard floor for the emperor and his grand retinue. Peer through the intricately crafted windows into the shady palace suites and picture them filled with the talk and laughter of the harem as the women float excitedly through the rooms and corridors draped in a kaleidoscope of fine silks and muslins. It was meant to be a magnificent, showcase capital city, but Fatehpur Sikri was abandoned 15 years after completion due to an inadequate supply of fresh water. Today it just takes a little imagination to bring this beautiful ghost city to life.

Above: Door of one of the Taj Mahal's minarets

Main: View of the Taj Mahal seen from the Gate House as the sun rises

Below: Beautiful calligraphy and inlay work around one of the doorways to the Taj Mahal

MUGHAL DIARY

Its name in Sanskrit means "paradise", and indeed Agra comes close to just that in February. The blissful weather is perfect for enjoying the majestic buildings of the Mughals. But they left more behind than just monuments – the Mughal legacy lives on in the creativity and energy of the people, and a delicious, aromatic cuisine.

A Six Day Trip to Agra

On arrival in Delhi, take a pre-paid taxi to your hotel. Spend the day either lounging by the pool or exploring the sights such as India Gate and Humayun's Tomb.

After breakfast, it's off to Agra and a visit to the Taj Mahal. Take your time to let the beauty sink in and have your picture taken in the love seat. If possible, try also to see the Taj by moonlight or get up early the next morning for a dawn viewing.

A 40-km (25-mile) drive from Agra, Fatehpur Sikri is a stunning red sandstone complex containing nine different monuments, but now eerily deserted; it definitely warrants a day trip.

Back in Agra, pry yourself away from the Taj Mahal for a while to see more Mughal sights – the mighty Agra Fort blends Hindu and Muslim architecture. Or see the exquisite craftmanship of Itimad-ud-Daulah's tomb.

Go shopping – local handicrafts include marble and stone inlay, and leather products. The main shopping destinations are the Taj Mahal Complex, Kinari Bazaar, Raja-ki-Mandi, Sadar Bazaar and Sanjay Place.

The next day, eat a hearty breakfast at your hotel as you gaze at the Taj Mahal. Then, it's time to head back to Delhi. En route, stop at Sikandra city to see the tomb of Emperor Akbar, another architectural gem.

Dos and Don'ts

✓ Always carry your own supply of mineral water. If you buy it in Agra, ensure that it's properly sealed.

✗ Don't plan a trip to the Taj Mahal on Friday – the mausoleum is closed on that day of the week.

✓ Remember that if you want a night-time tour, the Taj Mahal can only be seen on the nights around a full moon.

✗ Don't take your mobile phone to the Taj Mahal – they're not allowed within the main enclosure, and you'll have stand in a long queue to check the phone in at the collection booth.

✓ Haggle with all taxi drivers and agree a price beforehand as they don't use a meter.

JAN
FEB
DAY 1
DAY 2
DAY 3
DAY 4
DAY 5
DAY 6
MAR
APR
MAY
JUN
JUL
AUG
SEP
OCT
NOV
DEC

But the Mughals' best craftsmanship was reserved for funerary architecture. The mausoleum of Akbar the Great, completed in 1605 at Sikandra, is a perfect study in symmetry and marks the transition between the older architectural style of red sandstone and the newer style of more decorative white marble. Itimad-ud-Daulah's jewel of a tomb built in 1628 was a forerunner to the Taj Mahal, with its delicate lattice work, *pietra dura* (stone inlay), mosaics, and gilded niches.

Finally, you come to the Taj Mahal, a monument to the love of Shah Jahan for his wife Mumtaz, and one of the most famous buildings in the world. As familiar as it may be, nothing compares to experiencing it in real life at different times of the day. The marble absorbs and transforms in the light – a sleepy pink in the rosy dawn, white and pristine in the noon sun, dusky and sensuous in the shadows of evening, and ethereal and ghostly in the moon's diffused beams.

Perhaps a faint memory of the deft handiwork and skills that created these timeless monuments lives on in the marble inlay bric-a-brac and fine gold-thread embroidery found in the bazaars that are filled to overflowing with all the chaos of a bustling and energetic India.

Below: Washerman laying saris out on the bank of the Jamuna to dry

GETTING THERE
The Florida Keys are a chain of islands extending 180 km (112 miles) from the southern tip of Florida in the USA. Miami has the region's largest international airport which is about an hour's drive from the Upper Keys. Cars are available for hire at the airport.

GETTING AROUND
Car is the best way to travel between keys. Key West is great for walking, but parking is limited. You can take the shuttle or a taxi across town.

WEATHER
February is warm and sunny with occasional rain. The average high temperature is 24°C dropping to around 19°C at night.

ACCOMMODATION
Rock Reef Resort, Key Largo, is a beachfront resort with gardens and fishing pier; family rooms from £90; www.rockreefresort.com

Eden House Hotel in Key West is nice and quiet; family rooms from £180; www.edenhouse.com

The Gardens Hotel is a small historic hotel with gardens, near Duval Street in Key West; family rooms from £290; www.gardenshotel.com

EATING OUT
Seafood and Caribbean cuisine are the staples but key lime pie is the dessert to try. Blue Heaven is a local favourite, around £10, offering legendary banana pancakes for breakfast.

PRICE FOR A FAMILY OF FOUR
£240–280 per day including accommodation, food and car hire.

FURTHER INFORMATION
www.fla-keys.com

Nuestra Señora de Atocha
On 20 July 1985, the legendary treasure hunter Mel Fisher discovered the treasure of the *Nuestra Señora de Atocha*. A Spanish galleon heavily laden with New World riches, the *Atocha* sank off Key West during a hurricane in 1622. The ship's cargo included incredible wealth from Peru, Mexico and Colombia; precious metals and stones; as well as everyday articles from the 17th century. Today hundreds of pieces from the *Atocha* are on display in Key West at the Mel Fisher Maritime Heritage Society Museum.

KINGDOM OF COOL

A HALCYON HIGHWAY TO THE MYTHICAL KINGDOM OF COOL, the incredible 180-km (112-mile) long trip down the Florida Keys' Overseas Highway leads to a world so different in style and temperament from mainland America that it feels like a country all its own. The road itself is one-of-a-kind, connecting the curved line of lush, green islands that form the keys like a string of tropical pearls; its causeways crossing vast stretches of open water that offer dazzling, 360-degree vistas of the Caribbean-blue sea. Every mile marker you pass beckons you to shed stress and inhibitions, while pleasant stops along the way give you time to culturally decompress.

The road itself is one-of-a-kind, connecting the curved line of lush, green islands that form the keys like a string of tropical pearls.

John Pennekamp State Park on Key Largo protects one of America's few coral reefs and lures visitors to put on mask and fins and spend an afternoon exploring the kaleidoscope of colours below the waves. Key Largo offers the opportunity to take a ride on the original *African Queen* boat, a working prop from the 1951 Bogart and Hepburn movie of the same name. Farther along, Bahia Honda Park with its fabulous strand of flour-like white sand, offers a place to stroll and wade in the azure water and feel the truly tropical breezes flow across your skin.

But the ultimate destination is the weirdly wonderful other world of Key West that awaits at the end of the road. Actually, despite its reputation, Key West is only as weird and wild as you want it to be. It all depends on where you look. Those with partying in mind will want to join the boisterous throngs along Duval Street. And everyone should experience the carnival-like atmosphere of chainsaw jugglers and stilt-walkers that appear at sunset on Mallory Square.

Families can find plenty of attractions here too. The island's seafaring history comes alive in the cases of treasure on display at Mel Fisher's Maritime Museum. And the Hemingway House preserves the aura of Key West in the 1930s when the famous author lived here and wrote *To Have and Have Not*. Today, the laid-back, near mystical paradise that once lured him and so many others is alive and well. . . and waiting.

Main: Crowds gather around a fire juggler in Key West
Inset: Florida Key deer
Below (left and right): Captain Tony's Saloon in Key West; the road stretches through Marathon

ISLAND DIARY

February is the best time to explore the Florida Keys. While the rest of North America is experiencing the winter, the Keys are wrapped in sunny warmth and tropical breezes. Four days allows plenty of time to see the highlights, with an optional fifth to visit the National Park or enjoy relaxing on your favourite key.

Five Days in the Keys

On Key Largo, snorkel or scuba dive in the waters of John Pennekamp Coral Reef State Park, where the reef teems with 260 varieties of tropical fish.

Later, take a ride on the *African Queen*, famous for its role in the 1951 Humphrey Bogart film.

Swim and play with Atlantic bottlenose dolphins during an amazing Dolphin Encounter at the non-profit Dolphin Research Centre on Grassy Key.

Hike on trails through tropical forests at Crane Point Hammock Botanical Preserve, and visit the Museum of Natural History of the Florida Keys.

Kayak through quiet tidal lagoons and exotic mangrove forests to see wildlife on a guided eco-tour from Marathon or Big Pine Key.

Visit some of Key West's famous museums, including the Ernest Hemingway Home, Mel Fisher Maritime Heritage Museum, Audubon House and Garden, and the Key West Shipwreck Historeum.

Join the fun at Mallory Square as street performers provide fascinating entertainment, then watch the sunset and take part in the applause.

Fly on a seaplane or take the ferry to Fort Jefferson and Dry Tortugas National Park for a fascinating day trip on these remote islands

Dos and Don'ts

☑ Make reservations early as the best accommodation fills up quickly and the Dolphin Encounter sells out in advance.

☒ Don't forget that the sun is very intense, so wear a hat and sunglasses, and use plenty of sunblock.

☑ Read the regulations for fishing and diving, which can be obtained from the Florida Marine Patrol. Florida is very serious about coral reef protection, fish management and regulation enforcement.

JAN

FEB

DAY 1

DAYS 2–3

DAYS 4–5

MAR

APR

MAY

JUN

JUL

AUG

SEP

OCT

NOV

DEC

Below: Coral reef teeming with fish at Key Largo

TASMAN SEA

Auckland
Rotorua
Napier
WELLINGTON
NEW ZEALAND
Christchurch
PACIFIC OCEAN
Dunedin

GETTING THERE
New Zealand's North Island sits between the Tasman Sea and the South Pacific Ocean. Most international flights to the North Island arrive in Auckland. Wellington, the capital, is mainly served by domestic and Australian flights.

GETTING AROUND
Car hire is available from all major towns and airports and is the best way to explore the country. New Zealand also has an excellent public transport system, especially coaches.

WEATHER
February is warm with average temperatures hovering around 24–30°C and low rainfall.

ACCOMMODATION
Coromandel Colonial Cottages Motel in the Coromandel has a family cottage from £80; www.corocottagesmotel.co.nz

Rotorua Top 10 Holiday Park has two-bedroom units from £60; www.rotoruatop10.co.nz

Waiwhenua Farm and Homestay in Napier welcomes camper vans and has a cottage that sleeps six; from £55; www.waiwhenua.co.nz

EATING OUT
You can get a good meal for around £14 a head throughout the country. The Chocolate Fish Café in Wellington is a quirky seaside café – a favourite with the *Lord of the Rings* film crew.

PRICE FOR A FAMILY OF FOUR
£200–250 per day including accommodation, food, entrance charges and car hire.

FURTHER INFORMATION
www.newzealand.com/travel

Treaties and Traditions

6 February is Waitangi Day, a public holiday that celebrates the signing of the 1840 Treaty of Waitangi between Maori chiefs and the British Crown. Although the treaty remains a contentious issue, awareness of Maori heritage has increased in recent years. This has resulted in a rebirth of traditional crafts, such as wood carving, which continue the Pacific island traditions of Maori forefathers.

ISLAND OF PLENTY

IMAGINE A LAND WHERE EVERYONE LIVES WITHIN EASY REACH OF UNSPOILED BEACHES, lush forest trails, gently rolling farmland and sparkling rivers. Where mountains are shrouded in legend and the surrounding islands are sub-tropical idylls, rich in rare flora and fauna. Where the inhabitants have some of the world's best culinary ingredients and finest wines right on their doorstep. New Zealand's North Island has all of this, coupled with a sunny summer climate that is hard to resist.

At its volcanic heart, vast lakes are cradled in ancient craters and towering volcano cones are powerful reminders of the landscape's turbulent past. In this geothermal paradise, the land itself seems alive; geysers spout plumes of boiling, mineral-rich water, steam drifts eerily across a lunar landscape, silica terraces provide a kaleidoscope of colour, and slurping cauldrons of bubbling mud plop lazily, creating ripples in ever-increasing circles. These natural phenomena are key to the ancient Maori culture that flourishes on the island, an intrinsic part of the land.

Below (top to bottom): Art Deco architecture in Napier; thermal pool at Rotorua; Auckland skyline at night

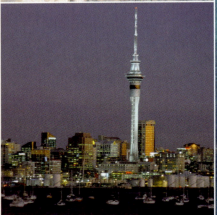

There's a real sense of openness here, in the landscape and the friendly people, making it a great place for families. Hiring a car or a camper van to tour the North Island will enable you to really experience all that is on offer. Cities and seaside towns have themed attractions; there are museums, like Te Papa (Maori for "Our Place") in Wellington, that will captivate children with their hands-on displays and unusual exhibits; while farm stays allow children to get a true sense of rural life here. From endless activities at self-catering holiday parks to toy baskets in cafés and kids menus in family restaurants, there is always much to entertain the children, and its small size means that travelling distances will never be too much.

Most of all, it is nature's attractions that will capture young imaginations. Where else can you walk in a rainforest, watch mud boil, find gemstones on a beach, dig your own mineral pool in the sand, and eat the freshest fish and chips ever in the shade of giant kauri trees, all over the course of just a few days? The North Island will astound you with opportunities for exploration and excitement, filling your mind with countless picture-postcard scenes of incredible landscapes.

Main: Urupukapuka Island in the Bay of Islands

Above (top to bottom): Enjoying the stunning countryside by camper van; whitewater rafting at Rotorua; Skyline Gondola luge ride in Rotorua

Below: Waikawau Bay on the Coromandel Peninsula

SCENIC DIARY

February is summertime, which means great weather for exploring. In three weeks you can discover the diversity of land and activities that the North Island offers. Distances are not great, but roads can be winding. Between activity-filled Auckland and Wellington lie brilliant beaches, vast lakes, forests and mountains.

Three Weeks Touring the North

In Auckland, cruise Waitemata Harbour, shop in trendy Parnell, catch the ferry to Devonport, picnic on a Hauraki Gulf island and visit the brilliant Kelly Tarlton's Antarctic Encounter and Underwater World.

North of Auckland, the Bay of Islands will enchant you with its beautiful beaches. While here, visit the Waitangi Treaty Grounds, where Maoris and government leaders gather each year on 6 February to mark Waitangi Day.

Head south to the Coromandel Peninsula to enjoy more idyllic beaches. Visit Waiau Kauri Grove, snorkel in Mercury Bay or dig a thermal pool at Hot Water Beach.

Head for Rotorua for scenic lakes, Maori culture and a geothermal extravaganza. Highlights include the sheep-shearing show at the Agrodome, the Skyline Gondola luge ride and Ohinemutu Maori Village. Then see the terraces and Pohutu geyser at Te Whakarewarewa.

Drive through Urewera National Park to Gisborne, the Chardonnay capital of New Zealand. Further on, in Napier, see Art Deco buildings, dinosaur footprints in the Hawkes Bay Museum and dolphins at Marineland.

Follow the spectacular coast to the gannet colony at Cape Kidnappers, or do a vineyard wine trail in Hawkes Bay.

Drive to Wellington through rolling farmland and country towns. Stop at Pukaha Mt Bruce for a rainforest walk and views of rare native birds. Spend a day at the exciting Te Papa museum and take the cable car up to the Botanic Gardens.

Dos and Don'ts

☑ Take off your shoes when entering a Maori meeting house, even when it is in a museum. Always ask permission before looking around a *marae* (Maori meeting grounds).

☒ Don't forget to wear sunscreen, sunglasses and a hat. With low air pollution, UV rays are very strong in the summer.

☑ Bring back Maori crafts. Children love pendants carved in traditional motifs, and they are light and easy to pack; wood carvings are heavy but make unusual souvenirs.

☑ Experience a traditional Maori *hangi*, where food is cooked on hot rocks in an authentic earth oven.

Below: Farmland and the Tukituki Hills at Hawkes Bay

JAN

FEB

DAYS 1–3

DAYS 4–6

DAYS 7–9

DAYS 10–12

DAYS 13–15

DAYS 16–17

DAYS 18–21

MAR

APR

MAY

JUN

JUL

AUG

SEP

OCT

NOV

DEC

GETTING THERE
Salvador lies on Brazil's northeastern coast. The international airport, Deputado Luis Eduardo Magalhães, is 34 km (21 miles) north of the city. Taxis from the airport to Pelourinho are around £15, the bus is £1.25.

GETTING AROUND
Taxis are recommended in the evening for safety, during the day visitors can get around on foot quite easily.

WEATHER
During Carnival expect hot, sunny days with an average maximum temperature of around 30°C.

ACCOMMODATION
For Carnival, you should reserve your accommodation 3–6 months ahead of time and there is usually a minimum stay of 5 nights.

Salvador Ibis, Rio Vermelho, is a budget option; doubles from £20; www.accorhotels.com.br

Pousada do Pilar is a beautifully restored heritage building in Pelourinho; doubles from £40; www.pousadadopilar.com

Monte Pascoal Praia hotel sits on Barra beach; doubles from £60; www.montepascoal.com.br

EATING OUT
Local cuisine focuses on seafood, often served in *moqueca* stews, with coconut milk, spices and palm oil. A large meal will cost around £9.

PRICE FOR TWO
£100–125 per day including accommodation, food and entrance charges.

FURTHER INFORMATION
www.bahiacarnival.com

The Room of Miracles
Salvador's symbolic church, Nosso Senhor do Bonfim, is famous for its power to perform miracles. Inside, in the *Sala dos Milagres* – Room of Miracles grateful worshippers have hung replica heads, limbs and organs to give thanks for miracles performed curing their afflicted body parts. The ostensibly Catholic church is also frequented by followers of the Afro-Brazilian religion *Candomblé*, which combines seemingly unreconcilable elements of Catholic worship with African spiritualist traditions.

Main: Celebrating Carnival in style, hundreds and thousands of partygoers dance in the streets
Above (top to bottom): Historic upper town of Pelourinho; woman in traditional Bahian dress; endless sandy coastline of Bahia

CARNIVAL!

Forget the feathers and floats and girls in tiny bikinis, and forget all notions of being a merely passive observer. The Salvador Carnival (Carnaval to the locals) is all about participation. Two million revellers flock to the Bahian capital to celebrate in an extravagant week-long street party. Hundreds of musicians, many of them Brazil's biggest names, perform musical marathons, singing and dancing for many hours, night after day after night.

Each band, or *bloco*, performs on a massive sound truck called a *trio elétrico*, a stage and multi-gigawatt monster sound system combined. Pied-piper like, the performers are followed by supporters, often dressed in specially co-ordinated outfits, and an excited crowd dancing in a musical frenzy as the truck slowly wends its way through narrow streets. Behind, in front and all around the *trios*, hundreds of thousands of people gather for the sheer fun of it – to drink, sing and dance, to kiss a perfect stranger, make instant friends and the next day do it all over again.

Above: Elaborate gilded interior of Igreja São Francisco Salvador da Bahia

Below: Costumed dancer representing the God of Medicine in a ritual *Candomblé* dance

SALVADOR DIARY

Carnival, is a last wild celebration before the 40 days of Lenten abstinence. The dates change every year due to the lunar cycle, but Carnival always takes place in February or early March. If you stay for the full five days you'll be able to join in the fun but relax and rest as well.

The Biggest Party in the World

Explore the historic Pelourinho quarter, the Afro-Brazilian museum and the Convent of São Francisco.

Early in the evening, locals and musicians will start to gather for the more traditional *blocos* which parade through the narrow streets from about 7pm to 2am.

Save your energies for a full evening of Carnival and spend a leisurely day at one of the ocean beaches such as Stella Maris or Flamengo.

Enjoy a late lunch of *moqueca* to fuel up. In the evening, grab your *abadá* (the t-shirt that admits you to a *bloco*), and get dancing.

Enjoy some of the traditional sights around downtown. Starting with the Bonfim church then stop in at the Mercado Modelo for some fine souvenir shopping.

Head over to the nearby Solar do Unhão. This restored 18th-century sugar mill and mansion now houses Salvador's Museum of Modern Art. Come sundown, you still have your *abadá*, so go and dance again.

Spend a day on the water by taking a schooner tour of the islands around the Bay of All Saints.

Around 5pm head to the Barra Lighthouse to catch the sunset and secure yourself a good spot to watch the evening's *trios* as they parade past.

On the last night of Carnival don't miss the "Meeting of the Trios", a final musical get together which takes place in the small hours of the morning of Ash Wednesday at the Praça Castro Alves.

Dos and Don'ts

✓ Wear comfortable shoes, shorts or a skirt with a pocket and a light t-shirt. Leave your valuables at home and carry only enough cash for the day.

✗ Don't procrastinate. Those visiting Salvador for Carnival should book their flights and hotels at least three months ahead of time, if not more, as they fill up quickly.

✓ See as many different *blocos* as possible. Even if you buy an *abadá* for one *bloco* or *trio*, you can still mix and match to experience a number of others.

✗ Don't sleep in too late if you want to do some sightseeing. The easiest time to get around before the crowds gather is between 10am and 2pm.

Below: Papayas, pineapples and bananas hang from a street stall.

JAN

FEB

DAY 1

DAY 2

DAY 3

DAY 4

DAY 5

MAR

APR

MAY

JUN

JUL

AUG

SEP

OCT

NOV

DEC

If you want, you can buy an *abadá* (a t-shirt-cum-ticket) that allows access to a large roped off area immediately behind the stage truck. Dozens of rope-carriers hold the rope ensuring that the cordon stays intact as the throng moves through the streets. Or you can opt to be a *pipoca* (a popcorn) and bop around in the slightly more unruly crowd on the fringes of the roped-off area.

As well as the big names of Brazilian music that perform regularly at Carnival, including Daniela Mercury, Gilberto Gil and Carlinhos Brown, there are dozens more traditional, community-based *blocos*. The Afro-Brazilian *bloco* Ilê Ayê kicks off Carnival with a Candomblé ceremony the night before the parade. The Filhos de Ghandi (Sons of Ghandi) are a popular all male *bloco*, who parade dressed in white Ghandi robes to the sound of African Afoxé drumming.

On Shrove Tuesday, the very last night of Carnival when most of the rest of Brazil is already sleeping, Carnival in Salvador comes to a dramatic close with the "Meeting of the Trios". In the early hours of Ash Wednesday morning, all the *blocos* that are still parading head to Praça Castro Alves and join together for a last joint concert, one that ends just as the sun rises over Salvador.

MARCH

Where to Go: **March**

The start of spring in the northern hemisphere brings a time of birth and renewal. Green shoots begin to appear and the temperatures start to improve. Around the world there are festivals celebrating rebirth and the end of winter. In the USA and Canada, the Spring Break sees thousands of college kids hit the beaches to party. Be warned it's a riotous affair, so you may wish to avoid their favourite spots like Florida, Cancun and Acapulco. In the reversed seasons of the southern hemisphere, Australia is entering autumn, although the northern part of Australia is in the Tropics so it really only has two seasons – wet and dry. To help you choose, you'll find all the destinations in this chapter below, as well as some extra suggestions to provide a little inspiration.

FESTIVALS AND CULTURE

YUCATÁN Temple of the Warriors at Chichén Itzá

UNFORGETTABLE JOURNEYS

HIMALAYAS The majestic peaks of Makalu

NATURAL WONDERS

NINGALOO Colourful sea starfish

YUCATÁN
MEXICO, NORTH AMERICA

See the Mayan pyramids for the descent of Kukulkan

As well as the ancient pyramids there's also great beaches, fresh-water cave systems (cenotes) and even a dense green jungle.
See pp64–5

ANTIGUA
GUATEMALA, CENTRAL AMERICA

A joyful celebration of Semana Santa in a pretty colonial city

Carpets of petals cover the streets for processions of religious statues carried by the joyful locals. Enjoy too the colonial architecture.
See pp84–5

ROUTE 66
USA, NORTH AMERICA

"Go west" may be a cliché but some clichés are worth doing

The urge to travel west is ingrained in the psyche of the USA – it has historically been a trip of promise and it still delivers on that.
www.historic66.com

HIMALAYAS
NEPAL, ASIA

An amazing journey hiking and rafting down mountains

The beauty of so many high peaks takes your breath away (as does the altitude), so will the other sights of this magical kingdom.
See pp68–9

"Discover a vibrant array of corals, manta rays, turtles, clownfish and sea stars, suspended in pristine harmony."

NINGALOO
AUSTRALIA, AUSTRALASIA

A vast pristine reef, home to a colourful fish and corals

Snorkel or dive with the 18-m (60-ft) whale sharks and other marine life as they follow the trail of eggs from the spawning coral.
See pp78–9

BERLIN
GERMANY, EUROPE

A weekend of great culture and cutting-edge nightlife

It may have great museums and history but Berlin's racing into the future with hip clubs, restaurants and top modern architecture.
See pp74–5

"Young art galleries and boutiques sprout up next to sombre-looking museums loaded with highbrow culture."

VICTORIA COAST
AUSTRALIA, AUSTRALASIA

Classic camper-van country for koalas and penguins

Drive along the south coast to see the penguins on Phillip Island and kangaroos and koalas in the Wilson's Promontory NP.
www.parkweb.vic.gov.au

AZORES
PORTUGAL, EUROPE

Go whale watching on these beautiful volcanic islands

These islands were once home to whale hunters and are now one of the best places for whale- and dolphin-watching.
www.azores.com

SARAWAK
BORNEO, ASIA

Meet your red-haired relatives, the great orang-utans

Set in virgin rainforest, Sepilok Rehabilitation Centre is a great place to watch primates learn to fend for themselves.
www.visitborneo.com

IZMIR
TURKEY, EUROPE

Ideal base for exploring many Roman and Greek sites

By the glorious Aegean Sea, some of the best preserved ancient ruins in the world can be found nearby – Ephesus, Pergamon and Hierapolis.
www.allaboutturkey.com

DOURO CRUISE
PORTUGAL, EUROPE

Cruise down the beautiful Douro valley – Port to Port

Dine in fabulous *pousadas* while following the port wine route to Porto. See monasteries, cathedrals and 16th-century gardens.
www.visitportugal.com

KWAZULU-NATAL
SOUTH AFRICA, AFRICA

A perfect beach that attracts more than sun worshippers

The 40-km (25-mile) beach is so quiet that turtles lay their eggs there and it is great for snorkelling, diving or horseback riding.
www.rocktailbay.com

BARSANA
INDIA, ASIA

Marking the onset of spring, Holi festival is literally a riot of colour

Northern India explodes with dusty clouds of coloured paint in an exuberant celebration. See the sights of Delhi on the way back.
See pp80–81

E & O EXPRESS
SINGAPORE, ASIA

Enjoy the historic and elegant Eastern & Oriental Express

Travel in comfort from Singapore via Georgetown, Fort Cornwallis and the infamous bridge over the River Kwai to Bangkok.
www.orient-express.com

ISLA FERNANDO DE NORONHA
BRAZIL, SOUTH AMERICA

Isolated tropical islands

Enjoy the small-scale tourism on these volcanic islands and go diving to explore the unique marine ecosystem.
www.noronha.com.br

Previous page: Devotees wave incense through the streets during Holy Week in Guatemala

Weather Watch

❶ The weather in the Canadian Rockies is a little warmer than midwinter but there's still good snow for skiing and a few sunny days.

❷ The Yucatán peninsula is hot at this time of year, as is much of South America, but low humidity and rainfall just about keep it pleasant and it's perfect for relaxing on the beach.

❸ Berlin's easterly position and proximity to Russia mean that there's little evidence of spring warmth, but at least it's usually the driest month.

❹ In Morocco, the Atlas Mountains keep out the dry heat of the Sahara and allow the temperature on the coast to remain at pleasant Mediterranean levels.

❺ The weather in Nepal depends on where you are – up in the Himalayas, it's snow and ice, while in the lowlands it is sunny and warm.

❻ Millions of Ningaloo corals spawn at the same time just after the full moon and when the water temperature is right for corals, it's also perfect for snorkelling and diving.

LUXURY AND ROMANCE

MARRAKESH The luxurious interior of a *riad*

ACTIVE ADVENTURES

WHISTLER Skiing the majestic slopes

FAMILY GETAWAYS

CHICAGO Colourfully dressed Irish dancers

THE ISLES OF SCILLY
ENGLAND, EUROPE

Luxurious hotels, lush gardens and a relaxed pace of life

It just feels different and romantic – you fly over by helicopter and there are beautiful sea views everywhere, topped off with a temperate climate.
www.simplyscilly.co.uk

CASTLE LESLIE
IRELAND, EUROPE

History, grandeur and a healthy dash of eccentricity

This castle has entertained the great and good – and even ghosts and UFOs – with cookery classes, riding school and fishing.
www.castleleslie.com

WHISTLER
CANADA, NORTH AMERICA

Heli-ski from the highest peaks through perfect deep powder

Whistler's two huge and scenic mountains provide unforgettable skiing and snowboarding and a lively and fun après-ski too.
See pp76–7

SOUTH DOWNS
ENGLAND, EUROPE

A bracing walk through the picturesque rolling countryside

Often ignored by commuters rushing to London from Brighton this quaint and historic area has pretty villages and cosy pubs.
www.visitsouthdowns.com

> "Pumping out clouds of gunpowder smoke, the fireworks explode with such ferocity that the ground literally judders."

VALENCIA
SPAIN, EUROPE

Paella, hot chocolate, dough-nuts and fireworks galore

Fallas festival involves burning huge papier-maché puppets, watching explosive firework displays and non-stop partying.
See pp66–7

MARRAKESH
MOROCCO, AFRICA

The rose city is awash with colours, aromas and romance

On a historic trade route, this city provides an intoxicating mix of spicy bazaars, peaceful Atlas mountains and luxurious *riads* (traditional hotels).
See pp72–3

SEYCHELLES
INDIAN OCEAN

Idyllic archipelago of over 100 islands in the Indian Ocean

Home to some of the most perfect beaches in the world, these fantastic palm-covered islands are washed by deliciously warm blue water.
www.seychelles.com

TIGNES
FRANCE, EUROPE

Top ski resort that also caters for snowboarders

Nice and high so it gets plenty of snow, this huge expanse of terrain has exhilarating powdery bowls and some over-the-top nightlife.
www.tignes.co.uk

CHICAGO
USA, NORTH AMERICA

St Patrick's Day – enjoy the parades and the Guinness

Take part in the *craic* in this most Irish of American cities. Too much Guinness though and you'll match the colour of the river – green.
See pp70–71

CAMARGUE
FRANCE, EUROPE

A magical part of France with pink flamingoes and cowboys

Lots for children here from the wildlife of the marshes to Crusader forts and the distinctively attired cowboys and their black bulls.
www.camargue.fr

PERHENTIAN ISLANDS
MALAYSIA, ASIA

Get away from it all on quiet, castaway beaches

Palm trees, white sand and clear water make these islands a deliciously indulgent destination.
See pp82–3

BONAIRE
DUTCH ANTILLES, CARIBBEAN

Regularly voted the best diving destination in the world

Set in a Marine Park, the coral reefs and clear water – little rain to disturb the view – make it great for underwater photography.
www.geographia.com/bonaire

FOSSIL RIM
USA, NORTH AMERICA

Overnight in this vast safari park near Fort Worth, Texas

This extraordinary park brings the sights, sounds and smells of Africa to you. Plus you're not far from lots of rodeo and sports action.
www.fossilrim.com

> "This is a paradise, where you can spend hours watching turtles do their own thing and…forget the problems of the world you left behind."

BERMUDA
NORTH ATLANTIC

Golf is an important part of daily life on this island

There's a higher density of golf courses here than anywhere else and the weather is great. Afterwards enjoy the pink sand beaches.
www.bermuda.com

NORFOLK
ENGLAND, EUROPE

Explore the springtime beauty of this eastern county

Follow the miles of footpaths along historic waterways and through quiet countryside for a taste of rural life.
www.visitnorfolk.co.uk

GETTING THERE
The Yucatán Peninsula is in SE Mexico between the Gulf of Mexico and the Caribbean. Cancún airport handles most international flights, Merida mostly domestic ones.

GETTING AROUND
First-class buses are a good way of getting between the main destinations in Mexico, but a car is essential if you want to explore more freely.

WEATHER
Tropical and hot, with an average daytime temperature of 31°C, cooler at nights (19°C).

ACCOMMODATION
Some of the more enjoyable hotels have wonderful Spanish colonial architecture.

Chan-Kah Village Palenque hotel has a lovely pool; doubles from £60; www.chan-kah.com.mx

Hacienda Chichén is next to Chichén Itzá's ruins; doubles from £80; www.haciendachichen.com

Hacienda San José Cholul, elegant luxury; doubles from £175; www.haciendasmexico.com

EATING OUT
Hacienda hotels all have restaurants, open to non-guests, serving refined local cooking in lovely settings. Mérida has plenty of charming restaurants, and by the coast there are always a few good seafood cafés. In Palenque, there are likeable places to eat around the town square. You can eat well for £10, or a good deal less.

PRICE FOR TWO
£120–160 per day including accommodation, food, car hire and entry to sites.

FURTHER INFORMATION
www.yucatantoday.com

The Mayan Ball Game

Dating back over 3,000 years, the Mayan Ball Game is one of the oldest sports known to man. There are courts in all the ancient Mexican cities, but the Great Ball Court of Chichén Itzá at 160 m (525 ft) long is the largest. Here, opposing teams of seven players had to get the ball through stone rings on either side using only the hips, shoulders, head or chest – and the ball couldn't touch the ground. It appears the game played a major part in Mayan religion, and losers were sometimes killed as human sacrifices.

Above (left to right): Windsurfing boards on Cancún beach; Celestún mangrove swamp; Hilton Hotel, Cancún behind Las Ruinas del Rey
Main: Temple of the Inscriptions at Palenque

MAYAN MYSTERY TOUR

BRILLIANT SUNLIGHT PICKS OUT THE TAIL OF A GIANT FEATHERED SERPENT carved alongside the great north staircase of El Castillo, the massive pyramid at the heart of the ruined Mayan city of Chichén Itzá. As the afternoon moves on, seven triangles of light form a zigzag on the great pyramid's steps and bring the serpent to life; as the sun moves across the sky, they expand to join up in another zigzag that seems to slither slowly down the ramp, all the way to the gaping jaws of the monstrous head at the stairway's foot. Across the grass plaza around the pyramid thousands of patient onlookers watch the spectacle, awestruck. This phenomenon – the Descent of Kukulcán – happens every year on the spring equinox. Aligned with sun and stars with extraordinary precision, El Castillo was built around AD 800. With 365 steps around its four sides, one for each day of the year, it is in effect a supersized clock, a representation in stone of the intricate Mayan calendar. More of the complex, surprising culture of the ancient Maya can also be seen across Mexico's

"In the romance of the world's history, nothing ever impressed me more forcibly than the spectacle of this once great and lovely city."

ohn L. Stephens writing on Palenque

Yucatán peninsula – from the elegant architecture of Uxmal to the ruins of Palenque, with its labyrinthine Mayan palace and temples rising up the hills amid the thick rainforests of Chiapas. The Maya are also very much alive in the Yucatán today and are very welcoming and charming hosts. This same charm extends into the region's towns and its capital, Mérida, a tropical Spanish colonial city of tranquil squares, shady colonnades and intimate patios. In the rest of the Yucatán, the landscape is equally special, with long white sandy beaches washed by warm seas; verdant forests alive with birds, from hummingbirds to flocks of flamingos; and the cenotes. These unique features are natural "sinkholes" in the local limestone that lead down to underground rivers of crystalline fresh water. To the ancient Maya they were gateways to the underworld, but they're also blissfully cool and magical places to swim.

Inset: Pool in a naturally formed limestone cave or *cenote*
Below (left and right): Serpent on the El Castillo steps, Chichén Itzá; Temple of the Warriors, Chichén Itzá

MAYAN DIARY

Yucatán has many flavours but a week or so will allow an insight into Mayan culture – sun worshippers, nature lovers or divers may want a few more days swimming, touring, or diving at Cozumel. The Descent of Kukulcán can be seen from mid-February into April, but is at its best at the equinox, on 20 and 21 March.

Eight Days in the Yucatán

Arriving in Cancún, try out the 23-km (15-mile) beach and maybe lunch in a beachside restaurant. The next day, have another morning on the beach, pick up the car, and drive 200 km (125 miles) to Chichén Itzá.

Look around Chichén Itzá ruins – but get back to the main plaza by at least 12 noon to pick a good spot to see the Descent of Kukulcán, at its best around 4pm.

Drive west to Izamal and its golden ochre buildings; there's a Spanish colonial monastery here built among the remains of Mayan pyramids. Continue on to Mérida.

Wander around Mérida's Plaza Mayor then take a cab to the Paseo Montejo which has an excellent museum of Mayan relics. Eat at one of its great terrace restaurants.

Make the 1-hour drive to Uxmal before touring other Mayan sites – Kabah, Sayil, Xlapak and Labná – in the bird-filled woods of the Puuc Hills. Descend into the awesome caves at Loltún before returning to Mérida.

In the morning, drive to Celestún to explore the mangrove lagoon, a must for any bird watchers, or simply relax on the beach at Progreso. Then hand back the hire car and fly to Villahermosa for a two-hour transfer to Palenque.

Make the most of your last day by getting to Palenque early as the ruins are often shrouded in an atmospheric mist. Climb as many pyramids as you can before exhaustion sets in. Cool off in a hotel pool before heading back to Cancún and flying home.

Dos and Don'ts

✗ Don't forget to book early for the equinox dates – hotels are always very busy at that time of year.

✓ Enjoy tropical fruit juices, fresh from the *juguerías* (stands). They're refreshing in the heat and keep vitamin levels up.

✗ Don't plan on driving at night. There is little lighting, and potholes and bicycles can be hard to see.

✓ Ask your hotel to make you a packed lunch for the Descent of Kukulcán as the nearby cafés will alll have big queues.

JAN	
FEB	
MAR	
19th–20th	
21st	
22nd	
23rd	
24th	
25th	
26th	
APR	
MAY	
JUN	
JUL	
AUG	
SEP	
OCT	
NOV	
DEC	

Below: Mérida, Mercado Municipal (city market)

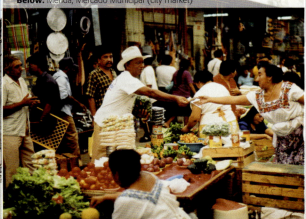

The Origins of the Fallas

The earliest *fallas*, in the 13th or 14th century, were simply huge piles of wood shavings and scrap wood from carpentry workshops burnt in a fiery celebration of the end of winter. Over time, the *fallas* evolved into satirical, almost cartoonish works of art. A *falla* refers to the whole wooden construction on which the *ninot* or figure is placed.

FIREWORK FRENZY

PUMPING OUT CLOUDS OF GUNPOWDER SMOKE, the fireworks explode with such ferocity that the ground literally judders and shockwaves of earshattering noise physically jar your insides. The explosions get louder and louder until you think you just can't take any more. Then it's over and the crowd, partly out of delight and partly out of relief, bursts into spontaneous applause. Today's *mascletà* – a daytime firework display that is not exactly something you see, more something you feel – is over, and tomorrow's will probably be even louder. This is part of the Fallas Festival in Valencia, a three-week-long boisterous celebration of fireworks, explosions and processions in honour of St Joseph, the patron saint of carpenters.

> Today's *mascletà* – a daytime firework display that is not exactly something you see, more something you feel – is over, and tomorrow's will probably be even louder.

After a week of colourful processions, traditional music and nightly firework displays, the most famous part of the festival begins (15–19 March) when over 300 huge elaborate papier-maché sculptures – the *fallas* – are set up in the streets to be inspected and judged on their artistic merit. Throughout the festival there is an air of unruly celebration that slowly builds to a crescendo of hysteria and anarchy. Traditionally, the revellers are sustained by creamy hot chocolate (made with real melted chocolate) and delicious sugar-dusted *churros* (a straight, deep-fried type of doughnut), while the more hardcore partygoers seek stronger stimulation around the clock in the fashionable bars and restaurants of the Barrio del Carmen.

On the final night, and with the crowd's eager encouragement, the firework-packed sculptures are set alight by local girls, the Fallas Queens, who are dressed immaculately in traditional costumes. As the flames greedily consume each work of art, the ecstatic onlookers pull back to avoid the heat and firefighters nonchalantly hose down the windows of neighbouring flats, occasionally flicking great plumes of water over the spectators. Within minutes, each sculpture, which typically take six months to create, has been burned to the ground in a spectacular fiery climax of wanton destruction and wood smoke. By the next morning, everything is back to normal, barring the odd scorch mark or spent rocket.

Main: *Falla* sculpture, or *ninot,* in the Playa de La Reina burning fiercely on the last night of the festival
Below (left and right): Firecrackers waiting to be lit; restaurant in the fashionable Barrio del Carmen, specializing in paella
Inset: Detail of colourful *ninot* before the final burning

FALLAS DIARY

Although the festival lasts three weeks, the key events occur between 17 and 19 of March. Five days should be enough time to enjoy the festivities as well as to see what else this cultured city has to offer. March brings ideal weather for getting out and about, as the days are warm and it seldom rains.

Five Days of Celebrations

Climb the tower of the Gothic cathedral for an excellent overview of the old town.

Eat a leisurely paella lunch, washed down with *agua de valencia* (cava and orange juice).

Tour the ancient silk market, a beautiful monument to the wealth brought by trade with the east.

Wander around town admiring the comic artistry of the short-lived *fallas* sculptures. Experience your first *mascletà* before seeing Moorish-influenced crafts at the Ceramics Museum.

Enjoy the aromas of the Ofrenda Virgen ceremony, when children in traditional dress strew millions of flower petals around a statue of the Virgin Mary.

Carry on the sensory overload with a visit to the Central Market, full of sumptuous local produce.

Admire the skill of Spanish masters such as Goya, Velasquez and El Greco at the Fine Arts Museum. Eat lunch in the Barrio del Carmen before experiencing the big *mascletà* in the Playa Ayuntamiento.

Alternatively, take a tram to one of Valencia's expansive sandy beaches and enjoy some peace and quiet.

Visit the City of Arts and Sciences – walk via glass tunnels through the shark tanks in the aquarium, or marvel at the stars in the planetarium.

Remember to have a siesta to prepare you for the last night of festivities – the spectacular burning of the *fallas* and the final fireworks display and party.

Dos and Don'ts

✓ Join the locals and get into the habit of taking a siesta – it's the only way to survive the partying.

✓ Make sure your restaurant is cooking your paella from scratch – they should tell you it will take 20 minutes.

✓ If you want to do a tour of the *fallas* sculptures get up early, as the city gets busy after 11am.

✗ Don't drive your car into the city during the festival as heavy traffic and no parking will make the journey a nightmare.

JAN
FEB
MAR
15th
16th
17th
18th
19th
APR
MAY
JUN
JUL
AUG
SEP
OCT
NOV
DEC

Below: L'Hemisferic planetarium and cinema in the City of Arts and Sciences

GETTING THERE
Nepal is a landlocked mountain country between India and China. International flights arrive into Tribhuvan International Airport, 6 km (4 miles) from the capital, Kathmandu.

GETTING AROUND
To travel around Kathmandu, hire a car and driver, auto-rickshaw or bicycle. The best way to reach Lukla, at the start of the trek, is by domestic flight.

WEATHER
In February it is fairly mild and dry at lower elevations, averaging around 11°C. It is a lot colder at higher altitudes, often dropping below freezing at night. The weather can change suddenly.

ACCOMMODATION
An excellent budget option is Kathmandu Guest House; doubles from £10; www.ktmgh.com

Shanker Hotel, a heritage hotel located in a century-old Rana palace in Kathmandu; doubles from £50; www.shankerhotel.com.np

Hotel Yak and Yeti is Kathmandu's leading deluxe hotel; doubles from £95; www.yakandyeti.com

EATING OUT
The staple food of most Nepalis – and the most easily available, especially on treks – is *dal bhat tarkari* (lentils, rice and lightly curried vegetables). *Gundruk*, a tangy dish made of dried and fermented vegetables, and *tama* (bamboo shoots) are also popular.

PRICE FOR TWO
£100–130 per day including accommodation, guide, local travel and internal flights.

FURTHER INFORMATION
www.welcomenepal.com

The Legend of the Yeti

Although tales of a large, hairy, ape-like creature wandering in the snowy reaches of the Himalayas only reached the outside world during the days of British rule in India, the yeti has been a central figure in Sherpa and Tibetan folk tales for hundreds of years. The frequency of reported sightings increased in the 20th century and interest peaked in the 1950s when British explorer Eric Shipton took photographs of prints in the snow, said to be the yeti's. While sceptics dismiss the yeti as a legend, it endures in the imaginations of many.

JOURNEY INTO THE CLOUDS

NEPAL IS THE CROWN OF THE INDIAN SUBCONTINENT, set against a stunning backdrop of the Himalayas, which stretch like a spine across the north of the country. It is a "must-see" destination for all those who want to walk, trek or climb difficult mountain terrains. There are many treks to choose from, which are all well organized, with comfortable camp sites en route. Wander across flower-strewn meadows, walk along dramatic ridges and wade through mountain steams. At night, warm your energized but physically tired body and liberated soul by a crackling bonfire in a pristine Nepalese village where the country's cultural roots are still very much intact.

Nepal is a wonderful and fascinating amalgam of two great faiths and cultures – Hindu and Buddhist. Temples, roadside shrines and *gompas* (monasteries) appear in the remotest of places, from the plateaus to towering mountain ranges and around high altitude lakes. The Nepalese are a hardy and hospitable people, shaped by their difficult landscape, yet ever ready to make you feel at home,

Main: The stupa of Bodhnath Temple near Kathmandu

which is always a surprising comfort on a strenuous trek or climb. Any mountain experience you have in this fascinating country will undoubtedly be coloured by the warm hospitality of the locals.

The Himalayas are an intrinsic part of any trip to Nepal, looming over the country with their snow-capped peaks that often seem to disappear into the sky. Of the country's eight Himalayan mountains, Everest is, of course, the main draw. Although undoubtedly hard work and only for the fit, the trek to Everest Base Camp is a memorable experience, one that pays dividends once you have seen the stunning views of the mountain at the end. The base camp is the furthest that you can go without mountaineering equipment, and the trek from Lukla to the camp takes around seven days, which includes vital time to acclimatize to the high altitude. Passing through surprisingly lush valleys that are filled with wildflowers and spending the night in Sherpa villages where the traditional culture of these mountain people still flourishes, you will be constantly surprised by all that this mountain kingdom has to offer. Nepal is a treasure trove of trails and climbs that are unmatched in the world, a land that embodies the mysticism and magic of the east.

BASE CAMP DIARY

Stretching for 800 km (500 miles) and home to eight of the world's 10 highest mountains, the majestic Himalayas are the prime attraction for most visitors to Nepal. March is a good time for trekking, with mild spring weather, wildflowers in bloom and spectacular rhododendrons blanketing the hillsides.

Two Weeks in the Himalayas

Arrive in Kathmandu and spend the afternoon exploring the atmospheric lanes and temples of the old town. Later, take the short trip to Bodhnath to see the incredible stupa, built by Tibetan B uddhists.

Fly on to Lukla, to find your guide before trekking the 3 hours to Phakding, a small village. After a night here, walk for 5 hours to Namche Bazaar, nestled in a horseshoe-shaped bowl. Apart from equipment, this Sherpa "capital" sells anything a trekker might conceivably need.

Have a day in Namche Bazaar to acclimatize. Next, head northeast to Tengboche, 5 hours away. Amid juniper forests, the town offers a fantastic view of Ama Dablan peak and a lovely monastery. The trail continues to Dingboche, another 5 hours away.

Spend another day acclimatizing, either at Dingboche or with a trip to the Chukung Valley with its excellent views of Makalu Peak. The next day, follow the trail as it bends north past the incredible Khumbu Glacier and on to Lobuche. After a night here, a 4-hour trek leads from Lobuche to Gorak Shep, which has the last few teahouses on the trail. Then make your way across the Khumbu Glacier to Everest Base Camp, which sits at an altitude of 5,380 m (17,600 ft). Appreciate the astounding views before turning back to Gorak Shep to spend the evening celebrating the feat.

Retrace your steps back to Lukla and on to Kathmandu ready for your return journey.

Dos and Don'ts

✗ Don't forget to take your rubbish off the mountain with you – littering is big problem here and negatively affects the environment.

✗ Don't point with a single finger; use a flat extended hand, especially if indicating a sacred object or place.

✓ Walk around temples and *stupas* in a clockwise direction – anti-clockwise is regarded as inauspicious.

✓ Use two hands rather than one when giving or receiving something, even money, to show appreciation and respect.

JAN	
FEB	
MAR	
DAY 1	
DAYS 2–3	
DAYS 4–6	
DAYS 7–9	
DAYS 10–15	
APR	
MAY	
JUN	
JUL	
AUG	
SEP	
OCT	
NOV	
DEC	

Above (top to bottom): Trekkers on their way to Everest Base Camp; wooden door decorated with the Buddha's eyes in Kathmandu; colourful market stalls in Kathmandu

Below: Sacred cows lying in the street in Kathmandu

Below: The majestic peaks of Makalu in the Himalayas

GETTING THERE
Chicago is located on Lake Michigan in the US Midwest. It is the 3rd largest city in the USA and one of the country's main transportation hubs. Most international traffic arrives at O'Hare Airport, 32 km (20 miles) northwest of the city centre.

GETTING AROUND
Chicago's elevated railway is a cheap and easy way to get around the city. Over the St Patrick's Day celebrations, the city will be difficult to negotiate with a car so stick to public transport.

WEATHER
March is often overcast in with average daytime high temperatures of 8°C sinking to 0°C at night. Rain is frequent with occasional snow.

ACCOMMODATION
Hotel Burnham is a contemporary hotel; family rooms from £130; www.burnhamhotel.com

The Peninsula Chicago is considered one of the finest hotels in the country; family rooms from £280; www.peninsula.com

Drake Hotel is a Chicago classic since 1920; two double rooms from £370; www.thedrakehotel.com

EATING OUT
For an out-of-the-ordinary experience, tuck into a massive steak at favourite Gibsons (£35) or sample the nationally acclaimed, progressive fare at Alinea (12–24 courses £65–95).

PRICE FOR A FAMILY OF FOUR
£300–320 per day including accommodation, food and a five-day Go Chicago pass.

FURTHER INFORMATION
www.chicagostpatsparade.com

Dyeing the River Green

The tradition of dyeing the Chicago River green was started in 1962, when the mayor allowed a local pipefitters union (sponsors of the parade since 1957) to pour 45 kg (100 lb) of green vegetable dye into the river. These days, the dye is actually an orange colour which then turns to a green after a few seconds in the water, leading some to claim that a leprechaun is at work. The river is dyed at 10:45am and can be best viewed from the upper level bridges at Michigan Avenue or Columbus Drive.

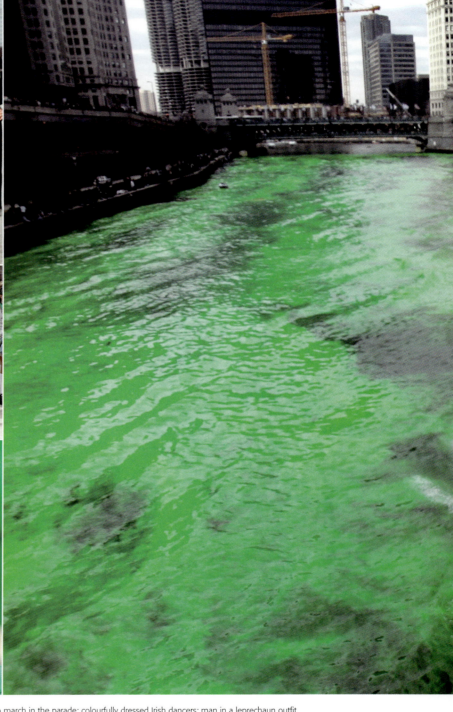

Above (top to bottom): Pipe band prepares to march in the parade; colourfully dressed Irish dancers; man in a leprechaun outfit
Main: Thousands of people line the banks of Chicago's river to watch the water being dyed emerald green for the St Patrick's Day celebrations

A TASTE OF IRISH AMERICA

Hundreds of green, white and orange flags flap in the wind; Irish dancers in skirts and white stockings pound out a rhythm on the asphalt, feet flying faster than the eye can follow; and in the distance, the droning wail of bagpipes, a mournful, dirge-like sound that's a jarring contrast to the happy shouts of face-painted children clad in shamrock green waving American and Irish flags.

It's March in Chicago, and for one rowdy weekend mid-month, the city feels more Irish than Ireland itself. Nearly a million local residents proudly claim the Irish sod as their heritage – back in the mid-19th century, immigrants from Ireland literally built this city – which may explain the fervour with which St Patrick's Day is celebrated here. Chicago hosts not one but two grand parades in honour of Ireland's patron saint on the Saturday and Sunday before the official holiday, drawing hundreds of thousands of Irish people (and Irish-for-a-day) from

Above: Children at the parade waving flags and singing on a float

Below (top and bottom): Interior of the State of Illinois building; high rise office blocks beside the river illuminated in the dusk

PARADE DIARY

Despite the chilly weather, crowds pack Chicago the weekend before St Patrick's Day. Five days is plenty to get a taste of the city's culture, museums, theatre scene and nightlife. Visitors should note that unless the holiday falls on a weekend, the holiday itself can be an anticlimax after the events of the preceding weekend.

Five Days in the Windy City

Stroll through Millennium Park, the city's acclaimed new green space, whose chief attraction is Anish Kapoor's *Cloudgate*, a huge elliptical sculpture of stainless steel. You can also visit the Boeing Galleries.

Admire the view from the skydeck of the Sears Tower, one of the tallest buildings in the world, then grab a steak at Gibsons in the Gold Coast neighbourhood.

Sample the city's incredible 20th-century architecture on a Chicago Architecture Foundation bus tour.

Laugh until it hurts at the Second City, famous for their sketch comedy shows. Order a Chicago-style hot dog from the famously abusive staff at Wieners Circle.

Stuff yourself with the local speciality – gooey, tomatoey deep-dish pizza. Stroll the lake shore path, a great spot for photos of the city skyline. Visit the free Lincoln Park Zoo, one of the oldest zoos in the country.

Enjoy the festive, family-friendly atmosphere of the city's official downtown parade. Head to one of the many Irish pubs to enjoy a post-parade pint.

Wake up early to get down to the South Side before the Sunday parade begins. Then later, catch the Uptown Poetry Slam at legendary jazz hang-out The Green Mill in North Broadway.

Dos and Don'ts

- ✓ Get in the habit of taking public transportation – riding the train, "the El", is a great way to get to know the city and mix with the locals, and it's much less expensive than a taxi.
- ✗ Don't drive into the city on parade day – traffic will be particularly busy.
- ✓ Dress warmly, and in layers, especially during the downtown parade, when wind whips off Lake Michigan.
- ✓ Get off Michigan Avenue and explore the city's many neighbourhoods, from Lincoln Park to Wicker Park and Lincoln Square, they are where the real character of the city lies.

JAN

FEB

MAR

WED

THU

FRI

SAT

SUN

APR

MAY

JUN

JUL

AUG

SEP

OCT

NOV

DEC

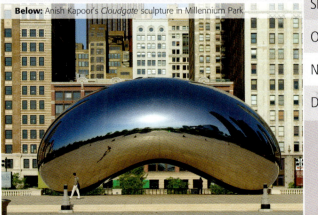

Below: Anish Kapoor's *Cloudgate* sculpture in Millennium Park

the world over. Held on Saturday, the city's official parade is a family affair, a visitor-friendly downtown event complete with an appearance from the mayor, plus thousands of marchers – kilt-clad bagpipers, heritage groups, even the official St Patrick's Day Queen herself, waving cheerily from her float. Sunday witnesses the more local South Side Irish St Patrick's Day parade held in the Beverly neighbourhood, where the increasingly boisterous party goers inside the pubs can make for a more interesting show than the marching bands and floats rolling past.

Indeed, the parades are only part of the story. As early as Friday morning, revellers can already be found queuing up outside the doors of the city's countless Irish bars, which swell with Guinness-drinkers as the weekend begins. Once the first parade is over, the partying truly begins, as parade spectators flood into bars across the city. The celebration doesn't flow into the streets (it's too cold), but by Saturday night, green beer is flowing, fiddlers and bodhran players are sweating through musical extravaganzas and the bacchanalian mood has reached a fever pitch – until the next morning, when everyone gets up, treks to the South Side, and does it all again.

GETTING THERE
Marrakesh is in central Morocco, North Africa. International flights arrive into Menara International Airport, 6.5 km (4 miles) from the city centre, which is 10 minutes by *petit taxi* (£4–7).

GETTING AROUND
The city is best seen by foot or bike but there are plenty of taxis around or you can try the romance of a *calèche* – a horse-drawn carriage.

WEATHER
By March, Marrakesh is heating up, with daytime temperatures of around 23°C, although they drop considerably at night.

ACCOMMODATION
Tchaikana, a beautiful and peaceful *riad*; doubles from £75; www.tchaikana.com

Riad El Cadi has 12 charming rooms and a small swimming pool; doubles from £105; www.riyadelcadi.com

Maison Arabe, a stylish *riad* built around flower-filled courtyards; doubles from £130; www.lamaisonarabe.com

EATING OUT
The two staples of Moroccan cuisine are the *tagine* (a slow-cooked stew of meat and vegetables) and couscous (steamed grains of semolina, served with vegetables and meat). Eating at the markets is a great way to sample different types of Moroccan food.

PRICE FOR TWO
£120–175 per day including accommodation, food and local travel.

FURTHER INFORMATION
www.visitmorocco.com
www.ilovemarrakesh.com

The Red City

In accordance with a law introduced during the time of French colonial rule, all buildings in Marrakesh must be painted red ochre. This is the colour of the earth on which the city was founded, traditionally used as a building material. The law also dictates that no new building in the Medina may be taller than a palm tree, while in the new quarters no building may rise above five storeys, so as not to compete with Marrakesh's landmark tower, the minaret of the Koutoubia Mosque.

Above (left to right): Brass lamps for sale in Souk Addadine; water seller; brightly coloured pyramids of herbs and spices

A FEAST FOR THE SENSES

ONE OF THE MOST EXOTIC PLACES ON EARTH, the ancient market town of Marrakesh was born as the first stop after the Atlas Mountains for trading caravans heading further into North Africa. Life in this old walled city revolves around the medieval minaret of the Koutoubia Mosque that stands high above all other buildings, a beacon to new arrivals. As an attraction however, it's put in the shade by the spectacular Jemaa El Fna, the main open space in Marrakesh. This is the heart of the city, throbbing day and night with an extraordinary carnival of snake-charmers, toothpullers, storytellers, acrobats, transvestite dancers and mystical musicians, drawing enthralled crowds. In the evening, the square becomes one giant open-air restaurant as hundreds of stalls sell traditional favourites, from simple hard-boiled eggs and delicious flame-grilled meats to *harira* (a thick lentil and chickpea soup) or – for those wishing to have a truly Moroccan experience – boiled sheep's head. Simply sit back on one of the many benches around the square and enjoy the sizzling, smoke-filled hustle and bustle of it all.

But there's still more to this romantic old trading city. Head for the ancient souk – a vast area of higgledy-piggledy cupboard-sized shops and stalls filling dozens of narrow alleyways. A delicious mix of heady aromas draws you further into the endless maze of lanes, where stalls are laden with bunches of fresh mint, jars of plump olives infused with lemon and garlic, mounds of succulent Mehjool dates and bright pyramids of spices. Intricately tooled leather, metalwork, inlaid boxes, brass lanterns, carpets and jewellery are all here in abundance. Each area of the souk specializes in a particular item, so one street might be filled with canary-yellow leather *babooshes* (slippers), the next with sparkling glazed pottery. "Hey my friend," cry the stall-holders as you pass, "for you I give special price". Whether you are buying or not, it is a wholly entrancing and magical experience.

> A delicious mix of heady aromas draws you further into the endless maze of lanes, where stalls are laden with bunches of fresh mint and bright pyramids of spices.

Main: Colourful skeins of wool drying in the Dyers' Souk.
Inset: Colourful *babooshes* (leather slippers)
Below (left to right): Jemaa El Fna Square in the evening; luxurious *riad* interiors

AROMATIC DIARY

Marrakesh is short on monuments and traditional sightseeing opportunities, but its pleasures lie elsewhere. A visit here is all about the romance of this magical city – soaking up the sights, sounds and fragrances of a vibrantly coloured, exotic marketplace that sits at the gateway to sub-Saharan Africa.

Three Days of Spices and Souks

Get your bearings and soak up the ambience by taking a leisurely horse-drawn *calèche* tour around the city.

Experience bustling Jemaa El Fna, the nerve centre of Marrakesh – in the mornings a large market is held here, selling medicinal plants and an array of nuts and confectionery. Afterwards, admire the striking façade of Koutoubia Mosque (closed to non-Muslims) or, for a little tranquillity, visit the palaces and tombs of the Kasbah quarter.

When night falls, head back to Jemaa El Fna to sample some local fare at the market stalls and watch the lively and varied performers.

Marrakesh's souks are utterly fascinating so plan to spend at least a morning here. Many of the souks are known by the name of whatever is sold there – head to the Dyers' Souk to see vivid skeins of freshly dyed wool and silk hung out to dry in the sun, or to Souk Addadine for intricately decorated lanterns.

Spend the afternoon in the Marrakesh Museum, housed in an old palace, then have a look next door at the Ben Youssef Medressa, a 16th-century religious school with gorgeous tiling and carved woodwork.

Hire a car and driver for a day-trip up into the Atlas Mountains. It's just a couple of hours' drive to the crumbling, mud-brick fortress of Kasbah Telouet, once home to the rulers of southern Morocco.

Afterwards, wash off the mountain dust and relax your weary limbs in the sensuous aromatics of a traditional *hammam* (Turkish bath).

Dos and Don'ts

☑ Shop around and don't accept the first price that you are given in the souks – bargaining is an expected practice.

☒ Don't go overboard on the lanterns, rugs and brass platters; they look fantastic in the setting of the souk but not quite as effective in a Western domestic setting.

☑ Stay in a *riad* (traditional residence) in the Medina (old city) – boutique accommodation is what Marrakesh does best.

☒ Don't be bullied into accepting a guide to accompany you into the souks – they are unnecessary.

JAN
FEB
MAR
DAY 1
DAY 2
DAY 3
APR
MAY
JUN
JUL
AUG
SEP
OCT
NOV
DEC

GETTING THERE
Berlin is the capital of Germany, situated in the east of the country. International flights arrive into Tegel airport, 15–25 minutes from the city centre by taxi.

GETTING AROUND
The comprehensive public transport system is made up of subway, commuter trains, buses and trams (only in the eastern part of town). Taxis are surprisingly inexpensive.

WEATHER
In March, Berlin has average high temperatures of around 8°C, dropping to 0°C at night, and rainfall is quite low.

ACCOMMODATION
Pension Dittberner, full of old charm in western Berlin; doubles from £65; www.hotel-dittberner.de

Hotel Savoy stylishly combines antique and modern furnishings; doubles from £115; www.hotel-savoy.com

Hotel Adlon for luxurious surroundings; doubles from £300; www.hotel-adlon.de

EATING OUT
For food on the go, a must is the local favourite, *currywurst* (sausage with tomato sauce and curry powder). Berlin's culinary scene has become a lot more sophisticated and multicultural in recent years, and now includes a number of Michelin-starred restaurants.

PRICE FOR TWO
£190–250 per day including accommodation, food, entrance charges and local travel.

FURTHER INFORMATION
www.berlin.de

A City Reunited

For almost 40 years, Berlin was one of the hot spots of the Cold War, a city divided in two by the infamous concrete Berlin Wall. The old German capital was reborn after the fall of the Wall on 9 November 1989 and since then the city has unified again, with only a few traces of the Wall left in the Kreuzberg district and along the Spree River. In central Berlin, a narrow cobblestone line marks the Wall's former location.

Main: Domes of Berlin Cathedral with the Television Tower illuminated in the background
Above (top to bottom): Siegessäule (Victory Column); Reichstag, designed by Norman Foster; interior of the Jüdisches (Jewish) Museum

A CITY REDISCOVERED

B ERLIN IS AN EVER-CHANGING CITY, A CULTURAL BLEND of German-Prussian traditions and proud history, with an insatiable longing for new, daring architecture, art and music. Life in the German capital has always been on the cutting edge – from the wild days of 1920s cabaret and the horrors of World War II, to the menacing Wall and the sudden reunification and reinvention of this metropolis. Culture, art and festivals have always been a means to cope with life here, along with the quirky, cheeky humour and slang of Berliners.

Walking through the streets of historic but hip Scheunenviertel, alongside scruffy buildings that haven't seen paint since 1920 and are still freckled with bullet holes, then suddenly coming across a brand-new glass and steel architectural gem by Helmut Jahn or Jean Nouvel is like taking a rollercoaster ride through European history. Culture is in continuum here, as art galleries and boutiques sprout up next to sombre-looking museums loaded with highbrow art.

Above: Ballet performed at the Staatsoper Unter den Linden

Below (top and bottom): Colourfully decorated old Trabant on the streets of Berlin; dancing the night away at Felix nightclub

BERLINER DIARY

Berlin is undoubtedly one of the world's leading cities for museums and art, due in large part to its historic past and many rulers. In addition, the city has lively districts and an exuberant nightlife scene. Three days will allow you to experience the multi-faceted nature of the city and to glimpse both its past and its future.

A Lively Weekend in the Capital

Begin in western Berlin, with a walk down the city's most elegant boulevard, Kurfürstendamm, to the heart of old West Berlin. Visit Kaiser-Wilhelm-Gedächtniskirche, a ruin of a church bombed in World War II, now a memorial to the horrors of war.

Drop by Schloss Charlottenburg to explore one of Europe's grandest Baroque palaces and gardens.

For fresh air in the middle of the city, take a walk in the vast Tiergarten park, where you can visit the Zoologischer Garten (zoo) and see the Siegessäule (Victory Column). To explore Berlin's varied history, head to the centre of old East Berlin. Here you can tour the Reichstag parliament building, see the famous Brandenburg Gate and visit the Holocaust Memorial, or head further south to Checkpoint Charlie and the new Jüdisches (Jewish) Museum.

Be sure to check out Potsdamer Platz, a reborn, modern city quarter between East and West Berlin. Once a no-man's land in the shadow of the Wall, the area is now a celebration of 20th- and 21st-century architecture.

Spend a day exploring the city's many fascinating museums. Head to the Kulturforum for fine art in the Gemäldegalerie, magnificent 20th-century art in the Neue Nationalgalerie, and an orchestral performance at the Philharmonie. Alternatively, visit Museum Island to see the cathedral and the famous antiquities collection of the Pergamonmuseum and the Neues Museum.

In the evening, enjoy Berlin's lively nightlife in the many pubs and bars around Kurfürstendamm and Savignyplatz, or see an opera at Staatsoper Unter den Linden.

Dos and Don'ts

- ✗ Don't let the antiques merchants in the city's many markets fool you – polite bargaining is part of the deal, even where a fixed price is given first.
- ✓ On weekend nights, stay up late to enjoy Berlin's nightlife, which tends to kick off around 10 or 11pm.
- ✗ Don't linger on the red-paved bicycle paths found throughout the city; Berlin bicyclists are known for their extremely fast and aggressive cycling.

Below: Lion mosaics on the Ishtar Gate in the Pergamonmuseum

JAN

FEB

MAR

DAY 1

DAY 2

DAY 3

APR

MAY

JUN

JUL

AUG

SEP

OCT

NOV

DEC

Due to the Cold War division of the city, there are two clusters of world-class museums, situated in what was once divided as East and West Berlin. The more historic centre on Muse um Island (*Museuminsel*) is a massive, grey colossus started in the late 19th century, home to the famous Pergamonmuseum. Its West Berlin counterpart, the Kulturforum, near lush Tiergarten park, holds the Philharmonie, a tent-like showcase of 1960s architecture that shimmers golden in the sunlight, and the Gemäldegalerie, which has an exceptional collection of fine art. The Hohenzollern monarchs who amassed the city's treasures once lived nearby, in surprisingly playful palaces such as Schloss Charlottenburg, which has been restored to its former glory, reflecting the long-ago excesses that present a stark contrast to the grey post-war years.

But Berlin is at heart a youthful city, especially at night when the latest European hip hop, techno, electro pop and other computer-based beats can be heard in its clubbing and bar scene. This is a city throbbing with new-found energy and life, shaking off its history to emerge at the heart of modern Europe.

GETTING THERE
Whistler is in western Canada, in British Columbia. International flights arrive into Vancouver airport, 120 km (75 miles) from the resort. A shuttle bus transports visitors from the airport and downtown Vancouver to Whistler. Car hire is also available.

GETTING AROUND
A free village shuttle bus provides transportation from hotels to the ski lifts, and runs every 10 to 12 minutes during the day.

WEATHER
Average daytime temperatures in Whistler are 2°C in March, but it is colder on the mountain.

ACCOMMODATION
Glacier's Reach has a number of apartments with full kitchens; one-bedroom apartments from £85; www.resortquest.com

Executive Inn, chalet-style rooms with a Jacuzzi; double from £120; www.executiveinnwhistler.com

Fairmont Château Whistler, with complete luxury and ski in/ski out facilities; double from £200; www.fairmont.com/whistler

EATING OUT
A mid-range three-course meal in Whistler costs under £20 a head. For a treat, try the seafood and other stylish west coast fare at Araxi, or the award-winning Bearfoot Bistro.

PRICE FOR TWO
£250–300 per day for accommodation, food, equipment, ski-passes and entertainment – heli-skiing costs an additional £300 per person.

FURTHER INFORMATION
www.tourismwhistler.com

Olympic Whistler
Whistler's Olympic dream has taken nearly 40 years to happen. The resort was developed in the 1960s, with the hopes of landing the 1968 Winter Games. But the Rocky Mountain resort of Banff submitted Canada's bid for the 1968 and 1972 games, and Whistler's 1976 bid came to naught when the Summer Games were awarded to Montreal. In 2010, Whistler will share the honour with Vancouver, hosting the downhill and cross-country ski races, as well as ski-jumping, luge and bobsleigh events.

Main: Snowboarder performs a cliff jump above the ski lift at Whistler

Above (left to right): Skiers and snowboarders making sure they start from the very top of the ridge; dogsledding through the Whistler woods; skier at speed gets a little air after going over a bump

WHISTLER WONDERLAND

IT'S ALL ABOUT THE GREAT OUTDOORS – winter in Whistler. If you can't climb up it, race down it, stride through it or suspend yourself from it, most visitors aren't interested. Everyone, from toddlers to octogenarians, is clad head-to-toe in bright Gore-Tex and carries ski poles or snowshoes.

This pretty resort village of around 10,000 permanent residents is cradled in one of the most scenic spots on Canada's west coast. The Whistler and Blackcomb mountains – with a combined total of 38 lifts, more than 200 ski runs, 34 sq km (13 sq miles) of skiable terrain and one of North America's longest lift-serviced vertical descents – dominate the landscape. Quiet trails through thick forests of fragrant pine and cedar beckon alluringly to cross-country skiers and snowshoers. The icy surface of the frozen Green Lake seems purpose-made for ice skating. And then there's the heli-skiing. Whistler is a prime centre for this extreme activity with a superb choice of pristine deep-powder runs that are only accessible by helicopter. When you've been the

> When you've been the first to ski an almost vertical slope of feet-thick unpacked powder …then you know you've really skied the mountain.

first to ski an almost vertical slope of feet-thick unpacked powder, or carved smooth, floating turns through fresh snow as it sprays up around your ears, you know you've really skied the mountain. Then you're hooked – normal skiing or snowboarding will never be the same again.

There are few winter sports that someone here hasn't tried, from ice climbing to snow tubing. And a bit of snow and wind doesn't deter daredevils from other year-round activities like ziplining or bungy jumping.

Whistler is a surprisingly cosmopolitan place, with a lot to offer even those with no interest in hurtling headfirst down mountains. With the award-winning Bearfoot Bistro restaurant cellar holding 2,100 labels, and shops selling Cuban cigars and French lingerie, the town has evolved far beyond its backcountry roots – but it remains at its most charming when under a blanket of snow.

Inset: A bit of Whistler nightlife at Dusty's Bar and BBQ
Below (left to right): Above the clouds – ski lift at Whistler; cross-country skiing through the delightful countryside; cabins set in the mountain forest

DEEP POWDER DIARY

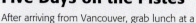

Whistler has one of the longest snow seasons in North America, and March is a great time to visit because temperatures are mild but snow is still plentiful. Because of the excellent conditions, rooms sell out quickly, so book ahead. Ski fanatics could easily spend two weeks here, but others will probably find five days ideal.

Five Days on the Pistes

After arriving from Vancouver, grab lunch at a mountainside restaurant and unpack. Spend the afternoon soaring over the tree-tops on a zipline tour, or strap on your skis and hit the slopes. In the evening, enjoy illuminated night-time snowboarding (early March, Thu–Sat only).

If you're a beginner or feeling a little rusty, brush up your skills with a lesson at the Whistler Blackcomb Ski and Snowboard School, then spend the rest of the day on the mountain. Afterwards, ease those aching muscles with a massage at one of the resort's spas and maybe a drink or two in one of the local bars.

Strap on some goggles and go snowmobiling along forested mountain trails, or spend a more leisurely day strolling through the village to shop for artwork, jewellery and other luxury goods – there are more than 200 shops in the resort. In the evening, take a horse-drawn sleigh ride around Green Lake, followed by an indulgent fondue dinner.

For a truly memorable experience, blaze your own track through the waist-deep, unmarked virgin powder of Whistler's spectacular backcountry on an exciting heli-skiing excursion. Finish the day with a dinner at one of Whistler's excellent restaurants.

Explore the beautiful Whistler countryside beyond the ski resort by trying your hand at cross-country skiing or learning to mush a team of Alaskan racing huskies along a snowy wilderness route.

Dos and Don'ts

- ✓ Buy a Fresh Tracks ticket, which will let you ski in pristine powder at sunrise, before the crowds arrive.
- ✓ Try skate-skiing, which combines elements of inline skating and cross-country skiing. Lessons are available at Lost Lake.
- ✓ Save money by booking self-catering accommodation – the village has a great selection of apartments.
- ✗ Don't think that you aren't good enough to heli-ski. If you can ski down a blue run you can do it – and you will never forget the experience (get a DVD of the trip made too).

JAN
FEB
MAR
DAY 1
DAY 2
DAY 3
DAY 4
DAY 5
APR
MAY
JUN
JUL
AUG
SEP
OCT
NOV
DEC

GETTING THERE
Daily flights operate to Learmonth Airport, 37 km (23 miles) from Exmouth – the gateway to Ningaloo Marine Park. Ningaloo is two days drive from Perth, 1,270 km (790 miles) south. Coaches depart daily from Perth and Exmouth.

GETTING AROUND
Hire a 4WD vehicle to take advantage of all the track roads in this area. There is also a limited bus service available.

WEATHER
Exmouth has a warm climate all year round with no wet season. March has temperatures of around 28°C. Annually, the water temperature ranges from 18 to 28°C.

ACCOMMODATION
Ningaloo Lodge is relaxed and friendly; doubles from £45; www.ningaloolodge.com.au

Ningaloo Caravan and Holiday Resort offers budget self-contained chalets; from £65; www.exmouthresort.com

Ningaloo Reef Retreat offers a safari experience, with luxury wilderness tents; doubles from £330; www.ningalooreefretreat.com

EATING OUT
Bundegi Beach Shack can pack a great gourmet hamper to take with you on your daytrip, from £20. Also, make sure you don't miss fish and chips for under £4, at Darcy's Café in Exmouth.

PRICE FOR TWO
£250–300 per day including accommodation, food and a reef tour package with dives and snorkelling with whale sharks.

FURTHER INFORMATION
www.exmouthwa.com.au

The Cape Range Peninsula
Twenty million years ago, the northwest corner of Australia was covered by a warm shallow sea. When the crust of the earth crumpled it resulted in the Cape Range Peninsula. Bushwalkers can often find fossil-bearing limestone on the walk to Mandu Mandu Gorge. Archeological digs have discovered artifacts from Aboriginal inhabitants of 34,000 years ago. Ningaloo is an Aboriginal word meaning promontory. Cape Range Peninsula is the promontory and Ningaloo Reef runs parallel to its western coast for 260 km (162 miles).

SWIM WITH WHALE SHARKS

Behind the blue curtain of the deep, Ningaloo's wonders beckon you to discover a vibrant array of corals, manta rays, turtles, clownfish and starfish, suspended in pristine harmony before you, as you float in a marvellous silence above reefs just seconds from the crystal white beach.

The glorious warm temperature of the water keeps you buoyed as you hover above a truly remarkable leviathan – the whale shark. Often over 15 m (50 ft), you can't quite believe that this harmless creature is so near as you snorkel alongside its giant body. Its massive metre-wide mouth takes a gulp of plankton, and as its speed gets the better of you, you watch its tail glide away into the blue. You have just had a close encounter with one of nature's rare and gentle giants.

For three months of the year off the coast of Western Australia, the opportunity to swim with the mighty whale shark awaits you. Attracted by the plankton feast of the March coral blooms, the docile leviathan returns annually to feed at Ningaloo Reef. Coral spawning occurs just days after the full

Main: School of beautifully coloured fish at Ningaloo Reef

moon in both March and April, and this event in itself is something of a spectacle. Imagine diving into the champagne fizz of millions of coral eggs as they float through the warm ocean, a pink phosphorescent glow heralding the rebirth of the reef.

Ningaloo Marine Park teems with life for 260 km (162 miles). A day of fishing on a chartered boat will result in a prize catch of coral trout, spanish mackerel, red emperor and the local delicacy, snapper. Maybe you'll see the energetic leap of the marlin or sailfish. Dive at one of the world's top dive sites – Navy Pier – and watch white-tipped reef sharks sleep undisturbed on the ocean floor.

Contrasting the aquatic splendour of Ningaloo, nearby Cape Range National Park offers a rugged wilderness for bushwalking, camping and birdwatching. Cruise the gorge of Yardie Creek and see the colony of black-footed rock wallabies, or spot the cornflower-blue plumage of a wren.

All year round, Ningaloo offers interactions with nature's most beautiful creatures – humpback whales are seen on their migration from July to November, and turtles nest from November to February. One of the world's largest fringe reefs, it is Australia's best kept secret.

Left panel (top to bottom): Imposing whale shark in Ningaloo Reef; kayaking in the calm waters above the reef; pelican sunning itself on the beach

Top: Camouflaged wobbegong shark surrounded by baitfish

Above: Hawksbill turtle swimming in the reef

Below: Colourful sea starfish

LEVIATHAN DIARY

The best time to visit Ningaloo is just around the coral bloom, when the whale sharks arrive. A visit in March will allow you to see the incredible sight of the coral spawning. Humpback whales and manta rays are common from July to November. Turtle nesting season is December to February.

A Week on the Reef

Hire a 4WD vehicle in Perth and drive to Exmouth, at the entrance to Ningaloo reef. This allows for two days of coastal exploration, or hire a car at Learmonth airport and drive to Coral Bay. Watch the magnificent sunset while tucking into some fish and chips.

Hire your own snorkelling gear to give you access to more experiences than just the tours. Explore the reef and its coral and fish species. Try some fishing off the beach, or head out to sea with a fishing charter.

In the morning, drive to Exmouth, either by the 150-km (93-mile) sealed road or by 4WD access terrain. Use the town as your base for the next few days. Spend the afternoon with a dive boat, exploring the Murion Islands, Lighthouse Bay or Navy Pier.

Choose a cruise company and go snorkelling beside the majestic whale sharks.

Try sea-kayaking to experience snorkelling further out. Enjoy a beach walk around Surfer's Beach, 17 km (10 miles) north of Exmouth, a reef break for the serious surfer or just sit back and watch.

Watch for emus, lizards and kangaroos as you journey to the northern tip of North West Cape by 4WD. Head up to Vlaming Head Lighthouse for incredible views.

Visit Yardie Creek Gorge, 90 km (56 miles) south of Exmouth to see the local wildlife then trek around the cape towards Exmouth to begin your journey home.

Dos and Don'ts

⊗ Don't touch coral – human interference can upset the very delicate eco-system.

✓ Pay heed to local environmental laws that forbid you to touch the whale sharks. The sharks' regular return every year is under speculation.

⊗ Don't use lights when observing turtles laying eggs, or during hatching. Allow your eyes to adjust to the moonlight.

Below: Flock of galahs fly over Cape Range

JAN

FEB

MAR

DAY 1

DAY 2

DAY 3

DAY 4

DAY 5

DAY 6

DAY 7

APR

MAY

JUN

JUL

AUG

SEP

OCT

NOV

DEC

GETTING THERE
Most international flights land in Delhi, India's capital. Barsana is about 100 km (62 miles) southeast of Delhi.

GETTING AROUND
The easiest way to reach Barsana is to hire a car. In Delhi, use taxis and auto-rickshaws.

WEATHER
March is sunny with temperatures reaching 30°C, dropping to around 16°C at night.

ACCOMMODATION
If you want to stay close to the festivities, the town of Mathura has a good selection of hotels.

Hotel Sheetal Regency is situated in the heart of Mathura and has doubles from £22; www.hotelsheetalregency.com

Best Western Radha Ashok has all mod cons; doubles from £35; www.bestwestern.com

In Delhi, the Oberoi offers luxurious surroundings; doubles from £185; www.oberoihotels.com

EATING OUT
Vegetarian food is prominent in the area; a typical meal might include *dal* (spiced lentils), *aloo sabzi* (curried potatoes), and breads such as *poori* and *paratha*. A meal in a restaurant will cost between £3–6 per head, a meal at a roadside eatery (*dhaba*) will cost around 25 pence.

PRICE FOR TWO
£75–90 per day including accommodation, food, entrance charges and car hire.

FURTHER INFORMATION
www.incredibleindia.org
www.up-tourism.com

The Krishna Cult

Lord Krishna, the eighth incarnation of Vishnu the Preserver, is the embodiment of love. This most human of all gods is still very much a real entity in the area around Mathura, where he was born, and Brindavan, where he lived. The temples around these towns all glorify the Krishna cult and there are many places that relate to episodes in his life – such as his dalliance with the milkmaids and his beloved Radha, who was born in Barsana. Holi was one of Krishna's favourite festivals, which is why it is celebrated with such enjoyment in Barsana.

Main: Covered in *gulal*, revellers celebrate the Holi Festival
Above (top to bottom): Decorated elephant in Brindavan; sacks of *gulal*; clouds of *gulal* billow above the crowds

A RIOT OF COLOUR

BURSTING ONTO THE CALENDAR TO HERALD THE ARRIVAL OF SPRING, Holi, the "Festival of Colours", is celebrated with infectious joy and frivolity. During this exuberant festival, the country erupts into a rainbow of colour and noise as everyone takes to the streets with handfuls of *gulal* (coloured powder) and reckless abandon.

Nothing encompasses the spirit of Holi better than the colours that are thrown about with such pleasure, symbolizing the change from drab winter into bright spring. In the days before the festival, vendors sit on street corners with pyramids of *gulal*. This is either used dry and smeared onto people, or mixed with water and splattered from water pistols and balloons. Every conceivable shade of pink and orange appears, blending into each other to create a riot of colour that could only ever exist in India. On the night before Holi, large *hola* (bonfires) are lit and an effigy of the demon Holika is burnt, signifying the triumph of good over evil. The mood is jubilant, but it is as dawn

Above: Intricately embroidered silks on display in Delhi

Below (top and bottom): Crowded street scene in Delhi; auto-rickshaw with passengers speeding through the streets of Delhi

HOLI DIARY

Although celebrated throughout the country, Holi is particularly important in North India, where the seasons are more pronounced. During the festival, the streets fill with people sprinkling coloured water and powder (*gulal*) on one another. Combine your trip with a visit to the Taj Mahal in Agra (*see pp52–3*).

Five Vibrant Days

Arrive in Delhi, where you can admire the grand Raj buildings on Raisina Hill, especially the President's impressive residence, Rashtrapati Bhavan. Browse the arcades, stalls and kiosks of Connaught Place or spend an afternoon exploring the museums.

Spend the morning in Old Delhi, exploring the Red Fort or Jami Masjid, India's biggest mosque. To stock up on *gulal*, head for the bustling alleys of Chandni Chowk, in particular Kinari Bazaar. For dinner, try a traditional *thali* (a platter of small dishes).

Head out of the city on the day before Holi to visit Mathura, where you can see Krishna's reputed birthplace and the 25 *ghats* (steps) along the river front. Every evening at sunset, oil lamps are floated on the river – watch this serene display and then stay in town to watch the burning of the effigy.

Head to Barsana first thing in the morning as the festivities start early. Join the fun in the streets and enjoy the lively atmosphere – but remember not to wear your best clothes. Once the proceedings have calmed down, enjoy a typical North Indian vegetarian meal, before visiting the village of Brindavan, with its impressive temples.

Back in Delhi, take an early morning walk around the gem-like Humayun's Tomb, or visit the Crafts Museum, where you can see local craftspeople at work. Browse the antique and jewellery shops in Sundar Nagar market. Alternatively, spend a few days in nearby Agra and revel in the glory of the Taj Mahal.

Dos and Don'ts

✓ Fix a rate with taxi and auto-rickshaw drivers as meters are rarely used, even though it is required by law.

✗ Don't be horrified if someone throws colour on you – make sure you wear old clothes and join the festivities.

✗ Don't be tempted to join groups where *bhang ki thandai* is being passed around. *Bhang* is a drink made with the leaves and flowers of the cannabis plant mixed with almond, spices and milk. It can often lead to strange hallucinations.

Below: Humayan's Tomb in Delhi

JAN

FEB

MAR

DAY 1

DAY 2

DAY 3

DAY 4

DAY 5

APR

MAY

JUN

JUL

AUG

SEP

OCT

NOV

DEC

breaks the next day that the festival erupts. People of all ages swarm onto the streets, splashing and smearing brightly coloured *gulal* on each other, and decorated elephants push through the crowd to the constant beat of *dholaks* (drums).

Linked to the lunar cycle and the changing of the seasons, the festival has long been presided over by mischievous Lord Krishna, whose roots in Uttar Pradesh give the festivities an increased fervour in the village of Barsana. The festival here follow a distinct tradition, in which the women of the village take control, armed with long bamboo sticks, forcing the men to dress up in saris and dance for the rest of the village. This takes place as the village is consumed by the eruption of colours and festival songs celebrating Krishna's beloved Radha ring out.

Clouds of flame red, turmeric orange and electric yellow powder cover the streets in a technicolour smog; this is a quintessentially Indian festival, which abounds with sensuality and joy. As the festivities draw to a close, men, women and children return home, drenched in a rainbow of colours and rejoicing in life.

Above (left and right): Boat pulled ashore on a sandy beach in the Perhentian Islands; jungle path to Flora Bay on Perhentian Besar

PALM-FRINGED PARADISE

WELCOME TO THE WORLD OF RAINFORESTS AND CORAL REEFS – two extraordinarily diverse natural habitats. The Perhentians are, in fact, two islands in the South China Sea – Perhentian Besar and Perhentian Kecil. Dense and lush rainforests are protected here by unending sandy beaches lined with swaying palms. Beyond them lies the clear and calm sea. If you love pristine and pure spaces, this is a wonderful retreat.

Scuba diving and snorkelling provide unforgettable underwater vistas of colourful carpets of soft and hard coral, home to thousands of mesmerizing reef fish. These smaller reef animals do attract the larger predators like barracudas, kingfish, blacktip sharks and nurse sharks – not necessarily dangerous, but deserving your careful respect. As you emerge from this world where you are the intruder back to your familiar beach terrain, you may even discover one of the rare nesting sites of the giant leatherback turtle.

These turtles have been inhabitants of the earth for more than a million years, surviving the dinosaur extinction. The green turtle, soft, pudgy and too often featuring on restaurant menus, is found in abundance in Malaysia, as is the hawksbill turtle with its hard and beautiful shell that has been prized for jewellery for hundreds of years. Rampant poaching of this species has led it to now be classed as an endangered species. However, the Perhentians are one of the few places in the world where sightings of this ancient species' nesting sites are possible.

This is a paradise, one where you can spend hours watching turtles do their own thing and for that short period of time forget the tiresome problems of the world you left behind. Or you can delve back into the magical underworld of marine life savouring its myriad colours, fluid movement and ethereal qualities.

Whether you want to go hiking through challenging tracks in the jungle-covered interior, have a wild time partying on the white-sand beaches until the sun rises over Perhentian Kecil, or lie gently swinging in a hammock watching the sun go down over the crystal-clear South China Sea, these islands have it all.

Main: One of the islands' many isolated beaches, perfect for lounging the day away
Below (left and right): Clownfish weaves in and out of an anemone; large plates of staghorn coral at a diving site off the Perhentian Islands

GETTING THERE
The Perhentian Islands lie off the northeastern coast of Peninsular Malaysia. The nearest international airport is in Kuala Lumpur (KL). Fly from KL to Kota Bharu or Kuala Terengganu and catch a bus to Kuala Besut – boats run to the Perhentians from here.

GETTING AROUND
On the islands, the easiest way to island-hop or go from beach to beach is by water taxi.

WEATHER
In March, expect sunny weather, with average high temperatures of around 31°C.

ACCOMMODATION
Perhentian Kecil has Impiani Beach Resort on the lovely beach of Pasir Petani; doubles from £25; www.watercoloursworld.com

Perhentian Island Resort, Perhentian Besar's most luxurious option, has beachfront suites from £40; www.perhentianislandresort.net

Perhentian Kecil's Bubu Long Beach Resort has doubles from £45; www.buburesort.com.my

EATING OUT
Regional specialities include *nasi dagang* (rice with coconut cream, eaten with tuna curry) and *otak otak* (fish in coconut and spice paste, in a banana leaf, cooked over charcoal).

PRICE FOR TWO
£55–65 per day including accommodation, food and water taxis.

FURTHER INFORMATION
www.tourism.terengganu.gov.my

The Green Turtles
The Perhentians are a major nesting site of green turtles, that come to the waters off these islands to mate and lay eggs. While some lucky visitors may just find themselves swimming near a turtle, they should be very careful not to approach these slow, cautious animals too closely or to disturb them in any other way. The green turtles are a protected species whose numbers declined rapidly last century due to hunting for their shells, meat and eggs.

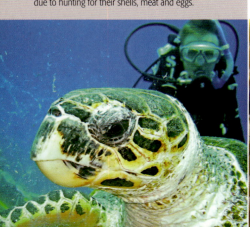

ISLAND DIARY

The Perhentians are among the loveliest islands in the region, covered with lush rainforest, fringed by palm-shaded white sand beaches, and surrounded by clear turquoise waters. The islands are encircled by coral reefs which provide habitat for a range of colourful fish and are perfect for diving and snorkelling.

JAN

FEB

MAR

Six Days in the Sun

Take an early morning flight to Kota Bharu or Kuala Terengganu to get to the Perhentians for lunch. Paddle about the islands by canoe, or spend the afternoon in a hammock under the casuarina trees on the beach. Apart from the putter of the occasional passing boat, few reminders of hectic urban life will disturb you.

DAY 1

Spend the morning snorkelling in the shallower reefs, then head off for a diving trip either around Terumbu Tiga off Perhentian Besar or Tokong Laut off Perhentian Kecil. Terumbu Tiga offers occasional sightings of the blacktip shark.

DAY 2

Set off for a trek across one of the islands. The toil of clambering through gnarled roots and heavy foliage will make that next dip in the sea all the more rewarding. Later, join an afternoon dive to Teluk Kerma off Perhentian Kecil. This site features hard coral gardens, and divers are likely to sight green turtles.

DAY 3

After a leisurely morning on the islands, take the boat to Kuala Besut and head back to Kuala Lumpur to explore this interesting and bustling city.

DAY 4

Spend the morning in atmospheric Chinatown to experience the country's diverse heritage at Chan See Shu Yuen Temple and Sri Mahamariamman Temple. Have a lazy lunch before browsing the colourful local art and craft stalls at nearby Central Market.

DAYS 5–6

Head to the Petronas Towers first thing to see the great views from the Skybridge. Spend the afternoon in the peaceful Lake Gardens and the Islamic Arts Museum.

Dos and Don'ts

✓ Bring plenty of money from the mainland as it's difficult to change money on the Perhentians and a number of resorts don't acccept credit cards and traveller's cheques.

✗ Don't touch or break off any coral. It is strictly prohibited as the islands belong to a national marine park.

✓ Carry a small flashlight. Power on the islands is provided by generators, and power cuts are not unusual.

APR

MAY

JUN

JUL

AUG

SEP

OCT

NOV

DEC

Below: Restaurant on one of the western beaches of the Perhentians

Tikal
BELIZE
MEXICO
GUATEMALA
HONDURAS
ANTIGUA ⊙ ● Guatemala City
San José
PACIFIC
OCEAN
EL SALVADOR

GETTING THERE
Antigua is in Guatemala, in Central America. It lies 26 km (16 miles) from Guatemala City, where international flights arrive at La Aurora airport. Shuttle buses and taxis connect to Antigua (45 minutes).

GETTING AROUND
Frequent 55-minute flights on TACA Airlines connect Guatemala City to Flores, 60 km (37 miles) from Tikal. Transfers are included in most tours or easily arranged on arrival.

WEATHER
March is in Guatemala's dry season and the temperature stays between 15°C and 27°C.

ACCOMMODATION
Casa Santo Domingo Hotel in Antigua is set in a colonial monastery; doubles from £100; www.casasantodomingo.com.gt

Central Posada de Don Rodrigo Hotel in Antigua has comfortable doubles from £50; www.posadadedonrodrigo.com

Hotel Jungle Lodge in Tikal is surrounded by forest and has bungalows from £30; www.junglelodge.guate.com

EATING OUT
Beans, tortillas and grilled meats play an important role in the cuisine of Guatemala. The kitchen of Casa Santo Domingo in Antigua is among the most sophisticated in Central America.

PRICE FOR TWO
£140–220 per day including accommodation, food and internal flights and entrance to Tikal.

FURTHER INFORMATION
www.visitguatemala.com

Carpets of Flowers

Alfombras, the brilliant carpets of flowers that pave the way for the sombre processions, are a tradition that dates back to colonial times, blending Spanish Catholic and Mayan influences. The streets are first covered with a bed of pine needles, the edges marked by temporary wooden frames. Intricate patterns are repeated hundreds of times in fine sawdust to form the borders, while bright tropical birds and Mayan motifs fill the centres. Once popular throughout the Spanish world, the tradition remains today in only a very few places.

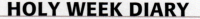

Main: Children wave incense through the streets to commemorate Holy Week
Above (left to right): Marchers in traditional costume in the Holy Week procession; young boy participates in the festivities; produce market in Antigua

FAITHFUL FESTIVITIES

L IVELY STRAINS OF SALSA AND MARIMBA MUSIC, the rhythmic pat, pat, pat of hands forming tortillas, the soft voices of Mayan ladies urging you to buy the bright woven *huipils* (traditional blouses) that turn every market stall and courtyard into a vivid kaleidoscope – this is Guatemala's former colonial capital of Antigua, one of Latin America's most beautiful cities.

For one week each spring the city takes on a whole new dimension, a sense of calm overlaying its usual lively buzz as residents pause to remember the most solemn of seasons in the Christian faith: Holy Week. The predominantly Catholic Guatemalans devoutly decorate the paving stones of their streets with intricate mosaics of bright blossoms and coloured sawdust. Over these ephemeral carpets, robed men bear heavy statues of Christ in penance for their year's transgressions. The scene is both beautiful and moving, an unselfconscious statement of faith encompassing sorrow as participants remember the Via Dolorosa – the Way of Tears that Christ travelled to Calvary – and hope for a new beginning at Easter.

At the other end of Guatemala, an untamed wilderness of jungle and swamps stretches between Mexico and Belize. The only bumps in this landscape are the temples atop Mayan pyramids, which break through the lush rainforest canopy; enigmas that have confounded archeologists since the dense coverings of vines were first torn away to reveal their stones. Once a thriving, sophisticated city, Tikal was suddenly abandoned a millennium ago and is remarkable for its scale and eerie desolation. Ponder its mysteries as you wander its winding paths, greeted by the cries of brilliant tropical birds and raucous howler monkeys playing high-wire acrobatics in the branches overhead. Climb at least one of those dizzyingly steep pyramids and be rewarded by views across the jungle to other temples, like stone islands in a leaf-green sea.

> Lively strains of salsa and marimba music, the rhythmic pat, pat, pat of hands forming tortillas, the soft voices of Mayan ladies urging you to buy …this is Antigua.

Inset: Antigua's Plaza Mayor with the Agua Volcano in the background
Below (left and right): Mayan ruins rise out of the twisted vines at Tikal; detail of a male figure from a Mayan ceramic from Tikal

HOLY WEEK DIARY

The air is filled with fragrances – earthy corn tortillas toasting, meat sizzling on a wood-fired grill, and the soft scent of frangipani. Late March and April are ideal for visiting Guatemala, when the weather is balmy. The date of Holy Week changes each year – time your visit carefully to coincide with the festivities.

A Week of Traditions

At noon, 80 robed *cucuruchos* (bearers) raise the statue of Jesus Nazarano at La Merced Church, carrying it through flower-carpeted streets until after midnight.

Explore old Antigua, especially Plaza Mayor and the cathedral with its roofless nave and bishop's palace. Visit Guatemala's most important jade-carving studio, Casa del Jade, and see weavers at Casa del Traje Antiguo.

Depart early for the airport in Guatemala City and fly to Flores. Head to the World Heritage site of Tikal and climb at least one of the temples to enjoy the views – Temple IV is great for a sunset view but be sure to take a torch so that you can find your way back.

Arrive early while the wildlife is most active to continue exploring Tikal, or head to the newly-uncovered temples of Yaxha. Return to Antigua on an afternoon flight.

Watch the processions as they weave through Antigua's flower-covered streets or take a day-tour to Chichicastenango's vibrant weekly market.

Antigua's most solemn procession starts at 6am. Observances of the Crucifixion begin at the cathedral at noon, followed by processions until 3am. Visit San Francisco Church and its convent to see the museum and extensive ruins – climb the walls for views of the cloister garden and nearby Agua Volcano.

Fit in a carriage ride through Antigua before flying home. Alternatively, extend your trip with a few days relaxing on one of neighbouring Belize's beautiful beaches.

Dos and Don'ts

✓ Best buys are thick wool blankets, woodcarvings and brilliant hand-woven fabrics.

✗ Don't forget to have a good supply of US$1 and $5 bills, or small denomination Quetzales, both welcomed by vendors.

✓ Coffee is sold everywhere in brightly coloured woven bags. The best place to buy it is in Antigua, opposite the cathedral, where you can sample a cup at the coffee bar before buying.

✗ Don't pay the first price (except in shops) as friendly bargaining is expected. Expect to pay 60–75 per cent of the asking price.

| JAN |
| FEB |
| **MAR** |
| PALM SUN |
| MON |
| TUE |
| WED |
| HOLY THU |
| GOOD FRI |
| SAT |
| APR |
| MAY |
| JUN |
| JUL |
| AUG |
| SEP |
| OCT |
| NOV |
| DEC |

Below: Collared Aracari in the dense jungle at Tikal

APRIL

Where to Go: April

While the temperate climes of Europe and North America have not warmed up fully, April still brings an explosion of colour to the northern hemisphere as the flowers and trees break out in bloom – spring is in full swing. This makes it the perfect time to sample the romantic delights of Paris, or to hike the Cinque Terre trails. In the reversed seasons of the southern hemisphere (see pp328–9), however, summer is but a memory, so water sports enthusiasts should consider somewhere tropical, where the seas are always warm. Remember too, Easter is a moveable feast and it can fall in March or April (see p327); this is always a busy time for travelling. Below you'll find all the destinations in this chapter, as well as some extra suggestions to provide a little inspiration.

FESTIVALS AND CULTURE

ISTANBUL Roman ruins at Yerebatan Saray

UNFORGETTABLE JOURNEYS

AMSTERDAM Keizersgracht (Emperor's Canal) at dusk

NATURAL WONDERS

IGUAÇU Torrential water at the Iguaçu Falls

STRATFORD
ENGLAND, EUROPE

Parades, parties, falcons and medieval weapons

April 23rd combines Shakespeare's birthday parade with St George's Day. Visit Warwick Castle for deft falconry and siege engines in action.
www.shakespeare-country.co.uk

SAVANNAH
USA, NORTH AMERICA

A city that is rich in history and Southern hospitality

Savannah's gardens bloom in April, making it most picturesque. Visit the annual Garden Expo and stroll through the elegant squares.
www.savannah-visit.com

AMSTERDAM
NETHERLANDS, EUROPE

Explore the canals in this characterful capital

Canals, tulips and cafés set in wonderful architecture cannot fail to inspire. Don't miss the carnival that is the Queen's Birthday.
See pp112–13

SAMARKAND
UZBEKISTAN, ASIA

A week exploring the ancient Silk Road trading towns

Marvel at Timur's glorious capital at the centre of the Silk Road before exploring the medieval towns of Bukhara and Khiva.
See pp98–9

"Crashing and splashing from clifftop to rock shelf to swirling whirlpool, spinning for a time before gravity tugs them back."

IGUAÇU FALLS
BRAZIL, SOUTH AMERICA

See the power of the largest waterfalls on the planet

One of the greatest natural wonders of the world, the falls are in a National Park that can be visited from both Brazil and Argentina.
See pp96–7

ISTANBUL
TURKEY, ASIA

One of the fabulous termini of the ancient Silk Road

See the Great Bazaar, the original shopping mall, and Ottoman gems like the Topkapi Palace, and the Suleymaniye and Blue Mosques.
See pp106–7

FJORD CRUISE
NORWAY, EUROPE

See the dramatic Norwegian coastline from a working ship

These fjords are natural wonders of the world. The Hurtigruten may not provide club class luxury but the views are priceless.
See pp90–91

BANFF NATIONAL PK
CANADA, NORTH AMERICA

Melting snows bring the animals out into the open

Banff's combination of lakes, mountains and forests makes it an animal haven. See bald eagles, caribou, grizzlies and birds galore.
www.banffnationalpark.com

MADAGASCAR
AFRICA

In April the forest growth will be thick and very luxuriant

Madagascar has a huge variety of animal species, most of which are unique to the island, including 30 different types of lemur.
www.madagascar-travel.net

KYOTO
JAPAN, ASIA

A holiday of traditions, nature and cutting-edge modernity

Visit this ancient capital during Sakura Matsuri (Cherry Blossom Festival) and witness Japan's special reverence for tradition.
See pp102–3

SHANGHAI
CHINA, ASIA

Hundreds of unforgettable journeys in this city

Walk down the historic Bund; take a lift to the top of a skyscraper; go back in time in the Old City; enjoy the views from a river cruise.
lyw.sh.gov.cn/en

GALÁPAGOS
ECUADOR, SOUTH AMERICA

A group of volcanic islands with unique flora and fauna

April is the best month to see the legendary giant tortoises as well as sea turtles, baby sea lions and island flowers.
See pp104–5

LESBOS
GREECE, EUROPE

This beautiful island is a paradise for migrating birds

With mountains, wetlands and saltpans, the island is a haven for birds such as flamingoes, great reed warblers and little bitterns.
www.greeknet.com

CUMBRIA
ENGLAND, EUROPE

Enjoy a host of golden daffodils just as Wordsworth did

See the flowers as immortalized by the poet on the shores of Ullswater. The Lake District is beautiful at this time of year, and not too busy.
www.ullswater.co.uk

CABOT TRAIL
CANADA, NORTH AMERICA

This Cape Breton drive is wild, rugged and beautiful

This route follows Cape Breton's northern shore before climbing to a high plateau. See fish eagles, moose and pods of whales.
www.cabottrail.com

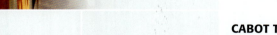

Previous page: Beautiful tiles on the interior walls of the Blue Mosque in Istanbul

Weather Watch

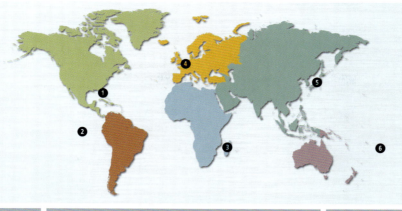

① April really is a good time to visit Florida. The temperature range is pleasant all day and night, more bearable than in summer, with less rain.

② Despite being almost on the Equator, the Galápagos Islands are relatively dry and cool. The temperature is moderated by the plankton-rich sea that attracts fish and marine animals.

③ The end of the rainy season in Madagascar has left the country lush and green, with more pleasant, but still very warm, temperatures.

④ Amsterdam is never going to attract people with fine weather – the chilly North sea makes sure of that. However April is one of its pleasantest months – mild, little rain and a fair bit of sun.

⑤ Kyoto is in sub-tropical Japan and receives a healthy mix of sun and rain – good for cherry blossom Expect mild sunny weather with occasional showers.

⑥ Tahiti's tropical oceanic climate means that it enjoys high temperatures throughout the year. Brief downpours often take place in the afternoons or evenings but provide respite from the humidity.

LUXURY AND ROMANCE

PARIS Waiters inside Brasserie Flo

ACTIVE ADVENTURES

CINQUE TERRE Walking the coastal path at Riomaggiore

FAMILY GETAWAYS

FLORIDA Shamu the killer whale in Sea World

PUERTO VALLARTA
MEXICO, NORTH AMERICA

Playground of legendary lovers Liz Taylor and Richard Burton

PV, as the locals call it, still retains an aura of Hollywood glitz but you can find delightful beaches away from the bright lights if you must.
www.visitpuertovallarta.com

DJIBOUTI SEATREK
DJIBOUTI, AFRICA

The horn of Africa is redolent of tales of pirates and derring-do

Relive those adventures with a "seatrek". You'll camp on the shore, meet the locals and have clear waters, reefs and beaches all to yourselves.
www.explore.co.uk

PARIS
FRANCE, EUROPE

A long weekend to rekindle the flames of romance

Springtime in Paris may be a cliché but it's a wonderful time to see the City of Light and to enjoy top-notch food, wine and art.
See pp110–11

TAHITI
POLYNESIA

These tiny islands make for the perfect romantic getaway

For those who want a bit of time to themselves, Tahiti offers intimate resorts, peaceful villages and miles of quiet sandy beaches.
www.tahiti-tourisme.com

OKAVANGO DELTA
BOTSWANA, AFRICA

Get up close and personal with an elephant-back safari

African wildlife is far more tolerant of elephants than of jeeps. Luxury tented camps for sundowners and the best sunsets you'll ever see.
www.okavango-delta.net

> "Paris…the glory of France, and one of the noblest ornaments of the world."
>
> **MICHEL DE MONTAIGNE**
> 1533–92

CINQUE TERRE
ITALY, EUROPE

Hike the coastal path of this picturesque part of Italy

This stretch of coastline is so well preserved it is a World Heritage Site. Hiking trails offer an aerobic workout with fantastic views.
See pp94–5

BUCKSKIN GULCH
USA, NORTH AMERICA

A classic hike via sculpted underground caverns

A different type of hike that offers a subterranean tour through the spectacular and colourful striations of Colorado's longest slot canyon.
www.americansouthwest.net

ANDAMAN ISLANDS
INDIA, ASIA

An aquasports paradise in virtually uncharted waters

These 600 islands shimmer in the clear waters of the Bay of Bengal. Home to some excellent surfing and world-class fishing and diving.
www.diveindia.com

PETRA
JORDAN, MIDDLE EAST

Act the intrepid explorer and "discover" the lost city of Petra

Explore the ancient city of Petra, hewn out of pink rock in a desert landscape. Camp out under the myriad stars in magical Wadi Rum.
See pp92–3

ISCHGL
AUSTRIA, EUROPE

Skiing at Ischgl is a brilliant option for all the family

Ischgl is high enough to have snow still at this time of the year – the season winds up with a huge party at the end of the month.
www.ischgl.com

PICOS DE EUROPA
SPAIN, EUROPE

Discover drama and adventure in these stunning mountains

Spain's most beautiful natural playground. Take a cable car to the peak and climb down. Explore the river Deva by kayak.
www.asturiaspicosdeeuropa.com

ATHENS
GREECE, EUROPE

The city's art and philosophy has shaped the world today

See the monuments and museums by day, and restaurants, clubs, and bars by night. Greek Orthodox Easter is a very important festival.
See pp100–1

> "Most visitors find Greece's capital nothing short of captivating these days."

FLORIDA
USA, NORTH AMERICA

Plenty of fun for everyone in this family-friendly state

Take the family to see Mickey and friends at Disney World and other theme parks, as well as enjoying long stretches of sandy beaches.
See pp108–9

LEVI
FINLAND, EUROPE

See what Santa Claus gets up to after Christmas

One of the top ski resorts in Finland also has a terrific all-year Santa theme park. Plenty of activities such as reindeer- and dogsledding.
www.visitfinland.com

PROTARAS
CYPRUS, EUROPE

Follow in the footsteps of the Greek goddess Aphrodite

Cyprus combines ancient ruins and frescoed churches for the grown-ups, with beaches and outdoor activities for the children.
www.visitcyprus.org.cy

CAIRO
EGYPT, AFRICA

Pyramids and mummies to fascinate all ages

This capital has much to offer the visitor – the Pyramids and the Cairo Museum are enough for any would-be Indiana Jones.
www.touregypt.net

Left: Colourful wooden-fronted shops and houses along the waterfront in Bergen

Right (left to right): Fishing boats lined up in a busy harbour; waterfall near Stryn, southeast of Ålesund; houses on the Lofoten Islands; Hurtigruten ship

Below right (top and bottom): Birds nest above the window of a typical house; sunset over Kvaloya Island, west of Tromsø

GETTING THERE
The starting point of the Hurtigruten ships, Bergen, can be reached by air, either direct or via Oslo, and by ferry from Newcastle, in the UK.

GETTING AROUND
Flesland airport is 20 km (12 miles) from Bergen city centre – journey time by airport bus, 25 minutes. The city has good public transport.

WEATHER
April may be spring in Bergen at 6°C, but it's still winter in Bodø (3.3°C) and Tromsø (1.1°C). Expect sunshine, rain and snow above the Arctic Circle, and 13–15 daylight hours.

ACCOMMODATION
En suite cabins on the 11 modern Hurtigruten ships range from standard inside cabins to suites with a private balcony; www.hurtigruten.com

Neptun Hotell, Bergen, a comfortable hotel full of contemporary art, has two good restaurants and doubles from £90; www.neptunhotell.no

Strand Hotel in Bergen has a harbour-front location with one of Bergen's best views; double rooms from £85; www.strandhotel.no

EATING OUT
On the Classic Round Voyage, all meals on board are included. A meal in Bergen will cost from £13 a head, without wine.

PRICE FOR TWO
Classic Round Voyage holidays cost from £1,990 for two, including the 11-night voyage in a shared twin cabin, full board on the ship, plus one night hotel, with breakfast, in Bergen.

FURTHER INFORMATION
www.hurtigruten.com

Bird Lore
April is early spring in Norway, when millions of seabirds return to the dramatic coast to breed. Legend says that the Atlantic puffin arrives on the island of Gjesvaer in the far north at 5:45pm on 14 April every year. You can actually book a specialized Hurtigruten trip (www.hurtigruten.com) which coincides with the puffins' return to see if there is any truth in the local lore. This special trip includes onboard lectures on the various seabirds and their colonies and plenty of opportunities to see the 1.5 million pairs of Atlantic puffins.

Main: Geirangerfjord, known as the "Pearl of the Norwegian Fjords"

COASTAL ODYSSEY

Norway's dramatic coastline is one of the world's natural wonders. Forest-coated mountains sit with their feet in the water and their snowy peaks raked with cloud. Waterfalls plunge into pristine fjords and glaciers crown cols between mountains. Sea eagles soar, cormorants dive from lichen-covered rocks, kittiwakes swoop and gulls skim dark waters that glisten with silver light.

Zigzagging among a pattern of islands, weaving in and out of narrow inlets, manoeuvring through gaps between rocky islets, the ships of the Norwegian Coastal Voyage reveal both the captivating scenery and the rich life that lies ashore. In brightly coloured hamlets, neat wooden houses are painted in spice shades of mustard and cinnamon and bells ring out from traditional wooden churches, calling residents to Sunday prayer. Russet barns dot the farmland, fishing boats bring home their catch and, in the cities, history sits alongside a 21st-century lifestyle.

CLASSIC VOYAGE DIARY

The 11-night Classic Round Voyage leaves Bergen daily at 8pm and calls at 34 ports. The journey north, from Bergen to Kirkenes, takes six nights; and the voyage south is five nights, arriving back in Bergen at 2pm. Summer schedules start in mid-April. The days are long and the light and scenery spectacular.

Eleven Days in the Fjords

Spend some time in Bergen – take the mountain funicular or cable car for panoramic views, explore the old Hanseatic quarter of Bryggen, and check out the lively fish market before boarding your ship.

DAY 1

Today's highlight is Ålesund with its Art Nouveau architecture. A Geirangerfjord excursion offers memorable views of Norway's most scenic fjord.

DAY 2

An early breakfast, then into historic Trondheim to see its charming old wooden buildings and Norway's biggest medieval church. The ship then passes farmsteads through wide Trondheimsfjord, into the open sea.

DAY 3

Be on deck by 7am to spot the globe that marks the Arctic Circle. The scenery is spectacular, from island landscape to the jagged Lofoten mountain range. Go ashore at Bodø for museums, or take a trip in a boat to get close to the world's strongest tidal current.

DAY 4

At Tromsø, see the stunning Arctic Cathedral and the Polaria Arctic Experience Centre. It is possible to husky-sled from here until late April.

DAY 5

Honningsvåg has the fascinating North Cape Museum, and the world's largest bird cliff is nearby. Take the excursion from here to see the North Cape rising a sheer 307 m (1,007 ft) out of the ocean.

DAY 6

Kirkenes, close to the Russian border, is the turning point of the Norwegian Coastal Voyage. Stay aboard for the southbound journey, or fly from Kirkenes to Oslo.

DAYS 7–11

Dos and Don'ts

✓ Pack for all weathers. A rain- and wind-proof jacket and good walking shoes are essential; layers are ideal. Take binoculars.

✗ Don't forget to spend some time in Bergen, before or after the fjord voyage – it is a beautiful city.

✓ Remember you can also hop on and off the ships, staying in towns along the way. It's important to plan the journey and book ahead.

✗ Don't look for wines and spirits on supermarket shelves – they're sold in state shops called *Vinmonopolet*. Alcohol is very expensive in Norway – you may wish to bring some supplies.

JAN
FEB
MAR
APR
DAY 1
DAY 2
DAY 3
DAY 4
DAY 5
DAY 6
DAYS 7–11
MAY
JUN
JUL
AUG
SEP
OCT
NOV
DEC

Every day of the year, a Hurtigruten (Coastal Voyage) ship leaves Bergen for Kirkenes, way above the Arctic Circle and close to the Russian border. The 11-day round-trip takes in 34 ports, delivering passengers, freight and essential supplies to big towns and remote island communities. Ports visited at night on the northbound route can be seen in daylight hours on the journey south, which is when the full splendour of the craggy-peaked Lofoten Islands is revealed.

Although many of the ships are newly built and each has its own character, they don't pretend to be glitzy cruise liners, which is undoubtedly part of their charm for travellers more interested in the northern lights than light entertainment. They are, however, very comfortable, with excellent restaurants and public spaces hung with fine Norwegian art. While on board, there are many opportunities to savour the extravagant beauty of land and sea from the panoramic-view lounges. Step ashore and there is always much to explore, including intriguing little museums in the towns. Varied excursions take passengers on city tours, into glacier country, husky dogsledding or on encounters with the Saami way of life. The trip is truly a unique voyage of discovery.

Below: Busy fish market in Bergen

GETTING THERE
The archeological site of Petra is in Jordan, 250 km (155 miles) south of the capital Amman, which has an international airport. Regular buses connect Petra with Amman. You can hire a taxi for four people for around £35.

GETTING AROUND
Explore the site on foot or by donkey, camel or *calèche* (horse-drawn carriage) if you get tired.

WEATHER
April has a temperature of around 20–24°C in the daytime and is mild at night.

ACCOMMODATION
For budget travellers, the Al-Anbat offers great value and free transport to the site; doubles from £15; www.alanbat.com

Most of the mid-range hotels in Wadi Musa are block-booked by tour groups so reserve well in advance. Try the Petra Palace, very close to the main entrance to the site; doubles from £40; www.petrapalace.com.jo

Petra's accommodation is usually located in the nearby town of Wadi Musa, but the Mövenpick hotel is right beside the gate to the site; doubles from £90; www.movenpick-petra.com

EATING OUT
There are a few restaurants in Wadi Musa – the Cleopetra and The Petra Kitchen are worth trying (from £10). The restaurants at the Mövenpick (from £20) are also recommended.

PRICE FOR TWO
£80–140 per day including accommodation, food, entrance charges and local travel.

FURTHER INFORMATION
www.visitjordan.com

Who were the Nabataeans?

The Nabataeans were a nomadic tribe who migrated west from northeastern Arabia in the 6th century BC. They grasped the potential of a position on the trade routes between Arabia and the Mediterranean and by the 1st century BC, their city of Petra had grown rich on the profits of silk, perfumes and oils. The Romans, feeling the threat of these people, took over the city in AD 106 and the Nabataeans ceased to be an identifiable group.

JAN
FEB
MAR
APR
DAY 1
DAY 2
DAY 3
DAYS 4–5
MAY
JUN
JUL
AUG
SEP
OCT
NOV
DEC

Above (left and right): Bedouin woman; camel caravan trekking through the barren landscape of Wadi Rum
Main: First glimpse of Petra from the Siq

THE ROSE-RED CITY

There are those of the world's great monuments that, when you finally stand before them, disappoint. They look exactly like they do in the photographs, and no more than that. Petra is the opposite. It surpasses all expectations – to call it dramatic is an understatement. Petra could easily have been dreamed up in some film studio.

Leaving behind a scorched and bleak stony landscape, you enter a narrow canyon known as the Siq, squeezed between vertical rock walls that are in places so narrow you can barely see the sky. This is the secretive entrance to a city that remained hidden to the outside world for over half a millennium, until it was rediscovered in 1812 by Jacob Burckhardt, a Swiss adventurer masquerading as an Islamic scholar. Advancing along the Siq, the sense of anticipation grows. It is easy to imagine that you are that early explorer about to stumble upon the lost city – if it wasn't for the crowds of your fellow visitors. But nothing takes away from the first magical glimpse of Petra, as you round the last bend to come face-to-face with the famous rose-pink façade of the Treasury, chiselled out of the solid rock wall. No magazine photo comes close to capturing this. The sensation is of absolute wonder, as if you've stepped into a passage from an Edgar Rice Burroughs adventure novel. To the right, the canyon widens, its glowing veined walls sculpted with façades of columns, pediments and ornate doorways. A little further on stands a theatre carved into the hillside, and beyond, a sandy-floored main street.

If that was it, it would be staggering enough, but it's not. From here you clamber up rock-hewn staircases and passageways to more tombs and monuments, to the ruins of a Crusader castle, and to a great altar known as the High Place of Sacrifice, with fantastic views of the mountains and desert beyond. Petra is far more than just an archeological site, it's a breathtaking adventure.

"Match me such a marvel save in Eastern clime, A rose-red city – half as old as Time"
John William Burgon

Inset: Roman Theatre, c.100 BC– AD 200
Below (left to right): Aaron's Tomb; Treasury of Petra; detail of sandstone

DESERT DIARY

The core of Petra with the most famous sites can be visited in a day. However, having come this far it would be a pity not to explore more of this unique capital of a vanished civilization. Five days will allow you to cover most of Petra, with time for some wilderness hiking and a trip to the desert splendour of nearby Wadi Rum.

Five Days in the Lost City

Explore the main areas of the site, including the Siq and Outer Siq and the Old and Modern Museums.

In the afternoon, make the mildly strenuous climb up to the Monastery, a colossal temple that is reminiscent of the Treasury building.

Make an early start for the hike up to one of the best preserved of Petra's many places of sacrifice, the High Place of Sacrifice. The ascent, while gradual, requires stamina and a good head for heights – it's at an altitude of 1,035 m (3,400 ft).

It is worth visiting Petra by a different route (via Madras, Wadi Muthlim or Wadi Turkmaniyeh) to see it from a different perspective. Serious trekkers may also wish to see the sublime views from Aaron's Tomb, at 1,050 m (3,450 ft) on the highest peak in the area.

Take a car, or hired taxi, first thing and visit Wadi Rum as a stop off en route to Aqaba and its airport. The desert landscape is filled with huge ochre-coloured rock pinnacles, rising up 600 m (2,000 ft) from the sandy valley – an inspiring memory to take home. You might even consider spending another day here and taking a camel trek into Wadi Rum and camping out under the most star-filled sky you've ever seen.

Dos and Don'ts

✗ Don't pass up the opportunity for a camel ride – touristy yes, but also an appropriate way to experience the ruins of this deserted trading city.

✓ Sign up for one of the guided walks around Petra by night, when it is even more enchanting and magical than usual.

✗ Don't imagine that you'll be able to gallop down the Siq on horseback just like Indiana Jones – Spielberg probably paid a fortune to ensure that the canyon was empty of tourists.

✓ Get your hotel to prepare you a packed lunch each day. There are not many options at Petra itself and it will only cost a couple of pounds a day.

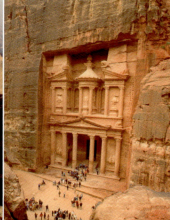
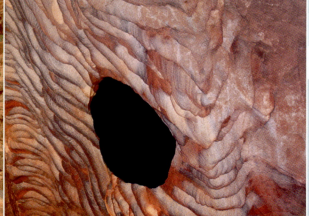

GETTING THERE
Squeezed between the French Riviera and the Tuscan coast, the Cinque Terre are best reached by flying to Genoa or Pisa and catching the coastal train to Riomaggiore (1½ hours).

GETTING AROUND
There is still no road that links all "five villages" of the Cinque Terre. If you get footsore on the paths between the villages, catch a train or boat. Frequent trains stop at the five villages, and motorboats also link them, weather permitting.

WEATHER
By April, the weather is warm and fairly settled; perfect for walking, although the sea is still cool for bathing.

ACCOMMODATION
In Vernazza, a good choice is Barbara, with simple, clean rooms overlooking the square; doubles from £45; www.albergobarbara.it

In Manarola, try Ca' D'Andrean, a short walk from the sea with a shady garden and doubles from £60; www.cadandrean.it

Monterosso's upmarket options include Porto di Roca, in a spectacular position on a promontory; doubles from £130; www.portoroca.it

EATING OUT
Expect to pay at least £20 for fish dishes, the region's speciality. Try Ristorante Belvedere in Monterosso for traditional Ligurian cuisine.

PRICE FOR TWO
£110–150 per day for accommodation, food and local travel.

FURTHER INFORMATION
www.turismoinliguria.it

WALK THE LIGURIAN COAST

A WALK ALONG THE OLD CINQUE TERRE MULE TRACK takes you through a landscape handcrafted over the last thousand years out of an uninhabitable rocky coast. The ochre and dusky pink houses of the "five villages" tumble down to the sea from clifftop promontories, piled up between tiny harbours and medieval forts. These fortified coastal hamlets were defended by the powerful Genoese navy against the Saracen raids of the first millennium and sheer isolation preserved them for most of the second, keeping them as a true record of past times.

Over the centuries, the isolated inhabitants have scraped an existence from the fish of the sea and the land that they created out of the Mediterranean bush. Dry-stone walled terraces line the hills that plummet into the sea, in mile upon mile of neatly contoured lines; on these are grown the vines that produce the local wines, in particular the famous *sciacchetrà* (sweet wine), and the groves of lemons and olives that cling to the steep hills and glisten in the Italian sun.

Below (top to bottom): Boats lined up at Vernazza; street in Corniglia; boarding the ferry at Corniglia

Regional Dishes

Fish, seafood and fresh pasta are the region's specialities: *tegame di acciughealla vernazzese* (fresh anchovies baked with potatoes, tomatoes and spices) is a famous fish dish, but unusual combinations like *trenette ai ricci di mare* (pasta with sea urchins), or the classic *grigliata mista di pesce* (mixed grilled fish) can also be found. For dessert, the delicious *monterossina* is made of cream, marmalade and chocolate. To wash it all down, try *sciacchetrà*, a dessert wine made with grapes withered on the vine.

Until the 19th century the only way in or out was by boat, or by mule over the steep tracks. It was only with the advent of the industrialized age that this rugged, inhospitable land became truly accessible. Italian engineers blasted tunnels through the rock and all of a sudden the railway linked Monterosso al Mare, Vernazza, Corniglia, Manarola and Riomaggiore to Lévanto in the west, La Spezia in the east – and beyond – putting it on the map for the Grand Tour.

This landscape suspended between sky and sea, the sundrenched *macchia* (thicket) with its scent of thyme and marjoram, the geckos scurrying for shelter in the shade of baking hot rocks, were immortalized in the poetry of Eugenio Montale as the villages were added to the trail of the Grand Tourists. As Montale said, many more "without knowing their name, discovered the Cinque Terre in flashes, segments and lightning, dazzling fragments, in the few portholes that open in the tunnel." For him, it was a mysterious, impenetrable landscape; even on a sunny day, when all you want is to wander through the spring flowers and gaze out at the expanse of emerald sea, it retains that mystical, unknowable edge.

MULE TRACK DIARY

April is the ideal time to walk the Cinque Terre; the weather is more settled than early spring, but temperatures have not yet reached the searing highs of summer. Five days is enough to walk the coastal path, spending a night in each village, with plenty of time for detours, mountain-biking, boating and diving.

Five Days in Five Towns

DAY 1
From the station at Riomaggiore, follow the Via dell'Amore to Manarola (30 minutes) – a famously romantic path carved into the rock. If you want more activity than just sipping a cool drink on a shady terrace, catch a bus up to Volastra to see the Romanesque sanctuary of Nostra Signora delle Grazie e di San Bernardino, or bike the Volastra circuit.

DAY 2
From Manarola the path ascends slightly and then follows a mule track through terraced vines until it reaches the steep descent to Corniglia (1 hour) and a dive site, La Franata di Corniglia. Alternatively, explore Corniglia's Roman origins.

DAY 3
From Corniglia, follow the path that skirts the coast until you descend into Vernazza (1½ hours), with its 14th-century Castello Doria and defensive walls. Walk up to the Santuario della Madonna di Reggio to see the amazing display of sailors' religious offerings.

DAY 4
The longest section of the walk is from Vernazza to Monterosso al Mare; here the path ascends to 180 m (590 ft) before descending precipitously to Monterosso (2 hours), where you can see the crenellated *campanile* (bell tower) of the Gothic church of San Giovanni Battista.

DAY 5
Wander around the Parco Montale to see the places that inspired the poet, and laze on the beach before boarding the train home.

Dos and Don'ts

☑ Remember that you are in a national park bordered by a marine reserve; respect both the wildlife and the dry-stone walled terraces of vines, lemon and olive groves created by hand over hundreds of years.

☒ Don't think you can see it all better from a car window: the *litoranea* road is single lane through tunnels where traffic lights turn green for 5 minutes an hour in each direction.

☑ Climb the steep path from each village to its clifftop sanctuary to admire the medieval architecture and breathtaking views.

Main: The tiny harbour at Riomaggiore, one of the Cinque Terre villages

Top: Coastal path at Riomaggiore

Above: Relaxing with a coffee in a peaceful piazza

Below: Turquoise waters at Monterosso al Mare

Below: Terraced vineyard near Monterosso al Mare

JAN
FEB
MAR
APR
DAY 1
DAY 2
DAY 3
DAY 4
DAY 5
MAY
JUN
JUL
AUG
SEP
OCT
NOV
DEC

GETTING THERE
Foz do Iguaçu (the town) is in southwest Brazil, about 2 hours by plane from Rio de Janeiro and São Paulo. Overland entry is possible from Argentina and Paraguay.

GETTING AROUND
Buses, taxis and tourist vans are the best ways to get around Iguaçu and the National Park. The bus to the park from the town is cheap but slow – taxis are quicker and cost around £10. Car hire is possible, for the adventurous.

WEATHER
Iguaçu in April is pleasantly warm during the day with an average temperature of about 18°C.

ACCOMMODATION
The only hotel inside the park is the Hotel das Cataratas, set in pleasant grounds; doubles from £155; www.hoteldascataratas.com.

The San Rafael is good value; doubles from £40; www.sanrafaelhotelfoz.com.br

Bourbon Cataratas is situated close to town and has many activities on offer; doubles from £90; www.bourbon.com.br

EATING OUT
A good meal should cost under £10 a head. For excellent steak try Búfalo Branco, or Zaragoza for superb Spanish cuisine. The Porto Canoas restaurant, overlooking the falls, is good for lunch.

PRICE FOR TWO
Around £175 per day including accommodation, food, local travel, souvenirs and entry to the park.

FURTHER INFORMATION
www.cataratasdoiguacu.com.br

The Itaipu Dam
The Itaipu Dam is perhaps the inevitable human response to the natural grandeur of Iguaçu Falls. The colossal manmade construction produces about a quarter of Brazil's total supply of electricity. Visitors are shown a video on the dam's construction and are then taken by bus to an observation point on the mid-point of the massive structure. For a more in-depth look, book the Special Tour ahead of time, which gets you into the dam's control centre and production building.

Main: The torrential and mighty rush of water at the Iguaçu Falls

AT THE DEVIL'S THROAT

Though there are other great waterfalls in the world, none can match Iguaçu's combination of towering heights, soul-churning flow and pristine rainforest setting. "Poor Niagara. . .", was Eleanor Roosevelt's comment upon seeing Iguaçu Falls for the first time. The falls straddle the border between southern Brazil and northern Argentina, where the powerful but slow Iguaçu River approaches a 3-km (2-mile) wide precipice. At the cliff edge, the river shatters and the shards of water seek hundreds of different pathways down to the gorge below. Some take the 70 m (230 ft) drop in a series of steps, crashing and splashing from clifftop to rock shelf to swirling whirlpool, spinning for a time before gravity tugs them back on their journey down. Others spill in gossamer threads so thin they turn to mist before they even touch the ground. The main body of the river hurtles into a huge horseshoe shaped defile, a boiling cauldron of water and foam known as *El Garganta del Diablo*, the Devil's Throat.

"Poor Niagara…" was Eleanor Roosevelt's comment, upon seeing Iguaçu Falls for the first time

WATERFALL DIARY

The falls are at their most dramatic in April, when they are swollen with summer rainfall. Four days is enough time to see both sides of the falls and have a day for some additional activities. Extend your holiday with a stay in Brazil's beautiful Rio (see pp322–3), or Argentina's lively capital, Buenos Aires (see pp264–5).

Four Days at the Falls

Start your visit on the Brazilian side, where you can learn about the park's natural history at the visitor centre. At the falls, check out all the trails, get wet on the boardwalks and take time to let the spectacular views sink in. Make sure to take the thrilling Macuco Safari jetboat ride to the very foot of the cascade. Afterwards, enjoy a delicious meal on the Porto Canoas restaurant terrace.

Set out early for the Argentinian side. From the main visitor centre, catch the narrow-gauge railway to the platform that takes you all the way up to the very lip of the incredible Devil's Throat. Get into the jungle on one of the many walking trails or, if you missed the jetboat ride up the river on the Brazilian side, you can get much the same wet and thrilling ride on the Argentinian side.

Use this day to explore some of the attractions beyond the falls. For nature lovers, there are interesting boat tours on the Iguaçu River where you can see cayman sunning themselves on the river bank.

Bird lovers will adore the Iguaçu Bird Park, on the Brazilian side, just outside the park. This houses an amazing variety of Brazilian bird species, many of them in large walk-through aviaries, while anyone with a technical bent should take a trip to see the mammoth Itaipu Dam.

Spend your last day relaxing, do some last minute sightseeing, or get one more look at one of the most spectacular natural wonders of the world.

Dos and Don'ts

✓ Pack a light raincoat and a plastic bag for your camera. The park itself is a rainforest and even on dry days you can get very wet.

✓ See the falls from both the Brazilian and the Argentinian sides and judge for yourself which is best.

✓ If you decide to hire a car, remember to tell the agency that you will be taking it across a border and that you will need the appropriate paperwork.

✗ Don't feed the cute and persistent little coatis (South American raccoons) that will accost you on the walking trails.

JAN
FEB
MAR
APR
DAY 1
DAY 2
DAY 3
DAY 4
MAY
JUN
JUL
AUG
SEP
OCT
NOV
DEC

Below: Dusky swifts swooping around the falls

Neither mist nor haze block your view of this spectacular display of nature, and on sunny days perfect rainbows form above the sparkling surface of the water. Encircling the falls is a lush subtropical rainforest, large and pristine enough that spotted jaguars still slink stealthily beneath the tree canopy. Although you are unlikely to encounter any of these big cats, you will almost certainly see the clouds of dusky swifts swooping in the updrafts from the falls and colourful, large-beaked toucans flopping from tree to tree with their cumbersome bills. Butterflies are everywhere, including the giant blue morpho, whose 15-cm (6-in) wings flash a striking iridescent blue as they flit and flutter away through the over-sized forest plants.

An intense national rivalry between Brazil and Argentina has only improved the falls in recent years, as both nations upgrade their facilities to make their side of the falls the best. Visitors should experience the falls in all its settings: from the water, from the air, by train and on foot, from distant vantage points that provide long sweeping views, and on viewing platforms almost within touching distance of the water, where the spray from the falls blasts its way into your soul.

GETTING THERE
Samarkand is in Uzbekistan, 275 km (170 miles) from Tashkent, the capital, which has an international airport. It takes 5 hours by bus from Tashkent to Samarkand although the latter, like Bukhara and Khiva, has a local airport.

GETTING AROUND
For travelling around the country, buses are cheaper and more frequent than trains; for trips into the countryside, hire taxis for the day.

WEATHER
In April the weather is very pleasant with an average daytime temperature of 22°C, with the odd cloudy day. Rain is unusual.

ACCOMMODATION
Amelia, 1 Bozor Hoja St, Bukhara is a privately owned guesthouse; doubles from £15.

Malika Samarkand Hotel (there is also another branch in Khiva); doubles from £25; www.malika-samarkand.com

Newly built Hotel President Palace, 53 Shokruh St, Samarkand; doubles from £80.

EATING OUT
Food is not really a highlight of a trip to Uzbekistan. Hotels serve mostly Russian food while the local restaurants sell *plov* (pilau rice), mutton *shashlik* (kebabs), discs of soft bread, green tea and watermelon. You can eat well for a few pounds but the food will vary little.

PRICE FOR TWO
£90–120 per day including accommodation, food and local travel.

FURTHER INFORMATION
www.samarkand.info

The Legacy of Timur

Born in 1336 near Samarkand, Timur (also known as Tamerlane) raised an army of Turkic-speaking Mongols and created an empire that extended from the Euphrates to the Indus. He brought together the best artisans from all corners of his empire to transform Samarkand into one of the most beautiful cities in the world. The tiles above, from the Registan, show Timur represented as a lion and are unique in Islamic art which forbids figural art in a religious context.

Above (left to right): Sher-Dor Madrassah, Registan, Samarkand; Uzbek trader; old, ornate doorway, Samarkand
Main: Blue dome of the Bibi-Khanum Mosque, Samarkand

CROSSROADS OF HISTORY

O NE OF THE MOST ROMANTIC NAMES of the trading stops along the Silk Road, Samarkand is still rich in the architecture that made it a remarkable outpost of medieval civilization. The city luxuriates in a golden sunlight that causes everything to glitter, from tomb mosaics and vivid lapis-blue tiled cupolas, to the gold and silver threads that run through the scarves of the local women. The central, unmissable sight is the Registan – a vast square, framed on three sides by a trio of 16th-century *madrassahs* (religious colleges). These great monuments are decorated with the most intricate and delicate patterns imaginable; floral, calligraphic and geometric motifs in dazzling blues, greens and golds. The scale and beauty of Samarkand's monuments is breathtaking but daily life in the Old Market is just as fascinating; women in colourful headscarves sell their wares amid piles of green and yellow watermelons and the air is filled with the aromas of spices and *shashlik* (mutton kebabs) sizzling over glowing charcoals cooked by bearded men in skull caps.

> "All I heard about the beauty of Samarkand appeared to be true, but the fact is: she is even more beautiful than I could have imagined."
>
> Alexander the Great

These scenes have barely changed from the era of the Silk Road, even if some of the wares on sale – instant coffee and plastic toys – reflect more modern tastes.

Some travellers prefer the more walkable intimacy of Bukhara, 240 km (150 miles) west along the Silk Road. This venerable town resembles an idealized desert oasis, riddled with narrow, winding alleys and dilapidated monuments crowned with scruffy storks' nests. At the heart of the Old Town is Lyab-i-Hauz, a cooling pool of water shaded by leafy mulberry trees and surrounded by tea houses with intricately carved divans where you can sit and gossip with the locals, while drinking green tea and dreaming of owning a hundred caravans of fine silk and gold. Another 320 km (200 miles) further west lies Khiva, the last outpost before the desert. Smaller still, the whole town is a living museum where time truly seems to have stopped during the Middle Ages.

Inset: Detail of the tile-work on one of the Registan buildings
Below (left to right): Ark Fortress, Bukhara; Kalyon Minaret, Bukhara; interior of the Juma Mosque, Khiva

SILK ROAD DIARY

April is the perfect month to visit Uzbekistan, before the extreme summer heat and sandstorms. A week is the minimum time required to travel this part of the fabulous route. Another Silk Road highlight is Istanbul (*see pp106–7*), one of its western termini, or China, its eastern origin (*pp132–3*).

A Week in Uzbekistan

There's little to see in Tashkent so, depending on the time of your arrival and whether or not you desperately want to experience some modern Uzbek-Russian nightlife, it's best to make the 5-hour journey on to Samarkand as soon as possible.

The Registan in Samarkand merits several visits as its exterior interacts beautifully with the changing light at different times of the day. The Old Market is nearby and can be seen in a combined visit.

See the Bibi-Khanum Mosque; although somewhat dilapidated it still conveys its original grandeur. Hire a taxi for the afternoon for a trip to the countryside to the town of Shakhrisabz, Timur's birthplace.

Head for Bukhara after an early morning visit to the Registan. Rest after the journey with a relaxed evening sipping tea or something stronger at the Lyab-i-Hauz.

The next day is a full-day's sightseeing: the Kalyon Minaret, the impregnable-looking Ark Citadel and the 10th-century Ismail Samani mausoleum.

Make an early start for the ancient town of Khiva by bus (6 hours) – spend the afternoon wandering on foot round the maze of alleyways surrounding the mosques and minarets, always a delight.

There's just time for a quick visit to the Juma Mosque and the Emir's Palace and Harem before flying back to Tashkent for transfer home or an onward flight.

Dos and Don'ts

✓ Drink bottled mineral water only and always check the seals before opening. Be wary even of the delicious looking fruit – make sure you peel everything.

✗ Don't wear shoes when entering someone's house or sitting down in a *chai-khana* (teahouse) – you should keep your socks on though.

✓ Be prepared to haggle over the price of just about everything. It's not rude, it is a way of life, although after thousands of years of practice they will be better at it than you.

JAN
FEB
MAR
APR
DAY 1
DAYS 2–3
DAYS 4–5
DAYS 6–7
MAY
JUN
JUL
AUG
SEP
OCT
NOV
DEC

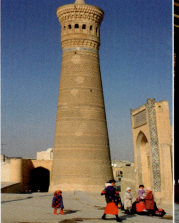

GETTING THERE
Athens is the capital of Greece. The international airport is 30 km (18 miles) from the city centre, about 45 minutes by taxi.

GETTING AROUND
The best and easiest way to get around is on foot – the city centre sights are closely packed. The bus and trolleybus network is comprehensive and there is also a useful Metro system.

WEATHER
In April, the weather is sunny with an average maximum temperature of 20°C.

ACCOMMODATION
Airotel Parthenon is excellent value in the heart of old Athens and has family rooms from £75; www.airotel.gr

Achilleas is a small hotel on a quiet street; family rooms from £100; www.achilleashotel.gr

The Electra Palace is within walking distance of the Acropolis; family rooms from £135; www.electrahotels.gr

EATING OUT
Dining out is a national pastime, with big portions and fresh ingredients. Expect to pay £6–12 per person for a traditional taverna dinner; £35 each for a high-end meal. Don't miss the Psyrri district, where live *bouzouki* music often accompanies late dinners.

PRICE FOR A FAMILY OF FOUR
£220–270 per day including accommodation, food, excursions, local travel and entrance charges.

FURTHER INFORMATION
www.gnto.gr

Return to Former Glory

The projects completed for the 2004 Olympics have transformed the historic centre – its long-standing reputation as one of the most chaotic and polluted cities in the world is now undeserved. The famous natural light is again apparent, and the city has a great liveliness about it. Smoke no longer belches from cars and buses, ring roads and the Metro keep traffic at bay, Neo-Classical buildings have been painted and lit up, and a promenade unifying Athens' ancient sites continues to spark life into neglected pockets along the route.

GRECIAN HOLIDAY

W HETHER ARRIVING SOLO OR WITH CHILDREN IN TOW, most visitors find Greece's capital nothing short of captivating these days. The majestic Parthenon continues to dominate the city from its position on top of the imposing Acropolis, while the cleaned-up cobblestone streets bustle with people enjoying the lively atmosphere in street-side cafés.

Children are welcome almost everywhere in Greece, at all hours, and there are many ways to occupy curious minds in this ancient city. The historic centre is an open museum, with railed-off ruins and Byzantine churches sitting alongside apartment buildings and office blocks.

Follow the shady paths through the National Gardens, one of the most peaceful spots in the city, then head towards the all-marble Panathenian Stadium, where the first modern Olympics were held in 1896 – a real draw for any budding athletes. The Agora, the site where democracy was born and the political heart of the city, is utterly fascinating for both young and older minds.

Away from the historical sites, children will enjoy the amusement parks, adventure tours and Spata's enormous zoo. Or, do as many Athenians do – walk along the promenade in the coastal town of Flisvos, stopping to board the *Averof*, a cruiser that dates back to around 1911.

Those lucky enough to be in Greece at Easter (*Pascha)* are in for an extra treat. This is the highlight of the Greek calendar and its traditions are observed by most of the native population. Holy Week begins on the Monday before Easter with a strict fast and houses traditionally get their yearly whitewash on the Tuesday. On Good Friday, church bells toll eerily all day long, and at around 8pm candlelit processions begin behind each church's *epitaphios* (decorated funeral bier), winding slowly through the streets. The following day, at midnight, people gather outside churches with *lambades* (candles) that are lit by priests carrying the holy flame from Jerusalem, which signals Christ's Resurrection. This occurs against a backdrop of fireworks set off by local children. The celebrations culminate on Easter Sunday with Greek music resounding through the streets and parks, and the smell of lamb permeating the air from rooftop spit-roasts.

Main: The Parthenon atop the Acropolis

Top: Detail from the fresco of boxers in the National Archeological Museum

Above: Overlooking Athens from a restaurant on Lykavitos Hill

Below: Guards at the Tomb of the Unknown Soldier

ATHENIAN DIARY

Greece is especially beautiful during springtime, when the temperatures are perfect for comfortable strolls through the historic city centre, ancient ruins and nearby hills. Orthodox Easter is Greece's biggest holiday and usually falls one week later than Western Easter. For exact dates *see p327*.

A Week in the Ancient City

Get your bearings with a wander through the streets of Plaka, the historic heart of the city. Visit the whitewashed suburb of Anafiótika, which resembles an island village. Follow the locals and have a late dinner in the lively Psyrri district or Monastiráki Station's famous kebab street.

Walk through the ancient Agora to visit the iconic Parthenon, which sits impressively on the Acropolis. On the way back, detour to the ancient Kerameikos cemetery or, if it's a Sunday, check out the flea market at Monastiráki. After dinner, enjoy the warm evenings in the café/bar district of Thissio with a nightcap in the child-friendly square, where you can gaze up at the flood-lit Acropolis and Lykavitos Hill.

Plan to spend at least 3 hours at the superb National Archeological Museum, where Greece's most important antiquities are housed. Be sure to stop by Parliament to see the Changing of the Guard on the hour in front of the Tomb of the Unknown Soldier. If you fancy shopping, head to pedestrian Ermoú for high-street bargains; Athinas and surrounding streets for bric-a-brac; or the Kolonaki district for top-of-the-line artifacts.

Take a bus to Cape Sounion to see the famous sunset at the Temple of Poseidon, and return via Piraeus to sample a seafood dinner at Mikrolímano harbour.

Book a day trip to magnificent Delphi, the navel of the earth according to Greek mythology.

Take a three-island cruise to nearby Aegina, Poros and Hydra with their picture-perfect ports.

Dos and Don'ts

☑ Check the opening times of museums and sites, which change around Orthodox Easter and October – they may close for a national holiday on Easter Sunday.

☒ Don't forget to look both ways when crossing even one-way streets; drivers regularly ignore red lights.

☑ Be on guard when taking a taxi from the airport. If the driver quotes more than £20 or is evasive, move on.

☑ Enjoy Athens after dark. Dinner hour starts at 10pm, and streets in the centre are lively and safe throughout the night.

Below: Busy harbour of Mikrolímano, near Athens

JAN

FEB

MAR

APR

DAY 1

DAY 2

DAYS 3–5

DAY 6

DAY 7

MAY

JUN

JUL

AUG

SEP

OCT

NOV

DEC

Left: Meditating in a Zen temple

Right (left to right): Shinto shrine, Heian-jingu; strolling along the Path of Philosophy; the Torii gates at the Fushimi Inari Taisha shrine

Below right: View from Nijo Castle

Inset: Zen garden at Tofuku-ji Temple

GETTING THERE
Kyoto is the hub of the Kansai area and is served by Kansai International Airport. The Haruka Airport Express train connects the airport to the city (1¼ hours). Kyoto is also 2½ hours from Tokyo by bullet train.

GETTING AROUND
The city's small subway system includes the convenient north to south Karasuma line.

WEATHER
In April, the weather is sunny and mild with an average high of 17°C.

ACCOMMODATION
For a taste of authentic Kyoto, include at least one night in a *ryokan*, a traditional guesthouse.

Ryokan Yuhara is a simple but friendly guesthouse with an 11pm curfew; doubles from £38; tel. (81) 75 371 9583.

The Sun Hotel Kyoto is a reliable mid-range option favoured by business travellers with doubles from £60; tel. (81) 75 241 3351.

The coolest place in town is currently the Hyatt Regency; doubles from £120; www.hyatt.com

EATING OUT
Kyoto is known for a local version of the highly ritualized *kaiseki* cuisine, around £25 for a large meal, but not all dining is about strict protocol – cheap noodle bars and sushi joints also abound.

PRICE FOR TWO
£100–150 per day for accommodation, food, local transport and entrance fees.

FURTHER INFORMATION
www.seejapan.co.uk

The World of the Geisha

At the age of 16, young women traditionally start the five-year training that takes them from *maiko* (apprentice). Only after graduation will their hair be ceremoniously cut and they can wear the kimono and *geta* (clogs) of a full geisha. However, the geisha are declining in numbers. At their peak in the early 19th century, Kyoto had around 700 teahouses with 3,000 working geisha. Today, there are about 200 geisha working in the five districts of Kyoto, plus around 50 *maiko*, with ten new entrants to the profession each year.

Main: Cherry trees in full blossom in Kyoto

TRADITION IN BLOOM

ANCIENT KYOTO IS THE YIN TO MODERN TOKYO'S YANG, providing the ultimate glimpse of traditional Japan. Elegance and philosophy permeate every sweep of a raked-pebble temple garden, every swish of a sliding *shoji* door at a discreet teahouse and every staccato clip-clop of a geisha's *geta* (wooden clogs) as she hurries to work. It is, unarguably, the bastion of Japan's rich cultural heritage, with 17 UNESCO World Heritage Sites around the city – 13 Buddhist temples, three Shinto shrines and Nijo Castle. Take it easy on the cultural pilgrimage, though. With so much to soak up, it's easy to overdose on shrines.

Springtime is awaited in Japan with keen anticipation and nowhere more so than in Kyoto when the cherry blossom season, celebrated for centuries in public and private spaces, brings everyone together to contemplate the majesty of the delicate blossom. The meteorological agency even monitors the so-called "cherry blossom front"

> Kyoto is synonymous with geisha…who make their home amid the narrow sidestreets and ancient shrines of the Gion district.

CHERRY BLOSSOM DIARY

Kyoto comes alive in the springtime when the cherry blossom season provides a magical backdrop to the city. Five days is long enough to visit Kyoto's numerous shrines and temples, including time for activities such as hiking in the nearby mountains and some shopping. Extend your trip by visiting Tokyo (see pp286–7).

Five Days in Old Japan

DAY 1 Start in the main downtown area, following up on a morning stroll in the Imperial Palace Park with a visit to Nijo Castle. In the afternoon, check out the latest exhibition at the Museum of Kyoto before heading east to the Gion area at dusk to admire the geisha.

DAY 2 Continue to explore the temples and shrines around the centre – Kiyomizu-dera and Kodai-ji are the main draws – before taking a stroll in nearby Maruyama-koen park, perfect for cherry blossom viewing. After dark, catch a kabuki theatre or geisha dance show.

DAY 3 Start the day with a stroll along the Path of Philosophy, soaking up the scent of cherry blossoms en route to Ginkaku-ji (the Silver Pavilion). After lunch on the go, head to Tofuku-ji Temple to admire the classic Zen garden. For dinner and a taste of old Kyoto, seek out the restaurants on lantern-lit Pontocho.

DAY 4 Spend the day browsing for antique souvenirs along Shinmonzen-dori and watching the world go by in a traditional coffee shop on Kamo-gawa. In the evening, transfer to a *ryokan*, don your *yukata* (gown) and enjoy the ritual of the experience of a slap-up dinner followed by futon beds.

DAY 5 Time to chill out by walking in the countryside around Kyoto – try the twin Kurama and Kibune valleys for fresh air and open spaces. Finish up at the Funaoka Onsen, a gloriously traditional hot springs with a cypress-wood tub and an outdoor dipping pool.

Dos and Don'ts

- ✓ Cash is still king in Japan, so carry around a bundle of notes in mixed denominations.
- ✗ Don't be afraid to slurp your noodles – it shows that you enjoyed the meal.
- ✓ Everybody in Japan has a *meishi* (business card). The etiquette is to offer and accept *meishi* with both hands.
- ✓ At public bath houses make sure you wash outside the bath, using the bath itself purely for soaking.
- ✓ If you are invited to a social event, do take a small gift such as flowers, green tea or a bottle of sake.

allowing the public to follow the festival throughout the season. Meanwhile, geisha stage special cherry dances in performance halls throughout April and pilgrims take to the Path of Philosophy, a pleasant canal-side trail lined by cherry trees, which leads to Ginkaku-ji (the Silver Pavilion).

Kyoto is synonymous with geisha, the "arts person" who makes her home amid the narrow sidestreets and ancient shrines of the Gion district. With dusk falling and the lights of Gion reflecting in puddles, Pontocho, a tiny, narrow street crammed full with exotic restaurants, comes alive with red lanterns illuminating the entrances. Camera-clutching tour groups congregate to indulge in their favourite sport of geisha-spotting, hoping to see a shadowy, kimono-clad figure shuffling along to an appointment at a local teahouse. In reality, however, catching sight of a bona fide geisha in Gion is not easy as geisha are shy and, increasingly, a dying breed.

Traditions still run deep in Kyoto. The city may have succumbed to the noisy mechanical diggers of so-called progress with the development of the area around the train station, but the values of a more refined former age are very much alive behind the city's discreetly closed doors.

JAN
FEB
MAR
APR
MAY
JUN
JUL
AUG
SEP
OCT
NOV
DEC

Below: Apprentice geisha dancers performing at the Pontocho Theatre

GALÁPAGOS ISLANDS

Isla Pinta
Isla Marchena
Isla Genovesa
Isla San Salvador
Isla Fernandina
Isla Isabela
Puerto Ayora
Isla Santa Cruz
Isla Santa Fe
PUERTO BAQUERIZO MORINO
Isla San Cristóbal
Isla Santa María
Isla Española
PACIFIC OCEAN

GETTING THERE
The 13 large, and innumerable smaller, islands of the Galápagos archipelago straddle the Equator, 1,000 km (600 miles) off the coast of Ecuador, South America. International flights go to Quito and Guayaquil in Ecuador, then take a flight to a domestic airport in Santa Cruz.

GETTING AROUND
Small cruise ships and charter boats offer organized excursions around the islands.

WEATHER
Pleasantly warm with temperatures averaging about 27°C. Feb–Apr are the rainiest months, when the islands are at their most verdant.

ACCOMMODATION
Sea views from Hotel Galápagos, Santa Cruz; doubles from £35; www.hotelgalapagos.com

Nemo, sleek catamaran; 12 passengers, from £915 (per person) for 8 days.

Cachalote I, charming schooner; 16 passengers, from £1,025 (per person) for 8 days.

Galápagos Explorer II, luxury cruise yacht; 100 passengers, from £1,590 (per person) for 7 days.

EATING OUT
Seafood is a speciality, try the amazing ceviche. Avoid lobsters, due to their over-fishing. Catered meals are included on boat charters.

PRICE FOR TWO
£225–375 per day including accommodation, food, cruise and entrance fee to the islands.

FURTHER INFORMATION
www.galapagos.org

The Origin of Species

When naturalist Charles Darwin visited the Galápagos in 1835, he noted how each of the 13 islands had a unique species of finch. Darwin speculated that they were all descended from one mainland species and isolation had encouraged the origin of individual species adapted to their unique environments. In 1859, using evidence he collected in the Galápagos, Darwin upset the established view of creation with the publication of his evolutionary theory in *The Origin of Species*.

Above (left to right): Galápagos tortoise resting; colourful Sally Lightfoot crab, San Cristobal Island; blue-footed booby displaying
Main: Brown pelican plunges to catch a mullet

FAR SIDE OF THE WORLD

N O-ONE HAS EVER SUGGESTED THAT THE GALÁPAGOS ISLANDS ARE A TROPICAL PARADISE. One could hardly imagine a more forlorn piece of earth. Darwin called them "the gardens of Hell". In these volcanic islands, the youngest – those furthest west – are still rising from the sea, the product of a "hot spot" hundreds of miles below the ocean floor. The older isles – about five million years old – are softly worn down, in contrast to the newer, more rugged isles. Even the coconut palm, the supreme emblem of the Pacific, is missing. Yet people come back from these islands speaking of marvels and exotic encounters: the islands' namesake ("*Galápagos*" is Spanish for tortoise), the giant tortoise, heaving its 275 kg (610 lb) weight up the beach, sea lions that let you lie down beside their newborn pups and Galápagos hawks that land on your head.

The islands, which owe their unique quality to their isolation, were set aside as a national park in 1959. Visits are strictly regulated and a licensed naturalist guide accompanies each cruise boat to enforce the park rules and educate tourists on the unique ecology, geology, flora and fauna of the fascinating and fragile archipelago.

Everywhere, lava lizards dart back and forth and iguanas lie torpid on shoreline lava floes like prehistoric flotsam washed ashore.

Huge manta rays glide shadow-like under the boat while bottlenose dolphins break the water's surface beside you. On Floreana and Jervis islands, go ashore to watch flamingoes wading in pink-tinged, oozy mud. You can dive with hammerhead sharks off Bartolomé Island or snorkel with penguins off Fernandina. Everywhere, lava lizards dart back and forth, iguanas lie torpid on shoreline lava floes like prehistoric flotsam washed ashore, marine turtles' eggs are hatching and female frigate birds wheel overhead as their mates proudly puff up their vermilion chests. You don't need to be interested in evolutionary theory to be thrilled by these islands, where 90 percent of the reptiles, 80 percent of land birds, and 40 percent of plants are unique.

Inset: Satellite image showing the craters on the islands of Isabela and Fernandina
Below (left to right): Isolated cove on Bartolomé island; diving among a school of striped salema; watchful marine iguana

NATURALIST'S DIARY

The Galápagos are unique for offering spectacular eye-to-eye encounters with wildlife: most of the animals and birds show no fear of humans. The islands are best explored on an organized cruise, departing from Puerto Ayora, Santa Cruz. It's worth adding a few days for exploring Quito and the Andean town of Otavalo.

Nine Days Exploring the Islands

Visit the Charles Darwin Research Station in Puerto Ayora to view the giant tortoise breeding programme.
DAY 1

Explore the verdant Santa Cruz highlands, keeping a look out for its giant tortoises.
DAY 2

Depart by boat for Española (Hood). Commune with marine iguanas, sea lions on sandy beaches and colonies of albatrosses and blue-footed boobies.

On nearby Floreana, watch flamingoes and snorkel with marina turtles and sharks at Devil's Crown. Leave your mail in the "Post Office Barrel".
DAYS 3–4

Hike through the misty highlands of Isabela and swim with sea lions and Galápagos penguins at Tagus Cove.

Look for dolphins and whales in the Bolivar Channel. On Fernandina, photograph cormorants and hike to the summit of a spectacular crater.

After the long haul to Genovesa (Tower), anchor in spectacular Darwin Bay for fabulous birding plus a chance to snorkel with Galápagos fur seals.

Next stop – Bartolomé for a hike to the summit of Pinnacle Rock and panoramic views. Continue to South Plaza, to see the enormous sea lion colony.
DAYS 5–8

Go snorkelling at Santa Fe. Look out for its land iguanas and prickly pear cacti.

Return to Santa Cruz to begin your homeward journey.
DAY 9

Dos and Don'ts

✓ Stay on the trails. The ecosystem is delicate and wandering off the trails can do lasting damage.

✗ Don't touch the creatures – it is strictly forbidden.

✓ Travel by small boat (fewer than 20 passengers is ideal), which offers a more intimate experience.

✗ Don't overdo it if you fly in to Quito on your first day – you may need some time to adjust to the 2,850 m (9,350 ft) altitude.

JAN
FEB
MAR
APR
MAY
JUN
JUL
AUG
SEP
OCT
NOV
DEC

Above (left and right): Decorative tile from the Topkapi Palace; interior of the New Mosque
Main: The domed roof of the Blue Mosque overlooking the Bosphorus

GETTING THERE
Ankara is the capital, but Istanbul is Turkey's largest city. It is served by Atatürk International Airport. A bus service connects the airport to Taksim Square, the heart of modern Istanbul. The journey takes 30 minutes and costs around £2.50.

GETTING AROUND
It is possible to walk around most sights but there is also a large network of tram and metro lines and there are plenty of taxis.

WEATHER
By April days are clear and mild with temperatures between 7°C and 15°C.

ACCOMMODATION
For traditional lodgings, try the Empress Zoe; doubles from £80; www.emzoe.com

Ottoman-style opulence in a renovated wooden townhouse at Yeşil Ev; doubles from £140; www.hotelyesilev.com

Regularly voted one of the top hotels in Europe, Istanbul's Four Seasons has doubles from £300; www.fourseasons.com

EATING OUT
The waterfront districts of Kumkapi and Ortaköy are full of seafood restaurants, try the *balık köftesi* (hot fish cakes). For *meyhanes*, the Turkish equivalent to tapas bars, go to the narrow alleyway of Nevizade Sokak.

PRICE FOR TWO
£180–220 per day including accommodation, food and a Bosphorus boat trip

FURTHER INFORMATION
www.istanbul.com

Constantine's City

In the 4th century, the Roman Emperor Constantine moved his capital from Rome to this city on the Bosphorus. After the division of the Roman Empire, Constantinople became the capital of the Byzantine Empire, lasting until the Ottoman conquest of 1453, after which the city became Istanbul. Hagia Sophia is the most magnificent Byzantine monument with its mosaics featuring many Byzantine emperors *(below)*.

MINARETS AND BAZAARS

ISTANBUL, WITH ITS BEAUTIFUL SPIKY SKYLINE of delicate minarets and onion domes, is a city adorned with fantastic palaces decorated with riches gained in conquest. Visitors can see the city's roots as a trading post with foreign lands in the magnificent Grand Bazaar with its miles of covered passageways and literally thousands of glittering shops and stalls. Here, you can lose yourself for hours and, if you are prepared to haggle hard enough, there are still bargains of jewel-coloured carpets and precious sapphires, rubies and emeralds to be had.

Downhill from the Bazaar, you will find the waters of the Golden Horn, spanned by the Galata Bridge that links the old city with the new – although this being Istanbul, new means at least a century old. The main street, Istiklal Caddesi, and the network of lanes around it are a haven of boutiques, cafés, restaurants, bars and clubs. It's here that you'll find the best food in town – creamy *tarama* – red caviar, delicious mussels stuffed with rice and spices, and the obligatory kebab. You'll also discover the Galatasaray fish market with not only fresh fish but many delicatessens with meats, cheeses, sweetmeats and pickles. One of the most pleasurable ways of dining is to feast on *meze* – portions are small so you can choose between a quick snack of *pide* (small Turkish pizzas) or a grand banquet of dishes that highlight the historic influence of Greece, the Balkans, the Caucasus and the Levant. This heady mix, accompanied by the anise-flavoured spirit *rakı* and a serenade by musicians playing the melancholic *saz*, makes it a cultural experience to rival a visit to the grandest of ancient monuments.

However, as a former capital of not one but two major empires – the ancient Byzantine and Ottoman Turkish – Istanbul is rich with imperial history and monuments that are an awesome sight to behold. The promontory of land known today as Sultanahmet was developed under centuries of emperors and sultans, its great walls enclosed long-since vanished palaces and some of the world's earliest Christian religious establishments. Today, among the many archeological treasures, you can explore the magnificent Topkapi Palace, the Blue Mosque and the remnants of the great hippodrome used for chariot races.

Below (left and right): Bustling crowds at the Grand Bazaar; Roman ruins at Yerebatan Saray

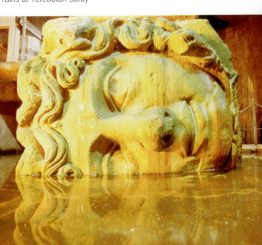

ANCIENT CITY DIARY

To really enjoy Istanbul means crossing the Golden Horn and exploring the 19th-century city centre neighbourhoods where the locals work and play. It's also worthwhile getting out on the water and taking a trip up the Bosphorus; not only is the boat ride enjoyable but Istanbul looks its best when seen from the water.

Four Days by the Bosphorus

Visit Istanbul's premier attraction, the Topkapi Palace, the seat of the Ottoman sultans and the hub of imperial power for three centuries. With four courts, numerous halls showcasing collections of jewellery, arms and armour, ceramics and silverware, plus the harem quarters, a full visit takes the best part of a day.

Explore the Blue Mosque and Haghia Sophia, two exquisite pieces of architecture.

Walk to the nearby spectacular underground Byzantine cistern, which is en route to the Grand Bazaar, where anybody inclined to shopping could lose days, if not weeks, of their lives.

Rummage around the Egyptian Bazaar down on the shore of the Golden Horn in search of bargains.

Cross the bridge over to the Galata Tower for marvellous views back towards historic Sultanhamet. Stop and have a drink in the area around the tower, old Pera, the 19th-century city, full of beautiful European-style architecture and streets filled with pavement cafes and bars.

Take a trip on a ferry from Eminönü up the Bosphorus. The standard cruise takes 6 hours return with a 2-hour stop off in a small fishing village — time enough for a fish lunch and a quick walk before returning to Istanbul.

Dos and Don'ts

✓ Haggle in the bazaar. It is expected and if you don't, be assured you will end up paying way over the odds.

✗ Don't think about getting an early night because Istanbul buzzes until the early hours of the morning.

✓ Be careful when buying street food; oysters in particular can quickly go off when displayed in hot weather.

✓ Check your change carefully when using taxis as Istanbul's cab drivers are notorious for taking advantage of tourists.

✓ Take your shoes off when visiting mosques – you won't be allowed in otherwise.

JAN
FEB
MAR
APR
DAY 1
DAY 2
DAY 3
DAY 4
MAY
JUN
JUL
AUG
SEP
OCT
NOV
DEC

Below: Colourful carpets at the Grand Bazaar.

GETTING THERE
Orlando is in central Florida, about 56 km (35 miles) inland from the east coast beaches.

GETTING AROUND
Orlando International Airport is about a 30-minute drive from Lake Buena Vista, home to Walt Disney World®, or to central Orlando.

WEATHER
Warm and pleasant – April has an average high temperature of 29°C.

ACCOMMODATION
Nickelodeon Family Suites offer free transport to other theme parks; suites from £60; www.nickhotel.com

Hampton Inn and Suites is a moderate, good value choice – from £75 for four; www.hamptoninnlbv.com

Guests of Walt Disney World® resorts or Universal Studios® hotels get perks specific to the theme parks; two doubles from £80; www.disneyworld.disney.go.com www.universalorlando.com

EATING OUT
Hundreds of choices for all budgets – fast food abounds. But sophisticated palates won't starve either – famous American chefs, such as Emiril and Wolfgang Puck, have restaurants here.

COST FOR A FAMILY OF FOUR
£280–335 per day including accommodation, food and a five-day Park Hopper pass for two adults and two children.

FURTHER INFORMATION
www.orlando.com

Kennedy Space Center

The Kennedy Space Center, home to NASA's space launch programme, has exhibits tracing the history of space exploration. The island was chosen for missile experiments in 1949 as it faced out to the Atlantic and was as close as you can get to the Equator in the USA – the rockets get a boost from the earth's rotation. The Center's highlights include a bus tour of the launch sites, seeing actual rockets and the Firing Room Theater simulating a rocket launch. Check the website: www.kennedyspacecenter.com

Above (left to right): Rafting on Castaway Creek, Walt Disney World®; Mickey Mouse; Shamu the killer whale, at SeaWorld®
Main: Spectacular firework display lights up the Magic Kingdom in Walt Disney World®

FUN FOR ALL THE FAMILY

MEETING MICKEY AND HIS MANY FRIENDS is the highlight of anyone's visit to Disney World. And that means everybody. After watching the excitement growing in the adults and children ahead of you in the queue for a bit of up-close and personal interaction, a quick hug from the six-foot-something hyperactive rodent is guaranteed to melt the heart of even the most cynical adult. On the way in to the park as you go through the turnstiles, they must sprinkle pixie dust on you or something but you really do turn back into a child and start grinning – along with all the other happy people. At times it may seem as though the green dollar, not pixie dust, makes Disney World the magical place it is but whatever it is, it works. Even when the place is heaving, Mickey and his animated chums still manage to create a good time for all.

Orlando was a sleepy town surrounded by citrus groves until 1971 when Walt Disney's Magic Kingdom arrived. Now it is the world's most popular holiday destination with over 20 million

visitors annually, rollicking through a non-stop parade of attractions, nausea-inducing rollercoasters and astonishing wildlife and water parks. The Magic Kingdom is just one of six parks that comprise the enormous Disney World. Universal Studios and SeaWorld seem to grow bigger every year. There is truly something for everyone from small tots to grandparents; the only challenge is fitting all the excitement into a single visit.

But there's more to Florida than theme parks so try a couple of days of Disney-detox at the wonderful sandy beaches to the east that stretch on for miles (it can be windy and the sea is somewhat fresh). Daytona Beach (north) and Cocoa Beach (south) are perfect for blowing out the pixie dust. Chill out at a natural theme park – a beach: splash in the waves, build your own castle out of sand and eat at the shrimp shack as the sun sets. Now that's magical and not a mouse in sight.

. . . as you go through the turnstiles, they must sprinkle pixie dust on you or something but you really do turn back into a child. . .

Inset: Universal Studios® rollercoaster
Below (left to right): Shuttle launch from the Kennedy Space Center; Harry P Leu's gorgeous gardens; rolling surf and golden sands at Daytona Beach

JAN

FEB

MAR

APR

MAY

JUN

JUL

AUG

SEP

OCT

NOV

DEC

FAIRY-TALE DIARY

No destination offers more family fun than Orlando. Besides Walt Disney World®, Universal Studios® and SeaWorld®, you can enjoy the beach or get into space at the Kennedy Space Center. April is prime time for a visit, before summer heat sets in and while many schools are on Easter holidays.

A Week of Childish Delights

DAY 1
Start with the classic, Disney's Magic Kingdom®. Ride Space Mountain's rocket and enjoy a spooky trip through the Haunted Mansion – and, of course, meet the Mouse and his equally famous friends.

DAYS 2–3
There's so many parks to choose from: you could go around the world at Epcot® or see the stars at MGM Studios®, for stunt shows and more thrill rides. Alternatively, go for a safari in the vast African Wildlife Park at Disney's Animal Kingdom® before finally cooling off at Disney's Blizzard Beach waterpark on a 90-kph (55-mph) water slide.

DAYS 4–5
Head to Universal Studios® for movie-theme fun, plus the chance to see how films are made. Universal's Islands of Adventure, a separate park, provides the ultimate in superhero thrill rides. SeaWorld marine park offers dolphin shows and the chance to meet Shamu the killer whale, the star of the park.

DAY 6
Five days at the parks should be enough fun for most people so do try and see what else the area has to offer – gardeners would enjoy Harry P Leu's peaceful gardens nearby in Orlando, while beach aficionados should drive east to the cooling ocean and recover on one of the impressive beaches.

DAY 7
Spend the last day exploring space – planning future holidays perhaps – at the Kennedy Space Center. If you are really lucky you may see a rocket launch.

Dos and Don'ts

✓ Plan your day out as thoroughly as possible – the parks are huge and wandering aimlessly will lead to frustration.

✗ Don't drive at rush hour if you hire a car; Orlando has only one major artery, I-4, and it gets jammed with local residents going to and from work.

✓ Arrive at the parks early, before the biggest crowds arrive and to get the most out of your day.

✓ Consider paying extra for Express Pass service at Universal or a Disney FastPass during busy periods to save long waits (and whines) in the sun.

GETTING THERE
Paris has two airports – Orly and Charles de Gaulle. Trains from Charles de Gaulle to Gare du Nord take 45 minutes, and from Orly to Quai d'Orsay it is 30 minutes.

GETTING AROUND
The metro and RER lines are an easy way to get around town. Taxis are readily available.

WEATHER
In April, the average temperature is 12ºC. Days are usually bright and sunny but evenings can be cool and the weather changeable.

ACCOMMODATION
Hotel du Jeu de Paume is a hideaway on the Île Saint-Louis; doubles from £140; www.jeudepaumehotel.com

Murano Urban Resort, the hippest spot in the Marais, with a spa and hammam; doubles from £275; www.muranoresort.com

Ritz Paris, for luxurious decadence; doubles from £550; www.ritzparis.com

EATING OUT
Paris is renowned for its luxurious food: buttery brioche, sumptuous patisserie, rich sauces and ripe cheese. For lunch, try La Palette, Rue de Seine, an atmospheric café on the Left Bank. In the evening, savour aphrodisiac oysters at Le Bar à Huître; www.barhuitre.com

PRICE FOR TWO
£270–320 per day, including accommodation, food, local transport and entrance charges.

FURTHER INFORMATION
www.parisinfo.com

Cimetière du Père-Lachaise

Situated on a wooded hill overlooking the city, is Paris's most prestigous cemetery. The land was bought by order of Napoleon in 1803 to create a new cemetery and was so popular with the city's bourgeoisie that it was expanded six times during the 19th century. The elaborate graves and interesting monuments make this a pleasant place for a leisurely stroll. Particularly of interest are the graves of Simone Signoret and Yves Montand, Edith Piaf, Jim Morrison and Oscar Wilde.

Main: The Eiffel Tower illuminated in the Parisian dusk.

Above (left to right): Enjoying the colourful café society in Montmartre; cheeky gargoyle adorning Notre-Dame Cathedral; waiters inside Brasserie Flo.

ROMANCE IN THE SPRING

WITH CHESTNUTS IN BLOSSOM AND HOLIDAY TABLES UNDER THE TREES, it seems that Paris and April were made for each other. Romance has been in the Parisian spring air at least since the 12th century when Pierre Abélard fell for his student, Héloïse Fulbert, resulting in such an enduring love story that Napoleon's Josephine had their remains reunited in the Père-Lachaise cemetery some 700 years later. A cemetery is not a usual tourist sight in a city, but this one attracts thousands every year because so many of its interrees are romantic figures – Bizet, Rossini, Apollinaire, Sarah Bernhardt, Maria Callas, Modigliani, Piaf, Proust, Jim Morrison and Oscar Wilde.

Couples in search of romance have much to see in Paris, from the view at the top of the Eiffel Tower to dinner cruises on the Seine. But real romantics will be content just to stroll through the spring sunshine along the blossom-strewn Left Bank streets, the ancient Marais quarter, or along the lanes of Île Saint-Louis. They will find a corner of the Jardin du Luxembourg or the Canal

> Real romantics will be content just to stroll through the spring sunshine along the blossom-strewn Left Bank steets, the ancient Marais quarter, or along the lanes of Île Saint-Louis.

St-Martin for a quiet moment, or declare their love with a kiss in the middle of Pont Neuf. A *café au lait* can be lingered over in street-side cafés, and intimate meals shared in a candlelit bistro. The literati will visit Shakespeare & Company, the famous Left Bank bookshop of Hemingway and Joyce, the arty will see what's on at the Beaubourg. Those interested in the haunts of Paris's bohemians will battle the Montmartre crowds to see the Moulin Rouge or perhaps catch a cabaret.

There is evening entertainment everywhere, whether you want to dress up in your finery for Charles Garnier's sumptuous opera house, inspiration for the spooky *Le Fantôme de l'Opéra*, or attend a concert in one of the city's atmospheric ancient churches. There is also excellent live jazz in bars and clubs around the city, perfect for rounding off another fabulous night in the most romantic city in the world.

Inset: Windows of the prestigious jewellery shop Cartier
Below (left to right): Art Nouveau Métro entrance sign; Pont Alexandre III; detail of Rodin's marble masterpiece *The Kiss*

SPRINGTIME DIARY

April in Paris is where you meet the charm of spring face to face. It is the start of the summer season of eating alfresco and the first outdoor concerts. Beneath cloud-scattered blue skies you can appreciate architecture and outdoor sculptures, stroll among the Montmartre painters and see blossom everywhere.

Five Days in the City of Lights

DAY 1
A great place to start is the heart of the city, on Île de la Cité, where you can climb to the top of Notre-Dame for a first sight of all of Paris, before taking a cruise from the quay beneath Pont Neuf.

Afterwards, wander through Île Saint-Louis and visit Bertillon for the best ice cream in Paris. Alternatively, head out of the city to the Cimetière du Père-Lachaise.

DAY 2
On the Left Bank, visit the Musée National du Moyen Age to see the enchanting Renaissance tapestry series, *Lady and the Unicorn*, then linger at the famous Left Bank cafés and check out the Shakespeare & Company bookshop.

Picnic under the trees in the Jardin du Luxembourg, then see 19th-century French art at the Musée d'Orsay.

DAY 3
Take a trip to the Marais, one of the most intimate districts of Paris. Visit the apartment of Victor Hugo, leading light of the Romantic Movement, in elegant Place des Vosges.

DAY 4
Make an early start to make the most of the Louvre. Afterwards, stroll through the Tuileries admiring Maillol's bronze nudes, before heading towards Rue de Rivoli for some of the city's best shops. Wander over beautiful Pont Alexandre III as the sun sets.

DAY 5
Stroll through Montmartre, then visit beautiful Sacré-Coeur. Later, take the Metro to visit the Musée Rodin, where you can see *The Kiss* and the lovely rose garden.

As the sun goes down, take a lift to the top of the Eiffel Tower for a memorable last glimpse of the city.

Dos and Don'ts

☑ Buy *Pariscope*, the essential weekly listings magazine, to keep an eye on what's happening around town.

☒ Don't forget that museums are often closed on Mondays and sometimes Tuesdays.

☑ Remember that the Beaubourg (Pompidou Centre) stays open until 10pm.

JAN
FEB
MAR
APR
MAY
JUN
JUL
AUG
SEP
OCT
NOV
DEC

Below: Bateau Mouche in front of Notre-Dame Cathedral

AMSTERDAM · Zwolle
NORTH SEA · NETHERLANDS · GERMANY
BELGIUM · Maastricht

GETTING THERE
Amsterdam, capital of the Netherlands, lies just inland from the North Sea. It is served by Schipol International Airport,

GETTING AROUND
The city lies 18 km (12 miles) from the airport, or 20 minutes by train. Buses, trams and walking are the best method of getting around the old town centre.

WEATHER
Daytime temperatures in April average around 13°C with occasional spring showers.

ACCOMMODATION
The city is popular year-round so reserve accommodation as early as possible.

Quintessentially Dutch, the Hotel Brouwer is simple but elegant; doubles from £75; www.hotelbrouwer.nl

The Seven Bridges Hotel is centrally located; doubles from £90; www.sevenbridgeshotel.nl

Amsterdam's best designer hotel, Seven One Seven with amenities and prices to impress; doubles from £335; www.717hotel.nl

EATING OUT
Amsterdam's colonial heritage means you'll find some exotic delights, particularly from Indonesia, or try the traditional *stampot* (a smoked sausage stew with puréed potato).

PRICE FOR TWO
£160–180 per day including accommodation, food and entrance charges.

FURTHER INFORMATION
www.amsterdamtourist.nl

The Night Watch

The most famous Golden Age painting, Rembrandt van Rijn's *Night Watch* marked the beginning of the end for the artist's career. Painted in 1642, Rembrandt illuminated the characters of the departing militia that he saw as key and put the rest in shadow – displeasing some of the powerful men who'd paid to be included. Soon after, his career went into decline and by 1656 he was bankrupt.

Pleasure boats glide through its lacy canal system, the sunlight glinting off their buffed wooden hulls onto opulent town houses.

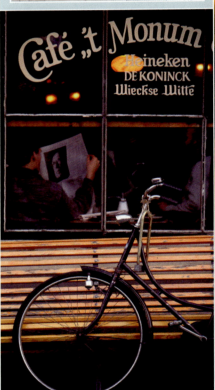

Main: Dusk descends on the Keizersgracht (Emperor's Canal)
Above: Relaxing in one of Amsterdam's "brown" cafés, so called because of their gloomy interiors of dark woodwork and tobacco smoke
Inset: Gilded clock over the Centraal railway station

TRAVEL THE WATERWAYS

GEERT MAK, THE DUTCH HISTORIAN AND JOURNALIST, argues that poverty saved Amsterdam's splendid centre from destruction, leaving it preserved "like Sleeping Beauty in a glass coffin". It is hard to imagine that this vibrant city was ever ready for embalming. Pleasure boats glide through its lacy canal system, the sunlight glinting off their buffed wooden hulls onto opulent town houses, the pride of the colonial merchants. Cyclists toting briefcases and fragrant bouquets whizz over the cobblestones, dodging visitors stunned by the elegance of a 17th-century façade. It is not monumental scale but fine details that lend these handsome edifices their ageless charm: a statuette, a gable topped with a wedding-cake cornice, a curlicued inscription by its original stonemason. This is a mine of renewable delight, as you wander along the same canal and find a surprise at every turn. Make your way to the Golden Bend on the Herengracht for a stretch that is particularly rich in detail.

Above: Revellers on the streets of Amsterdam celebrating Queen's Day, a national holiday; colourful tulips in bloom in the fields of the Keukenhof

Below: Typical fine architectural detailing with red brick and stone on the Huis Bartolotti, Amsterdam

ART-LOVER'S DIARY

Late April is the best time to see blooming tulips, Golden Age paintings and beautiful canals with a shot at good weather. You can also party with thousands of others in the Dutch Queen's birthday festivities. Five days are enough to cover most things including a jaunt to the Keukenhof fields.

Five Days Touring the Canals

Start with the Old Masters, getting up early to beat the crowds at the Van Gogh Museum, the Stedelijk or Rijksmuseum, home of the *Night Watch*.

View the red light district from a canal boat tour and admire the beautiful houses in the southern canal belt.

Pick up a pungent Gouda and home-made bread at the farmer's market on Noordermarkt. Shop in the quirky boutiques in the Negen Straatjes district, and relax with a drink at one of the many waterfront cafés.

Later, picnic in the sun at the Vondelpark then burn off the excess by dancing until the early hours in a club.

A full day out: flee the city, camera in hand, for the stunning tulip fields of the Keukenhof near the town of Haarlem, just north of the capital.

Visit the Netherlands Maritime Museum and see what life on board an 18th-century schooner was like.

Linger in a picturesque spot – perhaps the Seven Bridges on Reguliersgracht and savour the view.

Wander the café-filled Jordaan district or do as the Dutch do and cycle through the canal belt.

Join in with the Dutch Queen's birthday celebrations (*Koninginnedag*) usually on, or around, 30 April, when thousands of people gather in the city's streets to party and sell their wares in a huge open market.

Dos and Don'ts

✗ Don't smoke marijuana on the street – that is what coffee shops are for.

✓ Dress casually for most occasions, even the opera. Save your formal attire for the Queen.

✗ Don't even think about driving a car in Amsterdam. The one-way system is confusing and parking is a nightmare.

JAN

FEB

MAR

APR

DAY 1

DAY 2

DAY 3

DAY 4

DAY 5

MAY

JUN

JUL

AUG

SEP

OCT

NOV

DEC

Stop to peer up at the ceiling-high windows of these homes and you'll see the curtains are open to reveal a hand-carved bookcase or a brass chandelier – likely the greatest show of personal wealth you'll see in Amsterdam. Its inhabitants have bounced from colonial riches to squalor and back and know the trick isn't in making wealth but keeping it. For newcomers to the city, this can be an intriguing source of amusement; is that poised gent in the threadbare jacket an academic, a wealthy landlord, or perhaps both?

The Dutch Golden Age (1584–1702), when Holland's liberal regime allowed an influx of religious and political exiles, generated not just pots of wealth but also a plethora of breathtaking art. In Rembrandt's day, fine paintings were so common that they hung in the cottages of tradesmen and were even bartered for poultry. Today, Amsterdam treats these treasures with a touch more respect, yet the masterpieces in its Rijksmuseum and Van Gogh Museum, two of the world's most valuable collections, are pleasingly accessible to visitors.

Below: 18th-century schooner the *Amsterdam*, Shipping Museum

MAY

Where to Go: May

This is usually a pleasant month the whole world over. Winter hasn't yet hit the southern hemisphere, while the north finally delivers on its spring promise and the weather is consistently better. The Mediterranean warms up enough to get in the water without too much fuss and flowers bloom in abundance; even the far reaches of northern USA reach relatively comfortable temperatures. May Day was the traditional festival that marked the end of winter and beginning of summer. These days much of the world is more likely to celebrate May Day – 1st May – not as the beginning of summer but as International Workers' Day. To help you choose, you'll find all the destinations in this chapter below, as well as some extra suggestions to provide a little inspiration.

FESTIVALS AND CULTURE

PRAGUE Atmospheric mist on the Charles Bridge

UNFORGETTABLE JOURNEYS

SILK ROAD Rug salesman displays his wares

NATURAL WONDERS

VICTORIA FALLS Sunset over the falls, from the Zambian side

PRAGUE
CZECH REPUBLIC, EUROPE

Musical city with a splendid array of beautiful buildings

Prague is a marvellous repository of Medieval, Baroque and Renaissance buildings and in May these ring out with the sound of music.
See pp134–5

BRIGHTON
ENGLAND, EUROPE

"London-on-sea" throws a great arts festival all month

The town has much going for it in the way of art, culture and nightlife, with hundreds of interesting venues including the Pavilion.
www.brightonfestival.org

SILK ROAD
CHINA, ASIA

Follow the legendary trading route between east and west

Capture the romance of travel on the road from Xian, ancient capital of China, through harsh deserts and high mountains, to the West.
See pp132–3

WEST COAST
SCOTLAND, EUROPE

Through a landscape that has inspired poets and painters

The West Coast's legendary beauty is perfectly matched with great hospitality and this trip lets the visitor enjoy a bit of both.
See pp128–9

> "Dream-like spires of rock and delicate wind-carved arches stand in silence above stunning desert tableaux."

COLORADO PLATEAU
USA, NORTH AMERICA

Drive through the amazing Colorado Plateau landscapes

Take a camper van through the National Parks of the Southwest – see Bryce Canyon and the big one, the Grand Canyon.
See pp120–1

BOSTON
USA, NORTH AMERICA

A pretty and historical centre, good pubs and good food

Small and compact, Boston's historical centre is rich with Colonial history, fine Irish pubs and many examples of cultural and intellectual excellence.
See pp126–7

> "A citadel of quiet charm and tradition whose pretty streets and neighbourhoods cry out to be explored on foot."

CAMINO DE SANTIAGO
SPAIN, EUROPE

The medieval pilgrims' way

Walk, cycle or even ride a horse through Northern Spain, staying at traditional and hospitable inns along the way.
www.caminodesantiago.me.uk

RHODOPES
BULGARIA, EUROPE

A wild and unspoiled corner of Europe waits to be explored

The Rhodope Mountains are most famous for their raptors – eagles, vultures and buzzards – but spring sees their wildflowers bloom too.
www.rodopi-bg.com

VICTORIA FALLS
ZAMBIA & ZIMBABWE, AFRICA

One of the most spectacular waterfalls in the world

The mighty Zambesi river pours into a huge rip in the African earth with an awesome roar. See it up close with some whitewater rafting.
See pp130–1

ST LUCIA
CARIBBEAN

Come just after the peak season for beach fun and jazz

St Lucia expands on the usual Caribbean repertoire of great beaches, sunshine and warm water, with a very respectable Jazz Festival.
stlucia-guide.info

RIVER SHANNON
IRELAND, EUROPE

Cruise the longest stretch of navigable waterway in Ireland

A gentle cruise is the best way to appreciate the country and its incredibly beautiful landscape, slower pace of life, and pubs.
www.shannonregiontourism.ie

VANCOUVER ISLAND
CANADA, NORTH AMERICA

Watch whales galore in the Pacific Rim National Park

May is a good time for spotting migrating grey whales with their young – also killer and minke whales – off the west coast.
www.pc.gc.ca

GARDENS OF ENGLAND
EUROPE

Magnificent stately homes and their gardens in full bloom

Splendid architecture in perfect settings. Many are near to London, but to make the most of them, hire a car and go on a tour.
See pp118–19

KOKODA TRAIL
PAPUA NEW GUINEA, AUSTRALASIA

A tough trek in the rainforest

Linking the north and south coasts of Papua New Guinea, this trek goes via mountains, dense rainforest and friendly villages.
www.kokodatrail.com.au

NEW FOREST
ENGLAND, EUROPE

Ancient forest with a wide variety of plants and animals

As well as native ponies in this pretty forest, there's plenty of wildlife – especially hawks, reptiles, dragonflies, deer and wildflowers.
www.thenewforest.co.uk

Weather Watch

❶ New York suffers from hot sultry summers and bitterly cold winters so visit sometime in between – temperatures should be comfortable during May and the crowds will be light.

❷ Although it lies in the Tropics, La Paz is so high that its autumn temperature stays fairly moderate and it should be sunny every day.

❸ One of the best months to visit the south of England; temperatures are mild with plenty of warm sunny days. But there's always the chance of rain.

❹ In May the temperature can get quite high in Zambia and Zimbabwe, but there's little rainfall and the overall humidity is also nice and low – so the heat feels more bearable.

❺ In Xian, May brings comfortable and warm temperatures, but also a little rain. However, further west along the Silk Road the area becomes very arid and windswept – with temperature extremes likely.

❻ The tropical climate in Bali means there's rain throughout the year but, with lashings of sunshine, short warm showers are good for clearing the air.

LUXURY AND ROMANCE

BALI Exotic pink flower in bloom

ACTIVE ADVENTURES

LA PAZ Visitors take a break on a 4WD journey

FAMILY GETAWAYS

CRETE Venetian fort on Spinalonga

BALI
INDONESIA, ASIA

A deliciously relaxing spa break on this Indian Ocean jewel

With lush scenery, luxury spas and soft-sand beaches in abundance, it's no surprise that this island paradise is a favourite of honeymooners.
See pp124–5

LAKE KARIBA
ZIMBABWE, AFRICA

It's a Tarzan adventure living among the hippos and crocs

Stay on the reserve in a luxurious houseboat where the wild beasts are literally on your doorstep – it's a real romantic jungle adventure.
www.zambiatourism.com

FUJI FIVE LAKES
JAPAN, ASIA

Chain of five peaceful lakes to the north of the iconic Mt Fuji

Walk round the lakes to visit the Buddhist shrines dotted in the pretty woods. Relax afterwards in hot springs while enjoying the view of Mt Fuji.
www.japan-guide.com/e/e6906.html

BUZIOS
BRAZIL, SOUTH AMERICA

A hot spot first "discovered" by Brigitte Bardot in the 1960s

Buzios, a couple of hours' drive north from Rio, forms a peninsula from which the sea has scalloped many delightful beaches.
www.braziltour.com

NEW YORK CITY
USA, NORTH AMERICA

Brash and exuberant, this is a city for modern lovers

Show your loved one you have your finger on the pulse in this cutting-edge city of fashion, culture and entertainment.
See pp138–9

"The city has been so well documented in films that even if it's your first visit, you'll feel as if you know it already."

LA PAZ
BOLIVIA, SOUTH AMERICA

High-altitude holiday that will literally take your breath away

Hike around La Paz – the highest capital in the world – and Lake Titicaca, taking in traditional culture, markets and Inca ruins.
See pp136–7

ATLAS MOUNTAINS
MOROCCO, AFRICA

Hike among the wildflower trails of the high mountains

Not overly strenuous, this involves hiking through wonderful mountain scenery and camping out in Bedouin-style tents.
www.visitmorocco.org

PEAK DISTRICT
ENGLAND, EUROPE

Breathtaking landscapes offer great rock climbing and caving

The limestone karst geology provides perfect opportunities for caving and climbing amid some of the UK's best natural scenery.
www.cressbrook.co.uk

NORTH ISLAND
NEW ZEALAND, AUSTRALASIA

Head north from Auckland and learn to surf in style

The waves are consistent, the climate subtropical and the beaches remote and unspoiled. Best of all you're unlikely to meet any sharks.
www.newzealandsurftours.com

UMBRIA
ITALY, EUROPE

Cycle through beautiful and historic hilltowns and country

Less well known – and quieter – than Tuscany, Umbria, the "green heart of Italy" is stunningly pretty, and has even better food and wine.
www.italiantourism.com

"This island is wonderfully alive and fertile, with millions of dark green olive trees, leafy grape vines, fragrant orange groves and pink oleander."

BELIZE
BELIZE, CENTRAL AMERICA

Surprisingly affordable tropical destination for kids and adults

With a good priced flight this is great for families that are interested in Mayans, marine parks, jungle adventures and shady hammocks.
www.belizenet.com

LANZAROTE
CANARY ISLANDS, EUROPE

With much to offer families – especially out of season

Venture beyond the developed area to explore the volcanic island, in year-round sun with ideal beaches and converted haciendas.
www.turismolanzarote.com

CRETE
GREECE, EUROPE

Perfect time for a holiday on this beautiful island

Find your way around the maze-like ruins of the Palace of Knossos, or hike the Samarian Gorge and cool off in crystal clear seas.
See pp122–3

LAKESHORE
USA, NORTH AMERICA

Old-fashioned Minnesota lake-side camp with family cabins

Plenty for adults to do – fishing, golf, resting – and even more for children who will love the outdoors being literally just out the door.
www.lostlake.com

DORDOGNE
FRANCE, EUROPE

Outstanding natural scenery of farms, hills and winding rivers

Budding historians, gourmets and Olympic stars will love the prehistoric caves, exquisite French cuisine and opportunities for outdoors sports.
www.dordognebreak.com

GETTING THERE
The Cotswolds, Hampshire, Sussex and Kent are in southern England, within 160 km (100 miles) of London, which has two international airports.

GETTING AROUND
Most of these stately homes are within a 1-hour train journey from London, with a taxi or bus from the nearest station. Alternatively, rent a car and combine visits to make a complete tour.

WEATHER
May is generally warm and dry with average temperatures of about 12ºC. Occasional showers usually pass quickly.

ACCOMMODATION
Traditional English-style, Mermaid Inn in Kent; doubles from £80; www.mermaidinn.com

Impressive, fortified Amberley Castle, West Sussex has elegant doubles from £155; www.relaischateaux.com

Beautifully decorated, Le Manoir aux Quat'Saisons, Oxfordshire; doubles from £395; www.manoir.com

EATING OUT
You can dine well for £15 per head, although the fine dining establishments can cost more than triple that. For a special treat, try Le Manoir aux Quat'Saisons (see accommodation) or The Fat Duck in Berkshire, for their creative fare.

PRICE FOR TWO
£200–300 per day including accommodation, food, car hire and entrance charges.

FURTHER INFORMATION
www.visitbritain.com
www.nationaltrust.org.uk

Stately Home Hotels
In the past two decades, dozens of stately homes, palaces, castles and manors have opened their doors as luxurious country hotels, harking back to the days when their original owners invited friends down for a weekend or longer. Now restored to their former haughty grandeur for a paying clientele, these exquisite properties satisfy clients' nostalgia for historic surroundings and the refinement of days past, with stateliness and civilized comfort as keynotes.

Above (left to right): Barnsley House's colourful gardens; Long Gallery in Syon House; Longleat's challenging maze
Main: Row of statues overlooking the water terrace at Blenheim Palace

GARDENS AND GRANDEUR

SPARKLING WITH TREASURES, the sumptuous interiors of England's stately homes are still redolent of the patrician lifestyle, with their gleaming dark hardwood staircases, carved marble fireplaces, suits of armour, and galleries of precious paintings. The great Elizabethan palaces and the grand homes of the 18th and 19th centuries were a deliberate statement of wealth, when it was necessary for nobles to maintain a house in the royal style to cater to Britain's peripatetic monarchs. For those now converted into hotels, such as Cliveden, guests sleep in bedchambers once slept in by dukes, earls, kings and queens. A magnificent setting overlooking the River Thames adds to Cliveden's supreme expression of stateliness. Other homes, such as Petworth and Blenheim, also prove the adage that a fine house, like a jewel, is made complete by its setting. Many are located in an idealized Arcadian landscape, half-park, half-rolling pasture. No flowers. Just trees and bushes and grass and water and, occasionally, cattle as rural ornaments beyond a dry ditch. At Stourhead, England's premier 18th-century landscaped garden, the classical-theme paintings of Nicolas Poussin and Claude Lorrain became models for imitation in the real world so you literally can step into a painting.

In the 19th century, extraordinary botanical specimens flooded in from every part of Britain's expanding empire and plants became paramount. Roses are everywhere, thriving in the heavy soils. The flowering meadows of Great Dixter create a character of quintessential Englishness thanks to a diversity of soils and climates quite remarkable for so small a country. Without extremes of conditions or temperature, the climate encourages an immense variety of plants, as at Sissinghurst, the ultimate garden for enthusiasts. This large garden, nestled amid the rolling hills of Kent, is a riot of colour with an intoxicating blend of scents difficult to dampen in even the wettest of weather.

"A garden is the greatest refreshment for the spirits of man… There is nothing more pleasant to the eye than green grass kept finely shorn."

Sir Francis Bacon

Inset: Delicate Wisley rose
Below (left to right): Stourhead's magnificent gardens; sculptural detail at Hampton Court; Chartwell in Kent

STATELY DIARY

Many of the finest of Britain's stately homes and gardens are in southern England, in the Cotswolds, Hampshire, Sussex, Wiltshire and Kent. Most gardens are at their most luxuriant in spring, when England is bright and lush. The following suggestions are some of the highlights to choose from over a ten-day visit.

Ten Days in England's Past

Using London as your base for the next couple of days, take a riverboat to Hampton Court, with sumptuous state rooms and Britain's premier formal gardens.

Visit Syon House in Brentford, then drive down to Cliveden in Berkshire with its delightful water garden.

Head to the Cotswolds and explore Oxford before continuing to Blenheim Palace, the most palatial of the stately homes with huge parklands designed by "Capability" Brown, or visit Broughton Castle.

Travel through lovely thatched villages to Barnsley House and Hidcote Manor, famous for its old roses.

Journey on to Wiltshire to explore the splendid 18th-century Longleat House and Stourhead – considered to be England's finest landscape garden.

Visit Salisbury Cathedral before choosing either Broadlands, in Hampshire, former stately home of Lord Mountbatten or, for nature-lovers, head towards the New Forest to Exbury, featuring vast parks of colourful azaleas, magnolias and rhododendrons.

In the southeastern leg of your tour, travel to 17th-century Petworth House in Sussex, overlooking an exquisite, landscaped park. Continue into Kent to Great Dixter, a 15th-century manor house with a natural garden designed by writer Christopher Lloyd.

Alternatively, visit Sissinghurst, considered the jewel in the crown of English gardens, then return to London via Chartwell, once home to Sir Winston Churchill.

Dos and Don'ts

☑ Take an umbrella – you never know when you'll need it for England's famously fickle weather.

☒ Don't visit homes over the weekend if you can avoid it – tour groups and amateur gardeners descend en masse.

☑ Live it up like a blue blood with at least one stay overnight at a stately home-turned-hotel.

☒ Don't forget to check the opening times before you visit to avoid disappointment – stately homes are often closed for several days during the week.

JAN
FEB
MAR
APR
MAY
DAYS 1–2
DAYS 3–5
DAYS 6–8
DAYS 9–10
JUN
JUL
AUG
SEPT
OCT
NOV
DEC

GETTING THERE

Las Vegas airport is the most conveniently placed for exploring the Colorado Plateau and is well served by international and domestic airlines. From here, it is a 3-hour drive to the closest national park, Zion.

GETTING AROUND

The best way to get around is by Recreational Vehicle (RV), which allows you to explore at your own pace. RVs can be hired from several tour operators in Las Vegas.

WEATHER

Sunny, warm days and cool evenings are typical for late May, and rain is rare.

ACCOMMODATION

The national parks have camp sites that can accommodate small RVs, but they have limited facilities and some have length restrictions.

Many people use the private grounds, which are located outside the parks and have extra amenities such as swimming pools. Expect to pay from £6 in national parks and from £12 in private grounds.

EATING OUT

All RVs have full kitchen facilities so that you can pull off the road in a scenic location and enjoy a meal with a view. Restaurants can be found in, or just outside, most of the national parks. The superb Hell's Backbone Grill in Boulder, Utah, is worth seeking out.

PRICE FOR TWO

£100–180 per day, including accommodation, food, entrance charges and RV hire.

FURTHER INFORMATION

www.nps.gov

Ancient Anasazi Peoples

The Colorado Plateau is a land steeped in legends. One of the largest mysteries surrounds the disappearance of the Ancient Pueblo people, or Anasazi, who inhabited much of the southeastern plateau. They built the magnificent cliff dwellings at Mesa Verde and Hovenweep, sophisticated communities that were abandoned abruptly between about AD 1250 and AD 1350. War, drought, famine and disease have all been offered as possible reasons for their disappearance.

Top (left to right): Travelling by camper in the Petrified Forest National Park; entrance gate to Tombstone; dream catchers for sale, Monument Valley; desert cactus

CANYON COUNTRY

There's a reason they call it the Grand Circle. Condensed into this unforgettable multi-day loop-drive around the Colorado Plateau are some of the most jaw-dropping examples of landscapes to be found anywhere. Dream-like spires of rock and delicate wind-carved arches stand in silence above stunning desert tableaux, while ancient rivers run through mile-deep canyons whose towering red rock walls hold a record of the past fifty million years. Some landscapes, such as the buttes and mesas of Monument Valley, have appeared in countless images, making them instantly recognizable. Others, like Zion's river-carved canyon, are startlingly new and fresh. Even the Grand Canyon offers refreshing vistas when viewed from the North Rim. Over 600 m (2,000 ft) higher than the more famous and desert-like South Rim, the North Rim is blanketed in cool green forest, and from the canyon edge, the Colorado River appears as an almost-hidden glimmer 1,500 m (5,000 ft) below.

"The glories and the beauties of form, colour, and sound unite in the Grand Canyon…"

John Wesley Powell

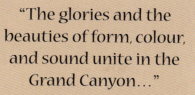

Main: View from Mather Point, Grand Canyon National Park.
Inset: Newspaper Rock, Canyonlands National Park
Above: Beautiful rock formation, Arizona

WESTERN DIARY

The Colorado Plateau is pleasantly cool in late May, perfect for hiking and long drives in the desert. The parks are at their greenest and the summer crowds have not yet arrived. It is possible to see the main sights in 10 days, which will give you a chance to further explore favourite parks and take guided trips.

Ten Days Exploring the Plateau

DAY 1 Arrive in Las Vegas and pick up your Recreational Vehicle (RV). Explore the glitzy casinos of the Strip.

DAY 2 Travel on to Zion National Park. From the visitors' centre, a park shuttle will take you to the lush canyon.

DAY 3 Drive to Bryce National Park and take the Park Shuttle along the canyon rim. The best way to admire the valley's wind-carved pink spires is on foot.

DAY 4 Begin the day by watching the spectacular sunrise from deceptively named Sunset Point. Explore Bryce Canyon further before taking Route 12 to Capital Reef National Park to see the Fremont Canyon petroglyphs.

DAYS 5–6 Take a scenic drive through Arches National Park and visit stunning Canyonlands National Park. Alternatively, hire mountain bikes for the trails around Moab, or go whitewater rafting on the Green and Colorado rivers.

Drive around Chapin Mesa to view the spectacular cliff dwellings, then take the tour to Balcony House.

DAYS 7–9 Visit Hovenweep National Monument or explore Monument Valley.

On your way to the Grand Canyon, stop to visit the Petrified Forest National Park. There are two approaches to the Grand Canyon – the desert-like South Rim is open all year, while the forested North Rim is open from mid-May until November.

DAY 10 Complete the Grand Circle by returning to Las Vegas, or continue south to take in legendary Tombstone.

Dos and Don'ts

- ✓ Remember when selecting a rental RV that a smaller one is easier to drive and park.
- ✗ Don't leave a national park without checking road conditions and confirming reservations for the next camp site.
- ✓ Camp near the rental agency on your first night in case you have any questions about the operation of the RV.
- ✗ Don't forget to dress in layers as temperatures can change quickly. Wear sturdy hiking shoes and carry at least 2 litres (4 pints) of water per person.

Below: Grand Canyon West Ranch, Arizona.

JAN

FEB

MAR

APR

MAY

JUN

JUL

AUG

SEP

OCT

NOV

DEC

The Colorado Plateau offers some of the most spectacular wilderness in the world – perfect for exploring on foot or even horseback. At Zion, red rock trails lead to hidden desert sanctuaries where translucent green pools are fed by misty waterfalls. In Bryce, trails lead through the weirdly wonderful landscape of red stone towers, sculpted by the wind, and at the Grand Canyon, the Rim Trail, true to its name, wanders for mile upon mile along the edge of the canyon.

But hiking is just the start of the outdoor adventures here. This is mountain bike heaven, and the area around Moab is legendary for its Slickrock cycling trails. For paddlers, both the Colorado and Green Rivers offer unforgettable rides through raging whitewater rapids or tranquil floats through rusty sunlit canyons. One of the very best ways to experience this country is in a Recreational Vehicle, which offers unparalleled freedom to explore at your own pace. There is nothing like enjoying the day's first coffee in the early morning crispness of the desert air, or camping a few steps from the edge of the Grand Canyon, watching the sunset paint its warm pastels across the vast and ancient canvas of stone, as nightfall turns the sky into a dazzling sea of stars.

GETTING THERE
Crete is a Greek island 45 km (280 miles) south of Athens. Its has two international airports: Irakleio in the centre, and Chania in the west.

GETTING AROUND
Inexpensive buses serve all the towns and resorts. Taxis are cheap and operate all over the island. Cars can be hired at both airports.

WEATHER
Crete's summer starts in May, with daytime temperatures of around 25°C.

ACCOMMODATION
Amphora is a traditionally decorated historic mansion set on Chania's quayside; family rooms from £95; www.amphora.gr

Santa Marina Plaza is a beachfront hotel at Aghia Marina in western Crete; family rooms from £140; www.santamarina-plaza.gr

Elounda Beach offers world-class luxury in seafront gardens, near Aghios Nikolaos; family rooms from £380; www.eloundabeach.gr

EATING OUT
Allow £10–15 per person for a full meal with wine at most restaurants and tavernas. Traditional Cretan dishes include *choirinó kritikó* (tender pork cutlets), *stifádo* (casserole with beef or rabbit) and *loukoumádes* (deep fried doughnuts soaked in honey syrup).

PRICE FOR A FAMILY OF FOUR
£210–260 per day for accommodation, food and local transport.

FURTHER INFORMATION
www.heraklion-city.gr
www.aghiosnikolaos.gr

Multicultural History
Crete has had a long and turbulent history. After the destruction of the bull-leaping Minoan civilization by earthquake in around 1500 BC, Crete became part of the Hellenistic (or Greek) civilization, but remained independent. Next taken over by the Romans, then by Arabs, and for 400 years part of the Venetian empire, Crete was then conquered by the Turkish Ottomans in the 17th century. Throughout the 19th century, Crete's Christians rebelled against Ottoman rule. The Ottomans withdrew in 1898, and Crete finally joined the Greek state in 1913.

LAND OF THE MINOANS

CRUCIBLE OF ANCIENT CIVILIZATIONS, Crete is as close to Africa as to Athens. Wherever you go on the island, you are constantly reminded of the wide range of cultural influences on its past, from Minoan frescoes to Venetian fortresses. During the long, hot summer that begins in May, Crete basks under deep blue, rainless skies. Yet this island is wonderfully alive and fertile, with millions of dark green olive trees, leafy grape vines, fragrant orange groves and pink oleander growing wild.

Crete's history reaches back to a time of myths and mysteries, vividly brought to life by the frescoes at the ruins of the 4,000-year-old Minoan palace at Knossos, legendary home to the underground labyrinth that imprisoned the Minotaur. Treasures found here and at Crete's other Minoan sites are on display at the Archeological Museum, one of Europe's great collections, in the busy waterfront capital, Irakleio.

East of here is Aghios Nikolaos, a lovely fishing village with a delightful inner harbour and a buzzing atmosphere. Even further east is a rustic, unspoiled Crete that tourists have yet to reach.

Below and bottom: Busy tavernas by Rethymnon's harbour; Samaria Gorge

Western Crete is greener, with the best of the beaches and a string of elegant, fortified ports built when the island was ruled by Venice. Loveliest of them all is Chania, one of the prettiest little harbour cities in the whole Mediterranean. Tall Italianate houses edge its U-shaped quayside, where bar and restaurant tables look across the water. Dramatically framing the town are the crests of the beautiful snow-topped White Mountains.

Cross these high hills to reach quieter south coast resorts like Paleochora. On the way, look out for eagles and the ibex-like wild goats called *kri-kri*. There's good walking in the hills, most famously the spectacular Samaria Gorge, a demanding 16-km (10-mile) hike to the south coast and one of the most striking areas of natural beauty in Greece. Eventually walkers emerge near the small village of Agia Roumeli after passing through the towering rock walls of the *Sideresportes* (Iron Gates).

Easier is the Therisso Gorge, south of Chania. A tiny road, almost traffic-free and edged by wild flowers, threads this narrow ravine. Butterflies flutter around, and from high on the cliffs the sound of goat bells seems to come from the immeasurable past.

Main: Swimming in the turquoise waters in the Gulf of Merabello near Aghios Nikolaos

Top: Weather-worn door in the morning sun

Above: Venetian fort in Spinalonga

Below: Natural sponges on display in Rethymnon

SUNSHINE DIARY

Crete's summer begins with warm May days when the lowlands are draped with colourful wild flowers – the perfect weather for a week of touring. Look out for sheep-shearing fairs, art exhibitions and late May's patriotic commemorations of the Battle of Crete, which took place in 1941, during World War II.

A Week of Island Exploration

Get acquainted with Chania, the most charming of Crete's harbour towns. Wander the lanes of the Old Town and visit the covered market. In the evening, enjoy a leisurely dinner at a quayside table.

Visit Chania's waterside fort and the Naval Museum. Alternatively, head over the White Mountains to the quiet resort and excellent beaches of Paleochora.

Make an early start for a mountain trek. The awesome 16-km (10-mile) Samaria Gorge is open from May (closed if it rains). If this is too strenuous for the children, a walk through pretty Therisso Gorge is easier.

Leave Chania and head east to Irakleio (or Heraklion) on the seafront road, pausing at sights on the way, such as the beautiful Allied World War II cemetery at Souda; the village resorts of Kalives, Almirida or Georgiopoli; and Rethymnon's fortress.

Relax at the picturesque resort of Elounda. If the weather's good, it should be warm enough to sunbathe and swim in the sea. Children will enjoy exploring the nearby fortress island of Spinalonga.

For more history, visit Irakleio's remarkable Archeological Museum and lunch in the walled Old City, before continuing to Knossos. Otherwise, spend a relaxing day in Aghios Nikolaos.

If there is time before returning to the airport, visit Panagia Kera church, in the hills 15km (8 miles) from Aghios Nikolaos, or spend your last hours enjoying the sunshine.

Dos and Don'ts

- ✓ On the main highway, move over to the hard shoulder to let faster drivers pass – normal practice on Crete.
- ✗ Don't forget to slap on the sun cream and drink lots of water – Crete is as far south as Tunisia.
- ✓ Dress modestly away from the beach, especially at churches and religious sites.
- ✗ Don't call locals "Greeks" – they are "Cretans", and proud to be so. But call their coffee "Greek", never "Turkish"!

Below: Calm waters at the harbour of Aghios Nikolaos

JAN
FEB
MAR
APR
MAY
DAY 1
DAY 2
DAY 3
DAY 4
DAY 5
DAY 6
DAY 7
JUN
JUL
AUG
SEP
OCT
NOV
DEC

GETTING THERE
Bali's Ngurah Rai International Airport (Denpasar) is served by carriers from a number of key cities in Australia and Asia. Transport from the airport is via taxi or hotel pick-up services.

GETTING AROUND
Public transport ranges from air-conditioned taxis to crowded buses. Alternatively, it is easy to rent a vehicle with a driver, or car/motorcycle. Be aware that driving in Bali can be dangerous.

WEATHER
May is the beginning of Bali's dry season. Expect sunshine and temperatures around 30°C. The mountainous regions are a cooler alternative.

ACCOMMODATION
The atmospheric Hotel Tugu at Canggu showcases rare cultural artifacts and antiques; doubles from £135; www.tuguhotels.com

Luxurious Four Seasons at Jimbaran and Sayan; doubles from £235; www.fourseasons.com

Aman Resorts at Nusa Dua, Ubud and Manggis; doubles from £380; www.amanresorts.com

EATING OUT
Bali's endless dining possibilities range from simple *warungs* (casual restaurants, usually outdoors) from around £1.50 to world-class gourmet restaurants (around £15–30). Look out for Seminyak's famous "Eat Street".

PRICE FOR TWO
£300–350 per day including luxury hotels, food and entrance charges (costs will be significantly less in lower-end accommodation).

FURTHER INFORMATON
www.balitourismauthority.net

Balinese *Boreh*

Boreh is a traditional remedy that has been used by Balinese villagers for many generations to relieve muscular aches and pains and boost circulation. Warm spices such as powdered sandalwood, cloves, ginger, cinnamon, coriander seed, turmeric, pepper and nutmeg are blended with rice powder into a fragrant paste and applied to the body as a healing masque. As a spa treatment, *boreh* is one of the most luxurious experiences available; great not only for its relaxing and curative properties but also for exfoliating and softening the skin.

Above (left to right): Infinity pool at the Four Seasons Hotel; detail of a demon statue; Balinese dancer in traditional attire
Main: Verdant flooded rice fields in Bali

MORNING OF THE WORLD

THE ISLAND OF BALI, NESTLED WITHIN THE INDONESIAN ARCHIPELAGO, is one of the world's most romantic holiday destinations. An ever-prevailing sense of harmony is combined with a vibrant theatre of dance, mystery and natural splendour. From the moment of arrival, visitors are assailed with an intense concentration of colour, sights, smells, sounds and tastes. Few places on earth celebrate life with such vitality. The gentle, friendly Balinese people refer to tourists as *tamu* – meaning guests – and immediately make everyone welcome.

Exotic and diverse, the island is picturesque to the point of resembling a painted backdrop – volcanoes climb into clouds and terraced rice fields cascade down to the ocean. It's not surprising that the great Indian statesman, Jawaharlal Nehru, named it "the Morning of the World".

Bali blends its beautiful nature with the glamour of world-class hotels, chic cocktail bars and internationally acclaimed restaurants. The island also hosts the highest concentration of spas in the whole of Southeast Asia. These timeless havens of serenity are dedicated not only to pampering the body but also to restoring inner equilibrium, and are therefore a magnet for those in search of something that will ease fatigue, stimulate the senses and awaken the spirit.

Behind the carved wooden doors of exclusive hideaways, where relaxation is the order of the day, honeymooners and lovers will be waited on by personal butlers. Romantic packages include everything from frangipani garlands to champagne and strawberries at the edge of the Indian Ocean. Sunset cocktails and candlelit dinners in bougainvillea-covered pavilions are followed by rose-petal baths under the stars in sunken marble tubs. There are also many ways to get married here; you just need to let your imagination run wild – make an entrance on an elaborately decorated elephant or have a ceremony in a glass cliff-top wedding-chapel.

> Sunset cocktails and candlelit dinners in bougainvillea-covered pavilions are followed by rose-petal baths under the stars.

Inset: Balinese Ubud painting
Below (left to right): Gunung Batur volcano, Bali; fishing boats anchored as the sun sets; exotic pink flower in full bloom

RELAXATION DIARY

May brings clear skies and a welcome respite from the tropical storms of Bali's rainy season. Now is the perfect time of year to enjoy land, sea and air tours, alfresco dining and other outdoor activities. Visitors will need at least one week to unwind and absorb the magic of this remarkable little island.

A Week on the Island of Gods

Relax aboard a luxury sailing boat with a day cruise to Lembongan Island, off Bali's southern coast.

See Bali from the air by helicopter or seaplane. Fly over the incredible scenery of rice fields, river gorges, lakes and even the craters of active volcanoes.

Visit Ubud, the cultural centre of Bali. Browse the market, art galleries, museums, and shops selling handicrafts of every description. Relish a body massage at a fabulous riverside spa and finish with a Balinese dance performance at the Royal Palace.

Renew your wedding vows or reaffirm your love and commitment to your partner with a Hindu karmic cleansing ceremony on the beach. Later, feast on a delicious six-course jungle supper served under a sky flickering with the light of hundreds of fireflies.

Go on a big bike cruise as pillion passengers on a pair of classic Harley Davidson motorcycles, in the capable hands of two experienced Harley jockeys. Visit the market town of Bedugul and Lake Bratan with its mystical tiered temple.

Ride an elephant through the Taro jungle. The elephants were rescued from Sumatra's diminishing forests.

Embark on a therapeutic journey through the water massages and aqua-beds of the Aquatonic Pool at the Ritz Carlton Thalasso & Spa. Then try the ultimate pampering experience in the dreamy offshore pavilion, the "Spa on the Rocks".

Dos and Don'ts

☑ Show your respect by wearing a sarong and a sash when entering temples and holy places.

☒ Don't use your left hand to give or receive things; the Balinese consider the left hand to be unclean and may be offended.

☑ Guard against the intense equatorial sun by wearing a hat and using waterproof sunscreen at all times.

☒ Don't go home without purchasing some local artwork, silver jewellery, woodcarvings, stylish homewares, batik fabrics, and the numerous other handicrafts that Bali has to offer.

JAN
FEB
MAR
APR
MAY
DAYS 1–2
DAY 3
DAY 4
DAY 5
DAYS 6–7
JUN
JUL
AUG
SEPT
OCT
NOV
DEC

GETTING THERE
Boston is a major seaport in Massachusetts in the USA. Its airport, Logan International, is 6 km (4 miles) from the city centre.

GETTING AROUND
Downtown Boston is compact and very walkable, but you can also get a 3-day Visitor's Passport for unlimited travel on the MBTA subway.

WEATHER
Summer is on the way but the weather is warm and very pleasant with an average temperature of around 20°C – perfect for walking.

ACCOMMODATION
Boston has many fine hotels, few budget ones.

Basic lodgings in the Irish South End at Best Western Roundhouse Suites; doubles from £80; www.bestwestern.com

The Lenox has an old-world ambience; doubles from £175; www.lenoxhotel.com

At the top of the elite list is the Four Seasons; doubles from £265; www.fourseasons.com

EATING OUT
Expect to pay £20–30 per person at better restaurants in Boston, though there are many less formal (and cheaper) alternatives. Try the clam chowder at Legal Sea Foods and the Corned Beef and Cabbage dinners at Durgin Park.

PRICE FOR TWO
£240–260 per day including accommodation, food, travel and entrance fees, but budget hotels and dining can nearly cut that in half.

FURTHER INFORMATION
www.bostonusa.com

Irish Influence
Boston's Irish heritage stems from immigrants fleeing the Great Famine in the mid-19th century. As a result the city probably has the most Irish pubs this side of Galway Bay. The best provide entertainment with traditional corned beef dinners and, of course, a glass of Guinness. Try the Black Rose *(below)*, Tiernans, Hennessy's, Ned Divine's, Coogans and The Last Hurrah, haunt of the city's Irish politicians.

INDEPENDENCE DAYS

DESPITE ITS LIVELY REVOLUTIONARY HISTORY, the heart of Boston remains a citadel of quiet charm and tradition whose pretty streets and neighbourhoods cry out to be explored on foot. The townhouses and cobbled streets of Beacon Hill, topped with gas-lit Louisburg Square, are the perfectly preserved Boston of the 1840s. Victoriana reigns along the elegant boulevards of the Back Bay area and huge swan boats glide gracefully on the lake in the Public Garden as they have since 1877. Yet this city is also non-stop action and excitement – sculls and sailboats glide by on the Charles River, joggers and skaters puff past on the Esplanade; the crowds fall eagerly onto the delicious wares displayed in the food stalls of Quincy Market and shoppers vie

. . . the heart of Boston remains a citadel of quiet charm and tradition whose pretty streets and neighbourhoods cry out to be explored on foot.

for the best bargains in Filene's Basement; rowdy sports fans cheer on the city's hockey team and much loved – and fairly successful – Red Sox baseball team.

Boston is also a bastion of highbrow culture with a world-renowned symphony orchestra and a great many important museums of art, science and history, but, thanks to over 100 colleges and universities, it is saved from stuffiness. Thousands of students make the place a lively city of eternal youth, filled with cafés, quirky book shops and independent fashion boutiques. Worth a special visit are the Cambridge campuses of Harvard, which has produced seven US presidents, and the Massachusetts Institute of Technology (MIT), boasting over 50 Nobel Prize winners. Families are not forgotten either; the city's many pleasures include the spectacular New England Aquarium, the Boston Children's Museum, a computer museum and the Boston Tea Party Ship. And then there's the pubs – after a few nights of traditional hospitality you'll enjoy the fresh sea breezes afforded by some island hopping and trekking.

While you can't see it all in a few days, Boston is a compact, easily walkable city that allows you to sample many of its pleasures on a short visit, although it would be such a shame to rush through all this at a Paul Revere-style gallop.

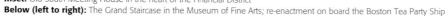

Main: View of the Victorian brownstone town houses of Boston's Back Bay area from the John Hancock Tower
Inset: Old South Meeting House in the heart of the Financial District
Below (left to right): The Grand Staircase in the Museum of Fine Arts; re-enactment on board the Boston Tea Party Ship

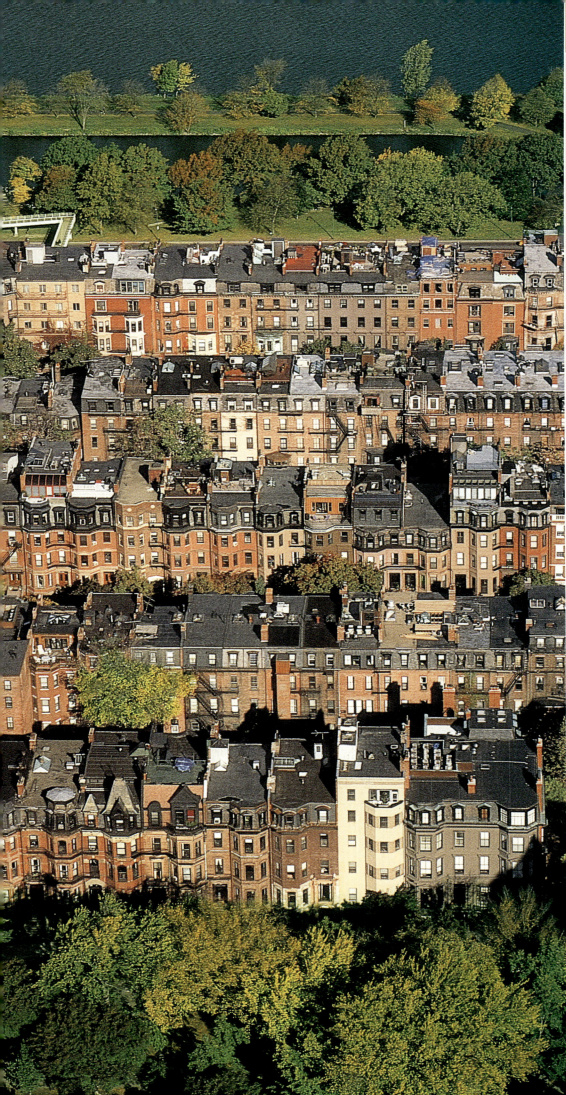

POST-COLONIAL DIARY

May is a great month to explore New England's largest city. The weather is great and there's lots to see and do. Four days is enough to see the main sights but, to really get to grips with this historic and vibrant city, stay longer in town and also see some of the outlying areas such as Lexington and Cape Cod (see pp188–9).

Four Days of Historical Charm

Start with the classic Freedom Trail around downtown Boston: from the golden-domed Massachusetts State House to the Quincy Market area followed by lunch at a nearby Irish pub such as the Black Rose. Serious boat buffs can carry on past Paul Revere's House, over the bridge to Charlestown Navy Yard. Try to get tickets to see a Boston Red Sox baseball game.

See more fine architecture while shopping around Copley Square and the Back Bay area, starting at the Prudential Centre and walking down Newbury Street. This has top-dollar designer outlets, hip indie shops and significant public buildings and churches. Pick up a picnic from Delucca's for the Public Garden and Boston Common. The afternoon could be spent at the Boston Tea Party Ship, the entertaining Children's Museum or the excellent New England Aquarium.

Museum lovers will enjoy the Museum of Fine Arts which could take days to explore properly (don't miss the Japanese Garden behind the museum); those wanting a more intimate experience will love the Venetian-style palazzo housing the Isabella Gardner Museum, while intellectuals may want to visit Harvard campus – chock full of museums and architecture. At night, music lovers should head for Symphony Hall, home to the renowned Boston Symphony Orchestra.

Even though there's a lot more to see in the city, why not take this chance to get out on the water with a visit to George's Island, which runs ferries to the other Boston Harbor Islands – good for nature, hiking trails and beaches. Or you could simply get out of town with a train trip to Salem of witch trial and sea-trading fame.

Dos and Don'ts

✗ Don't drive! Many Boston streets are narrow and winding with unexpected dead ends and one-way signs. Use the "T" – the convenient subway system – or grab a cab.

✓ Get a Boston City Pass and save up to 50 percent on entrance to six of the main attractions; and a Visitor's Passport for unlimited travel on subways and buses for 1, 3 or 5 days.

✗ Don't leave your mobile phone on when dining. Many restaurants – even the more informal ones – have banned "cellphones" so switch it off!

JAN
FEB
MAR
APR
MAY
DAY 1
DAY 2
DAY 3
DAY 4
JUN
JUL
AUG
SEPT
OCT
NOV
DEC

Below: Longfellow Bridge, the Charles River and Boston at night

GETTING THERE
Ayr, on the southwest coast of Scotland, is 66 km (41 miles) south of Glasgow International Airport and 8 km (5 miles) south of Glasgow Prestwick Airport.

GETTING AROUND
There is a rail link from Ayr to Glasgow and from there on the West Highland Line to Mallaig. The best and sometimes the only practical way to tour the west is by car.

WEATHER
May is wet and mild with sunny days. Expect temperatures of around 14°C.

ACCOMMODATION
Belhaven Hotel is in the vibrant West End of Glasgow; double rooms from £55; www.belhavenhotel.com

Old Racecourse Hotel, Ayr, is a small, family run hotel close to the town centre; doubles from £80; www.oldracecoursehotel.com

Westin Turnberry in Ayrshire is one of Scotland's best hotels; double rooms from £175; www.turnberry.co.uk

EATING OUT
Food outlets are plentiful throughout Scotland, from cheap and cheerful fish and chip shops to gourmet five-star restaurants. The west coast is famed for its seafood. Try The Buttery in Glasgow, its oldest and most celebrated restaurant, tel. (0141) 221 8188.

PRICE FOR TWO
£200–250 per day including accommodation, food and car hire.

FURTHER INFORMATION
www.visitscotland.com

Robert Burns

Robert Burns was born on the 25 January 1759. A true internationalist, his song *A Man's A Man for A' That*, inspired by the French Revolution, was sung at the opening of the Scottish Parliament in 1999. That universal anthem of parting, *Auld Lang Syne*, which he contributed to the Scots Musical Museum, is one of the most sung songs in the world.

Main: The dramatic scenery of Glencoe is reflected in the tranquil waters at Lochan

TAKE THE HIGH ROAD

THE SUN SINKS SLOWLY TO THE HORIZON, a golden red orb lighting liquid gold ripples across the darkening Firth of Clyde. As it disappears behind the islands, the rich glow of a west coast sunset remains in an indigo sky. The Kintyre peninsula, island of Arran and the granite outline of Ailsa Craig stand silhouetted in the foreground against the fiery sky. As the glow fades, the night sky is suddenly alive with a brilliance of colour from a series of explosions. People crowd onto Ayr's Low Green while others line the promenade along the beach, enjoying the fireworks and the music that is the finale of the Burns An' A' That! festival.

It's the culmination of ten days (20–29 May) celebrating the life and works of Scotland's most famous poet, Robert Burns, as well as a showcase for contemporary Scottish culture. One of the great strengths of this festival is its choice of venues. Every event provides the opportunity to journey through another part of this historic region.

Top: Musicians in Babbity Bowster's pub in Glasgow

Above: Highland cow, a common sight in the countryside

Below: Fisherman repairing his nets at the busy fishing harbour of Mallaig in the Highlands

WEST COAST DIARY

In May, lots of festivals take place around West Scotland. Traditional music can be found at the Girvan and Moniaive festivals, literature at Wigtown and wildlife on the Isle of Arran. The Scottish Pipe Band Championships are in Dumbarton while the Burns An' A' That! festival celebrates Scottish culture.

A Week in the Glens

Walk through Culzean Country Park then head for the Burns National Park. Make sure that you don't miss the finale of the Burns An' A' That! festival in Ayr, the culmination of over a week's worth of partying.

Head north through picturesque Ayrshire villages. In Tarbolton visit the Bachelors' Club founded by Burns then lunch at Poosie Nancie's tavern in Mauchline.

Continue to Glasgow and visit the recently refurbished Kelvingrove Museum to see its fascinating displays.

Visit the Burrell Collection gifted to Glasgow by a millionaire shipping owner.

Drive up to the "Bonnie Banks" of Loch Lomond to climb Ben Lomond then head to Oban for a spectacular west coast sunset.

Head through atmospheric Glencoe to Fort William then take the historic "Road to the Isles" to Mallaig. Stop at Glenfinnan where Bonnie Prince Charlie raised his standard in 1745 and the "Hogwarts Express" crossed the Viaduct in the Harry Potter Movies.

Cross by ferry to Skye. Visit the Museum of Island Life then the Talisker Distillery to see how the "water of life" is made. Then take the ferry from Uig to Harris.

Drive the Golden Road to Stornoway and on to the Butt of Lewis, visiting the Standing Stones of Callanish and the Arnol Black house on the way. Take the ferry to Ullapool then return via Inverness to Glasgow.

Dos and Don'ts

- ✓ Find a traditional music session taking place in one of many pubs throughout Scotland.
- ✗ Don't light up a cigarette, cigar or pipe. Smoking in enclosed public spaces has been illegal in Scotland since 2006.
- ✓ Do make sure you have an effective insect repellent. Otherwise the Scottish midge, a gnat-like insect of legendary biting power, will make your trip miserable.
- ✓ Do sample traditional Scottish foods like haggis, Scotch broth, *cullen skink* (smoked fish soup) and *cranachan* (dessert of cream, toasted oatmeal and raspberries).

Below: Admiring the paintings in Kelvingrove Museum and Art Gallery

JAN	
FEB	
MAR	
APR	
MAY	
DAY 1	
DAYS 2–3	
DAY 4	
DAY 5	
DAY 6	
DAY 7	
JUN	
JUL	
AUG	
SEP	
OCT	
NOV	
DEC	

From Girvan in the south of the county of South Ayrshire to its northern extremities there are readings, tastings, sessions, concerts, walks, funfairs and storytelling. Activities include the back room of a village pub with a few musicians one night, tasting fine malt whiskies in Rabbie's Drams in Ayr next morning, the funfair on the Low Green in the afternoon and then a concert of classical music in the magnificent Adam-designed Culzean Castle at night.

Burns was a man who liked to party and if he were alive today there is no doubt that he would be among the singers and musicians in the pubs, swapping stories in houses and joining the crowds on the Low Green for the fireworks and the music.

Once the fireworks are over, you can make your way up the west coast, enjoying the contrasting tranquillity of Loch Lomond and the eerie solitude of the standing stones of Callanish. Wind your way past tiny picturesque fishing villages and spectacular dramatic glens, savouring similar undisturbed views to those that inspired Burns all those years ago.

GETTING THERE
International flights arrive into Victoria Falls and Livingstone airports. There are daily flights from South Africa and other neighbouring countries.

GETTING AROUND
Both airports are accessed by shuttle bus or taxi. Taxis from either side of the falls will get you to the respective border posts, but the no-man's-land between the two posts will require a walk or a change of taxi.

WEATHER
The wet season is over by May, and the weather is warm and sunny. Water levels will be high enough for excellent views of the falls.

ACCOMMODATION
The historic Victoria Falls Hotel, Zimbabwe; doubles from £200; www.victoriafallshotel.com

Victoria Falls Safari Lodge, Zimbabwe, offers luxurious surroundings and stunning views; doubles from £200; www.zambezi.com/vfsl

Natural Mystic Lodge, by the Zambezi in Zambia; doubles from £75; www.naturalmysticlodge.com.

Luxurious Tongabezi Lodge, Zambia; doubles from £400, including meals; www.tongabezi.com

EATING OUT
There are local eateries and steakhouses on both sides of the falls. A unique open-air choice is The Boma at Victoria Falls Safari Lodge.

PRICE FOR TWO
£250–400 per day, including accommodation, food and excursions.

FURTHER INFORMATION
www.zambiatourism.com
www.zimbabwetourism.co.zw

The Name Game
When David Livingstone "discovered" the falls, the local Makololo tribe called them Mosi-oa-Tunya, the "smoke that thunders". In renaming them the Victoria Falls, the explorer was simply the latest in a long line of name-givers. The first known name was Shongwe, or "rainbow", given by the Tokaleya tribe; when the Ndebele moved to the area, the falls were christened Amanza Thunquayo, or "water rising as smoke". In fact, the Makololo name wasn't given until the mid-19th century, after the South African tribe invaded the area.

Above (left to right): Whitewater rafting in the Zambezi; seeing wildlife from the Zambezi by canoe; male dancers performing a traditional dance
Main: The largest curtain of water in the world, Victoria Falls

THRILLER IN THE MIST

A S NOTED IN THE WRITINGS OF AN AWESTRUCK DAVID LIVINGSTONE, the first European to see it, there's nothing to prepare a visitor for their first view of this overpowering natural wonder.

Victoria Falls straddles an international border and demonstrates two distinct personalities. In Zimbabwe, the falls remain at a distance, viewed across the gorge from a lush rainforest park created by the perpetually thick mist that's pumped out by the falling water. A more intimate relationship with the falls is available on the Zambian side. Here, visitors can saunter right up to the lip where the seemingly hell-bound Zambezi plunges over the edge, or negotiate a series of mist-soaked trails and catwalks for near-total immersion in the experience.

The schizophrenic nature is also evident in the two border towns' differences. Although Zimbabwe's reputation has suffered of late, Victoria Falls town steams ahead regardless of the country's turmoil. Saturated with hotels, guesthouses, steak joints, casinos and tour agencies, it is fuelled by tourism. However, having hit rock bottom several decades ago, Zambia is now enjoying the fruits of its political reforms – and Zimbabwe's downhill slide – in the shape of an evolving tourist scene. On the Zambian side, development in the immediate vicinity is limited to a five-star hotel and a small national park, while a growing collection of tourist-oriented enterprises awaits 11 km (7 miles) away in the real town of Livingstone.

Whichever side you choose, once you've seen the falls, there's still plenty to do. Soak yourself on a raft trip through the gorges or a microlight flight through the mist. Bungy jump off the bridge or enjoy a leisurely cruise on the hippo- and croc-infested river. Photograph elephants, lions and antelope on a horseback safari or try rock-climbing in the gorges. Bargain in the markets or just relax with a cold Zambezi Lager and toast the good fortune that brought you to Africa in the first place.

"with the ceaseless roar of the cataract...as if pouring forth from the hand of the Almighty… souls should be filled with reverential awe"

David Livingstone

Inset: Lobby of the Victoria Falls Hotel
Below (left and right): Steam train going over Victoria Falls Suspension Bridge; wooden bowls on sale at a local craft market

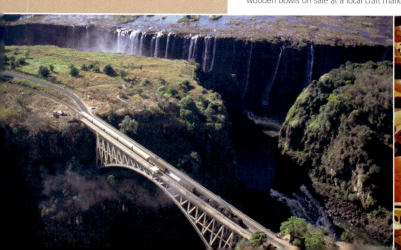

WATERFALL DIARY

The Zimbabwe side has a greater variety of places to stay and more opportunities to explore than the Zambian side, and the following itinerary reflects this. Five days at the falls will allow you time to enjoy some of the other activities on offer, such as a safari.

Five Days of Awesome Views

Explore Victoria Falls town (Zimbabwe), where you can shop for inexpensive curios. Stroll through the rainforest park along the gorge to enjoy overall views of the falls. Don't miss the most inspiring vantage point, Cataract View.
DAY 1

Cross over to the Zambian side and enjoy the quieter pace. Thoroughly explore the whole falls area, following one of the mist-soaked trails for a fantastic up-close experience of the falls.

Afterwards, head into Livingstone, a short distance from the falls, and visit the National Museum.
DAY 2

Make a splash on a thrilling whitewater rafting trip through the Zambezi Gorges below the falls. The trip begins further upstream, on the Zambian side, and offers an opportunity for even better views of the falls.

Alternatively, take a taxi out to Makuni, 18 km (11 miles) from Livingstone. This village is home to 7,000 Leya people and offers an insight into their traditional way of life. The small admission fee goes towards funding community projects.
DAY 3

Devote this day to two or three "adrenaline" activities – microlighting, abseiling, bungy jumping, or canoeing on the upper Zambezi – or opt for tamer choices such as the "Flight of the Angels" fixed-wing flight and an upper Zambezi cruise.
DAY 4

On your last day, take a horseback or motorized wildlife-viewing safari through Zambezi National Park on the Zimbabwean side or Mosi-oa-Tunya National Park on the Zambian side.
DAY 5

Dos and Don'ts

☑ Take advantage of the free Zambian visas offered to those who pre-book hotels or activities on the Zambian side.

☒ Don't approach wildlife along the forest tracks around the falls. Baboons in particular can be quite violent.

☒ Don't even think about swimming in the Zambezi above the falls unless you'd like to see a crocodile from the inside out.

☒ Don't deal with street moneychangers. Most travellers who do wind up with a sandwich of two legitimate bank notes enclosing a stack of clipped newspaper.

Below: Victoria Falls at sunset from Zambia

JAN
FEB
MAR
APR
MAY
DAY 1
DAY 2
DAY 3
DAY 4
DAY 5
JUN
JUL
AUG
SEP
OCT
NOV
DEC

GETTING THERE
Xian is the modern-day start for the Chinese leg of the Silk Road, and Xian airport is served from throughout China; most visitors come via Beijing.

GETTING AROUND
The most rewarding way to make the journey is by train, but there are airports in Lanzhou (albeit an hour's drive from town), Jiayuguan, Dunhuang and Kashgar.

WEATHER
May has an average high temperature of 21°C. The summers are blazing and the winters bitter.

ACCOMMODATION
Xian has a full range of accommodation, from dormitories to luxury; everywhere else it will be a mixture of mid-range to pretty basic.

Xian Hyatt Regency has double rooms from about £50; xian.regency.hyatt.com

Elsewhere, most hotels should have decent double rooms from £25.

EATING OUT
In Xian and Lanzhou the cuisine is still Chinese, although the street food has Islamic influences. Beyond Lanzhou, Islamic food is the norm – kebabs, yoghurt, flat bread and watermelon. For a couple of pounds you can eat well.

PRICE FOR TWO
Budget travel (dormitories, hard class on trains), should cost on average about £35 per day. For mid-range accommodation and travelling by plane, allow about £75 per day.

FURTHER INFORMATION
www.travelchinaguide.com
www.silk-road.com

The Story of Marco Polo

In the 13th century a trader, Marco Polo, claimed he had travelled to China and visited the great Kublai Khan. His descriptions of items like paper money, tigers, the Mongol Army and the Chinese postal system fired the West's imagination. However, many think the stories could have been picked up from Arabs with whom Marco Polo traded.

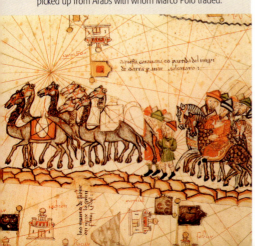

Above (top and bottom): Face of a Terracotta Warrior, Xian; Temple of the Big Wild Goose Pagoda, Xian

Below: Jiayuguan Fort in front of the Qilian Mountains

Right panel (top to bottom): Entrance to a cave at Mogao, Dunhuang; rug salesman displays his wares, Kashgar; view of Lake Karakuli and the Pamir Mountains

Main: Camel train crossing the sand dunes at Dunhuang

TRAVEL THE SILK ROAD

Xian was the beginning of the Silk Road, the ancient trading route that linked the East and West, and it still makes a good starting point. Each leg of the journey is a matter of minutes by plane but taking the train is good if you have the time – the sense of an epic journey is much better captured watching the changing landscape and architecture through a carriage window. In Xian, there are several reminders of its importance as an ancient destination for travellers. The Big Wild Goose Pagoda was built to house Buddhist sutras brought from India, whilst the Great Mosque services a large Muslim population, a foretaste of the different China that lies ahead.

From Xian the route heads northwest through the Hexi corridor to Lanzhou, on the turbid Yellow River. A large industrial city, Lanzhou reveals few clues as to its past, except for the exquisite Flying Horse in the city museum and the Buddhist caves, out in the countryside. It's best not to linger here but to continue to the oasis towns

WESTBOUND DIARY

To fully appreciate the Chinese part of the Silk Road, two weeks is an ideal amount of time if travelling by train. By plane, a week is the minimum time you'll need. If entering China via Beijing you might want to spend at least a couple of days sightseeing there *(see pp228–9)*.

Two Weeks on the Silk Road

Fly to Xian from Beijing – about an hour's flight – and take a transfer to town. Spend an afternoon exploring the old town with its huge city walls, Big Wild Goose Pagoda and Great Mosque. Spend at least another day here to see the amazing Terracotta Warriors before taking the overnight train to Lanzhou.

There's not much to see in Lanzhou – just the Yellow River and the Flying Horse in the Provincial Museum before catching the overnight train to Jiayuguan.

Next it's a trip out of town into the barren, stony desert to see the Ming Dynasty fort and the westernmost outpost of the Great Wall. Stay overnight.

To Dunhuang by plane. Join a tour for the beautiful cave paintings at Mogao. In the evening, take a trip to the nearby dunes and a hard climb to the top. The Mogao Caves deserve a second visit before taking a minibus to Liuyuan and a train to Turfan.

Turfan is a real oasis, and there's plenty to do and see, especially the market, with piles of glittering cloth and sheep carcasses. Spend some time sightseeing (by donkey cart) but make sure you enjoy a day of dozing in the shade of the grape trellises. Take at least a day to enjoy the beautiful scenery at the Heavenly Lake, Urumqi, before flying to Kashgar.

Kashgar – if you time it right you'll see the famed Sunday market, an astounding melée of donkeys, sheep, carpets, melons and knives. Otherwise there are smaller markets, mosques and tombs and wild scenery to enjoy before you fly back to Beijing.

Dos and Don'ts

☑ Take a torch and ask permission to use it in the Mogao Caves. You won't see much without one.

☒ Don't expect orderly queues. Buying train tickets requires determination and sharp elbows or ask your hotel to get them.

☑ Leave plenty of time to get anywhere. Trains and planes in China are generally efficient and punctual but west of Lanzhou things happen at a more relaxed pace.

☒ Don't attempt to take photographs where photography is forbidden – especially at military or religious sites.

JAN
FEB
MAR
APR
MAY
DAYS 1–3
DAY 4
DAYS 5–6
DAYS 7–8
DAYS 9–12
DAYS 13–14
JUN
JUL
AUG
SEP
OCT
NOV
DEC

beyond, strung across the dry, inhospitable plains. Jiayuguan marks the end of the Great Wall and, for the ancient Chinese, the end of civilization. The town's imposing fort, barring the way between mountain and desert, is a magnificent piece of architectural drama.

Still in Gansu province, the next stop is Dunhuang and the Mogao Caves, the richest collection of Buddhist art in China – murals painted by Buddhist monks over several centuries until the coming of Islam. Indeed, from Dunhuang, the route continues into Xinjiang, the homeland of China's Muslims. This is a region of mosques, desert, oases, flat bread and Arabic script. The Silk Road splits north and south of the Taklamakan Desert; go north to pass through Turfan, where trellises are laden with grapes and donkey carts trundle the dilapidated, dusty streets.

The two trails meet again at Kashgar, perhaps the most evocative of the Silk Road towns. Amid the acres of palms, against a fabulous backdrop of the forbidding Pamirs, the fabulous Sunday Market, raucous, dusty and hot, transports the traveller back to the Silk Road's heyday.

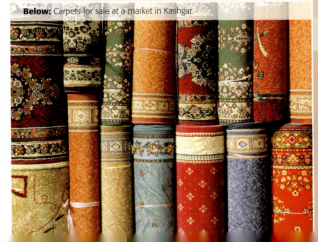

Below: Carpets for sale at a market in Kashgar

GETTING THERE
Prague's Ruznye Airport is 10 km (6 miles) from the city centre. Official taxis wait outside the arrivals hall and charge around £12.50 for the 20 minute ride into the centre of the city.

GETTING AROUND
Prague's compact centre suits travelling on foot. A ticket valid for 24 hours on all public transport costs around £1.50 and can be bought from newsstands in the airport arrivals hall.

WEATHER
May is usually sunny with an average high temperature of 18°C and it rarely rains.

ACCOMMODATION
Prague's hotels can be cheap but Sir Toby's comes with great service and immaculate interiors; doubles from £44; www.sirtobys.com

The quirky but delightful Hotel Sax is ideally located between the Old Town and the Castle district; doubles from £115; www.sax.cz

Views of the Charles Bridge and luxurious rooms at the Four Seasons; doubles from £250; www.fourseasons.com/prague

EATING OUT
Prague is home to some excellent restaurants. Fashionable Kampa Park is where the jet set dines on international food. More homely, Století has an innovative way with traditional dishes.

PRICE FOR TWO
£220 per day including accommodation, food, local transport and entrance to attractions.

FURTHER INFORMATION
www.pis.cz
www.dpp.cz

Black Light Theatre
An outcrop of the Dada movement, Black Light theatre – mime performance art, where actors wearing fluorescent costumes perform with fluorescent props in darkness – became popular in Prague during the cultural thaw that accompanied the political Prague Spring in 1968. Dismissed as decadent by the communist regime, it has seen a revival since 1989, and there are now more than 10 Black Light theatres in Prague. Try the Image Black Theatre at Pařiszka 4. Performances daily at 8pm.

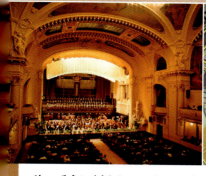

Above (left to right): Smetana Concert Hall; medieval astronomical clock, Old Town City Hall; Mucha Art Nouveau window in Obecní Dům
Main: Dome of the Church of St Francis and the steeples of the Church of St Nicholas rise above the historic city of Prague in the Old Town district

THE HEART OF EUROPE

MOZART ONCE SAID "MY ORCHESTRA IS IN PRAGUE", and during the city's legendary Spring Music Festival it appears that every great orchestra in the world has joined it. While for many the words "Prague Spring" sum up images of student protesters throwing Molotov cocktails at Soviet tanks during the political upheaval of 1968, the far more serene Prague Spring International Music Festival actually predates those violent events by more than two decades. Since 1946 the festival has hosted only the world's very best performance artists, symphony orchestras and chamber music ensembles, all performing in Prague's finest venues.

The finest of the lot is the Obecní Dům, completed in 1911: a concert hall, ballroom, café and restaurant with such a whimsical and exuberant design that the staid and venerable 15th-century Powder Gate next to it appears almost offended at the flamboyant upstart. Built at the height of the Art Nouveau period at the turn of the 20th century, the building is embellished with delicate stucco and heaps of statuary, and above the main entrance is a gargantuan mosaic by Karel Spillar entitled "Homage to Prague", portraying allegorical figures of serenity and permanence. There's an equally permanent Art Nouveau café on the ground floor, where, under the glimmering chandeliers – as they have for a century – over-efficient waitresses in starched white aprons serve coffee and cakes to penniless literary hopefuls, dreaming of writing the next great Prague novel. In the Smetana Concert Hall, at the core of the building, the ornate, glitzy decoration of Alfons Mucha leaves the concert goer breathless, and doubtful that any performer could live up to such over-the-top surroundings. Time and again, however, conductors and soloists find themselves inspired to outdo the setting, as though they were in competition with each other. It is this mix that produces the greatest series of annual concerts in Europe.

> Mozart once said "my orchestra is in Prague", and during the city's legendary Spring Music Festival it appears that every great orchestra in the world has joined it.

Inset: Ornate stucco decoration in Neruda Lane
Below (left and right): Atmospheric mist on the Charles Bridge; musicians performing near Prague Castle

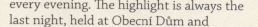

MUSIC LOVERS' DIARY

By day, enjoy the sights of Prague, by night, the Spring Festival concerts: this really is the best time to visit Prague. Throughout the festival (from mid-May to early June), there are performances every evening. The highlight is always the last night, held at Obecní Dům and devoted to the music of Beethoven.

Four Days in the Czech Capital

Walk up to the Castle District for a whirlwind tour of Prague's most famous sights: Golden Lane, St Vitus' Cathedral, Lobowicz Palace and St George's Convent.

Take a gentle walk down winding Nerudova and have coffee and cakes on the terrace at Little Quarter Square. Come back across historic Charles Bridge.

Visit Prague's former Jewish Quarter, in Pařiszka and Široka, admiring the ornate synagogues, Jewish cemeteries and the haunts of writer Franz Kafka. See also the Museum of Decorative Arts.

Shopaholics will love browsing in Pařiszka's expensive designer boutiques and jewellery stores.

Take the metro to Mustek for the classic view of Prague's grand Wenceslas Square. From here, head into the Old Town and leisurely tour its cobbled streets, with medieval courtyards, galleries, museums, and historic churches.

Don't miss the Town Hall's Astronomical Clock in action, every hour on the hour. Check inside the hall to see if a Spring Festival concert is taking place.

The best views anywhere in Prague are those from the top of the 19th-century observation tower, Petřín hill, on the western bank of the Vltava. There are plenty of children's attractions up here, as well as gentle walks and picnic sites. All reached by a funicular railway, it makes a great break from the bustle of the city below.

Dos and Don'ts

☑ Buy tickets for all festival performances well in advance: try the central booking agency at the Rudolfinum (Nám. Jana Palacha, Praha 1, tel. 227 059 234).

☒ Don't visit Prague over the weekend, if possible . It fills up with drunken and often boorish "stag" parties from other countries.

☑ Make sure you see some of the younger performers at the festival. Prague Spring is one of the few classical music festivals in the world to showcase young talent.

☒ Don't eat anywhere on or around Old Town Square unless you have a reliable recommendation. Almost all of these places prey on unsuspecting tourists, serving poor food at high prices, and charging for hidden extras. Adding a premium for sitting outside is the most common scam.

JAN
FEB
MAR
APR
MAY
DAY 1
DAY 2
DAY 3
DAY 4
JUN
JUL
AUG
SEP
OCT
NOV
DEC

GETTING THERE
El Alto International Airport lies about 10 km (6 miles) from the city centre, taking about a half hour by taxi and slightly longer by minibus.

GETTING AROUND
Local public transport in La Paz is provided by inexpensive taxis, *trufis* (collective taxis), *colectivos* (collective minibuses) and *micros* (buses). Taxis display their destinations prominently in the front window.

WEATHER
In May, lofty La Paz normally experiences dry, mild days of 12–20°C and cool evenings, with temperatures as low as 5°C.

ACCOMMODATION
In La Paz, the atmospheric colonial-style guesthouse Residencial Rosario has doubles from £25; www.hotelrosario.com

La Paz's Five-star Hotel Radisson Plaza has a central location and doubles from £60; www.radisson.com/lapazbo

In Copacabana, the Egyptian-themed La Cupula overlooks the lake; doubles from £10; www.hotelcupula.com

EATING OUT
Bolivian food tends to focus on meat – try *lomo montado* (pork with eggs, rice and banana). La Paz's finest eateries are around the So Pocachi district, the Lower Prado and the Zona Sur.

PRICE FOR TWO
£100–120 per day including accommodation, food and local transport.

FURTHER INFORMATION
www.boliviaweb.com

Poor Houses, Rich Views

In most cultures, the higher properties with the best views are owned by the wealthy, while the working classes huddle in the lower, less inspiring parts of town. In La Paz, however, per capita income is inversely proportional to the elevation. Above the canyon floor, the poorest *Paceños* (La Paz residents) enjoy the finest views, while the wealth is centred in the well-heeled Zona Sur, which lies below the central business district.

ABOVE THE CLOUDS

THANKS TO THE ALTITUDE AND SPECTACULAR SETTING of Bolivia's de facto capital city, those arriving by air will enjoy a breathtaking introduction to La Paz. The international airport, in the burgeoning suburb of El Alto – "the heights" – sits on the lung-stifling 4,000-m (13,125-ft) high Altiplano, the wind-swept high plain that dominates southwestern Bolivia.

While the altitude, elevation changes and undisciplined crowds make La Paz physically challenging to explore on foot, there's no better way to immerse yourself in the sights, sounds and smells of this distinctly Andean metropolis. Over half the city's population is of Aymara or Quechua heritage, and *cholas* – indigenous women wearing long plaits and clad in bowler hats and multi-layered dresses – crowd the bustling footpaths, street corners and pungent local markets, selling

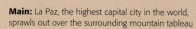

Main: La Paz, the highest capital city in the world, sprawls out over the surrounding mountain tableau

Left: Locals sit in the sunshine outside the Iglesia de San Francisco

Right (left to right): Visitors take a break on a 4WD journey; a local woman attending her stall; the sandy shores of Lake Titicaca; pre-Inca archeological site of Tiahuanaco near Lake Titicaca

everything from snacks and produce to practical items and magic remedies. "*Comprame*" (buy from me), they call out to shoppers threading through the maze of vendors, hoping to engage them in a session of spirited haggling over potential purchases.

Accompanied by the incessant din of horn-blaring traffic, this scene is the essence of the La Paz experience. Fortunately, plenty of quiet coffee shops, enjoyable restaurants and diverse museums provide respite, and the city's spectacular hinterlands offer even greater scope for relaxation. Hiking opportunities abound in the surrounding Andes, and the pre-Inca site, Tiahuanaco, makes a rewarding day trip. On the shores of Lake Titicaca, west of La Paz, the town of Copacabana has a lively atmosphere and easy access to the ancient wonders of Isla del Sol. Alternatively, the lush and leafy village of Coroico, three hours downhill from La Paz, entices visitors with a tropical ambience, and a rich and refreshing breath of flower-scented lowland air.

ANDEAN DIARY

May is an ideal time to visit La Paz and its surrounds as the weather is pleasant and mild. At such extreme heights, the effects of any exertion are greatly multiplied and a simple tour of the sights becomes an active holiday in itself. The empty hillsides round La Paz and Lake Titicaca are ideal for activities.

Eight Elevated Days

DAY 1 Take it easy and spend the first day acclimatizing to the altitude in your hotel or relaxing in a local coffee shop.

DAY 2 Stroll along the main thoroughfare, the Prado, visit the Museum of Contemporary Art, or admire the Iglesia de San Francisco, with its enigmatic blend of indigenous and Spanish Colonial design. Then hop on a sputtering local bus uphill to experience the teeming and nerve-shattering markets of upper La Paz.

DAY 3 Take a guided tour of the pre-Inca ceremonial centre of Tiahuanaco and wander around the site's many intriguing stone structures and carvings.

DAYS 4–5 Jump on a local bus to the holiday town of Copacabana and spend a day or two here. Organize a hike along the shore of beautiful Lake Titicaca. In the evening, enjoy a dinner of the delicious local trout.

DAY 6 Take a day tour to Isla del Sol (Island of the Sun) and spend the day hiking around the island, exploring the ruins that represent the birthplace of the sun.

DAY 7 Return to La Paz in the morning and spend the afternoon shopping along Calle Sagárnaga. Take in a *peña*, a Bolivian folk music programme.

DAY 8 Make a dramatic mountain bike descent down the Yungas Road, the "World's Most Dangerous Road", to refill your lungs in the tropical village of Coroico.

Dos and Don'ts

✓ Ask permission before photographing local people, especially bowler-hat clad *chola* (indigenous) vendors, who are often quite vociferously camera shy.

✗ Don't join or photograph local demonstrations, as you may be associated with unpopular Western policies concerning coca cultivation in Bolivia.

✓ Support the local economy by patronizing street vendors whenever possible. Besides, at a street stall, most things cost a fraction of what is charged in the shops.

✗ Don't exert yourself for the first few days. At 3,600 m (11,800 ft), a debilitating case of *soroche* (mountain sickness) may cause new arrivals to feel decidedly low.

JAN
FEB
MAR
APR
MAY
JUN
JUL
AUG
SEP
OCT
NOV
DEC

Below: Yungas road, connecting La Paz with Coroico below

GETTING THERE
New York is on the northeastern coast of the USA and has three airports – La Guardia for domestic flights; JFK and Newark for both domestic and international. Buses and taxis connect the airports to the city centre.

GETTING AROUND
New York is a great city to walk around. The subway system is comprehensive, and there are also buses and taxis available, although traffic can be heavy.

WEATHER
May is usually sunny, with average daytime temperatures of around 22°C, 12°C at night. There can be cold spells, so pack plenty of layers.

ACCOMMODATION
For budget accommodation, try B&B services such as City Lights Bed and Breakfast; doubles from £40; www.citylightsnewyork.com

Comfort Inn Midtown is conveniently located; doubles from £130; www.applecorehotels.com

Sofitel New York, close to 5th Avenue; doubles from £190; www.sofitel.com

EATING OUT
Whether you want a spaghetti dinner for £8 or a gourmet meal for £50 – New York has it all. For a taste of New York's famous Italian community, you can't beat Carmine on Carmine Street, main courses from £7.

PRICE FOR TWO
£175–200 per day including accommodation, food, local travel and entrance charges.

FURTHER INFORMATION
www.nycvisit.com

New York for Free
You can spend a king's ransom in New York – but with a little planning you can also enjoy many of the city's pleasures absolutely free. Take the Staten Island Ferry for perfect views of the skyline and the Statue of Liberty; head to Central Park for a guided park tour (www.centralparknyc.org); take a tour of Grand Central Station on Wednesdays or Fridays at 12:30pm (starts at the Information Desk); MoMA has free admission on Fridays from 4pm to 8pm; and the Juillard School and Manhattan School of Music both put on free concerts.

LIGHTS, CAMERA, ACTION!

THE PULSE AND THE PACE ARE DAUNTING AT FIRST, but the relentlessly fast rhythm of city life can't be ignored. Before you know it, you are dashing around like a local, talking fast, eating on the run and sharing in the excitement. New York can be anything you want it to be: stylishly chic or cutting-edge trendy; a high temple of culture or a hive of commercialism. Contrary to what some visitors expect, getting your bearings and getting around is easy as central Manhattan is on a straight grid, with avenues running north and south, and streets going east and west. Most are one-way, so you can hop on a bus assured of where you are heading.

Exploring is an unending pleasure because every neighbourhood offers a different mood and architecture, from the dazzle of Broadway neon and the cast iron landmarks of SoHo to the glittering skyscrapers of the financial district. Stroll the Upper East Side for Beaux Arts mansions and dozens of museums, including the Whitney

Main: New York life reflected in one of Saks Fifth Avenue's shop windows

Top: A legendary pairing – the Staten Island Ferry and the Statue of Liberty

Above: Street performers entertain visitors in front of the colossal Metropolitan Museum of Art

Below: Dramatic song and dance at the Schoenfeld Theater on Broadway

BIG APPLE DIARY

One of the world's most exciting cities, New York is full of cultural riches – art, theatre, music and museums – alongside world-class food and shopping. Late spring is a great time to visit, with mild days and not too many tourists. Five days will give you a good taste of the city.

Five Days of City Pleasures

Fifth Avenue is a great place to start – from here you can visit the Rockerfeller Center, window shop at Tiffany & Co and browse the goods at legendary Saks Fifth Avenue. Finish on 34th Street and take the lift up to the top of the Empire State Building for fantastic views. In the evening, take your pick of the Broadway shows.

Spend the morning among the treasures of the Museum of Modern Art (MoMA). In the afternoon, head to the cobbled streets of Greenwich Village and check out the eclectic shops. Stay in the area for dinner and an off-Broadway show.

Take your pick from "Museum Mile": the striking Guggenheim; historical objects in the Jewish Museum; priceless art in the Frick Collection; American art in the Whitney Museum of Modern Art; or the excellent Metropolitan Museum of Modern Art. Alternatively, spend a relaxing day exploring nearby Central Park, where the Conservatory Gardens are at their best.

In the evening, seek out a cosy trattoria in Little Italy, or take in an opera, ballet or concert at the Lincoln Center.

Take the ferry to Ellis Island to see the Statue of Liberty. Back in town, admire the buildings around Wall Street. Enjoy a slap up dinner amid the colourful streets of Chinatown or in the hip Meatpacking District.

Your choice: cutting edge art galleries in Chelsea, shopping in SoHo, or (depending on the day) a visit to the Greenmarket in Union Square or the flea market on Columbus Avenue. Finally, a last toast to the city lights from the 65th floor of the Rockerfeller Plaza, in the Rainbow Room.

Dos and Don'ts

- ✗ Don't be intimidated by the subway. It's safe (except late at night) and the quickest way to cover ground.
- ✓ Save money by joining the queue at Broadway's TKTS booth for half-price same-day seats to shows.
- ✓ See a TV show for free – but write well in advance for tickets. Find out more at www.nycvisit.com
- ✓ Bring comfortable walking shoes. The best way to appreciate the city is up close and personal – on foot!

JAN
FEB
MAR
APR
MAY
DAY 1
DAY 2
DAY 3
DAY 4
DAY 5
JUN
JUL
AUG
SEP
OCT
NOV
DEC

Below: Guggenheim Museum of Art designed by Frank Lloyd Wright

Museum of American Art, old masters in a mansion at the Frick Collection, Frank Lloyd Wright's landmark Guggenheim and the Jewish Museum. Head to the Upper West Side for classic Art Deco apartments and even more museums. The city has been so well documented in films that even if it's your first visit, you'll feel as if you know it already. The best way to see the city is on foot, which allows you to appreciate the fantastic architecture, and there are many great walking tours on offer.

To really feel the flavour of the city, share some other favourite pleasures with New Yorkers. Watch street performers and the passing parade from the steps of the Metropolitan Museum of Art on weekend afternoons. Browse the stalls of the farmers' Greenmarket in Union Square on Wednesday, Friday and Saturday. Walk the East River Promenade from the World Financial Center through Battery Park, with the Statue of Liberty in view all the way. Take in a show or two or check out the Sunday flea market at Columbus Avenue and 77th Street. Join the locals getting their daily exercise and jog around the Central Park reservoir or bike the roadways on weekends when cars are banned. You'll quickly understand why so many love calling the Big Apple home.

JUNE

Where to Go: **June**

Marking the start of summer in the northern hemisphere, June brings sunny weather and longer days. This is a good time to explore Europe and the USA, with natural beauty in abundance. Winter is starting in the southern hemisphere and the cooler weather makes this ideal for a visit to Australia's Northern Territory, which can be unbearably hot for much of the year, and Machu Picchu, where the cooler weather is great for hiking. The Middle East and North Africa are too hot to visit as are many parts of Asia – particularly the Indian subcontinent and southeast – although if you stick to the beach resorts, there should be a cooling sea breeze. To help you choose, you'll find all the destinations in this chapter below, as well as some extra suggestions to provide a little inspiration.

FESTIVALS AND CULTURE

BARCELONA Gaudí's rooftop sculptures on Casa Milà apartment block

UNFORGETTABLE JOURNEYS

ULURU Aboriginal man dressed in traditional costume

NATURAL WONDERS

KRUGER NATIONAL PARK Zebra drinking from a watering-hole

BARCELONA
SPAIN, EUROPE

Top destination for great culture, nightlife and beaches

Something for everyone – art and architecture (Gaudí, Picasso, Miró), shopping and nightlife and, when that gets too much, beaches to relax on.
See pp144–5

MONTREAL
CANADA, NORTH AMERICA

Check out the largest jazz festival in the world

Enjoy summer in this multi-cultural city as it literally jumps with jazz from around the world. Plus it's easy to get out and about in the countryside.
See pp164–5

> "This gourmet's paradise has over 5,000 eateries – more per head in North America than anywhere else save New York."

NASHVILLE & MEMPHIS
USA, NORTH AMERICA

Two musical centres – homes to country music and blues guitar

See the Grand Old Opry House, pay your respects to the King at Graceland and just enjoy the birthplace of Delta Blues.
See pp160–61

BATH
ENGLAND, EUROPE

Britain's premier Georgian spa town goes festival mad

Roman baths, the Royal Crescent and rolling countryside look perfect in summer sun. Enjoy the Fringe and International Music Festivals.
visitbath.co.uk

CUSCO
PERU, SOUTH AMERICA

Inti Raymi, Festival of the Sun, a summer solstice celebration

Fireworks, festivities and excited locals make pretty Cuzco – half Inca, half Spanish Colonial – a very lively place to stay.
www.andeantravelweb.com/peru

GREEK ISLANDS
GREECE, EUROPE

Make your own odyssey on an island-hopping holiday

Many hundreds of islands dot the seas around mainland Greece, and there's an extensive ferry network so you can always find a quiet spot.
www.greekisland.co.uk

JEFFERSON NATIONAL FOREST
USA, NORTH AMERICA

On the Appalachian Trail

The west-central Virginia section of the trail passes through some outstanding displays of azaleas and rhododendrons in this month.
www.appalachiantrail.org

HALONG BAY
VIETNAM, ASIA

A sailing trip between some of the 3,000 limestone isles

Cruise through this hauntingly beautiful seascape of dramatic limestone peaks and caves, coral reefs, and sandy beaches.
halong.org.vn

ULURU (AYERS ROCK)
AUSTRALIA, AUSTRALASIA

It's a drive of a lifetime to see this big, red rock

A 4WD-truck is needed to navigate the harsh outback, touring among the natural wonders of Australia, to this place sacred to Aboriginals.
See pp148–9

MACHU PICCHU
PERU, SOUTH AMERICA

A fantastic feat of construction on the side of a mountain

It's a strenuous high-altitude hike through the mountains, but the glorious views of this ancient city make the effort worthwhile.
See pp154–5

> "Hot springs, geysers, lonely mountains, wild rivers and innumerable waterfalls appeal to the crowd-weary tourist."

REYKJAVIK
ICELAND, EUROPE

Explore this beautiful land of ice, fire and the midnight sun

It's a geologist's paradise – the best way to enjoy it is to get out and about, amongst the glaciers, lava fields, thermal spas and waterfalls.
See pp158–9

KRUGER NATIONAL PK
SOUTH AFRICA, AFRICA

Go on safari in one of the largest game reserves in Africa

If it's the "big five" you're after – lion rhino, elephant, Cape buffalo and leopard – the Kruger is an excellent and varied safari destination.
See pp154–5

KODIAK ISLAND
USA, NORTH AMERICA

As the salmon run they attract the famously large bears

As well as huge bears you'll see moose with their calves, foxes, seals and maybe orcas – and an astonishing amount of birdlife.
www.kodiakisland.org

PANTANAL
BRAZIL, SOUTH AMERICA

The world's largest freshwater wetlands teem with wildlife

The animals here are far more visible than in the rainforest – see giant otters, tapirs, cayman, herds of capybara and many, many birds.
www.braziltourism.org

BUKK HILLS NATIONAL PARK
HUNGARY, EUROPE

Great for butterfly-spotting

In cave-riddled Bukk and Aggtelek National Parks you'll find an abundance of rare flora and fauna – as well as delicious local wines.
www.utikonyv.hu

Previous page: Vatnajökull Glacier, Jökulsarlon Lagoon, Iceland

Weather Watch

❶ Southern Canada is the warmest part of the country during the summer although rain is likely. By June temperatures have not reached their uncomfortable peak.

❷ Peru's weather is great this month. Machu Picchu will be noticeably warmer but also a lot wetter than Cusco. It can be cold at night too.

❸ During June, South Africa enjoys pleasant, warm sunny days and very little rain. But this is winter so the days are relatively short.

❹ Southern Europe comes into its own in summer. Barcelona, Rome and the Dalmatian Coast all bask in the warm sun. The sea breezes just about keep temperatures comfortable on the coast; but in Rome visitors can keep cool in the splendid churches.

❺ Although June temperatures are mild and pleasant in Yunnan, it is the start of the rainy season so pack a waterproof and expect some light rain.

❻ Much of the South Pacific is hot and rainy year-round but for Vanuatu, June is one of the coolest and driest months – and it's not cyclone season.

LUXURY AND ROMANCE

ROME View of St Peter's Basilica at dusk

MAURITIUS
INDIAN OCEAN

Stay at a luxury resort on a coral-fringed coastline

Luxury resorts at good prices, not that cost matters as you drift slowly through the colour-filled sea, or lie on white sand as soft as talc.
www.mauritius.net

LUDLOW
ENGLAND, EUROPE

One of the prettiest villages in the UK and with fine dining

Cobbled streets and crooked-timbered houses combine with a superb gastronomic offer to make a stay in the pastoral countryside a luxurious treat.
www.ludlow.org.uk

GRANADA
SPAIN, EUROPE

Stay at a traditional parador in the romantic Alhambra Palace

At the foot of the beautiful Sierra Nevada, this elegant palace was built as a paradise on earth – and you can still enjoy the nightlife in Granada.
www.parador.es

TURKS & CAICOS
CARIBBEAN

Deluxe spa treatments and long powdery-sand beaches

Choose between islands that are well-developed and provide pamperings and life's luxuries, and those that are deserted and simply divine.
www.turksandcaicostourism.com

ROME
ITALY, EUROPE

One of the most beautiful and romantic places in the world

There's so much history here it's amazing – it's everywhere you look. On top of this visual feast, you must enjoy the food, shopping and style.
See pp162–3

"Witness the glories of ancient Rome – the magnificent Forum, the Colosseum and the Palatine Hill."

ACTIVE ADVENTURES

VANUATU Scuba diver exploring the wreck at Million Dollar Point

VANUATU
MELANESIA, AUSTRALASIA

A string of volcanic islands that are a diver's paradise

The reefs are spectacular, but there's more here than just diving – try trekking, horseriding, caving, kayaking or volcano watching.
See pp146–7

YUNNAN
CHINA, ASIA

Walk the precipitous Tiger Leaping Gorge

Base yourself in Lijiang, one of the prettiest towns in China, with some remarkable sights before embarking on this famous hike.
See pp150–51

CARPATHIANS
ROMANIA, EUROPE

Take a horseriding and trekking holiday in the hills

Ride a local *hutzul* horse through the flower-covered meadows and foothills of the unspoiled Carpathian mountains and see Dracula's castle.
www.riding-holidays.ro

HADRIAN'S WALL
ENGLAND, EUROPE

Walk the National Trail next to this famous monument

Classic 135-km (84-mile) walk along the remains of this Roman monument through the rugged Northumberland countryside.
www.nationaltrail.co.uk

DAYTONA BEACH
USA, NORTH AMERICA

Learn to surf at a summer camp on Daytona Beach

Florida is underrated as a surf destination, and while there won't be awesome waves in summer, they should be perfect for learning.
www.surfline.com

FAMILY GETAWAYS

DALMATIAN COAST Brown fritillary on a lavender flower

"Emerald, cypress-clad isles are set in an aquamarine sea and exquisitely finished with red-roofed towns."

ILE DE RÉ
FRANCE, EUROPE

Bijou island getaway on the Atlantic coast near La Rochelle

Popular with affluent Parisians, it is quiet in June and, if you camp, not expensive. Sandy beaches, cycle paths and lots of atmosphere.
www.iledere.com

DARWIN
AUSTRALIA, AUSTRALASIA

Enjoy Darwin's outdoor lifestyle and harbour setting

Visit also the native artists of the Tiwi Islands, and Kakadu National Park – a mass of rivers, wetlands and forests, rich in Aboriginal art.
www.travelnt.com

DALMATIAN COAST
CROATIA, EUROPE

A coastline of crystal waters and quiet, picturesque islands

This Mediterranean riviera is still quite quiet, calm and unspoiled – so see it as soon as you can. Plenty of activities for the kids too.
See pp156–7

BIG ISLAND, HAWAI'I
USA, NORTH AMERICA

Off-season (June) is perfect for cheap deals and great weather

Explore the island's active volcanoes – with real hot lava flows – and snorkel in perfect, clear fish-filled water.
www.gohawaii.com

NIKKO & NARA
JAPAN, ASIA

Child-friendly destination that'll turn them into culture vultures

Kids will love how different it all is – throw in manga, Hello Kitty and monkeys and they'll be racing you to visit museums and temples.
www.japan-guide.com

GETTING THERE
Barcelona is on the Mediterranean coast in northeast Spain. The international airport, El Prat, is 30 minutes from the city centre, and is connected by bus, train and taxi.

GETTING AROUND
The city is easily explored on foot and there are excellent bus and metro connections.

WEATHER
The weather is reliably sunny in June, with an average daily temperature of 24ºC and warm nights. Rain is unusual.

ACCOMMODATION
Hotel Banys Orientals is a stylish hotel in one of the oldest parts of the city; doubles from £75; www.hotelbanysorientals.com

Hotel Mesón Castilla is a cosy hotel with a great central location near Las Ramblas; doubles from £90; www.mesoncastilla.com

Hotel Arts is a superb modern beachside hotel with every luxury and fabulous views; doubles from £250; www.ritzcarlton.com

EATING OUT
Catalan cuisine is rich and varied. Choose a selection of treats from a tapas bar, such as mouthwatering sardines, or tuck into a selection of cured meats, another Catalan speciality.

PRICE FOR TWO
£130–150 per day including accommodation, food and entrance charges.

FURTHER INFORMATION
www.barcelonaturisme.com

Antoni Gaudí
Barcelona's favourite architect, Antoni Gaudí, was an eccentric figure. His characteristic use of looping arches as the basis of a building was derived from natural models. They can be seen at their best in his apartment blocks, such as the giant rock-like La Pedrera, built without a single straight line. Profoundly religious, Gaudí devoted the last years of his life to his cathedral, the Sagrada Família. When he was run over by a tram in 1926, he looked so unkempt that no one recognized him, and he was taken to a paupers' hospital.

Above: The interior of bar So-Da in the Barri Gòtic; boats lined up in Barcelona's old port

Main: The interior of the Palau de la Music Catalana

Below: Fish for sale in busy Boqueria Market

DIFFERENT BY DESIGN

FEW CITIES ARE BETTER FOR STROLLING AND PEOPLE-WATCHING than Barcelona. The city is home to Las Ramblas – a spectacular mile-long promenade that runs down from the city centre to the sea, which is a real delight to walk along. The avenue gains a special verve in early summer as the last chills of spring are thrown off and fresh sunlight dapples the pavement and illuminates the roses stacked high in the street-side flower stalls. After dark, the soft, warm air invites you to linger at café tables long into the night.

Laid out like a giant stage set in the tight space between the Mediterranean and the two mountains of Montjüic and Tibidabo, Barcelona is a naturally theatrical city. Along Las Ramblas, everyone is part of the performance, and tourists join the human statues, dancers and other entertainers who form the resident cast. Winding streets lead off into the Barri Gòtic, the city's medieval core, with its heavy-columned churches, shaded

CATALAN DIARY

As well as offering Barcelona's best weather, June has a full cultural calendar, with the climax of the world-class opera and music seasons. The main draw is undoubtedly the huge all-night celebration, *Sant Joan*, on the 23rd. A five-day stay in the city will allow you to explore its many sights at a leisurely pace.

Five Days of Strolling

Wander along Las Ramblas from Plaça de Catalunya, stopping to savour the colours, scents and sounds of the fabulous Boqueria food market. Be sure to pause here and there to soak up the ambience.

Venture off Las Ramblas to see the cathedral and the surrounding alleys of the Barri Gòtic. Visit the nearby Museu d'Història de la Ciutat, with its Roman ruins, or check out the beautiful interior of the Palau de la Music Catalana.

Head to the Born district, where you will find Barcelona's most charming old street, Carrer Montcada, and some chic little design shops. While you are here, visit the Picasso Museum and the exquisite Basílica de Santa Maria del Mar, the city's finest Gothic church.

Immerse yourself in Gaudí – head up Passeig de Gràcia, past its many eye-catching shops, to visit the Casa Batlló and La Pedrera, his most extraordinary apartment blocks, then take the Metro to his stunning cathedral, Sagrada Família. Finish with a trip to the magnificent Parc Güell, for a ramble among its brilliant mosaics.

Head west of the city into the Raval, to discover the dazzling white spaces of the MACBA art showcase. In the evening head to the all-night *Sant Joan* party on the beach to watch the amazing firework display and dance the night away with the crowds.

Sleep off the last few days' adventures with a day on the beach, breaking off for a seafood lunch at one of the many restaurants by the old port.

Dos and Don'ts

☑ Get used to the local clock – lunch around 2pm and dinner after 9pm. Nightlife doesn't really get going until after 11pm.

☒ Don't even bother trying to use a car in town as parking is torture and public transport is much faster.

☑ Look out for the *Articket* and *Barcelona Card*, multi-entry tickets to museums and other attractions that can give big savings on admissions and transport.

☒ Don't mispronounce Gaudí – said gau-DEE, not to rhyme with howdy.

JAN	
FEB	
MAR	
APR	
MAY	
JUN	
20th	
21st	
22nd	
23rd	
24th	
JUL	
AUG	
SEP	
OCT	
NOV	
DEC	

doorways, elaborate gargoyles and countless other intriguing details. Tiny alleys suddenly open up onto romantic squares and sunstruck courtyards, giving stunning contrasts of light and shade. In the Born district, medieval palaces now contain art museums and lively tapas and cava bars. A short walk away are the dazzling open spaces of the old port and the long, elegantly curving beach. Dotted throughout Barcelona are the creations of Antoni Gaudí, with an individuality and sensuality so emblematic of this city that they have become its favourite icons.

Barcelona's street theatre is not a production set in the past – this is undoubtedly one of Europe's most stylish and culturally inventive cities. Medieval streets conceal cutting-edge design shops, ultra-hip clubs and chic modern restaurants, and mid-June sees the Sónar electronic music festival, three days of clubbers' heaven. However, the traditional climax to the month is *Sant Joan*, (St John) the "Night of Fire", on 23 June, when Barcelona is framed by giant firework displays on Montjüic and Tibidabo. Revellers gather on the beach to dance the night away around huge bonfires, before greeting the beautiful sunrise with a bracing swim.

Below: The hustle and bustle of city life on Las Ramblas

GETTING THERE
Air Vanuatu operates regular flights from Auckland, New Zealand and Brisbane or Sydney, Australia, to Port Vila's Bauerfield Airport 3 km (2 miles) from the city centre.

GETTING AROUND
Vanair operates a domestic air network connecting the various islands to Port Vila.

WEATHER
Vanuatu has a tropical climate. In June, day temperatures are around 25°C, dropping to around 19°C in the evening.

ACCOMMODATION
Evergreen Bungalows, Tanna Island, gives a real taste of Tanna; doubles from £45; www.evergreen-bungalows.com

Mangoes, Port Vila, is a child-free resort looking over the Erakor Lagoon; doubles from £90; www.mangoesresort.com

Bokissa Eco Resort, Espiritu Santo, is an away-from-it-all island resort 30 mins by boat from Luganville; doubles from £230; www.bokissa.vu

EATING OUT
Fresh local fish, beef, fruit and vegetables are plentiful. *Laplap* is Vanuatu's signature dish made with yam or taro roots soaked in coconut milk with pieces of pork, chicken or fish.

PRICE FOR TWO
£175–200 per day including accommodation, food, local travel, tours and inter-island flights.

FURTHER INFORMATION
www.vanuatutourism.com

Land Diving Ritual

Bungy jumping is the western world's version of land diving which developed as a coming of age ritual on Pentecost Island. This terrifying event takes place annually from April to June with male participants plunging headlong from a tower of branches anchored only by vines tied to their feet. The aim of the divers is to touch the ground with their shoulders to ensure fertility of the ground for the following year's yam harvest.

THE SLEEPING GIANT

VANUATU IS AN ARCHIPELAGO OF 83 VOLCANIC ISLANDS in the South Pacific. Here, alongside a natural adventure playground renowned for diving, lush jungle and active volcanoes, unique custom villages uphold a traditional way of life, preserving their ancient culture and also fostering tourism at a gentle pace.

Port Vila is the hub of Vanuatu and located on the main island of Efate. Here visitors will find agreeable resorts around the Erakor Lagoon, a rugged coastline, fast-flowing rivers and secluded sandy beaches. The interior is verdant rainforest cut only by a few walking tracks to remote weather and radio beacons, but it is the outer islands of Vanuatu that offer extraordinary adventures.

Known as the "Sleeping Giant", Espiritu Santo is a diver's mecca featuring stunning reefs, and wrecks from World War II when 100,000 American troops were based here. The *SS President Coolidge* sank after hitting US mines in 1942 and lies just 60 m (197 ft) below the surface. Million Dollar Point is a discarded jumble of military equipment tipped into the sea when the war ended.

Main: Watching the spectacular eruption of volcanic Mount Yasur on Tanna

In Santo's interior, there is a trek to a remote jungle cave. A 29-m (95-ft) bamboo ladder lashed with vines descends to a canopy of green where the cave is open-mouthed in a 15-m (49-ft) yawn. A dark eerie tunnel extends almost half a mile and the rock-strewn floor presents a watery obstacle course, cool and quiet, except for the intermittent chatter of flying foxes swooping above.

Torchlight illuminates the "Braille Trail" a step at a time, until you eventually emerge into dazzling sunlight beside the swift-flowing Vantar River. Sculpted into magnificent shapes and striations, sheer walls rise either side, waterfalls plummet in a massive exfoliating shower and you are swept along in a boat for two hours or more through this spectacular freshwater canal.

Yasur, is the world's most accessible volcano and located on Tanna, Vanuatu's "Island of Fire". Fascinated visitors can peer into Yasur's molten but still beating heart and feel a deep rumble shudder from its depths. At night they stand riveted by its sound and light show as embers fall around them like glow-in-the-dark confetti. Nearby, Tanna's custom villagers shun modern comforts to live traditionally in simple woven-palm huts.

Left panel (top to bottom): Millennium Cave in Espirito Santo; riding on the beach at Louantuiu, Tanna; kayaking on the Malo River, Espirito Santo

Top: Aerial view of a volcanic island, Vanuatu

Above: Dancers in traditional costume in Port Vila

Below: Grouper with a school of small fish

ACTIVITY DIARY

In June, you can see the spectacular land diving ritual performed by the local islanders. You can also enjoy the distinct atmosphere of each island – while the islanders (Ni-Vanuatu) are predominantly Melanesian, the islands have been influenced by Polynesian, French, British and Chinese settlement.

A Week Exploring the Islands

Arrive in Port Vila and settle into your resort overlooking the Erakor Lagoon. Explore the main street of the capital, including the colourful daily market.

Enjoy a day cruise on the restored ketch Coongoola, scuba dive and snorkel, barbecue on Tranquillity Island and visit a turtle hatchery.

Fly to Espiritu Santo, explore the capital of Luganville and transfer by boat to Bokissa Island. Circumnavigate the resort by outrigger canoe or kayak up the Malo River to a freshwater lake.

Dive the SS President Coolidge, Million Dollar Point or eight of the other magnificent Santo dive sites, with depths ranging from 6 m (20 ft) to 60 m (197 ft).

Visit Pentecost Island to see the locals participate in the annual land diving ritual by jumping off a wooden scaffold attached by vines.

Fly to Tanna Island to experience swimming with a dugong before testing your nerve on the rim of the active Yasur Volcano. Try to stay in traditional thatched village-style accommodation.

Return to Port Vila. Visit the Cascade Waterfalls and Ekasup Cultural Village to discover how the Ni-Vanuatu people live, including traditional food preparation, herbal medicines, hunting and dancing.

Dos and Don'ts

- ✓ Attempt some phrases of Bislama, the language of the islands. Locals love it if you make the effort.
- ✗ Don't rely on a public transport system – there isn't one.
- ✓ Look out for the special Vanuatu stamps and unusual post-boxes – there is even one under the sea!
- ✓ Make sure that you seek proper medical advice regarding malaria before visiting the outer islands.

Below: Scuba diver exploring the wreck at Million Dollar Point

JAN
FEB
MAR
APR
MAY
JUN
DAY 1
DAY 2
DAY 3
DAY 4
DAY 5
DAY 6
DAY 7
JUL
AUG
SEP
OCT
NOV
DEC

THE RED CENTRE

A PPROACHING THE ENORMOUS MONOLITH OF ULURU, you cannot help but be awestruck by the spectacle of this terracotta giant looming over the endless desert landscape. The rock is a guardian that governs the surrounding desert, a reminder that you are in the absolute centre of the Australian outback, standing beneath the oldest temple in the world.

Don't let the word "desert" fool you; the Uluru-Kata Tjuta National Park teems with wildlife and flora. Desert she-oak trees dot the landscape and birds of crimson and gold dance beneath them, feasting on flowering plants. At night, the howl of a dingo echoes eerily across the red sand landscape.

During the 4 hours that it takes to walk the circumference of Uluru, you will discover the water holes and ancient rock art that contribute to the site's sacred presence. Time your walk to end just

GETTING THERE
Uluru is in central Australia, 443 km (275 miles) by road from Alice Springs. Flights to Ayers Rock Airport depart daily from Alice Springs. The nearby town of Yulara services visits to Uluru-Kata Tjuta National Park.

GETTING AROUND
A free shuttle bus from the airport takes you to all the accommodation in the town of Yulara. You can also hire a car in Alice Springs but be sure to stay on the sealed roads around Uluru.

WEATHER
During June, temperatures at night can be as low as -5°C, reaching 20°C during the day.

ACCOMMODATION
All accommodation around Uluru is owned by Voyages, who provide a range of hotels.

The Lost Camel is the hip choice, with doubles from £80; www.ayersrockresort.com.au

Sails in the Desert for outback luxury; doubles from £110; www.ayersrockresort.com.au

Longitude 131 for perfect Uluru views; doubles from £410; www.longitude131.com.au

EATING OUT
The barbecue at the Outback Pioneer Lodge is a must for just £9. The Sounds of Silence Dinner, £60, takes in the sunset over Uluru, with a feast of crocodile and emu.

PRICE FOR TWO
£200–230 per day including accommodation, food, car hire, park charges and narrated tour.

FURTHER INFORMATION
www.uluru.com

The Origin of the Rock

Aboriginal people explain the world's creation through the exploits of mythical ancestors, plants and animals who lived in the *Tjukurpa*, or "Dreamtime". There are various Dreamtime stories about Uluru, although the local Anangu people believe that the monolith was created by two boys piling up mud. The route to the top of the rock has great cultural significance as it follows the sacred path taken by the ancestral Mala (hare wallaby) men for important ceremonies.

Main: Uluru glows deep red in the evening sun

Left: Adult wallaroo (wallaby/kangaroo cross) stands alert

Right (left to right): Tjukaruru Road leading towards the rock formations of Kata Tjuta; desert wildflowers near Alice Springs; Aboriginal man dressed in traditional costume

before sunset, then settle at one of the viewing spots to see the incredible colours that peel away from the rock as the sun drops behind it.

Kata Tjuta, which sits 32 km (20 miles) from Uluru, is thought by some to be an even more awesome sight. This otherworldly group of 36 domes, rising from the flat desert, is in fact bigger than Uluru. A 3-hour walk to the Valley of the Winds passes through gorges and valleys so hauntingly quiet that they evoke the huge spiritual significance of this strange landscape.

With a 4WD vehicle, the opportunities for exploring the vast wilderness are unlimited. Marvel at the high walls of Ormiston Gorge as you walk along the riverbed. Float on your back in the Ellery Creek water hole and gaze at the ochre cliffs above. Camp among ghost gums by the Finke River, the oldest in the world, towered over by the ancient gondwana palms of Palm Valley.

A few days in the red centre will change your concept of time forever. Forget your watch, for it's impossible to measure the aeons of creation evident in this ancient land.

ABORIGINAL DIARY

If you are able to plan your trip around the full moon, the opportunity to see it rise up from behind the rock at sunset is the chance of a lifetime. Combine your visit to take in local events such as the Finke River Dirt Bike Race (second weekend in June) or the Alice Springs Beanie Festival (June-July).

A Week in the Desert

DAY 1 Arrive at Yulara and travel out to the Cultural Centre. Spend an afternoon learning about the local culture. Enjoy the evening with the Sounds of Silence dinner, taking in the colours of sunset over Uluru.

DAY 2 Spend your morning at the rock with a local Aboriginal guide for an introduction to the local Dreamtime stories. Walk the circumference of Uluru, or take a short walk to view waterholes and sacred sites from a distance.

DAY 3 Enjoy the changing colours of sunrise overlooking Kata Tjuta before doing the walk to the Valley of the Winds, unguided or with a group. In the evening, cook a kangaroo fillet at the Outback Pioneer Lodge barbecue.

DAY 4 Head to Alice Springs and visit the Old Telegraph Station, walking along the Todd River. The story of Australia's telegraphic lifeline will give you an insight into the country's modern history.

DAY 5 Hire a 4WD vehicle and head to the West Macdonnell Ranges. Visit Hermannsburg and learn about local art history. Trek and camp in the valleys around Finke River.

DAY 6 Driving to Ormiston Gorge, you will pass sacred Tnorala, where you can walk the meteor crater rim. At Ormiston Gorge, take the ghost gum walk then camp out.

DAY 7 Take a helicopter flight from Glen Helen Gorge over Ormiston Gorge and the surrounding area before driving back to Alice Springs.

Dos and Don'ts

✓ Obey local requests such as not climbing Uluru or entering and taking photos of sacred sites. The local Aboriginal people consider the rock sacred, so respect their traditional beliefs.

✗ Don't go four-wheel driving alone if you are inexperienced. It is best to take a guided tour if you are unsure.

✓ Use the Aboriginal names for locations, such as Kata Tjuta instead of The Olgas, and Uluru instead of Ayers Rock.

✓ If you are using the shuttle bus service to Uluru and Kata Tjuta for an unguided walk, your name and location are recorded. Always meet up with your return transport, or a search party will be sent out for you.

Below: Ormiston Gorge

JAN
FEB
MAR
APR
MAY
JUN
JUL
AUG
SEP
OCT
NOV
DEC

GETTING THERE
The Yunnan region of China is located along China's southwest frontier and is served by Kunming International Airport. Taxis are available at the airport for the city centre.

GETTING AROUND
Taxis are plentiful and cheap. For longer trips you can rent a car with a driver. A train runs between Kunming and Dali.

WEATHER
In June the weather is mild, with an average temperature of 19°C. Skies are clear.

ACCOMMODATION
The luxurious Green Lake Hotel in Kunming has panoramic views of the lake; doubles from £85; www.greenlakehotel.com

Sanhe Hotel in Lijiang is in the centre of the Old Town; doubles from £25; tel. +86 (888) 512 0891.

Sean's Guesthouse, Walnut Garden in Tiger Leaping Gorge (East side) for a decent hot shower; doubles from £5; tel. +86 (887) 880 6300.

EATING OUT
Yunnan's speciality is *qiguoji* (steam-pot chicken), cooked in a special vessel. Yunnan also differs from the rest of China in that cheese is produced here, try the mild *rubing*.

PRICE FOR TWO
£75–100 per day including accommodation, food and 7-day car hire with driver.

FURTHER INFORMATION
www.yunnantourism.com

The Naxi

Tiger Leaping Gorge is in the territory of the Naxi minority, descendants of Tibetan nomads who lived until recently in matriarchal families. They have their own language and their script *(below)*, called Dongba, is the only hieroglyphic writing system still in use. Their religion is polytheistic and mixes Daoism and Lamaism with older animist beliefs. They're known for their skill as gardeners, musicians and as craftsmen and falconers.

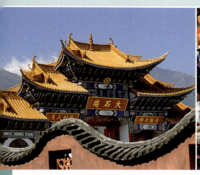

Above (left to right): Ornate roof of the Goddess of Mercy Temple; Naxi orchestra playing traditional instruments; canal and street in Lijiang
Main: Pagoda reflected in the Black Dragon Pool with Jade Dragon Snow Mountain in the background

WORLD'S DEEPEST GORGE

SAID TO BE THE WORLD'S DEEPEST GORGE, it splits snow-capped peaks. Yet it's so narrow that the sides of the mountains are almost vertical, and the fast-flowing river so tightly funnelled that – legend has it – a tiger once escaped from hunters by jumping it. This is Tiger Leaping Gorge, one of China's great natural wonders, where the Jinsha-Jiang, the River of Golden Sand, has sliced apart two 5,000 m (16,400 ft) high peaks, Jade Dragon Snow Mountain and Haba Snow Mountain.

Hiking along the narrow ridge above the gorge is like travelling through a Chinese scroll painting, with its characteristic tilted perspective; far below the river rages, high above, the cloud-draped mountain soars. Each turn reveals another facet of the sublime view and hikers completing the 32-km (20-mile) walk complain of tired necks as well as knees.

The path, an old miners' route that winds along the side of Haba Snow Mountain, is painted with arrows so that you don't get lost. It leads between three rustic hamlets – welcome huddles of

farmsteads whose eaves curl jauntily upwards. Some years ago, a farmer in Bendiwan village grew tired of exhausted hikers knocking at his door, so opened up a few rooms. Today the Halfway Guesthouse, as it is called, is one of a clutch of farms where weary hikers can rest while around them the family carries on laying chillis out to dry or threshing the harvest.

Towards the end of the walk, you can follow switchbacks all the way down to where the mythical tiger made its leap. Here, where the gorge is barely 30 m (100 ft) across, thunderous waters crash against jagged rocks. On the last leg of the trip, the verdant paddy fields of Walnut Grove are a glad sight just for being flat and placid, and it's a great place to rest weary legs, sip cool drinks under the trees, bask in a sense of achievement and reflect on the gorge's grandeur.

Hiking along the narrow ridge above the gorge is like travelling through a Chinese scroll painting, with its characteristic tilted perspective.

Inset: Naxi people in traditional outfits
Below (left and right): Narrow path in Tiger Leaping Gorge; tiger statue at the Gorge

YUNNAN DIARY

Yunnan is a very clement province of China throughout the year. In June, Tiger Leaping Gorge will be swollen with rain so that trekkers can see it in its full glory. To extend their trip, visitors could also visit Beijing *(see pp228–9)* which would give further insight into the contrasting nature of this enormous country.

A Week in Yunnan

Land in Kunming, Yunnan's capital and spend the rest of the day sightseeing around the city. Visit the lotus-filled ponds in Cui Hu Gongyuan and the colourful bird and flower market with its large selection of animals.

DAY 1

Make your way to picturesque Dali, a little town filled with cobbled lanes and stone houses.

Travel to the outskirts of town to see the famous San Ta (Three Pagodas). Then carry on your journey to Er Hai (Ear Lake) where you can watch the fishermen catch fish on the lake using their trained cormorants.

DAY 2

In the evening, enjoy the atmosphere of the town to the full by trying the local cuisine in a restaurant.

Travel on to Lijiang. Visit the pretty Old Town and admire the water wheels that mark the entrance. In the market square the locals gather to chat and play cards and occasionally show their falconry skills.

DAYS 3–4

Attend a traditional music concert by the Naxi people at the Naxi Music Academy in the evening.

Continue north to trek through Tiger Leaping Gorge, one of China's deepest gorges, named after a tiger that escaped hunters at its narrowest point. Three days allows for a leisurely pace although in places the track can be rather arduous. The well-marked trail has exceptional views and is dotted with small hamlets along the way so that you can stop for some refreshment. Fly back to Kunming from Lijiang.

DAYS 5–7

Dos and Don'ts

✓ Pick up one of the Tiger Leaping Gorge trail maps available from cafes and restaurants in Lijiang.

✗ Don't attempt the Gorge route in bad weather, especially not when it is wet as the area is prone to landslides.

✓ Try the local dishes. Yunnan has some of the best cuisine in China and its mellow climate means that vegetables are abundant all year round.

JAN

FEB

MAR

APR

MAY

JUN

DAY 1

DAY 2

DAYS 3–4

DAYS 5–7

JUL

AUG

SEP

OCT

NOV

DEC

Below: Jade Dragon mountain area in Lijiang

GETTING THERE
Machu Picchu is located around 80 km (50 miles) northwest of Cusco. The flight from Lima International Airport to Cusco takes 2 hours.

GETTING AROUND
It takes around 4 hours to get to Aguas Calientes (the nearest town to Machu Picchu) from Cusco by train, the price varies according to the standard of train. The Inca Trail is a 3–4 day hike from just outside Cusco.

WEATHER
June in Cusco is dry and sunny. The altitude keeps temperatures cool at around 13°C, dropping at night. Machu Picchu and Aguas Calientes have a wet and humid climate with average temperatures of 18°C.

ACCOMMODATION
The Machu Picchu Inn in Aguas Calientes is at the foot of the Inca ruins; doubles from £75; www.peru-hotels.com

The Sanctuary Lodge at the ruins has doubles from £400; machupicchu.orient-express.com

El Monasterio, is a sumptuous converted monastery in Cusco; doubles from £250; www.monasterio.orient-express.com

EATING OUT
Typical Peruvian cuisine usually consists of rice and beans served with a meat. Guinea pig, or *cui*, is a speciality as is the local grain, quinoa.

PRICE FOR TWO
£450–800 per day including accommodation, food, internal flights, local transportation and entrance charge to Machu Picchu.

FURTHER INFORMATION
www.machupicchu.org

Inti Raymi

On the day of the winter solstice, the ancient Incas honoured their Sun God. They sacrificed a llama to him to ensure a plentiful harvest in the coming year. The festival was suppressed by the invading Spaniards as a pagan ritual but today it has been revived and is one of the most spectacular of its kind in South America. On 24 June, thousands descend on Cusco for the week-long celebrations to mark the Festival of the Sun. There are street parties, live music and shows and a procession to the Inca fortress of Sacsayhuamán, above the town.

Breathtaking views of the moutain draped in a shroud of morning mist… one of the world's most iconic sights, Machu Picchu.

Main: Ruins at Machu Picchu rise majestically out of the clouds

CITY IN THE CLOUDS

SET ON A RIDGE ABOVE THE ROARING URUBAMBA RIVER, this ancient Inca citadel is one of the most evocative sights in South America. The small fortress city sits majestically in a saddle between two mountain peaks in the subtropical Andean foothills, surrounded by dense vegetation and often shrouded in mist. The extraordinary stonework is a testament to the incredible skills of Inca stonemasons more than 600 years ago – vast grey granite blocks fitted together so exactly that a knife blade cannot be slipped between their joints. Invisible from below and entirely self-contained, Machu Picchu was not found by the Spanish Conquistadors who were wreaking havoc throughout the continent in the 16th century. The ruins were forgotten, and it was an American archeologist, Hiram Bingham, who stumbled upon them in 1911. Short hikes from the site give some sense of its extraordinary position. A perilous ascent up Wayna Picchu, the small peak beyond the city, offers dizzying views.

JAN
FEB
MAR
APR
MAY
JUN
DAY 1
DAY 2
DAY 3
DAY 4
DAY 5
DAY 6
DAY 7
JUL
AUG
SEP
OCT
NOV
DEC

PERUVIAN DIARY

Peru is incredibly diverse, with a long coastal stretch, dense Amazon jungle, colonial cities and Andean splendour. To make the most of Machu Picchu and the Cusco region, a week is the bare minimum, as you'll need some time to acclimatize to Cusco's rarefied air and to explore the ruins at your own pace.

A Week on the Inca Trail

Most flights into Lima arrive in the evening so rest and prepare yourself for your onward journey.

Try to get a window seat for some fabulous views of the Andes on the Lima to Cusco flight. Take it easy on your first day at altitude, by wandering around the cobbled streets of Cusco, enjoying its lively markets.

Make a visit to Pisaq in the Sacred Valley which has some extensive ruins as well as a wonderful textile market on Tuesdays, Thursdays and Sundays.

Take the Vistadome train to Aguas Calientes. The glass roofs of the Vistadome carriage allow you to enjoy the views of mountains and waterfalls. From Aguas Calientes it's a short bus trip to Machu Picchu. Stay over on-site or stay in Aguas Calientes and get the bus up the next day.

The ruins look magical in the sunrise and skies are often clearer in the morning than in the afternoon. Take some time to wander by yourself, before the tour groups arrive. Take the afternoon train back to Cusco.

Spend the day in Cusco, relaxing in one of its many cafés and watching the world go by. There are also numerous active excursions available from the town, such as rafting on the Urubamba River, and some excellent downhill cycling.

Fly back to Lima and do a final bit of souvenir shopping before heading homewards.

Dos and Don'ts

☑ Request a window seat on your flight to Cusco for a good view of the spectacular Andean scenery.

☒ Don't overdo it on your first day at altitude in Cusco. Avoid fatty foods, alcohol and any strenuous activity. Keep hydrated and drink the coca tea, a local remedy for sickness.

☑ Book early if you intend to walk the Inca Trail. New laws have restricted the number of people allowed on the trail at one time, and in peak season it can be booked up around three months in advance.

☒ Don't miss out on the local textiles. Beautiful hand-woven shawls are available in the markets at Pisaq and in Cusco.

Inset: Llama with traditional tasselled decoration

Left (left to right): People at a colourful Pisaq market; detail of the incredible stone-masonry skills of the Incas at Sacsayhuamán; Cusco at night; train winding its way through the fertile Sacred Valley

Right: Steep steps on the Inca Trail

Below: Traditional Andean fabric found in local markets

Machu Picchu is 4 hours by train from Cusco, a bustling and atmospheric colonial city, bursting with colour. Cobbled streets, busy markets filled with rainbow-hued textiles, museums and cafés make it a wonderful place to spend a few days relaxing and acclimatizing to the effects of the altitude and people-watching the ebb and flow of the visiting crowds. However, if you are keen to explore further, there are plenty of day trips to explore the small market towns nearby.

Later, a spectacular rail journey will wind its way through the fertile Sacred Valley, the breadbasket of the Inca civilization where maize, fruit and vegetables grow in abundance, with sheer mountain walls on either side, taking you to Aguas Calientes, a small, ramshackle town that is a base for travellers exploring the site. Aside from the train, the ruins are accessible only by foot, and the Inca Trail is a spectacular three-to-four-day trek to the ancient site. Hikers pass through the regimented Inca terracing, a huge diversity of lush vegetation and breathtaking views of the mountain draped in a shroud of morning mist to eventually arrive at daybreak to be greeted by one of the world's most iconic sights, Machu Picchu.

BIG GAME COUNTRY

T HE REGION IS NAMED "MPUMALANGA" – Land of the Rising Sun – which seems perfectly appropriate as another day dawns on the plain and animals begin to stir and sigh. On the grasslands around Satara, the herbivores are already hard at work. Huge herds of zebra breakfast on the savannah grass, tails swishing flies from their sleek flanks. The impalas, nervous and alert, jerk eyes and ears towards every sound. A pair of giraffes, stooped as though uncomfortable with their height, move off with slow and surprising grace. Meanwhile, a rhino can be heard crashing around in the woods between the Olifants and Crocodile Rivers. Suddenly, the park guide points a finger. A pair of pricked ears, possibly belonging to a large cat, can just be made out in the savannah grass behind the zebra . . . Kruger National Park has awoken.

Main: The early morning sun rises over Lower Sabie, Kruger National Park

GETTING THERE
Kruger National Park lies in the province of Mpumalanga in South Africa, around 500 km (310 miles) from Johannesburg. Jo'burg's international airport has direct flights from many European capitals.

GETTING AROUND
From OR Tambo International Airport in Johannesburg, it's a 4–5 hour drive to the park. The best way to get around is by car, but the internal flight network is also useful.

WEATHER
June is a great time to visit as the days are dry and sunny but cool (around 17°C), although it can get cold at night.

ACCOMMODATION
The Westcliff in Jo'burg has luxurious double rooms from £240; www.westcliff.co.za

There is a good range of accommodation at the park; 2-person bungalows at Berg-en-Dal Restcamp from £40; 2-person cottages at Bateleur Bushveld Camp from £71; www.krugerpark.co.za

EATING OUT
Try the ubiquitous local speciality *boerewors* (farmers' sausage). In Jo'burg, Gramadoela's has mains from £3 and is considered by some the best restaurant in town.

PRICE FOR TWO
£110–150 per day including accommodation, food and safari charges.

FURTHER INFORMATION
www.parks-sa.co.za
www.southafrica.net

Ancient Masorini

Masorini, near Phalaborwa Gate in the park, is a reconstructed hill village that was built on the site of an Iron Age settlement. The village offers an insight into the economy and technology employed by the hunter-gatherers and the later Iron Age peoples of the region, as it is possible to see the remains of the original iron furnace and implements from as far back as the Stone Age. There are also thatched huts and grain storage areas that date back to when the original village was inhabited by the northeastern Sotho tribe in the 19th century.

Left: Zebra drinking from a watering-hole

Right (left to right): Lioness hidden among the grass; crocodile stretches in the sun; colourful lilac-breasted roller; hippos keeping cool

Established in 1898, Kruger is one of the oldest, largest and most successful wildlife parks in the world. Boasting more varieties of animal than any other park in Southern Africa, it's one of the best places in the world to see the "Big Five": lions, leopards, rhinos, elephants and buffalo.

Kruger's remarkable range of wildlife is explained by its huge range of habitats. Amid the dimly lit riverine woodland, short-sighted white rhinos lurk. North of the Olifants River, on the dry and dusty veldt, elephants amble, returning again and again to feed on their favourite food, the mopane tree. By the rivers, a bird chorus of whoops, whistles and cries can be heard, interrupted by the occasional crashing in the water of a hippo or crocodile. Along the rich plains south of Olifants River, large herds of wildebeest, zebra, giraffe and antelope sweep rhythmically back and forth across the savannah. At sunset, the dust kicked up by the animals' hooves still hangs in the air. Catching the last rays of the setting sun, it turns this stunning scene crimson.

WILDLIFE DIARY

Although several months couldn't do real justice to this vast country, you *can* see a great deal over a short period: tour one of the most spectacular wildlife parks in the world, Kruger National Park; wonder at beautiful Cape Town and hectic Jo'burg; visit the striking wine country and indulge yourself with fantastic food.

Two Weeks of Exploration

DAYS 1–3

Fly into Johannesburg and take a day or two to experience the city. The city is continuing to change, and you will feel the pulse of the country. The Apartheid Museum is worth a visit.

When you've tired of the noise and excitement, head for Pretoria – nice, neat and nearby.

DAYS 4–10

From Pretoria, drive the N4 to the Kruger National Park. It's worth joining an extended tour of the park that includes safaris in an open 4WD truck and night-drives, which allow you to see the most incredible African night skies – all with an expert local guide to explain your surroundings and identify the animals.

Spend the nights in one of the camps deep within the park – cook around the campfire and experience first-hand the strange smells and wild sounds of the night.

DAYS 11–12

Fly onto Cape Town, with its stunning sea and mountain setting. Take a ride in a cable car – or try trekking – up Table Mountain to view both the Atlantic and Indian oceans. Find out more about the country's apartheid history with a trip out to infamous Robben Island, where ex-prisoners lead fascinating tours.

In the evenings, check out the bars, cafés and restaurants for superb food and excellent nightlife.

DAYS 13–14

Explore the small seaside towns of the Cape Peninsula and the strange and fascinating flora of the Cape of Good Hope Nature Reserve. Alternatively, head to the beautiful Winelands, where you can try some of South Africa's oldest and finest vintages.

Dos and Don'ts

✓ Pick up an animal identification booklet (£2.50) and a free map at the park entrance gates.

✗ Don't forget to book accommodation and guided trails well in advance if you're planning to visit the park at the weekend or during local school and public holidays. Places fill up fast.

✓ Try a "Wilderness Trail", a guided two-day walk through the park with a knowledgeable guide. You may see a smaller number of animals than from wheels, but you'll learn, smell and hear far more about them and their environment.

JAN
FEB
MAR
APR
MAY
JUN
JUL
AUG
SEP
OCT
NOV
DEC

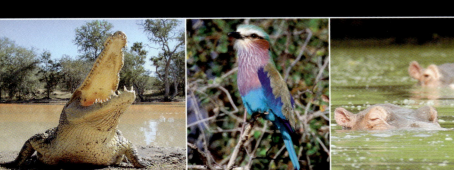

Below: Lion-spotting on safari

ADRIATIC JEWELS

DALMATIA, THE MOST VISITED DESTINATION IN CROATIA, has a full package of delights for any visitor – a happy combination of historic fortified towns, Roman ruins, Venetian palaces, Byzantine churches, miles and miles of coastline washed by crystal-clear waters and a constant, warm dry climate. And did we mention the islands? These are Croatia's jewels: the emerald, cypress-clad isles are set in an aquamarine sea and exquisitely finished with red-roofed towns. These look much as they did in medieval times when small city states vied for control of the area while the powers of Rome, Venice and the Ottoman Empire waxed and waned. Over the centuries, historic buildings have been absorbed into contemporary ones to create fascinating

A happy combination of historic fortified towns, Roman ruins, Venetian palaces, Byzantine churches and miles of coastline washed by crystal-clear waters.

archeological composites that are still kept alive as homes, restaurants or hotels. Stand-out examples include Diocletian's Palace, Split and Dubrovnik old towns, Trogir and Korčula: each has sections of Roman, Byzantine, Baroque and Renaissance buildings riddled with alleyways ripe for exploring. All this history works up an appetite and there's little food more acceptable to young palates than pizza and pasta. Italy may no longer lay claim to the area, but its cuisine has well and truly conquered it. For adults, there's not much that can beat freshly grilled fish, eaten on a shady seaview terrace and washed down with good local wine.

As for beaches, don't expect long stretches of soft sand, but do expect beautiful pebbled bays and coves. As you hop around from mainland to island to island you'll discover many spectacular spots to swim from – the beaches nearest to town may be busy but a little more effort will see you rewarded with somewhere splendidly isolated. You'll often find aromatic cypress and pine forests separated from the sea by a thin border of dark rocks – uncomfortably hot to start with, they make perfect diving platforms and, afterwards, there's something wonderfully restorative about warming up on a toasty flat rock – although choosing a body-friendly one does takes a bit of practice. When the heat gets too much you can retire to the shade of the trees for a simple picnic lunch of *pršut a paški sir*, local smoked ham and cheese.

Main: Beach next to the Dominican Monastery at Bol, on Brač Island
Below (left to right): Diocletian's Palace and Split's seafront; beach and fortifications of Dubrovnik; Korčula's winged lion symbol of Venice. **Inset:** Brown fritillary on a lavender flower, Hvar

GETTING THERE
Fly into Dubrovnik and out of Split, Croatia's two busiest Adriatic airports. Both are about 20 km (12 miles) from their respective towns and are situated on the beautiful southern Dalmatian coast.

GETTING AROUND
You can hire your car at one airport and drop it off at the other. For getting around the islands there are plenty of ferries but they can be pricey.

WEATHER
June is an ideal time to visit, with average temperatures around 21°C. This is also one of the driest months.

ACCOMMODATION
Hotel Peristil in Split is a small, comfortable hotel; family rooms from £100; www.hotelperistil.com

Hotel Pharia, Hvar, is a modern hotel in a quiet location; family rooms from £80; www.orvas-hotels.com

EATING OUT
Attractive outdoor fish restaurants and cheap and cheerful pizza/pasta places abound.

Konoba Menego in Hvar town, situated in an old, candle-lit stone house, is great for authentic local food.

Enjoy your last meal at Sumica in Split, under pine trees and looking out to sea.

PRICE FOR A FAMILY OF FOUR
About £280 a day including accommodation, car hire, food, excursions and ferries.

FURTHER INFORMATION
www.croatia.hr

Dalmatian Emperor
The Dalmatian coast was notorious in Roman times for a fierce pirate race, the Illyrians. Their attacks on Roman ships prompted an invasion in AD 12. Making Salona near Split, their capital, the Romans went on to build amphitheatres, roads, even cities. Centuries of Roman rule resulted in Diocletian, a Dalmatian, becoming Emperor of Rome, and then building his retirement palace at Split in AD 305, now the finest Roman site in eastern Europe. In the Middle Ages, his mausoleum was turned into a cathedral, claimed to be the oldest in the world.

COASTAL DIARY

In two weeks it is possible to cover more ground than here – but it's a holiday, not a race. The itinerary below is only a suggestion – if you find a place you like, stay a bit longer and miss out one of the stages. You can even base yourself in Split and take island excursions, but you'll miss out on the magic of staying on an island.

Two Weeks of Island Hopping

Cavtat, just south of Dubrovnik, is worth considering as a first base – it's nearer the airport, less overrun by tourists and the beaches are better. From here, you can take a boat to Dubrovnik for a walk around the ramparts and explore the architecture.

Drive up the coast and onto the picturesque Peljesac Peninsula to Orebić where you can get a ferry to the island of Korcula and its medieval town. There's plenty to explore on the island and some really good beaches.

From Korčula you can take a ferry to fashionable Hvar, the old centre buzzing with luxury yachts. Once you've had enough, head to quiet Sućuraj, at the other end of the lavender-covered island.

Take the ferry back to the mainland and drive up the coast towards Split. Options on the way include stopping at the popular resort of Makarska or trying Omiš for some whitewater rafting in the Cetina River.

At Split, you can spend a couple of days exploring Diocletian's Palace, the ruins of Salona and the Marjan Peninsula. Enjoy day trips to the island town of Trogir, or the famous, nearly sandy beach at Bol on Brač island.

If you're still restless you can drive on to Primošten, then on to Šibenik with its cathedral, churches and forts, and from where you can take excursions, kayak trips or snorkelling expeditions to see the beautiful Kornati National Park – barren islands in clear waters rich in marine life.

Dos and Don'ts

- ✗ Don't sound off on the war in the Balkans. Whatever your opinion, it's still a very emotive subject for many Croatians.

- ✓ Allow for traffic delays and make it to your ferry crossing in plenty of time. If you're too far back in the queue, you'll miss it.

- ✗ Don't expect to pay with a credit card everywhere you go. Have cash on you for smaller shops and restaurants.

- ✓ Look out for the local ferries, they can be much cheaper and run more regularly, but you may have to drive a bit further.

- ✗ Don't drive after even one alcoholic drink. Croatia has a zero tolerance policy and enforces it strictly.

Below: Kayaking in Kornati National Park

JAN
FEB
MAR
APR
MAY
JUN

DAYS 1–3

DAYS 4–5

DAYS 6–8

DAYS 9–10

DAYS 11–12

DAYS 13–14

JUL
AUG
SEP
OCT
NOV
DEC

GETTING THERE

International flights arrive into Keflavík International Airport, about 1 hour west of Reykjavík. There is a bus service that connects the airport to the town.

GETTING AROUND

Hiring a car in Iceland is extremely expensive. In summer, the bus system connects all main centres. For sights away from populated areas, use informal transport-only bus tours.

WEATHER

In June, Iceland enjoys mild temperatures. Although the island has a predominately wet marine climate, there are usually a fair number of rain-free days.

ACCOMMODATION

In Reykjavík, try the comfortable Hotel Vík, near the Botanical Gardens; doubles from £110; www.hotelvik.is

Also in Reykjavík is the luxurious Art Deco Hotel Borg; doubles from £225; www.hotelborg.is

At Landmannalaugar, a night in the communal hut costs from £13 per person. Guests must bring their own sleeping bags.

EATING OUT

Icelandic specialities include puffin, seal and whale. In rural areas, you'll probably be limited to self-catering or petrol station snack bars.

PRICE FOR TWO

£260–310 per day, including accommodation, food and local travel.

FURTHER INFORMATION

www.visiticeland.com

Wild in Reykjavík

The word "wild" applies to Iceland in more ways than one. In Reykjavík at weekends, throngs of free-spirited Icelanders and like-minded visitors wind their way though the city's bars, pubs and clubs in an unrestrained celebration of hedonism known as *runtur*. Beginning with a couple of drinks around 11pm, the enthusiasm and amorous energy of these early hours lapses into an increasingly stupefied crawl until the bright light of the non-dawn casts its unsympathetic rays upon the last vestiges of fun.

Main: Dramatic waterfall at Skogafoss in the south of the island
Above (left to right): Houses in Reykjavík overlooking the harbour; traditional fishing tools; calm waters near the port of Akureyri

GEOTHERMAL GLORIES

For its wild nature, Iceland is unmatched in Europe – although there is some question about whether it actually is European. In fact, this westernmost Scandinavian outpost claims bi-continental status, as evidenced by the diagonal rift that slashes across its interior, the geological boundary between Europe and North America. Culturally, the country combines the youthful *joie de vivre* and care-free attitude of Europe with the frontier spirit of North America.

Nearly everything ever written about Iceland refers to it as "the land of fire and ice" – although it is a rather tired old moniker, it's true that these natural forces represent some of the island's greatest assets. The country literally lives and breathes geology, from sheep pastures nurtured by the rich, volcanic soil and sparkling glacial run-off, to the distinctly aromatic geothermal heat and energy that powers the country. Its expansive glaciers, active volcanoes, hot springs, geysers, lonely mountains, wild rivers and innumerable waterfalls appeal to the crowd-weary tourist.

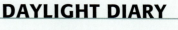

In summer, daylight becomes another Icelandic asset. From May to July, the island is bathed in round-the-clock sub-Arctic daylight (notwithstanding a good measure of North Atlantic rain). Visitors may complain about Iceland's prices, but they can take solace in the fact that for the money, they are getting two days in one. As the children of the Vikings discovered long ago, that's twice the time to indulge in Iceland's decadent offerings. Trot across the moors on a diminutive Icelandic horse, kick up your heels on a lonely white icefield, soothe your skin in the mineral-rich waters of the Blue Lagoon, sip a glass of bubbly in a luxuriant natural hot spring, or defeat the cold drenching rain with an open-air soak in a hot tub. And when you find yourself slouching towards reality, throw all caution to the wind, take out a second mortgage, and head back to Reykjavík for some serious eating, drinking and merriment.

> Iceland literally lives and breathes geology, from the sparkling glacial run-off to the geothermal energy that powers the country.

Below (left to right): The extraordinary Blue Lagoon, near Reykjavík; typical Icelandic corrugated iron church
Inset: Interior of the West Fjords Maritime Museum, Isafjordur

DAYLIGHT DIARY

With a week, it is possible to see the best of Iceland's capital, Reykjavík, and also take in some sights further afield. The following itinerary includes opportunities to see the country's eponymous ice, as well as its welcome natural heat. June is an ideal month to visit to experience the round-the-clock daylight.

A Week in the Great Outdoors

DAY 1
Spend a day exploring Reykjavík's sights. Visit the National Museum, pop into the unusual Icelandic Phallological Museum or warm up in the free hot tubs at the "hot beach" in Nauthólsvík.

DAY 2
Take the renowned Golden Circle Tour to see the dramatic Gullfoss waterfall, watch the world's original geysers at Geysir and stroll around intriguing Þingvellir, where the world's first parliament was born.

DAY 3
Head for a morning swim and soak in the warm waters of the Blue Lagoon. On your way back to Reykjavík, consider stopping at charming Hafnarfjörður, where you can explore the myths of Iceland's "hidden folk".

DAY 4
Join a day tour to the vast Mýrdalsjökull ice cap – the glacial ice is best explored by snowmobile.

DAY 5
Explore central Iceland's magnificent Fjallabak Reserve. Spend the afternoon soaking in the open-air hot springs and overnight in a rustic mountain hut.

DAY 6
Begin with an amble around the technicolour landscape at Fjallabak, through rhyolite hills and over lava fields. Alternatively, head south to see the dramatic waterfall at Skogafoss, or north to the port town of Akureyri.

DAY 7
Return to Reykjavík for some of Iceland's best dining at a cosy local seafood restaurant and a few beers in a local pub. If you have more time to spare, head to the wilds of the Western Fjords – ride horses in Dyrafjordur and explore Isafjordur's interesting Maritime Museum.

Dos and Don'ts

☑ Have a remedial shot of *brennivín* (literally, burnt wine) at hand if you intend to sample such Icelandic delicacies as *hákarl* (putrefied shark meat) or *súrsaðir hrútspungar* (pickled ram's testicles).

☒ Don't approach light-coloured soil around hot springs and fumaroles. The typically thin crust can collapse and anything that falls through will emerge hard-boiled (if at all).

☑ Have ready access to about twice as much money as you think you're going to need and then some more for a few necessary incidentals.

JAN
FEB
MAR
APR
MAY
JUN
JUL
AUG
SEP
OCT
NOV
DEC

Below: Horse riding in Dyrafjordur

GETTING THERE
Nashville and Memphis are in Tennessee, USA. Both have international airports, and although Nashville is the capital, Memphis offers more international flights. It is a 15-minute drive from Memphis International Airport to central Memphis. Nashville airport to the centre of Nashville is also 15 minutes.

GETTING AROUND
Car hire is available at the airports in Nashville and in Memphis. The drive between the two cities takes 4 hours.

WEATHER
June is warm, with 27°C to 32°C days and quite high humidity.

ACCOMMODATION
Stay at the Heartbreak Hotel in Memphis; doubles from £55; www.elvis.com

The Union Station hotel in Nashville has a stunning atrium lobby; doubles from £150; www.unionstationhotelnashville.com

The Hermitage Hotel, Nashville, has doubles from £175; www.thehermitagehotel.com

EATING OUT
In Nashville, the upmarket Capitol Grille serves Southern American cuisine for around £20 per person. Barbeque is king in Memphis with ribs and pulled-pork sandwiches for under £10 per person.

PRICE FOR TWO
£210–230 per day including accommodation, food, CMA festival tickets and car hire.

FURTHER INFORMATION
www.tnvacation.com

"The King" of Memphis

One day in 1954, the teenaged Elvis Presley walked into Sun Studios with the intention of making a record for his mother – the rest is musical history. Born in Tupelo and raised in Memphis, Elvis was brought up on the sounds of Beale Street – blues, gospel and soul. These influences pervaded his music throughout his early career but he developed a unique style. As he said when asked who he sang like, "I don't sound like nobody else". This sound came to be known as rock 'n' roll. Elvis died in 1977, but his legacy is still far-reaching.

Main: Dobro resonating guitars glisten in the lights of a shop display in Nashville
Above (top to bottom): Street musician in Memphis; Eddie "The Chief" Clearwater performs in Memphis; neon sign for BB King's Blues Club

TENNESSEE RHYTHMS

MUSIC, MUSIC AND MORE MUSIC! Where else in the world can you find two cities, so renowned for their musical styles, so vibrant and compelling, yet so different, just a half day's drive from each other? Nashville is the home of country music, and every June the city hosts the world's biggest party for country music fans. The fabulous Country Music Association (CMA) Festival brings together famous singers and groups like the Charlie Daniels Band and LeAnn Rimes along with scores of the hottest up-and-coming acts for a whirlwind of concerts, parties and autograph sessions. For these four days the city is one big party – so jump into the concert crowds, throw your hands up high, dance to the music and lipsync the words to your favourite tunes. Every night there are more concerts, events and parties than one person could attend in a week. During the day, make a pilgrimage to the Ryman Auditorium, original home of the Grand Ole Opry and the "Mother Church" of country music. The

Top: Dolly Parton sings to the crowds at the CMA festival in Nashville

Above: Audience member listens to the live music at the Wildhorse Saloon

Bottom: Piano-inspired design on the exterior of the Country Music Hall of Fame

JAN
FEB
MAR
APR
MAY
JUN

A TUNE A DAY DIARY

Nashville and Memphis offer great live music venues throughout the year; however for four magical days in June hundreds of the best country music stars come to Nashville to perform and meet their fans. Add on two days in nearby Memphis to visit Beale Street and the historic blues and rock 'n' roll sights.

Six Days of Musical Magic

In Nashville, visit the Country Music Hall of Fame then stop in at the Wildhorse Saloon for some live music.

Attend the opening night concert at the Coliseum and join the photo line to get that shot of a famous star.

DAY 1

Head over to the Nashville Convention Center in the morning to pick up an autograph-signing ticket.

Enjoy an afternoon of country music at Riverfront Stages then the night at the legendary Grand Ole Opry.

DAY 2

Visit the Hermitage, former President Andrew Jackson's antebellum mansion, before joining the crowds at the nightly concert at the Coliseum.

DAY 3

Take a river cruise on the General Jackson Showboat. Later, take a tour of the Ryman Auditorium, original home of the Grand Ole Opry. In the evening, watch the biggest stars play the finale at the Coliseum.

DAY 4

Drive down to Memphis and tour Graceland, Elvis Presley's mansion, then tour the Sun Records' studios, where Elvis, Jerry Lee Lewis and Johnny Cash started.

Do a blues crawl down Beale Street stopping in at BB King's Club and the Rum Boogie Café.

DAY 5

Visit the Memphis Rock 'n' Soul Museum, where a self-paced tour features over 100 classic rock tunes as you explore galleries filled with musical treasures.

Experience the STAX Museum of American Soul Music, and learn about the lives of renowned soul artists.

DAY 6

Dos and Don'ts

✓ Look out for tour operators offering CMA (Country Music Association) Festival packages that include accommodation, as well as tickets to the CMA Music Festival and other attractions – there can be some real bargains.

✗ Don't miss out on meeting your favourite star. Many stars host private parties for their Fan Club members. Check with the Fan Club for membership information and events.

✓ Stay in downtown Nashville where all of the major events are held. A car is helpful for attending late night Fan Club events which are scattered throughout the city.

JUL
AUG
SEP
OCT
NOV
DEC

Below: Still waters in downtown Nashville

other must-do is the Country Music Hall of Fame where you'll find all the latest on your favourite country stars, and more about the history of Country Music than you ever dreamed of.

If Nashville is the polished, professional centre of Country, Memphis is the down-home, elbows-on-the-table, eat-in-the-kitchen town that cooked up rhythm-and-blues and rock 'n' roll. The wonderfully historic Sun Records – where Jerry Lee Lewis, Johnny Cash and a kid that didn't sound like anyone else, named Elvis, got their start in the recording industry – is R 'n' B's fountainhead, but Graceland is its heart. More than 600,000 visitors every year wait in line to tour the splendid estate. You haven't really been to Memphis until you tour Graceland and see the green shag carpeting on the ceiling of the Jungle Room.

There are two more things you must do in Memphis: eat really good barbeque somewhere in town, and spend a night hitting the bars of Beale Street, famed as the place where blues got its start. In thumping clubs like BB King's Blues Club, dig into steaming plates of gumbo and barbeque ribs, drink ice cold beer and dance to some of the best blues in America.

GETTING THERE
Flights to Rome land at Leonardo da Vinci (Fiumicino) or Ciampino airport. Trains run from Fiumicino to the centre (30 minutes); from Ciampino there's a bus (about an hour). A taxi to the centre costs about £35.

GETTING AROUND
It's best to see Rome on foot, although you can use metro, buses and trams.

WEATHER
Temperatures usually hover around 25°C and there is little rain, making June one of the most pleasant months to visit.

ACCOMMODATION
Campo de'Fiori, near Piazza Navona; doubles from £120; www.hotelcampodefiori.com

Santa Maria, also central, has pleasant double rooms from £135; www.htlsantamaria.com

Casa Howard has two guesthouses in the centre; doubles from £135; www.casahoward.com

EATING OUT
You can get an excellent meal for £20–35, although simple but delicious pizzas can be found for much less. Try Da Giggetto for authentic Roman food (£25); Vecchia Locanda for great pasta (£20); or Gusto for food in cool, modern surroundings (£35).

PRICE FOR TWO
£220–240 per day including accommodation, food, entrance fees and local travel.

FURTHER INFORMATION
www.romaturismo.com

The Appian Way

If you have a little more time in the city you could explore the Appian Way (Via Appia Antica), which starts outside the huge Porta San Sebastiano by the old city walls to the south of the city. The famous ancient route, down which the Roman Empire's soldiers marched into southern Italy, is lined with catacombs, established here because burials were forbidden within the city walls. The walls and ceilings of the tomb chambers are covered in beautiful, well-preserved frescoes. The best day to come is on Sunday, when the road is closed to traffic.

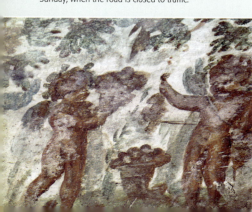

Main: Inside the dome of the Pantheon, which was built in AD 125
Above (top to bottom): The Mouth of Truth, Santa Maria in Cosmedin; Neptune's Fountain, Piazza Navona; view of St Peter's Basilica at dusk

ROMAN HOLIDAY

THE ETERNAL CITY HAS BEEN ATTRACTING VISITORS for many centuries, from medieval pilgrims visiting the shrines of St Peter and St Paul, to the 19th-century Romantic poets Byron, Shelley and tragic Keats – who died here aged 25; from those who went in search of the *dolce vita* after Fellini's classic film made headlines in the 1960s, to the many who flock here today, their visits made easy by frequent, inexpensive flights. Some come to witness the glories of ancient Rome – the magnificent Forum, the Colosseum and the Palatine Hill. Others consider a visit worthwhile just to see the beautiful ceiling of the Vatican's Sistine Chapel, Michelangelo's almost miraculous tour de force; while many come to browse covetously in the designer-label shops on the Via dei Condotti or simply to feast on the local cuisine – thin and crispy wood-fired pizzas, any of a hundred delicious spaghetti dishes, or the taste of summer – lightly-fried courgette flowers; and to finish, of course, some home-made *gelato* – ice cream.

Top: Enjoying lunch in a café in the Piazza Santa Maria in Trastevere

Above: A modern Roman icon – one of the ubiquitous scooters that zip around Rome

Below: Nuns walking in the city – a common sight in the capital city of the Catholic Church

LA DOLCE VITA DIARY

June is a lovely time to visit as it sees the start of the *Estate Romana* – Roman Summer. Three months of eclectic musical and theatrical events are held at outdoor venues all over the city, ranging from the Imperial Forum to the Villa Borghese gardens, as well as dozens of parks and piazzas. Five days should be enough time to enjoy the main attractions.

Five Days in the Eternal City

Start by visiting the Imperial Fora (the Roman Forum), Palatine Hill and the Colosseum, to immerse yourself in the ancient atmosphere. On Sunday, the main road linking the sites is closed to traffic.

Explore the attractive streets of the Trastevere district. In the café-lined Piazza Santa Maria, visit the church to see the splendid mosaics, then have one of Dar Poeta's famous pizzas before climbing Gianicolo Hill for fabulous views, a salute to the statue of Garibaldi. Enjoy an outdoor opera performance in a spectacular venue.

The Vatican Museums need a whole day. Don't miss the Raphael Rooms. Michelangelo's ceiling is a must-see too, although the Sistine Chapel is always busy. On the way to the Vatican you pass the Castel Sant'Angelo, from which Puccini's Tosca leapt to her death.

The Villa Borghese Gardens are home to three fine museums: the Galleria Borghese (Botticelli, Caravaggio, Titian); the Museo Etrusco (Etruscan Art); and the Galleria Nazionale d'Arte Moderna (Cézanne, De Chirico, Klimt). Lunch in the museum's Caffè delle Arte.

Start the day in the buzzing morning market in Campo de' Fiori, then wander the atmospheric alleyways of the old Jewish quarter. Cross over the road to the vast, Pantheon, where the great and the good are buried, then take a seat in elegant Piazza Navona to admire Bernini's fountains while you enjoy an ice cream.

Dos and Don'ts

- ✓ Go up to the Palatine Hill. Not only is it a great spot, but you get a combined ticket that allows you to bypass the lengthy queues to the Colosseum.
- ✗ Don't take photos in the Sistine Chapel. It's strictly forbidden.
- ✓ Ask at information offices about the various museum cards on offer, which can save you a considerable sum if you plan to visit a number of sites.
- ✗ Don't expect to get a late lunch (after 3pm) except in places catering for tourists, which often serve meals all day.

JAN FEB MAR APR MAY JUN DAY 1 DAY 2 DAY 3 DAY 4 DAY 5 JUL AUG SEP OCT NOV DEC

Whatever the reason for your own private pilgrimage, you can't walk far without stumbling upon something extraordinary, whether it is the Area Sacra, where the remains of ancient temples and the rumored site of Caesar's assassination, inhabited now by stray cats, sit in the middle of a noisy square; or Bernini's flamboyant sculptures cavorting in the fountains of the Piazza Navona and his kitsch little elephant outside the lovely Gothic church of Santa Maria Sopra Minerva.

Rome has been called a living museum, but it is also very much a living city. Strolling through the old Jewish quarter, around the Campo de' Fiori, peeking into *botteghe*, the artisans' workshops that still line many neighbourhood streets, or exploring the colourful narrow alleys of the bohemian Trastevere district, gives a delightful insight into Rome's daily life. Drinking coffee at an outdoor table in a lively square, while watching children chase the pigeons, noticing the warm glow of ochre-coloured buildings in the sunlight, or marvelling at the profusion of flowering plants crammed onto tiny balconies may stay in your memory longer than a visit to a museum.

Below: Opera performance among the ruins of the Caracalla Baths

IT'S A JAZZ THING

Montreal tries to be most things to most people – and with Gallic flair, it usually succeeds. While the city bills itself as a religious centre, it is also one of the world's great pleasure capitals. The nightlife is so amazing, in fact, that New Englanders come up on weekends to party. This bilingual riverport is conscious of its cosmopolitan freedoms in a deeply Catholic, nationalistic Quebec.

"This is the first time I was ever in a city where you couldn't throw a brick without breaking a church window," quipped Mark Twain on a visit in 1881. Nowadays you could say this about its restaurants as well. This gourmet's paradise has over 5,000 eateries – more per head than anywhere else in North America save New York, with an unimaginable variety of cuisines, from hot barbequed pork to traditional French. Throw in a new-found prosperity, fabulous mountainous scenery and streets full of pretty Victorian architecture, and you have an unbeatable formula for enjoyment for all. For the best of Europe and North America rolled into one, there's no place like it.

GETTING THERE
Montreal lies by the St Lawrence River in the province of Quebec, eastern Canada, 595 km (370 miles) north of New York City. Trudeau International Airport is a half-hour by taxi from the centre.

GETTING AROUND
In town, the superb Metro and bus network are the most efficient ways to get around.

WEATHER
Montreal is warm and sunny in late June, with average daytime temperatures around 20°C. Showers are frequent but pass quickly.

ACCOMMODATION
For something special, opt for a small European-style hotel in the Old Town district.

Victorian home via Downtown B&B Network; doubles from £42; www.bbmontreal.qc.ca

Auberge Bonaparte is a historic 30-room lodge in the heart of the Old Town; doubles from £85; www.bonaparte.ca

Hotel Gault, a designer's dream with sleek loft-style rooms; doubles from £150; www.hotelgault.com

EATING OUT
Montreal is a diner's paradise and the variety of great restaurants is truly staggering. You can order a great large meal for £15–30. Look out for Montreal's famed smoked meat.

PRICE FOR TWO
£120–150 per day including accommodation, food and local travel.

FURTHER INFORMATION
www.tourisme-montreal.org

Main: Looking over the bustling crowds at the International Jazz Festival

Above: Colourful Palais des Congrès

Below: Weathered dome of the Marie Reine du Monde church stands out in contrast against the surrounding modern architecture

Right panel (top to bottom): Place des Arts, the main events square at the festival; enjoying the Montreal café culture; performer at the jazz festival

Basilique Notre Dame

Montreal's soaring basilica was designed with anything but modesty in mind. Finished in 1829, the structure was for a while the largest church in North America, and its weighty bell, the Gros Bourdon, took 12 men to operate. The interiors are bombastic in the extreme; gilt stars shining from heavenly arches, a gargantuan organ (5,772 pipes), lavish wood carvings and a sanctuary backlit in wild colours. Its New York-born architect, James O'Donnell, converted to Catholicism so he could be buried in the vault.

JAN
FEB
MAR
APR
MAY
JUN

The Canadian summer is sweet and desperately short, but Montrealers are experts at making the most of it. When the snow melts, the city erupts into a seamless riot of festivals, street parties and celebrations. Any excuse will suffice: hand in a request, cordon off a sleepy *rue* and the jubilation begins. The mother of all shindigs is the *Festival International de Jazz*, held from late June to early July. From the outset it was conceived as a festival for the *peuple*, an 11-day extravaganza of 350 concerts held at open-air venues (free), music halls and jazz clubs. It's accessible to anyone and just about everyone comes, with crowds of around two million people gathering together to enjoy the music. Legendary jazz players from all over the world queue up to join in and share a stage with the local talent, making the festival one of the best parties on the planet.

Montreal also prides itself on its cultural exhibits. Visit the Pointe à Callière archeology museum for an intriguing history brought to life. For those lured by the great outdoors, the area is chock-a-block with natural wonders in the nearby ancient Laurentian Mountains. Plan ahead or not, it doesn't matter too much – the city is a mine of spontaneous enjoyment.

FESTIVAL DIARY

Montreal is a hotbed of fun in summer and the International Jazz Festival is its shining star. Best combine music-filled days with the lasting charms of this dynamic city – culture, shopping and nightlife galore, but also lush parklands and other outdoor diversions in and around the Laurentian Mountains.

Five Days by the St Lawrence

DAY 1 Wander around the Old Town and have your portrait sketched in the pedestrian Rue St Jacques. Take a ride in a horse-drawn *calèche*. In the evening, savour a French-style meal overlooking the Old Port.

DAY 2 Explore the shopping passages of the underground city then visit the magnificent Basilique Notre Dame.

Later, take in a jazz concert at the main events square, Place des Arts, before hitting the busy nightspots along Boulevard St Laurent.

DAY 3 Stroll along the waterside Promenade du Vieux Port and peruse the colourful Marché Atwater. Enjoy the panorama from the tilted Olympic Tower. Browse the hip boutiques along Ave du Mont Royal. Tap your toes at cosier Jazz Festival venues along Rue St Denis.

DAY 4 Make an early start, heading for the Laurentian Mountains for a day of hiking or biking along the leafy, rolling Parc Linéare through some of Quebec's prettiest villages. Catch a drag show at Mado Cabaret in the Village when you get back.

DAY 5 Delve into Montreal's past at the fascinating Pointe à Callière museum of archeology then bump along the St Lawrence rapids in a jet boat. Order some of the city's famous smoked meat and bagels and pack reserves for the home trip.

Dos and Don'ts

✓ Try your best French even if it's limited to *Parlez-vous anglais?* (Do you speak English?). Locals appreciate your effort and generally switch over.

✗ Don't address waiters as *garçon* (boy). A simple *s'il vous plait* (please) is how it's done in Francophone countries.

✓ Exchange two *bises* (kisses) as a familiar greeting – a peck on each cheek. Men mix handshakes and pecks.

✓ Bring a bottle of wine or bunch of flowers when invited to someone's home and show up an hour late to parties unless you like being first.

JUL
AUG
SEP
OCT
NOV
DEC

Below: Brightly lit up casino on Ile-Notre-Dame on the St Lawrence River

JULY

Where to Go: July

Summer is in full swing in the northern hemisphere, bringing long days, clear skies and bright sunshine. If you want to make the most of this from a beachside position, be prepared for crowds as it is the school holidays – even less obvious resorts in the Channel Islands or Corsica can get busy. This is a great time to experience some of the world's most vibrant festivals, including the Running of the Bulls in Spain, and the tropical Fiesta de Merengue in the Dominican Republic. Many parts of Asia are experiencing their monsoon season – the Indian subcontinent, in particular, is best avoided – and in the southern hemisphere it is winter. Below you'll find all the destinations in this chapter, as well as some extra suggestions to provide a little inspiration.

FESTIVALS AND CULTURE

MONGOLIA Mongolian family look over the vast plains

UNFORGETTABLE JOURNEYS

SPITSBERGEN Row of colourful houses in Longyearbyen

NATURAL WONDERS

SAN JUAN ISLANDS Brightly coloured starfish

THE GREAT STEPPES
MONGOLIA, ASIA

Try a traditional Mongolian tent on the wild steppes

The descendants of Genghis Khan certainly know how to let off steam at their colourful Nadaam festival – with wrestling, archery and horse racing.
See pp174–5

PAMPLONA
SPAIN, EUROPE

Run with the bulls in the Fiestas de San Fermín

The highlight of this annual nine-day festival is the famous bull-run through the medieval town, before partying in the streets.
www.sanfermin.com

SPITSBERGEN
NORWAY, EUROPE

A journey to the Arctic north, home of the polar bear

Only really accessible in summer, this arctic archipelago, rich in wildlife and scenery, evokes a true sense of adventure in the visitor.
See pp186–7

HUNZA VALLEY
PAKISTAN, ASIA

Spectacular mountains on the edge of the Himalayas

Limitless hiking and trekking, stunning mountain vistas and ancient forts – an ideal time of year to visit these remote valleys.
www.hunza.20m.com

> "Through the vapour, you can see the deep channel broken here and there by dark, tree-shrouded islands."

SAN JUAN ISLANDS
USA, NORTH AMERICA

Enjoy the great outdoors on these Puget Sound Islands

Escape to the wilderness of the San Juan Islands – savage but beautiful, like the killer whales that gather here each summer.
See pp184–5

PARIS
FRANCE, EUROPE

Official pomp and noisy fun combine on Bastille Day

Celebrate with dancing in Place de la Bastille on the 13th July, then enjoy military parades, fireworks and more parties on the 14th.
www.parisinfo.com

> "Curving through town, the glacial green Salzach River meanders off into great sweeps of verdant pastures."

SOUTH NAHANNI
CANADA, NORTH AMERICA

Canoe or raft through a real whitewater wilderness

Seaplanes take visitors to the lakes to begin an awesome river trip through giant canyons, rapids and forests, home to moose and bears.
www.explorenwt.com

MOUNT LUSHAN
CHINA, ASIA

One of the most astonishing natural sights in China

Famed in poetry and art, Mt Lushan rises out of misty lakes, rivers and waterfalls. Walk the Flower Path and see the Grand Heavenly Pool.
www.china-lushan.com

MALAWI
MALAWI, AFRICA

Experience the many charms of the "Warm Heart of Africa"

Malawi's landscape is at its best in June – ideal for hiking in the hills, water sports on vast Lake Malawi or bird and animal watching.
www.malawitourism.com

SALZBURG
AUSTRIA, EUROPE

Where the sound of Mozart echoes round every corner

This pretty city is filled with music lovers as visitors from around the world come to enjoy the Mozart Festival.
See pp172–3

SOUTH COAST
WALES, EUROPE

A string of imposing castles line this impressive coastline

These mighty monuments, set amid the softly rolling hills of South Wales and beautiful national parks, will fascinate adults and children alike.
See pp176–7

BOUNDARY WATERS
USA, NORTH AMERICA

The ideal place to find your own wilderness wonderland

A vast area of pristine forest in Minnesota, with hundreds of canoe routes through island-studded, crystal-clear, fish-filled water.
www.bwcaw.org

SANTO DOMINGO
DOMINICAN REPUBLIC, CARIBBEAN

Enjoy the Fiesta de Merengue

Visitors can dance till they drop at this annual festival, with high-energy bands playing hot tropical beats all along the city's historic waterfront.
www.godominicanrepublic.com

CANNING STOCK ROUTE
AUSTRALIA, AUSTRALASIA

Ultimate desert 4WD trip

An old drovers' track through one of Australia's emptiest, most remote desert regions. Superb landscapes, weird wildlife, endless solitude.
www.exploreoz.com

NERINGA
LITHUANIA, EUROPE

A special world of sea, forest and strange dune formations

A 100-km (60-mile) sand spit by the Baltic Sea, with endless beaches, strange dunes, pine woods and charming little resort towns.
www.visitneringa.com

Previous page: Chuckwagon racing at the Calgary Stampede

Weather Watch

❶ Summer brings hot and steamy weather to the Eastern USA. Washington, DC doesn't have the cooling sea breezes of Cape Cod and it could rain, but that won't hamper the July 4th celebrations.

❷ Mendoza has a pleasant climate – even in winter the weather is mild and sunny. But up in the Andes there should be fresh snow to ski on.

❸ The Mediterranean is even warmer in July – almost too hot – but the sea around Corsica cools swimmers by day and the air at night.

❹ Most of Malawi enjoys pleasantly warm weather with no rainfall during July, apart from the tropical lowlands, which are very hot and humid.

❺ The flat open steppes of Mongolia are obviously prone to winds, but these are welcome in summer as the daytime temperature rises considerably – however it drops again at night. A little rain is likely.

❻ Australia's winter brings cooler weather to most of the country. This is the ideal time to visit the outback – temperatures are still warm but lack the stifling humidity of the summer months.

LUXURY AND ROMANCE

CAPE COD The beautifully calm waters of Nantucket Harbour

ACTIVE ADVENTURES

MENDOZA Trekking in dramatic Aconcagua Park

FAMILY GETAWAYS

CALGARY Enjoying a fairground ride at dusk in Stampede Park

TAHITI & BORA BORA
POLYNESIA

The original island paradise beside dazzling turquoise seas

Seductive tranquillity in palm-roofed hotels. If you can tear yourself away, go canoeing, diving, or take a picnic to your own desert island.
www.tahiti-tourisme.com

TAORMINA
ITALY, EUROPE

The flavour of ancient Greece and secluded sunny terraces

Relax in a lovely villa hotel above Sicily's most elegant resort, with ancient ruins and fabulous views of the bay of Naxos and Mount Etna.
www.taormina.it

BURGH ISLAND
ENGLAND, EUROPE

Chic seclusion and an air of 1930s glamour

Put on the style at this beautiful, Art Deco hotel – a favourite of Noel Coward and Agatha Christie – on a tiny island off the Devon coast.
www.burghisland.com

ST TROPEZ
FRANCE, EUROPE

Spot celebrities and get to the heart of Riviera life

Stars descend on this famous spot in summer, but staying in the hills above town lets you take in the scene and cool off when you like.
www.ot-saint-tropez.com

CAPE COD
USA, NORTH AMERICA

Golden beaches, quiet islands and charming historic villages

Something for everyone – from chic, celebrity-filled Martha's Vineyard to the whaling town of Nantucket, and the wide open spaces of the Cape.
See pp188–9

MENDOZA
ARGENTINA, SOUTH AMERICA

Train like a champion at the ultimate Andes ski resort

Start off with some walking in the wine town of Mendoza before ascending to El Portillo, an exclusive ski resort in the Chilean Andes.
See pp180–81

THE MUNROS
SCOTLAND, EUROPE

Take your pick from a huge range of peaks and crags

Scotland has 284 "Munros" – peaks over 900 m (3,000 ft) high – from gentle hikes to rocky cliffs. You'll want to climb them all.
www.munromagic.com

"Mile after mile of sandy shores along the wave-tossed Atlantic."

GRAND CANYON
USA, NORTH AMERICA

Raft down this natural wonder for a different perspective

Thousands see the Canyon from above, but to get a real sense of its beauty take a boat along the bottom, camping at the riverside.
www.nps.gov/grca

GREENLAND
DENMARK, EUROPE

A unique landscape at the very top of the world

Take a tent into the wilderness with a dog sled, search for musk ox and polar bears, or take a boat trip to Disko Bay, visiting Inuit villages.
www.greenland.com

SARDINIA
ITALY, EUROPE

Porto Pollo is a world-class destination to kite- or windsurf

Super-consistent wind conditions, perfect beaches and wild reefs, mean experienced surfers can really let rip and have some fun.
www.planetwindsurf.com

"A real electricity descends on the city as fireworks explode over the striking Washington Monument."

CALGARY
CANADA, NORTH AMERICA

Action-packed rodeo and the flavour of the Wild West

The drama and skills on display at the Calgary Stampede are best appreciated live and up-close – fun and excitement for the family.
See pp178–9

CORSICA
FRANCE, EUROPE

A ruggedly beautiful island full of exciting things to do for all

Once perfect for hiding bandits, Corsica's landscape now provides sandy beaches, coves and the produce for some delicious food.
See pp182–3

WASHINGTON, DC
USA, NORTH AMERICA

Celebrate 4th July in style in the nation's capital

This elegantly laid out city is filled with world-class museums and historical monuments – all lit up by fireworks on Independence Day.
See pp170–71

CHANNEL ISLANDS
ENGLAND, EUROPE

Part of Britain, but with a definite French flavour

With bistros and baguettes, these sandy-bayed islands are closer to France than to England. Lots to see and do, from beaches to castles.
www.visitchannelislands.com

COPENHAGEN
DENMARK, EUROPE

Magic and enchantment in a wonderful waterside location

It is appropriate that the final resting place of the storyteller Hans Christian Andersen should be so full of child-friendly amusements.
See pp190–91

FOLKLIFE AND FIREWORKS

A HANDSOME CITY BUILT TO HUMAN SCALE, Washington, D.C., never fails to delight visitors. The highest points of the skyline will always be the gleaming Capitol dome and the slim shaft of the Washington Memorial, a profile that has been carefully protected by law. Standing at either end of the long lawns of the National Mall, they are part of the brilliant city plan of Frenchman Pierre Charles L'Enfant. Inspired by Paris, L'Enfant envisioned the city's wide avenues radiating from scenic squares and circles, adorned by sculptures and fountains, a unique design in America.

The only difficulty in Washington is deciding what to do first. The museums alone could fill days on end, and then there are the stately buildings of government – the US Capitol and the Supreme Court – which can be explored by guided visit. Even the President's home, the White House, may be toured.

Main: Red, white and blue balloons float in front of the Capitol

GETTING THERE
Washington, D.C., is situated near the east coast of the USA. The city is served by two international airports: Dulles and Baltimore-Washington. Taxis, metro rail and buses connect to the city centre.

GETTING AROUND
The Metro is a great way to get around, with five lines serving downtown D.C. Metrobuses are another quick and cheap mode of transport.

WEATHER
Washington can be hot and humid in summer, with average temperatures of 31°C.

ACCOMMODATION
Holiday Inn Capitol Hill is great for families, with a pool and free children's meals; family rooms from £75; www.holiday-inn.com

Embassy Suites, a spacious hotel between the White House and the Capitol; family rooms from £115; www.embassysuites.com

Hotel Palomar, a very stylish boutique hotel; family rooms from £170; www.hotelpalomar-dc.com

EATING OUT
The dining scene is eclectic, from traditional restaurants serving classic American dishes to a vast number of ethnic restaurants. Children will love eating in diners, which offer all-American fare such as hamburgers, fries and malt shakes.

PRICE FOR A FAMILY OF FOUR
£180–220 including accommodation, food, entrance charges and local travel.

FURTHER INFORMATION
www.washington.org

Smithsonian Institution

Despite never visiting the USA, James Smithson, a British scientist, left his entire fortune to found the Smithsonian Institution in Washington, upon his death in 1829. He would surely be amazed to see that his bequest has grown into the world's largest museum organization and a highlight for every visitor to Washington. The Smithsonian oversees 16 D.C. museums, plus the National Zoo and six research centres. All are free and open daily, and the holdings include art, history, natural science and the very popular Air and Space Museum.

Left: Performers playing Jazz at Blues Alley

Right (left to right): Studying the Vietnam Veterans' Memorial; elegant building façades in Georgetown; crowds at the Smithsonian Folklife Festival; colonial military demonstration at the Independence Day celebrations

Right panel (top and bottom): Interior of the National Archives; fireworks celebrating Independence Day with the Capitol in the foreground

July sees the city at its vibrant best, with two of its most important events taking place in close succession. The first, the Smithsonian Folklife Festival, celebrates cultural heritage and is an entirely free, open-air event. During the two weeks of the festival, the National Mall is filled with a colourful array of musicians, performers, artists, storytellers, cooks and craftspeople, creating an energetic celebration. This coincides with Independence Day on 4th of July, when a real electricity descends on the city, as fireworks explode over the striking Washington Monument.

Even when the heady excitement of these festival days has died down, there is still much to be enchanted by, from a ride on a mule-drawn barge on the C&O canal and watching elephant training in the National Zoo, to the exciting hands-on National Museum of Natural History and puppet shows in the Discovery Theater. There is nothing stuffy about this well-ordered, historic city – beneath its austere surface you will find a very modern heart.

Above: International Spy Museum in the Penn Quarter

BIRTHDAY DIARY

The two week Smithsonian Folklife Festival takes place at the beginning of July each year. Over a million visitors flock to the National Mall, which is filled with music, entertainment, crafts and food. The Independence Day festivities of the 4th of July always fall during this festival period, bringing a real vibrancy to the city.

Four Days in America's Capital

Head straight to the National Mall to enjoy the festival – watch the artisans at work, enjoy the wares in the food tent, dance to the lively music and browse the craft stalls. When you've had your fill, stroll down to the Tidal Basin to see the moving memorials to America's famous presidents – Thomas Jefferson, Abraham Lincoln and Franklin D. Roosevelt and have a look at the abstract Vietnam Veterans' Memorial.

Spend a day visiting some of the city's excellent museums. Start in the National Museum of Natural History for dinosaurs, an insect zoo and a living coral reef. Afterwards, choose from the National Gallery of Art, one of America's most important museums, or the popular National Air and Space Museum. In the evening, head to Georgetown for jazz at Blues Alley.

If you can face more museums, head for the Penn Quarter, home to the International Spy Museum, the Shakespeare Theatre and the Smithsonian American Art Museum and National Portrait Gallery. Otherwise, head to the Chesapeake and Ohio Canal (C&O) for a ride in a mule-driven canal clipper, or to the Discovery Theater for a puppet show. End the day watching the spectacular fireworks over the city as it celebrates Independence Day.

See the pandas at the National Zoo, the fish at the National Aquarium or the famous bonsai at the National Arboretum. Take a cruise on the Potomac or a tour across the river to Mount Vernon Estate, the home and gardens of George Washington.

Dos and Don'ts

✓ Get an insider's view of D.C. on a walking tour through Embassy Row, Georgetown and other interesting neighbourhoods (www.washingtonwalks.com), or consider a guided cycling tour of the sites (www.bikethesites.com).

✗ Don't miss out on the city's sporting heroes – Washington Redskins' merchandise make great souvenirs of the town.

✓ Be aware of the 14.5 percent tax levied on hotels in the city, which will be added to the bill at the end of your stay, on top of the room rate.

JAN

FEB

MAR

APR

MAY

JUN

JUL

2nd

3rd

4th

5th

AUG

SEP

OCT

NOV

DEC

GETTING THERE
Salzburg, in the Austrian province of the same name and close to the border with Germany, has good connections by air, road and rail. From W A Mozart airport, a bus goes to the railway station and Mirabellplatz, taking 25 minutes.

GETTING AROUND
The city is easily negotiated by foot. Alternatively, hire a bike or try a *fiaker* horse-drawn carriage ride.

WEATHER
July is a warm month, around 25–30°C, with lots of sunshine and showers.

ACCOMMODATION
Wolf-Dietrich offers traditional comfort in the heart of the old city; doubles from £100; www.salzburg-hotel.at

Arthotel Blaue Gans combines modern style with a historic Altstadt building; doubles from £120; www.blauegans.at

Try the luxurious Goldener Hirsch, which dates from 1407, a favourite with visiting royals; doubles from £150; www.luxurycollection.com

EATING OUT
You can get a good meal in Salzburg for around £14 a head. Traditional Austrian fare includes *Wiener schnitzel* (breaded veal escalopes), dumplings, apple strudel and luscious cakes.

PRICE FOR TWO
£170–200 per day including accommodation, food and local travel.

FURTHER INFORMATION
www2.salzburg.info
www.salzburgfestival.at

Salzburg's Riches

Salt was the so-called "white gold" that gave the city its name and its wealth. Under the rule of Prince-Archbishops, Salzburg became "the Rome of the North" and their architectural legacy can be found throughout the old town, which has been designated a UNESCO World Heritage Site. It is possible to take a tour of the salt mines by travelling up the mountain by funicular and entering deep into the mining tunnels.

Music is everywhere in Mozart's stylish, picturesque city. It rings out from carillons, fills the beautiful cathedral and drifts through cobbled squares.

Main: View of the old town of Salzburg overlooked by Hohensalzburg Fortress
Inset: Mozart chocolates on display
Above: Colourful floral display at the gardens of the Mirabell Palace

MOUNTAINS AND MUSIC

MUSIC IS EVERYWHERE in Mozart's stylish, picturesque city of spires and onion domes, narrow streets, graceful squares and pastel-painted façades. It rings out from carillons, fills the beautiful cathedral and drifts through cobbled squares where talented young musicians play impromptu concertos. Over 4,000 cultural events take place in Salzburg throughout the year, but the most coveted tickets are for the five-week Summer Festival, when packed concert halls, palaces and churches resound to thrilling performances by some of the world's greatest performers. Crowned and uncrowned heads of Europe descend on this most elegant and sophisticated of festivals; ball gowns are of course *de rigueur* for premières.

Ringed by craggy grey mountains and sheltered by tree-draped hills, Salzburg seems to inhabit a little world of its own. Grand and gracious architecture, a legacy of the powerful Prince-Archbishops who ruled here for over a

Left (left to right): View of the cupola inside Salzburg Cathedral; sundial at Mozartplatz; wrought-iron signs hanging from shops in the centre of Salzburg

Right: Traditionally crafted marionettes hang, waiting to be used in a theatre performance

Above: Mozart dinner concert at Stiftskeller St Peter

JAN
FEB
MAR
APR
MAY
JUN
JUL

FESTIVAL DIARY

During Salzburg's five weeks of festival, which spans late July and August, city evenings take on a truly elegant air. In four days you can visit museums, follow the Mozart trail, enjoy the music, soak up the atmosphere, and even have time to take a tour into the surrounding lakes and mountains.

Four Days of Mozart Mania

Explore the heart of the old town (*Altstadt*), with its fabulous cathedral and beautiful squares, then enjoy a cake on Café Tomaselli's terrace.

After lunch, ride the funicular to the fortress – the medieval apartments are spectacular. It is worth walking back down via the Nonnberg Convent, where you can hear the nuns sing at 5pm. A candlelit Mozart dinner concert at the Stiftskeller St Peter is the perfect end to the day.

DAY 1

Visit Mozart's birthplace, shop under the fancy signs, see the wonderful St Peter's Abbey and the soaring Franciscan Church. Or take the river boat to Hellbrunn, an Italianate pleasure palace. To see more of the countryside, join a leisurely cycle ride – tours leave from Mozartplatz at 5pm.

DAY 2

Head to the new town to indulge in delicious cakes at Fingerloos on leafy Franz-Josef-Strasse. Stroll through the Mirabell Gardens and Palace, or visit Mozart's Residence for an overview of his life.

Revive with a drink on the riverside terrace of the Hotel Sacher, walk off *Sacher Torte* (a rich, velvety chocolate cake) calories by climbing the steep steps from Steingasse for a panoramic city view or take an afternoon tour of the fascinating Festival Halls.

DAY 3

It's well worth going on a scenic lake and mountain half-day tour that includes pretty St Gilgen. Take the Mönchsberg Lift to the Modern Art Museum and its terrace restaurant to drink in the view.

DAY 4

Dos and Don'ts

✓ Buy a Salzburg Card. With free public transport, including the river boat and free entrance to museums, it is good value for serious sightseeing.

✗ Don't miss out on the glorious lakes and mountains – cycle *Sound of Music* country or walk on the Mönchsberg; return to the city mid-afternoon when the crowds have thinned.

✓ Go to a candlelit Mozart dinner concert at the Stiftskeller St Peter – good music and food in historic surroundings.

✗ Don't bother with the audio guide at the Hohensalzburg Fortress. Concentrate on the stunning rooms of the Archbishop's Palace and have a drink on the terrace.

AUG
SEP
OCT
NOV
DEC

thousand years, stands centre stage, while shops tempt and cafés invite. The Hohensalzburg Fortress has watched over the city since medieval times from atop its mountain, the Alps providing a dramatic backdrop. Curving through town, the glacial green Salzach River meanders off into great sweeps of verdant pastures – the familiar countryside of *The Sound of Music*.

Mozart mania engulfs the city; crowds besiege the narrow, old town lanes around the golden yellow-painted building where he was born. Mozart's image adorns everything, from chocolates to perfume, and all of the city's important buildings have Mozart connections. Baptized in the vast Cathedral, which boasts five organs, musicians' galleries and early Baroque decoration, he wrote a quarter of his work for this lovely building. He directed his famous Mass in C-Minor at the wonderfully Rococo St Peter's Abbey. Today, this soaring Franciscan church boasts a choir, two organs and two orchestras. Salzburg has always been a spiritual city at heart, drawing inspiration from the panoramic views that unfold from nearby mountain heights. Images of the city and its surroundings never fail to beguile, but music remains at its soul.

GETTING THERE
Mongolia is in Northern Asia. Flights arrive into Chinggis Khaan International Aiport in Ulan Bator, often via Beijing or Moscow. The Trans-Mongolian train line between Moscow and Beijing stops in Ulan Bator.

GETTING AROUND
MIAT offers a domestic air service throughout the country, including to Kharkorin. The railway is limited to one major line and a couple of spur lines and there is a somewhat erratic coach service. Jeep transfers can be arranged.

WEATHER
Mongolia has short, warm summers and average temperatures in July are around 21°C.

ACCOMMODATION
UB Guesthouse in Ulan Bator is a budget option; doubles from £8; www.ubguest.com

The Chinggis Khan Hotel, Ulan Bator, is a luxurious option with great views over the city; doubles from £60; www.chinggis-hotel.com

Accommodation in *ger* camps costs from £20 per person and can be arranged at tourist offices in Ulan Bator.

EATING OUT
Breakfast and lunch generally consist of fatty mutton with rice and yoghurt. In *ger* camps the food will consist of more palatable versions of traditional food.

PRICE FOR TWO
From £50–70 per day including accommodation, food and local transport.

FURTHER INFORMATION
www.mongoliatourism.gov.mn

THE LAND OF GENGHIS KHAN

Situated at the foot of a range of hills, Ulan Bator is, above all, remote. While it may have many of the trappings of a modern city, its quixotic mix of Soviet-inspired architecture, remnants of its pre-revolutionary history, and suburbs composed of neat rows of *gers* (traditional nomadic tents) lend it the charming air of a busy yet aimless outpost. Ulan Bator exemplifies the tension between city and country, for Mongolia and its people are essentially rural. Since before the time of Genghis Khan, beloved father of the Mongol nation, they've lived a semi-nomadic existence, staying in rural villages in winter and moving to *gers* on the grassy steppes in summer. Still there is enough to see in the city to merit spending a couple of days here, including a museum featuring the remains of dinosaurs found in the Gobi Desert, and the country's largest monastery, Gandantegcheling.

Main: Horse race at the Naadam Festival in Ulan Bator

The Mongolian Ger
The modern *ger*, the Mongolian nomadic tent, has many advantages – it is a flexible form of accommodation that is cheap yet durable, made to withstand the extremes of the Mongolian climate. The wooden framework is collapsible and consists of a trellis of poles over which layers of felt are placed, and finally a layer of canvas. There is a hole at the apex of the roof, which allows smoke from the stove to escape, and which can be covered in times of rain. A *ger* can be erected in less than an hour in expert hands.

Left (left and right): Woman archer at the Naadam festival; competitors take part in a wrestling match at the festival

Right (left and right): Mongolian family look over the vast plains; shepherds tending their flock

Getting into the countryside is the highlight of a visit to Mongolia, especially if it can be combined with a stay in a traditional *ger*. Most of this vast country is desert and grassland, and a major part of the population are still herdsmen of one sort or another, living as nomads.

At no time of year is this traditional lifestyle better seen than in mid-July, when the colourful Naadam Festival is held. For three days, from 11 to 13 July, this festival of games is celebrated throughout the country, with Ulan Bator being the main centre. This is an opportunity for the country's greatest athletes to compete in three classic Mongolian sports – horse racing, archery and wrestling. On the Mongolian steppe, horse racing is a cross-country event, which takes place over vast open grasslands and follows no set course. Dressed in Genghis Khan warrior-style costumes, the men and women who compete in these tests of stamina and strength illustrate the warrior spirit that is still intrinsic to the Mongolian character.

Above: Monastery in Kharkorin (Karakorum) in central Mongolia

NOMADIC DIARY

Naadam is held from the 11th to 13th of July every year. The festival is held throughout the country but the main event takes place in Ulan Bator. However, by venturing away from the capital you are able to combine the festival with an opportunity to experience traditional nomadic life, with a stay in a *ger*.

Six Days on the Steppes

Arrive in Ulan Bator. After checking into your hotel, explore the city on foot. Visit the Museum of Natural History, where you can see dinosaur eggs from the Gobi Desert.

Head out of the city to the nearby Gandantegcheling monastery, Mongolia's largest and the main site for Buddhist learning and worship in the country. Back in town, visit Choijin Lama temple, the National Art Gallery or Zaisan Hill War Memorial.

Take a jeep transfer to Kharkorin (Karakorum). Founded in 1220, the city sits at the crossroads of one of the Silk Roads and was the Mongol Empire's seat of power until 1439. The journey from Ulan Bator takes all day but the road is surprisingly good. Stay in a traditional *ger* – the tents are very comfortable, with a stove in the middle that warms the cool evenings.

Watch the opening festivities of Naadam, which begins with a colourful parade of monks, soldiers and athletes. Spend the rest of the day watching archery and wrestling. The wrestling is particular intriguing – the loser has to walk under the right arm of his vanquisher as a victory dance is performed.

Spend the day watching the horse racing, undeniably the most exciting event. The horsemanship of Mongolian riders cannot be bettered and many riders are frighteningly young – occasionaly as young as five.

Fly back to Ulan Bator and join in the merrymaking of the final day of the festival.

Dos and Don'ts

✓ Eat the wonderful local fermented yoghurt – usually made from either cattle or yak milk.

✗ Don't depend on finding vegetarian food outside of Ulan Bator as traditional Mongolian cooking is heavily meat based.

✓ A torch is invaluable as lighting can be poor – this is especially necessary if you are travelling into the countryside.

✗ Don't get into a car or bus if you think the driver is drunk – drink-driving is a big problem in Mongolia.

✓ Consider having a rabies jab before travelling – many of the nomadic population have dogs which may carry the disease.

JAN
FEB
MAR
APR
MAY
JUN
JUL
8th
9th
10th
11th
12th
13th
AUG
SEP
OCT
NOV
DEC

GETTING THERE
Wales is on the western coast of Britain, and shares a border with England. The capital city is Cardiff, 2 hours by train from central London.

GETTING AROUND
South Wales's finest coastline and castles can all be reached within a couple of hours' drive from Cardiff. Local buses are infrequent, as are the few trains, so car hire is recommended.

WEATHER
In July the weather in South Wales is pleasant, with average daytime temperatures of 20°C. You should be prepared for some rain though.

ACCOMMODATION
Llys Meddyg, Pembrokeshire, has lovely rooms and a restaurant; doubles from £90 per night; www.llysmeddyg.com

St Brides Hotel and Spa, Pembrokeshire, a newly refurbished hotel with sea views; doubles from £140; www.stbridesspahotel.com

St David's Hotel and Spa, Cardiff, a favourite with visiting celebrities; doubles from £230; www.stdavidshotelcardiff.co.uk

EATING OUT
There are some excellent restaurants and gastro-pubs, often using local produce such as black beef, lamb and seafood. Cheeses are also delicious. You can eat well for around £18.

PRICE FOR A FAMILY OF FOUR
£280–300 per day including accommodation, food, transport and entrance charges.

FURTHER INFORMATION
www.visitwales.com
www.castlewales.com

Rich Architectural Legacy
There are three types of castle in Wales. The earliest were built by the Normans when they tried to suppress the Welsh after the Conquest and are often sited on former Roman strongholds. Most of these are in the south. In the 13th century, when many factions were struggling for control of the country, Welsh princes built their own fortresses on isolated hills and crags, but few survive today. Finally, in the late 13th century, Edward I built a series of large and formidable castles to suppress rebellion in the north of the country.

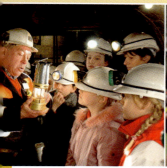

Main: Visitors admiring the impressive Laugharne Castle
Above (left to right): Tour of the Big Pit Mining Museum; battle re-enactment at Pembroke Castle; view over Cardigan Bay

Above: Walking along the beautiful River Wye

CASTLES AND COASTLINE

WITH ITS LUSH GREEN VALLEYS AND WINDSWEPT MOUNTAINS, South Wales is rich in natural beauty. There are few sights that beat the sunset at Rhossili, on the Gower peninsula, or the butter-soft beaches of Pembrokeshire. But this ancient land has man-made wonders too: a string of grey stone castles that stud the countryside like uncut gems. Some are crumbling ruins – providing a picturesque backdrop for family picnics and endless opportunities for games of hide and seek. Others look much as they did when they were first built – historic treasure troves with battlements, grand halls and mighty towers. All of them have a story to tell.

Chepstow Castle is particularly dramatic. Stunningly situated above the River Wye, on the border with England, it is a brooding reminder of a turbulent past. Built by the Normans in 1067 just after the Conquest, it was the first stone castle in Britain – a strategic base for aggressive raids into Wales. Then there's Caerphilly, a little town dominated by a castle so imposing that Tennyson declared: "It isn't a castle – it's a town in ruins." Built in the 13th century, it was a medieval masterpiece of military engineering, with impenetrable walls and formidable water defences. Cardiff Castle, by contrast, is noted for its flamboyant 19th-century interiors, created for the eccentric Marquis of Bute. Rooms are a Gothic fantasy of gilded ceilings, mirrors and elaborate carvings.

Travellers with an artistic streak love the romantic ruins of Laugharne Castle, favourite of the poet Dylan Thomas, while families with lively, budding historians might prefer Pembroke Castle, built by William the Conqueror's cousin. The birthplace of Henry VII, it is often used for energetic re-enactments of historic events.

The most striking sight of all is Carreg Cennen Castle, in rural Carmarthenshire. Perched precariously on a crag above the River Cennen, legend has it that one of King Arthur's knights lies deep beneath it – fast asleep.

"All that I heard him say of it was…that one of he castles in Wales would ontain all the castles that he had seen in Scotland."

James Boswell of Samuel Johnson

Inset: Exterior of the Wales Millennium Centre in Cardiff Bay
Below (left to right): Vaulted roof and stained-glass windows in Cardiff Castle; Worms Head at sunset from Rhossili Beach; Great Hall in Caerphilly Castle

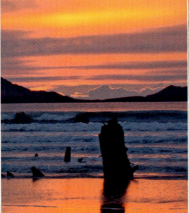

CASTLE DIARY

July is a lovely month to visit South Wales – the days are long, the countryside is lush and the sea is cool and inviting. Wales is a small country, but there's an extensive range of activities for families – so, while you can explore the south in a week, two would be even better.

A Week in South Wales

Start your trip in Cardiff, the lively capital. Take a tour around the Millennium Stadium, visit Cardiff Castle, or head to the wonderful Museum of Welsh Life. In the evening, watch a show at the Wales Millennium Centre.

From Cardiff, take a day trip and a picnic to Caerphilly, Chepstow or Carreg Cennen castles. Alternatively, head to the Valleys, where, at Big Pit Mining Museum, you can go for an underground tour with a former miner, before driving to nearby Blaenafon, a World Heritage Industrial Site.

Head west to Swansea market to try the famous cockles with vinegar and pepper, or an icecream at the Mumbles. Then make for the Gower Peninsula, a good overnight stop, and watch the sunset at Rhossili.

Leave the Gower and call in at the National Wetland Centre, near Llanelli, for birdwatching. Then continue to romantic Laugharne on the Carmarthenshire coast to visit its castle and Dylan Thomas's former home.

Drive westwards into Pembrokeshire. Explore lovely Tenby, a seaside town with a maze of medieval streets, sandy beaches and bustling bars and watch battle re-enactments at Pembroke Castle.

From Tenby it's easy to go for a full day's walk along the Pembrokeshire Coast Path.

Make an early start for a day on the superb beaches of St Bride's Bay. Try kite surfing or go on a dolphin-watching boat trip.

Dos and Don'ts

✓ Listen out for people speaking the lyrical Welsh language. It's still very much alive today.

✗ Don't miss out on the local specialities. Try laver bread if you see it – a type of seaweed, mixed with oatmeal, generally fried and eaten for breakfast with bacon.

✓ Make an early start for a day's sightseeing. The main roads get extremely busy in July.

JAN
FEB
MAR
APR
MAY
JUN
JUL
DAY 1
DAY 2
DAY 3
DAY 4
DAY 5
DAY 6
DAY 7
AUG
SEP
OCT
NOV
DEC

CANADA

CALGARY
Vancouver
Toronto   Ottawa
USA

GETTING THERE
Calgary is in Alberta, Canada. The International Airport is on the northeast edge of the city, 20 minutes from central Calgary.

GETTING AROUND
Calgary's Light Rail Transit system, called the C-Train, offers two stops at Stampede Park, and is a handy alternative to driving from your hotel.

WEATHER
Afternoon temperatures can hit 30°C in July, although the average high is closer to 24°C. Afternoon thunder showers are possible.

ACCOMMODATION
The Best Western Suites Downtown, with fully-equipped kitchens, has suites from £140; www.bestwestern.com

The Kensington Riverside Inn is just minutes from downtown and offers free parking; junior suites from £215; www.kensingtonriversideinn.com

The Fairmont Palliser Hotel – a historic hotel built in 1914 and restored to its original glory – has family rooms from £230; www.fairmont.com

EATING OUT
You'll find great meals available for around £7–10 per person. Try the 1886 Buffalo Café in downtown's Eau Claire Market for hearty breakfasts and stroll downtown to Stephen Avenue for pubs, bistros and fine restaurants.

PRICE FOR A FAMILY OF FOUR
£350–500 per day including accommodation, food, local transport and entrance charges.

FURTHER INFORMATION
www.tourismcalgary.com

WILD WEST STAMPEDE

I<small>T'S THE LONGEST EIGHT SECONDS IN THE WORLD</small> – an eternity ticking by, as a cowboy grips with hand and knees and heart to the bull or the horse that's twisting and turning beneath him, doing everything in its power to buck him off. It's grit and it's gumption and it's the Calgary Stampede – ten action-packed days when every second counts, whether it is the eight-second qualifying bell in bull, saddle bronc and bareback busting; the race against the clock in tie-down roping, steer wrestling and barrel racing; or the world-famous chuckwagon teams, emblazoned with colourful advertisements, thundering around the racetrack that's aptly known as the half-mile of hell.

They call the Stampede the greatest outdoor show on earth, and for good reason. It tempts the world's best cowboys and cowgirls to Calgary for the richest prize money in professional rodeo – and then it rolls out the red carpet for them, and for those who come to share in the action. In this most western of western cities, Stampede means that it's time to throw on hats and boots and offer a warm

Main: Chuckwagon racing at the Calgary Stampede

Top: Competing in a rodeo at the Stampede

Above: Enjoying a fairground ride at dusk

Below: Bar U Ranch National Historic Site

Head-Smashed-In Jump

A designated UNESCO World Heritage Site, Head-Smashed-In is the best preserved buffalo jump known. The native tribes, collectively known as the Blackfoot, were experts in the behaviour of buffalo. By predicting the movement of the herds, they were able to hunt the beasts by running them over the precipice in great numbers. The animals were then carved up and the flesh dried for the future months. There are still a great number of buffalo skeletons and marked trails to be seen, and a superb interpretive centre gives the site historical and cultural context.

welcome. But it's more than that – it is a celebration of the pioneer spirit and ranching history that helped to found this part of the world, a living legacy of the days when herding on horseback was the only way to make a livelihood.

You can feel the energy as soon as you enter Stampede Park, on the edge of downtown and bordered by the Elbow River. A neon-trimmed fair lines the grounds, with gravity-defying rides for cowboys and non-cowboys alike. The Stampede Casino kicks into full gear, providing a high-end cousin to the bar-room poker of the old west. Cattle and horses vie for blue ribbons in agricultural competitions, while the Indian Village showcases the culture of the region's five First Nations peoples, including arts, crafts and dancing. At the appropriately named Saddledome Stadium, and throughout the grounds, top music artists boost the excitement and noise.

You'll find the main events at the Grandstand where the itinerary goes almost as quickly as the wagons: rodeo in the afternoon and chuckwagon races in the early evening, followed by a high-energy musical show and topped off with fireworks. Prepare your best "yee-haw" – you'll need it.

Above: Aerial view of the Calgary Stampede's grounds

RODEO DIARY

Prepare to spend two days fully immersing yourself in the excitement of the Stampede. Then take some time to explore the rest of this interesting city – its historic and elegant sandstone buildings, pioneering western heritage, thriving arts scene and Olympic legacy. Calgary is also a gateway to four UNESCO World Heritage Sites.

A Week of Pioneer Spirit

Orient yourself with a trip up the Calgary Tower. Then hit the Stampede for the casino, midway, agricultural shows, Indian Village and, of course, the rodeo and chuckwagon events, plus the grandstand show.

Visit the Heritage Park Historical Village, on the edge of the sailboat-dotted Glenmore Reservoir, southwest of downtown. You'll find pioneer-era buildings, a steam locomotive and even a paddlewheeler.

There's plenty in town for the kids to enjoy – Glenbow Museum is a must-see for its permanent exhibits dedicated to the Blackfoot and other First Nations peoples. For thrills, try the Canada Olympic Park, with its mountain bike park and luge rides.

Just east of downtown, Fort Calgary re-creates the late-1800s home of the North West Mounted Police, while nearby Calgary Zoo has wildlife from Canada to Africa.

Visit Spruce Meadows in the city's southwest – consistently named the world's best outdoor show-jumping venue. From there, it's a quick trot down the Cowboy Trail to the Bar U Ranch National Historic Site.

Leave the city behind to appreciate the dramatic Alberta scenery – head to the mountain towns of Banff and Lake Louise, and then on to Jasper, past the ancient glaciers of the Columbia Icefield. Or, day-trip 90 minutes northeast to the renowned Royal Tyrrell Museum and the land of the dinosaurs in Drumheller, or head two hours south to the ancient cliff-site hunting ground at Head-Smashed-In Buffalo Jump.

Dos and Don'ts

☑ There's plenty of entertainment for adults too. At night, Calgary becomes the city that doesn't sleep while the Stampede's in town – try Stampede Park.

☒ Don't delay in booking your accommodation – hotels in and around Calgary start to fill up as much as a year in advance for the ten days of Stampede. The best rates and rooms go to those who make early reservations.

☑ Follow the cowboy example and wear a hat (and sunscreen) to protect yourself from the strong summer sun. Mountain breezes can fool you into thinking it's cooler than it seems.

JAN
FEB
MAR
APR
MAY
JUN
JUL
DAYS 1–2
DAY 3
DAY 4
DAY 5
DAY 6
DAY 7
AUG
SEP
OCT
NOV
DEC

GETTING THERE

Mendoza is in west Argentina. International flights arrive into Buenos Aires, 1,060 km (660 miles) away, and connecting flights to Mendoza take about 2 hours. El Portillo is in Chile, around 150 km (93 miles) from Santiago.

GETTING AROUND

Public buses will take you across the Andes and the Chilean border from Mendoza to El Portillo. The hotel in El Portillo has a shuttle to Santiago.

WEATHER

In Mendoza, the temperature hovers around 8°C in July. This is a great time to visit El Portillo, with bright sunshine and plenty of snow, and temperatures as low as -5°C.

ACCOMMODATION

In Mendoza, the large, modern 4-star Hotel Aconcagua has doubles from £50; www.hotelaconcagua.com

A stay at the Gran Hotel El Portillo includes full board and lift passes; doubles from £1,940 for the week; www.skiportillo.com.

EATING OUT

In Mendoza, try the *parilla* (grilled meats) at Trevi or the vegetarian buffet at The Green Apple; both from around £7.

Meals at El Portillo include exceptional Chilean seafood and the best Argentinian beef.

PRICE FOR TWO

In Mendoza, expect to spend £90 per day including accommodation, food and excursions. A stay at El Portillo costs around £280 per day.

FURTHER INFORMATION

www.mendoza.com

Main: Skiing on the crowd-free slopes of El Portillo in the Chilean Andes

Above: Trekking in Aconcagua Park, home to the highest peak in South America

Below: Thermal pools at Puente del Inca, Mendoza

Gran Hotel El Portillo

Rearing up from the mountain like a cruise ship, this hotel offers the only accommodation at El Portillo ski resort. All of the 123 rooms have magnificent views, facing either the mountain or the glacial lake, making the most of the wonderful location. Along with its extraordinary setting, the beauty of El Portillo is that queues and crowds are non-existent, so you will feel like you have this snowy, vertiginous paradise to yourself.

ANDEAN ADVENTURE

STROLLING THROUGH TREE-LINED STREETS AND PRETTY, LEAFY PLAZAS, the feeling is more Alpine than Andean. It is only when you glance up and catch a glimpse of the towering peak of Aconcagua (the highest outside the Himalayas) and its high-altitude neighbours that you realize you are somewhere of far greater extremes. In a fertile valley at the foot of the Andes, Mendoza, capital of the eponymous province, has a relaxed atmosphere, good restaurants and a temperate climate, all of which make it an attractive place for exploring the surrounding area.

Nearby is the extraordinary Puente del Inca, a natural, wide stone bridge over the Mendoza River which was created by glaciers. Its eye-catching golden-copper hue has been coloured by the minerals in the water, and just upstream you can bathe in the bubbling waters of a thermal spring, with views over a dramatic landscape of steep-sided mountains. Mendoza is famous as the centre of the flourishing Argentinian wine industry. The satisfying symmetry of the vineyards

Above: Wine cellar of an Uco Valley wine producer, Mendoza

SOUTHERN SNOW DIARY

Mendoza is the starting place for this trip and a lovely little town in which to spend a few days among great alpine scenery. Explore the surrounding countryside and vineyards before making the crossing into Chile (you will need to allow a full day for this), then spend an unforgettable week skiing in El Portillo.

Twelve Days Among the Peaks

Flights into Buenos Aires usually arrive in the morning so you can fly onto Mendoza the same day. Spend the afternoon exploring the squares and tree-lined boulevards of the city. — **DAY 1**

From Mendoza, take a trip to the Puente del Inca and enjoy a bath in the thermal springs or a trek at the foot of Aconcagua, the highest peak in South America.

Be sure to visit one of the wineries of the Uco Valley, where you can taste and purchase the excellent wines. — **DAYS 2–4**

Travel through the Andes by bus via the beautiful Upsallata Valley into Chile – enjoy the spectacular views of peaks thick with snow as you climb up and up. Check into the Gran Hotel El Portillo and unwind in the Jacuzzi or with a drink in the living room. — **DAY 5**

Spend your first day at ski school – this will help everyone, regardless of ability – beginners will learn the basics of powder skiing and experts will learn the best places to go.

Enjoy days of exhilarating skiing, refuelling with lunch overlooking the picturesque lake. Show off what you've learned during the week in the "Sol del Portillo" race – all abilities and ages can take part in the fun.

On Fridays at 8pm, a torchlight parade descends the mountain, making an impressive sight, before an evening of celebrations as the week draws to a close. — **DAYS 6–11**

Check out of the hotel and enjoy the winding journey through the Andes to Santiago. — **DAY 12**

Dos and Don'ts

☑ Check the weather forecast before setting off from Mendoza. Heavy snow may block the Andean crossing.

☒ Don't overdo it on your first day – El Portillo sits at 2,855 m (9,370 ft) and the altitude takes some getting used to.

☑ Take some smarter clothes for the evening. Dress in the restaurant is "smart casual", with shirt collars for men and no open sandals for women.

☑ Look out for visiting Olympic teams – the US, Austrian and Canadian teams have all trained here in the past.

JAN
FEB
MAR
APR
MAY
JUN
JUL
AUG
SEP
OCT
NOV
DEC

characterizes the landscape here, and fascinating tours of the wineries provide insight into this important industry, as well as a chance to taste the best wines inexpensively.

From Mendoza, a full-day drive across the Andes and the Chilean border will deliver you to the continent's most famous ski resort, El Portillo. Nearly 3,000 m (9,800 ft) above sea level, amid jaw-dropping Andean peaks, the resort is situated on the shores of Laguna del Inca, a vast glacial lake that freezes over completely during the winter months. The frequent snowfall comes in short, intense bursts of deep, fresh powder, and the narrow, sheer passes make for fantastic skiing. Clear blue skies and brilliant sunshine intensify the landscape of one of the most impenetrable mountain ranges in the world.

There is no town at El Portillo, just one hotel with 123 rooms, so runs are often completely clear without the queues for lifts or crowded runs that are common in European and North American resorts. Bouncing through powder down a deserted run against a backdrop of awesome Andean scenery is undoubtedly one of the most exhilarating feelings on earth.

GETTING THERE
The island has four airports: Ajaccio, Bastia, Calvi and Figari. Ferries from Nice take under 3 hours, while ferries from Livorno in Italy take 2 hours.

GETTING AROUND
Tour companies offer transport to many places and a train service runs across the island. Car hire is the easiest way to get around.

WEATHER
There are many microclimates on the island, but July is generally hot and dry. Temperatures on the beaches average around 30°C but it is cooler in the mountains.

ACCOMMODATION
Kalliste, in the centre of Ajaccio, is an attractive and friendly small hotel; family rooms from £96; www.hotel-kalliste-ajaccio.com

Hotel Dominique Colonna, Corte, has a wonderful countryside location; family rooms from £140; www.dominique-colonna.com

L'Alivi, a large 3-star hotel with a pool and beach, near Bastia on the north coast; family room from £170; www.hotel-alivi.com

EATING OUT
Corsican cuisine combines the ample produce from land and sea, seasoned with olive oil and herbs. Fish and seafood are most often served grilled, but look out for the local speciality, *aziminu* (seafood soup).

PRICE FOR A FAMILY OF FOUR
£200–250 per day including accommodation, food and car hire.

FURTHER INFORMATION
www.visit-corsica.com

MIDSUMMER PLAYGROUND

A LANDSCAPE SHROUDED IN MYTH, Corsica remains today a place of mysterious beauty. This is a craggy, wild land; its interior is peppered with 20 peaks, which are believed to have once been the land of giants and ogres, now home to an astonishing diversity that is unexpected in this part of the Mediterranean. It's no surprise that this, the fourth largest island in the Mediterranean, is so popular during the summer, for it combines sunshine with charming small towns, lush green forests, cool clear rivers and soft white sand beaches from which you can let the days drift past.

Despite being part of France since the 18th century, Corsica is closer to Italy, geographically and culturally, with graceful Baroque churches, Genoese fortresses and a cuisine that brings together both the Mediterranean and the mountains. The island's somewhat turbulent history has led to many fascinating tales of heroic struggles, bandits and long-running vendettas – the stuff of bedtime stories – which can be explored in the charming harbourside towns.

Below (top and bottom): Walking through the streets of Bonifacio; visiting the Scandola Nature Reserve by boat

Food and Wine
The best way to see what is on offer is to attend one of the country fairs. In July there is an Olive Fair in Montemaggiore in the Balagne and the weekend Corsican Wine Fair takes place in Luri on Cap Corse. The only *denominacion d'origen* cheese is *brocciu*. Made from the whey left after other cheeses have been produced, it is appreciated in a number of ways, from pastas to desserts. Olive oil is excellent, as is honey, particularly those from chestnut flowers or the maquis. Wines are produced everywhere, mostly rosé and dry whites, best drunk young.

Corsica is an ideal midsummer playground as its astonishing landscape is perfect for a huge range of exciting activities. Take a horse ride through the green hills of the Castagniccia or along the sandy shores of the lovely east coast, or hire bicycles and find the perfect picnic spot. Many of Corsica's rivers are quite spectacular, ideal for canoeing or an exhilarating rafting expedition. The many footpaths are perfect for discovering some of the island's 2,000 species of flora. When you've had your fill of activities and just want to laze in the sun and splash around in the sea, you are again spoilt for choice. Seek out the magnificent coves in the south, such as Rondinara Bay, where fine white sand leads down to unbelievably clear water, or take a boat to virtually inaccessible Saleccia Beach in the north. And when enjoying the sun and scenery isn't enough to occupy you, take a boat trip around the rugged coast and the small rocky islands that lie off it, explore the beautiful diving sites or utilize the good breezes by windsurfing off the north coast. The islanders have a reputation for being rather aloof to visitors – but show respect for their captivating island and you will be rewarded with typical Mediterranean warmth.

Above: Climbing on board a diving boat in Corsica

COASTAL DIARY

July is high season in Corsica but it doesn't get as crowded as other Mediterranean destinations and there are many activities on offer for families to enjoy. Base yourself in one place and hire a car for trips to the coast and the interior – don't be too ambitious though as the roads are slow and winding.

A Mediterranean Week

Spend a day in Ajaccio, the island's administrative capital. Visit the market, which sells excellent local produce such as cheese, oil and honey. Enjoy a coffee in an outdoor café before heading to the Musée d'Histoire to find out more about the island's history.

Visit Calvi, in the north of the island, which has a wonderful medieval citadel and 6 km (4 miles) of sandy beaches nearby. To see dolphins and seals, take a boat to the Scandola Nature Reserve, or hike into the beautiful Balange region.

Visit the ethnographic museum and Genoese dungeons in Bastia. To the north is Cap Corse, which is dotted with watchtowers. Take your pick of the many activities on offer – hire bikes to explore, join a diving trip or a rafting expedition on one of the rivers, or take a boat to isolated Saleccia Beach.

Corte lies at the heart of the island and is the best base for exploring the mountains – walk up the Gorges du Tavignono or horse ride through the green hills. Nearby are the beautiful glacial lakes around Monte Rotondo.

Bonifacio, the most Italian of Corsica's towns, is sited on a limestone cliff 200 m (650 ft) above the sea. From the old port, where there is an aquarium, take a boat to the *grottes marines* (sea caves), which are spectacular, or to the Îles Lavezzi archipelago and nature reserve where rare wildflowers flourish. Seek out beautiful Rondinara Bay and enjoy its soft sands and clear waters.

Dos and Don'ts

✓ Take a rattling train ride on the narrow-gauge railway which links Ajaccio, Bastia and Calvi via Corte, with dramatic views of the Corsican landscape.

✗ Don't light matches or throw away cigarettes in the countryside – summer fires are very easily started.

✓ Make sure you try the local *Pietra*, a chestnut beer that is made by the only Corsican brewery.

JAN
FEB
MAR
APR
MAY
JUN
JUL
DAY 1
DAY 2
DAYS 3–4
DAY 5
DAYS 6–7
AUG
SEP
OCT
NOV
DEC

Main: Secluded cove at Roccapina near Bonifacio

Above (top to bottom): Bonifacio's old town perched above the sea; daisies in bloom

Below: Diving in the clear waters off Corsica

GETTING THERE
The San Juan Islands are in Puget Sound, off the coast of Washington State, USA. Friday Harbor in San Juan is 45 minutes by seaplane from Seattle, which has an international airport. There are also excellent inter-island ferries.

GETTING AROUND
Scooters, mopeds, bicycles and cars are all available for hire on San Juan Island.

WEATHER
July is sunny, with an average high of 21°C. Although July is the driest month, rain is likely.

ACCOMMODATION
July is high season in the islands, so make reservations up to a year in advance.

San Juan Central Reservations provides details of many of the small inns and B&Bs; www.sanjuanisland.com

Tucker House Inn offers comfort and charm; doubles from £80; www.tuckerhouse.com

Friday's Historic Inn, built in 1891, has double rooms from £80; www.friday-harbor.com

EATING OUT
On the islands you'll find a wide variety of fresh seafood and locally grown fruits and vegetables. Duck Soup Inn (www.ducksoupinn.com) has a creative seasonal dinner menu of fresh Pacific seafood from around £15 per person.

PRICE FOR TWO
£130–160 per day including accommodation, food and a whale-spotting excursion.

FURTHER INFORMATION
www.guidetosanjuans.com

Orca Whales

More than 80 of these graceful black and white mammals spend the summer in the cold waters to the west of San Juan Islands. Orcas are highly intelligent and hunt in pods. Their skill in pursuing salmon and other marine animals has given them the name killer whales. They live in all of the oceans of the world, but thrive in the cold waters of Antarctica and the Pacific Northwest.

Above (left to right): Boats lined up in Friday Harbor; harbour seal lounging on a beach, San Juan Islands; biking on the islands
Main: Sea kayakers paddle as the sun sets with Mount Baker in the distance

Above: Lighthouse of Lime Kiln Park

ORCAS AND ISLANDS

THE EARLY MORNING CHILL BRINGS CURTAINS OF SILVERY MIST OFF THE WATER, and your paddle makes soft, liquid sounds as the kayak glides over the mirror-calm water. Everything else is eerily silent. Through the vapour, you can see the deep channel broken here and there by dark, tree-shrouded islands. Above the low-lying mist, the air is diamond-clear, and on the distant horizon a volcanic peak rises, its snowy cap made brilliant in the warming light.

Suddenly, a deep whoosh of air sounds behind you and you turn to see a spout of spray turning golden in the sun. A second whoosh and you see the fin – no, fins – two, then four then six; jet black and each bent and notched uniquely. A pod of killer whales. They are in no hurry and you paddle along beside them, slowly closing the distance as they dive and feed. The small wakes they leave behind belie the tremendous size and strength of their bodies. This is not Shamu and some tame friends, these are the worlds largest predators; a honed and voracious hunting pack in the wild, natural setting of Puget Sound.

Set against the stunning backdrop of the snow-capped mountains of the Olympic and Coastal Mountain Ranges, the emerald green San Juan Islands offer up a world of outdoor adventure and unforgettable sights. Kayaking is at the top of the activity lists in the islands, but it isn't the only thing to do. On Orcas Island, Moran State Park offers hiking trails that lead into the heart of the mountainous island, with old growth forests and panoramas where the views across the sound go on forever. Some islands, like quiet Lopez, are relatively level and offer gentle roads that are perfect for cyclists.

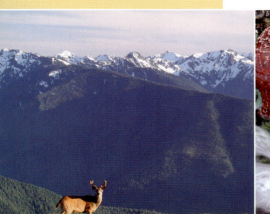

The air is diamond-clear, on the distant horizon a volcanic peak rises, its snowy cap made brilliant in the warming light.

For gentler adventure, there are plenty of small villages to explore, such as historic Friday Harbor on San Juan Island, where narrow streets are lined with galleries and quaint inns and virtually every restaurant serves fresh seafood with a view of the boat-filled harbour.

Inset: Seattle's skyline illuminated at night
Below (left and right): Mule deer at Olympic National Park; colourful starfish

PACIFIC DIARY

The weather is at its best in July, the month with the least rain and the warmest days. The spectacular orca whales are a common sight, and the salmon fishing is great. And although this is the busiest season, the worst of the crowds can be avoided by staying in the quieter Friday Harbor.

Five Days in Puget Sound

Spend the day in Seattle. Take a walk around Green Lake in Discovery Park and lunch at Pike Place Market. In the evening, visit the landmark Space Needle and view the city from the observation deck.

Fly to the Islands by seaplane for fantastic views, arriving at Friday Harbor in the early morning.
Take a naturalist-led whale-watching tour to see the amazing orca whales and bird life of Puget Sound. Explore the shops and waterfront in Friday Harbor, and enjoy dinner with a panoramic water view.

Join a guided kayak tour and paddle through the clear blue waters of Puget Sound. Visit the Whale Museum in Friday Harbor to learn about the orcas found in the San Juan Island waters.

Take a salmon fishing charter and spend the day fishing. Bring your camera to capture incredible memories and a cooler to take home the tasty catch.

Rent a moped or two-person motorized scooter and explore the gently rolling hills or walk along the shore past pretty Lime Kiln State Park to the Olympic National Park. Explore the seaside village of Roche Harbor.

Get an early start and take the inter-island ferry to Orcas Island for the morning. Ride the shuttle bus to Moran State Park for the short climb to the top of Mt Constitution for the stunning vistas of Puget Sound. In the afternoon, take the ferry to Lopez Island and rent a bicycle to tour the sandy beaches.

Dos and Don'ts

✓ Travel light and dress casually for the islands, but take along a rain jacket and warm clothes as it is cooler on the water.

✗ Don't forget to check the luggage restrictions for the seaplane, and pack accordingly. Alternatively, fly to San Juan Island with a regional airline.

✓ Be aware that cars must wait in line for 2–3 hours to get on the ferries in July, while walk-on passengers and bicycles can arrive shortly before departure.

✗ Don't miss out by not booking in advance, reservations are essential at this time of year.

JAN
FEB
MAR
APR
MAY
JUN
JUL
DAY 1
DAY 2
DAY 3
DAY 4
DAY 5
DAY 6
AUG
SEP
OCT
NOV
DEC

ARCTIC OCEAN

SPITSBERGEN

Longyearbyen

GREENLAND
SEA

BARENTS
SEA

NORWAY

GETTING THERE
Spitsbergen's hub, Longyearbyen, is accessible by plane from Tromsø, Norway, about 1,000 km (600 miles) to the south. It's also a stop on some Arctic cruises.

GETTING AROUND
Flights from Longyearbyen serve Ny Ålesund, and other sites of interest can be reached on organized tours and cruises. Taxi services are available around Longyearbyen, or you can hire a car or bicycle.

WEATHER
July is mostly dry, with temperatures ranging from near freezing to around 18°C, but any wind makes it feel much colder.

ACCOMMODATION
Gjesthuset 102, in Longyearbyen has doubles from £50; tel. (47) 790 256 60.

The Radisson SAS Polar Hotel, Longyearbyen, offers a dining room, sauna and solarium; doubles from £130; www.radisson.com

Atmospheric Spitsbergen Basecamp, Longyearbyen; doubles from £120; www.basecampexplorer.com

EATING OUT
The restaurant at Huset, in Longyearbyen, does reindeer steaks, whale, seal and local fish. The dining rooms at the Radisson SAS Polar Hotel and Spitsbergen Hotel offer international fare.

PRICE FOR TWO
£300–325 per day including accommodation, food and six-day cruise around Spitsbergen.

FURTHER INFORMATION
www.svalbard.net
www.spitsbergentravel.com

Journey to the Pole
Throughout the 20th century, Spitsbergen served as a jump-off point for polar expeditions. Norwegian explorer Roald Amundsen set his sights on being the first to fly over the North Pole and on 11 May, 1926, Amundsen, along with American financier Lincoln Ellsworth, Italian adventurer Umberto Nobile and Norwegian pilot-navigator Hjalmar Riiser-Larsen, left northern Spitsbergen aboard the airship *Norge* and 16 hours later, dropped the US, Italian and Norwegian flags at the North Pole.

Main: Female polar bear steps gingerly onto the melting ice

ARCTIC EXPLORATION

Bathed in the perpetual sunlight of midsummer, Spitsbergen in July presents an unrivalled and comparatively accessible glimpse of the polar north. After most of the pack ice has retreated and snow has melted in low-lying areas, migrating birds return to nest on towering sea cliffs, and tiny wild flowers emerge to splash colour across the lonely, treeless tundra of this high Arctic archipelago.

The Spitsbergen experience begins in Longyearbyen, which nestles near the foot of two glaciers at the mouth of relatively luxuriant Adventdalen valley. In this Arctic "metropolis" and former coal mining centre, 1,500 hardy people create a microcosm of mainland Norwegian society and a base for forays into the archipelago's icy hinterland. Perhaps because the sun is visible around the clock between mid-April and late October, the tempo of life remains upbeat in the summer with visitors and locals partying in the town's lively weekend night spots.

Above: Row of colourful wooden houses in Longyearbyen

Below (top to bottom): Trekking over a rocky outcrop; purple saxifrage; Arctic terns nesting

Above: *MS Europa* in Isfjorden, Spitsbergen

POLAR DIARY

Spitsbergen enjoys the 24-hour sunshine of the Arctic summer in July. Although this wildlife-rich archipelago represents the most accessible point of the polar north, it's not on any main tourist routes. Visitors will probably want to spend at least nine days to include a cruise that takes in the best of this wonderland.

Nine Days in the Wild North

DAY 1 Explore the tiny and colourful Longyearbyen. After calling in at the small art gallery and historic graveyard, hike the Burma Road and head for the town museum.

DAY 2 Join a hiking tour to Longyeardalen or Bolterdalen to hunt for fossils of ancient tropical plants followed by a tour of Coal Mine No. 3, where the deep permafrost preserves a gene bank of over 7,000 seed varieties.

DAY 3 Choose between a tour by wheeled dogsled, sea kayaking through icy Arctic waters, or a horseback expedition to the Platåberget mountain to experience the highlands and appreciate the wide-ranging views.

DAYS 4–9 Take a cruise around the islands. Most cruises visit the Russian coal-mining settlement of Barentsburg on the first day where Norwegian sovereignty is evident only in the post office signage and the kroner used to pay.

Cruise north to 80°N latitude and see the walrus breeding site on Moffen Island. En route, enjoy Zodiac (rubber dinghy) landings at lovely Magdalenefjord and the historic sites at Amsterdamøya island and Virgohamna, on Danskøya island.

Visit the scientific post of Ny Ålesund, the northernmost civilian community on earth. It boasts the world's northernmost locomotive and ethereal views of the spectacular Kronebreen glacier.

Cruise back to Longyearbyen via the calving face of Lillehöökbreen glacier, with landings at Ebeltoftbukta and the dramatic cliffs at the head of Krossfjorden.

Dos and Don'ts

✓ Remove your shoes when entering a Longyearbyen home, office, hotel or museum, as local custom requires.

✗ Don't move or collect archeological relics. Even rusting drums at historic campsites are protected artifacts.

✓ Pack clothing for a range of temperatures and conditions, from frozen to moderate. Include light summer clothes, windproof shells, warm jumpers, and winter jackets.

✓ Join organized tours for hikes outside developed areas. Hungry polar bears are dangerous and tour groups are required by law to speak softly and carry guns.

JAN FEB MAR APR MAY JUN **JUL** AUG SEP OCT NOV DEC

Just outside the town however, the wilderness begins, and in the surrounding hills and valleys the sound of rushing meltwater and the solitude of open tundra inspire an overwhelming sense of adventure and discovery. On one of the popular cruises along the island's west coast, the typically biting wind carries the cries of thousands of sea birds – puffins, guillemots, cormorants, fulmars, auks, gulls and others – that occupy cliff-hugging nests, rearing the season's chicks. At the head of iceberg studded fjords, skyscraper-sized chunks of ice crash down from towering glacier faces with a thunderous roar as they plunge into the Arctic waters.

Along tamer shorelines, it's a joy to wander over the landscape in search of tundra wild flowers and the rusting remnants of adventurers past. There's always a chance of spotting a squat Svalbard reindeer or a wandering Arctic fox. However, no wildlife experience can compare with the heart-stopping thrill of seeing a polar bear lumbering across the tundra or hunting amid the grinding pack ice that it shares with the seals that is its main prey and, given that in the archipelago there are more polar bears than people, it is not such an unlikely sighting.

GETTING THERE
Cape Cod is in Massachusetts, in the northeast USA. Flights arrive into Hyannis airport, which is connected to Boston and New York.

GETTING AROUND
Hiring a car is a great way to explore, but visitors to the islands are advised not to take cars. Ferry services to the islands operate from Hyannis or Woods Hole. On the islands, taxis and island buses operate and bicycle hire is available.

WEATHER
Temperatures in July average around 26ºC – ideal beach weather.

ACCOMMODATION
Nauset House is a lovely bed and breakfast in Cape Cod; doubles from £45; www.nausethouseinn.com

Nantucket's Cliff Lodge is a whaling master's home turned B&B; doubles from £100; www.clifflodgenantucket.com

On Cape Cod, Ocean Edge Resort offers a beach, pool, tennis and golf; doubles from £200; www.oceanedge.com

EATING OUT
Try local favourites like clam chowder, lobster and scrod (young cod or haddock, often fried with breadcrumbs) – freshly caught and delicious eaten with a New England beer.

PRICE FOR TWO
£170–200 including accommodation, food and car hire.

FURTHER INFORMATION
www.capecodchamber.org

Beaches and Marshes

Declared a National Seashore in 1961 by John F. Kennedy and maintained by the US National Park Service, the Cape Cod National Seashore includes not only boundless beach but 42 sq miles (110 sq km) of marshes, meadows, ponds, uplands, cranberry bogs and trails. The Seashore provides recreation and beauty for swimmers, surfers, hikers and bikers or anyone who simply wants to sit on an uncrowded beach and contemplate the rhythms of the sea.

Beyond the town is a vision for romantics, a wild untamed landscape of heather-covered moors, bound by great expanses of sandy beaches...

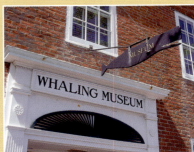

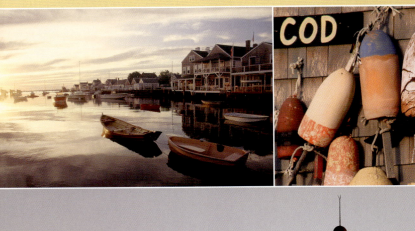

Main: Wood End lighthouse in Provincetown
Inset: Whaling Museum in Nantucket
Above and Top (left to right): Boats in Provincetown harbour; Nantucket harbour; lobster buoys at Rock harbour; boating on the lake; coffee shop, Edgartown

JOURNEY BACK IN TIME

THE BEACHES ARE THE FIRST ATTRACTION, mile after mile of sandy shores along the wave-tossed Atlantic and the warmer, gentler waters of Nantucket Sound. But "The Cape", as it is fondly known to its many admirers, has many other lures. Villages with a history dating back over 350 years are filled with vintage grey shingled cottages, windmills and lighthouses; picturesque remnants of an earlier time. Along Route 6A, once known as the King's Highway, many homes now house antique shops and art galleries, a great opportunity to do a spot of browsing. Running for miles, this road is America's largest historic district, where the past is lovingly maintained.

Provincetown sits at the north tip of the Cape and, as the first landing place of the Pilgrims in 1620, boasts not only a fascinating history but outstanding scenery that has inspired eminent writers and artists, including Eugene O'Neill and Edward Hopper. At the colourful harbour, bustling with working fishing boats, visitors can join a

Above: Tail of a humpback whale breaks the water.

CAPE DIARY

Cape Cod, Nantucket and Martha's Vineyard are home to some of America's most exceptional scenery. Villages of historic charm border miles of magnificent beaches. Deservedly popular in July for sunning, shopping, fine dining and charming lodging, each destination still manages to maintain a faraway feel.

A Week by the Water

Arrive in Hyannis, pick up a hire car and drive up the Cape to your hotel. After checking in, head to the nearest beach. Later in the day, drive up Route 6A and browse the shops and galleries, before enjoying a lobster dinner.

DAY 1

Begin the day with a few more hours on the beach, then pick your pleasure: a hike or bike ride along National Seashore trails, a round of golf, a dune tour or a whale-watching cruise in Provincetown. Alternatively, stay on the beach and enjoy a swim and a good book.

DAY 2

Drive back down to Hyannis, from where you can take the ferry to Nantucket Island. Relax on the beach before taking a stroll around town, home to the highest concentration of pre-1850s houses in the country.

DAY 3

Hire bicycles and tour the island – have lunch amid the colourful fishermen's cottages in Siasconset then visit Nantucket's Whaling Museum.

DAY 4

Take the 70-minute Hyline Inter-Island Ferry from Nantucket to Oak Bluffs on Martha's Vineyard. Have a look at the colourful gingerbread cottages and shops, and the pretty Flying Horses Carousel, before taking the island bus to Edgartown.

DAY 5

Check out Edgartown's shops or rent a bike and explore the island's picturesque western shoreline.

DAY 6

Spend the morning on the beach, before taking the 45-minute cruise back to Hyannis to pick up your car and head for the airport, or travel on to Boston.

DAY 7

Dos and Don'ts

✓ You need a car on Cape Cod but do consider hiring a bicycle to get around on the islands. Fares for car ferries are high and parking places are few. If you aren't a cyclist, it's still cheaper to rent a taxi for an island tour.

✗ Don't miss the Cape Cod National Seashore Visitor Centers in Eastham and Provincetown for some of the most breathtaking views of sand and sea.

✓ Visit a typical casual Cape Cod "lobster shack", where you order at the window, your lobster is cooked to order and you eat at outdoor picnic tables.

JAN
FEB
MAR
APR
MAY
JUN
JUL
DAY 1
DAY 2
DAY 3
DAY 4
DAY 5
DAY 6
DAY 7
AUG
SEP
OCT
NOV
DEC

whale-watching cruise and spend the day spotting humpback whales and viewing the beautiful coastline. For a more leisurely day, follow the dunes that stretch endlessly outside the town.

Just offshore are the celebrated islands of the Cape. Martha's Vineyard, the closest, is a land of opposites, with the pastoral beauty of the English countryside in the interior and the pleasures of the sea on its shores. The towns are also delightfully diverse and ideal for strolling, stopping for lunch at a lobster shack to sample the local delicacy. Edgartown is filled with stately white clapboard sea captains' homes; Oak Bluffs is high Victorian; West Tisbury, classic colonial with the requisite white-spired church; and Menemsha is a fishing village with a picturesque harbour.

The more remote Nantucket is remarkably unchanged from the days when it was the whaling capital of the world. The town's cobbled streets, seamen's cottages and sea captains' mansions make up America's largest living colonial town. Beyond the town is a vision for romantics, a wild, untamed landscape of heather-covered moors, bound by great expanses of sandy beaches that make it easy to understand why the locals say that once you get Cape Cod sand in your shoes, you will surely return.

GETTING THERE
Copenhagen, on Denmark's eastern coast, straddles the islands of Sjælland (Zealand) and Amager. It has excellent connections by air, rail, road and sea. Frequent trains shuttle from Kastrup airport to the city centre in 14 minutes.

GETTING AROUND
There's a superb public transport system of buses, metro, waterbuses and trains (two children under 12 travel free with one adult fare) plus free-to-borrow city bikes.

WEATHER
Copenhagen enjoys four distinct seasons. July is usually the sunniest month, with long days and an average temperature of 22°C.

ACCOMMODATION
The Square is a very family-friendly design hotel, located on City Hall Square, with family rooms from £175; www.thesquarecopenhagen.com

DGI-Byens Hotel, near Tivoli, has modern decor and guests can use the Swim Centre; family rooms from £105; www.dgi-byen.dk

Danhostel is a central hostel, with en-suite family rooms from £65; www.danhostel.dk

EATING OUT
Stylish Copenhagen boasts many Michelin-starred restaurants and wine is seriously expensive. A good, child-friendly restaurant is Peder Oxe, around £15 per person for a meal.

PRICE FOR A FAMILY OF FOUR
£210–260 per day including accommodation, food and local travel.

FURTHER INFORMATION
www.visitcopenhagen.com

Carlsberg Contributions

The giant Carlsberg company is probably Denmark's most famous brand. In its philanthropic past, family wealth made a big contribution to the city's cultural assets, including the fabulous art and sculpture collection of the Ny Carlsberg Glyptotek. The company funded the creation of the Little Mermaid statue, ran Tivoli until a few years ago and paid for the restoration of the magnificent 17th-century Fredericksborg Castle in Hillerød, as well as founding the Museum of National History there.

MAGICAL AMUSEMENTS

WITH TIVOLI, THE WORLD'S MOST MAGICAL AMUSEMENT PARK, at its heart, canal boat sightseeing, city beaches, free bicycles to borrow, children's menus in restaurants, and museums with sections just for the kids, compact Copenhagen is a truly family-friendly city. Add fairytale castles and stories by Hans Christian Andersen and you have an ideal package for a great holiday.

Every summer, beach life opens up around the harbour – the city's water is clean enough to swim in – and teenagers can revel in a guided kayak trip that drops in on the "free city" of Christianshavn. Should it rain, the Experimentarium makes science huge fun (for adults, too) and the state-of-the-art Vandkulturhuset has great swimming pools and a spa. The Louisiana Museum of Modern Art has a children's wing, the National Museum a dressing-up box, the Danish Film Institute shows special children's movies and under-fours eat free in its café. The Tycho Brahe Planetarium is a must – home to the world's largest digital 3-D screen, its presentations of the night sky are utterly captivating.

Below (top to bottom): Children's wing in the Louisiana Museum of Modern Art; Rosenborg Palace; Changing of the Guard at Amalienborg Slot

The city's main draw is Tivoli, with more rides than you can fit into a day – from simple carousels to the twisting, towering, Demon rollercoaster, the heart-thumping Golden Tower vertical drop and the nail-biting Star Flyer – and traditional funfair attractions. It also has a lake, a marooned pirate ship, theatres, concert stages, restaurants, cafés, a stunning new aquarium and the most wonderful gardens. At night, 100,000 soft-glow lights (no neon here) turn the whole place into a fairyland. Tivoli brings out the child in everyone and it's right in the centre of town.

This magical city, with its medieval cobbled streets, trendy and traditional neighbourhoods, and leafy, café-lined squares is also a thriving cultural hub of spectacular art galleries and museums. The mile-long, pedestrianized Strøget, with its smaller off-shoot roads filled with wonderful treasure troves of beautifully designed goods, is a shopping heaven. Surrounded by green parks and flower-filled gardens, stately historical buildings and royal palaces sit comfortably alongside dynamic modern architecture – witness the Black Diamond, the daring waterfront addition to the 17th-century Royal Library, a perfect example of how old and new complement each other.

Above: The Oresund Bridge that stretches between Denmark and Sweden

SIGHTSEEING DIARY

July is peak season and sees the lively international Jazz Festival – ten days of free outdoor concerts and street parades city-wide. The Sand Sculpture Festival at Amager Beach Park also runs throughout July. You can see the main Copenhagen sights in three days, but to get a real feel for the city, five days is better.

Five Child-Friendly Days

Tivoli opens at 11am. Food is expensive inside, so take a picnic. If you want a break, be sure to get a return entry stamp. Tour the city by bike and visit the dramatic Black Diamond (part of the Royal Library). Return to Tivoli in the evening, when it is truly magical.

If the shops on Strøget don't grab the youngsters' attention, the street acts will. Turn off at Købmagergade for the Rundtårn, an observatory tower with great views. Café Hovedtelegrafen, in the Postal Museum, has crates of toys. Then head for Nyhavn and a sightseeing Netto boat tour to see the Little Mermaid.

Rosenborg Palace has a fairytale air and houses the Crown Jewels. Nearby, the National Gallery features a gallery for children, and the lake-filled park behind it has playgrounds. *Kongens Have* (King's Garden) is heaven for under-fives, with a playground and a puppet theatre in the afternoon (except Monday).

Visit another country! The elegant Oresund Bridge links Denmark with Sweden, and it is just 35 minutes by train to Malmö, a fascinating city. Alternatively, travel the 35 km (22 miles) north of Copenhagen to Humlebæk to see the Louisiana Museum of Modern Art, which has a fantastic children's wing.

Consider the superb National Museum or Danish Maritime Museum (fabulous model ships), but be sure to be at the Royal Palace, Amalienborg Slot, by noon for the Changing of the Guard. Spend the afternoon at the zoo, on a city beach, at the trendy Vandkulturhuset pools or gazing at the stars in the Planetarium.

Dos and Don'ts

☑ Remember that many museums are free on Wednesdays, and so is Ny Carlsberg Glyptotek on Sundays; none of the churches or parks charge entrance fees; there are free summer concerts on Friday evenings in Tivoli.

☒ Don't cross the road on red – Danes always wait for the little green man signal.

☑ Learn a few words of Danish – like *"hej"* (pronounced *"hi"*) for hello, and *"tak"* for thank you. Beer is *"øl"* (*"ool"*).

☑ Explore the side streets and squares off Strøget. Some of the most interesting little shops are minutes away from the main pedestrianized shopping street.

JAN
FEB
MAR
APR
MAY
JUN
JUL
DAY 1
DAY 2
DAY 3
DAY 4
DAY 5
AUG
SEP
OCT
NOV
DEC

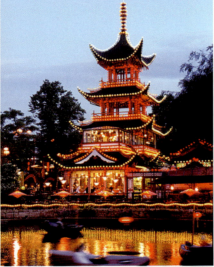

Main: Enjoying the bustling restaurants in the Nyhavn waterfront area

Top: Lights magically twinkle on the pagoda in Tivoli Amusement Park

Above: The Little Mermaid statue commemorating Hans Christian Andersen's famous tale

Below: Bikes lined up ready for use in the city centre

AUGUST

Where to Go: **August**

Across the northern hemisphere the long summer days continue. Get relief from the heat by visiting forests and lakes – they're not only picturesque but also help keep the temperature down a little. North Africa and the Middle East swelter at this time of year, making a visit often unbearably hot, but parts of the southern hemisphere such as Mozambique provide ideal warm, winter hideaways in beautiful surroundings. August also sees one of the world's greatest spectacles – the wildebeest migration on the Masai Mara in Kenya – and the world's largest and most famous celebration of the arts – the Edinburgh Festival. Below you'll find all the destinations in this chapter as well as some extra suggestions to provide a little inspiration.

FESTIVALS AND CULTURE

KANDY Performer at the Festival of the Tooth

UNFORGETTABLE JOURNEYS

BLACK FOREST Waterfall at Gutach

NATURAL WONDERS

MANU RAINFOREST Violet-fronted brilliant hummingbird

KANDY
SRI LANKA, ASIA

Colourful parades and dancing at the Festival of the Tooth

At the festival, Kandy's elephants are dressed in impressive finery, and torchlight parades light up the pretty city under the full moon.
See pp214–15

BOROBUDUR
INDONESIA, ASIA

An impressive Buddhist monument in central Java

A huge monument beautifully carved with stories from the life of Buddha – there's an incredible, misty view at sunrise and sunset.
See pp206–7

BLACK FOREST
GERMANY, EUROPE

If you go down to the woods today you're in for some fun

More welcoming than its name may suggest, the Black Forest is perfect for a driving tour, stopping off for walks, rich cakes and spas.
See pp204–5

THE AMALFI COAST
ITALY, EUROPE

A road that seems impossible, until you see it

Twisting madly around cliffs, with the Mediterranean laid out below, this is the definitive coast road – you need a head for heights.
www.divinecoast.com

> "The vistas here are as wild and visually captivating as they were when the park was first discovered."

MANU RAINFOREST
PERU, SOUTH AMERICA

Few parks can match Manu's incredible variety of wildlife

This is one of the most important national parks in the world – filled with sights to amaze – giant otters, caymans and flocks of macaws.
See pp196–7

LUCERNE
SWITZERLAND, EUROPE

Enjoy the International Music Festival in a breathtaking location

Ringed by the Alps and sitting beside a beautiful lake, this charming city is the perfect host for this renowned and enjoyable festival.
See pp200–1

> "Flower-carpeted meadows dotted with wooden chalets, leading down to the lakeside town."

TIEN-SHAN
KYRGYZSTAN, ASIA

Glaciers and soaring peaks on the roof of Asia

Treks lead you into an awesome knot of mountain ranges and remote valleys, camping beside vast, exquisite glacial lakes.
www.tien-shan.com

YELLOWSTONE
USA, NORTH AMERICA

A huge area of wilderness in the heartland of the USA

Yellowstone National Park is a great place to see bears, wolves, eagles, elk, steamy geysers and also herds of great thundering bison.
See pp202–3

BURNING MAN
USA, NORTH AMERICA

The ultimate festival of everything alternative

Every year 25,000 people create a temporary "city" in the Nevada desert for a week of art, dance, performance and participation.
www.burningman.com

NORTH CAPE
NORWAY, EUROPE

Under the midnight sun, at the far edge of a continent

Travel by ship up the Norwegian coast to Europe's most northerly point and take a midnight boat trip round its dramatic cliffs.
www.nordkapp.no

GLACIER BAY
USA, NORTH AMERICA

An inhospitable terrain, rich in flora and fauna

Amazing Alaska scenery: icebergs, glaciers and mountains – home to bears, deer and summer flowers.
See pp212–13

EDINBURGH
SCOTLAND, EUROPE

Non-stop entertainment at the world's largest arts festival

For three weeks, Scotland's capital is full of passion, creativity and fun, with everything from world-class performers to new comedy.
www.eif.co.uk & www.edfringe.com

TRANS-SIBERIAN
RUSSIA, EUROPE

Not just a railway, but a spectacular experience

The definitive train ride – lasting at least 10 days, through 12,880 km (8,000 miles) of Russia, Mongolia and China.
www.trans-siberian.co.uk

THE DOLOMITES
ITALY, EUROPE

The most spectacular summer alpine region in Europe

A world of steep, jagged crags, where in summer you can hike and climb the "iron ways" – precipitous mountain paths.
www.dolomiti.it

MASAI MARA
KENYA, AFRICA

A natural spectacle that is one of the world's great wonders

August is the peak time of the annual wildebeest migration, when over half a million animals pass through this giant reserve.
www.masai-mara.com

Weather Watch

❶ In August, Yellowstone should be warm during the day but chilly at night – even colder at high elevations. Risk of lightning storms in the afternoons.

❷ The dry season for Manu runs from Jun–Sep. In August at low altitudes it will get warm but it is more comfortable higher up. At any time of year it can go cold and rainy for a couple of days.

❸ Costa de la Luz sees a lot of sun – 12 hours a day in August. This may be just what you want but some may find it too much even with sea breezes.

❹ Mozambique's rainy season runs from November to March – August is warm and pleasant with cooling sea breezes, so not too hot at night either.

❺ Sri Lanka has a hot humid climate all-year round, but August is a drier month than most for Kandy and the monsoon rains are a couple of months away.

❻ It's winter in the southern hemisphere and Queenstown's position in the south of New Zealand's South Island means it experiences cool and probably damp weather at low altitudes but plenty of snow up in the Southern Alps.

LUXURY AND ROMANCE

MOZAMBIQUE Turquoise waters of the Bazaruto Archipelago

SIERRA DE GREDOS
SPAIN, EUROPE

Delicious summer evenings in green mountain valleys

One of Spain's secrets, these steep mountains contain castles and convents, beautiful old villages and lovely hotels in superb locations.
www.turismocastillayleon.com

VERONA
ITALY, EUROPE

A magical opera season in a Roman amphitheatre

Sit under the stars to hear classic Italian opera in an ideal setting – the giant Roman arena of Romeo and Juliet's city, Verona.
www.arena.it

THE HAMPTONS
USA, NORTH AMERICA

Celebrity-spot and shop till you drop on the Long Island shore

The little towns and superb beaches of Long Island are where the New York media crowd head each summer – rent a house and join the scene.
www.hamptons.com

MENDOCINO
USA, NORTH AMERICA

A beautiful, tranquil peace of old America

This wonderfully preserved little town on the California coast has hotels full of charm, fine food, a laidback feel and fabulous sunsets.
www.mendocino.com

MOZAMBIQUE
MOZAMBIQUE, AFRICA

White sands, romantic island hideaways and exotic culture

Relatively undiscovered by tourism, Mozambique has a unique mix of colonial history and ethnic culture as well as pristine beaches and coastline.
See pp210–11

"Brilliant turquoises and deep blues swirl together with jade tones, in contrast to the shimmering white sand beaches."

ACTIVE ADVENTURES

QUEENSTOWN Skiing at Cardrona Alpine Resort

QUEENSTOWN
NEW ZEALAND, AUSTRALASIA

The ultimate action and adventure holiday destination

If adrenaline thrills are what you're after, this is where you should be for skiing, white-water rafting, jet boating, bungy jumping and more.
See pp198–9

RIO SELLA
SPAIN, EUROPE

One of Europe's liveliest whitewater rivers

Every year an international kayaking race is held on this steep, vibrant river in Northern Spain, a real test of skill and speed.
www.descensodelsella.com

KNOYDART
SCOTLAND, EUROPE

Heather-clad hills, broad lochs, the essence of the Highlands

Hike across the hills to this peninsula, and Britain's only village with absolutely no road to it – though there are hotels and a pub.
www.knoydart-foundation.com

MOUNT COTOPAXI
ECUADOR, SOUTH AMERICA

A breathtaking test for the adventurous cyclist

Explore the stunning region around Mount Cotopaxi by mountain bike, where you can descend up to 3,000 m (9,800 ft) in one day.
www.ecuadorexplorer.com

FAMILY GETAWAYS

SLOVENIA Watching the sunset at Lake Bohinj

"The unspoiled countryside boasts everything from lush farmland and gushing rivers to thundering waterfalls and pristine lakes."

COLUMBIA RIVER
USA, NORTH AMERICA

A gorgeous inland utopia for windsurfers

The gorge of the Columbia in Oregon creates unique conditions for windsurfing – drawing fans and beginners from around the world.
www.el.com/to/hoodriver

SLOVENIA
SLOVENIA, EUROPE

Great value camping holiday in an undiscovered country

With a network of well-equipped camps in delightful woodland and simple rural settings, Slovenia is fully geared for camping holidays.
See pp216–17

COSTA DE LA LUZ
SPAIN, EUROPE

Undiscovered coastline that has much to offer

Ideal for an active holiday for children – but there's a lot for adults to enjoy: food, wines and culture galore.
See pp208–9

SENTOSA ISLAND
SINGAPORE, ASIA

Rides, beaches, shops and gardens on a pleasure island

Cable cars carry you to Singapore's theme-park island, with every kind of attraction – from Underwater World to lovely Orchid Gardens.
www.sentosa.com.sg

HOLY ISLAND
ENGLAND, EUROPE

A tiny island lost in time on the Northumbrian coast

Cut off at high tide, this little islet with its ancient ruined monastery is the highlight of a coast rich in castles, beaches and wildlife.
www.lindisfarne.org.uk

BRYCE CANYON
USA, NORTH AMERICA

Weird and wonderful scenery that never fails to fascinate

Famed for its bizarre stone pillars or "hoodoos", this Utah canyon can be seen by car or on paths that are a great first-taste of hiking for kids.
www.nps.gov/brca

For sheer wilderness, it doesn't get much better than this.

GETTING THERE
The closest international airport is Lima. From there, Cusco is a 40-minute flight. A further 40-minute flight aboard a small twin-engined plane will get you to Boca Manu. Then a motorized canoe takes you on the 90-minute trip down the Madre de Dios River to the lodge.

GETTING AROUND
In Cusco you can explore on foot. In the Park all your trips, on land or water, will be with a guide.

WEATHER
This is the dry season, and Park temperatures can reach a humid 31°C, with lows of 18°C. In Cusco, daytime temperatures average 20°C but drop sharply at night.

ACCOMMODATION
In Cusco, the centrally located Picoaga Hotel has doubles from £80; www.picoagahotel.com

The Manu Wildlife Center has accommodation in rustic cabins, with en suite facilities. The lodge offers 3-night packages for the round trip from Cusco for £650 per person, on a full-board basis; www.manu-wildlife-center.com

EATING OUT
Peruvian dishes include *arroz con pollo*, a spicy chicken and rice dish, and *lomo salteado*, fried beef with tomatoes, onions and potatoes. Food will be provided when staying in the park.

PRICE FOR TWO
£185–220 per day including accommodation in Cusco and in Manu National Park, food, and internal flights to the park.

FURTHER INFORMATION
www.peru-explorer.com

Giant Otters

One of the world's most endangered species, the giant otters that are found in Manu National Park are actually quite ferocious animals – fending off jaguars and killing caymans that cross into their nesting territory. The park was made a UNESCO World Natural Heritage Site in 1987. This has helped in some ways to stave off the reduction in numbers of these otters over the years, maintaining the clean water and fish stocks that are essential for the survival of the species.

Main: Group of red and green macaws take off from a claylick in Manu National Park
Above: Overlooking the misty rainforest **Inset:** Tufted capuchin in acrobatic pose
Top (left to right): Typical lodge accommodation; violet-fronted brilliant hummingbird; roots of palms in Manu Park; steering through the Madre de Dios River

LAND OF THE GIANT OTTER

The view over Manu National Park from the small, twin-engine plane that takes you to Boca Manu is humbling. Nearly 8,095 sq km (3,125 sq miles) of dense lowland tropical jungle and misty cloud forest, sloping up into the Andes, stretch out around you, crisscrossed by the sludgy brown waters of the Manu and Madre de Dios rivers. Manu National Park is the largest tropical park in South America, and home to an extraordinary diversity of plant and wildlife. More than 1,000 species of bird including the flamboyant, strutting Cock-of-the-Rock, 200 species of mammal, such as the giant otter, tapir and majestic jaguar, and more than 15,000 species of plant are found in this verdant jungle. All of this is remarkably preserved in pristine condition due to the inaccessibility of the area and careful controls and monitoring of the numbers now allowed to visit. The park is so isolated in parts that several indigenous groups from within have never had contact with outsiders.

Above: Manu River meanders through Manu National Park

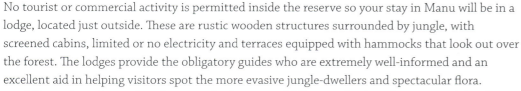

JAN
FEB
MAR
APR
MAY
JUN
JUL
AUG

PERUVIAN PARK DIARY

You will need at least three nights in Manu in order to fully experience all that the jungle has to offer. August is also an excellent time of year to visit the Andean region, so it's worth exploring the pretty colonial streets of Cusco. You could extend your trip with a visit to the Inca citadel of Machu Picchu (see pp152–3).

A Week in the Rainforest

DAY 1
Flights tend to arrive into Lima in the evening; if there's time, explore some of the capital's excellent museums.

DAY 2
Fly over the Andes to Cusco and spend the day exploring its churches and colourful markets.

DAY 3
A 40-minute flight aboard a small twin-engine craft will take you to Boca Manu, a small frontier town on the banks of the Manu River. From here a motorized canoe ploughs deep into the forest along the Madre de Dios River, to the Manu Wildlife Center. In the afternoon, explore the jungle in search of monkeys.

DAY 4
A pre-dawn start for the 25-minute boat trip to the macaw lick to see Amazon parrots and large macaws feasting on the clay. Later, climb the 34-m (110-ft) high platform over the rainforest canopy to observe the frantic dusk activity of the jungle fauna. Take a night hike to a tapir lick to watch them feed.

DAY 5
Head out onto the nearby Blanco Oxbow Lake in search of the resident giant otter family, and take a night-time boat trip on the Madre de Dios River, following the reclusive black caiman.

DAY 6
Emerging from the jungle by canoe at Boca Manu, take a flight back to Cusco and enjoy the dry air and laid-back atmosphere of this bustling town.

DAY 7
Fly back to Lima, or you could choose to extend your trip with a visit to the hidden Inca city at Machu Picchu.

Dos and Don'ts

☑ Make sure you take a good insect repellent and long-sleeved clothing. Mosquitoes here are large and persistent.

☒ Don't expect luxury. Accommodation here is basic, but you'll feel like you are in the heart of the jungle.

☑ Bring a good pair of binoculars. You may not get close enough to see some of the more elusive birds and mammals.

☑ Bring several changes of clothes for your time in the jungle – nothing dries in the humidity!

SEP
OCT
NOV
DEC

No tourist or commercial activity is permitted inside the reserve so your stay in Manu will be in a lodge, located just outside. These are rustic wooden structures surrounded by jungle, with screened cabins, limited or no electricity and terraces equipped with hammocks that look out over the forest. The lodges provide the obligatory guides who are extremely well-informed and an excellent aid in helping visitors spot the more evasive jungle-dwellers and spectacular flora.

Hiking along forested trails in search of tapir, and following the faint footprints of the elusive jaguar, brings out the adventurer in visitors. On the river, the boat becomes a silent viewing platform as everyone waits with bated breath for the slick head of a rare giant otter to emerge from the water, or for a black cayman to catch the light as it slides from the bank and into the mud. Ploughing deeper into the reserve aboard a long slender motor-canoe, the foliage becomes thicker, the humidity more intense, and the chattering of monkeys and birds and the steady hum of insects almost deafening. The scale and density of the jungle is breathtaking here. For sheer wilderness, it doesn't get much better than this.

AUGUST

TASMAN
SEA

Auckland

Wellington

NEW ZEALAND

Christchurch

PACIFIC
OCEAN

QUEENSTOWN   Dunedin

GETTING THERE
Queenstown is in Otago, on New Zealand's
South Island. International flights arrive into
Christchurch, where you can catch a domestic
flight on to Queenstown or hire a car.

GETTING AROUND
To really explore, you will need your own
transport – a 4WD vehicle is ideal. Walking is
the best way to get around the towns and cities,
and shuttle buses run out between the resort
towns and the ski slopes.

WEATHER
August is the peak of the ski season in the
Southern Alps, with reliable snow cover and
temperatures of -3°C to 15°C.

ACCOMMODATION
The award-winning Heritage Hotel, Queenstown,
is comfortable and has doubles from £70;
www.heritagehotels.co.nz

Cardrona Hotel in Wanaka is one of New
Zealand's oldest; doubles from £75;
www.cardronahotel.co.nz

Nugget Point, Queenstown, looks over
Shotover River, with doubles from £177;
www.nuggetpoint.co.nz

EATING OUT
The Bathhouse (www.bathhouse.co.nz) has
mains from around £25 and serves excellent
cuisine on the lakeshore.

PRICE FOR TWO
£190–230 per day including accommodation,
food, ski passes and hire car.

FURTHER INFORMATION
www.queenstown-nz.co.nz

The Arrowtown Gold Rush

Twenty minutes' drive from Queenstown is the old
gold-mining settlement of Arrowtown, where you can
still see many of the historic buildings of the 1860s
gold rush. Gold was discovered in the Arrow River in
1862, and within months the town's population grew
to 7,000, due to tales of fortunes made there. When
gold was found in the Shotover River, 5,000 men
turned up in the space of a few weeks, some venturing
on inland in search of the mother lode. When the
Europeans moved on to the West Coast in 1865,
Chinese miners moved in.

Main: Bungy jumping from "The Ledge" above Queenstown
Above (left to right): Parasailing on Lake Wakatipu; biking on The Remarkables; jet-boat on the Shotover River

Above: Shotover Street in Queenstown

ADRENALINE RUSH

WELCOME TO QUEENSTOWN, ADVENTURE CAPITAL OF THE WORLD. This place is a vast natural theme park where thrill-seekers can enjoy action-packed adventure; bungy jumping, white-water rafting, jet-boating and countless other head-rush experiences. The town is also the southern hemisphere's premier ski destination. A snow sports playground, set amid spectacular scenery, this buzzing lakeside resort town is the jump-off point for The Remarkables and Coronet Peak ski areas. An hour's drive along the twisty-turny Crown Range Road will take you to Wanaka – a more charming, less developed town on the shore of another deep, serpentine lake. From here you can reach further ski areas – Snow Park, Snow Farm, Cardrona and Treble Cone.

There is a good range of runs for all abilities across the Southern Alps, from adrenaline-pumping heli-ski, max vert and ungroomed powder to exhilaratingly steep chutes and undulating trails for intermediate skiers and long, groomed trails and sheltered bowls for beginners. The terrain parks at Cardrona and Snow Park are favourites with boarders; features include a super pipe, beginner pipe, ride wall and a snow skate area. Snow Farm is great for cross-country skiing, while Cardrona is famous for its excellent disabled ski facilities.

All this inspiring terrain action is set against the picture-postcard backdrop of lakes Wakatipu and Wanaka, The Remarkables mountain range and Mount Aspiring National Park. It is well worth making a detour for the scenery alone – try exploring Wanaka's back country areas by horse or mountain bike, kayaking along the winding rivers and across lakes, or travelling up through rugged Mackenzie Country to Aoraki (Mount Cook) – New Zealand's highest mountain. And when you tire of the slopes, which stay open until 10pm, you can bus back down to Queenstown to enjoy the appropriately lively après-ski – top-notch cuisine, bars, pubs and partying.

> A vast natural theme park where thrill-seekers enjoy action-packed adventure; bungy jumping, white-water rafting and countless other head-rush experiences.

Inset: Skiing at Cardrona Alpine resort
Below: Panorama of the Coronet Peak ski field

ADVENTURE DIARY

August is the best time to ski and board in the Southern Alps as it's the most reliable month for snow. Ten full days on the South Island will give you enough time to sample the ski fields of Queenstown and Wanaka and enjoy the spectacular scenery en route. For an extended trip, combine with a visit to the North Island (*see pp56–7*).

Ten Days of Southern Snow

Fly into Christchurch and rent a 4WD vehicle. Drive the 91 km (56 miles) up to Methven, where you can hit the slopes straightaway at Mount Hutt, then unwind in the town's cosy pubs, bars and restaurants. Spend the next day or two here, skiing or boarding.

Drive up to Mount Cook through Mackenzie Country, a 284-km (175-mile) journey through some of New Zealand's most spectacular scenery. Here you can take a scenic flight over the Southern Alps or heli-ski the Tasman Glacier.

It's an easy 212-km (130-mile) drive on to Wanaka for more skiing and boarding. Once there, you have a choice of four ski fields: Treble Cone, arguably one of the most spectacularly scenic resorts in the world; Cardrona, a high mountain renowned for its inspiring terrain and dry natural snow; Snow Park and Snow Field. For a break from the snow, there are some breathtaking walking tracks in nearby Mount Aspiring National Park.

Drive the 70 km (45 miles) to Queenstown via the Crown Range. Most of Queenstown's adrenaline-inducing activities can still be enjoyed in winter, including jet-boating, rafting and bungy jumping. If you haven't yet tired of all the snow, the ski fields to try here are Coronet Peak, the oldest and most developed, and The Remarkables, a true alpine area. Enjoy drinks overlooking Lake Wakatipu in the evenings.

Drive back to Christchurch, or extend your trip and either drive over Haast Pass to the West Coast glaciers, or head south to the cultured Victorian city of Dunedin.

Dos and Don'ts

✓ Bring your own ski clothing, but rent equipment to save you carrying it – unless you're a style-conscious snowboarder.

✗ Don't attempt to drive up high mountain roads and over passes without a 4WD vehicle and snow chains (you can rent them from petrol stations).

✓ Wear goggles and use sunscreen as reflected sunlight can be intense.

✓ Watch out for the cold southerly winds and remember that the north-facing slopes get the most sun.

JAN
FEB
MAR
APR
MAY
JUN
JUL
AUG
DAYS 1–2
DAYS 3–4
DAYS 5–6
DAYS 7–9
DAY 10
SEP
OCT
NOV
DEC

COSMOPOLITAN FAIRYTALE

WITH ITS FAIRYTALE TURRETS AND COVERED WOODEN BRIDGES, medieval Lucerne is one of the world's most beautiful cities. Surrounded by mountains on the western shore of the lake that shares its name, there can be few festival towns that enjoy such a setting.

The city's reputation as one of the leading international organizers of classical and contemporary music festivals is well established, as host of the renowned Lucerne International Festival of Music. Each year, during August and September, over 30 symphony concerts and up to 60 other events are held here, including plays and opera at the Lucerne Theatre. The striking waterside concert hall, the KKL, symbolizes the surprisingly cosmopolitan character of this charming medieval city. A modernist structure made of glass and steel, the KKL juts out into the lake, creating a most exciting and memorable concert experience. The terrace here is a great place from which to see the city, especially at night, when it really comes alive with the festival.

Below (top and bottom): Cogwheel railway; fresco on the exterior of a building in the Old Town

GETTING THERE
Lucerne (Luzern in German) is in the centre of Switzerland. International flights arrive into Zurich Airport, 60 km (37 miles) away. The journey takes one hour by car or train.

GETTING AROUND
Buy a Swiss Pass for all travel before you leave home. The city is well served by transport but is best explored on foot. Use the rail and ship network for trips to Mounts Pilatus and Titlis, and other lakeside towns.

WEATHER
August has an average daily temperature of 25°C with occasional cloudy days.

ACCOMMODATION
Art-Deco Hotel Montana has doubles from £160; www.hotel-montana.ch

Hotel Palace is one of the Leading Hotels of the World, with views of the Alps and doubles from £200; www.palace-luzern.ch

Grand Hotel National is a legendary hotel created in the 1870s by César Ritz and Auguste Escoffier; doubles from £230; www.national-luzern.ch

EATING OUT
Forget fondue and try *raclette*, a less well-known cheese and potato dish, at a traditional restaurant. Try Restaurant Schiff at Unter der Egg for traditional specialities; tel. (041) 418 52 52.

PRICE FOR TWO
£280–320 per day for accommodation, food, travel passes, tickets and entrance charges.

FURTHER INFORMATION
www.luzern.org
www.myswitzerland.com

The Sad Lion

Carved out of a cliff face by sculptor Bertel Thorvaldsen in 1819 is the Löwendenkmal, or Lion Monument. This commemorates the 700 Swiss Guards that were killed by the French in 1792 as they defended the Tuileries Palace in Paris during the French Revolution. Situated just northeast of Löwenplatz, the lion is depicted dying upon his shield, with a broken spear piercing its chest. The sad lion is one of Lucerne's biggest tourist attractions, so try to go early to avoid the large crowds that assemble later in the day.

Aside from the festival's many performances, diversions can also be found in cabaret shows, beer kellers and some exquisite shops. There are enough high-quality restaurants here to excite the most discerning gourmet, and museums to please the most ardent culture-seeker. This is a most manageable city, a delight to wander through on a bright, late-summer day.

Lucerne's much photographed landmarks, the Chapel Bridge and the Water Tower, originally formed part of the city's fortifications, and it is lovely to walk across the bridge, admiring the series of pretty painted panels that hang beneath the eaves. The old town is a good place to stop for a glass of wine or *Kafi Zwetschgen* (coffee and schnapps), especially on one of the three main squares, which are surrounded by historic houses with colourful frescoes.

Festival fatigue can easily be dispersed by a trip to the mountains, especially Mount Pilatus, which can be reached by the slow climb of the world's steepest cogwheel railway. At the top, gasp at the panorama laid out before you – flower-carpeted meadows dotted with wooden chalets, leading down to the lakeside town, where, as dusk falls, myriad lights begin to twinkle.

Above: Traditional steamer on Lake Lucerne

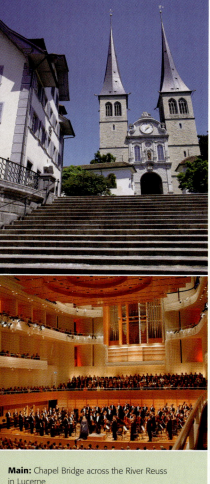

Main: Chapel Bridge across the River Reuss in Lucerne

Top: Renaissance Hofkirche

Above and below: Lucerne Festival Orchestra

MUSICAL CITY DIARY

To get the most out of a visit, you need at least five days, which will allow you to enjoy the Festival's concerts, take trips on the lake steamers and visit some of the outlying towns and the snow-covered mountains. The main events of the Festival commence with a grand firework display.

Five Days of Festivities

Cross the Chapel Bridge, originally erected in the 14th century and faithfully reconstructed after it was destroyed by fire in 1993. Walk through the old town, have a beer or a coffee beside the river, and then walk the city wall or visit the Picasso Museum. Later, enjoy a symphony, opera or ballet performance in the KKL centre.

For wonderful views, visit the summit of Mt Pilatus – take the trolley to Kriens and then the cable car to the summit. Come down via the world's steepest cogwheel railway to Alpnachstad, then return to Lucerne by rail or lake steamer. In the evening, enjoy another Festival event or eat out by the lake in one of the city's traditional hostelries.

Visit the Lion Monument, which Mark Twain described as "the saddest piece of stone in the world", then, perhaps, the nearby Glacier Garden, a geological phenomenon. After lunch, shop alongside the River Reuss before taking in another concert, ballet or light opera, or enjoying a leisurely sunset cruise on the lake.

To make the most of Lucerne's setting, take the train to Engelberg – from here, catch the funicular to Gerschnialp then two cable cars to Trübsee and Titlis-Stand. If you have the stomach for more, you can take another cable car across the glacier to Titlis where there is a panoramic restaurant.

Walk around the lake to the excellent Transport Museum. Afterwards, enjoy a lake cruise before trying out the lively bars of the Old Town in the evening.

Dos and Don'ts

✓ Sit on the left-hand side of the train from Zurich to Lucerne for a wonderful panorama of the Zürichsee.

✗ Don't be late – the Swiss take efficiency and service very seriously, so if you make appointments, be on time.

✓ Try the largely unknown but surprisingly good Swiss wines; Lizard and Faendant are two recommendations.

✓ The Lucerne Festival Academy often invites the public to watch opening rehearsals and concerts, free of charge.

JAN
FEB
MAR
APR
MAY
JUN
JUL
AUG
DAY 1
DAY 2
DAY 3
DAY 4
DAY 5
SEP
OCT
NOV
DEC

GETTING THERE
Yellowstone National Park is in the Rocky Mountain Range, USA. It is mainly located in the state of Wyoming. The closest major international airport is in Salt Lake City, Utah.

GETTING AROUND
Cars can be rented at the airport for the 515-km (320-mile) drive to Yellowstone. There are small airports closer to the park, with a 1–2 hour drive. Regional airports are found in Cody and Jackson, WY; Bozeman and Billings, MT; and Idaho Falls, ID. The West Yellowstone, MT airport is open from June–September.

WEATHER
August has daytime temperatures of up to 30°C but can drop below freezing at night. Thunderstorms are frequent.

ACCOMMODATION
All of the accommodation in the park is managed by Xanterra Parks and Resorts, with rooms in historic lodges, motels and cottages. Old Faithful Inn, Mammoth Hot Springs Hotel and Yellowstone Lake Hotel are popular choices; doubles from £75; www.xanterra.com

Budget accommodation, from £35 a night, may require sharing a bathroom.

EATING OUT
Restaurants range from elegant lodge dining to an Old West Cookout. There are many cafeterias and grills which also offer packed lunches.

PRICE FOR TWO
£115–150 per day including accommodation, food, car hire and park entrance charge.

FURTHER INFORMATION
www.nps.gov/yell/home.htm

Wonders of Yellowstone
Known as "Mi tsi a da zi", or "Rock Yellow River" to the Minnetaree tribe of Native Americans, the region's name was simplified by early fur trappers to Yellowstone. It took a major exploration by a forerunner of the US Geological Survey in 1871 to introduce the world to the wonders of the park. Accompanying that expedition were photographer William H. Jackson and artist Thomas Moran. Their images helped convince President Grant to set aside the land as the world's first National Park in 1872.

Main: Aerial view of the Grand Prismatic Spring in Yellowstone – the spring is around 120 m (380 ft) in diameter

WHERE THE BUFFALO ROAM

THE DUST RISES AS HEAVY HOOVES FALL, the older males stand guard, young calves stay close to their mother's side. Time comes to a standstill as you count ten, then twenty, then a hundred thundering herbivores; and you realize you are witnessing a primeval scene that once had all but vanished from the planet, but is now slowly returning – North American buffalo or bison on the move. You wait till the herd disappears into the valley below, then continue on your way, forever changed by the sheer magnitude of the wild beauty of Yellowstone National Park.

More than half a million years ago, a gargantuan volcanic explosion blanketed western North America in ash and scooped out a vast caldera 80 km long and 50 km wide (50 miles by 30 miles wide). Today that caldera, located just north of the spectacular Grand Teton Mountains, is green and lush with landscapes and ecosystems that are unique in the world. Stunning tableaux of green mountain meadows, wild rivers, azure lakes and snow-capped

Left (left to right): Majestic bull elk; plains buffalo grazing in the park; stripy least chipmunk stands alert; signpost for the Continental Divide – the ridge of mountains that runs from Alaska in the north to Mexico in the south

Left panel (top and bottom): Visitors on a horseback tour through the park; Old Faithful geyser

Above: Canary Spring, named after the yellow algae growing at its edge

JAN

FEB

MAR

APR

MAY

JUN

JUL

AUG

DAY 1

DAY 2

DAY 3

DAY 4

SEP

OCT

NOV

DEC

WILDERNESS DIARY

August days are long and warm, with the chance to participate in ranger-led tours and activities. It is possible to see the park's highlights in four days. Try to escape the crowds and explore the spectacular wilderness. Guided fishing and boating trips, naturalist-led outings, photo-safaris and overnight hikes are all available.

Four Days in the Parkland

Watch the spectacular eruption of Old Faithful, Yellowstone's most popular geyser, early in the morning when crowds are thin.

Stroll along the walkways at Upper Geyser Basin to see spouting geysers, steaming pools and bubbling springs. Be sure to see the colourful Morning Glory Pool.

Drive, or if you are feeling energetic walk, along the 32-km (20-mile) Grand Canyon of the Yellowstone, stopping frequently for breathtaking views of the waterfalls and magnificent, coppery-orange canyon.

Visit lovely, marshy Hayden Valley in the early morning and watch for herds of bison. Elk, grizzly bears, wolves, bald eagles and geese may also be seen from the road.

In the afternoon, join in one of the ranger-led daytime programmes offering guided nature and history walks. There are also evening slide-shows and talks offered at a variety of locations throughout the park.

Drive the length of Lamar Valley starting as the sun comes up, stopping frequently to look for bison, pronghorn antelope, bear and wolves in the valley and along the gently rolling hills.

Dos and Don'ts

✓ Stop in visitors' centres for park maps and brochures, get the latest information on wildlife viewing, and peruse the exhibits on this incredible wilderness park.

✗ Don't try to see too much in one go – limit your exploration to one section of the park each day and take along a packed lunch or have meals close-by.

✓ Try to be outdoors at dawn when there are no crowds, getting out of the car often to walk, hike, take tours and attend the ranger programmes available at the park.

✗ Don't be caught out by the changeable weather; dress in layers as it may be below freezing at dawn and over 30°C by mid-afternoon with a late-afternoon thunderstorm.

✓ Drive slowly, be patient and watch closely everywhere you go. Sometimes animals can be seen very close to the road.

peaks set the backdrop for an otherworldly landscape of 10,000 steaming fumaroles, geysers, bubbling mud pots and psychedelically coloured thermal springs (the colour is caused by pigmented bacterial growth in the cooler water at the edge of the pool).

This huge park preserves one of the most intact ecosystems in the United States. August is an ideal time to visit because although tourists are present in large numbers, they tend to congregate in the popular areas, so discovering the real wilderness beauty of Yellowstone is as simple as getting off the beaten path anywhere in the park. A walk along the South Rim Trail east from busy Artist Point leads you up a brief steep ascent that takes you far from the crowds and plunges you into a pristine world leaving civilization far behind. Following the gentle terrain of the canyon rim, the trail offers stunning views of the canyon, the Yellowstone River and the cascading cataract of lower falls. A turn on the short Lily Pad Lake Trail takes you further into the outback to the unspoiled splendour of the lily-covered lake where moose, bear and elk roam freely and the vistas here are as wild and visually captivating as they were when the park was first discovered.

FAIRY-TALE FOREST

GETTING THERE
Baden-Baden is the main entry point for the Black Forest. International flights arrive into Frankfurt, 170 km (106 miles) away and connected by train and bus.

GETTING AROUND
Germany has an excellent railway system – it is possible to explore this region entirely by trains and buses. However, the best way – with most flexibility – is to hire a car from the airport.

WEATHER
Temperatures vary between the mountains and the valleys but average between 15 and 20°C in August with sunny and mild days.

ACCOMMODATION
In Baden-Baden, Brenner's Park Hotel & Spa is one of Europe's grand old spa hotels; doubles from £270; www.brenners-park.de

Zum Hirschen Hotel in Staufen is a small, traditional hotel; family apartments from £120; www.hirschen-staufen.de

Hotel Brugger am See, beautifully set on the shores of Lake Titisee; family rooms from £100; www.hotel-brugger.de

EATING OUT
Try the local specialities such as *Schwarzwälder Schinken* (smoked bacon) – nothing tastes better than those sold in the gourmet delicatessens and butchers in the small villages.

PRICE FOR A FAMILY OF FOUR
£250–280 per day including accommodation, food and car hire.

FURTHER INFORMATION
www.blackforest-tourism.com

I F YOU EVER WANTED TO SEE THE ARCHETYPAL DARK LOOMING FOREST, somewhere out of a fairytale, the *Schwarzwald* (Black Forest) is your best opportunity. It is a remote and quaint yet friendly place to visit; a dreamy countryside with gentle rolling hills, torn apart by mountainous ridges and deep river gorges, then surprising you again with crystal clear lakes and welcoming traditional villages and farms. The area is a paradise for outdoor enthusiasts who want a great nature adventure – and it's perfect for families too. With a car you can get off the beaten track a little and cover a lot of ground, but try and combine the driving with a bit of walking – it's the only way to really see the countryside.

To make this easier, Germany has more than 20,000 km (12,425 miles) of walking trails and thousands of *Wandervereine*, free associations of people who regularly meet to walk the trails. The Black Forest is in a region rich in traditional German culture and there are hundreds of miles of well-marked hiking paths: do as the Germans do and enjoy some short walks, staying the night in village

Main: The Black Forest blooming with wildflowers

The Cuckoo Clock

The first cuckoo clock was built near Triberg in 1750 by Franz Anton Ketterer. The handcrafting of the clocks was a winter pastime for farmers, most of whom were traditionally wood-carvers, and this evolved into a huge industry around Triberg in the 19th century. The *Uhrenträger*, the traditional merchant who carried the clocks he made over winter across the Black Forest to city markets, can still be seen today, and there are *Uhrenträger* paths that you can follow for hikes.

inns. For longer hikes, you can even have your luggage transported ahead of you – a comfortable way of exploring the forest called *Wandern ohne Gepäck* (Hiking without Luggage). Many trails follow century-old paths; some of the more famous are loop trails that follow the paths – from Triberg via Titisee-Neustadt and then back to Triberg via Villingen-Schwenningen. Other great trails can be found in the nature preserve around the Feldberg or in the wooded valleys surrounding Baiersbronn. Along the way, you can discover the wildlife, visit museums or the traditional glass-blowing manufacturer at Wolfach, and stumble upon charming villages. Then there are the many beautiful lakes, especially the glacier lakes Titisee and Schluchsee, surrounded by spectacular mountains and each offering plentiful sports that will keep everyone entertained for hours.

If you make it into the mountains, this area is also famous for its hot springs and healthy waters, with top-notch spa retreats in Baden-Baden, Bad Dürrheim, Bad Herrenalb and Bad Liebenzell, to name just a few. Here you can indulge your weary limbs with an invigorating massage, relax in a steam sauna or simply float in a hot tub, drifting away into your own fairytale.

Above: Waterfall at Gutach in the Black Forest

JAN
FEB
MAR
APR
MAY
JUN
JUL

AUG

TOURING DIARY

August is the perfect time to visit the Black Forest as wildflowers are in bloom and the weather is sunny – great for getting out and about in the hills and mountains. When you tire of all this activity you can retreat to a luxurious spa and realise why this area used to be known as the "summer capital of Europe".

A Week in the Wild Wood

DAY 1

Start in Baden-Baden, one of the oldest towns in Germany and an elegant spa resort. Have a wander through the old town to marvel at the architecture. Indulge in spa luxury while you are here – enjoy the Kurhaus and other magnificent 19th-century spa buildings. Later, have a night out in the Baden-Baden casino, the setting for Dostoevsky's novel *The Gambler*.

DAYS 2–5

A leisurely drive through the Black Forest leads you southwest to quaint, dreamy villages such as Baiersbronn, Freudenstadt, Gutach, Staufen, Todtnau and Todtmoos, with its lovely Baroque church. Stop to explore as many of these as you want, taking in the beautiful surroundings. Near Todtnau is Hanglock-Wasserfall, one of the most beautiful waterfalls in the Black Forest.

Venture off the main roads to seek out walking trails, such as the loop from Triberg via Titisee-Neustadt and Villingen-Schwenningen, or try hang-gliding on the slopes of the Feldberg. For something a little more sedate, visit the open-air museum at Gutach, which offers a fascinating look into the region's rural history.

DAYS 6–7

Take a swim in the crystal clear waters of lakes Titisee and Schluchsee, where you can also enjoy a number of beach and water sports.

Spend a day at Europa-Park, a huge theme park with roller coasters such as "Enzian" – sure to thrill both young and old alike. Drive on to Freiburg, a hip but romantic university town with inviting pubs, restaurants and a breeze of French *savoir-vivre*. Alternatively, relax in another of the region's spa towns – Bad Dürrheim, Bad Herrenalb or Bad Liebenzell.

Dos and Don'ts

✓ Look out for good *Schwarzwälder kirschtorte*, Black Forest gateau – moist and not too sweet, made with fresh whipped cream and cherries – at a *konditorei* or café, where cakes are always homemade.

✗ Don't drink too much of the *Kirschwasser* offered in souvenir shops, restaurants and bars: it may taste pleasantly fruity, but is, in fact, a quite strong cherry-based schnapps.

✓ Do buy a cuckoo clock, even if it is much more expensive than at home. This is as authentic as it gets and most local products are much more tasteful than the ones for export.

SEP
OCT
NOV
DEC

Top: Women dressed in the national costume of the Black Forest

Above: Dining on the streets of Freiburg

Below: Traditional timber-framed houses

Left panel (top to bottom): Trekking near Waldau; paragliding in the Black Forest region; families enjoying the alpine rollercoaster "Enzian" at Europa-Park

GETTING THERE
Borobudur is on the island of Java, in Indonesia. International flights arrive into Jakarta, which is linked to Yogyakarta and Solo domestic airports, both about 40 minutes from Borobudur by car.

GETTING AROUND
Frequent local bus services run throughout the region and metered taxis can be hired. The site itself is best explored on food and a shuttle train runs from the entrance, around the temple.

WEATHER
The temperature in Java varies little, averaging around 27°C.

ACCOMMODATION
Duta Guest House, Yogyakarta, is set in tropical gardens and has been traditionally decorated; doubles from £7; www.dutagardenhotel.com

Grande Mercure Yogyakarta, a colonial-style hotel with large, bright rooms; doubles from £30; www.mercure.com

Amanjiwo is a super-luxurious resort, with beautiful views of Borobudur; doubles from £350; www.amanresorts.com

EATING OUT
Rice is an intrinsic part of Indonesian cuisine. *Warung* (food stalls) are a great place to try local food such as *sate* (grilled meat) and *mie goreng* (fried noodles) – dishes usually cost less than £1.

PRICE FOR TWO
£40–60 per day including accommodation, food and entrance charges, although it can rise to much more.

FURTHER INFORMATION
www.tourismindonesia.com.

Mount Merapi
Nearby Mount Merapi, the dramatic volcano viewed from Borobudur, means "Mountain of Fire" and is revered as sacred. It is 2,914 m (9,616 ft) high, and plumes of smoke are often visible. There was considerable fluctuating volcanic activity during May 2006 causing thousands of villagers to flee the area. It stabilized after a lava dome that was forming at its peak collapsed. Merapi is thought to have erupted in the 9th century, causing ash to cover Borobudur, which left it undiscovered for a thousand years.

Main: Temple of Borobudur looking towards Merapi volcano
Above (top to bottom): Detail of the stone carving at Borobudur; large Buddha image with stupas in background; monks at the shrine; intricately carved entrance at Borobudur

MONUMENTAL ADVENTURE

Travelling through the lush plantations and terraced rice fields of central Java, you don't see Borobudur until you arrive at the gateway to the monument. Then, through the flame trees and palm groves, it suddenly materializes, a solid mass of grey stone. It's only as you climb the first of nine levels of the huge structure that you make out its towers, niches and carved panels, topped by 72 stupas and a final, enormous central stupa.

Borobudur is one of the world's largest religious monuments. It represents Mount Meru, the mythical Hindu cosmic mountain. This earthly manifestation of the universe was built with a million-and-a-half blocks of volcanic andesite in the 8th century; a magnificent feat of devotion. You can circumambulate it in stages, as pilgrims do, starting at the five square terraces, proceeding around three circular ones and culminating at the uppermost stupa, where you can breathe in the beauty of the surrounding green countryside.

Above: Food for sale in the market at Borobudur

JAN

FEB

MAR

APR

MAY

JUN

JUL

AUG

JAVANESE DIARY

Although it is often humid, the skies in August tend to be clear as the rains have long finished. Yogyakarta is a good place to base yourself during your visit as it is only 40 minutes away from the site and will enable you to explore the surrounding region. To extend your trip, Bali is easy to reach from Java *(see pp124–5)*.

Four Days Among the Ruins

Get to Borobudur before 6am, so that you can enjoy the mystical ambience that surrounds it at sunrise. Spend the day walking the 5 km (3 miles) around the levels. Walk clockwise and look at the reliefs in the lowest sphere, which depict daily life. Hold off getting to the top until lunchtime, when the tour groups disperse. This will allow you to contemplate the empty stupa in relative peace.

Spend the rest of the day exploring the surrounding countryside, perhaps by elephant. Return to the temple before 6pm to see the beautiful sunset.

Spend the day exploring Yogyakarta. Head first to the old city, where you will find the Kraton, an elegant palace still in use today. Enjoy lunch at a *warung* (food stall) before exploring the shops – the town is a major centre for Javanese art so a great place to pick up batik. In the evening, watch a traditional puppet show or seek out a music or drama performance.

Head back into the countryside to visit the small temple of Candi Mendut, which is thought to have been built as a pointer to Borobudur. From here, you can travel on to the Hindu temple of Prambanan. From May to October, during the full moon, there are performances of the *Ramayana* from 7:30pm – 9:30pm. If you are there during this time, stay to watch the traditional dancing and soak up the lively ambience.

Return to Borobudur to further explore the ruins or visit the quiet town of Surakarta, home to two royal palaces and the biggest batik market on the island.

Dos and Don'ts

✓ Remember the gates don't open until 6am so consider taking a special sunrise tour to enable you to enter early.

✗ Don't forget that this is a sacred Buddhist monument, even though Java is now Islamic.

✓ Dodge the tour groups by taking a snack and staying on site when they go to lunch.

✓ Take a local guide to describe the carvings – this will help you gain a more thorough understanding of the monument.

Covered in volcanic ash and jungle for a thousand years before it was rediscovered by Thomas Stamford Raffles in 1814, Borobudur's power lies in its five levels of sublime carvings. Be prepared for a long walk (5 km/3 miles) as you examine the images at the lower levels, which depict daily life in the 8th century, showing village activities, fishermen, animals, cooking and washing. Further up are dedications to the life of the Buddha, who is shown wearing earrings and necklaces as worshippers bring him gifts and musicians play their instruments. At the upper levels, the smaller stupas contain meditating Buddhas but, at the top, the central stupa is mysteriously empty, suggesting *nirvana*, the ultimate state of nothingness. Emerging from this, with just the sky above you and the plains stretching out below towards the awesome Merapi volcano, the most active on earth, you will suddenly feel liberated.

The serenity is shortlived as Indonesians come here to play music or stroll with friends – it is the country's most popular site and no longer a religious monument. But, as you return through the tropical countryside, you cannot help but feel that you have had a vision of the divine.

GETTING THERE
The Costa de la Luz is at the southernmost tip of Spain, facing the Atlantic, about 130 km (80 miles) from Seville. The airports at Seville and Jerez both receive international flights.

GETTING AROUND
There are good fast train services between Madrid, Seville, Jerez and Cádiz, but to get further you need to hire a car.

WEATHER
August is one of the hottest times of the year, with an average temperature of 29°C, but the strong Atlantic winds provide cool nights at around 18°C. There are also occasional storms.

ACCOMMODATION
Hotel Sindhura is situated in the hills above Cádiz, with beautiful views of the surrounding countryside; family rooms from £75; www.hotelsindhura.com

Hotel Casa Grande is a charming place to stay in the historical centre of Jerez; family rooms from £95; www.casagrande.com.es

Hotel Porfirio is a short walk from Zahara Beach, with an excellent traditional restaurant; family rooms from £115; www.hotelporfirio.com

EATING OUT
A highlight of the local cuisine is the great fresh fish and seafood, especially tuna, straight out of the sea and cooked simply.

PRICE FOR FAMILY OF FOUR
£200–240 per day including accommodation, food, entrance charges and car hire.

FURTHER INFORMATION
www.andalucia.com

The Sherry Story
Sherry's distinctive flavour is traditionally attributed to the rare white *albariza* soils found around the mouth of the River Guadalquivir, and real sherry is only produced in Jerez and nearby towns like Sanlúcar de Barrameda, Chipiona and Puerto de Santa María. Large-scale production has always been associated with Britain, hence the English names of many of Jerez's sherry barons and their bodegas. Heavier sherries like *olorosos* and *amontillados* have traditionally been mainly for export, with locals preferring the lighter, dry *finos*.

Main: Kite-surfing on the Costa de la Luz
Above (top to bottom): Arcos de la Frontera perched on a hilltop; steep staircase winds up a narrow street in Arcos de la Frontera; horses in the wetlands of the Coto Doñana

ANCIENT ANDALUCÍA

Tight clusters of old, square-edged white houses and churches, from a distance looking like a child's building blocks, cling to the tops of lonely hills and crags across southern Andalucía, their whiteness and their red-tiled roofs picked out sharply in the fierce heat against a brilliant blue sky. These are the *pueblos blancos*, the "white villages", all uniformly whitewashed in line with old Moorish tradition. The words *de la Frontera* in many place names refer back to the times when this was indeed the frontier between Christian and Muslim Spain, and these villages were built – by one side or the other – as semi-fortresses, huddled together for safety in locations that sometimes seem to defy all logic. Each village is a maze of narrow lanes that wind, climb and fall, their whiteness offset by vibrant red flowers. And, far below, is what is now called the Costa de la Luz, in recognition of its exquisitely clear light – a line of great, broad beaches facing the windy Atlantic and washed by crashing surf.

Above: Playing in the clear waters near Cadiz town

JAN

FEB

MAR

APR

MAY

JUN

JUL

AUG

COASTAL DIARY

This area offers a unique combination of open beaches, surf, wild landscapes, whitewashed hilltop villages, rich Andalucían culture and great cuisine. It is at its liveliest in high summer, but is not usually overcrowded. A week's visit will provide ample time to enjoy the region's most special attractions.

A Week of Sun and Beaches

Get into the mood with a day in Jerez: make your way to the Spanish Riding School by 11am for a tour of the stables before the "Equestrian Ballet" at noon.

Have a long lunch accompanied by some chilled *fino* (a very dry sherry). Later, visit the Cathedral and the Moorish castle before joining the evening *paseo* (stroll).

DAY 1

Drive to Sanlúcar de Barrameda to catch the 10am boat for the trip upriver into the Coto Doñana Nature Reserve, which you can explore on a guided walk. Afterwards, continue down to the charming little port of Chipiona.

Spend the afternoon touring some of the *pueblos blancos* that are scattered across hilltops and often-sheer crags: head east to Arcos de la Frontera then climb through the oak woods around El Bosque to Ubrique. Alternatively, seek out one of the great beaches for sandcastle-building and swimming in the sea.

DAYS 2–3

Head south through Medina Sidonia to Vejer de la Frontera, with its old Moorish town gates. Spend the afternoon on the endless beach at Zahara de los Atunes, to the south.

Drive down to Tarifa and take a whale-watching trip in the Straits of Gibraltar. Afterwards, try windsurfing or go for a horse ride in the dunes.

DAYS 4–5

A day for total relaxation by the beach. In the evening, enjoy freshly cooked fish by the sea.

DAY 6

Head towards the airport for your flight home, via Cádiz for a last late lunch overlooking the port and the clear-blue sea.

DAY 7

Dos and Don'ts

☑ Get in tune with the local clock – lunchtime is from 2pm, and restaurants serve dinner after 9pm.

☑ Use plenty of high protection-factor sun lotion. The combination of sun and Atlantic winds can be very powerful.

☑ Try to visit the Spanish Riding School in Jerez on a Tuesday, Thursday or Friday, when there are spectacular performances of traditional horsemanship.

☒ Don't be put off by the full-time windsurfing cognoscenti at Tarifa – have a go at it yourself.

Much less well-known than Spain's Mediterranean coasts, this area nevertheless offers one of the most distinctive mixes of character and landscape anywhere in Andalucía. Its two main towns offer a complete contrast – Jerez de la Frontera, once a Moorish fortress, but long the capital of sherry and now filled with elegant *bodegas* that give it a special air of gracious living; and Cádiz, the oldest city in western Europe, a salty sea port with streets full of echoes of voyages of discovery. Just to the north across the River Guadalquivir is the Coto Doñana, a vast expanse of wetland that is home to some of Europe's rarest wildlife, including lynxes and flamingoes. Southwards, the long beaches run down to the old Moorish citadel of Tarifa. The meeting of the Atlantic and Mediterranean in the straits is also a prime feeding-ground for whales and dolphins, and a trip from Tarifa out to see them, with the mountains of Morocco as a backdrop, is an unforgettable experience.

Beyond all these attractions, the Costa de la Luz is also an ideal place just to relax. Beach towns like Zahara de los Atunes, "Of the Tuna", are still fishing villages, and as you sample the local delicacies you can find an easygoing friendliness that often seems lost elsewhere.

ARCHIPELAGO TREASURES

Long one of southern africa's least known destinations, Mozambique is rapidly gaining a reputation as one of the continents most upmarket and alluring destinations. Its magnificent coastline is fringed by pristine islands, their white sands dotted with palm trees and crisscrossed by centuries-old footsteps from trading centres as distant as Goa, Macau and Arabia.

The colours of the Bazaruto Archipelago – the most accessible of the island groups – are truly mesmerizing. From above, brilliant turquoises, aquas and deep blues swirl together with green and jade tones, all in stunning contrast to the shimmering white sand banks and beaches.

About 1,400 km (870 miles) north is the Quirimbas Archipelago, a chain of remote islands and islets strewn offshore in Mozambique's uppermost corner. Renowned in ancient times as trading hubs for ivory and ambergris, these islands now attract divers and visitors to a handful of exclusive and romantic luxury lodges. Daily life continues here much as it has for centuries. Women clad in brightly coloured *capulanas*

Main: Fishermen's nets lie out to dry outside a church on Mozambique Island

GETTING THERE
Mozambique is situated on Africa's southeastern coast. The closest major international airport is in Johannesburg, South Africa. There are frequent flights connecting Johannesburg with Maputo, Mozambique's capital.

GETTING AROUND
From Maputo, internal flights connect to the Bazaruto Archipelago and the northern town of Pemba, from where the Quirimbas islands are an easy onward hop via charter boat or small plane.

WEATHER
Mozambique in August is sunny, dry and warm, with daytime temperatures averaging 24°C.

ACCOMMODATION
Hotel Polana, Maputo offers colonial-style luxury; doubles from £90; www.serenahotels.com

Benguerra Lodge in the Bazaruto Archipelago has intimate and luxurious island chalets; doubles from £450, full board; www.benguerra.co.za

O Escondidinho on Mozambique Island has simple accommodation; doubles from £30; www.ilhatur.co.mz

Vamizi Island Lodge in the Quirimbas Archipelago is wonderfully romantic and remote; doubles from £370 full board; www.vamizi.com

EATING OUT
Delicious grilled seafood is available from £5. On the islands, lodges offer the best dining.

PRICE FOR TWO
£150–300 per day including food, entertainment and accommodation.

FURTHER INFORMATION
www.mozambiquetourism.co.za

Mozambique Island

Mozambique Island is a melting pot of cultures, with 17th-century colonial buildings overshadowing modest reed huts, while mosque calls echo near Hindu temples and dhows sail along ancient sea routes. The island's prosperity lasted until the late 19th century, when gold and diamond booms in South Africa and the development of new ports put the island into a slow decline. The island quietly crumbled until 1991, when it was designated a UNESCO World Heritage Site.

(wraps) and headscarves wade out into the shallows to harvest clams; skilled craftsmen build dhows using age-old techniques; fishermen haul their catches onshore using handwoven nets; the days begin gently, with the soft pink hues of sunrise filling the Indian Ocean skies.

Floating on its own along the expanse of coastline between the Bazaruto and Quirimbas archipelagos is tiny Mozambique Island, once an affluent port stop along the trading routes to the east. Today, the empty streets of old Stone Town echo with the footsteps of bygone centuries, while cobwebbed churches keep watch over now-quiet *praças* (squares), their silence broken only by the occasional sounds of children playing and the calls of a nearby mosque.

Well removed geographically and culturally from Mozambique's tropical island idylls is the modern coastal capital, Maputo. Here, wide avenues are lined with flowering trees, and colonial-era buildings peek out between bland block-style apartments. At night, a fusion of Latin and African rhythms fuels the city's legendary nightlife, filling the streets with an addictive beat. Still a little-known jewel on a vast continent, Mozambique's many treasures are just waiting to be discovered.

Above: Turquoise waters at the Bazaruto Archipelago

ISLAND LUXURY DIARY

One of Africa's most exciting destinations, Mozambique is still relatively undiscovered by tourism, which adds to its charms. Allow at least seven to eight days to get a taste of the country and relax on the islands. In addition to great weather, August also offers favourable conditions for diving.

Eight Days of African Delights

DAY 1
Arriving in Maputo, rest up at your hotel before setting off in a *laranjinha* – one of Maputo's bright yellow and red, impeccably-maintained tuk-tuks – for a sightseeing jaunt around town. The city is great for craft shopping – the market in front of Hotel Polana is a good place to start, but bargain hard. Later on, soak up the lively atmosphere from a street-side café.

DAY 2
Visit the National Museum of Art, the Núcleo de Arte or the studio of famed artist Malangatana in the outlying suburbs. Charter a vintage *habana* car for a guided evening out sampling Maputo's famed nightlife.

DAY 3
Head to the airport early for an island connection to the Bazaruto Archipelago, where you may have the chance to see dugong (large marine mammals). Alternatively, fly north to Pemba, from where you can continue on to the Quirimbas Archipelago, formed of 32 stunning coral islands. For a cheaper alternative, stay in Pemba and take day trips to the islands.

DAYS 4–5
Relax on the islands, diving, beach walking, sunbathing or lazing in a hammock, followed by evening candlelight dinners on the beach. Enjoy fantastic fresh seafood and the quiet isolation of it all.

DAYS 6–8
Take a charter flight to Mozambique Island. Stroll around the island's northeastern tip at sunset, when the massive walls of São Sebastião fort and the restored governor's palace are bathed in light. Visit the island's southwestern tip at sunrise, when the beach bustles with fishermen repairing their nets. Explore old Makuti Town before heading back to the mainland.

Dos and Don'ts

☑ Most lodges come with billowing mosquito nets over the beds – be sure to sleep under them.

☑ Take a Visa card if possible as it is often the only card accepted at ATMs.

☑ Many hotel staff speak English, but learning a few phrases in Portuguese (the official language) is helpful and appreciated.

☒ Don't wear skimpy beachwear away from the beach – be sure to cover up in town.

☑ Mozambique is large, so if time is limited, focus on either the south or the far north, rather than trying to see both.

Top: Central market in Maputo

Above: Makua woman in traditional white face-paint

Below: Diving with a potato cod and a lionfish off the Mozambique coast

Bottom: Young impala feeding

JAN
FEB
MAR
APR
MAY
JUN
JUL
AUG
SEP
OCT
NOV
DEC

GETTING THERE
Gustavus airport, 16 km (10 miles) from Bartlett Cove Park, is accessed via Juneau International Airport, 95 km (60 miles) away. Ferries connect Juneau, Gustavus, and Bartlett Cove, but many visitors arrive by cruise ship.

GETTING AROUND
Shuttle buses connect Gustavus with the Bartlett Cove Park, for forest hiking, but the best wildlife viewing is from cruise ships, tour boats and kayaks.

WEATHER
In August, Glacier Bay is cool and often rainy, with occasional sunny periods.

ACCOMMODATION
Nearby Gustavus offers a selection of B&Bs, guesthouses and lodges such as Annie Mae Lodge; doubles from £80; www.anniemae.com

Apart from camping, park accommodation is limited to the Glacier Bay Lodge at Bartlett Cove, from £200 per person including all meals and a Glacier Bay day cruise; www.visitglacierbay.com

In Juneau, try the fabulous Alaska Wolf House B&B, from £65; www.alaskawolfhouse.com

EATING OUT
Meals are available at Glacier Bay Lodge, as well as on cruise ships and day tours, and Gustavus has a couple of small eateries and food shops.

PRICE FOR CRUISES
Cruise packages cost between £125–250 per day. Independent travellers should expect to pay from £150 per person per day (not including £75–125 for return ferries or flights), but can choose their own itinerary.

FURTHER INFORMATION
www.nps.gov/glba

Disaster in Lituya Bay
After a magnitude 8.3 earthquake on 9 July 1958, the occupants of three fishing boats saw a huge mass of the Gilbert Inlet rock wall collapse into Lituya Bay, creating the highest tsunami in recorded history. The wave may have been as high as 500 m (1,700 ft) and travelling at 320 km per hour (200 mph). Two ships, the *Badger* and the *Dunmore*, were picked up by the wave and smashed to pieces and only the crew of the *Badger* survived. The *Edrie*, seeing the danger just in time, turned into the wave, miraculously riding over the top.

Main: Alaska cruise ship in Glacier Bay

Above (left to right): Exploring Alsek Lake by kayak; hiking near Fern Harbor, Glacier Bay National Park

Above: Humpback whales breaching in unison, Reid Inlet.

BACK TO THE ICE AGE

HAD HE BEEN INTERESTED, Captain George Vancouver, who charted the waters of Icy Strait in 1794, could have seen all of Glacier Bay in about an hour. In those days, however, this 8-km-long indentation in the 160-km (100-mile) long, 32-km (20-mile) wide, and 1,350-m (4,450-ft) thick Grand Pacific Glacier was considerably less intriguing than it became over the next two centuries. By the time John Muir reached the site in 1879, that indent had grown to about 50 km (31 miles) long and today, due to further melting, Glacier Bay now stretches about 115 km (72 miles).

The dynamic ecosystems created by such a dramatic two-century meltdown demonstrate the natural cycles working to recolonize landscapes recently released from the grip of an icy blanket. As a result, a trip up Glacier Bay today becomes a journey back to the last Ice Age. At Bartlett Cove, near the entrance, mature spruce and hemlock trees shelter a layer of rich, decomposed vegetation. Cruising up the bay, however, the pioneer plant communities grow younger and sparser and the rock becomes more prominent until the boat approaches the face of the Grand Pacific Glacier, land-bound behind a field of barren glacial moraine.

These ever-emerging landscapes also create a changing wilderness tableau, and on an optimum day, cruise passengers will see the spouting and splashing of breaching whales, hear the cries of sea birds, watch comical sea otters play and bald eagles wheel overhead and perhaps even a brown bear methodically plodding along the shore. But, when the boat pulls up to Margerie Glacier, the real thrills begin as a massive block of ice dislodges from the glacier face and slides silently into the sea. A second or two later, comes the thunderous crack of the breaking ice, followed after a few more seconds by a line-up of swells that cause the boat to bob up and down like a cork. It's probably safe to say that a lesson on wave physics has never been more captivating.

> *"I saw the berg-filled expanse of the bay… a solitude of ice and snow and newborn rocks – dim, dreary, mysterious."*
>
> John Muir

Below (left to right): Brown bear foraging on the shoreline, Glacier Bay; sweetpeas in bloom, Glacier Bay **Inset:** Glacier calving with a spectacular splash

GLACIER DIARY

Glacier Bay is famed for its interest to environmentalists as a glimpse of post-Ice Age development. But, for the visitor, little can compare to seeing a house-sized block of ice crashing into the water or huge humpback whales seemingly defy gravity as they break the surface of the water. August is a great time to visit the Bay as the days are long and cool.

Five Days in the Icy Bay

DAY 1 Explore Juneau, Alaska's capital city, visiting the Alaska State Museum and the Last Chance Mining Museum.

Later, ride the Mount Roberts tramway for unrivalled views of Juneau's surrounding peaks and waterways.

DAY 2 Splurge on a thrilling morning helicopter tour to the Juneau Icefield, then head for the Mendenhall Glacier, north of town, perhaps stopping en route at the Alaska Brewing Company and the lovely Glacier Gardens.

DAY 3 Fly to Gustavus or take a ferry to Bartlett Cove and spend the afternoon exploring the rainforest trails to look for wildlife and scan the sea for a glimpse of passing humpbacks, minke whales and orcas.

DAY 4 Enjoy a day cruise up Glacier Bay, past towering cliffs and frosted peaks, to the face of Margerie Glacier, where you can marvel at the sight and sound of great ice blocks calving into the sea.

DAY 5 Join a guided kayaking tour to the Beardslee Islands to explore small, secluded coves and get really close to nature. Under your own steam you get to see bears, seals and colourful tide pools from a different perspective.

Dos and Don'ts

✓ Understand a bit about ice and glacier dynamics. When a glacier calves, it doesn't much care what's admiring it from below. Boaters – especially kayakers – should stay at least 500 m (1,600 ft) from glacier faces.

✗ Don't cover yourself with pepper spray hoping to repel bears. The product is only meant to be sprayed into the bear's eyes as a last resort.

✓ Remember to bring a good, strong bug repellent, which will preserve your sanity amidst the swarms along the shoreline.

✓ Advise park rangers of your itinerary before hiking or kayaking in the park backcountry.

JAN
FEB
MAR
APR
MAY
JUN
JUL
AUG
SEP
OCT
NOV
DEC

Above: Panoramic view of a tea plantation in the hills of Matale near Kandy

GETTING THERE
Kandy is in central Sri Lanka. International flights arrive into Colombo, the capital, 116 km (72 miles) away. Buses, trains and taxis connect to Kandy from Colombo airport.

GETTING AROUND
Kandy is easy to navigate on foot. Alternatively, tuk-tuks and taxis are useful for getting around.

WEATHER
In August, the temperature ranges from 21–28°C. Kandy is cooler and more prone to rain than the coastal areas.

ACCOMMODATION
Spica Holiday Home, a small and homely guesthouse with beautiful panoramic views; doubles from £13; www.spica.go2lk.com

The Hotel Tree of Life is an eco-friendly resort with a unique architectural design; doubles from £45; www.hoteltreeoflife.com

Mahaweli Reach, close to the Temple of the Tooth, has lovely rooms with river or garden views; doubles from £75; www.mahaweli.com

EATING OUT
Sri Lankan food typically comprises hot curries, rice and chicken- and fish-based dishes. These are often accompanied by *sambol* (a mix of coconut, chillies, and spices). A typical meal will cost around £2.

PRICE FOR TWO
£60–110 per day including accommodation, food, local transport and entrance charges.

FURTHER INFORMATION
www.kandycity.org

The Legend of the Tooth

The Temple of the Sacred Tooth Relic (Sri Dâlada Mâligâwa) is Kandy's prime attraction. It houses the most revered Buddhist object – the left canine tooth of the Buddha. Legend has it that after the Buddha was cremated the tooth was salvaged from his funeral pyre. In AD 313, to protect the tooth from enemies, the King of Kalinga concealed it in the hair of his daughter who took it to Sri Lanka.

HONOURING THE TOOTH

The ANCIENT RELIGIOUS CAPITAL OF BUDDHISM IN SRI LANKA, Kandy is home to the famed Temple of the Tooth, which enshrines within its sanctum the canine of the Lord Buddha. Pilgrims, clad in white, unstitched (and therefore unpolluted) cloth and bearing white blossoms, visit throughout the year. The temple itself was originally built of wood and sponsored by the Kandyan kings between 1687 and 1707 but it was destroyed during the colonial wars of the 18th century and later rebuilt in stone. Serenely positioned at the edge of Lake Kandy, the cluster of buildings with their sloping red tiled roofs are unobtrusive and austere. Their interiors are a sharp contrast – elaborate in design, they make use of lacquer, ivory and wood with inlay work. The tooth itself sits in a gold lotus flower, encased in a jewelled casket on a throne that is protected by two elephant tusks. The erstwhile palace of the king is also in the same compound, so there is much to savour here.

In the past, during the full moon in late July or early August, the tooth was carried in a ceremonial procession, led by elaborately decorated elephants and flanked by smaller ones, for all to see and celebrate. Today, the tooth does not leave its sanctum and instead the procession of torchbearers, fire dancers, jugglers, musicians, elephants, acrobats, noblemen and women in traditional dress, all move towards the temple to venerate the sacred object. On the tenth and last night of the festival, millions of devotees enter the temple, each holding a lit candle, and circumambulate the shrine to pay their respects. It is a spectacular sight, made vibrant by the colours and devotion of the pilgrims – a truly once in a lifetime event for visitors.

This festival of Esala Perahera is the largest Buddhist celebration in the world and draws into its fold nearly a million people each year. Tamil Hindus and Christians also take part in the festival, which has become part of a shared heritage and political leaders also have a ceremony where they dedicate themselves to the service of the people and the protection of the relic. Representing both Mahayana and Theravada Buddhism, Kandy's unique nature as a sacred site was recognized in 1988 when it was designated a UNESCO World Heritage Site.

Main: Bedecked in their finery, elephants line up for the Esala Perahera procession
Below (left to right): Elephants drinking in the water at Pinnewala Elephant Orphanage outside Kandy; traditional Kandyan dancing with a *Geta Bera* drum; Temple of the Tooth behind Kandy Lake

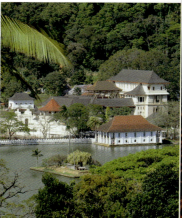

Above: Performer twirling his flaming torch in the Esala Perahera festival

FESTIVAL DIARY

August is a great time to visit as the rains have eased and the city is abuzz with the Esala Perahera festival. A highlight of the event is the vibrant procession of elephants, drummers and dancers through the streets. Although it lasts for ten days, six days in Kandy will be ample time to enjoy the festival and the local sights.

Six Days in the Hills

Arrive in Colombo and take a taxi or intercity bus to Kandy. Take in the lovely setting of the town, before having a wander around the peaceful lake.

Spend the day in Kandy, exploring. This is a laid-back, historical town – have a look at the distinctive architecture and explore the markets and old shops of the town centre. After lunch, pay a visit to the Temple of the Sacred Tooth to watch the ceremonies.

Hire a car to take you to Pinnewala Elephant Orphanage, 40 km (25 miles) west of Kandy. Home to the largest group of captive elephants in the world, the orphanage not only rears orphaned elephants but is also a breeding centre. Return to Kandy to watch the evening's festivities.

Begin your day with a visit to the Peradenia Botanical Gardens, Sri Lanka's largest gardens and home to 4,000 different tree species. Afterwards, find a good spot from which to watch the procession to the temple and enjoy the lively ambience.

Dedicate a day to exploring the surrounding tea plantations – they are stunning, especially those near Ella village and Nuwara Eliya.

Pay a visit to some of Kandy's other temples, including Hindagala Vihara, which has a beautiful setting, and Natha Devale, the oldest shrine in Kandy. In the afternoon, shop for souvenirs before enjoying a traditional Sri Lankan dinner.

Dos and Don'ts

✓ Buy some avocados from local fruit stalls if they are in season – they're cheap and delicious.

✗ Don't get into a tuk-tuk without first negotiating the fare – these nimble motorized rickshaws are not metered.

✓ Take home some pachyderm paper, locally produced from elephant dung.

✗ Don't pose in front of, or beside, a statue of the Buddha – the locals see this as a sign of disrespect.

JAN
FEB
MAR
APR
MAY
JUN
JUL
AUG
DAY 1
DAY 2
DAY 3
DAY 4
DAY 5
DAY 6
SEP
OCT
NOV
DEC

AUGUST

GETTING THERE
Slovenia is located in central Europe, between Italy, Austria, Croatia and the Adriatic. Its international airport is in the capital, Ljubljana.

GETTING AROUND
An efficient bus network links most places to Ljubljana. Buses from Ljubljana take 1¼ hours to Bled, 1¾ hours to Bohinj and 3¾ hours to Bovec. Rail services are more limited.

WEATHER
Temperatures regularly reach the mid-20s°C during August, falling to a pleasant 12°C at night. It can get a lot colder at higher altitudes.

ACCOMMODATION
Camping Bled is a family centred site near Bled; from £6 per adult; www.camping-bled.com

Kamp Danica is a riverside campsite with family entertainment onsite; from £5 per adult; www.bohinj.si/camping-danica

Kamp Polovnik is near Bovec in the Soča Valley; from £4 per adult; www.kamp-polovnik.com

EATING OUT
You can get a good meal in Slovenia for around £13 a head. Freshwater fish dominate menus close to Slovenia's rivers and lakes. Don't miss the award-winning Restaurant Topli Val, Kobarid near Bovec (£27).

PRICE FOR A FAMILY OF FOUR
£100–160 per day including accommodation, food, local travel, entrance charges and two guided activities.

FURTHER INFORMATION
www.slovenia.info

The Soča Front
It is hard to believe that some of the bloodiest battles of World War I raged through the tranquil Soča Valley, or that young Italian and Austro-Hungarian soldiers could survive in this unforgiving mountain terrain during the winter. Established in May 1915, the Soča Front, which extended from Slovenia's Adriatic coast all the way to Mount Rombon, was the site of fierce combat until the Italian line was brutally put down in October 1917, when the German commander Erwin Rommel employed the ultimate weapon – gas – to quell the opposition.

EXHILARATING WILDERNESS

Blessed with voluminous snow-capped mountain peaks and glacial valleys, Slovenia is perfect for families seeking a camping holiday in the great outdoors. Nowhere is this dramatic mountainscape better encapsulated than in the country's only national park, Triglav, where hiking 2,864 m (9,400 ft) to the Triglav summit has become something of a rite of passage for young Slovenes. But you don't have to be a climber to get active in Slovenia – the unspoiled countryside boasts everything from lush farmland and gushing rivers to thundering waterfalls and pristine lakes.

One of the most iconic images of the country is the ethereal Lake Bled, lauded by local poet France Prešeren as "this second Eden, full of charm and grace". Admiring its mist-shrouded island church, which reclines under the protective eye of Bled Castle and the vaulting mountain peaks of the Julian Alps, it is hard to disagree. The array of gondolas and rowing boats plying the lake and scenic walks promise to keep every member of the family happy away from the tent.

Main: Water sports on the Soča River

Local adventure tour operators also organize excursions into the national park with everything from hiking and trekking to mountain biking, caving and canyoning on offer. In nearby Bohinj you will find more unspoiled countryside and Slovenia's largest lake, the eponymous glacial Lake Bohinj. Like its Bled sibling this stunning expanse of Alpine water is framed by the hulking Triglav mountains, with lake cruises and a range of outdoor sports like paragliding, kayaking and horse riding available during the long summer days.

South of the Julian Alps in the Soča Valley, a water wonderland awaits, where, amid rugged mountain peaks and leafy forest, the brilliant emerald-coloured Soča River, the ultimate destination for whitewater rafters from all over Europe, is the real attraction. If a white-knuckle ride on the river isn't for you then try a family-orientated canoe or mountain bike trip.

Slovenia's campsites tend to be large and well-equipped with hot showers and laundry facilities, and many have the added benefit of multi-purpose sports courts and activities for children and families. Above all, camping offers the chance to really get a feel for this alpine land.

Above: Tables laid out for dinner on Stari Street in Ljubljana

ALPINE CAMPING DIARY

August in Slovenia is perfect camping weather. The good weather allows you to get out and about in the country's dramatic alpine environment. If you want to spend time walking or cycling in the mountains, cruising on its lakes, or hurtling down whitewater rapids, then you will need at least a week to explore.

Seven Days of Adventure

After arriving in Ljubljana, meander through the cobbled streets of its old town admiring the distinctive flair of architect Jože Plečnik who graced the city with ornate bridges, a colonnaded central market and fortified riverbanks.

Travel to Lake Bled – stroll around the lake and savour the beauty of its position in the Julian Alps. Picnic by the lake before catching the tourist train to the castle, or go across the water to St Mary's Church.

Immerse yourself in the great outdoors and hike or mountain bike in Triglav National Park – Tolminska Ravine and the picturesque village of Pokljuka are particulary worth a visit.

Head south to Bohinj. Cruising on dramatic Lake Bohinj is very popular – to escape the crowds, take a hike up to the Savica Falls, which pound the rocks 78 m (260 ft) below. Alternatively, travel to the top of the Vogel Cable Car for a mesmerizing aerial view of this vast mountain wilderness.

Travel to Slovenia's adventure capital, Bovec, in the Soča Valley. Join a heart-stopping whitewater rafting trip down the emerald river – zooming down this with water spraying in your face is truly exhilarating.

Explore the valley's World War I history. Start in the Kobarid War Museum for an overview of the Soča Front, before taking the World War I walking tour, or walk around the front lines outside Bovec. Travel back to Ljubljana for your return flight home.

Dos and Don'ts

☑ Make a good impression and look Slovenes in the eye when shaking hands or raising a toast.

☒ Don't raft on the Soča River unless you have booked a trip with a local tour operator. The water is dangerous after heavy rain and no self-respecting Slovene will take you out.

☑ Leave a tip of at least 10 percent if you eat in a restaurant or risk incurring the wrath of your waiter.

☒ Don't head into the mountains unprepared. A compass, map, bad weather gear, survival shelter and plenty to eat and drink are all essential. Slovenia's mountains are seriously high so take a local guide along too.

JAN
FEB
MAR
APR
MAY
JUN
JUL
AUG
DAY 1
DAY 2
DAY 3
DAY 4
DAY 5
DAYS 6–7
SEP
OCT
NOV
DEC

Top: Pokljuka in the Julian Alps

Above: Hiking in Triglav National Park

Below: Sunset at Lake Bohinj

Left panel (top to bottom): Novelty boats on Lake Bled; hiking in the Tolminska Ravine; Bled Castle overlooking Lake Bled

SEPTEMBER

Where to Go: **September**

This is a great month for trying out some of Europe's southern hotspots, now the crowds have left the beaches – the lovely summer sunsets in Greece and Turkey will be unforgettable. But all evidence of summer has not yet gone – Provence's cuisine and even Vermont's colourful leaf display are legacies of summer; you could claim that the beer at the Oktoberfest is summer in a glass (well you could try). Elsewhere, in India and southeast Asia, the torrential rains of the monsoons are diminishing in power, but not yet over; and the southern hemisphere is entering spring, making it a great place for wildlife-spotting, particularly in southern Africa. Below you'll find all the destinations in this chapter as well as some extra suggestions to provide a little inspiration.

FESTIVALS AND CULTURE

BEIJING Performer at the Chinese opera

UNFORGETTABLE JOURNEYS

SOUTHERN TURKEY Anchored wooden *gulet* in Fethiye

NATURAL WONDERS

NAMIBIA Silhouetted quiver trees at sunset

GALWAY
IRELAND, EUROPE

International shindig fuelled by oysters and Guinness

The Galway Oyster Festival draws crowds from all over. See record-breaking shellfish shucking before eating, drinking and dancing aplenty.
See pp222–3

MUNICH
GERMANY, EUROPE

Probably the finest beer festival in the world

The Oktoberfest was moved to late September because the weather's better – if that matters inside a beer tent.
See pp224–5

VERMONT
USA, NORTH AMERICA

Catch the autumn on a tour of the northeast back roads

The prime place to see all the colours of the New England autumn: maple, beech and ash frame picture-perfect villages.
See pp230–1

BHUTAN
BHUTAN, ASIA

Be one of the few to explore this Himalayan kingdom

Only 18,000 tourists are let into Bhutan each year; the rewards are ancient temples, fabulous festivals and wonderful trekking.
www.kingdomofbhutan.com

> "The crisp, clear desert air makes the Namib night sky a thing of shimmering, awe-inspiring beauty."

NAMIB-NAUKLUFT
NAMIBIA, AFRICA

You could be on a different planet, the terrain is so weird

Despite the extreme environment, these huge, ochre-red sand dunes are home to a surprising amount of extraordinary wildlife.
See pp240–1

LONDON
ENGLAND, EUROPE

A vibrant cultural melting pot – museums, markets and musicals

Although famous for its magnificent museums and ancient pageantry, London's restaurants, pubs and entertainment are world-class too.
See pp232–3

> "The parks are mellow, and the lively buzz of pubs and cafés can be enjoyed outside."

SOUTHERN TURKEY
TURKEY, EUROPE

Sail from cove to cove on a *gulet* following the Lycian Way

Fresh fish barbecues, secluded swims and remarkable historic ruins coupled with clear water and fine hospitality make this a winner.
See pp226–7

LAKE DISTRICT
ENGLAND, EUROPE

Deep-green hills and glittering ribbons of water

Hike up onto the fells to get a real feel of some of Britain's finest landscapes, beloved of Wordsworth and Beatrix Potter.
www.lake-district.gov.uk

BAY OF FUNDY
CANADA, NORTH AMERICA

The awesome power of the sea in a unique environment

The world's highest tides come and go in this huge bay, creating whirlpools and bizarre rocks, and attracting a great range of wildlife.
www.bayoffundytourism.com

BEIJING
CHINA, ASIA

A culture steeped in tradition yet galloping into the future

Plenty to delight the visitor, old – Forbidden City, Summer Palace, and the Great Wall – and new – the stunning Olympic buildings.
See pp228–9

THE RHINE
GERMANY, EUROPE

Relax on a cruise down Europe's greatest river

Boats cruise through Germany, from Switzerland to Holland, past historic towns, wine villages and the treacherous Lorelei rock.
www.germany-tourism.de

HIGH TATRAS
SLOVAKIA, EUROPE

A breath of fresh air in unspoilt mountains

Little known outside Slovakia, the Tatras are home to chamois and eagles, and offer space to hike, glide, ride or swim.
www.tanap.sk

SEATTLE
USA, NORTH AMERICA

America's biggest and brightest pop-culture fest

Summer's over, but Seattle makes up for it with the USA's biggest new music and arts festival, hosting a range of international performers.
www.bumbershoot.org

NAZCA
PERU, SOUTH AMERICA

Fly above the most enigmatic creations of ancient America

Only from a plane can you fully see the Nazca Lines, mysterious figures and patterns marked in the desert over 1,000 years ago.
www.peru.info

HERMANUS
SOUTH AFRICA, AFRICA

World capital for whale-watchers

Every year whales come to Walker Bay in amazing numbers to calve, and thousands of people meet up on the cliffs to see them.
www.whalefestival.co.za

Weather Watch

❶ Autumn weather in Vermont is cool and crisp, although there's a chance of rain too – very rarely this combines with strong winds and strips the trees of their colourful leaves.

❷ September is spring in South America and temperatures are comfortable. Nazca is in Peru's coastal desert, and will be a little hotter.

❸ The Kalahari desert is in southern Africa and so it is hot and sunny in the interior – but very cold at night. The coast is generally cooler.

❹ September is the perfect month for southeastern Europe. The sea is as hot as it gets, the air temperature is more bearable than at the peak of summer – but it's still very hot so those with fair skins should be careful.

❺ This is a good month to visit China as it's nice and warm with very little rain. Autumn's clear skies keep the wind and dust that blights spring away. But if there's no wind, air pollution can build up.

❻ Tropical destinations are hot and wet all year – but there's often plenty of sunshine in between warm showers. September is one of Borneo's driest months.

LUXURY AND ROMANCE

SANTORINI The cliff-side village of Fira at night

ACTIVE ADVENTURES

BORNEO The open seed pods of a sterculia tree

FAMILY GETAWAYS

PROVENCE Family cycling through the countryside

DEAUVILLE
FRANCE, EUROPE

The essence of indulgent luxury and Gallic style

Stroll the beachfront at this classic resort, before some pampering at the beauty centre, a gourmet meal and a night at the casino.
www.deauville.org

SANTORINI
GREECE, EUROPE

An extraordinary landscape with romantic sunsets

The vibrant colours – blue seas, red sunsets, shining white houses – lend the island a dreamlike quality, perfect for newlyweds.
See pp242–3

TAOS
USA, NORTH AMERICA

A town with a special mix of cultures and atmospheres

Wander through the historic pueblo and its art galleries and new age centres, or just chill out in the hot springs and many lovely B&Bs.
www.taosvacationguide.com

MILAN
ITALY, EUROPE

Shop and people-watch in Italy's fashion capital

City life picks up in Italy after the long summer: visit the designer stores and artists' studios, and eat beside the Naviglio Grande canal.
www.ciaomilano.it

MADEIRA
PORTUGAL, EUROPE

This prettiest of islands is a botanist's dream.

Nature abounds here, from rugged coast and volcanic caves to the mountainous interior and lush vineyards.
See pp236–7

"A paradise of flower-filled evergreen forests, tumbling waterfalls and safe, sunny natural harbours."

TABARKA
TUNISIA, NORTH AFRICA

Fine diving in an ancient Arab town

With some of the best coral and diving waters in the Mediterranean, this little town hosts a "Coralis" diving festival every September.
www.tourismtunisia.com

BORNEO
SOUTHEAST ASIA

The biggest adventure is seeing an orang-utan

Borneo's amazing array of habitats are ideal for taking part in many active adventures – and seeing a great variety of flora and fauna.
See pp234–5

CYCLE WALES
WALES, EUROPE

Get a new angle on Wales's green hills and valleys

Wales has some of the world's best mountain-biking routes, throughout the country – along hilltops with limitless views.
www.mbwales.com

COLORADO
USA, NORTH AMERICA

Discover your inner cowboy on a dude ranch

Try a real outdoor adventure, learning how to really ride on a western ranch – and hike, fish and go climbing and rafting too.
www.coloradoranch.com

THE PYRENEES
FRANCE/SPAIN, EUROPE

Hike it from the Atlantic to the Mediterranean

Winding paths on either side – French or Spanish – allow you to walk the length of these fascinating mountains, or just a short stretch.
www.pyreneesguide.com

"The summer heat has left the skies clear, the fields golden and the grapes bursting to be picked..."

PARC ASTERIX
FRANCE, EUROPE

A distinctive French take on the theme park

A change from the everyday theme park, this is based around cartoon character Astérix and his fellow Gauls – and it's great fun.
www.parcasterix.fr

COUNTY CORK
IRELAND, EUROPE

Magnificent beaches, towering crags and lovely fishing villages

A blend of beauty and tranquillity – explore the Cork coast's empty beaches and meet Fungie, Dingle Bay's resident dolphin.
www.county-cork.com

PROVENCE
FRANCE, EUROPE

Inspiration to artists, historians and bon viveurs

Explore Roman monuments, enjoy Renaissance architecture, and get lost among vineyards and hills for a well-provisioned picnic.
See pp238–9

MALLORCA
SPAIN, EUROPE

A mellow month on this famous holiday island

After the summer crowds have left, this is a lovely time to sit in cafés, swim in still-warm seas and explore lesser-known corners.
www.illesbalears.es

LAKE GEORGE
USA, NORTH AMERICA

An inland sea in upstate New York

In the heart of the Adirondacks, this giant forest lake is ringed by campsites, fine hotels and places to swim, hike, sail and more.
www.visitlakegeorge.com

OYSTERS AND THE BLACK STUFF

OYSTERS AND GUINNESS ARE THE STAPLE DIET OF GUESTS at the Galway Oyster Festival, which hits this charming Irish city at the end of every September.

The "cracking" Guinness World Oyster Opening Championships is a highlight at the four-day festival, which goes into its 54th year in 2008. The emphasis rests on fun, food, and, of course, filling up with Guinness – the national drink. After months of summer festivals and *fleadhs* (music festivals), there is always more than enough *craic* (fun) to go round at the last festival of the season. And its line-up continues to draw crowds from overseas every year – the official festival events are guaranteed sell-outs, hardly surprising as the festival is often called one of the best in the world.

The main attraction of the festivities is the oysters, which are carefully selected from beds within Galway Bay where the native oyster still grows wild. After suffering at the hands of eager men frantically trying to beat the world record at the oyster opening championships on the Saturday

Main: Revellers enjoying the *craic* in the marquee at the Galway Oyster Festival

GETTING THERE
Galway is situated on the west coast of Ireland, 215 km (135 miles) from Dublin. Galway airport is 6 km (4 miles) from the city centre and is accessible by internal flights from Dublin airport. The city is also well serviced by train and bus links.

GETTING AROUND
There are taxis and buses in the city and the centre is small enough to cover easily on foot. Hire a car to travel further afield.

WEATHER
September is generally a mild month with an average temperature of 13°C, and is often sunny, but rain is not unusual.

ACCOMMODATION
Sea Breeze Lodge is a cosy guesthouse overlooking beautiful Galway Bay; doubles from £75; www.seabreezelodge.org

Jurys Inn has a central location close to the Spanish Arch; doubles from £100; www.jurysinn.com

The g Hotel is a new and very stylish 5 star hotel; doubles from £150; www.theghotel.ie

EATING OUT
Seafood is a speciality and a highlight of a stay here. Try McDonaghs on Quay Street (mains from £15) or leave the city for its surrounds and visit St Cleran's in Craughwell.

PRICE FOR TWO
£190–230 per day including accommodation, food, local travel and festival tickets.

FURTHER INFORMATION
www.galwayoysterfest.com

The Claddagh Ring
The Claddagh Ring is a distinct design with two hands joined together to support a heart. The ring is a monument to love and friendship, and how you wear it depends on your love life. When worn on the right hand with the heart facing outward to the nail, it signifies the heart is free. When the heart is facing inward on the right hand, it indicates the heart is no longer available.

afternoon, the oysters are served in all their glory in the festival marquee, which rests at the mouth of the Claddagh – one of the oldest parts of the city, and home of the famous Claddagh Ring. Glamour plays a big part in the whole affair, with high heels and *haute couture* aplenty seen walking past the Spanish Arch to Nimmo's Pier where the marquee is erected.

Galway is so conveniently located in the heart of the west of Ireland, that most of the 12,000 or so visitors to the festival make the most of their journey and venture beyond the folds of the marquee in search of a real sense of Irish life.

The Aran Islands, Connemara, and The Burren are all on Galway's doorstep awaiting your discovery. Take the ferry over to Aran, an archipelago of three tiny islands where the primary language is Irish and life has a more traditional pace. A walk along the dramatic rocky coast will certainly awaken your Guinness-dulled senses as you stroll past fields that have been tamed over the years by the locals constantly working the craggy land. Afterwards, stop off in a cosy bar to warm up and get ready to start the *craic* all over again.

Above: Busy streets of Galway during the Oyster Festival

Above (top to bottom): Looking over onto Claddagh Quay; the Twelve Ben mountain range in Connemara; festival staples – oysters and Guinness

Below: Competitors shuck the oysters at the World Oyster Opening Championship

SEAFOOD DIARY

The Galway Oyster Festival is said to be Ireland's longest running festival, and it remains very popular, providing one last hurrah for revellers after the summer. The festival itself lasts for four days, but a week in Galway will allow you plenty of time to enjoy the town and the beautiful surrounding area.

A Week in West Ireland

Stroll around the town and get familiarized with the pedestrian Shop Street and Quay Street, walk under the Spanish Arch, and take a 10-minute stroll out to Salthill to breathe in some fresh sea air.

Visit buildings of note – the cathedral, the university, and the largest medieval church still in use in Ireland, St Nicholas's Collegiate Church.

Leave town to take a trip out west to the heart of Connemara. See the Twelve Ben mountains and the unspoilt beauty of Letterfrack and Leenane.

Visit the Aran Islands, Europe's westernmost point, and make it back just in time to watch Irish oyster openers vie for a place in the World Oyster Opening Championships in The Quays Bar at 8pm.

Browse the art galleries, museums, and arts and craft shops dotted all around the city. In the evening, make your way to the marquee for jazz and seafood.

Visit the eclectic Galway Market which sets up outside St Nicholas's Church every Saturday, then head to the official opening of the festival in Eyre Square. The fun is centred around the marquee with the Guinness World Oyster Opening Championship. The Oyster Festival Gala Ball is held on the Saturday night.

The party continues at the marquee on the Sunday, but if you are full to the brim of Guinness you could have a windsurfing lesson at Rusheen Bay.

Dos and Don'ts

✓ Enjoy the *craic* (fun) with the locals. Irish people really are very friendly and love meeting new people.

✗ Don't expect people to always be on time for things – Irish time runs at a more relaxed pace.

✓ Buy tickets and book accommodation in advance. Galway is quite a small city and fills up quickly.

✗ Don't park your car without being sure it is parked legally – clampers are in operation all over the city.

JAN
FEB
MAR
APR
MAY
JUN
JUL
AUG
SEP
MON
TUE
WED
THU
FRI
SAT
SUN
OCT
NOV
DEC

GETTING THERE
Munich is the capital of Bavaria, south Germany.
The Franz-Josef-Strauss International Airport is
40 km (25 miles) northwest of the city. The
40-minute transfer to Munich via S-Bahn line 8
is fast and cheap. Most other connecting flights
arrive from Frankfurt am Main.

GETTING AROUND
The extensive public transport system makes
getting around Munich easy. Taxis are plentiful
and the centre can easily be explored by foot.

WEATHER
In September, Munich is sunny and dry with
average maximum temperatures of 18°C.

ACCOMMODATION
There are many homely, traditional *gasthäuser*
(inns) and boutique hotels in Munich.

The cosy Hotel Leopold has doubles from £80;
www.hotel-leopold.de

Family-run Alphenhotel München; doubles from
£140; www.alpenhotel-muenchen.de

Luxury hotel the historic Bayerischer Hof has
doubles from £215; www.bayerischerhof.de

EATING OUT
Bavarian cuisine is hearty and heavy on meats
like pork knuckle, sausages – and beer. An
authentic choice is the Hofbräuhaus,
www.hofbraeuhaus.de, where dishes start at £7.

PRICE FOR TWO
£250–300 per day for accommodation, food
and entrance charges to the opera and theatre.

FURTHER INFORMATION
www.oktoberfest.de

Bavarian Beer

Munich likes to dub itself the beer capital of the
world – and as a city with six traditional breweries,
there is probably no other place on earth where
you can enjoy so many different kinds of beer on
tap. All beers – from the light, golden shining
Weizen to the dark bocks – are brewed according
to the Reinheitsgebot from 1519, which only allows
water, barley and hops to be used. Among the
historic beer gardens are the famous Hofbräuhaus,
the Paulaner and the Augustiner-Keller.

Main: Beer tent filled with the Oktoberfest crowds

GERMANY'S UBER PARTY

A SPECTACULARLY COLOURFUL PARADE of horse-drawn floats and more than 40 brewery carriages laden with
giant kegs rumble down the elegant streets of Maximilian- and Residenzstrasse. They are led by the *münchener
kindl*, the hooded figure on the city's official coat of arms, and followed by some 8,000 traditionally dressed practitioners
from oompah bands, folk dance groups, *Schützenvereine* (shooting associations) and other Bavarian groups. Next
come the *Wiesn-Wirte* – the innkeepers of the Oktoberfest beer tents – and they make their way down to the
festival grounds on Theriesenwiese. This joyful spectacle takes place on the first Sunday of the Oktoberfest, after it
has been opened at midday. The party officially starts when Munich's mayor taps the first keg of beer shouting
"*O'zapft is*" ("It's tapped"), and drinks to a successful Oktoberfest. The locals join in with vociferous cheers and
enthusiastically set about quenching their thirst, while millions watching on TV throughout Germany do the same.

Left (left to right): Musicians parade at the Oktoberfest; waitress in a traditional outfit; getting dizzy on the merry-go-round

Right (clockwise from left): National Theatre, home to the Bavarian State Opera; Alte Pinakothek, one of the largest art collections in Munich; Antiquarium in the Munich Residenz

Inset: Munich's coat of arms

Above: Looking towards the Liebfrauenkirche from the steeple of Alter Peter

This is one juggernaut of a party – and the world's biggest festival.

BAVARIAN DIARY

Munich's Oktoberfest (mid-September–early October) is the world's biggest beer festival, a boisterous yet charming celebration of German *Gemütlichkeit* (sociability), with beer, *Brez'n* (sausages) and partying for a full 16 days. Try to make the opening parade for the festival – an unforgettable experience.

Three Days at the Oktoberfest

Start with a full day on the *Wiesn* (meadows) as Bavarians simply call the Oktoberfest tents, and enjoy the festival as the locals do – just walk slowly from tent to tent absorbing the atmosphere and sampling the different beers and food.

Give the liver a rest and take a stroll through the late medieval and Renaissance downtown surrounding the City Hall on Marienplatz. Take a peek inside one of the city's most beloved landmarks, the Liebfrauenkirche.

Spend the afternoon shopping on one of Europe's most expensive shopping streets, Maximilianstrasse.

In the evening, dress in your finery and attend the city's "see and be seen" ballet at the Bavarian State Opera.

Explore Munich's fascinating museums such as the Alte and Neue Pinakothek and the Pinakothek der Moderne, a world-class cluster of art galleries with paintings ranging from Rembrandt, Titian and Dürer to Manet and Warhol. Also admire the incredible Renaissance interior of the 66-m (215-ft) Antiquarium in the Munich Residenz.

Later, explore the Deutsches Museum, the world's biggest (and most fascinating) museum for technology, science and transportation.

Dos and Don'ts

✓ Stay a while on Marienplatz to enjoy the carillon at the Neues Rathaus daily at 11am, noon, and 5pm – a colourful parade of wooden, medieval characters swirling around to traditional tunes.

✗ Don't eat a *Weisswurst* (type of sausage) after noon, as these traditional sausages are eaten for breakfast and have often been on display since early morning.

✓ Walk across Viktualienmarkt, a traditional food and fresh produce market, in the morning and watch a city awakening. Don't forget to sample the delights of the many food stalls.

The Oktoberfest is not for the faint-hearted, non-beer lovers or vegetarians. With 6 million visitors a year, some 60,000 hectolitres (10,500,000 pints) of beer, half a million chickens, and close to 400,000 sausages, this is one juggernaut of a party – and the world's biggest festival.

Don't be late though; the Oktoberfest, despite its name, usually starts in mid-September. The name harks back to the first Oktoberfest which was held in 1810 in honour of the Bavarian Crown Prince Ludwig's marriage; festivities began on October 12 and lasted for five days. With Teutonic pragmatism, it was later moved to September, as the autumn sun makes it easier to party alfresco.

The Oktoberfest has evolved as one of the country's premier events, where the rich and beautiful, policy and business leaders have to see and be seen. The favourite tents enjoy such incredible hype that you have to be on a guest list. But what do you expect at an uber party like this?

Once you've had your fill and partied yourself out, do step out and explore the sights of Munich. At festival time the streets really buzz with excitement and life.

JAN
FEB
MAR
APR
MAY
JUN
JUL
AUG
SEP
DAY 1
DAY 2
DAY 3
OCT
NOV
DEC

Above (left and right): Anchored wooden *gulet* in Fethiye Bay; enjoying the sun on Ölü Deniz beach lagoon

GETTING THERE
Between Greece and the Middle East, Turkey bridges East and West. International airports include Antalya, Bodrum, Dalaman and Izmir.

GETTING AROUND
Excellent bus services operate between towns. Car hire is available from airports. *Gulet* (traditional Turkish boat) cruises can be tailored to include alternative stops.

WEATHER
September has warm, sunny days averaging high temperatures of around 24°C.

ACCOMMODATION
For smaller groups, or individual travellers, Yacht Doğan provide cabin charters; from £40 per day, full board; www.yachtdogan.com

Vira have a large selection of luxury *gulets* to choose; from £70 per person, per day, full board; www.virayachting.com

Exclusive Escapes provide private charters; from £95 per person, per day, full board and flights (from UK); www.hiddenturkey.com

EATING OUT
With fresh seafood, and local fruit, veg and herbs, eating on a *gulet* cruise is excellent. On land, Korsan Restaurant in Kalkan (around £10) makes old Ottoman recipes.

PRICE FOR TWO
Depending on the trip and boat size, prices for full-board *gulet* cruises can vary greatly (see accommodation).

FURTHER INFORMATION
www.tourismturkey.org

Lycian Tombs
Ancient Lycia, a federation of 19 independent cities, lay in the mountainous area between Dalaman and Antalya. Burials must have held an important role in the beliefs of the Lycians, for they cut hundreds of tombs into the cliff faces and crags that can be seen throughout the area. They were probably copies of domestic architecture, intended as houses for the dead. Most have carved doors, beam ends, pitched roofs and prominent lintels.

THE LYCIAN COAST

SOUTHWESTERN TURKEY IS BELIEVED TO BOAST MORE ANCIENT RUINS area for area than any other region in the world. Since time immemorial, conquerors, traders and travellers have beaten a path to the mighty monuments, yet the sites still never fail to impress. And, gliding through the calm waters past these wonders as the sun sparkles on the sea and you enjoy a meal of fresh fish cooked to order on board your *gulet*, the feeling of total relaxation cannot be surpassed.

Set spectacularly on hillsides, carved into coastal outcrops or set in fertile valleys, the scenic surrounds only add to the drama and romance of the ruins. However large and loud the crowd (particularly during the local school holidays), the ancient sites never seem overwhelmed or overawed. Huge, majestic and serene the monuments loom over everything, colonized only by the wildflowers and butterflies that make their homes here. On a mighty column atop a colossal Corinthian capital, a stork shapes a shabby nest. As the sun begins to sink in the sky, the coach parties vanish and the ruins are suddenly all silent and sullen again. Turned crimson by the last rays of the setting sun, and highlighted against a darkening sky, the scenery seems as tremendous, timeless and enduring today as it must have done millennia ago.

The boat continues through the turquoise waters, past pine-forested land, with the occasional stop for a refreshing swim or to go ashore to a pretty little town to sip tea in a picturesque square. You may see a shepherd marshal his woolly charges along a narrow road, or farmers with black moustaches patiently hawking little jars of amber honey from the roadside as women in heavy skirts and patterned headscarves gather wild herbs from the meadows. And at sea, around another spit of land, a sheltered cove or beautiful beach beckons from the foot of a towering cliff. The Mediterranean, set against the bleached blocks of old stone, looks almost luminous in its blueness as a couple of *gulets* slowly drift by, shimmering and hazy in the heavy heat of the afternoon sun.

Main: Wooden *gulets* anchored in a quiet bay
Below (left and right): Colourful slippers for sale in Fethiye Bazaar; Gulf of Kekova with its sunken ruins

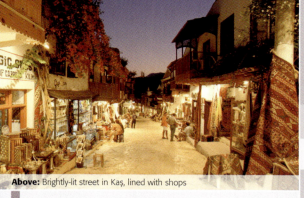

Above: Brightly-lit street in Kaş, lined with shops

JAN

FEB

MAR

APR

MAY

JUN

JUL

AUG

SEP

OCT

NOV

DEC

COASTAL DIARY

With the weather warm but not too hot, September is a great time for a *gulet* cruise in Turkey. Trips can be tailored to suit the preferences of the group. A week is sufficient to tour the highlights of southwestern Turkey but ten days would be more leisurely and allow time also for some walking, diving and snorkelling.

A Week on a *Gulet* Cruise

Travel the 50 km (30 miles) from Dalaman to Fethiye and spend the morning visiting the Fethiye Museum. Later, explore the market and look up to the cliffs above with Lycian tombs carved into the rock. Join your *gulet* cruise to begin your journey south.

DAY 1

At Ölü Deniz stop off to admire the impossibly turquoise sea at the Blue Lagoon. Close by, visit Butterfly Valley named after the Jersey Tiger butterflies that colonise the valley in thousands during the summer.

DAY 2

Next stop, Patara, an endless stretch of soft, white sand, perfect for enjoying the gently rolling waves and relaxing on the beach.

DAY 3

Located near Kalkan, discover the beautiful Kaputas Beach within swimming distance of Mavi Mağara (Blue Cave), the largest sea cave in Turkey. Then on to Kaş where you can sip Turkish tea on the main square with the locals and watch the sun go down.

DAY 4

Sail over the sunken city of Kekova and on to nearby Üçağiz and Simena with pretty coves and ancient ruins.

DAY 5

At the market town of Finike, see the fertile orchards brimming with oranges and lemons. Visit Olympos to see the Yanartaş (burning stone), a vent of natural gas that is permanently alight.

DAY 6

Spend your final day in Antalya exploring the palm-lined boulevards and Old Town. There are plenty of excellent shops, beaches and restaurants to enjoy before heading homewards.

DAY 7

Dos and Don'ts

☑ Take care if driving. Turkey's terrible road record has finally provoked the police into action. To avoid accidents as well as high speeding fines, drive slowly!

☒ Don't forget to book your cruise as early as possible to take advantage of the considerable discounts available.

☑ Keep a careful eye on your bags and pockets in towns.

GETTING THERE
Beijing is the capital of China, the world's most populous nation (1.3 billion people). It is served by Beijing Capital Airport

GETTING AROUND
There are no convenient public transport links between Capital Airport and central Beijing; a taxi to the city centre takes 40 minutes to an hour depending on traffic and costs around £4–5.

WEATHER
September sees relief from the extreme heat of summer. Expect temperatures of around 20°C and just the odd day of rain.

ACCOMMODATION
For character, try Lusong Yuan Binguan; doubles from £55; www.the-silk-road.com

For reasonable rates in a central, modern hotel there's the Novotel Peace Beijing; doubles from £45; www.accorhotels-asia.com

New luxury hotels open all the time. One of the best is the Grand Hyatt; doubles from £135; www.beijing.grand.hyatt.com

EATING OUT
Dining out is one of the highlights of Beijing and it's cheap – a filling meal need not be more than £5 a head. Highlights include Peking duck, Hakka fish dishes and the Xinjiang-style kebabs from the street markets.

PRICE FOR TWO
£100–130 per day including accommodation, food and local travel.

FURTHER INFORMATION
www.cnto.org

Design by Numbers

The importance of numbers in Chinese design is down to the pervasive influence of the harmonious principles of *yin* and *yang*. *Yang* is represented by odd numbers, and these also indicate the masculine element associated with the emperor. Therefore the ultimate odd number – nine – is repeatedly seen in architectural details. The Forbidden City is said to have 9,999 rooms and the doors for imperial use often have brass studs in a nine-by-nine formation.

HUTONGS TO HIGHRISES

LIKE CHINA ITSELF, Beijing makes few concessions to the visitor. It is a vast, uncontainable city teeming with people. They throng the downtown neighbourhoods, spill out from restaurants and cafés, crowd into the city's many landscaped parks and, in their cars, jam highways and flyovers. The sheer size of the population is reflected in the absurd scale of the ancient imperial palaces and temple complexes – the Forbidden City is an entire world enclosed within its own towering four walls; vast courtyards linked by elaborate gateways are filled with lavish buildings whose roofs are topped by a gilt menagerie of dragons, phoenixes and other mythological beasts. Although matching the Forbidden City in scale, the bleak concrete expanse of Tian'an Men Square, the biggest public space in the world, sprawls austerely outside the palace gates with a markedly contrasting drabness.

中华人民共和国万岁

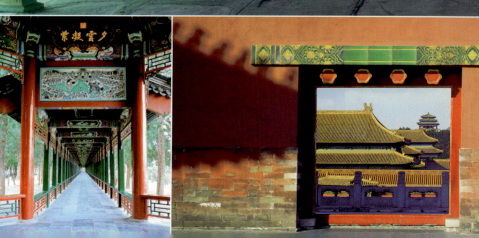

Main: Brightly lit Tian'an Men (Gate of Heavenly Peace), Beijing

Right (left to right): Long corridor in the Summer Palace; window on to the Forbidden City; opera performer; busy Wangfujing street

However, not far from the seething crowds, busy streets and honking cars, there is tranquillity among the ancient *hutongs*, meandering alleyways that are as old as the Forbidden City and often accessible only by rickshaws and bicycles. These untidy lanes and their timeless, crumbling courtyards form a communal living space for the locals where they can sit out and observe the world going by, gossip with their neighbours, play with their pets – whistling finches and mynah birds and the occasional Pekinese dog – and enjoy games of Chinese chess, mahjong and cards.

But what is a *hutong* today could well be a skyscraper tomorrow as the city races headlong into the future. The encircling rings of city walls were knocked down a half century ago, replaced by vast multi-lane ringroads, and there has been no let-up in Beijing's insatiable appetite for change since. Top international architects are currently reshaping the city with a handful of iconic new super-buildings that will continue Beijing's ancient tradition of building to excess.

Above: Performer at the Chinese opera

ORIENTAL DIARY

Not only is Beijing a vast and sprawling city containing a long list of unmissable sights, there are also the essential nearby attractions of the Ming Tombs and the Great Wall, both full day-trips from the city. A week is the bare minimum required to see even just the highlights of the Chinese capital.

A Week in the Imperial City

DAY 1
Start off at Tian'an Men Square, arriving early for the morning opening of Mao's Mausoleum, then spend the bulk of the day in the Forbidden City.

DAY 2
Explore the Summer Palace – a vast landscaped imperial park in the northwest of the city with enough monuments and features for a full day of sightseeing.

DAY 3
In the morning, wander around the Temple of Heaven, one of the largest temple complexes in China.
Later, take a walk to the nearby main shopping street of Wanfujing and its famed "night market", a street of open-air food stalls that set up as the sun goes down.

DAY 4
Take a trip out to Simatai – the most spectacular access point to the Great Wall from Beijing.

DAY 5
Visit the splendid Ming Tombs. This can be combined with a trip to the Great Wall but it makes for a less hurried, and more worthwhile, trip on its own.

DAY 6
Spend the day at Bei Hai Park – a smaller but no less beautiful version of the Summer Palace that links with the area of Hou Hai, a lake surrounded by *hutongs*, the characteristic alleys of old Beijing.

DAY 7
See the Lama Temple, a vast Tibetan temple complex with enough halls and courts to fill half a day.
Then move from idols to covetables, with a trip to the Silk Market, an emporium of cut-price (fake) designer-labels.

Dos and Don'ts

- ✓ Be adventurous when ordering food – flame-grilled grubs don't taste as bad as you might think.
- ✗ Don't for one moment think that the Gucci bag you just paid five pounds for is going to fool anyone.
- ✓ Expect to spend lots of time in traffic jams, and always carry a book.
- ✗ Don't give credence to the "art students" around central Beijing who are always on the look-out for gullible foreigners to pay over the odds for "Chinese art".
- ✓ Carry plenty of small denomination notes because taxi drivers never have change.

JAN
FEB
MAR
APR
MAY
JUN
JUL
AUG
SEP
OCT
NOV
DEC

GETTING THERE
Vermont is in New England, in the northeastern corner of the USA. Vermont's major airport is in Burlington, 124 km (77 miles) from St Johnsbury. More international flights arrive into Boston, 240 km (150 miles) away.

GETTING AROUND
Hiring a car is the best way to tour the Northeast Kingdom, as public transport can be very time-consuming.

WEATHER
The weather is mild but changeable in September, with temperatures of 10–20°C.

ACCOMMODATION
Willough Vale Inn, on the shores of Lake Willoughby, has doubles from £70; www.willoughvale.com

Inn at Mountain View Farm in East Burke has lovely hilltop views; doubles from £90; www.innmtnview.com

Wildflower Inn, Lyndonville, has great vistas and cheery rooms; doubles from £100; www.wildflowerinn.com

EATING OUT
The state's 1,500 dairy farms provide cheddar cheese and rich ice cream. Maple syrup is a speciality found on every breakfast menu.

PRICE FOR TWO
£160–200 including accommodation, food and car hire.

FURTHER INFORMATION
www.travel-vermont.com

Autumnal Shades

Leaves look green because of pigments known as *chlorophylls*, which dominate during the growing season. As autumn approaches, the chlorophylls dwindle, allowing other colours to show. These are the *carotenoids* – shades of yellow, brown and orange. Brighter colours come from pigments called *anthocyanins* that only develop in late summer.

FOLIAGE FESTIVALS

WITH ITS MIX OF MOUNTAINS AND MEADOWS, Vermont is a special scenic corner of America, blessed with an abundance of sugar maple trees that not only produce the state's famous maple syrup but are responsible for the distinctive bright red leaves that make this one of autumn's most colourful destinations.

The unspoiled rural northeast corner of the state is the place to enjoy country pleasures and scenery, especially during the annual Northeast Kingdom Foliage Festival, which rotates from town to town for a week during late September and early October. Proceeds from back-road school bus tours and local church suppers and concerts benefit worthy local causes.

A walk to the top offers a view that sweeps all the way from New Hampshire's White Mountains to Vermont's Green Mountains and the valleys that nestle in between.

Craft stalls sell beautiful hand-stitched quilts, hand-knitted items and home-made wooden toys and puzzles. Each town gets its own day and offers its own activities. Pretty Peacham, founded in 1776, makes for great photos, with its venerable white clapboard buildings and church spire contrasting beautifully against the autumn colours. A guided "ghost walk" through Peacham's cemetery tells of the town's founders, and a walk to the top of the cemetery hill offers a view that sweeps all the way from New Hampshire's White Mountains to Vermont's Green Mountains and the valleys that nestle in between. A wander through the town will provide visitors with sights such as the local blacksmith at work in the forge. In Cabot, visitors tour the town's famous cheese factory, and local musicians perform at the turkey supper in the United Church and Masonic Hall. In Walden, a festival map pinpoints places of interest, including an alpaca farm, a home bakery and a collection of antique engines and tools, and there's usually a hymn sing and ham dinner at Walden Church. Groton draws big crowds on its festival day, which is also Homecoming Day, with a parade and a "Famous Chicken Pie Supper".

In towns like these you are far from the tourist track, mingling with local people and sharing their old-fashioned pleasures with family and friends.

Main: Vivid colours of the autumn trees on Burke Mountain
Inset: White church spire through the forest, Peacham
Below (left to right): Boats on Lake Champlain, Burlington; autumn in East Topsham; the Athenaeum Art Gallery, St Johnsbury

Maple Grove Farms, St Johnsbury

JAN

FEB

MAR

APR

MAY

JUN

JUL

AUG

SEP

MAPLE DIARY

The flaming reds and golds of maple and other hardwood trees, set against a backdrop of deep green pines, create an annual autumn spectacular in Vermont, drawing visitors from around the world. Visiting the "Northeast Kingdom" allows you to enjoy the colours without the crowds found elsewhere in the state.

Three Days Viewing the Leaves

Start in St Johnsbury, the unofficial capital of the "Northeast Kingdom", which sits at the convergence of the Moose, Sleeper and Passumpsie rivers. The town's handsome Athenaeum Art Gallery is well worth a visit, or take a tour of Maple Grove Farms, the largest maple confectionery factory in the world.

After lunch, head north towards Lydonville, stopping wherever possible to view the colours and take some great photos. In the evening, check into a country inn, where you can enjoy a homely meal.

DAY 1

There are some incredible views in Vermont, especially during autumn, so make time for a driving tour to take these in. The sweeping vistas from Darling Hill and Burke Mountain are especially worth a stop.

Continue on north towards Lake Willoughby, a narrow glacial lake that is flanked by soaring cliffs, earning it the nickname of the "Lucerne of America". There are hiking trails that lead around both promontories and, if warm, it's a lovely place to swim.

DAY 2

From Lake Willoughby, drive southwest to Craftsbury Common, with its typical New England village green, flanked by handsome clapboard homes. Further south you'll come to towns like Walden, Cabot, Peacham and Barnet, where the annual Foliage Festival is in full swing. Stop the car at any of these little picturesque villages and stay to enjoy the fun-filled atmosphere and beautiful surroundings.

Head back towards Burlington, stopping to visit Lake Champion, or continue south to take in other Vermont towns such as East Topsham.

DAY 3

Dos and Don'ts

☑ Check out the state's country stores – a New England tradition, they sell local products, crafts and home-made foods that make great souvenirs.

☒ Don't rush. This is a relaxing journey best savoured with country drives, strolls through small towns and enjoying the local festivities.

☑ Do get current schedules of local festivals and special events before you go, so that you don't miss out.

☑ Be sure to book accommodation as early as possible – inns and hotels tend to get booked up months in advance for key weekends during this season.

GETTING THERE
Most international flights arrive into Heathrow and Gatwick airports, both of which are well linked by public transport to central London. Eurostar (trains) from St Pancras International connect to the European high-speed railways.

GETTING AROUND
The comprehensive Underground network is easy to use. Buses are cheaper and frequent. Black cabs are available throughout the city.

WEATHER
September is generally a mild and pleasant month in London, with temperatures around 14°C and the occasional shower.

ACCOMMODATION
Travel Inn at County Hall, by the London Eye; doubles from £104; www.premiertravelinn.com

Covent Garden Hotel, intimate and luxurious; doubles from £235; www.firmdale.com/covent

Claridges, one of London's most glamorous hotels; doubles from £480; www.claridges.co.uk

EATING OUT
London is a great place for food, and the influence of generations of immigrants can be seen throughout. A meal for two can cost from £40 including wine, but many restaurants offer cheaper pre-theatre menus, which are worth seeking out. Most pubs serve food, with main courses starting from around £6.

PRICE FOR TWO
£230–300 per day including accommodation, food, local transport and entrance charges.

FURTHER INFORMATION
www.visitlondon.com

Shakespeare's Globe

Opened in 1997, Shakespeare's Globe is a painstakingly faithful reconstruction of the original Globe Theatre, which William Shakespeare helped found in 1599. Rebuilt using specially made Tudor bricks, oak pegs (instead of nails), thatching reeds from Norfolk and plaster made from goat's hair, sand and lime, the theatre's central space is uncovered, leaving it open to the elements. As well as seating tiers, there is space for 500 standing spectators (known as "groundlings"), just as there would have been in Shakespeare's day

Main: Interior courtyard of the British Museum combining the old and the new
Above (top to bottom): Fresh flowers on display at Columbia Road Market; fountain in Trafalgar Square; view of the Houses of Parliament from the London Eye

POUNDING THE STREETS

THE ART CRITIC JOHN BERGER ONCE DESCRIBED LONDON as "a teenager, an urchin, and, in this, it hasn't changed since the time of Dickens". To describe this great city of culture as an urchin is to get to its heart, because it is the scruffy and mercurial streets that have long been London's driving force. The rough houses of Southwark produced the theatres in which Shakespeare thrived; the squalor of the city streets and river led to Hogarth's brilliant paintings and Dickens' excoriating tales. In the 20th century, the seediness of Soho inspired Francis Bacon and Lucien Freud while punk was sown on Chelsea's streets, making Vivienne Westwood a fashion queen, and the untidy East End produced the BritArt pack. Teenage urchins don't care for rules – jaywalking is not illegal, speech is free, everyone is welcome and change is good. This is not contradicted by the popularity of London's great pageants – the Changing of the Guard, the liveried City guildsmen, the Tower of London's Ceremony of the Keys. While these

Top: Guards stand to attention at the Changing of the Guard ceremony at Buckingham Palace

Above: Customers enjoy a drink outside a typical London pub, The Sherlock Holmes

Below: Canary Wharf business centre viewed from the River Thames at dusk

Above: Conductor enthusiastically guiding musicians at the Proms

BIG SMOKE DIARY

The riches amassed in London's museums and galleries should be savoured, so combine them with strolls along streets and squares. If you are in town over a weekend, London has some fantastic markets – Columbia Road Market in the East End and Borough Market in Southwark are just two worth a visit.

Five Days Savouring the Sights

Start with the main attraction: the Houses of Parliament and dazzling Westminster Abbey. Walk back up Whitehall, past Churchill's War Rooms and Horse Guards, to Trafalgar Square and the National Gallery to feast on art. Spend the evening like Londoners do, sitting with a pint outside a pub.

Changing of the Guard starts at 11:30am at Buckingham Palace, so make that your first stop. Drop in at Fortnum & Mason's on Piccadilly for coffee or lunch and check out the sumptuous food hall. Then shop your way up Bond Street to Oxford Street, or, if the weather is nice, spend the afternoon relaxing in nearby Hyde Park.

Spend a morning in Covent Garden, browsing the market and the shops. Visit colourful Neal Street Yard or sit out on the terrace at the Amphitheatre Restaurant at the Royal Opera House. Spend the afternoon marvelling at the riches of the British Museum in nearby Bloomsbury.

Begin the day with a spin on the British Airways London Eye. Then continue along the South Bank, where you can check out the Royal Festival Hall, National Theatre, Tate Modern and Shakespeare's Globe. If you can, buy tickets for the evening performance at the Globe.

Start early to avoid the queues at the Tower of London. Afterwards, appreciate the elaborate beauty of Tower Bridge before catching a boat from Tower Pier to Greenwich for lunch in a riverside pub. Greenwich is a UNESCO World Heritage Site, home to the Royal Observatory, the Maritime Museum and the Cutty Sark.

Dos and Don'ts

- ✓ Book tickets in advance to sights such as the Tower of London to avoid lengthy queueing.
- ✗ Don't hire a car, it's not worth the frustration, and public transport is comprehensive and easy to use.
- ✓ Look out for free lunchtime concerts in City and West End churches.
- ✗ Don't light up a cigarette, cigar or pipe. Smoking in enclosed public spaces has been illegal in England since 2007.

JAN
FEB
MAR
APR
MAY
JUN
JUL
AUG
SEP
DAY 1
DAY 2
DAY 3
DAY 4
DAY 5
OCT
NOV
DEC

have indeed remained unchanged for hundreds of years, they are applauded because, long-removed from their original context, they have become unconventional and eccentric, a quality much admired.

September is an ideal time to be on London's streets. The temperature is good for walking, for open-top bus rides and river trips. The parks are mellow, and the lively buzz of pubs and cafés can be enjoyed from outside. There are the last weeks of outdoor theatre, too, at Shakespeare's Globe, and the Proms in the Park brings the finale of the world's largest classical music festival to the masses in Hyde Park, one of the city's finest open spaces.

One of the best things about London is that many of its major museums and galleries are free. In September, visitors benefit from Open House weekend, when architecturally significant buildings not normally open to the public throw wide their doors, free – from the Royal Opera House and the Courts of Justice to stunning new landmark buildings in the city.

And who cares if it rains a little? Urchins certainly don't. In fact, the architectural melting pot of London's streets and buildings positively sparkle when it's wet.

Sumatran Rhinoceros

The Sumatran Rhino once roamed almost the entire island of Borneo but is now rarely sighted, with little evidence to show that the decline in numbers is stabilizing. Currently on the critically endangered list, with less than 300 remaining in the wild, the rhino is illegally hunted for its horn for ornamental and mythical medicinal uses. Also known as the hairy rhino, the Sumatran can be recognized by its long hair and reddish-brown skin.

RAINFOREST ADVENTURES

WITH ITS ROCKY PINNACLES AND MISTY RAINFORESTS, raging rivers, mangrove-encrusted shores and coral reefs, Borneo is a living Eden. The third largest island in the world, it boasts a rich biodiversity and is home to around 15,000 species of flowering plants, including many rare orchids and the huge rafflesia, which measures a metre (over 3 ft) in width and emits a foul, pungent odour. Known as "The Island in the Clouds", Borneo is the centre of evolution for many endemic forest species including the Asian Elephant, the Sumatran Rhinoceros and the Clouded Leopard. The rainforest, home to trees that tower up to 75 m (246 ft), is also the natural habitat of the endangered Bornean orang-utan, while the island's

Envisage a lush dripping landscape, peat swamp forests, and traditional villages with bamboo longhouses resting on stilts.

surrounding coastal waters support a magnificent ecosystem that abounds with marine life, corals and species of turtle, including the hawksbill and the green.

It's no surprise then that Borneo sets the scene for intrepid adventure, presenting great opportunities for wildlife observation, mountain climbing, rainforest trekking and river rafting. Diving is particularly good off the islands of Sabah in northern Malaysia. Consider climbing Mt Kinabalu – you will need to allow two days to climb and descend the mountain, and if you are lucky enough to have a clear morning sky, the views from the summit are amazing. If you want to explore the island further, Brunei is home to Ulu Temburong National Park, the tiny sultanate's "Green Jewel", while Kalimantan (Indonesia) is quintessential jungle and parts of it remain unexplored even to this day. Envisage a lush dripping landscape, peat swamp forests, and traditional villages with bamboo longhouses resting on stilts. Imagine coming face to face with Borneo's legendary head-hunters, the Dayak tribesmen, who inhabit Kalimantan's deep interior highlands. Although they live in much the same way as they have for the last millennium, they thankfully no longer practise head-hunting. A trip to Borneo feels like you have stepped back in time to a land that is still being discovered, opening up countless opportunities for exhilarating adventures.

Main: Orang-utan carries her baby through the jungle
Inset: The open seed pods of a Sterculia tree
Below (left to right): Bamboo bridge in Sarawak, Malaysia; green sea turtle, Pulau Sipadan, Malaysia; hikers on Mt Kinabalu

Above: Gunung Mulu National Park in Sarawak at dawn

ISLAND DIARY

Borneo is made up of Brunei and Malay and Indonesian enclaves. In order to make the most of your time it is best to focus on just one area. Malaysian Borneo, particularly the state of Sabah in the north, is perhaps the most accessible of the three, but if you have more time to spare then it is well worth exploring further.

Ten Days Exploring Sabah

Arrive into Kota Kinabalu. Stroll up Signal Hill for a view over the bay, shop for souvenirs at the Filipino Market and visit the State Museum. Jump on a boat to the lovely islands of nearby Tunku Abdul Rahman Park. Catch a bus to beautiful Kinabalu National Park.

Get up early to climb Mt Kinabalu. The climb takes two days, with an overnight stop at Laban Rata. Alternatively, follow the walking trails through the rainforest and enjoy a relaxing soak at Poring Hot Springs.

Head to Sandakan, a good base for nearby sights. Travel out to the world-famous Sepilok Orang-utan Rehabilitation Centre. Take a river safari on Sungai Kinabatangan, Sabah's longest river, or spend a day whitewater rafting on the wild Padas River through the spectacular gorge. Vist Turtle Islands National Park to spot turtles in the water or on the beach.

Head south to Semporna, from where you can catch a boat out to beautiful Pulau Sipadan. This is a small island – it only takes an hour to walk around – and it's a great site for diving. If you don't dive but want to, you can take a course here.

Head back to Kota Kinabalu or, if you have more time, continue exploring – head south to Sarawak (another Malay State) to visit the vibrant town of Kuching and beautiful Gunung Mulu National Park, or to the tiny sultanate of Brunei to see the "Green Jewel" of Ulu Temburong National Park, or into Kalimantan (Indonesian Borneo) to experience the traditional highland villages of head-hunters.

Dos and Don'ts

☑ Check your shoes before putting them on when you are staying in the jungle. Some creatures like to hide in them.

☒ Don't feed or touch orang-utans – it undermines their ability to fend for themselves in the wild. Touching them may expose them to human illnesses to which they are highly susceptible.

☑ Be gentle when diving or snorkelling around coral reefs. Living corals are easily damaged by contact with divers and their equipment.

JAN

FEB

MAR

APR

MAY

JUN

JUL

AUG

SEP

DAYS 1–2

DAYS 3–4

DAYS 5–7

DAYS 8–9

DAY 10

OCT

NOV

DEC

> "Madeira's seasons
> are the youth,
> maturity and old-age
> of a never-ending,
> still-beginning Spring."
>
> Henry Nelson Coleridge

GETTING THERE
Madeira International Airport is about 30 minutes from the capital, Funchal. Madeira is also a popular port of call for cruise liners.

GETTING AROUND
Cheap buses reach most parts of the island but car hire gives maximum flexibility. Taxis can be hired by the day for excursions.

WEATHER
In September, Madeira has average temperatures of 22°C, with low rainfall.

ACCOMMODATION
Quinta da Penha de Franca set among tropical gardens, close to the centre of Funchal; doubles from £60; www.penhafranca.com

Suite Hotel Eden Maris located by the sea in Funchal, and all rooms have kitchenettes; doubles from £85; www.portobay.pt

Reid's Palace, world-renowned luxury overlooking the Bay of Funchal; doubles from £250; www.reidspalace.com

EATING OUT
Freshly caught fish, simply grilled, is the staple of most menus, along with *espetadas* (grilled beef cubes), the food of Madeiran festivals. You can get a good meal for less than £16 per person.

PRICE FOR TWO
£170–200 per day including accommodation, food, entrance charges and car hire.

FURTHER INFORMATION
www.madeiratourism.org

Madeira Wine

Madeira is one of the world's great wines, with a unique depth and complexity of flavour. This was once thought to be the result of the rocking motion on board ships, as Madeira wine came back from long voyages magically improved. Nowadays, Madeira is matured on dry land in attics that are warmed by the sun, as experiments showed it was heat that did the trick. Genuine Madeira has to be made from medium dry Sercial and Verdelho or sweeter Bual and Malmsey.

Main: Beautiful Penha de Águia near Faial on Madeira's north coast
Inset: *Protea cynaroides* in the Botanical Gardens
Above: Fresh fruit and vegetables in Mercado dos Lavradores

GARDEN OF DELIGHTS

Rising from the Atlantic like the mythical Atlantis, Madeira sits a surprising 1,000 km (620 miles) from Portugal's capital, Lisbon. In 1419, Portuguese adventurers set out from Lisbon to explore the coast of Africa. In his diary, Captain Zarco recorded the fear experienced by his sailors as they headed for what they thought was the monster-infested rim of the ocean. What they found instead was a paradise of flower-filled evergreen forests, tumbling waterfalls and safe, sunny natural harbours.

Though storm-tossed sailors had visited Madeira before, nobody had yet settled there, and the fertile virgin soil proved perfect for crops of grapes and sugar cane. Lavishly decorated churches, luxurious rural mansions and elegant townhouses are the legacy of Madeira's early wealth, as are the vibrant religious paintings that adorn the island's churches. The Madeiran landscape is as impressive as this renowned art and architecture: tiny

Above: Wine barrels ready for the festivals

Above (top and bottom): Wine tasting at Funchal's wine festival; delicate Madeiran embroidery

Below: The dramatic beauty of Ponta de São Lourenço

FLOWER-FILLED DIARY

September is a great time to visit Madeira as the weather is still at its best, the crowds have disappeared and the countryside looks beautiful. September also sees lively wine festivals in Funchal and Estreito de Câmara de Lobos, the latter of which is particularly worth seeking out as it has a real local feel.

A Week of Botanical Charms

Spend the morning strolling through the pleasant streets of Funchal. Visit the Mercado dos Lavradores ("market of the workmen") to see the bountiful displays of fruit and flowers, before heading to the 15th-century cathedral and the Museum of Sacred Art.

Head first to the lovely Botanical Gardens before taking the cable car up to Monte to explore the Monte Palace Tropical Gardens. Head back downhill by traditional wooden toboggan, which was invented here in 1850.

Visit Câmara de Lobos and its neighbouring villages, nestled among the vines. From here it is just 10 km (6 miles) to Cabo Girão, the second highest sea cliff in Europe, at 589 m (1,932 ft) above sea level.

Head west to Rabaçal, the starting point for two magical *levada* walks. The more demanding walk takes two to three hours and leads to the beauty spot known as Vinte e Cinco Fontes (25 Springs).

Follow the footpaths from Ponta de São Lourenço which meander from one clifftop to another, past wild flowers growing in the sheltered hollows.

Drive the spectacular north coast road from Faial (taking in the beautiful Penha de Águia) to Porto Moniz for a seafood lunch. Return via the wild moorland heights of the Paúl da Serra.

Drive up to Pico Ruivo, the island's third highest mountain, passing through hillsides cloaked in fragrant eucalyptus and bay laurel.

Dos and Don'ts

☑ Take a cruise to Porto Santo. Madeira's smaller neighbour has one of Europe's best sandy beaches – 11 miles of unbroken golden sand.

☒ Don't spend all your day by the pool – discover Madeira's lovely scenery and wildlife by walking the island's footpaths.

☑ Visit an embroidery factory, where you can learn about this traditional craft and admire the exquisite needlework.

JAN
FEB
MAR
APR
MAY
JUN
JUL
AUG
SEP
DAY 1
DAY 2
DAY 3
DAY 4
DAY 5
DAY 6
DAY 7
OCT
NOV
DEC

terraces cling to the near vertical valley sides, watered by *levadas* (irrigation canals), which form a vital 2,150-km (1,335-mile) network around the island.

As moisture-laden Atlantic air reaches Madeira, it rises through the cloud forest before falling as rain in the cool high mountains at the heart of the island. Seeping through the porous volcanic soil to emerge at countless springs, the life-giving water travels for huge distances through tunnels and along rock-cut channels to feed the sun-drenched vineyards, fields, orchards and banana plantations. Best of all for the visitor, the paths that run alongside these contour-hugging *levadas* provide access to waterfalls, pools, forested ravines, dramatic viewpoints and the awesome geology of deeply eroded valleys and dramatic sea cliffs.

The island's sub-tropical climate promotes a rich variety of flora, mixing indigenous and foreign plants to create a horticulturalist's heaven, and even the dry and stony coastline erupts with colour from exotic blooms. In September, as the colours of the landscape begin to change and visitors become fewer, Madeira has the air of a secret garden, just waiting to be discovered.

GETTING THERE
The main airports are Marseille Marignane and Nice Côte d'Azur. There are also airports at Aix-en-Provence, Avignon, Grenoble, Nîmes and Toulon. The TGV (express train) from Paris takes 2 hours 40 minutes to Avignon.

GETTING AROUND
The coast is served by reliable bus and train networks, but hire a car if you want to see more of the region.

WEATHER
During the day, temperatures average around 24°C. Evenings are cool.

ACCOMMODATION
Hôtel d'Arlatan, a fine mansion in the centre of Arles; family rooms from £70; www.hotel-arlatan.fr

Hotel Danieli, Avignon, is a traditional hotel in the town centre; family rooms from £85; www.hoteldanieli-avignon.com

Hotel Durante, Nice, is a small and conveniently located hotel; family rooms from £115; www.hotel-durante.cote.azur.fr

EATING OUT
Provence's cuisine makes use of the abundant fruit and vegetables of the region, alongside fresh fish and seafood. Hiély-Lucullus in Avignon is one of the region's top restaurants.

PRICE FOR A FAMILY OF FOUR
£190–220 per day including accommodation, food and car hire.

FURTHER INFORMATION
www.provenceweb.fr

Frédéric Mistral

Provençal, the local language, had no real literature until the 19th century when concerned literati formed the Félibrige society. Its leading light was the poet Frédéric Mistral, whose writings won him the Nobel Prize for literature. He used the prize money to open the Museon Arlaten in Arles, which shows the traditional Provençal way of life.

Main: Sun-bleached door and window in a small village in Provence
Above (left to right): Herbs on display in Nice; Roman aqueduct, the Pont du Gard; detail of the façade of le Paillon de Vendome, Aix-en-Provence

The village of Les Baux at dusk

PROVENÇAL LIFE

IT WAS DURING THE SEPTEMBERS OF 1887 AND 1888 that Vincent Van Gogh completed his famous pictures of sunflowers in Arles. It's no surprise – this is a glorious time to be in the south of France, when the full summer heat has left the skies clear, the fields golden and the grapes bursting to be picked, while the soft sand of the emptying beaches is lapped by the Mediterranean at its warmest. Bee-eaters and roller birds brighten the meadows, flamingoes gather in the Camargue and the last bullfights take place in Nîmes and Arles.

The diversity of sights is vast, from monumental Roman remains at Arles, Nîmes and Orange to the Palace of the Popes in Avignon and Good King René's fountain-filled Aix-en-Provence. Some places will forever be associated with writers and artists: F. Scott Fitzgerald's Juan les Pins, Picasso's Antibes, Matisse's Nice. You can visit the home of Cézanne near Mt Victoire and Renoir in Cagnes. Those in search of 20th-century art will love the Fondation Maeght, just outside of the classic medieval village of St-Paul-de-Vence.

> The full summer heat has left the skies clear, the fields golden and the grapes bursting to be picked.

Provence also means good food: garlicky *pistou*, oily *ratatouille*, fishy *bouillabaisse*, or a fresh catch with just a squeeze of lemon. Then there's the wine: classic Côtes du Rhone as well as the lighter, refreshing local Provençal rosés, which are just right for a picnic. Fill your basket with treats from the markets: fresh vegetables, local cheese and late summer fruits; and take them to the hills or the beach for alfresco dining at its best.

Provence's *villages perchés* (hilltop towns) are made for lazy strolling. Les Baux-de-Provence is more of a citadel than a village, a dramatic high spot where troubadours became famous for their Courts of Love. By September the narrow, gallery-filled streets will be freer from tourists. Buy a painting, Provençal troubadour music or the brightly patterned fabrics of Arles to echo the sunshine of the south long after your tan has faded.

Inset: Rural road near St-Rémy-de-Provence
Below (left and right): Family cycling through the countryside of Provence; Carlton Hotel overlooking the beach in Cannes

TOURING DIARY

There are festivals and wine fairs throughout September, particularly the Grape Harvest Festival in Nîmes and the Rice Festival – with a distinct Spanish flavour of bullfights and sangria – in Arles. Hire a car to really explore Provence and get a good taste for this beautiful region.

A Week of Autumn Sun

Begin in Marseille, France's premier port and oldest major city. Wander through the old town to see the lovely Vieille Charité and the impressive Palais Longchamps. Enjoy the famed *bouillabaisse* for lunch, before heading on to Aix-en-Provence with its grand boulevards, interesting museums and cosmopolitan ambience.
DAY 1

Visit Arles, which is centred around a huge Roman amphitheatre. Explore the ancient sites and enjoy a coffee in the Café Van Gogh. Afterwards, head to Nîmes, another Roman town – the third weekend in September celebrates the *vendange* (grape harvest), with bullfights in the arena. Alternatively, visit Les Baux, with its dramatic fortress site and views across to the Camargue.
DAY 2

Spend a leisurely couple of days exploring the beautiful Vaucluse region – blessed with vines, lavender, truffles and melons. The area is home to the historical towns of Avignon and Orange, both well worth a visit.
DAYS 3–4

Head through the relatively undiscovered region of Alpes-de-Haute-Provence, which still has a very rural way of life. Stop for a picnic on your way to the coast. Once in Cannes, wander the famous Boulevard de la Croisette and take tea at the Carlton Hotel. Swim in the sea and laze on the beach, or visit the perfume factories in Grasse.
DAYS 5–6

Spend the morning in Nice for the market in Cours Saleya. From here you can head out to St-Paul-de-Vence for the Fondation Maeght, to Cagnes-sur-Mer for the Musée Renoir, or further along the coast to Menton and Monte Carlo.
DAY 7

Dos and Don'ts

☑ Take the narrow-gauge Train des Pignes from Nice up into the Alps to admire the wonderful views.

☒ Don't forget to pack your suntan lotion – the sun is still very strong at this time of year.

☑ Make sure that you pick up a leaflet from the French Tourist Office that shows what festivals are taking place in the area.

JAN
FEB
MAR
APR
MAY
JUN
JUL
AUG
SEP
OCT
NOV
DEC

ANGOLA
Rundu •
NAMIBIA
Swakopmund •
• Windhoek
BOTSWANA
NAMIB-NAUKLUFT
NATIONAL PARK
ATLANTIC
OCEAN
SOUTH
AFRICA

GETTING THERE
Namibia is in southwest Africa on the coast. The international airport, Hosea Kutako, is 42 km (26 miles) from the capital, Windhoek.

GETTING AROUND
Windhoek, Swakopmund and Sesriem are all interconnected by roads, some sealed and others dirt but suitable for driving. All three points are also connected by daily flights.

WEATHER
Namibia has a typical desert climate but September is in spring so is unlikely to be extremely hot or to drop below zero at night.

ACCOMMODATION
In Windhoek, Olive Grove Guesthouse offers luxurious and tranquil accommodation; doubles from £80; www.olivegrove-namibia.com

Sam's Giardino, in Swakopmund, is a friendly and comfortable retreat; doubles from £60; www.giardino.com.na

The exclusive Kulala Lodge is near Sesriem; doubles from £210, including dinner and breakfast; www.namibweb.com/kulala.htm

EATING OUT
Along the coast there is a strong emphasis on fresh seafood, and inland, beef and lamb dishes are popular. Try the southern African staple *mieliepap* (a maize porridge).

PRICE FOR TWO
£150–225 including accommodation, food and car hire.

FURTHER INFORMATION
www.namibiatourism.com.na

Namibian Rock Art

Namibia forms an important repository for the fine rock paintings and engravings executed by the hunter-gatherers that once inhabited most of Africa. Whether primarily of mystical or ritual symbolism, the paintings have great significance as the sole surviving testament to a hunter-gatherer culture more complex than ever acknowledged by the European settlers who exterminated it.

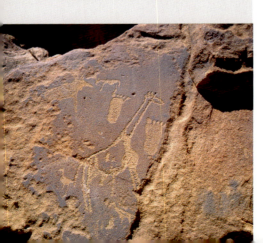

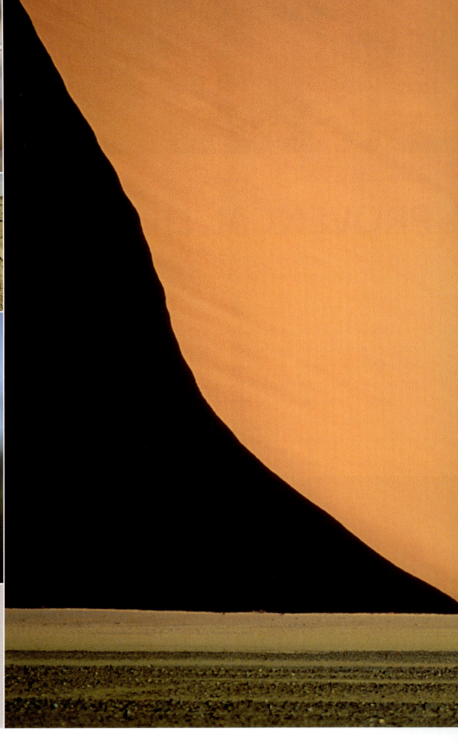

Main: Apricot-coloured sand dune catches the evening light in Sossusvlei, in the heart of the Namib Desert

Above (top to bottom): The Bushmen (also known as Khwe Khoe or Basarwa) people of Namibia; parched welwitschia in Welwitschia Drive in the Namib-Naukluft National Park; meerkat scanning the landscape in Namib-Naukluft National Park

DISCOVERING THE DUNES

N AMIBIA MUST RANK CLOSE to being the emptiest non-polar nation on the planet. Dominated by the Namib Desert, whose parched sandy soils are teased by less than 2.5 cm (1 inch) of rain annually, this immense land is too desiccated to sit comfortably with adjectives such as pretty or beautiful. And yet there is a vastness to the Namibian landscape, a ravaged majesty that is at once humbling, breathtaking and profoundly liberating.

The most compelling of Namibian landscapes, Sossusvlei lies on the eastern border of Africa's largest national park, the 50,000-sq km (19,000-sq miles) Namib-Naukluft. Here you'll find the world's tallest dunes: rippled apricot mountains whose curvaceous "scorpion tails" tower above a series of seasonal pans that fill with water once or perhaps twice in a decade. Here, too, you'll find the aptly named Deadvlei, its embalmed floor of cracked dried mud hosting a spectral medieval forest, a relic of the days when this parody of a lake received water more regularly.

Above (top to bottom): Colonial architecture in picturesque Swakopmund; tented bedroom overlooking the Namibian dunes; flamingoes wading in Walvis Bay

Below: Cape fur seal colony at Cape Cross

Above: Unmistakeable silhouettes of quiver trees at sunset

JAN

FEB

MAR

APR

MAY

JUN

JUL

AUG

SEP

OCT

NOV

DEC

DESERT DIARY

The loop through southern Namibia might be explored over 4–5 days or longer, extending the trip to include Fish River Canyon near the South African border. With more time, at least another week, you could tag on northwest Namibia, with its superb rock art sites and amazing desert-adapted elephants.

Five Days in the Apricot Sands

DAY 1
Drive from Windhoek to the port of Swakopmund, arriving in time to enjoy a late lunch by the beachfront.

Spend the afternoon exploring the town centre, with its German colonial architecture, museum, aquarium, snake park and terrace cafés.

DAY 2
In the morning, drive north to Cape Cross, named after the cross erected by Diego Cão in 1485. Here, you'll find the world's largest permanent seal colony – around 100,000 animals – sunbathing and squabbling.

Spend the afternoon relaxing and shopping, birdwatching and dolphin-spotting at nearby Walvis Bay Lagoon, or quad-biking in the surrounding dunes.

DAY 3
Take the scenic route through the Namib-Naukluft Park to the Sesriem area, starting with Welwitschia Drive, where you'll find some of the largest and oldest specimens of these weird semi-subterranean desert conifers. Then head to the freakily isolated settlement of Solitaire, a good place to fill up the car and grab a snack and a drink.

DAY 4
Full day exploring the Sesriem area, in particular Sossusvlei and Deadvlei, which are best viewed in the soft early morning or later afternoon light, the afternoon being far quieter in terms of tourist traffic.

DAY 5
Half-day drive back to Windhoek, leaving you the morning free for a horseback excursion into the dunes or a flight above them. Alternatively, explore the museums and art galleries of the capital.

Dos and Don'ts

✘ Don't exceed 80 km/h (50 mph) on unsurfaced roads – as the road quality can suddenly change from good to bad.

✓ Carry plenty of water – you could be in for a long, hot wait in the event of a breakdown.

✓ Fill up when there is an opportunity or carry a filled jerry-can – distances between fuel stations are often measured in hundreds of kilometres/miles.

✓ Stop the car to enjoy the scenery once in a while – it's amazing how often you'll notice an antelope or beautiful bird you might otherwise have sped past.

Come dusk, you might see a herd of oryx antelope filing regally across a dune crest, a meerkat (a type of mongoose) family standing to attention in the dying light, or a spiky quiver tree silhouetted against the emerging sun. The crisp, clear desert air and absence of competing light sources makes the Namib night sky a thing of shimmering, awe-inspiring beauty. No less memorable is the silence of the Namib on a windless night: so close to absolute that it becomes almost tangible, an enveloping presence broken sporadically by the gentle chatter of a gecko or the demented whooping of a distant hyena or jackal.

By way of surreal contrast, the German-built port of Swakopmund rises in bizarre isolation from the dunes that surround it on three sides, and the chilly waves that beat down on it from the fourth. With its distinctive colonial architecture and memorable location on what is effectively a beach the size of a small European nation, this surprisingly lively town is the ideal base from which to explore the magical Namib, as well as more remote coastal spots such as the flamingo-filled Sandwich Harbour to its south and the immense Cape Cross seal colony to the north.

GETTING THERE
Santorini is the southernmost island of Greece's Cycladic group in the Aegean Sea. Santorini can be reached by air – its airport is served domestically from Athens, Thessaloniki, Crete, Rhodes and Mykonos. The island can also be reached by ferry from Athens (6–12 hours), Thessaloniki and other Greek islands.

GETTING AROUND
Get around the 96-sq km (37-sq mile) island by bus, taxi, car or scooter.

WEATHER
September is sunny, warm and dry with an average temperature of 24°C.

ACCOMMODATION
Armonia Hotel at popular Kamari Beach; doubles from £40; www.kamaritours.gr

Panorama Hotel is located on the cliff in Fira; doubles from £85; santorama@otenet.gr

Museum Spa Hotel, situated in a converted mansion/museum in Oia, has studios from £120; www.hotelmuseum.net

EATING OUT
Look out for the local specialities *apoxti* (cured ham), capers and stuffed courgettes, as well as delicious seafood. The local Vin Santo dessert wine is also a must.

PRICE FOR TWO
£180–250 per day including accommodation, food, sunset cruise, boat excursion, car hire and entrance charges.

FURTHER INFORMATION
www.santorini.com

Volcanic Santorini
Santorini has changed shape 12 times over the last 400,000 years – from a single land mass to small islands that were joined and then split apart again. The cataclysmic Minoan eruption around 1630 BC spewed out 90 billion tons of magma over just a few days. Geologically, Santorini is part of an arc formed together with the volcanic islands of Milos, Nisyros in the eastern Aegean, the Methana peninsula near Athens and Mt Etna in Italy.

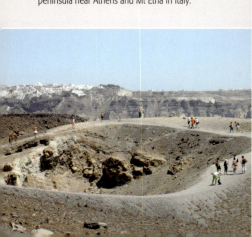

Above: Dinghies tied up in the harbour at Oia

Main: Church bells at sunset on Santorini Island
Above (left to right): Pool overlooking the sea at Fira; flowers with Santorini's volcanic landscape in the background; church domes in Oia

VOLCANIC PARADISE

LIKE DELPHI'S GLORIOUS ANCIENT THEATRE or Meteora's otherworldly rocks, the Greek island of Santorini must be seen to be believed. The raw and elemental beauty of the volcanic landscape is adorned by the gleaming, gravity-defying villages to great effect.

Santorini emerges from the deep blue Aegean like no other landmass. It is easy to picture it as it once was: a round island with a central volcano whose cone imploded during an eruption, the resulting crater flooding with water. This deep void is the caldera and what now remains as Santorini, following numerous further eruptions, is the outer crust of the original island on three sides. The inner rim of this is a steep, dramatic cliff of black and red rock, to which the island's famous white villages cling. A small, smouldering cone juts out in the middle of what was the original island, now the startling blue Aegean, while another part, cut off from the outer ring on the far side of the volcanic cone, has emerged as the islet of Thirassia. It is the dramatic view from

on top of the inner rim, overlooking the caldera, that captivates all who see it. Though many have tried to paint and describe it, it is hard to capture the sense of peace and awe that the view creates.

In the precipice-clinging towns of Oia and Fira, art galleries and trinket shops line narrow, cobbled alleys with vibrant displays. Yet, despite obvious tourist trappings, tradition is not hard to find. Whitewashed buildings teeter on the edge while bells ring out from blue-domed churches and elderly villagers trot through the steep, sun-bleached streets on their donkeys.

This is undeniably an island of romance – for a most magical evening, take an unforgettable sunset cruise on a schooner. Santorini is famed for the dramatic colours of the slowly setting sun and a view from the water is an incredible way to see it. Later, over dinner on board, you will be able to see the twinkling lights of clifftop Oia as dusk descends over the island.

Whitewashed buildings teeter on the edge while bells ring out from blue-domed churches and elderly villagers trot through the sun-bleached streets on their donkeys.

Inset: Donkey stands against a whitewashed wall
Below (left and right): Eating at a traditional taverna; Fira at night

CALDERA DIARY

September see the crowds diminish, while the days remain sunny and the evenings balmy. The town of Fira is commercial and lively, while more traditional Oia perfectly complements the island's dramatic beauty. Extend your trip by adding a few days in Athens to the itinerary (see pp100–1).

Four Days with a View

Arrive at your caldera-view hotel and soak up the panorama and sunshine from your terrace. When you are ready for a little more activity, head into Fira or Oia to wander through the narrow streets and admire the traditional architecture and pretty churches. Be sure to seek out a good place to watch the sunset over drinks or a taverna dinner. — **DAY 1**

To explore the island like the locals, hire a scooter. Head to Fira for the museums, which contain finds from two local ancient settlements. Thira dates back to the 3rd century BC, while Akrotiri, the Pompeii of the Aegean, predates the AD 79 Vesuvius disaster by 1,700 years. Then head off to see one or both of these sites. Spend the evening back in town, after taking a sunset cruise around the caldera. — **DAY 2**

Go on a half-day boat excursion – climb the desolate volcano, swim at the hot springs, and have lunch in the cliff-top village on the islet of Thirassia. Alternatively, other tours available include wine-tasting, scuba diving, sea kayaking or horse-riding. Rest in the afternoon before heading out when it is a little cooler to explore the alleys and shops of Santorini's towns. Later, dine outside on a restaurant terrace to make the most of the warm evenings and lively ambience. — **DAY 3**

Head to one of Santorini's volcanic black or red sand beaches for the day, or combine it with an early morning trip to one of the ancient sites (both are near beaches). Spend your last afternoon/evening getting your fill of the spectacular view from your hotel or at a nearby restaurant or bar. — **DAY 4**

Dos and Don'ts

✓ Rent a scooter to zip around the island, but fill up in Fira – there are no petrol stations in Oia. Be a cautious driver as accidents are not uncommon.

✗ Don't go to Ancient Thira unless you are in good shape. The very young and the unfit will have great difficulty climbing the steep hill.

✓ Check that Ancient Akrotiri is open for the season before heading out there.

✗ Don't stay in Oia if mobility is a problem – the town is known for its steep steps, especially those leading up to it from the port.

JAN
FEB
MAR
APR
MAY
JUN
JUL
AUG
SEP
OCT
NOV
DEC

OCTOBER

Where to Go: October

October marks the middle of autumn in the northern hemisphere. The shortening of the days and importance of gathering in the harvest are reflected in the wine festivals that start to take place around Europe. Visit the vineyards in the Loire Valley or follow the celebrated Chianti route through Tuscany. There's still time to catch the autumn leaf displays of North America, or for something different, see the Japanese ones instead. Meanwhile, in the southern hemisphere, things are beginning to heat up as spring approaches – perfect for a tango in Buenos Aires, or a dive on the Great Barrier Reef. To help you choose where to go, you'll find all the destinations in this chapter below, as well as some extra suggestions to provide a little inspiration.

FESTIVALS AND CULTURE

LHASA Man wearing the traditional dress of Tibet

UNFORGETTABLE JOURNEYS

ROCKY MOUNTAINS Maligne Lake and Spirit Island, Canada

NATURAL WONDERS

KAUA`I Exotic pink frangipani flowers in full bloom

LHASA
CHINA, ASIA

Tibet is a spiritual place that is literally on a higher plane

Against the backdrop of the Himalayan mountains, Lhasa has long been secluded by its location in the world's highest area.
See pp258–9

PAPUA NEW GUINEA
AUSTRALASIA

Sail between faraway islands in pristine diving waters

Join a catamaran for an adventure cruise through the islands off New Guinea, stopping to dive, trek and visit traditional villages.
www.theimajicaexperience.com

WAHIBA DESERT
OMAN, MIDDLE EAST

Empty sands and all the remoteness of Arabia

Take a 4WD ride through Oman's untouched deserts, dropping from giant dunes into rocky wadis and camping under the stars.
www.omantourism.gov.om

"The garden isle is covered with lush, green forests, and a myriad colourful flowers."

KAUA`I
USA, NORTH AMERICA

Nature at its finest on the most beautiful of Hawaiian islands

There's more here than big waves and flower garlands – an incredibly varied environment ripe for exploration and filled with nature.
See pp248–9

BUENOS AIRES
ARGENTINA, SOUTH AMERICA

Combines European style with South American hedonism

A centre of culture and sophistication, and a vibrant exotic city characterized by the national dance – the tango. With quality food and wine to boot.
See pp264–5

"There is something for everyone in Buenos Aires – and it all mirrors the irrepressible spirit of Argentina."

BIG SUR
USA, NORTH AMERICA

The wild coastline on the road between San Francisco and LA

Driving between these two great coastal cities you'll see some of America's finest wind- and wave-lashed coastlines and a lot more.
See pp254–5

EDEN PROJECT
ENGLAND, EUROPE

A whole world of nature all in one place

A fascinating range of the world's natural environments, all recreated in vast transparent "biomes", and an exciting range of events.
www.edenproject.com

TAKACHIHOKYO GORGE
JAPAN, ASIA

Waterfalls and colourful cliffs

Japan's forests explode into beautiful colour in autumn as the *momeji* – Japanese maple tree – forests turn brilliant red.
www.jnto.go.jp

TIMBUKTU
MALI, AFRICA

A historic city whose very name conjures up a sense of mystery

Once a centre of Islamic teaching, Timbuktu's architectural glories have been taken by the desert, but the people and the romance remain.
See pp262–3

BUDAPEST
HUNGARY, EUROPE

Hungary's capital celebrates the arts in its Autumn Festival

Dazzling architecture, fine restaurants and an eclectic art scene make this elegant city one of Europe's trendiest destinations.
See pp266–7

COAST TO COAST
CANADA, NORTH AMERICA

A legendary train ride east to west over the mountains

Canada's interior is a land of wide vistas so there's a lot of superb scenery to enjoy, but the mountains are the highlight of the journey.
See pp252–3

CHURCHILL
CANADA, NORTH AMERICA

The undisputed polar bear capital of the world

Between the summer thaw and winter freeze hundreds of polar bears migrate past (or through!) this Arctic town.
www.townofchurchill.ca

KAIKOURA
NEW ZEALAND, AUSTRALASIA

Taste the ocean at the annual Seafest

The centre of a major wine-producing region, this waterside town hosts a fun celebration of food, wine and entertainment.
www.kaikoura.co.nz

KHYBER PASS
PAKISTAN, ASIA

A unique train trip into one of the world's wildest places

The "Khyber Steam Safari" takes you in a vintage steam train up the Khyber Pass to the Afghan border – with an army escort.
www.khybersteamsafari.com

PIEDMONT
ITALY, EUROPE

Autumn countryside and gourmet pleasures

See the Northern Italian woods at their best on a truffle hunt, as locals head for the hills in search of these rare delicacies.
www.enit.it

Previous page: Vibrant blue waves off the coast of Kaua`i, Hawai`i

Weather Watch

❶ Winter is approaching fast in Canada, so it's cold at night but clear by day – just right for a train ride. California is still pleasant and sunny and you'll notice it gets warmer as you drive south.

❷ Argentina, especially Buenos Aires, has a pleasant climate and spring is the best season – sunny and warm without summer's humidity.

❸ It is always hot in Mali. The only solace is that the rains have recently ended (in September) – so it feels a little fresher.

❹ Temperatures in Europe are falling, but still comfortable day and night in the south. Plenty of sunny days but the rain is increasing.

❺ Tibet has a harsh climate with seasonal storms of dust, sand or snow possible. This month, below 3,900 m (13,000 ft) it is mild during the day and cold at night; above this height, it is always icy cold.

❻ The area around the Great Barrier Reef has a tropical climate – hot and sunny all year round. The monsoon rains are still a month away, so the humidity is comfortably low – and the water, clear.

LUXURY AND ROMANCE

TUSCANY The wine cellar at the Castello Banfi Estate

ACTIVE ADVENTURES

QUEENSLAND Sailing around the Whitsunday Islands

FAMILY GETAWAYS

OAXACA Coloured carpet of sand for the Day of the Dead

MAFIA ISLAND
TANZANIA, AFRICA

A romantic escape for independent-minded dreamers

This cluster of tiny islands offers fantastic beaches, great diving, nature trails and the feel of a real tropical backwater far from the everyday.
www.africatravelresource.com

LA RIOJA
SPAIN, EUROPE

Fine wines and an array of architectural jewels

Spain's première wine region has a matchless range of atmospheric places to stay – from medieval mansions to luxury designer hotels.
www.spain.info

SAN FRANCISCO
USA, NORTH AMERICA

Sample the pleasures of one of America's special cities

Take in the views, the character and the fantastic cuisine of the city on the bay, then head up to the Napa Valley for a winery tour.
www.onlyinsanfrancisco.com

LOIRE VALLEY
FRANCE, EUROPE

Tour the Loire valley visiting the châteaux

See grand medieval and fantastic Renaissance architecture among the pretty river landscapes.
See pp260–61

TUSCANY
ITALY, EUROPE

Feast your senses on architecture, art and exquisite cuisine

With romantic landscapes cloaked in mist, splendid architecture rich in history, Tuscany is a prime destination for lovers of refinement and beauty.
See pp250–51

"Sublime art and breathtaking architecture vie for your attention amid vistas of incomparably romantic landscapes."

SOOMAA NATIONAL PARK
ESTONIA, EUROPE

Adventure in a watery world

A huge area of Estonia is made up of bogs, and "bog-walking" is a national pastime – a fascinating way to discover a rare landscape.
www.soomaa.com

ZAMBEZI RIVER
ZAMBIA, AFRICA

Test yourself on the wildest whitewater river in the world

Almost a mix of rafting and surfing, getting through the Zambezi rapids is truly hair-raising – but less taxing trips are also available.
whitewater.safpar.com

QUEENSLAND
AUSTRALIA, AUSTRALASIA

Scuba dive to see the treasures of the Great Barrier Reef

It's one of the most famous dive sites in the world, and still one of the best. You can also sail, kayak, or go river rafting and bungy jumping.
See pp256–7

YASAWA ISLANDS
FIJI, SOUTH PACIFIC

Island-hop around the South Seas under your own steam

These idyllic tropical islands are never more than a short distance apart, so are perfect for kayak tours of a few days or more.
www.south-seas-adventures.com

WADI RUM
JORDAN, MIDDLE EAST

The deep-red heart of the Arabian desert

Giant valleys with unearthly desert landscapes: try a camel trek with Bedouin guide, the only way to capture the desert silence.
www.rumguides.com

"The magical sight of a cemetery glittering with hundreds of candles and the dancing that accompany these reunions, lingers in the memory."

ALBUQUERQUE
USA, NORTH AMERICA

Brilliantly colourful balloons soar above New Mexico

Ballooning enthusiasts home in on Albuquerque for the USA's biggest hot-air festival – a ride is a must for the 100,000 or more spectators.
www.balloonfiesta.com

BLUE MOUNTAINS
AUSTRALIA, AUSTRALASIA

Get high above the fabulous New South Wales hills

Fly over ravines and waterfalls in the glass-bottomed Skyway, or take the Walkway through towering forests past breathtaking views.
www.scenicworld.com.au

OAXACA
MEXICO, NORTH AMERICA

Kids will enjoy the macabre but joyous Day of The Dead

Feast on skulls and other ghoulish delights – chocolate of course – as Mexican families honour their dead with parties and celebration.
See pp268–9

RHODES
GREECE, EUROPE

The crowds have gone, but the water's still beautifully warm

Ancient ruins, medieval Venetian fortresses, delightful towns and countless beaches – in October you can have them to yourself.
www.rhodesguide.com

EUREKA! HALIFAX
ENGLAND, EUROPE

Kids love getting to grips with the real world

This museum for children is totally hands-on, with all sorts of fun exhibits: later, burn more energy with a walk in the Yorkshire Dales.
www.eureka.org.uk

GETTING THERE
Kaua`i is the northernmost island of the Hawaiian archipelago, 3,827 km (2,375 miles) west of California. It is a 5-hour flight from the US mainland to Līhu`e, the main city on Kaua`i. Or fly to Honolulu then take the shuttle planes from there to Kaua`i.

GETTING AROUND
Once on the island, you will need to rent a car at the airport, as there is no public transport. You can also rent bikes or horses for shorter trips, but be aware of steep mountain slopes.

WEATHER
Kaua`i is warm in October with the temperature averaging 26°C. Rainfall is frequent but short-lived.

ACCOMMODATION
The Sheraton Kauai is near Po`ipū Beach; doubles from £215; www.sheraton-kauai.com

The Hyatt Regency Kauai Resort & Spa is one of the island's top luxury resorts; doubles from £230; kauai.hyatt.com

The Princeville Resort Kauai occupies a paradise-like setting above Hanalei Bay; doubles from £305; www.princevillehotelhawaii.com

EATING OUT
A favourite hang-out both for locals and tourists is quirky Brennecke's Beach Broiler, Po`ipū – a relaxed restaurant right on the beach. Try *kālua* pork – a whole pig baked in leaves.

PRICE FOR TWO
£250–300 per day including accommodation, food and sports activities.

FURTHER INFORMATION
www.kauai-hawaii.com
www.kauaidiscovery.com

Hawaiian Surfing
With the arrival of the missionaries, Hawaiian traditions (and the language) were outlawed or forgotten, and it was only at the beginning of the 20th century that Olympic gold medallist swimmer Duke Kahanamoku (1890–1968) revived surfing and developed the modern sport, making it popular again not only in the islands, but also in California and Australia. Hawai`i still offers some of the best waves in the world, and the giant waves off Maui, called "Jaws", present surfers with one of the highest-risk sports adventures on the planet.

Above (left and right): Sumptuous pink frangipani flowers on Kaua'i; aerial view of Hanalei Bay
Main: Rugged landscape of the Nā Pali Coast

Above: Hanakapi`ai Falls on the Kalalau Trail

JAN
FEB
MAR
APR
MAY
JUN
JUL
AUG
SEP
OCT
NOV
DEC

HAWAIIAN DREAM

Kaua'i is a scented dream of a tropical paradise. The garden isle is covered with lush, green forests and a myriad colourful flowers; it echoes with the twittering welcome of exotic birds while the hypnotic boom of waves crashing onto the golden beaches draws you into a spiritual neverland. To many *haoles* (strangers) who fly to the islands year after year, Kaua'i is the prettiest of all. Six million years old, this island, once a volcano rising from the sea, is certainly the oldest of all, and the most ecologically varied. It offers deep rainforest, deserts, plains and mountains, all thrown together in a breathtaking natural setting with the Waimea Canyon, the largest canyon in the Pacific, and the world-famous Nā Pali Coast – jungle-clad cliffs rising sharply from dark blue sea. Kaua'i is an intriguing place, created by the immense forces of nature, and still subject to them. Because of this, Hollywood has used the primeval and unruly landscape of the island as a backdrop in several films, including *Blue Hawaii*, *King Kong* and *Jurassic Park*.

The mountains, canyons and the beaches, especially on the Nā Pali coastline, are so unique that they deserve two different approaches – by sea and by land. Attacking the Kalalau Trail, through the Nā Pali Mountains, is a once-in-a-lifetime experience – but not for the faint-hearted. The paths lead through thick fern and rainforests, down to the sea through river rapids, and then on to the Hanakapi'ai Falls where you can swim in cool, clear water. The falls are 3 km (2 miles) into the trail, and anybody continuing needs a hiking permit to scramble the next 15 km (9 miles) to Kalalau, an isolated beach. It is an arduous journey, too much for one day, so camping at the falls is well-advised.

To get the sea view before you leave, take a kayak out and paddle round until the Nā Pali cliffs rear high above you. As you glide through the water you'll be confronted with the same breathtaking spectacle the first Polynesians saw when they stumbled upon this natural paradise.

> . . . deep rainforest, deserts, plains and mountains, all thrown together in a breathtaking natural setting.

Inset: Green turtle surrounded by surgeonfish
Below (left to right): The Spouting Horn; giant ficus trees; hula dancer

SURFER'S DIARY

It takes almost a full day to circle the island by car, so plan ahead when visiting areas – and never leave too late, as it can be difficult to find your way back in the darkness which comes quite early in these latitudes. Kaua'i is all about the sea and the lush green nature inland so kick back and indulge in this tropical paradise.

Five Days on Kaua`i

Take an early ride on one of the sailing catamarans such as HoloHolo Charters, to tour the sea off the Nā Pali Coast – occasionally clouds and strong winds may prevent you from seeing a picture-perfect Nā Pali Coast image, but the humpback whales in the water more than make up for it.

Drive up to Waimea Canyon to simply enjoy the view or, if you are feeling a little more energetic, book a walk or horse ride tour deep through this incredible 6-km (10-mile) canyon, the longest in the Pacific.

DAYS 1–2

Head south to Po`ipū beach and try to catch some waves on the surfboard or a body board; later enjoy the sun luxuriating on the tropical golden sands.

Tour the southern coastline to the west along to the Spouting Horn, a natural sea water geyser. In the evening, enjoy a *lū`au* at one of the luxury hotels.

DAYS 3–4

Get up at sunrise and head north to the trailhead of the Kalalau Trail. You can follow the narrow path through lush mountains several hundred feet above the sea while enjoying an entirely different view of these jungle-covered, 915-m (3000-ft) cliffs than from the sea. If you choose only to walk for 3 km (2 miles) (the first part of the trail), spend the afternoon in the Hanalei Bay area swimming. On your way there, stop by Tunnel's Beach, one of the most beautiful Hawaiian beaches with some great snorkelling.

DAY 5

Dos and Don'ts

✓ Try to hike the Kalalau Trail – it's certainly one of the world's most scenic walking routes.

✗ Don't remove any coral or other plants or sea life from the ocean and never touch anything underwater you don't know.

✓ Swim, surf, snorkel or scuba dive with someone else. In general, Hawaiian waters close to the shores are safe, but strong, unpredictable undercurrents, an occasional shark and large waves can be hazardous.

✗ Don't jump into a waterfall, lake or river from a cliff high above – water depths can be difficult to gauge.

GETTING THERE
Tuscany is a large region in central Italy and Florence is the capital. Florence's airport is 4 km (2 miles) from the city centre and is linked to the main train station by bus. Pisa's airport is the region's largest, 1 hour west of Florence.

GETTING AROUND
In cities, walk or use public transport. Hire a car to tour the countryside.

WEATHER
October is still warm at around 20°C; be prepared for some rain and autumnal mists.

ACCOMMODATION
Many Tuscan hotels were converted from historic residences, and therein lies their charm.

La Cisterna, an 18th-century palace in San Gimignano, has doubles from £80; www.hotelcisterna.it

Villa Vignamaggio in Greve in Chianti offers *agriturismo* luxury and doubles from £120; www.vignamaggio.it.

Certosa di Maggiano provides country elegance in Siena, with doubles from £300; www.relaischateaux.com/certosa

EATING OUT
For gourmet Tuscan cooking in a romantic setting, visit Badia a Coltibuono in Gaiole in Chianti; main courses are around £10; www.coltibuono.com

PRICE FOR TWO
£200–220 per day for accommodation, food, car hire and entrance charges.

FURTHER INFORMATION
www.turismo.toscana.it

Tuscan Firsts
In art and architecture, Tuscans reign supreme. As well as the mighty Michelangelo and Leonardo da Vinci, the region was home to many other artists, including Giotto, who introduced humanity to figure painting, and Donatello, who worked out perspective in sculpture. Tuscans gave Europe its first public library, founded the first banks and commissioned the first opera. Chianti was the world's first officially defined wine-producing region – the logo for Gallo Nero wines dates from the 14th century, so was arguably the world's first "brand".

SUBLIME TREASURES

TUSCANY IS A FEAST FOR THE SENSES. Sublime art and breathtaking architecture vie for your attention amid vistas of incomparably romantic landscapes. The vineyards that clamber among timeless hilltop towns provide rich red wines; the bountiful earth offers up food long enjoyed by both kings and peasants.

The region also boasts two of Italy's city highlights – Renaissance Florence and Gothic, brick-built Siena – and an array of handsome villages and ochre towns of fortresses and frescoes. Drenched in history, the narrow lanes of wide-walled towns bring surprises at every turn; Etruscan Cortona captivates with both the views from its steep streets and its medieval and Renaissance buildings. South of Siena, in a quintessential Tuscan landscape of cypress trees and thick-walled farmhouses, Montalcino shows off its Brunello wine and Montepulciano its Vino Nobile.

Tuscans, who love art, music, food and wine, find countless excuses to party. If the long hot days and balmy nights of summer induce a flurry of festivals, what better reason to celebrate in autumn

Below (top to bottom): The wine cellar at the Castello Banfi Estate in Montalcino; copy of Michelangelo's *David* in Piazza della Signoria, Florence; Ponte Vecchio, Florence

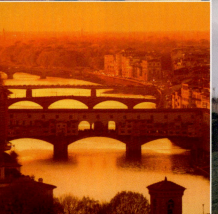

than *vendemmia* (the bringing in of the grapes) and the harvesting of olives? This is the season when sought-after *porcini* mushrooms and prized *tartufo* (truffles) flavour risottos and game appears on Tuscan menus – slow-stewed wild boar, or hare cooked with red wine and herbs and served with the region's wide *pappardelle* pasta.

Each area, each town even, has its own specialities. Think of *bistecca alla fiorentina* – thick steak, at its best sourced from the white cattle of the Valdiciana, drizzled with the finest olive oil and grilled over the embers of a chestnut wood fire; Prato's *cantucci*, biscuits made to be dipped in sweet Vin Santo; *pici* pasta from the hill towns around Siena; and that city's deliciously chewy *panforte* (spiced cake), packed with nuts and candied fruit.

Owners of grand Renaissance villas and medieval hilltop castles have opened up their homes to paying guests, and vineyards offer *agriturismo* (farm-stays) on a luxurious scale – 24-hour room service may not be on the menu, but when you wake up to glorious views, feast on the finest food and wines and visit some of the best galleries in the world, it seems like a fair exchange.

Above: Towers of San Gimignano illuminated at dusk

AUTUMNAL DIARY

October is harvest time for grapes and olives, the hunt is on for wild boar and truffles, and the countryside is draped in sunburned shades and romantic mists. The S222 from Florence to Siena is the classic Chianti trail and can be done in a day, but you would miss out on vineyards, towns and myriad back-road discoveries.

Six Days on the Chianti Trail

Spend a day in Florence – the centre is quite small and easy to see on foot. Admire the architectural genius of Brunelleschi's cupola on the cathedral and browse the jewellers that line Ponte Vecchio.

Leave Florence for Greve in Chianti. Feast your eyes on the hams and salamis at Macelleria Falorni on Piazza Matteotti. Explore the excellent vineyards and pretty villages nearby, such as tiny 14th-century Montefioralle, and Panzano for some wonderful sweeping views.

Explore hilltop Radda in Chianti and the ancient abbey in Badia a Coltibuono. Drive on to Siena and spend the evening in the sloping Piazza del Campo.

Marvel at Siena's 13th- and 14th-century architecture – seek out graceful Palazzo Publico, the sumptuous Museo Civico and the majestic Duomo. Visit the Museo Metropolitana to see its magnificent art.

Stay in Siena to enjoy a view of the city from the Museo dell'Opera, visit the Casa di Santa Caterina or feast on more Sienese paintings at the Pinacoteca Nazionale. Or head out to the countryside to explore the ruined abbey of San Galgano, superbly set in dense woodland.

On your way back to Florence, allow a day to see the medieval stone towers of San Gimignano and the frescoes in the Collegiata and Sant'Agostino. Alternatively, continue south to the quintessential Tuscan landscape that surrounds the wine-producing towns of Montalcino and Montepulciano, or visit the captivating Etruscan town of Cortona.

Dos and Don'ts

✓ Call into tourist offices for local information. Opening times of shops, churches, museums and restaurants can vary.

✗ Don't even think of taking your car into central Florence – the limited traffic zone covers most of the city centre.

✓ Go armed with a detailed map of the region. It's very easy to get lost in wooded Chianti country.

✓ Call ahead before visiting vineyards and wineries to check availability of tours and tastings.

✓ Allow plenty of time – with winding roads, long lingering lunches and vineyard stops, getting anywhere in the region usually takes twice as long as you first imagined.

JAN
FEB
MAR
APR
MAY
JUN
JUL
AUG
SEP
OCT
DAY 1
DAY 2
DAY 3
DAY 4
DAY 5
DAY 6
NOV
DEC

Main: Villa Il Belvedere in the Tuscan landscape

Top: Aerial view of Siena's terracotta rooftops and the 12th-century Piazza del Campo

Above: The stripey Gothic Duomo in Siena

Below: Eating al fresco in Siena's Piazza del Campo

GETTING THERE
Halifax is a small waterfront city on Canada's east coast. International flights arrive into the airport, 22 km (14 miles) from the city centre. There are also international flights to other major cities, including Vancouver, Toronto, Montreal and Edmonton.

GETTING AROUND
You can travel across Canada both east- and westbound by train, beginning in Halifax or Vancouver, and between other towns and cities.

WEATHER
Daytime temperatures average 18°C in Vancouver, 20°C in Toronto.

ACCOMMODATION
The most economical way to travel is in Via Rail's Comfort class, with a partially reclining seat and a shared bathroom; www.viarail.ca

On the Rocky Mountaineer route, choose from RedLeaf (economy) and GoldLeaf (luxury), over-nighting in hotels; www.rockymountaineer.com

The Royal Canadian Pacific trains through the Rockies offer pure luxury in vintage rail cars, with private cabins; www.cpr.ca

EATING OUT
Meals are served on trains and include regional ingredients like salmon, beef and local wines.

PRICE FOR TWO
Rail-only tickets between Toronto and Vancouver cost from £550 for a 3-day journey. A 17-day rail vacation package (Halifax–Vancouver) costs from £340 per day, including rail tickets, accommodation, local tours, meals and taxes.

FURTHER INFORMATION
www.canadatourism.ca

The Spiral Tunnels
In the late 1800s, near the mountain town of Field in British Columbia, the "Big Hill" and its dangerous 4.5 percent gradient caused many a heart to race – and several runaway train engines. To solve the problem, engineers began building the Spiral Tunnels in 1907. Still in use today (both the Rocky Mountaineer and Royal Canadian Pacific routes include them), the tunnels corkscrew into Mount Ogden and Cathedral Mountain, essentially doubling back on themselves inside the mountains and allowing a much more gradual slope.

RIDING THE RAILS

The twin ribbons of steel that stretch for thousands of kilometres across Canada have tales to tell of the travellers who have made history on this journey – Mounties and military men, royalty and roustabouts, pioneers and poets. More than a century ago, these rails united a nation still in its infancy, weaving together the threads of a landscape as varied as the people making their home within it. It's still an epic journey today, following the mighty St Lawrence River to the granite outcroppings of the Canadian Shield; across the great prairie plains and through pine and spruce in the Rockies; emerging from west coast cedar rainforests to greet the Pacific Ocean.

Ride the rails from sea to sea and you'll glimpse the old stories, set against the rhythmic sway of the train. Lobster traps piled on eastern wharves, the train slowing to a stop at the Great Lakes to let a party of canoeists off, the grain harvest waiting in the fields as the sun silhouettes a first glimpse of the Rockies.

Above: Sunrise on Maligne Lake and Spirit Island in Jasper National Park

Main: Rocky Mountaineer travels alongside the Bow River through Alberta

Above (left to right): Vintage Canadian Pacific poster; luxurious cabin interior on the Canadian Pacific; dining carriage on Via Rail; Union Station in Toronto; Rocky Mountaineer crossing the dramatic Stoney Creek Bridge; Peggy's Cove Lighthouse in Nova Scotia

Below: Entrance to one of the spiral tunnels in Yoho National Park in British Colombia

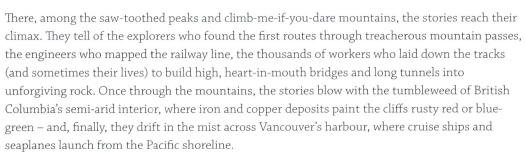

CROSS-COUNTRY DIARY

The train can transport you between Canada's east and west coasts in as little as five days, but this vast and varied country is worth a more in-depth experience – whether it's exploring the arts of Toronto, the dramatic Rocky Mountains, or the wave-washed shores of the Pacific and Atlantic coasts.

Two Weeks by Train

DAY 1
Fly into Halifax the day before the train departs to explore the historic wharves of the harbour, where tall ships often dock, and the rocky coast and dramatic lighthouse of Peggy's Cove, a nearby fishing village.

DAYS 2–4
Overnight on Via Rail's Ocean service between Halifax and Montreal, travelling alongside Canada's windswept Atlantic coastline to the St Lawrence River. Spend a night in Montreal to enjoy the boutiques and bistros of this cosmopolitan French-speaking city.

DAYS 5–6
Take the train to Toronto. Stroll the waterfront, hit the museums or head to the theatre district to enjoy Broadway shows. Then board Via Rail's The Canadian for the journey north of Lake Superior, a landscape known as the Canadian Shield.

DAYS 7–9
The Canadian then sweeps across prairie plains through Manitoba and Saskatchewan and on to Alberta, revealing the snow-capped Rocky Mountains. Take a self-drive or tour option between Jasper and Banff on the Icefields Parkway, past spectacular glaciers and through national parks. Alternatively, take another train on to Calgary, from where you can take the luxurious Royal Canadian Pacific to the Rocky Mountain resort of Banff.

DAYS 10–12
In Banff, join the Rocky Mountaineer for its two-day trip on the historic track through the Rockies into British Columbia's desert-like interior and on to lush Vancouver.

DAYS 13–14
Spend your last days in Vancouver on Stanley Park's waterfront, at the VanDusen Botanical Garden or exploring in Gastown and Chinatown.

Dos and Don'ts

✓ Take advantage of the friendly on-board atmosphere to strike up conversations with fellow travellers – it's part of the fun.

✓ Keep your eyes open for wildlife – deer and moose are often seen across the country, while elk and bears might be spotted in the Rockies.

✗ Don't underestimate distances in Canada: 6,300 km (3,915 miles) of railway tracks join Halifax, Nova Scotia, with Vancouver, British Columbia.

There, among the saw-toothed peaks and climb-me-if-you-dare mountains, the stories reach their climax. They tell of the explorers who found the first routes through treacherous mountain passes, the engineers who mapped the railway line, the thousands of workers who laid down the tracks (and sometimes their lives) to build high, heart-in-mouth bridges and long tunnels into unforgiving rock. Once through the mountains, the stories blow with the tumbleweed of British Columbia's semi-arid interior, where iron and copper deposits paint the cliffs rusty red or blue-green – and, finally, they drift in the mist across Vancouver's harbour, where cruise ships and seaplanes launch from the Pacific shoreline.

Many travellers choose a small portion of the cross-Canada route, focussing on the east coast, for example, or charting a grand circle through the Rockies. But the intrepid can cross the entire nation by rail between Halifax and Vancouver. So settle back in your seat, relax, and let the scenes unfold outside your picture window. This trip is all about the journey.

JAN
FEB
MAR
APR
MAY
JUN
JUL
AUG
SEP
OCT
NOV
DEC

GETTING THERE
San Francisco is in California on the west coast of the USA. The international airport is 20 km (13 miles) south of the city, and is linked to the city by train, bus and taxi.

GETTING AROUND
Renting a car is the best option, although buses and Amtrak's Coast Starlight trains operate between Los Angeles and San Francisco.

WEATHER
Usually sunny and warm, with temperatures from 20–30°C, although it can get a lot warmer inland.

ACCOMMODATION
Post Ranch Inn, a romantic hideaway by the coast, just off Highway 1; doubles from £280; www.postranchinn.com

Inn at Depot Hill in Capitola has pretty, individually decorated rooms; doubles from £175; www.innatdepothill.com

Inn at Morro Bay, halfway between San Francisco and Los Angeles; doubles from £80; www.innatmorrobay.com

EATING OUT
Seafood is the local speciality and many restaurants have coastal vistas. Prices range from £2 breakfasts to £50-per-head dinners. Two to try are Dorn's Original Breakers Café in Morro Bay, and Nepenthe on Highway 1.

PRICE FOR TWO
About £230 per day including accommodation, food and standard car hire – add about £100 extra per day for an open top (ragtop) Mustang.

FURTHER INFORMATION
www.visitcalifornia.com

CALIFORNIA DREAMING

Highway 1 (officially the Cabrillo Highway) snakes along wave-lashed seashores, hugging the Golden State's coast all the way from the beautiful vineyards of Mendocino to just south of the sprawling metropolis of Los Angeles. Pick up a hire-car at San Francisco and drive south 200 km (120 miles) to Monterey for the start of the most famous stretch of the drive. It's a classic route that winds on for another 400 km (250 miles) to surf-city Santa Barbara. Along the way you'll pass picturesque little seaside towns, forests of giant redwoods, Spanish missions that pre-date the state's founding, enchanting inns and resorts nestled against the roaring Pacific and the Big Sur, a rugged coastline of unsurpassed beauty. One minute you're skimming alongside a golden beach caressed by smoothly curving sets of waves and the next you're looking down onto thundering surf crashing into the cliffs 300 m (1,000 ft) below. At times the road seems suspended in mid-air before dropping you precipitously towards dancing blue waters and coves where bulky elephant seals bask in the sun.

Inset: Viewing pool in Monterey Bay Aquarium

Bottom: Climbing a giant redwood near the California coast

Dancing blue waters and coves where bulky elephant seals bask in the sun…

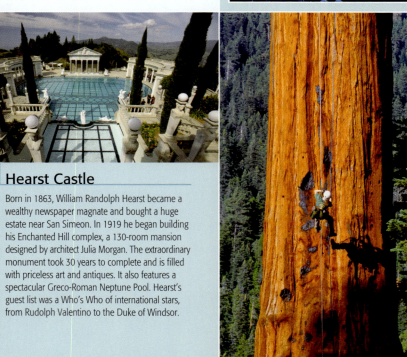

Hearst Castle
Born in 1863, William Randolph Hearst became a wealthy newspaper magnate and bought a huge estate near San Simeon. In 1919 he began building his Enchanted Hill complex, a 130-room mansion designed by architect Julia Morgan. The extraordinary monument took 30 years to complete and is filled with priceless art and antiques. It also features a spectacular Greco-Roman Neptune Pool. Hearst's guest list was a Who's Who of international stars, from Rudolph Valentino to the Duke of Windsor.

Many travellers like to linger in Monterey. Here stand well-preserved adobe structures and Cannery Row (of John Steinbeck fame), where the Monterey Bay Aquarium holds visitors spellbound with its tanks full of jellyfish, sharks and cavorting sea otters. But the drama begins immediately south at Carmel, with its sculpted cliffs studded with gnarled Monterey cypress, twisted by centuries of windy assault. Stands of majestic redwoods tower overhead as you wind along the spectacularly scenic Big Sur, where waves smash ashore at the base of soaring mountains.

Near San Simeon, Hearst Castle is a flamboyant counterpoint to the simple former whaling towns with their art galleries and antique stores. You might stop for impromptu picnics with sea views, or drive inland where vineyards abound, tempting you to sample their renowned wines. Further south, the landscape softens, the Coast Range mountains move inland, and the road sweeps across broad coastal plateaus, and redwoods and cypress give way to heat-loving bougainvillea and palms. Finally comes laid-back Santa Barbara, with its Mediterranean vistas, lovely homes in Spanish-Moorish style, and surfer-dude-chic. It's enough to inspire anyone to rent a ragtop.

Above: Surfing the central coast swells near Santa Barbara

HIGHWAY 1 DIARY

California's Highway 1 is hard to beat for sheer driving pleasure, with the 400-km (250-mile) section between Monterey and Santa Barbara the most thrilling. Although the journey can be made quicker, six days is ideal for savouring this stunning coastal highway, with time for forays to inland wineries, and exploring little fishing villages and San Simeon castle.

Six Days Driving the Big Sur

Set off early from San Francisco, heading south along Route 101. The first day is a long drive to Monterey, so enjoy the winding road – maybe stop off to see the elephant seals at the Ana Nuevo State Park.

DAY 1

Spend the morning in Monterey before taking the 17-Mile Drive through mist-shrouded pine groves and past homes of the rich and famous. It's not far to Carmel, and here you can amble the pretty streets dotted with galleries and dine in one of its fine restaurants.

DAY 2

In the morning see Carmel Mission (1783) where pioneering missionary Father Junipero Serra is buried. Set off down the Big Sur stopping for a half-day hike through the towering redwoods of Pfeiffer Big Sur State Park. Overnight in a cosy country inn.

DAY 3

Stock up with a picnic and head off again along the Big Sur. Stretch your legs at Julia Pfeiffer Burn's secluded cove – enjoy lunch to the sound of crashing surf, wherever takes your fancy, finishing up at San Simeon.

DAY 4

See Hearst's Castle then to Morro Bay for lunch before visiting Mission San Luis Obispo (1772). Carry on inland to La Purisima Mission State Historic Park before pushing on to Solvang, a quintessential Danish village.

DAY 5

Take a morning to explore (and, for the non-driver, taste) the wineries of the Santa Ynez Valley. Head on to a sandy beach near Santa Barbara for an afternoon marvelling at the surfing prowess of the locals, or explore charming Santa Barbara Mission (1786).

DAY 6

Dos and Don'ts

☑ Keep your distance from seals and elephant seals. They can give a devastating bite if you get too close.

☑ Take hiking shoes or sturdy trainers, a sunhat and plenty of water for exploring the redwood forests.

☑ Do make a reservation to visit Hearst Castle. Many visitors arrive without doing so and leave disappointed.

☒ Don't underestimate the danger of the roads. If you want to admire the view, stop at one of the many roadside stopping points. Mudslides, other drivers stopping in the middle of the road to admire the view and the steep winding roads all require your absolute concentration.

JAN
FEB
MAR
APR
MAY
JUN
JUL
AUG
SEP
OCT
NOV
DEC

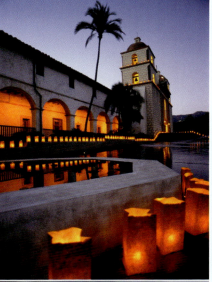

Main: Car lights on Highway 1, along the beautiful Big Sur coastline

Top: Spanish architecture of Santa Barbara mission

Above: Northern Elephant Seal alerting everyone to his presence on the Californian Coast

Below: Rows of vines growing in one of California's many successful vineyards

GETTING THERE
International flights arrive into Brisbane airport, 9 km (6 miles) from the city and connected by trains and buses. Cairns also has an international airport, 7 km (4 miles) from the centre.

GETTING AROUND
Hiring a car or a 4WD vehicle is the best option. Regular public buses connect the main towns, but the train network is less comprehensive.

WEATHER
Queensland has warm days and cool nights during October, with temperatures ranging from 20 to 30°C.

ACCOMMODATION
The Inchcolm, a heritage hotel in Brisbane; suites from £90; www.inchcolmhotel.com.au

Hayman Island, a luxurious private island resort in the Whitsundays; doubles from £280; www.hayman.com.au

Cairns Reef & Rainforest B&B, charming family-run accommodation close to Cairns; doubles from £70; www.cairnsreefbnb.com.au

EATING OUT
There are many excellent restaurants in the state serving modern Australian cuisine, making use of the abundant local produce. Immigrant populations have brought excellent Thai and Indonesian cooking to the region. You can eat well for under £12 a head.

PRICE FOR TWO
£160–260 per day including accommodation, food, transport and excursions.

FURTHER INFORMATION
www.queenslandholidays.com.au

Great Barrier Reef
The Great Barrier Reef is one of the natural wonders of the world. It is in fact not one reef, but a string of over 2,500 coral reefs, some of them thought to be up to a staggering 18 million years old, which stretch for 2,000 km (1,243 miles) up the Queensland coast. The multicoloured reefs burst with life and are home to over 400 different types of coral and 1,500 species of fish. It also teems with larger creatures like whales, turtles and sharks, although the latter usually stay well away from people.

Main: Diagonal banded sweetlips on the Great Barrier Reef
Above (left to right): Sailing around the Whitsunday Islands; koala resting in a tree; driving along the beach on Fraser Island

Above: Looking over Queensland's forested interior

REEF TO RAINFOREST

AN ABUNDANT PARADISE OF NATURAL ATTRACTIONS, Queensland attracts tourists, scientists, botanists and adventure junkies from all over the world. This sunbathed land ripples up the eastern Australian coast from just south of its energetic and youthful state capital, Brisbane, right up to the wild rainforests of Cape York at the very northern tip of the country.

Queensland ticks all the boxes for a sunny holiday destination, whether you are looking to relax on a soft white-sand beach or retreat to an island hideaway; though thrill-seekers may think that lounging around is a waste given the world-class adventure possibilities offered in abundance.

The coast overflows with opportunities for getting in and about the water, whether you are looking to get out on a yacht for a day to tour the sheltered waters of the Great Barrier Reef, or prefer to delve deep below sea level on a scuba dive. The scuba diving is world class, with divers bubbling back to the surface, enthusing about the spectacular delights encountered below; few return to land disappointed. Then there is also the snorkelling, sea kayaking, windsurfing and parasailing, all available up and down the long coast.

Inland, the fun continues, where lush rainforests await. Venture into the dense foliage and another Queensland unfolds, as exotic animal calls shriek out among ancient trees. Even here, activities are in abundance – you can tumble down raging rivers on a raft, ride the rapids on a kayak or even fling yourself off a ridiculous height with only a rubber bungy for company.

Then there is Fraser Island, a truly other-worldly escape. The largest sand island in the world, it will not fail to captivate you as you follow sandy paths to empty beaches and unbelievably clear lakes.

Reflecting the youthful spirit of Australia through the simple pleasures of sun, sea and sand, it is no surprise that Queensland is Australia's holiday state.

> Tumble down raging rivers on a raft, ride the rapids or fling yourself off a ridiculous height with only a rubber bungy for company.

Inset: Brisbane's skyline and harbour
Below (left and right): Feather duster tubeworm; diver swims behind a huge gorgonian fan coral on the reef

JAN
FEB
MAR
APR
MAY
JUN
JUL
AUG
SEP
OCT
NOV
DEC

HOLIDAY-STATE DIARY

Given the substantial travelling distances in this large state, you will need at least two weeks to really savour Queensland's epic scenery and enjoy the myriad activities on offer. Start in Brisbane and make your way north overland, but consider flying back from Cairns to Brisbane to save time.

Two Weeks up the Coast

Explore Brisbane – take in the Botanic Gardens, the Cultural Centre and the Lone Pine Koala Sanctuary.	**DAY 1**
Leave the city behind and head north up the Gold Coast to Urangan, where you can catch a ferry to Fraser Island. A 4WD vehicle is necessary for exploration – either self-drive or as part of a tour. Drive up 75-Mile Beach and through the interior to seek out the 200 or so shimmering lakes for swimming.	**DAYS 2–3**
Back on the mainland, continue north to Airlie Beach. From here you can join a boat trip to the beautiful Whitsunday Islands – be sure to visit Whitehaven Beach, recognized as one of the world's best beaches. Enjoy your first snorkel on the Great Barrier Reef.	**DAYS 4–6**
Continue up to Cairns, perhaps stopping to take in Magnetic Island and Mission Beach. Cairns is the region's activity centre and a great base for exploring the reef. Join a boat tour to snorkel or scuba dive, or explore Green and Fitzroy Islands. For adrenaline-fuelled activities, head inland for bungy jumping, sky-diving or freshwater kayaking.	**DAYS 7–10**
The Atherton Tablelands offer more adventure opportunities – try whitewater rafting on the Tully River. If you long for something a little more sedate, take the Kuranda Skyrail up the Tablelands for fantastic views.	**DAYS 11–12**
Head up to Port Douglas to join the big Quicksilver catamarans, which speed you right out to the extremities of the Outer Reef. Return to Cairns to fly back down the coast to Brisbane.	**DAYS 13–14**

Dos and Don'ts

✓ Check around for the best adventure activity operators, especially in Cairns and Airlie Beach, as you are spoilt for choice and shopping around often pays dividends.

✗ Don't mention the cricket if you are supporting the Poms (England)!

✓ Slip, slop, slap as the Australians do: slip on a t-shirt, slop on the sunscreen and slap on a hat to avoid the worst of the searing sun.

✓ Seek local advice before swimming anywhere as deadly box jellyfish can appear as early as October and saltwater crocodiles can be a problem in both the sea and rivers.

GETTING THERE
Lhasa is the main city of Tibet, set on a high Himalayan plateau in west China. Flights from international destinations usually connect in Chengdu, China or Kathmandu in Nepal. A new, but controversial train service to Lhasa operates from Qinghai.

GETTING AROUND
Tibetan roads are extremely rough, so hired 4WD trucks are the best way to travel around.

WEATHER
In October, temperatures range from 1 to 17°C, with mostly cloudless skies and cold nights.

ACCOMMODATION
Try to stay in a locally run guest house in the old town; the facilities are pretty basic but atmosphere and location are great.

Pentoc Hotel is clean and characterful; doubles from £10; tel: 891 632 6686.

Yak Hotel has a convenient location; doubles from £25; tel: 891 632 3496.

The Kyichu Hotel, a friendly family run hotel; doubles from £30; www.kyichuhotel.com

EATING OUT
Tibetan cuisine is basic but cheap – try Dunya on Beijing Dong Lu or Makye Ama behind the Jokhang. Expect lots of yak meat but try *momos* (dumplings) and yak-butter tea – if only once.

PRICE FOR TWO
About £100 per day for visa, accommodation, 4WD vehicle and driver hire, tips and food.

FURTHER INFORMATION
www.tibet.com

Main picture: Young trainee monk tends to the yak-butter candles

Tibetan Buddhism

Mahayana Buddhism, which emphasizes compassion and self-sacrifice, came to Tibet from India in the 7th century AD and adopted many of the aspects of the native animist Bon religion such as its deities and rituals. Like most Buddhists, Tibetans believe in reincarnation with the next life being better or worse depending on the *karma* or merit gained in the present life. Praying (by spinning a prayer wheel), circuits of holy sites (*koras*) or fully-fledged pilgrimages are all means of accruing merit.

LAND OF THE SNOWS

THE PERSPECTIVES ARE VERY SMALL AND ENCLOSED, within the city – prostrating pilgrims can barely be seen through the wisps of fragrant smoke rising from clumps of smouldering juniper; in the dim, flickering light escaping from yak-butter lamps, monks chant solemnly and rhythmically to the quiet click of rosary beads; narrow alleyways throng with visitors to the gentle creak of turning prayer wheels. Outside, the contrast could not be more spectacular – bright prayer flags flutter against an intensely blue sky; the wide-open expanses stretch on and on, framed by the jagged barrier of snowy peaks that seem to glow white-hot in the thin air. It could only be Tibet, the Land of Snows, the mysterious kingdom whose piety, isolation and grandeur have always captured the imagination of the West. Not so long ago, many western explorers died trying to penetrate the secrets of the capital, Lhasa. Today, under Chinese occupation, the place is open to the world.

Above: The huge 13-storey Potala Palace, Lhasa

Top row (left to right): Prayer flags fluttering beside Namtso Lake; creating a colourful sand *mandala* (symbolic representation of the cosmos); *mani* stones inscribed with prayer mantras; man wearing traditional dress; prostrate pilgrims performing a *kora* (circuit) around the Jokhang, Lhasa

Below (top and bottom): Monks practising debating at Sera Monastery; praying before a Buddha image

PILGRIM'S DIARY

As well as the magnificent sights of Lhasa, the high desert plateau of Tibet offers some of the most amazing views in the world. Take a trip by 4WD vehicle out of town to see the remote monasteries, spectacular Himalayan mountains, the deep azure-blue of Namtso Lake, and to get a glimpse of traditional Tibetan life.

Eight Days on the High Plateau

Take it easy on your first day to give yourself a chance to get used to the altitude – do nothing more than wander through the streets near your hotel and soak up the atmosphere.

DAY 1

See the Jokhang and admire the candle-lit interior. Join pilgrims as they walk the *kora* around the temple. Wander along the sacred pilgrim path, Barkhor, browsing the stalls and shops, or watching the pilgrims.

DAY 2

Climb to the fortress-like Potala Palace, once home of the Dalai Lama, Tibet's spiritual leader, and now a vast and dusty repository of holy Buddhist relics.

DAY 3

Pay a visit to Drepung, on the city's outskirts, one of the world's largest monasteries, where vast halls of statues resound to the hypnotic drone of chanting monks.

DAY 4

Hire a 4WD truck for a three-day tour of the Tibetan Plateau. Head first to Sera monastery, where you can watch one of the monks' lively debates. Afterwards, drive on to Ganden Monastery for great views and to Samye Monastery with its splendid valley setting.

Make the long and bone-shaking drive to Namtso Lake via a night at Tsurphu Monastery. The water at Namtso is an amazing azure blue and the scenery is spectacular. Afterwards, head back to Lhasa.

DAYS 5–7

Take it easy on this last day. Stroll through the Norbulingka, once the summer palace of the Dalai Lama and now a pleasant park; watch Tibetans singing and dancing, and soak up the excited atmosphere.

DAY 8

Dos and Don'ts

✓ You will probably feel mild altitude sickness when you arrive, so be sure to take it easy for a day or two.

✓ Always walk clockwise around religious buildings and pilgrimage circuits – anti-clockwise is considered bad luck.

✓ At this altitude, the sun is harsh, so bring high-factor suncream, a hat and sunglasses. Take a sweater or two for the chilly nights too.

✗ Don't be tempted to drink the local homebrew, *chang*, as it's made with unfiltered water.

Pilgrims flock to Lhasa, home of Tibet's most significant religious buildings – the Jokhang and the Potala; one a living, functioning temple packed with reverent worshippers and the other a magnificent and spectacular museum-piece. For many Tibetans, nomads from the wild plains, the city is just as exotic as it is to a western visitor. You'll see Khampa men from the east swaggering like cowboys with red braided hair and bejewelled daggers, and Amdo girls from the north bedecked in coral jewellery with their hair in 108 plaits. All will spend time spinning prayer wheels, chanting, praying and walking pilgrimage circuits, or *koras* – the more devout prostrating themselves for the entire 8-km (5-mile) journey of the Lhasa *kora*.

No visit to Tibet is complete without the excitement and adventure of an expedition by 4WD truck into the surrounding country – one of the world's least populated areas – whether to visit the country's great and historic monasteries, to experience fleetingly the harsh way of life of the Tibetan nomads or to see the magnificence of the greatest mountain range in the world, the Himalayas. Tibet offers an unbeatable wealth of natural wonders and a fascinating and unique culture.

JAN
FEB
MAR
APR
MAY
JUN
JUL
AUG
SEP
OCT
NOV
DEC

GETTING THERE
The Loire Valley is served by two airports – Nantes-Atlantique and Tours Val de Loire. Alternatively, the region can be reached by TGV from Paris, which takes 2 hours to Tours and 1½ hours to Angers. The region is about 2 hours from Paris on the A10 motorway.

GETTING AROUND
Public transport is limited, but tours to the major châteaux are organized in the larger towns. Hiring a car is a great way to travel around the region as you can set your own pace.

WEATHER
The Loire Valley has a mild climate, and the average temperature for October is around 16°C. Be prepared for a day or two of rain.

ACCOMMODATION
Hôtel St-Pierre, in Saumur, a charming hotel; doubles from £60; www.saintpierresaumur.com

Château de Pray, Amboise, overlooking the Loire; doubles from £100; praycastel.online.fr

Château des Briottières, close to Angers, has elegant period bedrooms; doubles from £125; www.briottieres.com

EATING OUT
The Loire region's forests provide the local specialities such as truffles, mushrooms and game. Try La Petite Marmite in Orléans, with its *menus du terroir* from £15.

PRICE FOR TWO
£150–200 per day for accommodation, food, château entrance charges and car hire.

FURTHER INFORMATION
www.loirevalleytourism.com

Renaissance France

The Renaissance in France reached its height during the 32-year reign of François I (1515–47). Brought up in the château at Amboise, he turned his hunting lodge into the Château de Chambord, where his court was known for its regular balls, concerts and mammoth banquets. A devotee of the arts, he persuaded Leonardo da Vinci to live in Amboise, and the Italian artist remained there for the last four years of his life. Da Vinci is buried in the Chapel of St Hubert in Chambord and his house in Amboise is now a museum.

Above (left to right): Formal gardens at Villandry; detail of statue from Cathédrale St Pierre et St Paul, Nantes; view of the Loire river

Above: Vineyards in the fertile Loire Valley

JAN
FEB
MAR
APR
MAY
JUN
JUL
AUG
SEP
OCT
DAY 1
DAY 2
DAY 3
DAY 4
DAY 5
DAY 6
NOV
DEC

THE GARDEN OF FRANCE

EUROPEAN ARCHITECTURE DOESN'T GET RICHER than the grand châteaux of the Loire Valley. Reflecting the decadent beauty of the Renaissance, more than fifty 15th- and 16th-century wildly extravagant mansions pepper the region. The greatest are undoubtedly the 440-room Château de Chambord, built for François I with the help of Leonardo da Vinci, and Château Chenonceau, home to a succession of aristocratic women, which seems to almost float upon the water on which it sits. "To sleep in the bed of Diane of Poitiers, even empty," said Flaubert of Chenonceau, "is much more exciting than sleeping in a bed with far more tangible realities." Though little more than the ghosts of the kings and queens of France may remain today, the illustrious past can still be discovered in these truly incomparable surroundings.

Yet the Loire Valley is not just about stunning art and architecture. Though the gentle landscape lacks drama, the French aristocracy chose this region because of its fertility and

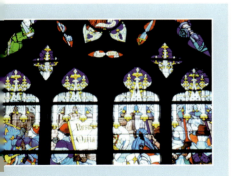

"Each step in this land of enactment allows the fresh discovery of a picture, the frame of which is a river or a tranquil pool..."

Honoré de Balzac

proximity to Paris. Dubbed "the Garden of France", it is dotted with small farms where flowers, corn, fruit and vegetables flourish. Look out for local apples and delicious pears, and of course the products of the Loire grapes, including great white wines such as Muscadet, Pouilly Fumé and Sancerre. The landscape includes extraordinary troglodyte caves around Vouvray and along the 42 km (26 miles) of riverside between Saumur and Angers. These tufa caves are ideal for growing the famous Saumur button mushrooms that fill the markets.

The Loire is France's longest river and, with its lakes and many tributaries, it is a watery playground where canoes and yachts can be hired and river trips made, though at this time of year water levels may be low. The valley is not a hilly place, which makes self-guide biking and walking tours an easy and popular way to discover the beauty of this region of France.

Main: Château de Chenonceau reflected in the Loire river
Below (left and right): Eating in the Caves de Marson; mushrooms on display
Inset: Stained-glass window in the Cathédrale Sainte-Croix, Orléans

RIVERSIDE DIARY

This six-day itinerary from Orléans to Nantes follows the right bank of the river. There is so much to see here that your journey could easily take two or three times as long. October is a good time to visit the region as the numbers of coach tours will have diminished and it is still warm enough to be outside.

Six Days in the Loire Valley

Spend a morning in Orléans, the capital of medieval France. Stroll up to the magnificent Cathédrale Sainte-Croix where Joan of Arc's story is told in stained glass, and visit the Musée des Beaux-Arts. In the afternoon, head to the fabulous Château de Chambord, the largest in the region.

Explore Blois, the most attractive town on the Loire, perhaps by horse-drawn carriage. Visit Robert Houdin's House of Magic and enjoy the view from Escalier Denis-Papin. In the afternoon, walk in the Sologne, the wooded marshes on the south side of the Loire, or visit nearby Château de Chaumont.

Head to Tours and explore its medieval centre around Place Plumereau, or visit the Touraine Wine Museum. Afterwards, take your pick from the beautiful châteaux at Villandry and Chenonceau.

Begin the morning with a visit to Saumur and its château. Afterwards, tour Rochemenier, a former troglodyte farming community, now a museum. Alternatively, you may prefer to spend the afternoon exploring the attractive wine region around Chinon.

Angers is the liveliest spot on the river, known for its festivals, flowers and massive 13th-century fortress. Explore its sites, including the château, which contains the longest tapestry in the world, the *Apocalypse*.

Drive on to the ancient port of Nantes. Explore the fashionable Quartier Graslin and later the flamboyant Gothic Cathédrale St Pierre et St Paul.

Dos and Don'ts

✓ Visit the local tourist offices to pick up audio guides – a great way of making sure that you don't miss out any hidden gems.

✗ Don't imagine that if you have seen one château you have seen them all as each has its own personality.

✓ Make the most of the fresh local produce from the markets by having picnics by the river.

GETTING THERE
Timbuktu is in Mali, West Africa. International flights arrive into the capital, Bamako, around 640 km (400 miles) from Timbuktu. Internal flights and river steamers connect to Timbuktu.

GETTING AROUND
Passenger boats down the Niger, buses and bush taxis are the main ways to travel around. It is possible to hire a 4WD vehicle to go out into the desert but it can be difficult and time consuming.

WEATHER
October is the end of the rainy season. Desert temperatures are hot – typically 38°C in Timbuktu cooling to 20°C at night.

ACCOMMODATION
Hotel La Colombe, a central hotel in Timbuktu; doubles from £30; tel: 223 292 1434.

Auberge Le Maafir, Djenné, has air-conditioning; doubles from £35; tel: 223 242 0611.

Hotel Sofitel l'Amitié, a recently renovated high-rise in Bamako; doubles from £95; www.sofitel.com

EATING OUT
Basic restaurants usually have rice, couscous, chicken and *sauce d'arachide* (peanut sauce). Camel may be served in Timbuktu. In the smaller Dogon villages, meals consist of gumbo and *tô* (okra with millet dough).

PRICE FOR TWO
£50–70 per day including accommodation, food and local transport (not flights).

FURTHER INFORMATION
www.officetourisme-mali.com

DOGON COUNTRY

EVERYONE HAS HEARD OF IT, few could place it on a map, and some doubt it actually exists at all. The sandy streets and alleys of the old town, the squat mud houses – some bearing the names of the explorers who stayed in them – and the piercing sound of the call to prayer floating out across the desert create an enchanting, otherworldly feel. But Timbuktu is no El Dorado, no Atlantis: the blinding heat, dusty winds and bread with a distinctly Saharan crunch are all things of the real world.

Only vestiges and faint memories remain of Timbuktu's glorious past. The conical towers of the Djingareiber Mosque rise like lighthouses in the desert, a monument to a time when Timbuktu was the centre of Islamic learning in West Africa. The brisk trade in gold that once fed the dreams of the explorers trying to reach the city has gone, replaced by vegetables in the *grand marché* (great market)

Streets Lined with Gold

Discovering a city so rich that the streets were said to be lined with gold was the goal of many an 18th- and 19th-century European explorer. Timbuktu's mythical reputation was born in the 1400s, when the city became the principal trading post for gold originating in the Akan forest in Ghana and bound for North Africa, and salt brought down from the mines in the Sahara by huge camel caravans or Azalaïs. The salt trade is still operating today with large slabs ferried about by *pirogue* (boat).

Main: Imposing Djenné Mosque, the largest mud building in the world

Right (left to right): Tuareg woman wearing the striking traditional robes; salt caravan trails through the Sahara Desert, Mali; detail of mosque minaret in Timbuktu; Dogon granary in Mali; ancient Islamic manuscript kept in the CEDRAB library in Timbuktu

and Tuareg salesmen hawking camel rides outside the hotels in between cups of sickly-sweet tea. Everyone comes to Timbuktu in search of a dream that has long since been swallowed by the sands.

Djenné, southwest of Timbuktu on an island in the Niger floodplain, was also a great centre of Islamic learning and trans-Saharan trade. Unlike Timbuktu, however, the town has found a modern-day niche as one of Africa's architectural gems – and site of the greatest mud building in the world. The vast Djenné Mosque, wide and low along one side of the main square, its smooth mud walls studded with wooden beams, resembles a giant brought down by a thousand arrows. This surreal sight is matched west of Djenné along the Bandiagara escarpment, where the resourceful Dogon people have built villages right into the cliff face at the most precarious of angles. Above the villages lie skeletons in dark caves, in a world governed by the type of strange customs and traditions that will have Mali romantics salivating with anticipation.

Above: Locals sell their wares at a bustling Dogon market in Mali

JAN

FEB

MAR

APR

MAY

JUN

JUL

AUG

SEP

OCT

DEC

NOV

WEST AFRICAN DIARY

Mali is one of the most interesting tourist destinations in West Africa – but it is also one of the largest. Road travel is slow and internal flights limited, so to do justice to the main sights – Timbuktu, Djenné and Dogon country – you'll need to stay at least ten days, considerably longer if you're not flying to Timbuktu.

Ten Other-Worldly Days

DAY 1
Acclimatize in Bamako, Mali's dusty capital, where you'll get your first peek at one of the world's legendary rivers, the Niger.

DAY 2
Fly to Timbuktu and make the Djingareiber Mosque your first stop – a great view of the city can be enjoyed from the roof. Head to the Centre de Recherches Historiques Ahmed Baba (CEDRAB), where you can see an amazing collection of ancient books and manuscripts.

DAY 3
Spend the day exploring Timbuktu. Most of the notable buildings in the old town are private houses, not museums, so you'll be out in the sun for most of the time. In the evening, take a camel ride in the desert.

DAY 4
Fly to the town of Mopti, a bustling place with a port full of traditional *pirogues* (boats) laden with slabs of salt and other valuable West African commodities.

DAYS 5–7
Travel by bus to the town of Bandiagara, from where you can organize a trip into Dogon country. Reserve three days to explore the many facets of Dogon life and culture, including, of course, the amazing cliff villages.

DAY 8
Take a bus to Djenné, where you can explore one of Mali's most colourful markets.

DAY 9
Djenné is small enough to see on foot in a day. Spend time admiring the Djenné Mosque, but don't neglect the other architectural gems.

DAY 10
Return by bus to Bamako (eight hours) and unwind before your flight home.

Dos and Don'ts

✓ Walk to the western and northern edges of Timbuktu and sit on sand dunes in the middle of nowhere.

✓ Take photographs of Djenné at the end of the day when the mud-brick architecture is bathed in a mysterious light.

✓ Employ the services of a knowledgeable guide, preferably Dogon themselves, to avoid committing cultural faux pas while exploring Dogon villages.

✗ Don't give items to children – but do give back to the country by making a donation to a charity, school or hospital.

The Origins of Tango

Tango originated, as the story goes, in the brothels of Buenos Aires in the late 19th century. Whether it was the lewd and explicit lyrics of the songs or the shockingly close bodily contact of the dance itself, tango took its time to emerge from the underground. During the beginning of the 20th century, the number of men – many of them newly arrived from Europe in search of work – far outstripped the female population in Buenos Aires, so the sight of men practising tango moves together was not an uncommon sight.

A CITY WITH SPIRIT

Buenos Aires, as guidebooks readily affirm, is a city of great restaurants, great museums, great shops, great parks, great nightlife and, after the 2002 devaluation of the peso, great prices. But there is something more to Buenos Aires, something more intangible.

You'll find it brushed in sensual strokes across the cobbled streets of the *barrio* (neighbourhood) of San Telmo by crowd-pleasing tango dancers. Passionate fans shout it out from the bleachers at one of the city's iconic soccer stadiums. It drifts in the smoke of roasting meat at a *parrilla* (steak house) and shimmers in a glass of Argentina's renowned wine. The venerable Café Tortoni on Avenida de Mayo, with its bow-tied waiters, mirrored walls and tables graced in former times by Jorge Luis Borges and company, has it in spades. It hangs poignantly over the silent weekly demonstrations of

Main: Dancing tango in the streets of San Telmo

Left (top to bottom): General Juan Lavalle monument; stained-glass window at the popular Café Tortoni; soda syphons in the antiques market in San Telmo

Right (left to right): Shop display in San Telmo; bright buildings in the La Boca district; Bombonera stadium before kick-off

Las Madres de Plaza de Mayo, a group established nearly 30 years ago to protest against the actions of the military dictatorship. Eva Perón embodied it back in the late 'forties and early 'fifties, her black tomb now guarded by cats in La Recoleta Cemetery. And the *porteños* (inhabitants of Buenos Aires) who patronize the trendy restaurants along the riverfront *barrio* of Puerto Madero and fill the Bohemian bars in Palermo Viejo give it a young, contemporary twist.

Buenos Aires combines European style and sophistication with the South American gift for knowing how to have a good time, a more reserved hedonism than Rio tempered by a fascination with arts and culture and strong European ties. The mansions along Avenida Alvear in the *barrio* of Recoleta would not be out of place in Paris, but the weekly Feria de Mataderos, with its livestock market and *gauchos* (cowboys) performing on horseback, certainly would be. There is something for everyone in Buenos Aires – and it all mirrors the irrepressible spirit of Argentina.

Above: Lunching at Jardin d'Hiver at Alvear Palace Hotel

TANGO DIARY

The diversity and cultural depth of Buenos Aires is enough to keep you busy for a couple of weeks, but four full days will allow you to see the main sights and get a feel for the place. Make sure that you're around on a Sunday, when several of the city's most atmospheric events take place, like the antiques market and dancing.

Four Days in the *Barrios*

Take a moment to soak in the history surrounding lovely Plaza de Mayo before heading up Avenida de Mayo for a coffee at Café Tortoni.

Spend the afternoon strolling along Calle Florida, shopping for Argentina's renowned leather goods and resting in the bookshops on Avenida Corrientes.

Enjoy the sunset by the river in the nearby *barrio* of Puerto Madero with a meal at a riverside restaurant – a great opportunity to try some of Argentina's famed beef.

Arrive at La Recoleta Cemetery at opening time (7am) when the elaborate graves are at their most peaceful and pay your respects to the grave of Eva Perón.

Avoid the midday heat by exploring the fantastic collections at the Museo Nacional de Bellas Artes, near the cemetery, and the Museo de Arte Hispanoamericano Isaac Fernández Blanco, a short walk past the grandiose mansions on Avenida Alvear. Afterwards, enjoy a classic afternoon tea at the Alvear Palace Hotel.

The *barrio* of Palermo is prime people-watching territory: sit back with a glass of wine on Plaza Cortázar in Palermo Viejo or find a shady spot in one of the parks. Several of the excellent restaurants, such as Club del Vino, have tango shows in the evening.

In the morning visit the *barrio* of San Telmo for the antiques market and street tango performances then continue a short way south to La Boca to see the blocks of brightly-coloured houses before touring – or perhaps catching an actual match – at Bombonera Stadium.

Dos and Don'ts

✓ Copy the locals and sit out the hottest parts of the day in one of the city's several attractive parks with a picnic.

✗ Don't stand too close to the barbecue in a *parrilla* unless you want your clothes to smell of meat for the evening.

✓ Have a snack in the late afternoon, since restaurants don't get going until around 10pm.

✓ Pick up free magazines such as *Buenos Aires Tango* and *El Tangauta* for listings of tango shows, schools and the like.

JAN
FEB
MAR
APR
MAY
JUN
JUL
AUG
SEP
OCT
NOV
DEC

THU
FRI
SAT
SUN

GETTING THERE
International flights arrive into Ferihegy Airport, 18 km (10 miles) from the city centre. Taxis and buses connect to the city.

GETTING AROUND
The city is pleasant to walk around and metro, buses and trams provide an easy way to get around the city. Taxis are not expensive but visitors should be wary of unlicensed cabs.

WEATHER
October is usually dry and sunny, with temperatures ranging from 7 to16°C. It can get chilly in the evenings.

ACCOMMODATION
Leo Panzió is a small family run pension near the city centre; doubles from £75; www.leopanzio.hu

The Gellért remains an outstanding hotel – both it and its thermal baths are living pieces of the city's history; doubles from £115 including entrance to the baths; www.gellerthotel.hu

Four Seasons Hotel Gresham Palace is a luxurious and exclusive hotel in a grand palace; doubles from £250; www.fourseasons.com

EATING OUT
Hungary has a rich culinary legacy, with game a speciality. Try *gulydsleves*, the traditional goulash served as a soup. You can get a great meal in Budapest for around £10.

PRICE FOR TWO
Around £190 per day including accommodation, food, local travel and entrance charges.

FURTHER INFORMATION
www.budapestinfo.hu

Bánk Bán

Hungary's national opera, *Bánk Bán*, was written by Ferenc Erkel and first performed in 1861. A classic tale of lust and revenge, it tells the tale of Bánk Bán, a Hungarian viceroy whose wife is seduced by Otto, brother of King András II. Bán takes his revenge by leading a rebellion against the King. The opera is alas rarely performed at the State Opera today, though performances are staged from time to time at the smaller Operetta Theatre on Nagymezo utca.

Main: The Art Nouveau splendour of the Gellért Baths

Above: Atmospheric view of the Chain Bridge and Parliament Building at night; detail of statuary at the Royal Palace; old town of Buda

GOOD CLEAN FUN

AN ELABORATE MULTI-TIERED CONSTRUCTION topped with figures, the Hungarian State Opera House resembles a huge wedding cake from the outside. Inside it is even richer, with deep red velvet banquettes, luxurious silk wall coverings, heavily gilded opera boxes (in fact, heavily gilded everything), and shimmering chandeliers – all in such pristine condition that you half expect Emperor Franz Josef, the last major Habsburg monarch, to come stomping grumpily down the stairs. Why would he be grumpy? Well, he'd probably be a bit upset that this upstart opera house rivals his own Vienna Opera House. In 1867, after nearly 150 years of dominating Hungary, the Austrian Empire was forced to do some power-sharing and become the Austro-Hungarian Empire, with Hungary emerging with its own parliament. This new found self-confidence released a wave of national exuberance, of ornate, gaudy, and even garish architecture, and pride in art as a statement of national intent. As a result, a rash of suitably over-the-top confections went up in Budapest aiming to outdo the splendour of Vienna's architecture – the Hungarian State Opera House, the majestic Parliament Building overlooking the Danube, the Millenary Monument, St Stephen's Basilica and City Park – all ripe for exploration today.

Prior to the Habsburgs, Hungary had been governed by the Ottomans, who left behind their taste for public baths. The Gellért Baths are an upmarket riot of Art Nouveau expression, where you can enjoy a fizzing soak, or face the warm, artificial waves of the open-air pool. Alternatively, you may prefer the more democratic Széchenyi Baths. Here, on the Pest side of town, you'll make waves with the ordinary people of Budapest as they enjoy their daily treat – a hot bath, a game of chess and a bottle of beer. No visit to a bath would be complete without an invigorating, if firm, massage, to help you really get under the skin of this city.

> This new found self-confidence released a wave of national exuberance, of ornate, gaudy and even garish architecture…

Inset: A traditional pastime – men playing chess in Széchenyi Baths
Below (left to right): Funicular railway to the Castle District; elegant café culture

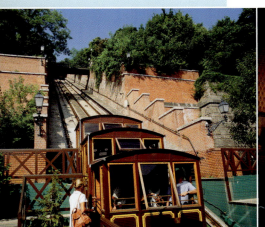

Above: Art Nouveau detail of the Post Office Saving Bank

OLD TOWN DIARY

Autumn is when Budapest is at its best. Visitor numbers fall and the city's cultural life resumes after the summer break. New seasons of cinema, music, opera and ballet get under way, and four days will enable you to see the best of the city's museums and galleries, while enjoying a selection of cultural events.

Four Days of Culture

DAY 1

Take the *sikló* (funicular) to the Castle District and enjoy the beautiful views. Stroll around the Royal Palace, the Hungarian National Gallery and the Fisherman's Bastion.

In the evening catch an organ concert at the Neo-Gothic-style Matyas Church.

DAY 2

Spend the whole day in lovely *Varosliget* (City Park). Go boating on the lake, or visit the circus, zoo or funfair. Then indulge yourself with a soak and a massage at the Széchenyi or Gellért thermal baths.

In the evening dine at Gundel, Hungary's finest restaurant, before walking down stylish Andrassy Utca and taking in an opera at the fabulous State Opera House.

DAY 3

Visit the Parliament building. To enjoy it in full, begin by viewing its astonishing façade from the opposite bank of the Danube. Then, cross the Chain Bridge and join one of the tours to see the building's highlights. If you are lucky, your visit will coincide with one of the occasional concerts held in Parliament's Dome Hall. Afterwards, wander around the old town in Buda and enjoy a break in one of the lovely old cafés.

DAY 4

Explore the former Jewish Quarter around Kiraly utca, today a loveable mish-mash of book- and antique shops, delicatessens and trendy cafés, Kosher eateries and expensive apartments. Visit Europe's largest synagogue and take in a concert at the Franz Liszt Academy of Music, built in 1906 and second only to the Opera House for opulence and acoustics.

Dos and Don'ts

☑ Buy tickets for all performances in advance: a central booking agency (Andrassy Utca 15, tel. 01 267 12 67) sells tickets for all of the city's cultural events.

☒ Don't speak to any of the over-friendly girls on Váci utca. They are not quite what they appear to be, and a drink with one of them could be the most expensive date of your life.

☑ Do visit the new Holocaust Museum on Pava utca, chronicling the tragic story of Budapest's Jews.

☒ Don't get into a taxi that doesn't clearly display which company it belongs to.

JAN
FEB
MAR
APR
MAY
JUN
JUL
AUG
SEP
OCT
NOV
DEC

GETTING THERE
Oaxaca is in Mexico, 400 km (250 miles) southeast of the capital, Mexico City. Oaxaca's airport has a few international flights from the USA, but travellers usually arrive via a domestic flight from Mexico City. Taxis and minibuses cover the 6.5 km (4 miles) between airport and city.

GETTING AROUND
Taxis, *colectivos* (shared taxis) and crowded, stop-anywhere buses run out to the villages and archeological sites outside the city.

WEATHER
By late October, summer rains are more or less over and temperatures reach a pleasant 25ºC by day, cooling to 13–15ºC at night.

ACCOMMODATION
Hotel Las Golondrinas is a lovely small hotel; two doubles from £70; tel. 951 514 3298.

Hostal de la Noria, a converted colonial mansion in the heart of Oaxaca; junior suites from £50; www.hostaldelanoria.com

Mision de los Angeles, a roomy hotel; family suites from £65; www.hotel-mision-oaxaca.com

EATING OUT
Specialities include the city's famed seven *moles* (sauces), grasshopper and even the corn mould called *huitlacoche*. Try the Restaurante Los Danzantes, which offers innovative dishes from £5 in an avant-garde setting.

PRICE FOR A FAMILY OF FOUR
£150–200 per day including accommodation, food, local travel and entrance charges.

FURTHER INFORMATION
www.visitmexico.com

Cults of the Dead
All of Mexico's many pre-Hispanic civilizations – the Aztecs, the Maya, the Zapotecs, the Mixtecs and others – believed in forms of afterlife and performed rituals in honour of the dead, often involving feasts and offerings to the departed. Spanish colonial missionaries were able to reinterpret these activities under the umbrella of All Souls' Day, when Catholics pray for departed souls – hence the 2 November date for the Day of the Dead. However, strong elements of the pre-Hispanic ritual beliefs still remain to this day in the way the fiesta is celebrated.

DAY OF THE DEAD

THIS MOST MEXICAN OF FIESTAS IS A TRULY SUPERNATURAL EVENT where the dead return to earth to commune with their living relatives. In the colonial city of Oaxaca, full of beautiful churches and mansions built by the Spanish colonists, and surrounded by indigenous villages where even more ancient beliefs still thrive, the celebrations are at their most vivid.

Mexicans generally consider death to be a continuity, a transition into another realm, rather than an ending. And, happily, the dead come back to visit their nearest and dearest every year on All Souls' Day (2 November) – more commonly referred to as *Dia de los Muertos* (Day of the Dead). In Oaxaca the deceased are believed to arrive back at 3pm on 1 November

In the gorgeous colonial city of Oaxaca … surrounded by indigenous villages where ancient beliefs still thrive, the celebrations are at their most vivid.

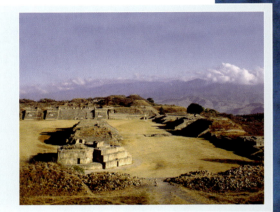

and they stay for 24 hours. The preceding 24 hours are for the return of those who died as children, known as *angelitos* (little angels).

The reunion between the living and the dead is at least as joyful as it is poignant, and the atmosphere in homes and cemeteries can be amazingly animated and happy. To welcome their dead, families create elaborate "altars of the dead" in their homes. A table is set under an arch of palm leaves, flowers and fruits, and is adorned with photos of the dead, saints' images, candles, flowers, favourite foods, drinks, even cigarettes, for the deceased to enjoy. And just to help returnees know they've found the right house, there'll be chocolate or sugar skulls, often inscribed with their names, and miniature skeletons engaged in the kind of things the deceased used to do – dancing, playing football, riding a bicycle.

Families also decorate loved ones' graves – with more flowers, candles, photos, drinks and miniature skulls and skeletons – and will spend hours in graveyards communing with the dead on the afternoon and evening of 1 November, even staying for night-long vigils and sharing food and drink with friends and relatives. The magical sight of a cemetery glittering with hundreds of candles, the buzz of talk among the crowds of excited, often joyful people, and the music and dancing that accompany these reunions, lingers in the memory.

Main: Traditional papier-mâché skeleton colourfully decorated with animals and plants
Inset: Zapotec architecture at Monte Albán near Oaxaca
Below (left and right): Carpet of coloured sand; costume parade in the Zócalo

Above: Child wrapped in local textiles at a market in Oaxaca

FIESTA DIARY

Oaxaca is the best place to see the Day of the Dead celebrations. Activities run from 31 October to 2 November; if you give yourself six days you can experience the essence of this unique event and explore the city and its fascinating surroundings, or extend your trip by visiting Yucatán (see pp64–5).

Six Days with the Spirits

Soak up the atmosphere in the Zócalo, the city's leafy central square. Stroll up Calle Alcalá to the lavish Santo Domingo church. See the Market of the Dead, where special flowers, foods, papier-mâché skeletons and chocolate and candy skulls are sold.

For a different perspective on the Day of the Dead Markets, head out of Oaxaca to one of the local villages. The biggest markets include those at Zaachila, Ocotlán and Tlacolula – but check what day they are held on as it does vary from place to place.

Back in town, the fascinating Museum of Oaxacan Cultures is worth a look, and take in any Day of the Dead dancing or theatre in the evening.

See the altars of the dead in your hotel and in local restaurants. After dark, visit the nearby village cemeteries of Santa Cruz Xoxocatlán and Santa María Atzompa – aglow with candles and full of people.

Experience the city's main cemetery, Panteón General, as people gather to decorate graves and celebrate. Later, enjoy the vibrant costume parade at the Zócalo.

To explore the area's fascinating history, head to the spectacular ruins of Monte Albán, the ancient Zapotec capital dating from around 200 BC–AD 700, which has a superb hilltop site. If you want to visit another cemetery in the evening, try the one in San Felipe del Agua.

Oaxaca has a fantastically vibrant indigenous crafts scene so spend your final day shopping for souvenirs or head out of town to see more of the area.

Dos and Don'ts

✓ Though the atmosphere in graveyards and around altars may be surprisingly happy and light-hearted, always maintain due respect as this is also a serious event.

✗ Don't take photos without asking, or unless you have been told it's okay by a guide or someone with authority.

✓ Join a class in altar-decoration or Day of the Dead cooking for a unique insight.

✓ Local agencies offer tours to cemeteries and markets, and a good guide will make everything more accessible.

JAN
FEB
MAR
APR
MAY
JUN
JUL
AUG
SEP
OCT
29 OCT
30 OCT
31 OCT
1 NOV
2 NOV
3 NOV
NOV
DEC

NOVEMBER

Where to Go: **November**

It's the start of winter in the northern hemisphere; travellers can embrace the cooling weather by taking to the ski-slopes of Europe or hide from it indoors with some pampering in a luxurious spa. November is a good time to visit the USA – just in time for Thanksgiving. The heat and humidity of the Mississippi has lessened and travellers can comfortably explore the river's historic towns.

Alternatively, head south to soak up the start of the southern hemisphere's summer season. Lounge on the beaches, explore the mangrove forests of Margarita Island or visit Ghana on Africa's Gold Coast, with its rich colonial history. To help you choose, you'll find all the destinations in this chapter below, as well as some extra suggestions to provide a little inspiration.

FESTIVALS AND CULTURE

GHANA Casting a net from the rocks on Labadi Beach near Accra

UNFORGETTABLE JOURNEYS

BURGUNDY Bottles of Domaine Laroche in a cellar

NATURAL WONDERS

AITUTAKI Threadfin butterfly fish in the tropical waters off Aitutaki

---

BRUSSELS
BELGIUM, EUROPE

Take a break in the sophisticated capital of the EU

Home to Tintin, Magritte, over 80 museums and a highly cosmopolitan population, this elegant city is also a great place to enjoy terrific food.
www.bruxelles.irisnet.be

MELBOURNE
AUSTRALIA, AUSTRALASIA

Put your shirt on a rider in the Melbourne Cup

Every first Tuesday in November Australia comes to a stop for the Melbourne Cup horse race, the start of an exuberant carnival.
www.melbournecup.com

NARIZ DEL DIABLO
ECUADOR, SOUTH AMERICA

An awe-inspiring rail route that's hard to believe is real

The world's most difficult railway to build, this line winds down the incredibly steep "Devil's Nose", from high mountain to rainforest.
www.ecuadorexplorer.com

BURGUNDY
FRANCE, EUROPE

A canal cruise in search of autumnal delights

Travel at a leisurely pace through the heart of the French countryside – because you mustn't rush such great food and wine.
See pp276–7

> "Such beauty and simplicity cannot fail to fill visitors with complete awe."

AITUTAKI
COOK ISLANDS, AUSTRALASIA

The bluest of blue lagoons filled with technicolour fish

Dancing, singing and fresh fish are what matter here. It's a perfect setting and one of the most natural places in the world.
See pp290–91

GOLD COAST
GHANA, AFRICA

Explore the dark history of the slave forts along the Gold Coast

After reflecting on this sombre history, learn about Ashanti culture, explore the roof of a nature-filled rainforest or take a safari to a National Park.
See pp292–3

> "A dynamic, modern country whose cultural and natural attractions make it an ideal destination for first-time visitors to Africa."

MISSISSIPPI CRUISE
USA, NORTH AMERICA

Take a paddlesteamer up the great river to the US heartland

Travel in a genuine "floating palace" from New Orleans past stately antebellum houses, historic plantations and Civil War sites.
See pp284–5

THE LOW COUNTRY
USA, NORTH AMERICA

Discover silent creeks and marshes alive with birds

Kayak through the wildlife-filled salt-marshes and rivers of the South Carolina Low Country, and stay in historic little island towns.
www.southcarolinalowcountry.com

YUCATÁN CENOTES
MEXICO, NORTH AMERICA

A unique underwater, subterranean world

The world's largest underwater caves, these cathedral-like caverns beneath the Yucatán are unforgettable places to dive.
www.visitmexico.com

VIETNAM
ASIA

Experience a beguiling mix of cultures in this country

Enjoy the chaos of Ho Chi Minh City, dawdling on the calm Mekong river, fun-packed beaches and ancient traditions.
See pp274–5

DRAA VALLEY
MOROCCO, AFRICA

High peaks to sandy desert and mud-walled kasbahs

Drive from Marrakesh across the High Atlas down into a world of date groves, oases and endless sands on the edge of the Sahara.
www.visitmorocco.org

MARGARITA ISLAND
VENEZUELA, SOUTH AMERICA

Perfect for snorkelling, watersports and nature

Find sandy beaches, a verdant and mountainous interior and a fabulous mangrove National Park teeming with wildlife.
See pp294–5

TYSFJORD
NORWAY, EUROPE

Sail between killer whales in a snow-ringed fjord

Just before the Arctic winter hundreds of orcas (killer whales) gather in this fjord in northern Norway, an astonishing spectacle.
www.tysfjord-turistsenter.no

TOKYO
JAPAN, ASIA

Futuristic city that is both cutting edge and traditional

The busy, crowded cityscape feels modern to the core, but traditional values such as an appreciation of the natural world are not forgotten.
See pp286–7

SICILY
ITALY, EUROPE

The wild heart of one of Europe's most special places

Follow back roads across the island from Palermo to Siracusa, through Enna, perched atop a massive rocky crag.
www.regione.sicilia.it

Previous page: Santa Maria delle Salute Church at sunset, seen from the lagoon, Venice

Weather Watch

1 This month (in fact most months) the Bahamas enjoy warm, sunny weather and low rainfall. It can still get a little chilly at night time though.

2 Margarita Island is almost a desert island and the temperature stays high – day and night. Small amounts of rain are likely at the end of the month.

3 Ghana is hot and humid all year round, although the dry season (Nov–Mar) is the best time to visit. Thanks to cool sea currents the coast is a little cooler and drier than the interior.

4 Temperatures are quite cool in Burgundy and it becomes noticeably colder in the evenings as the month goes on. However, there are still many bright, sunny days and rainfall is infrequent.

5 This is the driest month for Rajasthan, with low humidity and days that are sunny and warm, without being too hot – thanks to the passing of the monsoon.

6 Daytime temperatures are high all year for the Cook Islands, but there are cooling sea breezes. Rain is always possible, but it comes in short bursts that clear the sky and relieve some of the humidity.

LUXURY AND ROMANCE

VENICE Plush fabrics decorate the interior of a gondola

ACTIVE ADVENTURES

TASMANIA Rafting the challenging waters at Wild Rivers National Park

FAMILY GETAWAYS

BAHAMAS Colourful souvenirs for sale on the islands

BARBADOS
CARIBBEAN

Brilliant sunshine, and a rather cosy charm

Cricket, golf, driving on the right – it's often called a little piece of England, but has Caribbean beaches and buzzing nightlife too.
www.visitbarbados.org

RAJASTHAN
INDIA, ASIA

Take the sumptuous Palace on Wheels around the state

See the great forts and palaces of the once mighty Mughals by train; plus tiger sanctuaries, game parks and the serene Taj Mahal.
See pp288–9

VENICE
ITALY, EUROPE

A magical destination that must be seen to be believed

This watery city has romantic gondolas, grand coffee houses, magnificent churches, bustling markets, and wonderful art.
See pp282–3

MAR DEL PLATA
ARGENTINA, SOUTH AMERICA

Sample the scene in the smartest resort in the south

Argentina's holiday season starts here, in this stylish town with dynamic nightlife and long, beautiful beaches.
www.argentinaturistica.com

MONART
IRELAND, EUROPE

Banish the November blues with some real pampering

This lavish spa in the Irish countryside caters to every possible need – including gourmet cuisine, if you wish.
www.monart.ie

"Extraordinary beauty, laden with myths and mystery that has inspired artists, poets and film-makers throughout the centuries."

THE MILFORD TRACK
NEW ZEALAND, AUSTRALASIA

An unmissable hike through superb lakes and mountains

Book early to get a permit to walk this famous trail – access is controlled to preserve the pristine landscape.
www.milfordtrack.net

TASMANIA
AUSTRALIA, AUSTRALASIA

An island adventure holiday at the edge of the world

Cycle down mountains, kayak to empty sandy beaches, and trek through the alpine centre of an undiscovered wilderness.
See pp280–81

LA REUNION
INDIAN OCEAN

From mountain peaks and cascades to coral reefs

With its high peaks, this French island offers the chance to hike the mountains and dive in tropical waters – the same day.
www.la-reunion-tourisme.com

SALAR DE UYUNI
BOLIVIA, SOUTH AMERICA

Experience a moonscape in the High Andes

This huge space is the world's largest salt desert, high in the Andes – driving across its vast flatness is bizarrely disorientating.
www.andeansummits.com

LE CROTOY
FRANCE, EUROPE

Clear your head with a fast sail across the sands

Giant sand flats in the Somme Bay have made it a world centre for sand-yachting – and November is when the winds are sharpest.
www.noshoesclub.com

"Picture-postcard with its clapboard cottages in a pastiche of Caribbean pastels graced by gingerbread trim."

PLYMOUTH
USA, NORTH AMERICA

First landing site of the Pilgrim Fathers

Mark Thanksgiving where it all began – watch the parade, eat at the Pilgrim Village and visit the reproduction *Mayflower*.
www.plimoth.org

KURANDA
AUSTRALIA, AUSTRALASIA

The rain forest made accessible

Travel by cable car up to this town in Queensland's forest for a dazzling look at a landscape alive with birds, flowers and butterflies.
www.kuranda.org

BAHAMAS
NORTH ATLANTIC

Swim with dolphins or relax on gorgeous, safe beaches

Excellent facilities, genuine hospitality and idyllic beaches make these islands the perfect family destination.
See pp278–9

COSTA RICA
CENTRAL AMERICA

One of the most beguiling of tropical countries

Costa Rica offers a seductive mix of exuberant landscapes and wildlife, beaches and a very laid-back, friendly atmosphere.
www.visitcostarica.com

GAMBIA
WEST AFRICA

Perfect, unspoilt beaches and a rich African culture

Tropical sunshine is guaranteed – and when you need a change, there's an abundance of natural attractions and great markets.
www.visitthegambia.gm

GETTING THERE
Vietnam is in south Asia. Hanoi is the capital and is served by Noi Bai international airport 45 km (27 miles) from the city centre. Ho Chi Minh City is served by Tan Son Nhat airport, 7 km (5 miles) from Ho Chi Minh City. Both airports are well connected by bus and taxi.

GETTING AROUND
Cyclos, *xe om* (motorbikes) and metered taxis get you around towns; buses, trains and planes cover longer distances.

WEATHER
November is one of the cooler months (25–30°C), with lower rainfall; humidity is high.

ACCOMMODATION
Perfume Grass Inn, Nha Trang, is friendly and quiet; doubles from £15; www.perfume-grass.com

Ha An Hotel, Hoi An, a beautiful boutique hotel with lush gardens; doubles from £20; www.haanhotel.com

Majestic Hotel, Ho Chi Minh City, is an elegant riverfront hotel with spectacular views; doubles from £85; www.majesticsaigon.com

EATING OUT
Vietnamese cuisine is a travel highlight. Try Huong Lai, Ho Chi Minh City for excellent Vietnamese food in a lovely setting with a set menu for about £4 and Hong Phuc Restaurant, Hoi An which is famous for its fish cooked in a banana leaf. Dishes from around £1.50.

PRICE FOR TWO
£40–60 per day including accommodation, food, local travel and entrance charges.

FURTHER INFORMATION
www.vietnamtourism.com

The Cu Chi Tunnels
A massive tourist attraction, the 120-km (75-mile) network of tunnels made during the Vietnam War at Cu Chi has been preserved as a war memorial park by the government of Vietnam. Visitors can crawl around in the safer parts of the tunnel system with low-power lights installed in several of them. Underground conference rooms where campaigns such as the Tet Offensive were planned have been restored. However, a short crawl through these claustrophobic black tunnels today makes it difficult to conceive how people lived like this for years.

Main: Woman rowing in the calm waters near Hanoi
Above (top to bottom): Cao Dai Great Temple in Tay Ninh; family travelling on a cyclo; Presidential Palace in Hanoi; carrying fruit on Nha Trang beach

VISIONS OF VIETNAM

IN A BLEND OF MESMERISING SIGHTS, SOUNDS, SMELLS AND TASTES that is like no other, Vietnam delivers adventure and sensory overload. This is a land of picture-postcard images: a scattering of bobbing conical straw hats dot a patchwork landscape of emerald rice fields; graceful girls in their elegant white *ao dai* national dress, zipping around cities on their motorcycles; decorative pagodas and the dizzying colours of a Cao Dai temple.

The beguiling mix of cultures stems from a long and convoluted history. From a rich civilization with deeply held traditions has risen a country that has seen the future, and rushed headlong into it. However, the past is not forgotten whether it be still-revered ancient temples, or poignant sites of the terrible 20th-century wars.

Noisy, vibrant, chaotic and colourful, Ho Chi Minh City dazzles. District 1 (Saigon) has French colonial architecture and striking modern buildings, from skyscrapers to the eerie Reunification Palace. The War Remnants

Above: Cham ancient ruins near Hoi An

JAN

FEB

MAR

APR

MAY

JUN

JUL

AUG

SEP

OCT

NOV

DAYS
1–2

DAYS
3–5

DAY 6

DAYS
7–8

DAYS
9–10

DAYS
11–12

DAYS
13–14

DEC

TOURING DIARY

November is the start of the driest time of the year in the Vietnam. In two weeks you can pack in a mix of experiences and get a good feel for the country. Begin in cosmopolitan Hanoi then head down to Hoi An and enjoy the beaches along the coast before exploring the rural Mekong Delta and finishing in Ho Chi Minh City.

Two Weeks in Vietnam

Fly into Hanoi, Vietnam's capital, and spend a couple of days taking in the sights – the colonial architecture in the French Quarter, the beautiful Buddhist Temple of Literature and the Hoan Kiem Lake.

Make your way to Hoi An which delights with its old wooden houses, Japanese Covered Bridge and tranquil waterfront setting. Meander through the Old Town, watch craftspeople at work and join a half-day Vietnamese cookery course.

Head to Danang, visit the Museum of Cham Sculpture and relax on China Beach (My Khe). Alternatively, visit the caves and sanctuaries at Thuy Son.

Next, visit Nha Trang, Vietnam's beach party capital, to eat seafood, visit the Long Son Pagoda, Cham towers at Po Nagar, and take boat trips to the idyllic islands.

Go on a minibus tour (cheap and easy to organise) to the Mekong Delta, Can Tho is the main city. A boat ride through the canals and an early morning visit to a floating market are the must-dos.

Take a day trip to the Cu Chi Tunnels, a section of the vast, and legendary, underground network created by Viet Cong guerrillas. Most tours also include a visit to the colourful Cao Dai Great Temple in Tay Ninh.

Finish in Ho Chi Minh City. In the Saigon district, visit museums, markets and memorials, pagodas and parks; fill up on *pho* (noodle soup). Shop in Dong Khoi Street and try the bars in Pham Ngu Lau. Explore the Chinese temples and herbal medicine shops in Cholon.

Dos and Don'ts

- ✓ Take care of your possessions. Bag-snatching and scams are on the increase, especially in big cities and resorts.
- ✗ Don't leave your chopsticks in a V-shape in the bowl – it symbolizes death.
- ✓ Pack ear plugs if you want a good night's sleep – Vietnam can be very noisy.
- ✓ Wear shoes if you're swimming in the sea. Stonefish, stingrays and scorpion fish lurk in the shallows.

Museum pulls no punches about the horrors of the Vietnam War. You'll find relief in the shops selling colourful and sensuous silks to be tailored into anything you want; in market stalls overflowing with produce, and in the ornate temples of Cholon (Chinatown), wreathed with incense.

Tiny cafés line traffic-clogged streets, the smells of aromatic spices waft from countless restaurants and food stalls. The city's nightlife is memorable. Have a drink at the balcony bar of a high-rise hotel, and watch the city explode in a riot of neon – then get down there and join in.

By contrast the towns of the Mekong Delta feel a world away. The pace of life is much slower in this lush, watery world of rice paddies, fish farms and floating markets, where an intricate web of narrow canals links tiny green islands where tropical fruits grow in surprising abundance.

Vietnam has another special feature – its long coastline has some of the world's best beaches. Shaded by casuarina trees and coconut palms, long, empty stretches of fine sand are lapped by cool, clear water, and jungle-clad mountains fall into quiet bays. China Beach is a good example: a perfect beach stretching almost 30 km (19 miles) north from the edge of tranquil, old-world, Hoi An.

GETTING THERE
Dijon's airport is 6 km (4 miles) south of the city with international connections from Paris. The TGV from Paris stops at Montbard.

GETTING AROUND
Apart from travelling by canal, the main towns in the region are linked by bus. Car hire is available in larger towns for day trips. Excursions are often provided with cruise packages.

WEATHER
In November, the average temperature is 9°C and it can become quite cold in the evenings.

ACCOMMODATION
Crewed B&B and gîtes barges cost around £675 per person per week.

Smaller canal boats are available for self-drive holidays, with no licence needed, from around £945 for a four-berth boat per week.

Charters, including meals and often excursions, cost from £1,700–3,375 per person per week.

"Hotel Canal Barges" take up to 20 passengers for around £1,200 per person for six nights.

See www.holidaysafloat.co.uk for the above.

EATING OUT
Dijon vies with Lyon for the title of gastronomic capital of France. Le Pré aux Clercs in Dijon is about as good as it gets, around £55.

PRICE FOR TWO
With all-inclusive cruises, you will only need money for treats ashore. Otherwise allow £70 a day. If you self-skipper and eat on board with the occasional trip, £35 a day is sufficient.

FURTHER INFORMATION
www.burgundy-canal.com

The Canals of Burgundy
Completed in 1832, the Canal de Bourgogne is 242 km (150 miles) long and has 209 locks with an average of 1.3 km (1 mile) between each. From Lock No 1 at Escommes at the southern Saóne end, the canal climbs 299 m (980 ft) to Pouilly-en-Auxois past Dijon. After which it continues towards Migennes and the Yonne. As the Yonne eventually meets the Seine, which flows through Paris to the English Channel, the canal provides a direct link between the waterways of the north and south of the country.

AUTUMNAL RIVER CRUISE

B RIMMING WITH GOOD FOOD AND FINE WINE, Burgundy is the heartiest region of France. In November the hunting season is underway, mushrooms are being gathered and the grape harvest is being celebrated among the renowned Côte d'Or vineyards – it's a good time for a remarkable journey. The way to travel is by canal boat or barge, unhurried transports along the 242-km (150-mile) *Canal de Bourgogne*, the Burgundy Canal. This waterway cuts through the heart of the countryside allowing you to sample its bountiful delights as you go – from picnics to gourmet meals.

Whether you choose to splash out on a traditional barge with a crew, perhaps with full gourmet dining, or potter alone in a small pleasure craft, you can dictate your own pace, gliding through picturesque villages, with lock-keepers, homes, canal workers' cottages and other fascinating vestiges of water-borne life. At this time of year the oak and maple forests will be glowing like burnished gold, and the vine leaves will be taking on their ruddy autumn mantle.

Step off the barge to admire the villages, and appreciate their cafés; stretch your legs in the autumnal countryside, hire a bike for half a day or try your hand at fishing – licences are easily obtainable from local stores. Not far from the canal are châteaux that show just how rich Burgundy once was: it once ruled the continent from the Netherlands to Provence and its hefty red wine was drunk in all the royal courts of Europe. There are number of fine churches and abbeys, too, as this was the heartland of the Cistercian order.

Dijon, the region's capital, lies at the southern end of the canal – its famous mustard is made with the juice of unripe grapes. Among other delights of the table you will find hearty *boeuf bourguignon* from Charolais cattle, *coq au vin* from Bresse chicken fed on maize and whey, *escargots à la bourguignonne*, and wild mushrooms, newly gathered. As for the wines – Chablis, Côtes de Nuits and Côtes de Beaune – they are all divine. The annual charity wine auction in the medieval jewel, the Hôtel Dieu in Beaune with its multi-coloured glazed roof tiles, gives you a great opportunity to sample the delights of your winning bid in a perfect Burgundian setting.

Above: Bidders crowd the cellars at the Beaune charity wine auction

CANAL DIARY

Look out for local harvest festivals – November sees Dijon put on its annual International Gastronomic Fair at the Palais des Expositions and Beaune its Charity Wine Auction. Some smaller museums and châteaux may be closed for the season and Dijon's museums are closed on Tuesdays.

One Week on the Waterways

Arrive in Dijon and travel up to Sens to start your cruise. But first explore this ancient town, centred around St Etienne, the oldest of France's great Gothic cathedrals. Its treasury, one of the largest in the country, is part of the Museum of Fine Arts. — **DAY 1**

Start your cruise gently, Tonnerre makes a pleasant stop, with good shops, cafés and restaurants. A curiosity that draws visitors is Fosse Dionne, a mystic spring. Tonnerre's Hôtel-Dieu was founded in 1293. This is one of the few places that you will see vineyards beside the canal. — **DAY 2**

Montbard lies half way along the canal and it provides a hopping off point for several fine sites in the vicinity: the Renaissance Château d'Ancy-le-Franc (closes mid-November), the beautiful Romanesque Basilique Ste-Madeleine Vézelay and Abbaye de Fontenay, the oldest surviving Cistercian foundation in France. Hire a car to see them all in a day. — **DAY 3**

Travel down to Beaune, the wine capital of Burgundy, to visit the wine museum in the 16th-century Hôtel des Ducs de Bourgogne and the beautiful Hôtel Dieu, for the annual charity wine auction each November. — **DAY 4**

Dijon is a high spot of the journey and needs time to explore. Start by looking down on the medieval town from the top of the Philippe le Bon Tower. Visit Gustave Eiffel's covered market and lunch in the Bistrot des Halles. Shops along Rue de la Liberté include the Maille mustard store at no. 32 and the antiques quarter lies behind Notre Dame. — **DAYS 5–7**

Dos and Don'ts

✓ Hire a Segway (2-wheeled personal transporter) from the main tourist office in Dijon – a fun way to get around.

✗ Don't drink and drive; always have a designated driver when going on wine tours.

✓ Do buy some of the famous Dijon mustard when in the town, it makes a great gift.

JAN
FEB
MAR
APR
MAY
JUN
JUL
AUG
SEP
OCT
NOV
DEC

Main: Latricières-Chambertin Vineyard

Left panel (top to bottom): Dijon with the church of Notre Dame; chapterhouse in the Abbaye de Fontenay; Hôtel Dieu in Beaune

Above (top to bottom): Burgundy canal; bottles of Domaine Laroche; Moutarde Maille shop in Dijon

Below: Olive stall in Beaune market

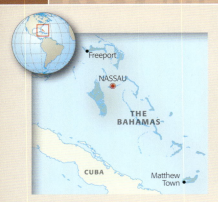

GETTING THERE
The Bahamas is a chain of 700 islands covering 259,000 sq km (100,000 sq miles) in the western Atlantic, southeast of Florida. Nassau has the main international airport. Ferries link Nassau with Eleuthera, and mailboats serve other islands.

GETTING AROUND
There are many modes of transport around the islands, including car, boat and hired bicycles. Taxis are readily available.

WEATHER
In November, the weather is sunny with cooling trade winds and temperatures of around 26°C.

ACCOMMODATION
Dillet's Guest House is a traditional house; two doubles from £130; www.islandeaze.com

Brightly coloured beach cabanas at Compass Point, New Providence; two-bedroomed hut from £215; www.compasspointbahamas.com

Beside the famous beach of the same name, Pink Sands on Harbour Island; two-bedroomed cottage £630; www.islandoutpost.com

EATING OUT
Seafood predominates, including swordfish, grouper, and conch, a clam-like staple usually grilled and served with a tomato sauce. Tropical fruits such as guava and papaya also feature.

PRICE FOR A FAMILY OF FOUR
£270–330 per day including accommodation, food and mailboat travel around the islands.

FURTHER INFORMATION
www.bahamas.com
www.atlantis.com

Bottlenose Dolphins
Bottlenose dolphins are common in warm, shallow Bahamian waters. Playful acrobats, these amazing marine mammals are capable of leaping 6 m (20 feet) out of the water. The streamlined creatures seem to enjoy contact with humans. Blue Lagoon, off New Providence, and UNEXSO, on Grand Bahama, let visitors enter enclosed lagoons to swim with Atlantic bottlenose dolphins while specialist tours offer opportunities to see wild dolphins in the oceans off Bimini and Grand Bahama.

Main: Boat passes the quiet Exuma Cays
Above (top to bottom): Typical Bahamian architecture; scuba diving with Barracuda; Atlantis Beach Resort in Paradise Island

FUN IN THE SUN

WHILE MANY PEOPLE THINK OF THE BAHAMAS AS ONE ISLAND, the nation actually comprises a chain of isles – some large, others tiny – sprinkled across a vast area of the perfectly blue-green western Atlantic waters. Each group is as distinct as a thumbprint. Island-hopping from one to the next, visitors discover that even the most Lilliputian island is blessed with gargantuan charm.

Nassau, the capital city with its plethora of hotels and restaurants, also follows a lifestyle wed to the sea, providing a perfect combination of fine beaches and aquatic adventures that appeal to the young and young-at-heart. Choose from aqua-biking to sunfish boat sailing at Cable Beach. Boats will whisk you to Blue Lagoon to swim with trained dolphins in a protected enclosed environment, and to Stingray City to snorkel with harmless rays. You can even take to the air for a bird's-eye view of Nassau and neighbouring Paradise Island. Atlantis, home to

Above: Brightly coloured souvenirs for sale at a beach stall

MARINE DIARY

Fringed by sand as soft as a pillow and waters of teal-blue perfection, the islands in the Bahamas are perfect in November for lazing by the sea. Exploring all the islands would require several weeks, but four or five days is sufficient to sample the best of Nassau and Paradise Island plus a trip to the Family Islands (the outer islands).

Four Days of Sand and Sea

Explore downtown Nassau by horse-drawn carriage then visit the interactive museum, Pirates of Nassau.

View the exhibits recalling the days of slavery at the Pompey Museum then wander around the nearby Straw Market to pick up some souvenirs.

Spend a full day at Atlantis, on Paradise Island, renowned for its vast water-park with plexiglass walkways for eyeball-to-eyeball encounters with sharks.

Experience the rush of the Leap of Faith water slide or savour a sedate Lazy River Ride. Children can enjoy the fully-equipped video game centres and teens can spend the evening at their own nightclub and lounge.

Take a boat trip to Blue Lagoon. Here, you can swim with dolphins and aquaplane across the lagoon. Younger children can wade into the waist-deep water while dolphins swim up to be petted.

Later, enjoy snorkelling and other water sports or laze in a hammock while the young ones dig in the sand.

Travel to Harbour Island on the high-speed ferry and explore the quaint village, then scuba dive or laze the day away on the long stretch of rose-pink beach.

Either spend the night in one of the exquisite hotels or return to Nassau on the afternoon ferry.

Dos and Don'ts

✓ Observe the rules for swimming with dolphins. They are wild creatures and their behaviour is unpredictable.

✗ Don't miss out on the fascinating and colourful underwater world; snorkelling is a great way to see marine-life up close.

✓ Go steady on the legendary Bahamian cocktails. There's a reason they have such names as the Jack Hammer and Goombay Smash.

Calendar (right column): JAN, FEB, MAR, APR, MAY, JUN, JUL, AUG, SEP, OCT, NOV, DAY 1, DAY 2, DAY 3, DAY 4, DEC

50,000 live sea animals, is the largest marine habitat in the world, enthralling children and adults alike. Here, visitors can journey through ancient Atlantis and partake of a week's-worth of water-slides and other educational and fun-filled activities. Nassau is also filled with quaint colonial buildings and plenty of things to do with the kids. Pirates of Nassau educates and entertains with an interactive museum where kids learn about the Golden Age of Piracy. And don't miss Junkanoo Expo, a museum honouring the unique and contagious Bahamas' heritage celebration.

Every island has pillow-soft beaches but few can rival Eleuthera's Harbour Island, famous for its pink sands merging into the electric-blue water, often voted as one of the most beautiful beaches in the world. One of the Family Islands, 'briland, as it is locally known, looks like it has fallen from its own picture-postcard with its clapboard cottages in a pastiche of Caribbean pastels graced by gingerbread trim. Visitors can peek into tiny churches, eat in traditional restaurants, and rent an electric golf cart to explore further afield. Although, of all the activities available, little can surpass swimming in the turquoise waters and drying out under the Bahamian sun.

GETTING THERE
Tasmania is separated from mainland Australia by the Bass Strait, a 250-km (150-mile) stretch of water flanking the northern coast of the island. There are flights to Hobart from Melbourne, Adelaide, Sydney and Canberra. Ferries make regular overnight journeys from Melbourne to Devonport on the north coast.

GETTING AROUND
Coaches travel between major tourist attractions. Touring is best done with a car.

WEATHER
November is springtime in Tasmania with an average daytime temperature of 20°C.

ACCOMMODATION
Diamond Island Apartments, overlooking the ocean at Bicheno, on the east coast; doubles from £90; www.diamondisland.com.au

Cradle Mountain Lodge offers a wilderness retreat; doubles from £70; www.cradlemountainlodge.com.au

The Islington for luxury just minutes from the centre of Hobart; doubles from £260; www.islingtonhotel.com

EATING OUT
Enjoy the great local produce: pick up a bag of crisp apples from a roadside stall, taste handmade cheese straight from the farm and buy your seafood fresh from the fisherman.

PRICE FOR TWO
£200–250 per day including accommodation, food, guided tours and local travel.

FURTHER INFORMATION
www.discovertasmania.com

The Penal Experiment

The British settled in Tasmania (known then as Van Diemen's Land) in 1803, but they had another use in mind for this outpost. With jails in Britain overflowing, the island was an ideal repository for the Empire's criminals. Transportation began in 1822 to the remote settlement of Sarah Island. The "success" of the island led to the establishment of further penal sites across Tasmania, including the infamous Port Arthur settlement (above). In all, some 74,000 convicts were sent here before the practice ceased in 1853.

PRIMEVAL WILDERNESS

IT IS EASY TO FEEL HUMBLED BY THE ENORMITY of Tasmania's wild and remote southwest. Virtually at the edge of the world, there's just the vast expanse of the mighty Southern Ocean separating this spectacular tract of wilderness from the Antarctic continent. To the west, it's some 20,000 kilometres (12,000 miles) to the next landmass – South America. Such isolation has been a lifeline for the island's native flora and fauna; it's also a blessing for adventure-seekers – Tasmania has millions of hectares of wild countryside to explore and an abundance of fresh air and water.

Australia's smallest state is also its greenest. A vast 13,800 sq km (5,330 sq miles) of Tasmania – around 20 percent – is protected as World Heritage Wilderness, an area of outstanding cultural and natural value that includes some of the last remaining temperate rainforests in the world.

Main: Sun setting over the unusual rock formations at Wineglass Bay

Left: The Painted Cliffs, Maria Island National Park

Right (left to right): Clambering through the forested interior of the island; camping in the wilderness; rafting in the Wild Rivers National Park; canoeing in the turquoise waters at Freycinet

Tasmania is covered in managed walking tracks, including the famed Overland Track – a 65-km (40-mile) 6-day walk through Tasmania's rugged alpine heart. On the Freycinet Peninsula, the short but thoroughly rewarding 45-minute uphill trek to the Wineglass Bay lookout provides a heart-stopping view of one of the planet's most spectacular stretches of sand.

On the island's west, in the glacial lakes and streams of the Franklin-Gordon Wild Rivers National Park, there lie links with the Permian period, some 250 million years ago. Primitive crustaceans still live here among the rivers and ferns they've called home for millions of years. The Franklin River, one of three major rivers that run through the park, is revered by Tasmanians for its natural, cultural and historical significance and is known for epic white-water rafting experiences.

Off the usual tourist trail, Tasmania is Australia's best-kept secret, offering endless possibilities for adventure in an ancient landscape that teems with life.

Above: Wineglass Bay lookout at Freycinet National Park

ACTION-PACKED DIARY

November is the ideal time for a trip around Tasmania, as the island enjoys mild spring days and long daylight hours. Tasmania's compact size – 315 km by 286 km (189 miles by 175 miles) – makes it the perfect self-drive destination. In two weeks you can travel around most of the island's beautiful sights.

Two Weeks of Adventure

Starting in the southern capital of Hobart, head for an adrenaline-pumping cycle down the city's local mountain, Mt Wellington. Soak up Hobart's maritime atmosphere at the magnificent waterfront, or explore the island's history in the excellent museums.

Just south of Hobart, Bruny Island's maritime wilds are best explored by an adventure cruise. Chances are you'll encounter a plethora of marine life, such as bottlenose dolphins, fur seals and migrating humpback and southern right whales.

DAYS 1–3

Head east to beautiful Maria Island National Park before travelling on south to the Tasman Peninsula, once home to some of Britain's worst criminals and exiled political revolutionaries, as well as the odd pickpocket. Port Arthur offers an insightful and interesting look back at the island's convict past.

DAYS 4–6

On the island's astonishingly beautiful east coast you'll encounter arc after arc of people-free white sand, framed by pristine waters. Kayaking is the best way to explore the coast's much-lauded Freycinet Peninsula.

DAYS 7–8

Inland and west to Cradle Mountain, Tasmania's natural icon and northern gateway to the Overland Track. Spend a few nights in the area before continuing west to Franklin-Gordon Wild Rivers National Park.

DAYS 9–12

Travel southwest, deep into Tasmania's World Heritage wilderness, past tannin-stained rivers and streams towards the remote west coast. Climb Mount Rugby for fantastic views of natural Bathurst Harbour, then cruise, raft or hike your way about these ancient wilds.

DAYS 13–14

Dos and Don'ts

- ✓ Pack a jumper and raincoat. Spring in Tasmania can mean temperamental weather.
- ✓ Drink the water from the tap! Tasmania has some of the cleanest, purest water in the world, thanks to its clean environment and mountain-fed water supplies.
- ✓ Ask a local – Tasmanians are friendly people and are usually able to offer useful advice or directions.
- ✗ Don't leave for a bushwalk without checking the weather forecast and preparing yourself accordingly.

JAN
FEB
MAR
APR
MAY
JUN
JUL
AUG
SEP
OCT
NOV
DEC

GETTING THERE
Marco Polo International Airport is 14 km (9 miles) from the city. Some flights use Treviso, which is 30 km (19 miles) from the centre. A bus runs from the airport to Piazzale Roma. A more expensive option is a water taxi from the airport to central Venice.

GETTING AROUND
In Venice, the most useful *vaporetto* (water bus) service is Line 1, which follows the Grand Canal. The city centre is small and is easy to traverse by foot.

WEATHER
November can be wet and misty but there are many days of pale sunshine. The average temperature is 13ºC.

ACCOMMODATION
La Calcina has lovely views of the Giudecca Canal; doubles from £110; www.lacalcina.com

Hotel Flora is a charming hotel with doubles from £115; www.hotelflora.it

Hotel Gritti Palace offers complete luxury, overlooking the Grand Canal; doubles from £350; www.hotelgrittivenice.com

EATING OUT
Venetian cuisine specializes in fish and seafood, together with more unusual ingredients like pomegranates, pine nuts and raisins, which reflect the city's past as a trading post. Outstanding but pricey food can be enjoyed at La Caravella.

PRICE FOR TWO
£220–300 including accommodation, food, local transport and entrance charges.

FURTHER INFORMATION
www.turismovenezia.it

Venetian Glass
In the 13th century, the Venetian glass industry was moved to the nearby island of Murano for fear of fire in the city. The glass-making inhabitants were confined to the island until the 17th century to keep the production methods a secret. Venetian glass is world-renowned, famed for the purity of its glass, ornate design and embellishment with glowing enamels. A stroll along any of the main streets on Murano will provide you with a colourful display of the island's famous wares.

"I stood in Venice on the Bridge of Sighs, A palace and a prison on each hand."

Lord Byron

Main: Dusk descends upon the Grand Canal
Inset: Detail from the roof of the Basilica di San Marco **Above:** Palazzo Contarini del Bovolo's beautiful spiral staircase

HISTORY IN REFLECTION

BUILT ON THE WATER, SLOWLY SINKING INTO THE SEA, Venice is one of the most romantic cities in the world, as well as one of the most distinctive. However many paintings or photographs of it you have been exposed to, the first view of Venice never fails to take the breath away – the reflections of Gothic and Renaissance palaces in the waters of the Grand Canal seem too perfect to be real, and St Mark's Square, which Napoleon called "the finest drawing room in Europe", has the stylized symmetry of a film set.

A place of extraordinary beauty, laden with myths and mystery, Venice has inspired artists, poets and film-makers throughout the centuries, and exerts an insidious power over everyone who has seen it. Everyone has their own idea of Venice, be it the raucous, colourful celebration of Carnival, or the sombre, dreamy allure of *Death in Venice*, the novel by Thomas Mann famously filmed by Visconti. Then there is the sophisticated café society of the

Left (left to right): Luxurious interior of a gondola; St Mark's Square during the *acqua alta* (high water); painted ceiling of the Sala Capitolare in Scuola Grande dei Carmini; colourful house on Burano Island; fresh fruit and vegetables on display at Rialto food market on the Grand Canal

Above: Exclusive Caffè Florian on St Mark's Square

JAN
FEB
MAR
APR
MAY
JUN
JUL
AUG
SEP
OCT
NOV
DAY 1
DAY 2
DAY 3
DAY 4
DAY 5
DEC

GONDOLA DIARY

November is a good time to visit Venice as there are fewer people, hotel prices are lower, and the pale wintry sunshine lends the city an ethereal air. If you come at a time of *acqua alta* (high water), you will have the experience of crossing St Mark's Square on duck-boards. Five days is sufficient to see most sights.

Five Days in the Sinking City

Take a *vaporetto* trip along the Grand Canal. A day pass enables you to hop on and off to visit palaces such as the Gothic Ca' d'Oro and the Baroque Ca' Rezzonico, both of which contain galleries. Take in the architectural beauty of the city, especially on the little island of San Giorgio Maggiore.

Start with coffee in the spendid Caffè Florian in St Mark's Square, then take a tour of the Doge's Palace. After a late lunch, wander around the beautiful Basilica di San Marco, or head to Museo Correr to see Bellini's *Pietà* and other Renaissance masterpieces. A little difficult to find, but well worth the effort, is Palazzo Contarini del Bovolo, with its fairy-tale exterior staircase.

Visit the huge, colourful Rialto market, near the famous bridge, then on to the Frari church to see Titian's *Assumption*. For more masterpieces, visit nearby San Rocco – its interior is covered with works by Tintoretto – returning later for a romantic recital of Baroque music.

Go by *vaporetto* to see the Accademia Gallery's wonderful collection of Venetian paintings. After lunch, head to the Guggenheim Collection of modern art in the Palazzo Venier, and the lovely La Salute church, or see the ornate ceilings at Scuola Grande dei Carmini before enjoying a hot chocolate in the Zattere.

Catch a ferry to one of the outlying islands: Murano, where the famous glass is made; or Burano, with its brightly painted houses. In the evening, take a gondola trip – an unforgettable way to experience Venice one last time before heading home.

Dos and Don'ts

- ✓ Visit Harry's Bar and try a Bellini cocktail (*prosecco* and peach juice).
- ✗ Don't forget mosquito repellent. Less essential in November than in summer, but mosquitoes can still be a nuisance.
- ✓ Buy a VeniceCard, which gives you 1, 3 or 7 days' free use of public transport, access to the municipal museum and discounts for visits to other museums, galleries and events.
- ✗ Don't attempt to visit St Mark's when it first opens in the morning – that is when it's at its busiest. Queues are much shorter in the late afternoon.

grand coffee houses of San Marco, where the ghosts of 19th-century literary figures such as Goethe, Proust and George Sand still linger; and the romance of a gondola trip, something to which even the most world-weary and cynical succumb, setting aside, for the duration of the ride, their views on commercialized tourist traps.

The glories of the Basilica di San Marco, the Doge's Palace, San Giorgio Maggiore and La Salute must be seen, however short your visit, and the Rialto Bridge simply has to be crossed, but there are also unsung delights. One of the joys of Venice is to wander over bridges and through quiet back streets first thing in the morning, when the place belongs to the Venetians, not the tour groups; when work-a-day gondolas are unloading essential goods, brought over from the mainland, and women are returning from markets, their bags bulging with fresh produce. Or do as the Venetians do, and stroll along the Zattere quaysides in the Dorsoduro neighbourhood, stopping for a hot chocolate if the winds blow cold. At times like these, La Serenissima, as the Venetian Republic was known, does indeed seem serene.

GETTING THERE
The Mississippi runs from Lake Itasca, Minnesota to the Gulf of Mexico. New Orleans is a good place to start a cruise and is served by Louis Armstrong International Airport, 15 km (9 miles) from the city centre.

GETTING AROUND
In New Orleans, the easiest modes of transport are cabs and streetcars. Tours from the cruise will be included as part of the package.

WEATHER
The average temperature in November is 16°C and mainly clear with the occasional cloudy day.

ACCOMMODATION
The Windsor Court Hotel in New Orleans is an Orient Express property; doubles from £180; www.windsorcourthotel.com

Mississippi River Cruises offer a variety of cruises and boats; doubles from £2,245 for seven days; www.mississippirivercruises.com

Majestic America Line have a variety of cruise packages on their luxurious boats; doubles from £2,843 for 5 days; www.majesticamericaline.com

EATING OUT
Excellent food will be served on board your ship but every trip should include a Po' boy sandwich for lunch, at Mother's Restaurant in New Orleans – about £7 for a fried shrimp sandwich with traditional jambalaya on the side.

PRICE FOR TWO
£340–360 per day including accommodation, food and all-inclusive cruise.

FURTHER INFORMATION
www.neworleansonline.com

Civil War on the Mississippi
The Mississippi played a pivotal role in the Union Army (the north) winning the American Civil War. The river was a lifeline for their army – valuable resources could be transported up and down the country, and steamboats were converted and used as naval boats alongside purpose-built gunboats. One of the biggest battles along the Mississippi was the Siege of Vicksburg in 1863; after Vicksburg was captured, the entire length of the river was under Union control.

Main: Paddle steamer on the Mississippi
Above (top to bottom): Interior of Oak Alley Plantation; morning mist on the river; antebellum architecture in Natchez; New Orleans jazz musicians

LIFE ON THE MISSISSIPPI

THE MIGHTY MISSISSIPPI RIVER is the largest river in the USA. Great literature and music have been created on and inspired by the river, but the true folklife of America has its roots in the lower Mississippi. From New Orleans, as you cruise along the river, the history of the South unfolds.

These days, the elegantly appointed, six-deck *Mississippi Queen* paddlewheel steamboat makes the journey from the port of New Orleans to Oak Alley Plantation – the grand residence used in the opening scene of the Deep South classic *Gone With the Wind*. Then she sails on to Natchez, the oldest civilized settlement on the Mississippi River. In Natchez, there are more antebellum homes (the style of architecture that preceded the American Civil War) than in any other city in the country. Step into 19th-century America, with authentic historic architecture, quaint restaurants at the river's edge and a distinctive downtown shopping area.

Above: New Orleans by the Mississippi

JAN

FEB

MAR

APR

MAY

JUN

JUL

AUG

SEP

OCT

NOV

DAY 1

DAY 2

DAY 3

DAYS
4–6

DAY 7

DEC

STEAMBOAT DIARY

November is a great time to travel down the Mississippi by steamboat. The weather is mild allowing you to enjoy the onshore activities to the full without the humidity of the summer months. Extend your stay by visiting one of the other US destinations covered in this book such as Nashville and Memphis (see pp160–61).

A Week on the Mississippi

Arrive in New Orleans and spend the day exploring the French Quarter. Have a traditional Creole lunch at one of the many restaurants that line the streets then round off your day with an evening in the birthplace of jazz with a glass of bourbon in an underground bar.

Head to your steamboat to begin your cruise. First stop along the river is Oak Alley, a historic plantation famed for its double row of oak trees that line the walkway to the historic house that has been used in several films.

St Francisville is the next port-of-call and is home to many picturesque plantations with grand gardens. For something a bit quirkier, visit the Myrtles Plantation, one of America's most haunted homes. Later, head back to the boat for an evening of entertainment and breathtaking views of the river.

Over the next three days, the steamboat will call in at Natchez, Vicksburg and Baton Rouge. Natchez is the oldest city along the river with a downtown area filled with antique shops and historic buildings. In Vicksburg, see the monuments highlighting its pivotal position on the river during the Civil War. Take a carriage ride through the main street and enjoy the hustle and bustle of the town. Then revel in the mixture of influences prevalent in Baton Rouge: Creole, Cajun and Caribbean. Try some of the delicious and distinctive local food, visit the Botanic Gardens and admire the design of the Magnolia Mound Plantation.

Spend your last day on the Mississippi returning to New Orleans to head back home.

Dos and Don'ts

✓ Feel free to ask locals for information and directions – they're used to it and they're generally very accommodating.

✗ Don't walk on quiet side streets downtown and in the French Quarter in New Orleans; like any other major urban area, New Orleans has its share of crime.

✓ Plan to do a lot of walking in New Orleans. The city is compact and visitor attractions are generally grouped within walking distance of one another.

After starting your visit to early America, the logical next stop is Vicksburg, Mississippi, where the National Military Park captures the spirit of the Civil War. In 1863, Vicksburg served as a key fortress guarding the Mississippi River. The fall of Vicksburg signalled the true end of the war, and victory for the North. The Vicksburg battlefield includes more than 1,300 monuments, fortifications and a restored Union gunboat and National Cemetery.

The cruise continues to St Francisville, home of six historic plantation homes, all open for touring. St Francisville is a walking town, with a charming downtown shopping district. Rosedown Plantation welcomes travellers to tour its exquisite main house with lush gardens.

Not far up the river lies Baton Rouge, the state capital. This city is full of places to visit including an award-winning zoo, water parks, botanical gardens, museums and more plantations. Magnolia Mound Plantation's separate open-hearth kitchen and crop gardens are much the same today as they were more than two centuries ago. Then it's time to return to the 21st century as the boat makes slow but steady progress back to New Orleans and the bustling streets of the French Quarter.

The Boiled Octopus
There are over 2,000 *onsen* (mineral hot springs) scattered across Japan. These rural retreats were traditionally places to ease the aching muscles of rice farmers with thrice daily bathing. Today, the *onsen* concept remains integral to Japanese culture. There are several old *onsen* in Tokyo and families still gather for an evening soak at communal public bathhouses. If you follow the *onsen* bathing etiquette correctly and have a good long soak, expect to be congratulated for attaining the state of *yude-dako*, the "boiled octopus".

Left: Panoramic view of Tokyo from the Roppongi Hills; tuna for sale at Tsukiji fish market

Right: Shrine maiden walking past sake barrels in the Tosho-gu Shrine; bullet train; Ginza Kabuki Theatre

Inset: Dressed-up teenagers in Harajuku

Swarms of worker-bee salarymen cross the Shibuya intersection…gabbling into high-tech mobile phones while animated advertising hoardings bombard them with flashing strobe-effect slogans.

Main: Busy Shibuya intersection in the centre of Tokyo
Above: Mori Art Museum

HIGH-TECH HEAVEN

NOWHERE IN THE WORLD COMBINES THE ANCIENT AND MODERN quite like Tokyo. On one hand, it's a futuristic neon cityscape, fast-paced and crowded with a high-octane lifestyle and a real, genuine buzz about it. Think swarms of worker-bee salarymen crossing the Shibuya intersection, all of them gabbling into high-tech mobile phones while animated advertising hoardings bombard them with flashing strobe-effect slogans. On the other hand, venture away from the neon glare and find quiet cobbled sidestreets that lead to secluded Shinto shrines, where Tokyoites can grab a rare moment of quiet contemplation. Reciting ancient incantations, they ring the temple bell out against the city noise before continuing about their busy daily lives.

A testament to Tokyo's insatiable appetite for self-reinvention and growth is the huge Roppongi Hills complex, a new "lifestyle" development in the heart of Tokyo. A sprawling behemoth of shops, galleries and restaurants, it is

Above: Countryside outside Tokyo with Mount Fuji in the distance

JAN

FEB

MAR

APR

MAY

JUN

JUL

AUG

SEP

OCT

METROPOLITAN DIARY

November is a great time to visit Tokyo, with pleasant days and blue skies. Allow a week to have enough time for day excursions to the shrines and temples of Nikko and to Hakone for spectacular views of majestic Mount Fuji. Extend your trip by visiting Kyoto (see pp102–3) to experience the slower pace.

A Week in the Electric City

NOV

Make an early start with a dawn excursion to the bustling Tsukiji fish market, followed by a traditional slap-up breakfast of raw fish at a nearby café. Then spend the afternoon taking a stroll in Yoyogi-koen Park to see some alfresco performances by local musicians.

DAY 1

Explore Tokyo's ancient side with a morning visit to the Meiji-jingu shrine – keep an eye out for the impromptu fashion shows by local teenagers from the Harajuku area. Later, explore Tokyo's historic geisha district, centred on the streets behind Asakusa temple.

DAY 2

Spend the morning exploring Akihabara's "electric town" – a heaven for gadget fans. Then head over to Roppongi Hills to admire the panorama from the Tokyo City View and an exhibition at the Mori Art Museum.

DAY 3

Take a half-day excursion to Studio Ghibli, Japan's leading manga animation studio, and its accompanying museum. Then, visit the Ginza Kabuki Theatre, spiritual home of Japan's traditional theatre.

DAY 4

Have a full-day excursion to Nikko, the shrine-filled mountain home of the unmissable Tosho-gu shrine.

DAY 5

Hakone to the west of Tokyo is tourist heaven, but it's worth braving the crowds for a glimpse of cloud-fringed Mount Fuji and the open-air art museum.

DAY 6

After visiting the Imperial Palace East Garden, head to Shinjuku for kitsch souvenirs and Ginza for classy ones. Finish at a temple flea market for cut-price kimonos.

DAY 7

Dos and Don'ts

DEC

☑ Be prepared to carry around a bundle of notes as credit cards are only accepted at major hotels and department stores.

☒ When out drinking, don't fill your own glass; Japanese drinking etiquette demands that you pour for the other person, and vice versa. When everyone's glass is full, Japanese for "cheers" is "*kampai*".

☑ Most people will bow when they are first introduced, but a short nod back will suffice to acknowledge their greeting.

☑ Slurping your noodles is actively encouraged to show enjoyment, as is bringing the bowl up to your mouth to drink the broth.

an urban planner's fantasy with offbeat, modern art sculptures splattered across a canvas of rampant consumerism. The Tokyo City View observation deck on the 52nd floor offers different perspectives of the Tokyo cityscape, while the Mori Art Museum captures the city's passion for contemporary pop culture.

But while shopping, dining and the bright lights of the entertainment district remain the superficial attractions of big-city Tokyo life, the city's most rewarding experiences are actually far simpler pleasures: admiring the chrysanthemums on a walk in the Imperial Palace East Garden, eating a hearty bowl of noodles at a street-side stall and watching children play with autumn leaves at a backstreet shrine. Such sights are a humble reminder that while Tokyo appears to be the ultimate 21st-century city, bustling and jostling into the future, scratch beneath the brash veneer of the concrete jungle and the traditional values of Japanese society – nature, family and philosophy – are actually still very much alive and kicking.

GETTING THERE
Rajasthan stretches across the west of India and borders Pakistan. Delhi is India's main entry point for visitors and its international airport is situated 5 km (3 miles) from the city centre.

GETTING AROUND
The Palace on Wheels travels from Delhi to Agra between October and March. In the towns and cities, local transport includes taxis, cycle rickshaws and auto-rickshaws.

WEATHER
In November, maximum temperatures are around 33°C, although they can be much higher in the desert.

ACCOMMODATION
There are 52 rooms on the train. Each carriage (saloon) is composed of four rooms and has a mini pantry and lounge so that guests can relax and enjoy hot and cold beverages. The rooms have been decorated in a traditional style and have hot and cold showers; www.thepalaceonwheels.com

EATING OUT
Indian, Rajasthani and Continental cuisine is available on board the train. Meals are served in the two restaurant cars – The Maharaja and The Maharani – and in the saloons. Lunch (included in the price) is often taken in converted palaces.

PRICE FOR TWO
The 7-night journey on the Palace on Wheels costs from £2,788 for a double room. This is a full package, which includes all travel, meals, entrance charges and entertainment.

FURTHER INFORMATION
www.rajasthantourism.gov.in

Jantar Mantar
Of the five observatories built by Sawai Jai Singh II, Jantar Mantar in Jaipur is the largest and best preserved. A keen astronomer himself, Jai Singh kept abreast of the latest astronomical studies and was inspired by the work of Mirza Ulugh Beg, the astonomer king of Samarkand. Built between 1728 and 1734, Jantar Mantar's 16 instruments resemble a giant sculptural composition. Some of the instruments are still used to forecast how hot the summer months will be.

Main: Man watches the world go by from a window in the Mehrangarh Fort in Jodhpur
Above (left to right): Mehrangarh Fort in Jodhpur; luxurious interior of the Palace on Wheels train; Bengal tiger in Ranthambhore National Park

Above: Jag Mandir Palace on Lake Pichola in Udaipur

THE ENCHANTING WEST

STILL A MAJESTIC LAND OF FAIRY-TALE PALACES AND VIBRANT LOCAL LIFE, Rajasthan fulfils all expectations of India, and there is no more appropriate way of travelling through the state than by train, on the luxurious Palace on Wheels between Delhi and Agra. Journeying leisurely across Rajasthan allows you to revel in the glorious scenery as you pass through lush fields, tropical forests, rocky landscapes and the endless sands of the Thar Desert, enabling you to gain a real sense of this diverse state and its distinct civilization.

This land continues to be home to rajas and maharajas, who today share their legacy, historical past, traditions and homes with visitors who wish to experience the past and present of Rajasthan. In this desert kingdom, fortresses wrap themselves around hills while below, in the plains, pleasure gardens surround serene lakeside palaces and royal settlements command imposing views over vast open spaces. Ornate palace doors have been flung open to welcome the outside world; the erstwhile rulers now invite the curious traveller into their homes, drawing them into another world that evokes an enchanting past.

These palaces are home to treasures that tell stories of those who have peopled these historic abodes through the generations. Luxury still pervades throughout – old retainers lead weary travellers through fan-cooled marble hallways; fine cuisine dominates the dinner table, often in the company of the raja and his *rani* (wife); and heirlooms and traditional decorations add to the intimacy of such a visit.

The pace of the train journey provides ample time to explore the state's memorable palaces – from the magical Lake Palace in Udaipur to the delicate beauty of Hawa Mahal in Jaipur. Pass through the gates of these palaces and you will find yourself stepping into folk traditions that tell the vivid history and legends of the region.

This land continues to be home to maharajas, who today share their legacy… with those who wish to experience the past and present of Rajasthan.

Inset: Interior of the Jag Mandir Palace, Udaipur
Below (left to right): Hawa Mahal in Jaipur; ornate balcony in Jaisalmer; crowds at Sadar Bazaar in Jodhpur

DESERT STATE DIARY

November is the ideal month for touring Rajasthan as the summer heat has passed and the weather is generally pleasant. You will be treated like royalty on the Palace on Wheels, which is ranked as one of the top ten luxury train journeys in the world. Consider extending your trip with a longer stay in Agra (see pp52–3).

Eight Leisurely Days by Train

DAY 1
The train departs from Safdarjung Railway Station in Delhi and guests are welcomed with music and garlands.

DAY 2
The "Pink City" of Jaipur is the first stop – explore its many forts and palaces including Hawa Mahal (Palace of the Winds) and the Amber Fort, then shop for jewellery and handicrafts. After lunch at the Rambagh Palace, visit the City Palace and the Jantar Mantar Observatory.

DAY 3
Spend a day exploring 12th-century Jaisalmer and its impressive sandstone fort. In the evening, join a camel safari into the Thar Desert for dinner under the stars.

DAY 4
The next stop is Jodhpur – visit the majestic Mehrangarh Fort, then descend to Umaid Bhavan Palace, said to be the world's largest Art Deco residence. Browse Sadar Bazaar for spices, jewellery and fabrics.

DAY 5
The train arrives in Sawai Madhopur, home of Ranthambhore National Park. Take an early morning trip into the park to spot tigers. As you lunch, the train travels on, allowing you to appreciate the countryside.

DAY 6
Today, visit the lake-side city of Udaipur. Lunch at the romantic Lake Palace Hotel, situated on Lake Pichola. Admire the stunning vistas of the City Palace along the lake, or take a boat ride to Jag Mandir Palace.

DAY 7
Arrive at Bharatpur to see the bird sanctuary at Keoladeo Ghana National Park. After lunch, marvel at the Taj Mahal before shopping in Agra.

DAY 8
Travel overnight to Delhi, where your journey ends.

Dos and Don'ts

✓ Carry your swimsuit if you want to take a dip at one of the luxury hotels during a stop.

✗ Don't forget to lock your valuables in your saloon before disembarking at every stop.

✓ Jaipur is famous for its beautiful traditional jewellery – make sure you have time to browse the shops and markets after sightseeing.

✗ Don't accept free gifts or food from strangers or other passengers you don't know well.

JAN
FEB
MAR
APR
MAY
JUN
JUL
AUG
SEP
OCT
NOV
DEC

GETTING THERE
Air Rarotonga has daily flights to Aitutaki from the international airport on Rarotonga. The main carrier to the Cook Islands is Air New Zealand. You can also get to Aitutaki by freight ship.

GETTING AROUND
The island is small so getting around on foot is possible but there are also cars, scooters, motorbikes and mountain bikes for hire.

WEATHER
Aitutaki enjoys warm weather throughout the year, with temperatures ranging from 20 to 27°C. The wet season is from January to May.

ACCOMMODATION
Josie's Beach Lodge has a fantastic beach and basic doubles from £11; tel. 682 31 111

Maina Sunset Motel is a small property with studio units from £60; www.soltel.co.ck

The luxurious Aitutaki Lagoon Resort & Spa is situated on a private island; doubles from £150; www.aitutakilagoonresort.com

EATING OUT
Dining on freshly-caught fish is a highlight of any stay on the island. The resort restaurants such as the Flying Boat Beach Bar & Grill at the Aitutaki Lagoon Resort and the superb Island Night buffet at the Pacific Resort provide reliably good food. Samade on the Beach (O'otu Beach) has the freshest fish and chips from £5.

PRICE FOR TWO
£100–170 including accommodation, food, a daily tour and evening entertainment.

FURTHER INFORMATION
www.aitutaki.com

The Art of *Tivaevae*

Tivaevae is a type of needlework that is peculiar to the Cook Islands. Often given as gifts, they are highly valued and often become family heirlooms. The technique originated from the European missionaries who came to the islands in the early 19th century, although the patterns now used have evolved to reflect local elements such as colourful flowers and animals. As it is a communal activity, *tivaevae* plays a large role in the social lives of the Cook Island women who participate.

Above (left to right): Threadfin butterfly fish; frangipani flower in full bloom; steering through the turquoise waters of the lagoon

TECHNICOLOUR PARADISE

I T'S SAID THAT THE COOK ISLANDS, AND PARTICULARLY AITUTAKI, are what Tahiti was 50 years ago; a place of such beauty and simplicity that it cannot fail to fill visitors with complete awe. A place where the islanders go about daily lives much as their parents, grandparents and great-great grandparents did, without lusting for the playthings of the outside world. A place where people are passionate about the things that matter: the joy of dancing and singing; how good the fishing is in the lagoon; how well they can belt out the intricately harmonized hymns of praise in their white sandstone churches on a Sunday.

Aitutaki sits at the apex of a vast lagoon dotted by tiny islands called *motus* that encircle the waters like a necklace of pearls. "Blue" is the colour usually applied to South Sea water but Aitutaki only begins at "blue" – the lagoon forms a quilt of unmodulated patches in every shade imaginable of blue and green: emerald, aquamarine, cobalt, Prussian blue, royal blue and periwinkle. Below the water, the colour palette turns psychedelic with vivid corals that are only eclipsed by resident fish that seem to have dipped themselves in a technicolour paintbox: reds, oranges, royal blues, canary yellows, turquoise – sometimes all on the same fish. On land, this riot continues: the bold, seductive reds of the immortelle trees; the sensual shades and perfumes in the *leis* (flower garlands) the locals throw around a visitor's neck upon arrival; and especially in the woven floral crowns that people still wear in their hair. A glimpse of this gentle simplicity and the hues of the island helps explain why the Impressionist artist Paul Gauguin saw the South Sea landscapes in such bold primary colours. If poor old Claude Monet could have joined his contemporary Gauguin in the South Pacific he might actually have found what he was searching for – a place, he said, "where the landscape is even crazier than my art".

The colour palette turns psychedelic with vivid corals that are only eclipsed by resident fish that seem to have dipped themselves in a technicolour paintbox.

Main: Snorkelling with fish in the Aitutaki Lagoon
Inset: Aerial view of Aitutaki Lagoon with its coral reef clearly visible
Below (left and right): Calm waters with a fishing boat silhouetted against the fiery sunset; local plays the ukulele in Aitutaki

Above: Dancing performance on O'otu Beach

LAGOON DIARY

November in Aitutaki maintains the warm weather enjoyed throughout the year in the Cook Islands. This is the end of "winter", before the wet season, and cyclones don't usually threaten until December, if at all. Consider combining your trip with a visit to New Zealand (*see pp56–7 and pp198–9*).

A Week in the South Pacific

A lagoon cruise is a great way to see the island and its surrounds – there are a number of companies on the island that organize trips. Snorkel in the lagoon, visit tranquil One-Foot Island for great views and picnic on the beach with freshly-caught grilled fish.

Water sports are everything here so take your pick: a day of scuba diving, kayaking, deep-sea fishing or snorkelling around the sand bars and coral ridges of the lagoon. End the day with a beer at the friendly and relaxed Aitutaki Game Fishing Club.

A circle-island tour is a great way to explore Aitutaki – choose one that has stops in villages along the way for a true taste of island life. Dine at the Pacific Resort and take in one of the best displays of Cook Island dancing available – the dancers of Aitutaki are considered the best of all the South Pacific islands.

Pack lots of water and a camera and climb to the top of Maungapu, the highest point on the island, for an incredible view. Talk an islander into taking you on a land crab hunt with torches at night-time – a real Polynesian experience that's fun and tasty too.

Relax on O'otu Beach where the snorkelling is great and lunch can be served on the sand. If it's a Sunday, there's a traditional *umukai* (Polynesian food cooked in an underground oven). A Sunday alternative is to take in a local church service to hear islanders exquisitely singing a capella. Extend your trip by exploring some of the other Cook Islands, or head further south to New Zealand.

Dos and Don'ts

✓ Pack your smile – Aitutakians react poorly to rudeness. Even if you're in a grumpy mood, remember that respect and friendliness are important values to Cook Islanders.

✗ Don't walk around in short shorts and bikinis when you're off the beach – Aitutakians are modest people.

✓ Be especially polite to elderly people and children as they are blindly adored on the islands.

✗ Don't bring your dog on holiday with you – they are not allowed on the island.

JAN
FEB
MAR
APR
MAY
JUN
JUL
AUG
SEP
OCT
NOV
DAY 1
DAY 2
DAY 3
DAY 4
DAYS 5–7
DEC

THE GOLD COAST

CAPE COAST CASTLE IS AN IMPOSING HULK. Founded in 1653, this one-time British administrative centre still towers above the rocky shoreline of Ghana's coast, its whitewashed façade and monolithic implacability lending an air of distinction to the port of Cape Coast.

Originally founded to service the prosperous trade that gave the Gold Coast its name, Cape Coast Castle had by the early 18th century become the hub of an altogether more predatory mercantile industry: the transatlantic slave trade from West Africa to the Americas.

There is little physical evidence of the horrors perpetrated within these grim stone walls, just a few desperate scratch marks. However, there's still an intangible something in the dank air, a chilling legacy of the millions who passed through the castle dungeons. After a few minutes' contemplation,

GETTING THERE
Ghana is situated along the Gulf of Guinea in West Africa. International flights land at the coastal capital city of Accra.

GETTING AROUND
The main tourist focus are the twin ports of Cape Coast and Elmina, which lie three hours from Accra along a road traversable by coach, minibus-taxi or rented car.

WEATHER
Hot and humid with an average maximum temperature of 34°C. November falls after the rainy season and before the dusty Harmattan winds blow in from the Sahara.

ACCOMMODATION
In Accra, Labadi Beach Hotel has spacious rooms and is close to the beach; doubles from £120; www.labadibeach.com

In Elmina, Coconut Grove Beach Resort has a peaceful position; doubles from £55; www.coconutgrovehotels.com.gh

In Kumasi, Four Villages Inn is a popular family-run guesthouse; doubles from £40; www.fourvillages.com

EATING OUT
Try a local "chop shop", where doughball-like staples such as *kenkey* (fermented maize) and *fufu* (mashed yams) are normally eaten with a light soup or groundnut sauce.

PRICE FOR TWO
£90–120 per day including accommodation, food and car hire.

FURTHER INFORMATION
www.ghanaweb.com

Land of Firsts

Historically, Ghana is a land of firsts. In 1482, Elmina became the first place in sub-Saharan Africa to host a permanent European settlement. Three centuries later, the formal creation of a British colony on the Gold Coast (as Ghana was known) pre-dated the widespread Scramble for Africa by several decades. In 1957, Ghana was again thrust into a pioneering role as the first African colony to gain independence, while the four coups between 1966 and 1981 foreshadowed the political turmoil that still scars several neighbouring countries.

Main: Cannons point out to sea at Cape Coast Castle

Left: Elmina Castle, also known as the Castle of St George

Right (left to right): Fishing *pirogue*; Ghanaian man at Kumasi market; canopy walkway in Kakum National Park; crowded Makola Market in central Accra

the urge to escape becomes overpowering. Succumb, and you'll most likely find yourself following an invisible but ancient path across the castle courtyard towards a quaint doorway that frames the swelling blue Atlantic. Innocuous-looking, even picturesque, this stone frame is the so-called "Door of No Return", the gate through which the captives would be bundled onto a slave ship to undertake a passage in conditions so awful that half the human cargo might be lost in transit.

Ghana, thanks to its rich reserves of gold, was actually a latecomer to the maritime slave trade. What distinguishes it today is not that innocent villagers were once captured and sold here, but that the structures where they were held still survive. Today, Cape Coast Castle and its counterpart at Elmina stand as harrowing shrines to the largest forced diaspora in human history. Yet they also form the springboard for wider travels in a dynamic, modern country whose cultural and natural attractions make it an ideal destination for first-time visitors to Africa.

Above: Casting a net from the rocks on Labadi Beach near Accra

ATLANTIC COAST DIARY

The somewhat breathless nine-day itinerary could easily be stretched over two weeks with a few additional diversions to make the most of the November climate. Visitors with more time at their disposal could dedicate a third week to Lake Volta and the green, waterfall-studded hills to its east.

Nine Days in Ghana's Past

DAY 1 Explore downtown Accra, with its wealth of colonial architecture and busy markets, or just kick back at Labadi Beach east of the city centre.

DAY 2 Drive past Cape Coast to Elmina and spend the afternoon absorbing the atmosphere of this small but antiquated fishing town, where the brightly painted *pirogues* (boats) that crowd the lively fishing harbour are placed in sober perspective by the insidious slave dungeons of the 500-year-old Elmina Castle.

DAYS 3–4 Start out early to get to beautiful Kakum National Park. Spend the day exploring the park (with its legendary wobbly canopy walkway).
Drive back to the port of Cape Coast and explore the winding alleys and brooding slave castle.

DAY 5 Drive inland to Kumasi, capital of the Ashanti Kingdom, dedicating the afternoon to the wealth of museums and other cultural sites that stud this bustling city.

DAYS 6–7 Drive through to Mole National Park and spend the morning game-walking. Expect excellent close encounters with elephants, baboons, antelope and dozens of brightly coloured birds. In the afternoon, take a look at the curvaceous Larabanga Mosque, built entirely from mud and sticks in the 15th century.

DAYS 8–9 Return southward towards Accra diverting en route to Boabeng-Fiema, an unfenced community-run sanctuary overrun by the mischievous mona and colobus monkeys held sacred by local villagers.

Dos and Don'ts

✓ Try to find out about any funerals that are taking place locally – these are surprisingly upbeat, colourful and welcoming affairs, often held months after a person's death.

✗ Don't swim without asking local advice – dangerous riptides and undertows are a common phenomenon in some areas.

✓ Kick back and enjoy a chilled beer and one of the delicious fiery meat kebabs served at local bars (rather delightfully called "spots") all around the country.

✗ Don't dress too skimpily or you risk offending most Islamic and many Christian Ghanaians.

✓ Watch your step on beaches close to villages as they may have been used as a communal toilet.

JAN FEB MAR APR MAY JUN JUL AUG SEP OCT NOV DEC

COLLAR OF ISLANDS

FLYING OVER THE CARIBBEAN FROM MAINLAND VENEZUELA, you will see a collar of islands, their lush, green interiors ringed by the whitish-yellow of their beaches and an outer circle of light turquoise where the sand is visible through the shallow waters of the sea. Margarita Island is the largest of the Minor Antilles, although at its longest it stretches a mere 62 km (39 miles), and is a bustling, diverse and beautiful place to spend an unforgettable holiday.

Mountainous and subtropical, the island is divided into two regions. Its eastern section is developed and populous; Porlamar is a thriving commercial city, and its status as a duty-free port draws in Venezuelan tourists who enjoy its nightlife, casinos, restaurants and cheap shopping.

GETTING THERE
Margarita Island is 23 km (14 miles) north of the Venezuelan coast. Flights from Caracas, Venezuela's international airport, take 45 minutes.

GETTING AROUND
Roads are good on the island and car hire is an excellent way to explore. Boat trips are available from most beaches and harbours to visit some of the offshore sights and islands.

WEATHER
Margarita Island enjoys average temperature of around 27°C, with a gentle sea breeze.

ACCOMMODATION
Luxurious Hesperia Playa El Agua is a modern complex on the beach; doubles from £125; www.hesperiaislamargarita.com

The colonial-style Hotel Costa Linda Beach is next to El Agua beach; doubles from £25; www.hotelcostalinda.com

The Hilton Margarita has a large swimming pool; doubles from £130; www1.hilton.com

EATING OUT
Tuna, snapper and lobster are typical local fare, as are tropical fruits. Look out for the national dish, *Pabellón Crollo* – shredded beef with black beans and fried plantains.

PRICE FOR TWO
£95–200 per day, depending on accommodation choice, including food, car hire and petrol, trips and activities.

FURTHER INFORMATION
www.islamargarita.com

…you can explore the labyrinthine channels that meander through the tangled roots of the mangroves, a dense green canopy blocking out the sun from overhead.

The west of the island in contrast, is quiet and unspoiled. The Macanao is an expansive, arid peninsula, shrubs and cacti pepper the landscape and wild hare dart across the path of your jeep. A string of verdant mountains makes up the interior encircled by wide, deserted beaches and dunes, with crashing surf and picture-book palms. Often the only people you will see here are local fishermen, rigging their hooks and setting off in search of tuna and red snapper which you can sample, freshly grilled in one of the small restaurants in town.

The narrow isthmus that connects these two regions is a sand spit that forms part of the Restinga National Park, an area of mangrove swamps filled with bountiful wildlife. Aboard a small wooden *peñero* – a traditional local fishing boat – you can explore the labyrinthine channels that meander through the tangled roots of the mangroves, a dense green canopy blocking out the sun from overhead. The crystal clear waters are a window onto some spectacular marine life, including green and leatherback turtles and the enormous oysters that cling to the underwater mangrove roots. For visitors wishing to prolong their experience of totally unspoiled Venezuelan sea-life, trips can be made out to the coral reefs of Los Roques, an amazing National Park of sandy beaches and waters that teem with colourful fish swimming between some of the best preserved reefs in the world.

Main: Aerial view of the coral reefs at Los Roques, Venezuela
Inset: Parrotfish, a common sight in the waters around Margarita Island
Below (left to right): Nueva Esparta; Playa el Agua; baby green turtles

Historical Margarita
The island has been the setting for many notable events in South American history. Christopher Columbus himself happened upon the island paradise in 1498, and the then inhabitants inevitably became slaves to the conquering Spaniards. In 1814 it became the first territory in Venezuela to rid itself of Spanish rule, and it was here that Simón Bolívar, famous liberator of the continent, was confirmed Commander-in-Chief of the new republic. Traces of Spanish influence can be seen throughout the island in the typical Spanish-style architecture in the towns.

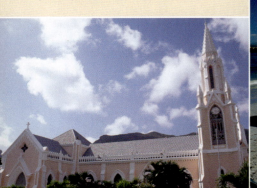

Above: A flock of scarlet ibis in a tree

ISLAND DIARY

November should bring clear skies, warm temperatures and a refreshing offshore breeze. The island is a manageable size for a week's stay with enough time to kick back and relax, view the wildlife and to enjoy the nightlife as well. Visitors can extend their trip by visiting the Angel Falls on the mainland.

A Week of Natural Wonder

Flights from Caracas arrive just outside Porlamar, so you can begin your trip visiting the duty-free port.

Spend the afternoon relaxing in the warm waters at El Agua beach and have a cocktail at a beachfront bar.

Take a day to explore Macanao, the unspoiled beaches of the eastern region then drive to Manzanillo, on the peninsula's northeastern tip, and watch the local fishermen unload their catch.

Try your hand at some water sports: the beach at El Yaque has some excellent windsurfing, while the tides and swell at Parguito make it good for surfing.

Take one of the daily boat trips from Margarita Island to the islands of Coche and Cubague. The former is a quiet fishing village, with white sand beaches, and Cobague has some excellent diving.

Visit the archipelago, Los Roques, a group of 42 coral reefs and beautiful sandy beaches. Wonder at the amazing variety of wildlife and try your hand at bonefishing with the locals.

Board a *peñero* to explore the mangroves of the Restinga National Park. Colourful sealife and bird life and beautiful natural scenery make this one of the undoubted highlights of a trip to Margarita Island.

Take the short flight back to Caracas to connect with your onward flight.

Dos and Don'ts

☑ Be careful of strong currents and tides. Some beaches are dangerous, even for strong swimmers; make sure you know the situation before you take the plunge.

☒ Don't underestimate the sun – a light sea breeze takes the edge off the heat, but the tropical sun is still very powerful.

☑ Get off the beaten track – the island still has many quiet corners and deserted beaches. Hire a car to explore, and you will be rewarded.

☒ Don't miss out on the tax-free bargains in Porlamar.

JAN
FEB
MAR
APR
MAY
JUN
JUL
AUG
SEP
OCT
NOV
DAY 1
DAY 2
DAY 3
DAY 4
DAY 5
DAY 6
DAY 7
DEC

DECEMBER

Where to Go: December

For much of the world, December brings a grand finale to the year, with celebrations announcing the end of one year and the beginning of the next. From fireworks over Sydney Bridge to wild revelry on Copacabana beach in Rio, the parties go with a bang. In chilly Europe, Christmas is celebrated in style in Vienna, where magical markets entice shoppers to join in the festive spirit, and in snowy Lapland, children can deliver their letters directly to Santa. But it is the other extreme as you head further south, where romancing couples can share a beach hammock in the Caribbean and adventurers can dive with manta rays in Yap. To help you choose, you'll find all the destinations in this chapter below, as well as some extra suggestions to provide a little inspiration.

FESTIVALS AND CULTURE

RIO DE JANEIRO Samba musicians on the streets of Rio

UNFORGETTABLE JOURNEYS

LAOS Steering a boat down the calm Mekong River

NATURAL WONDERS

YAP Traditional island dancers in costume

RIO DE JANEIRO
BRAZIL, SOUTH AMERICA

The beach is central to life in Brazil, especially at New Year

Millions, dressed in white, come to party on the beach, see amazing fireworks and float an offering on the sea for the year to come.
See pp322–3

MEKONG RIVER
LAOS, ASIA

Sail down the Mekong to see the best of Southeast Asia

Discover a fascinating world of carved wooden temples, colonial architecture, jungle-clad mountains and lively markets.
See pp302–3

> "In town you'll be greeted with constant smiles, the mouths stained a disconcerting red by the prolonged chewing of betel nut."

YAP
MICRONESIA

Tiny speck of an island where you can swim with manta rays

One of the best places to see these huge and magnificent rays; there are also reefs, and lagoons with tiger sharks and turtles.
See pp316–17

VIENNA
AUSTRIA, EUROPE

Christmas in a refined capital at the heart of Europe

Christmas markets bustle with shoppers enjoying mulled wine and gingerbread, before the New Year ball season takes off.
See pp318–19

> "A winter wonderland with lights twinkling in the frosty nights and open-air Christmas markets everywhere."

MALEALEA
LESOTHO, AFRICA

A chance to discover the "kingdom in the sky"

This great escape takes you by 4WD, horseback and on foot into the mountains of southern Africa, to meet the friendly Basotho.
www.malealea.co.ls

THE AMAZON
BRAZIL, SOUTH AMERICA

One of the truly great river journeys

Board your ship in the sultry city of Belem for a mind-broadening cruise up the great river to Manaus, or on to Iquitos in Peru.
www.amazoncruise.net

CHRISTMAS ISLAND
AUSTRALIA, AUSTRALASIA

A very seasonal destination – though it may not look it

Many species of birds are unique to this remote island of coral, giant crabs and forest – a birder's and nature-watcher's delight.
www.christmasisland.net.au

SAN BLAS ISLANDS
PANAMA, CENTRAL AMERICA

Explore the customs and landscape of Native America

Remote islands that are home to the Kuna indians, who guide visitors to the abundant wildlife with intimate knowledge.
www.explorepanama.com

LAS VEGAS
USA, NORTH AMERICA

A glitzy desert mirage where almost anything goes

Cruise the neon-lit strip lined with man-made wonders of the world, play the slots, and then clear your head in the desert.
See pp320–21

FROZEN ALASKA
USA, NORTH AMERICA

Get to the heart of the Arctic winter

Drive a 4WD through frozen woods from Anchorage to Fairbanks and back – with luck, you'll see the Aurora Borealis.
www.alaskatours.com

FALKLAND ISLANDS
SOUTH AMERICA

Many thousand more penguins than people

Albatross, giant petrels, elephant seals and five kinds of penguin all breed on the islands at this time – in giant, noisy colonies.
www.visitorfalklands.com

SYDNEY
AUSTRALIA, AUSTRALASIA

A top party city – see the best fireworks, surf off the headache

Sydney Harbour is gorgeous any time of year and the New Year fireworks are reputed to be the best in the world. Great beaches too.
See pp310–11

LILLE
FRANCE, EUROPE

Get set for the festivities with a real Christmas atmosphere

Lille hosts the biggest of northern France's Christmas fairs, with a funfair, lights, entertainment and scrumptious festive foods.
www.lilletourism.com

GLACIER EXPRESS
SWITZERLAND, EUROPE

See the Alps at their most magnificent – but in comfort

This famous train snakes through the Alps from Zermatt to St Moritz, beneath the Matterhorn – luxury with a hint of adventure.
www.glacierexpress.ch

KOMODO NATIONAL PARK
INDONESIA, ASIA

The home of the world's only real dragons

These three small islands are the only home of the world's largest lizard, the Komodo Dragon.
www.komodonationalpark.org

Weather Watch

❶ December is surprisingly cold in Santa Fe, with temperatures falling quite low at night (especially in the mountains). However, there is little rain, so days are clear, bright and sunny.

❷ Expect hot, humid days with afternoon rain showers in much of South America. As you head further south, it becomes cooler and wetter.

❸ Days are short and cold in northern Europe, getting colder the further north you go. In Finland, snow is guaranteed for Santa and his elves.

❹ The Red Sea temperature in December is relatively cool for Egypt – but still nice and warm. It is sunny every day and very warm in the interior.

❺ The end of the northeast monsoon leaves Kerala with cooler and more pleasant temperatures, and lower humidity – this is also seen across southeast Asia, with the end of the rainy season.

❻ Sydney's weather is agreeable in any season but is particularly good in December, with the water warm enough for swimming. Rain is possible throughout the year but is unlikely to be heavy in December.

LUXURY AND ROMANCE

TORTOLA Luxuriating in a beach hammock in the British Virgin Islands

TORTOLA
BVI, CARIBBEAN

Leave your cares behind on this Caribbean island paradise

Simply enjoy the talcum-soft sand between your toes, crystal clear water for swimming, freshly caught seafood and potent cocktails.
See pp300–1

COUNTRY HOUSES
ENGLAND, EUROPE

Combine the Christmas season with some gracious living

Celebrate Christmas or New Year in style by renting a country manor (and staff) for your own house party. There are houses throughout the UK.
www.uniquehomestays.com

TELLURIDE
USA, NORTH AMERICA

Winter sports with a very fashionable buzz

Every winter sport can be tried in the Rockies' most fashionable resort, or you can just enjoy the stunning view from a luxurious suite.
www.telluride.com

KERALA
INDIA, ASIA

Experience life on the water in this beautiful, lush destination

Travel on a houseboat down a network of canals, soothe your soul the Ayurvedic way, or just chill out on a beach.
See pp308–9

KOH SAMUI
THAILAND, ASIA

Look no further for winter sun and a tropical idyll

A wonderful escape, this is a place to find long white beaches, and palm-roofed cabins where you can sleep to the sound of the waves.
www.kohsamui.org

"Wooden boats meander through the waterways from which you can watch the sublime surroundings at a leisurely pace."

ACTIVE ADVENTURES

DOMINICA Aerial tram crossing the Morne Trois Pitons National Park

DOMINICA
CARIBBEAN

This pristine ocean rainforest is a great active destination

Try hiking, scuba diving and horse-riding and you'll be able to fully explore this wonderful natural wilderness.
See pp312–13

RED SEA
EGYPT, AFRICA

One of the world's most intriguing dive sites

Offshore there's great reef and wreck diving, while on land you can take a desert camel safari and visit Mount Sinai.
See pp306–7

GEILO
NORWAY, EUROPE

Skiing as it was first meant to be – cross-country

For Norwegians, skis are a means of getting around, and there are many cross-country skiing centres – and a network of skiing routes.
www.geilo.no

TORRES DEL PAINE
CHILE, SOUTH AMERICA

Granite pillars, crags, glaciers – a true wilderness

Rising up out of the emptiness of Patagonia, this mountain range has wonderfully dramatic scenery – treks take several days.
www.torresdelpaine.com

MARLBOROUGH
NEW ZEALAND, AUSTRALASIA

Explore a coastline of countless tree-lined inlets

Take a boat from Wellington to the South Island, then explore the Marlborough Sounds on foot or kayak, camping in secluded bays.
www.marlboroughsounds.co.nz

FAMILY GETAWAYS

LAPLAND Santa on his snowmobile

"Holiday sights, sounds and aromas fill the land: the excited squeal of children catching a glimpse of Santa, herring sizzling over glowing coals. . ."

SANTA FE
USA, NORTH AMERICA

Enjoy the unique Santa Fe Christmas experience

After a hard day's skiing, enjoy carol singing by the light of a thousand magical *farolitos* (lanterns).
See pp304–5

LAPLAND
FINLAND, EUROPE

Visit Santa's homeland for some old-fashioned snow fun

Kids will love Santa's workshop and reindeer, and will be able to skate, ski and hopefully wear themselves out in the snow.
See pp314–15

WAIHEKE ISLAND
NEW ZEALAND, AUSTRALASIA

A subtropical island with miles of varied coastline

Only a short ferry ride from Auckland, this seems a world away, with wineries, beaches and plenty of places to kayak, swim, hike and sail.
www.tourismwaiheke.co.nz

CAYMAN ISLANDS
CARIBBEAN

Some of the most laid-back spots in the Caribbean

Newcomers to tropical seas can see plenty of life in the Caymans' dazzling, placid waters with just a snorkel or just play in the waves.
www.caymanislands.ky

VIEQUES
PUERTO RICO, CARIBBEAN

Wonderfully unspoilt beaches and lots to do

Even though this little island has been getting better known, visitors can still have exquisite places all to themselves.
www.vieques-island.com

GETTING THERE
Tortola is the largest of the 60 islands that comprise the British Virgin Islands, in the Caribbean. Flights into Tortola connect in San Juan and other neighbouring islands.

GETTING AROUND
To get around Tortola there are plenty of taxis, or you can hire a car or Jeep. Water taxis, ferries and small charter planes link Tortola to the other islands.

WEATHER
In December, Tortola enjoys balmy weather. Temperatures average around 29°C and there are gentle, cooling trade winds.

ACCOMMODATION
Heritage Inn is a hilltop hideaway that looks out over Carrot Bay; doubles from £65; www.heritageinnbvi.com

Long Bay Beach Resort & Villas has beachfront cabanas and hillside cottages with great views; doubles from £100; www.longbay.com

The Sugar Mill Hotel & Restaurant is an intimate beachfront hotel; doubles from £170; www.sugarmillhotel.com

EATING OUT
Spicy Caribbean dishes such as curried goat are specialities, alongside grilled seafood. A good meal can be had for around £5 at beach bistros such as Coco Plums Bar & Grill in Apple Bay.

PRICE FOR TWO
£140–180 per day including accommodation, food and local transport.

FURTHER INFORMATION
www.bvitourism.com

The British Virgin Islands

Legend has it that upon seeing the islands for the first time in 1493, Christopher Columbus named them "Santa Ursula y las Once Mil Vírgenes", later shortened to "Las Vírgenes", as they reminded him of Saint Ursula and her 11,000 virginal handmaidens. In 1672, the English arrived and, after much struggle, took control of the 60 islands that make up the present day British Virgin Island group. They were finally named as such in 1917.

Main Image: Fiery sunset at Carrot Bay

SECLUDED PARADISE

WAVES GENTLY WASH OVER THE CORAL REEFS that act as a calming barrier to the Atlantic rollers, enticing you to swim and snorkel in the calm turquoise waters that teem with colourful fish. Tortola is a place of repose, with beaches rivalling in beauty and solitude those of anywhere in the world. The island is scalloped by secluded coves where the warm sand is like talc between your toes. The north shore is fringed with endless stretches of champagne-coloured beaches: Brewers Bay, Cane Garden Bay, Elizabeth Beach and Long Bay are just some of the nicest – making it hard to imagine a more satisfying place to luxuriate.

Carefree and casual, with a barefoot charm typified by the isle's lack of glitzy night spots and mega-resorts, Tortola is nevertheless blessed with many great restaurants and bars that are perfect for lingering lunches and alfresco candlelit dinners. Dine on velvety crab callaloo and johnny cakes (a spicy okra stew with cornbread) as you

Top: Yachting in the calm waters around Tortola

Above: Secluded sandy cove with turquoise waters

Below: Relaxing in a beach hammock enjoying the glorious view

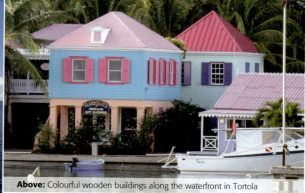

Above: Colourful wooden buildings along the waterfront in Tortola

BEACHCOMBER'S DIARY

Tortola possesses all the key ingredients for a romantic Caribbean getaway, not least great beaches and fabulous waters. Five days will allow you time to relax on the many beautiful beaches, as well as ample opportunities to hike, snorkel and boat, or explore the island's historical and cultural sights.

Five Romantic Island Days

Head straight to the beach, douse yourself in suntan lotion and spend the day soaking up the sun and swimming in the blissfully warm ocean. Watch the sunset over a drink and then enjoy a leisurely dinner at a beachside restaurant.

Take a tour of the island, which will give you the opportunity to explore Mount Healthy National Park with its sugar plantation-era windmill. Get a taster of the excellent local rums at Callwood's Rum Distillery.

Lunch in Road Town before exploring its sights, which include Fort Burt, Old Government House and the Folk Museum.

Get up early for a rewarding hike in beautiful Sage Mountain National Park, then head back to your hotel to enjoy a well-deserved rejuvenating massage on the beach.

Spend the afternoon lazing until sunset, then head to a beachside bar to kick-start your evening with a typically Caribbean cocktail.

Have your hotel prepare a picnic and hire a boat for a day's cruising. Head first to the Caves, a great place to snorkel, with its fascinating rock formations.

Afterwards, find an isolated beach to relax on before a casual drink on the Willie T, a converted schooner.

Spend an activity-filled morning snorkelling, windsurfing and kayaking. After lunch, pick up some souvenirs on Main Street, which is particularly good for silk-screened fabrics and hand-crafted jewellery.

Dos and Don'ts

✓ Be sure to use suntan lotion liberally as the trade winds can be deceptively cooling.

✗ Don't eat turtle, even if it turns up on your menu – marine reptiles are endangered and protected by law.

✓ Make sure that you have enough fuel if you hire a car to go exploring – you don't want to get stranded.

✗ Don't forget to start your conversations with a polite greeting as such niceties are very important to the locals.

JAN
FEB
MAR
APR
MAY
JUN
JUL
AUG
SEP
OCT
NOV
DEC
DAY 1
DAY 2
DAY 3
DAY 4
DAY 5

listen to the sound of lapping waves at your feet. Later, head down to one of the many beach bars scattered around the bays and, with a potent rum cocktail in hand, dance the night away on the shore to the calypso music that throbs across the moonlit bay.

When you feel rejuvenated from your beachside respite, take a trip to Road Town, Tortola's urban hub. Although home to modern banks and shops, the town is still steeped in its colonial past with elegant wooden houses and a rather old-worldy feel. Its centuries-old charm seems to fade slightly when the cruise ships arrive but the boats make a beautiful backdrop to the bustling harbour-town. Stroll down the central shopping strip, narrow Main Street, and pick up some of the beautiful gold, emeralds and shells that Tortola is famed for. Afterwards, take the weight off your feet with a long lunch at one of the many restaurants in the area. This popular cruise ship port is also a placid playground for yachters. Many of the sleek sloops and powerboats bobbing alongside the jetties can be rented to explore the neighbouring islands that seem to float invitingly on the horizon, tempting you to partake in another day of decadent relaxation.

GETTING THERE
International flights arrive into Luang Prabang, via Bangkok. Boats travel down the Mekong River to Luang Prabang from Ban Houei Xai on the Thai border.

GETTING AROUND
Buses link towns throughout the country and boats along the Mekong stop at points between the Thai and Cambodian borders. The towns are easy to get around on foot or bicycle.

WEATHER
December is dry with average daytime temperatures of 30°C.

ACCOMMODATION
The Apsara, Luang Prabang, has large rooms furnished in beautiful Lao textiles; doubles from £35; www.theapsara.com

La Residence Phou Vao, Luang Prabang, offers complete luxury in a wonderful hilltop position; doubles from £125; www.orient-express.com

Thongbay Guesthouse in Vientiane has a lovely, quiet setting and just 10 rooms; doubles from £8; www.thongbay-guesthouses.com

EATING OUT
Laos's national dish is *laap* or *larb*, a spicy mix of marinated meat or fish – try this at night market stalls – a meal will cost you less than £1.

PRICE FOR TWO
£80–100 per day including acommodation, food and local transport, but could be much less depending on the standard of lodging chosen.

FURTHER INFORMATION
www.visit-laos.com

Silk Weaving

Silk weaving is exceptionally beautiful in Laos and is a centuries-old tradition that has recently been revived. Textiles are more than an art form, they are a manifestation of cultural identity, and skills are handed down through families. The intricate designs and motifs are based on the weaver's region and ethnic group – there are 68 ethnic groups in Laos, each with their own patterns.

SAIL DOWN THE MEKONG

LUANG PRABANG WAS DESCRIBED AS A PARADISE by the French explorer Henri Mouhot, who came here in 1861 on an expedition to open up a route to China. More than a century later, this remote town of glittering Buddhist temples and saffron-robed monks still has an otherworldly atmosphere.

Situated high in the mist-shrouded mountains of northern Laos, Luang Prabang sits on a promontory on the broad Mekong river and was once the royal capital. It remains a treasure trove of 33 ornately carved wooden temples, covered with golden stencils and shimmering mosaics, with multi-tiered roofs that cascade almost to the ground. The most elaborate is Wat Xieng Thong, set amid shrines, stupas and crimson bougainvillea, built in 1559 by King Setthathirat. So exquisite are these temples that UNESCO made the whole town, including its elegant French colonial villas and secular buildings, into a World Heritage Site to preserve it.

Main: Intricately decorated Buddhist temple Wat Xieng Thong

Left (left and right): Reclining Buddha in Vientiane; woman selling handicrafts at a local market

Right: Sun setting over the Mekong River

JAN

FEB

MAR

APR

MAY

JUN

JUL

AUG

SEP

OCT

NOV

DEC

DAYS 1–2

DAYS 3–5

DAY 6

DAY 7

Climb the 328 steps to the top of Mount Phousi, in the centre, and behold a panorama unchanged since 1861 – just three traffic-free streets strung out with jewel-like temples, a white palace with a golden spire and wooden houses on stilts nestled amongst tropical greenery.

There is no better way to arrive in Luang Prabang than by boat on the Mekong, a magical journey that starts at the Thai border. Sailing down its brown, swirling waters, past sheer limestone cliffs and jungle-clad mountains, you can marvel at unspoiled landscapes, picturesque villages where hill tribes in traditional costumes descend to sell their produce, and sacred caves like those of Pak Ou, filled with Buddhas brought during pilgrimages.

From Luang Prabang, continue down the river to Vientiane, today's laid-back capital. Here, too, houses and offices are interspersed with temples. The peace is broken by tuk-tuks rattling along to the morning market where you can bargain for dazzling raw silk and silver jewellery. In the evening, head for Nam Phu Square to sip French wine and dine on delicious Lao cuisine. But first, watch the spectacular sunset turn the Mekong from red to gold and reflect on this little-changed land.

Above: Mekong River flowing past Luang Prabang

TEMPLE DIARY

In December, the air is clear and bright, perfect for travelling on the fast-flowing Mekong. Although you can fly into Luang Prabang, a river journey from the Thai border will allow you to really appreciate this beautiful country. Extend your trip by visiting Vietnam (*see pp274–5*), Thailand (*see pp22–3*) or Cambodia (*see pp40–41*).

A Week Along the River

Begin in Ban Houei Xai, on the Thai border. Here you can take a converted rice barge down the Mekong to Luang Prabang, 320 km (200 miles) away. The journey takes two days (although it can be done in 6 hours by longtail boat) and is quite magical, passing great limestone cliffs, forests of bamboo and tiny fishing villages.

Arrive in Luang Prabang – walk through the streets and enjoy its wonderful setting. In the evening, try some of the city's culinary delights.

The next day, visit some of the city's many *wats* (temples). Wat Xieng Thong is undoubtedly the most beautiful and is where royal ceremonies were held. Also worth visiting is Wat Mai, richly decorated with red and gold frescoes, and Wat Visoun, which is filled with ancient Buddhas. Alternatively, take a day trip out to see the sacred Pak Ou Caves.

Hire a bicycle to tour around the different markets and take in the sights. After lunch, head up Mount Phousi, where you can enjoy great views of the city and the surrounding area, and stay to enjoy the sunset.

Continue down the river towards Vientiane. The 400-km (250-mile) journey takes 8 hours by longtail speedboat. Spend your first evening in Vientiane dining in Nam Phu Square on fantastic local cuisine.

Visit the morning market to bargain for hill tribe jewellery. See That Luang, the most revered temple in Vientiane, originally built in 1566 but much rebuilt since. After lunch, visit Lao National History Museum, then watch the sunset over the river.

Dos and Don'ts

✓ Remove your shoes when entering a *wat* (temple) or a Lao home.

✗ Don't shake the hand of a monk or, if you are a woman, touch them in any way.

✓ Drive defensively. Few drivers have a licence and often turn right or left without warning.

✗ Don't point your feet at a Buddha image, it is seen as disrespectful.

GETTING THERE
Santa Fe is in New Mexico, in southwest USA. International flights arrive into Albuquerque, 105 km (65 miles) away. It is a 60-minute drive to Santa Fe from the airport.

GETTING AROUND
Rent a car if you plan to stay outside the town or want to ski. Otherwise, the city itself is best explored on foot.

WEATHER
December is sunny, with an average daytime temperature of 7°C, dropping to -7°C at night.

ACCOMMODATION
El Rey Inn offers friendly accommodation; family rooms from £65; www.elreyinnsantafe.com

La Posada de Santa Fe Resort & Spa offers luxury near the plaza; family rooms from £165; www.laposada.rockresorts.com

Just outside of town, Bishops Lodge Resort & Spa is a historic luxury retreat near Ski Santa Fe; family rooms from £180; www.bishopslodge.com

EATING OUT
Santa Fe is known for a unique spicy southwest cuisine that combines traditional Mexican and Native American foods with non-traditional spices, organic produce, fresh fish and meats. Great places to try this are Café Pasqual (mains from £11) and The Shed, both in central Santa Fe.

PRICE FOR A FAMILY OF FOUR
£250–290 per day including accommodation, food, local transport and entrance charges.

FURTHER INFORMATION
www.santafe.org

Santa Fe Firsts

Founded in 1607 by the Spanish, Santa Fe is the oldest capital city in the United States. It is also home to the oldest road in the nation, El Camino Real, which runs from Santa Fe to Chihuahua in Mexico, and was first travelled in 1581. The oldest public building in the USA is also here – the Palace of the Governors, built in the early 17th century.

Main: *Farolitos* decorate the Hotel Loretto in Santa Fe
Above (left to right): Woodcarving in San Miguel church; Navajo Native Americans sell their crafts; chilli decorations hang from a cow skull

Above: Skiing on the steep slopes of Ski Santa Fe

JAN
FEB
MAR
APR
MAY
JUN
JUL
AUG
SEP
OCT
NOV
DEC

GLITTERING NIGHTS

IT'S A SIMPLE THING REALLY, A CANDLE, IN A PAPER BAG, filled with sand. Light the candle at dusk and the little lantern, known as a *farolito*, glows with a warm, inviting light. Now multiply the *farolitos* by hundreds, and thousands, and tens of thousands. Imagine them lining this ancient town square and all the ledges and windowsills of the surrounding adobe buildings.

Christmas in Santa Fe is more, of course, than *farolitos*. It is the traditions that reach back hundreds of years and celebrate Santa Fe's powerful and captivating blend of Native American, Spanish and Anglo cultures. It is the cold, clear nights where the air seems so transparent that you can see forever, and the starlit night sky dazzles from horizon to horizon like an inverted bowl of celestial fairy lights. Christmas in Santa Fe is bonfires in the plaza and carollers strolling along glittering Canyon Road where the world-class galleries open their doors and welcome chilly celebrants with hot spiced cider and a chance to view some of the best art in North America.

It's the scent of *piñon* smoke hanging in the crisp winter air, magical Christmas train rides for the kids and adrenaline-filled ski runs for everyone. And it's curling up after the day's festivities with a warm drink in front of a crackling fire.

But the celebrations go much deeper. This is, after all, "The City Different". Perhaps it is that people have lived, loved and worshipped their gods here for so many centuries. Santa Fe was founded in 1607, but people were here thousands of years before that. In the *pueblos* (Native American villages) that surround Santa Fe, Christmas is a special time. Here, ceremonies blend Christian practice with traditional dancing and chanting, the origins of which stretch back to the beginning of human existence. Their echoes seem to be the ancient hymn of this startling land that lies on the high plateaus between snow-covered mountains and the endless western desert.

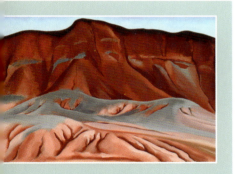

"The moment I saw the brilliant, proud morning shine over the deserts of Santa Fe, something stood still in my soul…"

D. H. Lawrence

Inset: Georgia O'Keefe's painting, *Purple Hills*
Below (left to right): Santa Fe Plaza twinkles in the night; house in Santa Fe traditionally decorated for Christmas

CANDLELIGHT DIARY

Although Christmas festivities, performances and activities occur throughout December, the unique Santa Fe experiences occur from 23 to 26 December. Four days allows time to explore a few of the many fine museums, galleries and shops, and to include a train excursion or a day of skiing.

Four Days in the City Different

Explore the dazzling merchandise and works by some of America's finest artists in the shops and galleries around the plaza and along Canyon Road.

23rd

Take the children on the "Polar Express", an early evening ride on the Santa Fe Southern Railroad. Children enjoy hot chocolate and cookies while the Christmas-themed book is read to them.

Head for the ski slopes at Ski Santa Fe, or hike the Dale Ball Trails. Afterwards, stop at Ten Thousand Waves for a refreshing soak in one of the hot tubs at this legendary Japanese spa.

Attend the beautiful Baroque Christmas performance at lovely Loretto Chapel before taking the traditional *farolitos* walk along Canyon Road. The street lights are turned off, cars are banned and the galleries host open houses with hot cider and treats, as carollers stroll along the streets.

24th

Attend Christmas Eve Midnight Mass at St Francis Cathedral – a Santa Fe tradition.

Many of the local Native American *pueblos* hold sacred dances over 24–29 December which can be watched by the public. Christmas Day is a great time to visit a pueblo and experience these traditions.

25th

Start your day with a leisurely breakfast. Explore the fine museums, which include the Palace of the Governors, Georgia O'Keeffe Museum and Museum Hill, or wander through the charming old town, stopping to look at the woodcarvings in San Miguel Church.

26th

Dos and Don'ts

✗ Don't forget that this is a very busy time of year – make reservations early as the best hotels, activities and performances are booked up quickly.

✓ Request a kiva fireplace in your hotel room when you make a reservation – this is a curved corner fireplace that is traditionally found in Southwestern homes.

✓ Plan to arrive early at deservedly popular lunch spots such as Café Pasqual and The Shed, or expect to wait.

✓ If you are driving into Santa Fe, try the parking lot located behind St Francis Cathedral.

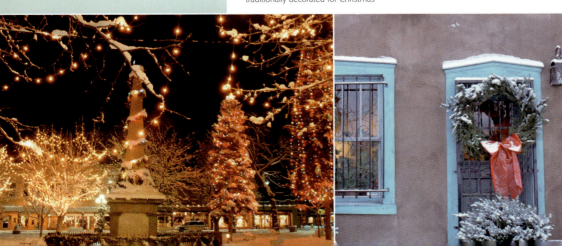

MEDITERRANEAN SEA

ISRAEL

Cairo

Mt Sinai Dahab

EGYPT **SHARM EL-SHEIKH**

LIBYA

RED SEA

SUDAN

Left: Typical airy hotel interior in Sharm el Sheikh

Right (left to right): Sun setting over Naama Bay; school of mullet fish; dolphin and calf swim together in the Red Sea; gazing through the clear waters at a school of sergeant major fish

Inset: Clown fish swims through a pink anemone, unhurt by the anemone's sting

GETTING THERE
The Red Sea fringes the east coast of Egypt and the southern coasts of the Sinai Peninsula. It is accessed by international airports at Hurghada and Sharm el-Sheikh. The airports are connected to the nearby resorts by taxi.

GETTING AROUND
Local taxis are cheap and plentiful. For longer trips, share a car and driver with other travellers.

WEATHER
In December, the Red Sea enjoys pleasantly warm temperatures of around 20°C.

ACCOMMODATION
The Hilton, Dahab has an onsite diving school; doubles from £65; www.hiltonworldresorts.com

Sonesta Beach Resort has been fashioned to look like a Bedouin village; doubles from £90; www.sonesta.com

Four Seasons Resort Sharm el-Sheikh has its own beach; doubles from £230; www.fourseasons.com/sharmelsheikh

EATING OUT
The hotels in Egypt's Red Sea resorts come with a plethora of restaurants, most of which specialize in seafood. Many of these restaurants also offer beachfront terraces, where the cooking is done on an open charcoal grill.

PRICE FOR TWO
£140–160 per day including accommodation, food and a one-day dive.

FURTHER INFORMATION
www.redseaexplorers.com
www.touregypt.com

Mount Sinai

On the summit of Mount Sinai, visitors will find the Monastery of the Transfiguration, better known as St Catherine's Monastery. The original building was built in the 4th century by a Byzantine Empress to mark the location where the burning bush appeared to Moses. Thanks to later fortifications, the monastery has managed to survive intact. Inside, there is a superb collection of icon paintings.

Main: Wreck diving in the Red Sea surrounded by anthias fish

MYSTERIES OF THE DEEP

IT USED TO BE THE COLOSSI AND COLUMNS OF THE PHARAOHS that drew travellers to Egypt, but in recent times the wonders of the ancient world are surpassed in the eyes of many visitors by the marvels of the undersea world.

Egypt has over 800 km (500 miles) of reef-lined Red Sea coastline, running around the Sinai Peninsula and down to the border with Sudan in the south. The sea fills a great rift in the earth's crust, where the African and Asian landmasses meet. In places, the seabed is well over a mile deep. Between the subterranean cliffs and the shore are shallow fringe reefs, and these constitute one of the richest ecosystems on earth, absolutely teeming with life. These coral reefs support more than 1,000 species of marine life, including a huge number of endemic species that are not found elsewhere. To dive in the Red Sea is to descend into a vast and well-stocked aquarium, where schools of stripey angel fish, turquoise parrotfish and gaudy clown fish swirl and wheel with the currents. Manta

Above: Stopping for a break in the arid desert

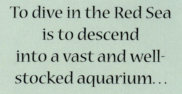

To dive in the Red Sea
is to descend
into a vast and well-
stocked aquarium…

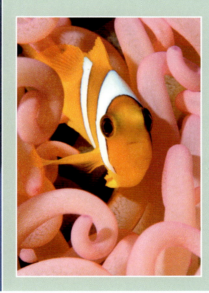

JAN

FEB

MAR

APR

MAY

JUN

JUL

AUG

SEP

OCT

NOV

DEC

DIVING DIARY

For some winter sun, the Red Sea in December is a great choice. It is a sun-baked region of burned, rocky landscapes, bleached blue skies and glittering waters, perfect for diving in the close-to-shore shallow reefs that teem with aquatic life. But there is also life beyond the beach.

Eight Days at the Red Sea

Grab your snorkel and plunge in for a look at the marvels of the Red Sea Reef. There is a bounty of fish accessible from the beaches at Sharm el-Sheikh, Naama Bay and Dahab. If you are inspired to explore deeper, most hotels have dive centres and many of the best dive sites are accessible by short boat trips.

DAYS 1–2

Just 30 km (18 miles) south of Sharm el-Sheikh is Ras Muhammad National Park, a reserve for the endangered wildlife of the region including gazelles and wild foxes. The beautiful craggy, sandy scenery is relieved with mangrove clusters and brilliant freshwater pools. Ras Muhammad is also one of the world's best diving spots with a well-preserved coral reef.

DAYS 3–4

Join an organized camel-trekking expedition into the interior or hire a car to drive up into central Sinai to the ancient, fortress-like St Catherine's Monastery nestled in the shadow of biblical Mt Sinai where Moses received the Ten Commandments.

DAYS 5–6

Finally, give in to the temptation to laze away a couple of days under the cloudless shimmering sky, before catching a flight back home.

DAYS 7–8

Dos and Don'ts

- ✓ Whether diving or trekking, there is one very simple rule: take nothing with you; leave nothing behind.
- ✗ Don't take risks; only dive with reputable companies, as the underwater world is not only beautiful but also dangerous.
- ✓ Make the effort to visit inland Sinai for its desert scenery and geological treats such as the sparkling coloured canyon.

rays up to 6 m (20 ft) wide glide over the sea bed, their wings gently undulating, while turtles make their stately way just below the surface and pods of dolphins play, hunt and socialize.

It isn't even necessary to get wet to appreciate this magical world. The fact that the seabed is so deep means that the sediment never rises, leaving the waters completely clear. Even from a boat it is possible to peer down and observe the kaleidoscopic explosions of fish below.

Capitalizing on the riches under the waves are recently developed resorts such as Sharm el-Sheikh, Naama Bay and Hurghada, which offer beachfront accommodation in international five-star hotels with direct access to the water. All have their own diving clubs and instructors, plus plenty of dry-land diversions. The backdrop to the resorts is either the bare mountains of the Sinai or the barren flats of the Eastern Desert, both of which can be explored; in either case, the visibly lifeless terrain makes the riches of the reefs all the more astonishing.

GETTING THERE
Kerala is a state on the southwest coast of India. International flights arrive into both Kochi and the state capital, Thiruvananthapuram (Trivandrum).

GETTING AROUND
Buses and trains are cheap and safe, or you can hire a car with a driver. When using unmetered taxis, be sure to agree on a figure beforehand. The only way to see the backwaters is by boat.

WEATHER
Temperatures are balmy in December, averaging around 30°C. The mild northeastern monsoon finishes in Kerala at the beginning of the month.

ACCOMMODATION
Old Harbour Hotel, Kochi, a beautifully restored heritage building with large rooms; doubles from £90; www.oldharbourhotel.com

Isola Di Cocco, near Trivandrum, has a lovely beach setting and can organize backwater tours; doubles from £45; www.isoladicocco.com

A stay on a *kettuvallam* costs from £35 for two per night, including a tour of the backwaters.

EATING OUT
Fish, rice and coconut are the most important components of Keralan cuisine, usually flavoured further with tamarind and curry leaves. Try a traditional meal on a banana leaf – best eaten with your hand.

PRICE FOR TWO
£70–90 per day including accommodation, food and local transport.

FURTHER INFORMATION
www.keralatourism.org

Kerala Ayurveda Massage

A classical text on medicine, the *Ashtangahridaya* was the foundation of Ayurveda in Kerala. Its author, Vagbhata, was the disciple of a Buddhist physician. Today, this holistic science of healing is practised throughout India. However, the Kerala method is famous for its five-pronged treatment, *panchakarma*, in which medicated oils, herbs, milk, massage and a special diet are used to cure all types of ailments.

SAIL THE BACKWATERS

STILL, GREEN WATERS, CHANNELLED THROUGH RICE PADDIES and dense coconut groves, only occasionally disturbed by the languid movement of a *kettuvallam* (rice barge): these are the palm-shaded canals and lakes that make up Kerala's 900-km (560-mile) network of backwaters, a patchwork of land and water – both of which are often at the same level. Life here has remained uniquely rural – villages have been built on thin strips of reclaimed land, often no more than a few paces wide, and the sloping roofs of the houses allow the monsoon rains to pour onto the earth. Within these small spaces, people keep animals – ducks and chickens, even cows – and farm small vegetable plots.

There is no more appropriate way to travel through these lush waterways than by *kettuvallam*, past centuries-old Chinese-style fishing nets and lush plantations. Originally used to carry rice and as

Main: Sailing throught the still, palm-fringed backwaters of Kerala in a *kettuvallam*, a converted rice boat

Left: *Kettuvallam* with its distinctive straw roof

Right (left and right): Santa Cruz Cathedral in Fort Cochin; women dressed in traditional yellow clothes at the beach

ferries, these attractive wooden boats now meander through the waterways as a kind of mobile home, from which you can watch the sublime surroundings at a leisurely pace.

One of the most fascinating aspects of a trip through the backwaters is the glimpse it offers of daily life, a world away from India's sprawling cities. In the mornings, the excited chatter of children pierces the humid air as they travel by boat to school. Mounds of cashew nuts and *coir* (coconut fibre, used to make ropes and floor coverings) are loaded into boats to be transported to other villages and beyond. Look closely at the towering coconut palms and you may see nimble-footed toddy tappers scaling their slender trunks for the sap, which is used in the local brew and sold along the waterways and in restaurants. As the sun sets over the backwaters, silhouetting the palms against the sky, a deep peace settles, broken only by the occasional shriek of a monkey – an utterly enchanting experience, unlike anything else on the subcontinent.

Above: Sailing through the tranquil backwaters

Top: Fishing nets at Fort Cochin

Above: Fishermen gathering their nets

Below: Kathakali dancer with traditional green face makeup

JAN

FEB

MAR

APR

MAY

JUN

JUL

AUG

SEP

OCT

NOV

DEC

DAYS 1–2

DAY 3

DAY 4

DAY 5

DAYS 6–8

DAYS 9–10

WATERWAY DIARY

Kerala is one of the most popular tourist destinations in India, with visitors flocking to the state throughout the year. It is during December that the region lives up to its nickname, "God's Own Country", as the northeast monsoon has left the state lush, with high water levels that are ideal for seeing the backwaters.

Ten Days in God's Own Country

Arrive in Kochi and spend a couple of days here. Wander around Fort Cochin and enjoy its old world charm. Head to the River Road to see the Chinese fishing nets, before having a look at St Francis Church, Santa Cruz Cathedral, and the narrow streets and antique shops that surround the Paradesi Synagogue in Jew Town. Try to see a Kathakali performance in the evening at the See India Foundation.

Make a trip to Munnar, a small hill town surrounded by sprawling green tea estates. Enjoy the excellent walks in the area and afterwards, ease your weary limbs with a traditional Ayurveda massage at your hotel.

Travel on to Periyar Wildlife Sanctuary, where you can see a variety of wildlife, including tigers, elephants, wild boars, deer, bison and monkeys.

Head to Alapphuzha, one of the main starting points for backwater cruises. On your way there, stop off at lovely Vembanad Lake.

Join a backwater cruise that travels from Alapphuzha to Kollam, staying overnight on a *kettuvalam* (rice barge). Enjoy the leisurely pace and beautiful surroundings.

From Kollam, head south to Thiruvananthapuram (Trivandrum), Kerala's capital, built across seven hills. While here, admire the exterior of the Anantha Padmanabhaswamy Temple and visit the museums. When you've had your fill of the city, spend a day or so shopping for handicrafts or soaking up the sun on Kovalam or Varkala beaches.

Dos and Don'ts

☑ Carry mosquito repellent at all times, especially while visiting the backwaters.

☑ Make sure that you dress respectfully, covering the tops of your arms and your legs.

☒ Don't drink water out of slow-flowing streams, lakes and dams, no matter how parched you may be.

The bridge literally explodes in flames as the best fireworks display in the world lights up the sky with an eyeball-searing intensity.

GETTING THERE
Sydney is in New South Wales, on Australia's southeast coast. International and domestic flights arrive into Sydney Airport, 9 km (6 miles) from the city centre.

GETTING AROUND
The city has an excellent network of buses, light rail and ferries – a travel pass lets you combine all three. Taxis are also cheap.

WEATHER
Warm weather virtually guaranteed in December, with average temperatures of 24–26°C.

ACCOMMODATION
Park Lodge Hotel, a cosy hotel just 5 minutes from the city centre; doubles from £35; www.parklodgehotel.com

Kirketon Boutique Hotel provides stylish accommodation in Darlinghurst; doubles from £105; www.kirketon.com.au

Sebel Pier One has an enviable harbour position and great views from every room; doubles from £115; www.mirvachotels.com.

EATING OUT
Sydney offers world-class dining, with a lot of Asian-Pacific influences. Head to Chinatown for an inexpensive but good meal (mains from around £5). Push the boat out for great views and a fantastic three-course meal at Modern Australia on Circular Quay (around £40).

PRICE FOR TWO
£140–170 per day including accommodation, food, local transport and entrance charges.

FURTHER INFORMATION
www.sydney.com.au

Sydney Opera House
One of the architectural wonders of the world, Australia's iconic structure was designed by Danish architect Jørn Utzon and completed in 1973. The expressionistic building comprises five theatres in a series of precast concrete shells shaped like upturned orange segments. The main concert hall features a 10,000-pipe organ. More than one million white granite tiles cover the gleaming exterior, while the interior is made of local hardwoods and pink granite. One-hour guided tours are offered, as are longer backstage tours.

Above: The futuristic-looking monorail near Darling Harbour
Inset: Koala in the trees at Taronga Zoo

NEW YEAR DOWN UNDER

WITH ONE OF THE WORLD'S MOST RECOGNIZABLE SKYLINES, Sydney is a beautiful city: set around a sparkling harbour graced by the Sydney Harbour Bridge and famous Opera House, its multi-peaked roof evocative of a ship at full sail. A cultural and postmodern metropolis, this has become one of the best places to enjoy New Year's Eve. On the big day, as the light slowly fades, the harbour fills up with twinkling, bobbing boats. The night's iconic image takes place at midnight, when the bridge literally explodes in flames as the best fireworks display in the world lights up the sky with an eyeball-searing intensity. A curtain of liquid fire drops 50 metres (164 ft) from the bridge to the water, while volleys of rockets release layer-upon-layer of coloured sheets of flame, a psychedelic starburst of colour. When it finishes, it's as though someone has turned the lights out, and the spectators go wild. There's no more Australian way to celebrate than with a barbeque and a few "tinnies" (cans of beer) – head to one of

---

JAN FEB MAR APR MAY JUN JUL AUG SEP OCT NOV **DEC** 30 DEC 31 DEC 1 JAN 2 JAN 3 JAN 4 JAN 5 JAN

Above: A vibrant Aboriginal bark painting; Sydney Aquarium's Open Ocean display

Main: Sydney Harbour Bridge bursts with colour on New Year's Eve

Below: Dining alfresco on Circular Quay

Above: Young surfers taking part in a surf carnival on Bondi Beach

SYDNEY DIARY

Australia's "Harbour City" is the country's party capital and New Year is the biggest party there is (although the camp and colourful Mardi Gras comes close). A week will give you plenty of time to explore the city's sights. Consider extending your visit with a trip up the sunny Queensland coast (see pp256–7).

A Week in the Harbour City

Orientate yourself with a morning city tour by open-air bus. Spend a leisurely afternoon on a walking tour of The Rocks or visit the Museum of Contemporary Art.

Enjoy a leisurely scenic harbour cruise. Back on land, take it easy in preparation for the night's festivities. There's a warm-up display of fireworks at 9pm (for the youngsters) but the spectacular climax is at midnight and the party goes on until dawn.

Head to Bondi Beach, where real party animals can sleep off the night before. If you have the energy, try your hand at surfing – a number of local surf schools run full- and half-day lessons.

Join an excursion to the Hunter Valley. Tour the wineries for tastings and gourmet food – particularly of note are the Rothbury Estate, Lindemans and McWilliams Mount Pleasant Winery.

See the Art Gallery of New South Wales, the Australian Museum or Sydney Aquarium. After a café lunch, tour Sydney Opera House, explore bustling Chinatown, or take the ferry from Circular Quay to Taronga Zoo.

For some fresh air and great scenery, explore the nearby Blue Mountains. See the Three Sisters, take the Scenic Skyway ride over the mountains from Katoomba and explore the Jenolan Caves.

Spend your last day relaxing in the beautiful Royal Botanic Gardens before heading to Darling Harbour for some fantastic shopping.

Dos and Don'ts

✓ Buy a two-, three- or seven-day adult or child Smartcard granting free admission to most attractions.

✗ Don't forget your zinc oxide! ZnO absorbs ultraviolet rays. A dollop on the nose is de rigueur for lazing on Bondi Beach.

✓ Heed the flags at the beaches – a red flag indicates no swimming. Dangerous rip tides and high surf are the most common dangers; sharks are another.

---

the official viewpoints as the unofficial ones, while usually very lively and entertaining, can get a little rowdy. For those who can, the parties go on till dawn – and beyond.

The next day, before the rest of the city wakes, the serious surfers line up across beautiful Bondi Beach, straddling their boards and waiting for the perfect wave. Each big wave's arrival is signalled by a burst of frantic activity, followed by the successful few riding the spinning blue tube of water effortlessly into shore. It's worth trying once, and even if you do no more than fall off spectacularly while gulping down seawater, the chances are you'll have also tasted the excitement.

Sydney was only founded in 1788, but the area's Aboriginal history goes back 40,000 years – trace this in the Australia Museum, before exploring the city's infamous convict past at the Museum of Sydney. The best way to see the city is on foot, which allows you to get a real feel for its vibrancy and character, especially at this time of year. Most travellers begin at The Rocks, the pedestrian-friendly site of Australia's first English settlement, now bursting with museums, art galleries, craft shops, historic pubs and delightful restaurants with the obligatory harbour view.

MOUNTAINOUS EDEN

YOUNGEST YET LARGEST OF THE WINDWARD ISLANDS, Dominica is a lush, mountainous Eden framed in a thousand shades of emerald green, famously captured on camera in the *Pirates of the Caribbean* films. You can almost sense the vegetation growing around you and perhaps suspect that a brash buccaneer might be lurking in the undergrowth. Most visitors choose to explore the rainforests, where the air is cool and dank and alive with the whistles and cooings of birds – 170 species in all, including two species of parrots found nowhere else. A popular site to birdwatch is the lower slopes of Morne Diablotin. Botanists, too, can have a field day. Dominica blazes with tropical flowers: showy torch gingers, bougainvillea as red as

GETTING THERE
Dominica is part of the Windward Islands chain in the eastern Caribbean Sea. It has two airports with service from Puerto Rico. Ferries connect it to Guadalupe and Martinique.

GETTING AROUND
There are plenty of car hire firms and taxi services available to get around the island. Be aware there is an additional driver's permit fee.

WEATHER
December is during the driest period. However, due to Dominica's topography and vegetation, temperatures vary widely. Rain falls year-round in the mountains.

ACCOMMODATION
3 Rivers Eco-Lodge, Newfoundland Estate, Rosalie – rainforest lodge with camping; 2-man tent from £15; www.3riversdominica.com

Garraway Hotel, Roseau – city hotel with views; doubles from £50; www.garrawayhotel.com

Jungle Bay Resort & Spa – cottages in the forest; doubles from £95; www.junglebaydominica.com

EATING OUT
African, Carib Indian, French and Oriental influences infuse Dominica's spicy cuisine, such as *buljow* – saltfish with peppers, chives and onions, cooked in coconut milk. While £5 will buy you a filling meal, expect to pay twice that amount for gourmet fare.

PRICE FOR TWO
£90–110 per day including accommodation, food and car hire.

FURTHER INFORMATION
www.dominica.dm

Dominica blazes with tropical flowers: showy torch gingers, bougainvillea as red as bright lipstick and hibiscus and heliconias in riotous colour.

bright lipstick and hibiscus and heliconias in riotous colour. With some of the wildest terrain in the Caribbean, this fecund island supports the only surviving tribe of Carib Indians, who live today on the eastern shores.

Dominica also boasts seven active volcanoes – more than any other neighbouring isle. Many craters are studded with clear mountain lakes and bubbling hot springs. A favourite destination for hikers is Valley of the Desolation, in Morne Trois Pitons National Park, where the spectacular cascades of Trafalgar Falls reward intrepid travellers with both hot springs and cool spring-fed pools. But, you don't have to be activity minded – the Rainforest Aerial Tram, for example, gives you a monkey's-eye view of life in the treetop canopies.

For divers too, the island is an aquatic heaven; a favourite dive site is Soufrière Crater, a sunken volcano brim-full of corals. Snorkellers don't need to venture far from shore to swim with groupers, wrasses, parrotfish and a swarm of smaller spectacularly coloured, polka-dotted, zebra-striped fish. These warm waters also host sperm whales year-round and humpbacks are predictable winter visitors. Marine turtles can be seen crawling ashore to lay their eggs for tomorrow's turtles. And sections of the coast are so wild that you can be the first to put your footprints on your very own black-sand beach, except for the pirates that is. . .

Main: Graceful rainforest tree ferns
Inset: Aerial tram crosses the Morne Trois Pitons National Park
Below (left to right): The Emerald Pool and waterfall; brightly coloured heliconia; rugged eastern coastline of the island

Dominica's Parrots
Dominica is home to two endemic parrots unique to the isle. The Imperial, known to locals as the Sisserou, is Dominica's national bird and proudly adorns the island's flag. Males grow to 50 cm (20 inches) and can weigh almost 1 kg (2 lb) – the largest of all Amazonian parrots. It has a purple chest, cobalt-green neck and rust-coloured head. The Sisserou's smaller cousin, the lime-green Jacquot or red-necked parrot, wears a blood-red bib. The best place to spot them is in the Northern Forest Reserve, near Syndicate.

Above: Horse-riding through the cooling waves

JAN

FEB

MAR

APR

MAY

JUN

JUL

AUG

SEP

OCT

NOV

DEC

JUNGLE DIARY

Known for the best preserved ocean rainforest in the Caribbean, Dominica is a nature-lover's delight and best suited to active travellers. In December, the island is at its driest. At least one week is needed to do the island justice, with time for snorkelling and other water activities, hiking and rainforest exploration.

A Week on a Tropical Island

Tour the capital, Roseau, and admire the New Orleans-style architecture. Visit the local museum to learn about Dominican culture and natural history.

Spend the afternoon snorkelling at Champagne Bay, where underwater vents blow bubbles into the sea.

DAY 1

Head to Morne Trois Pitons National Park. Hike to Trafalgar Falls and visit the Papillote Tropical Gardens.

Mid-afternoon explore the rainforest canopy aboard the Rainforest Aerial Tram. A guide will point out the birds and other wildlife.

DAY 2

In the morning scuba dive in the underwater caves of Soufrière Crater, a sunken volcano brim-full of corals. Non-divers will enjoy exploring Soufrière Marine Park. After, continue to Soufrière Sulphur Springs.

DAY 3

Have a full day out at Wacky Rollers Adventure Park, including horse-riding and Jeep safari.

Take a boat trip to get close to, or even swim with, humpback whales. Then relax on the beach.

DAYS 4–5

Hike up and along the island's mountain spine to aptly-named Boiling Lake, in the Valley of Desolation. En route, soak in the thermal pools.

DAY 6

Relax on the beach before transferring to the airport for your flight home.

DAY 7

Dos and Don'ts

✓ Take a sweater and rainproof jacket, as it can get chilly in the mountains and rain is always a possibility.

✗ Don't forget that traffic drives on the left-hand side if you rent a car.

✓ Try some of the local fruits such as barbadine, carambola, tamarind, guava, and soursop. They're delicious!

GETTING THERE
Helsinki is the capital of Finland. International flights arrive into Vantaa International Airport, 30 minutes from the city centre. Rovaniemi, in Finnish Lapland, is 834 km (518 miles) north of Helsinki and can be reached by an 11-hour train ride or a short flight.

GETTING AROUND
Buses, trams, trains and boats provide comprehensive public transport in Helsinki. In Lapland, travel around by dogsled or snowmobile for an exciting experience.

WEATHER
Helsinki's average December temperatures rarely drop below 5°C and light snow is frequent. Rovaniemi is much colder at around -5°C.

ACCOMMODATION
Scandic Grand Marina, a stylish modern hotel in a converted warehouse; family rooms from £160; www.scandic-hotels.com/grandmarina

Hotel Kamp, overlooking Helsinki's Esplanadi Christmas market, has luxurious family rooms from £165; www.hotelkamp.fi

In Rovaniemi, Rantasipi Pohjanhovi has family rooms from £145; www.rantasipi.fi

EATING OUT
HelsinkiMenu signs indicate seasonal menus featuring local produce. At G W Sundmans on Etelaranta, you can try reindeer (from £45).

PRICE FOR FAMILY OF FOUR
£250–280 per day including accommodation, food, entrance charges and local travel.

FURTHER INFORMATION
www.visitfinland.com

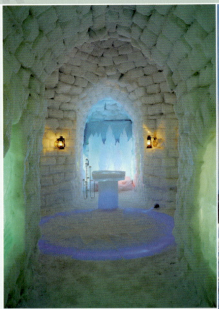

Main: Laplander in his reindeer-sledge, a convenient way of travelling through the snowy landscape
Above (top to bottom): Snow chapel in Rovaniemi; ski slope in Levi; northern lights flash across the Finnish sky

Festival of Light

Throughout Scandinavia on 13 December, Santa Lucia – the Festival of Light – is celebrated. A young woman is chosen to wear a crown of burning candles and bring the light into homes, places of work, hospitals and schools. Processions take place in all towns and villages with the Lucia Queen leading carol singers. The festival is also celebrated by families in their homes – a daughter is chosen to wake the family, dressed in the traditional white costume and bearing a tray of coffee and saffronbread.

SLEIGH BELLS IN THE SNOW

THE FINNS LOVE CHRISTMAS – AND WHY WOULDN'T THEY? After all, Santa's home is in a village just south of Rovaniemi, in Finnish Lapland. By early December, holiday sights, sounds and aromas fill the land: the excited squeal of children catching a glimpse of Santa, sausages and herring sizzling over glowing coals, the swell of voices rising in the chorus from *Finlandia*, the aroma of freshly baked honey cakes as you enter a café, mellow brass notes from a street musician's horn, the jingle of bells on a reindeer harness, and the hubbub of open-air markets filled with shoppers. Even nature seems to enjoy the season, painting the night sky with the colourful Northern Lights.

Between visiting Santa's workshop, meeting real reindeer and getting a sneak preview of Christmas toys in the markets, it's a sensory overload for kids. Add a real fortress to explore, a zoo with snow leopards, ice skating, skiing and a husky safari and it's a child's winter dream come true.

JAN
FEB
MAR
APR
MAY
JUN
JUL
AUG
SEP
OCT
NOV
DEC
DAY 1
DAY 2
DAY 3
DAYS 4–6
DAY 7
DAY 8

Above: Santa scoots past on a snowmobile

Below: Festive stall selling handmade decorations and gifts in Helsinki; looking up towards Helsinki Cathedral through the decorated streets

Above: Mammoth ice sculpture at the Helsinki Zoo

SANTA DIARY

December is filled with Christmas: Helsinki's broad Esplanadi is alive with bright market tents and shop windows glitter. Twinkling lights arch over the streets and all Helsinki seems to glow from within. A week allows time for the city and shopping, and a few days in Lapland to visit Santa's hometown.

Eight Days in a Wonderland

Get your bearings in the capital by exploring the small area that wraps around the harbour, before heading to the Art Nouveau Katajanokka neighbourhood for the Women's Christmas Fair (December 2–6).

Take a boat to Suomenlinna Island, a World Heritage Site and one of the world's largest sea fortresses. Back at the harbour, visit the Russian Uspensky Cathedral and stop for hot chocolate on the cosy sailing ship/café *Kathrina*. Spend the evening shopping in Esplanadi market.

Discover Helsinki's design district, with the Design Museum, Museum of Finnish Architecture and the Design Forum. Or, take the kids to Temppeliaukio Church, carved out of solid rock, or to see the snow leopards at Helsinki Zoo. Rent skates at Kallion Tekojäärata and glide across the ice.

Fly to Rovaniemi and learn about Lapland and its people with a visit to the Arktikum museum.

Meet Santa and his reindeer at Santa's Village, then visit a Sámi camp and earn your Reindeer Driving Licence on a reindeer sled.

Join a dogsledding safari into remote forests, with a traditional fire-grilled lunch in a Sámi tent.

Spend the day skiing in the beautiful rolling fells at Kittila or Levi, relaxing afterwards in a sauna.

Return to Helsinki and take a final spin around the Esplanadi market.

Dos and Don'ts

✗ Don't be afraid to ask strangers directions; almost everyone speaks English.

✓ Buy a Helsinki Card if you plan to visit museums and use the trams a lot; it's also useful for hotel discounts.

✓ Experience a sauna at least once. These will never be mixed-sex except when shared by families.

✓ Helsinki has an extensive and useful system of underground passages, connecting Metro stations, department stores and entire subterranean shopping arcades.

Shoppers will also find nirvana. Holiday handicraft markets are filled with beautiful woodcarvings, knitted sweaters, dolls, candles, wooden toys and puzzles, fur hats, blown glassware, straw reindeer and jars of shimmering lingonberry jam. Little red woollen elves perch everywhere and fleece is slipped into slippers, hats and cheery red apple decorations. At least one booth will have a steaming cauldron of *glogi*, a mouth-tingling brew of red wine, spices, raisins and blackcurrant juice that warms you to your toes.

It's not just Christmas; the Finns love winter too. They brag about it, revel in it and invite the world to join them on frozen ponds, ski slopes and trails, on dogsleds and reindeer sleds, in a world of glistening white, broken only by the intensely vivid colours of woolly winter hats, scarves and mittens. They make winter so much fun that it's an irresistible invitation, whether you long to feel the rush of icy air as you speed across a white landscape behind a team of yipping huskies, or to enter into the steamy warmth of a hide-covered Sámi tent.

GETTING THERE
Yap, part of the Federated States of Micronesia, is a stopover on the Guam to Palau route. There are no direct flights.

GETTING AROUND
There is no public transport as such. The capital, Colonia, is about 15 minutes from the airport by car. Rent a vehicle through your hotel or take a taxi around Colonia and to the airport.

WEATHER
Yap is warm and dry in December, and temperatures average around 27°C year-round.

ACCOMMODATION
ESA Hotel has basic double rooms from £50; www.yapesabayview.com

Manta Ray Bay Hotel is colourful and spacious; doubles from £80; www.mantaray.com

Traders' Ridge Resort is an upscale hotel; doubles from £115; www.tradersridge.com

EATING OUT
The best eating is at the hotels. The Manta Ray Bay's restaurant, actually an Indonesian fishing boat moored in the harbour, serves excellent seafood (mains from £8). The Veranda View (mains from £10), at Trader's Ridge, naturally has the best view, out over Chamorro Bay, as well as the "only professional Yapese chef on Yap". Try the delicious betel nut cocktails.

PRICE FOR TWO
£120–140 per day including accommodation, food, car hire, a half-day tour and a dive.

FURTHER INFORMATION
www.visityap.org

Ancient Banking

Yap's ancient *rai* – huge stone money – was quarried long ago on Palau's Rock Islands. The *rai* was then towed by canoe to Yap, 400 km (250 miles) away. Although the Yapese are masters of the sea, the awkward cargo could be lethal in bad weather – the value of the coin was therefore indexed to the difficulty of transportation. Today, *rai* is still sometimes used, although the money never moves, staying in pathside village "banks" *(below)*.

UNDERWATER TREASURES

I MAGINE THIS: you're a pressure-suit-encased plaything suspended in the void, bobbing about at the mercy of a shapeshifting blue mass. Looking up you can see a hazy lozenge of light illuminating scattered clumps of misshapen rock. You float over to a rock ledge surrounded by sheer vertical walls. The light grows dim as a large, deltoid shape blocks it from view. The shape, its wingspan almost tipping 5 m (16 ft), floats into close range, an unfamiliar mass of unnatural lobes and projecting eye sockets.

As it passes by the creature opens its huge mouth, almost brushing you with its wingtips. . . without realizing it you're holding your breath in awe. Are you an astronaut searching for life forms on an alien planet? No, you're 9 m (30 ft) under the western Pacific, diving the M'il Channel and communing with nature's very own devilfish – the famous manta rays of Yap.

JAN

FEB

MAR

APR

MAY

JUN

JUL

AUG

SEP

OCT

NOV

DEC

DAY 1

DAY 2

DAY 3

DAY 4

DAY 5

Tiny Yap might be the proverbial speck in the ocean, but its gentle, graceful and extremely large mantas are among the world's premier underwater attractions. Yet on land Yap is just as beguiling. If they're not diving, most people skip Yap on the way to Guam or Palau, but why miss the chance to explore Micronesia's most traditional state? Unusual sights will greet you, far removed from Western society: giant stone money, for example, up to 4 m (13 ft) wide; or loin-clothed men chewing betel nut, the seed of the areca palm, as they go about their business in the capital, Colonia.

At the miniscule airport, children crowd the runway to meet the planes, and in town you'll be greeted with constant smiles, the mouths stained a disconcerting red by the prolonged chewing of betel nut. At first, it may seem an alarming sight but the friendliness of the inhabitants will soon set you at ease and get you into the mood to discover some of the most colourful underwater treasures of the Pacific Ocean as well as some well deserved laid-back relaxation.

Above: Traditional dancers in colourful costume

DIVING DIARY

December through to February is the peak season for manta watching – a day or two should be plenty of time, especially as Yap is one of the best places in the world to see them. Four days is ample time to see the rest of Yap at a luxurious pace, unless you want to extend your stay with a trip to the outer islands.

Five Days Around the Island

Swim with the mantas – the best time is in the very early morning. In the afternoon, snorkel around Yap's wonderful reef, blue holes and shallow lagoon.

Hire a guide to take you to Bechiyal, a relaxed beachside village. Its ancient *faluw* (men's meeting house) is the oldest on the island. Later, visit the stone-money banks at Balabat, Okau and Wanyan villages. Glimpse local artisans at work in open-air workshops at the Ethnic Art Village. Sometimes there are dance performances, as well as demonstrations in carrying stone money and chewing betel nut.

Take a tour to the "forbidden island" of Rumung, a 20-minute boat trip from Bechiyal. Since the 17th century until very recently, Rumung had been closed to all foreigners. It still has no cars, roads or electricity – just stone paths and a strong feel of the past.

Hire a guide to show you the WWII relics scattered about Yap, including rusting cannon and shot-down fighter planes – a legacy of wartime occupation by the Japanese. Take a tour on a traditional sailing canoe, kayak through the mangrove channels, or mountain bike through lush jungle greenery.

Fly to the Ulithi atoll in the outer islands, an unspoiled, unhurried attraction. Spend a day or two snorkelling and diving: underwater attractions include tiger sharks, turtles and some interesting WWII wrecks.

Dos and Don'ts

- ✓ Ask the locals to show you how to chew betel nut. You'll make them laugh when you stain your nice new shirt with the gushing, bright-red saliva it produces.

- ✗ Don't sunbathe on the beach in a bathing costume – cover up with a sarong. Although some Yapese women go topless, it's shameful for females to display bare thighs.

- ✓ Carry a blade of grass when walking through a village – it's a sign of respect.

- ✗ Don't just walk anywhere without asking – every piece of land on Yap is privately owned, and to not seek permission is a deep insult.

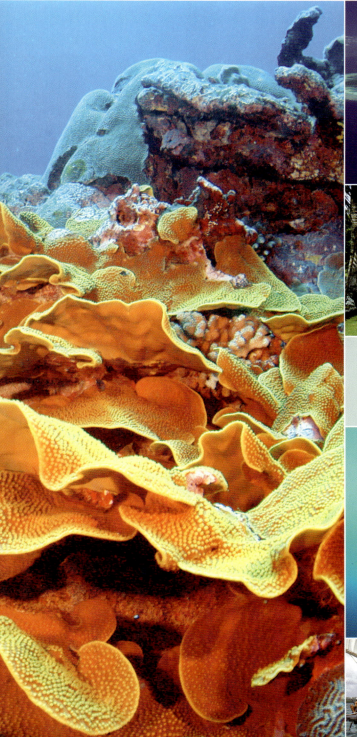

Above (top and bottom): Aerial view of Yap; a meeting hut – *faluw* – by the beach

Main: Diver swims among the coral off the coast of Yap

Below (top and bottom): Pair of manta rays in the waters around Yap; traditional outrigger canoe

GETTING THERE
Vienna is the capital of Austria. International flights arrive into Schwechat Airport, 20 km (12 miles) southeast of the city. The easiest way to get into town is by City Airport Train (CAT), which takes just 16 minutes.

GETTING AROUND
The best way to see Vienna is on foot. There is also an efficient subway system (U-Bahn), as well as buses and trams.

WEATHER
Vienna is cold in December, with temperatures ranging between -1 and 3°C.

ACCOMMODATION
Hotel Zipser, a family run hotel in a central location; doubles from £70; www.zipser.at

Hotel Altstadt Vienna is a stylish hotel with an intimate feel; doubles from £95; www.altstadt.at

The Grand Hotel Wien, a historic and luxurious hotel; doubles from £255; www.jjwhotels.com

EATING OUT
Dishes found throughout the city include *Wiener Schnitzel* (breaded veal escalopes) and *Bauernschamaus* (a country platter of hot meats and dumplings). Dinner typically costs between £12 and £20 per head. Vienna is also famous for its coffee houses, which serve decadent cakes, eaten as snacks between meals.

PRICE FOR TWO
£190–220 per day including accommodation, food, local transport and entrance charges.

FURTHER INFORMATION
www.aboutvienna.org

City of Music

Vienna is, and has always been, Europe's music capital – and never more so than at Christmas when the city spills over with sound and song. "Silent Night", composed in the village of Oberndorf near Salzburg in 1818, is a beloved choice for choirs at the Christmas markets, including the famous Vienna Boys Choir who perform a special repertoire of traditional carols in December. Other tickets in hot demand include the annual Christmas concerts at the Konzerthaus – if you want to attend, you will have to book ahead.

Main: The bustling Christkindlmarkt by night
Above (left to right): Decorations displayed at a market stall; Christmas market at the Schönbrunn Palace; coffee and cake at Café Stern

Above: Dome of the Michaelertrakt as dusk descends over Vienna

GINGERBREAD AND WINE

OF ALL THE CITIES IN EUROPE, Vienna has the merriest Advent and Christmas imaginable, one that lasts for weeks and weeks, starting with the arrival of St Nicholas and his scary sidekick Krampus at the Christkindlmarkt. Some say this love of Christmas harks back to the Habsburg emperors, passionate Catholics who saw the birth of Christ as the ultimate festival.

Each year for hundreds of years, Vienna has transformed into a winter wonderland with lights twinkling in the frosty nights and open-air Christmas markets everywhere, such as at the magical Schönbrunn Palace. The colourful markets sell a huge selection of beautifully made handicrafts, toys, decorations and tree ornaments, all carefully displayed. As you wander through the maze of stalls, the smell of traditional roasted chestnuts, *Glühwein* (hot spiced wine), *Punsch* (fruit punch spiked with wine) and *Lebkuchen* (a moulded gingerbread) will drift through the air tempting you to try the Christmas fare for which the Viennese markets are famed.

When it comes to tradition, Vienna pulls out all the stops – there are choirs from around the world that fill the air with song, special marionette shows and an immense display of Nativity scenes. After a traditional Christmas Eve and Christmas Day, the party just goes on and on. New Year's Eve in Vienna is one giant party rivalling New York City's Times Square – a huge New Year's market extends along a mile-long strip linking the city's squares, and the champagne flows. The heart of the party is in the plaza around St Stephen's Cathedral, where celebrants down their chilled champagne and waltz the night away like a professional after the free lessons available in the Neuer Markt.

And the party is not over yet – New Year's is merely a prelude to 300 balls that take place during January's Ball Season, a time that ensures no one forgets that this is the most musical city in the world.

"The streets of Vienna are paved with culture; in other cities they are paved with asphalt."

Karl Kraus

Below (left and right): Waltzers at the Vienna Opera Ball; Viennese Boys Choir
Inset: Sign glows Christmas tidings to all

FESTIVE DIARY

Christmas celebrations start in November and continue until the Ball Season in January. A visit over Christmas will give you a chance to enjoy the fantastic markets, but if you delay your visit until just before New Year, you can enjoy the open-air party in St Stephen's Square and the many balls that follow.

Four Days Celebrating Christmas

23rd Spend your first day getting your bearings in the city before heading to the Christmas markets (such as the one at Schönbrunn Palace) for tree decorations, wooden toys, hand-crafted gifts, honey cake and gingerbread. Dine at the food stalls on *Kartoffelpuffer* (potato pancakes) and *Glühwein*. In the evening, attend a Christmas concert.

24th Explore the city's imperial history with a visit to the glorious Hofburg Complex and the State Apartments in the Reichskanzleitrakt. Take an afternoon coffee break (known as *Jause*) to enjoy a slice of *Sachertorte* (chocolate cake) or *Dobostorte* (layers of sponge and buttercream).

Spend the evening at the famous Christkindlmarkt by the Rathaus, soaking up the festive atmosphere, before a traditional Christmas Eve meal of *Fischbeuschelsuppe* (creamy fish soup) and freshly fried carp.

25th Enjoy a relaxing Christmas Day with lots of decadent Viennese treats. Take the opportunity to have a wander through the city while it is near-empty and enjoy the old-world ambience.

26th Music-lovers should take a tram over to Zentralfriedhof Cemetery to pay tribute to Vienna's greatest composers who are buried here. Alternatively, check out the excellent art galleries, including the Museum of Modern Art's extensive collection and Austrian art at the Leopold Museum. Make sure you make time for more cake and coffee. In the evening, enjoy an opera at the world-famous Staatsoper.

Dos and Don'ts

- ✓ If invited over for dinner, bring a gift of chocolates or flowers, but not red roses – these are for lovers.

- ✗ Don't start your meal until the official cue to begin eating – when the hostess says "*Guten Appetite*" or "*Mahlzeit*".

- ✓ Leave your inhibitions at home since Austrians are not prudish about saunas. Here men and women share the heat *au naturel*.

- ✓ Children will enjoy the daily workshop in the Volkshalle (town hall), where they can make presents and bake Christmas cookies while their parents shop.

JAN
FEB
MAR
APR
MAY
JUN
JUL
AUG
SEP
OCT
NOV
DEC

Left: Chevrolet cruises down the Strip in Las Vegas

Right (left to right): Glitzy interior of the Tropicana; Red Rock Canyon in the Nevada Desert; slot machines at the Flamingo Casino; elaborately dressed showgirl at Bally's

Inset: The Venetian Hotel and Casino on Las Vegas Boulevard

GETTING THERE
Las Vegas is in southwest USA. International flights arrive into McCarran International Airport. Taxis run from the airport to the Strip.

GETTING AROUND
The best way to get around is by taxi, bus or the Monorail, which connects many of the major hotels along the Strip.

WEATHER
In December, daytime temperatures average around 16°C but can dip to -1°C in the evening.

ACCOMMODATION
Golden Nugget, a good-value vintage jewel situated downtown; doubles from £50; www.goldennugget.com

THEhotel is a swanky, quiet retreat on the southern Strip; large doubles from £80; www.thehotelatmandalaybay.com

Bellagio, an Italian palazzo on the central Strip; doubles from £90; www.bellagio.com

EATING OUT
A standard meal, including a drink, costs around £18. For a treat, indulge in a gourmet tasting menu (£45, wine extra) at Picasso in the Bellagio. Buffets are often the cheapest option (apart from the ubiquitous fast food) – the best in town is Carnival World Buffet at the Rio Las Vegas (from £7).

PRICE FOR TWO
£250–280 per day including accommodation, food, entertainment and local travel.

FURTHER INFORMATION
www.visitlasvegas.com

Bugsy's Town
Hollywood glitz and glamour, mob money and murder and legalized gambling. It fell to arch-mobster Benjamin "Bugsy" Siegel to connect these disparate dots and build a gambling and entertainment mecca in the scorching Nevada desert. Still with us today, his 1946 Flamingo Hotel was the rip-roaring wellspring from which Vegas sprawled. It took years for the casino-hotel to turn a profit, but when it did, "Sin City" was born.

Main: Dazzling neon sign outside Binion's Casino

VIVA LAS VEGAS!

I
T'S SAFE TO SAY THAT LAS VEGAS IS LIKE NOWHERE ELSE ON EARTH. It's alluring and repulsive, entirely artificial and mesmerizing, an American Dream of freedom without bounds blasting a cosmic hole in the darkness of the desert night. No other city has over 120,000 hotel rooms or a single hotel, the Wynn Las Vegas, that cost $2.7 billion to erect. Where once the legendary Strip played to waddling hinterlanders lusting for their favourite slots and gustatory orgies at cheap buffets, Vegas now croons its siren song for the wildly rich. Direct flights from as far as Narita, Japan, regularly dump waves of high-rollers, and room rates can soar into the ionosphere. Filthy lucre and luxury are once again the focus of Sin City.

To be in Vegas any time of day is an assault on the senses. The desert heat vaporizes sweat and the glaring sun brings on a perpetual Clint Eastwood squint. But it's at night when the "overwhelm quotient" has you doubting

JAN
FEB
MAR
APR
MAY
JUN
JUL
AUG
SEP
OCT
NOV
DEC
FRI
SAT
SUN

Above: Las Vegas' famed "Strip" glows as night descends

An American Dream of freedom without bounds blasting a cosmic hole in the darkness of the desert night.

SIN CITY DIARY

The best time to visit Las Vegas is at the weekends, when it is at its glitziest. Over the Christmas period the city becomes even more over-the-top and in-your-face. The city's position means that once you have fed your hedonistic cravings you can experience the beauty of the surrounding desert (see pp120–1).

A Lost Weekend in Vegas

Travel from ancient Egypt to New York, and from Polynesia to Venice as you explore the mega-hotels along the famous Strip. For breathtaking views, be whisked up the Stratosphere Tower aboard a high-speed elevator to a lofty 274 m (900 ft). In the evening, head downtown to marvel at the Fremont Street Experience, a high-octane light and sound spectacle, before taking your pick from one of the casinos, such as the Art Nouveau Tropicana, the famous Flamingo or the more traditional Binion's.

Head to Caesar's Palace, where you can ride the spiralling escalator, stroll down ancient Roman streets and throw a coin in the replica Trevi fountain. Alternatively, spend a couple of hours relaxing poolside at your hotel or treating yourself at a spa.

Enjoy a lively buffet dinner before seeing a mesmerizing show by the Cirque du Soleil, such as the aquatic O, or see the showgirls at Bally's. Afterwards, ride the glass elevator to the 64th floor of the THEhotel for a Martini at Mix before hitting one of the trendy clubs along the Strip.

Restore balance to the brain with heavenly sounds and the earthy cuisine of the American south during a lavish Gospel Brunch at the House of Blues. For a little culture, feast your eyes on masterpieces by the world's finest artists at the Guggenheim Hermitage Museum at the Venetian. Alternatively, head out to Red Rock Canyon on the city outskirts for a scenic drive through the desert park. Spend your last evening in the casinos, either joining in the hedonistic thrills or just observing if your wallet is feeling a little too light.

Dos and Don'ts

☒ Don't even bother getting up early – the city doesn't look pretty in the morning.

☑ When booking a room, request one on the upper floors overlooking the Strip. Unless the hotel is fully booked, staff will usually try to accommodate you.

☑ Make reservations early if want to get the best table, room or ticket. Many places now take reservations online.

☑ Distances along the Strip can be deceptive – wear comfortable shoes and carry a bottle of water.

your perceptions. Elvis clones in white jumpsuits huddle like albino penguins and hawkers proffer everything from "discreet" escort services to exorbitantly priced tickets to the latest must-see glamour show. The streets are jammed with Maseratis and pickup trucks prowling beneath mountains of screaming imagery and replicas of the Eiffel Tower and the Empire State Building. But it's inside the casinos where the wall of sound washing over you blots out any hope of rational thought. The clanging, blasting, ringing of the slots is akin to standing in the midst of a choir of lunatic munchkins under the baton of the Marquis de Sade.

But, hey baby, this is Vegas! What better way to celebrate the festive period of excess than to head for a weekend of undiluted pleasure? The place where Wayne "Mr Las Vegas" Newton gave his 25,000th performance – ten years ago. The city where even the tourism website encourages you to become anyone you want to be. So whatever your Rat Pack, mobster or *Fear and Loathing* fantasy might be, Vegas is the place to give in to it. And, most likely, no one will even notice.

GETTING THERE
International flights arrive into António Carlos Jobim Airport, around 20 km (12 miles) from the city. Travel into the city by taxi or shuttle bus.

GETTING AROUND
To get around Rio in the daytime, use a combination of buses and metro. Taxis are advisable for travel in the evenings.

WEATHER
In December, temperatures range between 34 and 42°C, often with fairly high humidity.

ACCOMMODATION
During Révellion, most hotels offer four-night packages at much higher rates than usual.

Martinique is an affordable hotel close to Copacabana beach; doubles from £45; www.windsorhoteis.com.br

Praia Ipanema faces Ipanema Beach and offers excellent ocean views; doubles from £100; www.praiaipanema.com

The famous Copacabana Palace has an enviable location and provides complete luxury; doubles from £345; www.copacabanapalace.com.br

EATING OUT
Rio offers a variety of restaurants. An average meal costs around £5–10. Try the archetypical Brazilian dish, feijoada blackbean stew, at Casa da Feijoada, Rua Prudente de Morais 10, Ipanema.

PRICE FOR TWO
£180–200 per day including accommodation, food, local transport and entrance charges.

FURTHER INFORMATION
www.riodejaneiro-turismo.com.br

Futbol Fever

A game of *futbol* (football) in Rio's Maracanã stadium may well be the greatest spectator sport experience on earth. Fans begin arriving at least 3 or 4 hours before the game starts, and the team percussion corps pounds out a samba beat to energize their fans. Brazilians put next to no premium on defence, so games tend to be open, flowing affairs, with plenty of fancy footwork and lots of shots on goal.

SAMBA CELEBRATIONS

THE SAND, GLITTERING WITH THOUSANDS OF CANDLES in horseshoe trenches, pounds with the heady beat of samba. On the dark water, small wooden boats, laden with flowers, jewellery and sweets float out to sea, watched by millions of people from the shore, their white costumes appearing out of the darkness like ghostly apparitions. This is *Reveillon*, Rio de Janeiro's New Year's Eve celebration, held in honour of Iemanjá, goddess of the sea and an important deity of the Afro-Brazilian religion, Macumba.

Throughout the city, regardless of colour, faith or wealth, people embrace the spontaneous character of this spiritual event, creating a surprisingly relaxed ambience. The festivities begin during the day, when the first people begin their pilgrimage, drifting onto the beach in white among the glistening sunbathers to build altars to the *orixá* (goddess) in the sand.

Main: Colourful fireworks explode over Copacabana Beach

JAN

FEB

MAR

APR

MAY

JUN

JUL

AUG

SEP

OCT

NOV

DEC

But it is as night falls that the celebrations really begin. Three huge sound stages blast out music to appeal to the varied crowd – rock, Brazilian popular music (samba and *choros*), and older music (*boleros* and old carnival songs). On the pavement that runs alongside the beach, makeshift tables announce fortune-tellers, artisans and food vendors, while white roses and gladioli perfume the air, sold on every street corner as offerings for Iemanjá. Just before midnight, religious devotees crouch at the water's edge to scatter these flowers in the sea, as the tiny wooden boats are pushed away from the shore. Legend has it that if your boat floats out to sea, you will have good fortune in the coming year, but if your boat returns, there will be disappointment.

Midnight is heralded by a spectacular firework display, launched from offshore boats, and the atmosphere becomes truly electric. The music and dancing continues well into the night, only beginning to fade away as the first rays of the new year's sun begin to snake across the sky.

Above: Statue of Christ the Redeemer looking down over Rio

NEW YEAR DIARY

For the biggest New Year party, Rio is hard to beat. Two million people from all over the world meet up to join in the celebrations and watch the fireworks explode over the sea. Six days will give you enough time to explore Rio at leisure as well as taking part in the exuberant partying on Copacabana Beach.

Six Days of Tropical Sun

28 DEC The best cure for jetlag is a trip to the beach – head to Copacabana or Ipanema and enjoy the sand and sun. When you've had your fill, take the cable car to the top of Sugar Loaf Mountain for the incredible views. In the evening watch a traditional *roda de samba* (samba band) at bar Bip Bip in Copabanana.

29 DEC A surprising number of heritage buildings still hide in nooks and crannies in Rio's otherwise modern downtown. Explore the streets around Praça XV, the city's original square, 19th-century Praça Floriano and the Fine Arts Museum.

30 DEC Take the funicular up Corcovado to see the statue of Christ the Redeemer, and marvel at the 360° views of the mountains, sea and city. On the way down, hire a tour company to take you through the Tijuca Forest, the world's largest urban rainforest.

31 DEC Spend the morning relaxing on the beach or by your hotel pool. Head to Copacabana once it is dark to join the dancing on the beach or attend one of the extravagant balls at the beachside hotels. Watch the fireworks from the beach at midnight.

1 JAN Spend the morning in bed, recovering. After a late lunch, head to Ipanema or downtown Rio for some souvenir shopping.

2 JAN Join a sightseeing schooner for a different perspective on the city and its beaches. On your return, visit the Museum of Modern Art before heading to Rio's elaborate 19th-century tearoom, the Confeitaria Colombo.

Dos and Don'ts

✓ Go to the beach dressed in white on New Year's Eve – this is an important part of the festivities and will help you blend in with the crowd.

✓ Wear sunscreen, even if you're just walking around downtown. The tropical sun is extraordinarily strong.

✗ Don't take your valuables with you – leave them at home or in the hotel safe. Put your camera in a small, inconspicuous bag and carry a copy of your passport rather than the real thing.

✓ Take the metro. It is cheap, clean, safe and air-conditioned and thanks to an integrated bus system it will take you almost anywhere you want to go.

Above: Woman performs religious ritual in honour of Iemanjá; local samba performers

Below: Crowded Copacabana Beach; lush Tijuca National Park, with Rio de Janeiro in the background

Above (left to right): Neon lights of crowded Nathan Road in Kowloon, Hong Kong; airport sign in Portugal; sign for Sunset Station Hotel and Casino in Las Vegas; entry stamps in a passport

Travel and the Environment

GETTING THERE

The impact of air travel and tourism on the global environment has been well publicized but there are ways to limit the damaging effects of your own travels. Consider trains and ships as alternatives to flying – you may be surprised by how quick they are, and the journey itself can be part of the fun. If flights are unavoidable, look at carbon offsetting or the trips offered by Better World, Responsible Travel and other ecologically aware operators.

CARBON OFFSETTING SCHEMES

These enable you to "offset" the effects of carbon emissions by planting sustainable forests or contributing to biodiversity schemes that notionally "match" the amount of CO_2 you've generated. Organizations like Better World, Carbon Neutral and Climate Care offer information on how to calculate your carbon impact and how to make an offset contribution. Many sustainable tourism operators include an offsetting contribution in their ticket prices.

HIGH- AND LOW-IMPACT TOURISM

Tourism also directly affects the ecology and local economy of the destination countries. Major resort complexes can damage the landscape and local infrastructure. Not all resorts are the same but don't be afraid to ask questions, such as what is the employment policy for local people? How is waste disposed of? Where does their energy come from?

Locally run hotels and tour operations, in contrast, often have a more positive impact, especially if they use zero-impact toilets and other environmentally friendly features. The best will work with local communities and guides – by spreading the income from tourism more widely, locals have alternatives to harmful practices like deforestation and strip-farming.

Trips to see wildlife and into remote areas should be made in small groups, with local guides, not in big bus tours. It is not only the environment that gains by this – intimate, small hotels in natural settings will also give you a far more memorable experience.

Think Global, Shop Local

Spread the financial benefits of tourism by shopping for souvenirs in local shops and markets, instead of hotel stores and large malls. A little research on the customs of the country you're visiting and a few courteous questions will reduce any language barriers. Do not assume that everything you buy should be very cheap because you're in a poor country: people have a right to be paid for their work. And – avoiding the cheapest, shabbiest places – eat in local restaurants rather than those set aside for tourists. The food will usually be more interesting.

TRAVEL INFORMATION

Travelling worldwide has never been easier – it is possible to head off to even the most exotic locations within just a few days of first getting the idea of going there. But to make the most of your trip, it's best to pay attention to a few details; by doing a little planning you can save yourself some money and minimize the chance of something going horribly wrong.

Health

MD Travel Health www.mdtravelhealth.com

Global health may have improved but inoculations against specific diseases are strongly recommended: typhoid, cholera, tetanus, polio and hepatitis are the most common. The precise list depends on the area to be visited; for current advice relating to your destination, check with your GP or a specialist travel medicine service, such as MD Travel Health, or the CDC in the USA. Tetanus shots last for 10 years, typhoid for three – so you may not need new ones before each trip.

Malaria is the most dangerous tropical disease – especially in much of central Africa and parts of India and Southeast Asia. There's no vaccine, but several anti-malarial treatments are available: these are strong drugs which affect people in different ways (especially pregnant women and anyone on medication), so it is essential to get advice from a medical specialist. You also need to start taking anti-malarials at least a week before entering a risk area, so plan ahead.

The most common medical problem for travellers, however, is diarrhoea and other stomach upsets. Minor upsets are hard to avoid when diets change, but stomach problems can be minimized by simple precautions. Drink only bottled water or, if unavailable, processed fizzy drinks; do not eat at the cheapest restaurants; if eating street food, ensure it is cooked in front of you; avoid salads and raw vegetables if you're not sure how they have been washed; only eat fruit you can peel yourself. Keep Imodium, Dioralyte or similar medications in your first-aid kit. If diarrhoea is extreme or persistent, see a doctor.

Insects can carry diseases (including malaria) so take precautions to avoid being bitten – a strong insect repellent, one containing DEET (diethyltoluamide) is recommended, preferably at least 50% concentration.

Medical facilities vary around the world so make sure that you have full travel insurance (see right). For lesser incidents, carry a basic medical kit containing insect repellent, stomach remedies, bite lotion, antiseptic cream and wipes, easy-to-use dressings and plasters for cuts and scratches.

Personal Security

Foreign & Commonwealth Office www.fco.gov.uk
US State Department www.travel.state.gov

For general information on crime risks in your destination country, check the travel advice on foreign ministry websites. If you are travelling into remote areas, check with other travellers, local guides, hotel owners and other people there about the risks. Let someone know where you're going – someone at home, your travel company, a reliable hotel owner in the nearest city – so that it will be noticed if you're late back.

The most common kind of crime affecting travellers is petty street crime. Its likelihood can be reduced by following a few precautions (see box below). Make photocopies of your passport, air tickets and important documents – carry these with you and leave the originals in your hotel safe and another copy at home.

If you are a victim of crime, report it immediately to the local police. It may be unlikely that your property will be recovered, but you'll need a copy of the police statement for an insurance claim. If you are left with no money or your passport is stolen, report this immediately to your consulate, contact details for which will be on the relevant government website.

Insurance

Columbus Direct www.columbusdirect.com
World Travel Center www.worldtravelcenter.com

British and Irish citizens are entitled to medical treatment in all European Union (EU) countries, provided they have a European Health Insurance Card (EHIC), available via health centres and post offices. The USA, Canada and Australia also have reciprocal health arrangements with some countries. This is sufficient for basic emergencies, but to cover you against all eventualities, it is essential to have a full travel insurance policy. This should cover cancellations, theft, lost property and passports, legal expenses and full medical treatment including air evacuation. "High risk" activities – skiing and most winter sports, rafting and scuba diving among others – and some countries and regions may need extra cover so check your policy very carefully.

All UK and European car insurance policies now include basic third-party cover which is valid in all EU countries, but if you drive it is highly advisable to also get fully comprehensive international cover from your insurance company – essential if you intend to take a car outside the EU. Please note that US and Canadian car insurance is not valid in Mexico for stays of over 24 hours. If you drive into Mexico you must get a Mexican policy and a temporary vehicle import permit at the border.

Passports and Visas

Project Visa www.projectvisa.com

Citizens of all EU countries, the USA and Canada do not normally require visas to visit each other's countries and many other parts of the world for up to 90 days, only a full passport. However, the exact requirements for crossing borders change periodically, so check with your own country's foreign ministry or with the embassy of the country you are visiting. For visa-free entry to the USA, all passports must be machine-readable (older passports may not be valid).

Countries that require most visitors to have a visa for each trip include Australia, Russia, China, India and Cuba. Some tourist visas (eg Australia) can now be applied for online; others can be obtained through travel agents or (for a fee) visa advisory services, but some countries still demand that you go to their nearest consulate in person.

Travelling with Money

Travelex www.travelex.com

Usually the most useful form of money is a major international credit or debit card. They are the best means of handling larger transactions like hotel bills, are essential for renting a car and can be used to obtain local cash through ATMs. Your card company will usually charge a fee for ATM cash withdrawals, but often you will get better exchange rates than you would from a local bank.

However, you cannot rely on ATMs and card terminals being available everywhere, so it's best to take along some cash and traveller's cheques as back-up. Outside Europe – especially in Latin America – cash and cheques should be in US dollars, although the euro is widely accepted in Eastern Europe and much of Africa. Local banks nearly always give worse rates for other less-familiar currencies, or may refuse to take them at all.

Some countries such as Tunisia, Morocco and China have currencies that you can only obtain within the country. In this case, take some cash and traveller's cheques (US dollars are usually best), change only as much as you absolutely need on arrival and keep exchange receipts as you'll need them if you want to change any money back at the end of your stay.

DIRECTORY OF USEFUL CONTACTS

GENERAL TRAVEL

The Adventure Directory
www.adventuredirectory.com
UK-based website with links to active sports around the world

Adventure Sports Worldwide
www.adventuresportsonline.com
Directory of adventure travel opportunities

Adventure Travel Trade Association
www.adventuretravel.biz
US-based organization with members worldwide

AITO – Association of Independent Tour Operators
www.aito.co.uk
A large range of UK-based tour companies

BootsnAll
www.bootsnall.com
Information and resources for independent travellers

Scuba Spots Diving Directory
www.scubaspots.com
Diving operators, courses and related facilities around the world

ENVIRONMENTAL TRAVEL

Better World Travel
www.betterworldtravel.com
US organization offering carbon offsetting and other green options

The CarbonNeutral Company
www.carbonneutral.com
UK company that offers a range of ways to offset the carbon footprint of your travels

Climate Care
www.co2.org
A variety of options for offsetting the carbon impact of travel

Ecotourism Australia
www.ecotourism.org.au
Providing a very good certification system that identifies genuinely eco-aware hotels

Responsible Travel
www.responsibletravel.com
UK-based agent for ecologically and socially aware travel

Tourism Concern
www.tourismconcern.org.uk
Pressure group that seeks to raise awareness of the effects of tourism

HEALTH

Centers for Disease Control & Prevention (CDC)
www.cdc.gov/travel
Comprehensive health information for travellers

International Association for Medical Assistance to Travellers
www.iamat.org
Worldwide non-profit organization

Nomad Travel
www.nomadtravel.co.uk
UK adventure travel shops that offer vaccination clinics

The Travel Doctor TMVC
www.traveldoctor.com.au
Travel clinics across Australia and New Zealand

PERSONAL SECURITY

Australian Deparment of Foreign Affairs and Trade
www.smartraveller.gov.au
Traveller's information website

Canadian Department of Foreign Affairs
www.dfait-maeci.gc.ca
Travel advice and full consular information

INSURANCE

Adventure Mexican Insurance
www.mexadventure.com
Insurance for all types of US and Canadian vehicles in Mexico

Dogtag Worldwide Assistance
www.dogtag.co.uk
UK-based sports and adventure-travel insurance specialists

World Nomad
www.worldnomad.com
Australian-based insurance service focused on independent and adventure travellers

PASSPORTS AND VISAS

My Visa Advisor
www.myvisaadvisor.co.uk
UK-based online service for help in obtaining visas

MONEY

Western Union
www.westernunion.com
Worldwide money transfers

GETTING AROUND

Eurail
www.eurail.com
Rail passes covering 17 European countries

European Rail Guide
www.europeanrailguide.com
Information and rail passes for the whole of Europe and the UK

The Man in Seat 61
www.seat61.com
A worldwide guide to trains and other alternatives to air travel

Pacific Air Travel Association
www.pata.org
A listing of companies and operators throughout Asia

INTERNET

DK Travel
www.traveldk.com
Destination guides and accommodation bookings

Travel Pod
www.travelpod.com
Create your own travel blog

MOBILE PHONES

Ekit
www.ekit.com
Mobile phones, phone cards and other communications that can be used in many countries

Below: Yellow taxis queueing on a New York street

Getting Around

Air pass www.interlineres.com/air-pass-search

If you book your own international flights, you will still need to work out how to get around once you're in the country. Domestic flights can be expensive but airpass systems can make economic sense as they give large discounts on condition that you take a certain number of flights. Buy them in advance of your trip, as they are not always sold within the relevant countries. They are common in – but not confined to – Latin America – Mexipass covers Mexico and parts of the USA and Central America, and the Mercosur Airpass covers Brazil, Uruguay, Argentina, Paraguay and Chile.

Rail passes giving unlimited travel for a fixed period are useful in countries and regions with extensive rail networks. Again, they must usually be bought before you travel, and are not always sold within the countries themselves. The Eurail pass, covering most of Europe, is well known, but other useful passes are Britrail for the UK and the Japan Rail Pass.

If you decide to hire a car, for most – but not all – countries you will get better rates by booking in advance through a car rental website than by hiring on the spot. In some countries, notably India and China, it's advisable to hire a car with a local driver rather than drive yourself.

PACKING TIPS

In addition to your first-aid kit *(see Health)* here are a few things to consider:
• Clothes that can bounce back and look decent after packing and unpacking
• Long-sleeved shirts, long trousers or long skirts – to protect against sunburn, scratches or bites and for modesty
• High-factor sun cream and sun block – best bought at home
• Suitable plug adaptors
• A small torch/flashlight
• A multi-sized bath plug
• A travel guide
• A sunhat, unless you're going to countries like Mexico or much of Africa, where you can buy excellent hats

Travel and the Internet

Jiwire www.jiwire.com

Email is an easy way to keep in touch while travelling, and in most countries it's not hard to find internet cafés. Email addresses with a major free email service, such as Hotmail or Yahoo, will be the easiest to access in places where unreliable internet connections may be an issue.

If you carry a laptop with Wi-Fi capacity, many hotels and other locations now offer a wireless internet service, but some hotels charge heavily for this service and you need to consider extra wireless security. The best sources of information on free Wi-Fi hotspots around the world are specialized sites such as Jiwire.

Even if you do not carry a laptop, you can still create your own travel blog or web diary from internet cafés through one of the many sites that now offer free space. Depending on the internet café where you're writing, there may also be the facilities to upload digital pictures.

Be aware that in some countries, notably China, Iran, Saudi Arabia and several other Arab countries, access to internet services may be censored or severely controlled.

Mobile Phones

GSM World www.gsmworld.com

There are four main GSM frequencies (Global System for Mobiles) in use around the world, so to guarantee your phone will work, use a quad-band phone. European tri-band phones will normally work in North America, but not in some parts of Asia; and, since the USA and Canada use two frequency bands, a North American tri-band phone may only have limited global coverage. Contact your service provider or check the GSM World website for a frequency guide.

To use your mobile phone abroad your network provider may have to enable the "roaming" facility on your phone. Before travelling, check with your network on the tariffs for using the phone abroad; every service provider has its own price structure, and costs can be very high. If you expect to use the phone a lot, it can be worth pre-buying "bundles" of international calls.

Other popular options are to get an international mobile phone through services such as Ekit, or to buy a local SIM card – the chip that links your phone to a particular network – and so use a local cellphone network. You can only do this if your handset is "unlocked" – some operators lock their phones to specific networks. A simpler alternative can be just to hire or buy a local mobile phone for the duration of your stay.

If you take your own phone, check your insurance policy to see if the phone is covered if it is lost or stolen, and keep your network provider's helpline number handy.

Travel Photography

Photography tips www.photographytips.com

Digital cameras are a convenient choice for most travellers. You can take many more pictures, review them immediately, and upload them to a disk, laptop or blog. If you don't expect to upload them straightaway, take several memory cards or a photobank or similar digital storage system – many MP3 systems allow you to upload pictures to them. Don't forget the connection cables, and at least two sets of batteries, so you can use one while the other is recharging. Film is now less popular, but still available in most countries.

Be aware that in many parts of the world people dislike being arbitrarily photographed by passing tourists. This is usually not due to any primitive fear of cameras but to resentment at being used as "source material". If you ask courteously and offer to show them your earlier pictures you may well get a better response.

Right panel (top to bottom): Internet café; Turkish telephone booths; busy shopping street in Quebec; trams waiting for a green light; an Art Nouveau entrance to the Paris Metro; exploring the Preah Khan temple in Angkor

FIVE-YEAR DIARY

This calendar of events shows the major religious festivals with varying dates and international sports events between 2009 and 2013. Religious festivals with fixed dates (such as Christmas) are not shown. For religious festivals that last more than one day, the start date is shown.

	2009	2010	2011	2012	2013
JANUARY	7 ASHURA (MUSLIM) 26 CHINESE NEW YEAR			23 CHINESE NEW YEAR	
FEBRUARY	21–24 CARNIVAL*	10 CHINESE NEW YEAR 12–28 WINTER OLYMPICS (VANCOUVER) 13–16 CARNIVAL*	3 CHINESE NEW YEAR	18–21 CARNIVAL*	8–12 CARNIVAL 10 CHINESE NEW YEAR 10 KUMBH MELA (HINDU)
MARCH	11 HOLI (HINDU)	1 HOLI (HINDU) 29 PESACH (PASSOVER)	5–8 CARNIVAL 20 HOLI (HINDU)	8 HOLI (HINDU)	25 PESACH (PASSOVER) 27 HOLI 29 GOOD FRIDAY 31 EASTER SUNDAY
APRIL	8 PESACH (PASSOVER) 10 GOOD FRIDAY 12 EASTER SUNDAY 14 KUMBH MELA (HINDU) 19 ORTHODOX EASTER	2 GOOD FRIDAY 4 EASTER SUNDAY 4 ORTHODOX EASTER	18 PESACH (PASSOVER) 22 GOOD FRIDAY 24 EASTER SUNDAY 24 ORTHODOX EASTER	6 GOOD FRIDAY 6 PESACH (PASSOVER) 8 EASTER SUNDAY 15 ORTHODOX EASTER	
MAY	9 WESAK (BUDDHIST)	27 WESAK (BUDDHIST)	17 WESAK (BUDDHIST)	6 WESAK (BUDDHIST)	5 ORTHODOX EASTER 25 WESAK (BUDDHIST)
JUNE	THE ASHES (UK)	27 JUN–12 JUL FOOTBALL WORLD CUP (SOUTH AFRICA)	15 TOTAL LUNAR ECLIPSE		
JULY	7 DHARMA DAY (BUDDHIST) THE ASHES (UK)	26 DHARMA DAY (BUDDHIST)	15 DHARMA DAY (BUDDHIST) 31 RAMADAN (MUSLIM)	3 DHARMA DAY (BUDDHIST) 21 RAMADAN (MUSLIM) 27 JUL–12 AUG OLYMPICS (LONDON)	9 RAMADAN (MUSLIM)
AUGUST	22 RAMADAN (MUSLIM) THE ASHES (UK)	10 RAMADAN (MUSLIM)	12–22 RUGBY UNION WORLD CUP (NZ) 29 EID AL-FITR (MUSLIM)	19 EID AL-FITR (MUSLIM)	8 EID AL-FITR (MUSLIM)
SEPTEMBER	18 ROSH HASHANAH 21 EID AL-FITR (MUSLIM) 28 YOM KIPPUR	8 EID AL-FITR (MUSLIM) 8 ROSH HASHANAH 17 YOM KIPPUR RYDER CUP (UK)	28 ROSH HASHANAH	17 ROSH HASHANAH 26 YOM KIPPUR RYDER CUP (USA)	5 ROSH HASHANAH 14 YOM KIPPUR
OCTOBER	17 DIWALI (HINDU) 20 WORLD SERIES (USA)**	20 WORLD SERIES (USA)** THE ASHES (AUS)	7 YOM KIPPUR 20 WORLD SERIES (USA)** 26 DIWALI (HINDU) CRICKET WORLD CUP (ASIA)	20 WORLD SERIES (USA)**	15 EID AL-ADHA (MUSLIM)
NOVEMBER	26 THANKSGIVING (USA) 28 EID AL-ADHA (MUSLIM)	5 DIWALI (HINDU) 15 EID AL-ADHA (MUSLIM) 25 THANKSGIVING (USA) THE ASHES (AUS)	5 EID AL-ADHA (MUSLIM) 24 THANKSGIVING (USA) 25 AL-HIJRA (MUSLIM)	13 DIWALI (HINDU) 14 AL-HIJRA (MUSLIM) 22 THANKSGIVING (USA) 24 ASHURA (MUSLIM)	3 DIWALI (HINDU) 4 AL-HIJRA (MUSLIM) 14 ASHURA (MUSLIM) 27 HANUKKAH 28 THANKSGIVING (USA)
DECEMBER	11 HANUKKAH 18 AL-HIJRA (MUSLIM) 27 ASHURA (MUSLIM)	1 HANUKKAH 6 AL-HIJRA (MUSLIM) 15 ASHURA (MUSLIM) THE ASHES (AUS)	4 ASHURA (MUSLIM) 20 HANUKKAH	5 HANUKKAH	

NOTE: Please be aware that the dates of festivals governed by the lunar calendar may vary slightly; always double check before making final plans.
*Mardi Gras falls on the last day of Carnival
**World Series takes place within 1–2 days of this date.

Weather Around the World

Simply put, weather is the result of areas of the earth receiving different amounts of radiant energy from the sun. As the planet is curved, the poles receive a more diffused heat than the equator. Surfaces such as forests, oceans and ice absorb heat at different rates; land masses heat up and cool down more quickly than the sea; differences in elevation affect how the heat is retained by the air – it is colder higher up. It is these differences in temperature that drive the weather. When air is heated it rises and draws in more air underneath; cooler, more dense air sinks, pushing what is beneath out of the way – this is how winds are caused. As water evaporates in the heat and becomes picked up by the air currents, it also precipitates as rain when the temperature cools.

GLOBAL CLIMATE ZONES

Weather is the daily changing process of heat and water distribution over the earth. Climate, however, is a description of the pattern of those events over time. When these patterns regularly recur in a predictable way, they can be plotted onto a map as climate zones (see illustration). You can then use these to predict broad weather patterns. Some examples of particular phenomena that are the result or cause of weather patterns have been highlighted and located on the map too.

The Sunny State

❶ California Coast

California's coastline climate is consistently pleasant and mild. It avoids the winter cold winds from Canada thanks to the barriers of the Rocky Mountains and the Sierra Nevada and is warmed by the heat-retaining sea. In summer the relatively cool Californian sea current moderates coastal temperatures, and also stops the formation of tropical cyclones.

Tornado Alley

❷ The Great Plains

These spiralling columns of air usually result from a severe thunderstorm when strong winds with different temperatures, moisture content and direction are combined. On the Great Plains, in central USA, cold dry winds from Canada meet warm moist winds from Mexico causing so many tornadoes that the area is known as Tornado Alley.

Hurricane Warning

❸ Tropical Atlantic Ocean

Hurricane season runs roughly from August to October. At the start of the season the Gulf of Mexico is the most likely hurricane zone. By peak season the zone has moved east to the Lesser Antilles, and finally moves back to the west Caribbean. However, in a three-year period only about five actually hit the US coastline, most petering out over the sea.

EL NIÑO – THE CHRIST CHILD

Normally, westward-blowing winds drive warm surface water from South America to Australia and Indonesia. Every two to seven years, these winds reverse and the warm water flows east. This reaches the South American coast around December – hence the name "El Niño", the name for the infant Jesus.

As the mass of warm water builds up, it also spreads north and south along the coast, blocking off deep, cold and nutrient-rich currents. All along the coast, fish and marine life die. This major environmental change has many knock-on effects around the world such as droughts and crop failure in Africa, South America and Southeast Asia; and flooding in Peru, Gulf States and the USA.

CLIMATE GRAPHS

These mini-graphs show the average high and low temperatures, the average daily number of hours of sunshine, and the average monthly amount of rainfall for each of the four seasons. Each one represents a type of climate according to the climate key and is marked on the map.

KUALA LUMPUR
MALAYSIA, ASIA

	Dec-Feb	Mar-May	Jun-Aug	Sep-Nov
°C (high)	32	33	32	32
°C (low)	22	23	23	23
sunshine	6 hrs	6 hrs	7 hrs	5 hrs
rainfall	183 mm	258 mm	131 mm	242 mm

BUENOS AIRES
ARGENTINA, SOUTH AMERICA

	Dec-Feb	Mar-May	Jun-Aug	Sep-Nov
°C (high)	28	22	15	21
°C (low)	17	12	6	10
sunshine	9 hrs	7 hrs	5 hrs	7 hrs
rainfall	83 mm	91 mm	59 mm	83 mm

ULURU
AUSTRALIA, AUSTRALASIA

	Dec-Feb	Mar-May	Jun-Aug	Sep-Nov
°C (high)	36	27	20	31
°C (low)	21	12	5	14
sunshine	10 hrs	9 hrs	9 hrs	10 hrs
rainfall	38 mm	18 mm	10 mm	19 mm

ROME
ITALY, EUROPE

	Dec-Feb	Mar-May	Jun-Aug	Sep-Nov
°C (high)	12	16	29	21
°C (low)	5	10	19	13
sunshine	4 hrs	7 hrs	10 hrs	6 hrs
rainfall	75 mm	51 mm	24 mm	97 mm

Key to Climate Zones

Tropical: High rainfall, consistently high temperatures and humidity, and a short dry season.

Subtropical/Equatorial: Broader temperature range than tropical climates, with wet and dry seasons of more equal lengths.

Arid: Low rainfall and large temperature fluctuations between night and day; slightly less extreme conditions at the edges.

Mediterranean: Warm temperate climate that results in hot dry summers and mild wet winters.

Temperate Maritime: Four distinct seasons, but proximity to the warm sea currents prevents extremes of temperatures.

Temperate: Four distinct seasons with fairly consistent rainfall throughout the year; summers can be very warm and humid, and winters very cold with plenty of snow.

Northern Temperate: Similar characteristics to Temperate Climate Zone but the winters are much longer, lasting up to nine months; snowfall is also heavier and covers the ground for much of the year.

Mountain: Temperatures diminish as elevation increases; mountain climates are also much wetter – low temperatures often give snow.

Polar: Extremely long and cold winter months, frequent snow; 24-hour days during short summers, but even then the temperature only manages to rise a little.

THE FOUR SEASONS

Summer in the south/winter in the north

Winter in the south/summer in the north

The earth spins round the sun on an axis of about 23.5 degrees making a complete orbit in a year. This means that for a location in the northern or southern hemisphere there are two extremes six months apart – one when it is most directly "pointing at" the sun (summer), and the other when it is most directly "pointing away" (winter). July sees summer in the northern hemisphere but winter in the south, and for December it is vice versa. The two midway points between these extremes designate spring and autumn. Thus there are four seasons. The central band between the tropics however, remains fairly consistently in the direct rays of the sun, and therefore has less obvious seasons – just wet or dry.

Map labels

ARCTIC OCEAN
SPITSBERGEN
LONDON
EUROPE
ROME
MEDITERRANEAN SEA
AFRICA
RED SEA
ASIA
ARABIAN SEA
KATHMANDU
5
BAY OF BENGAL
EAST CHINA SEA
PHILIPPINE SEA
SOUTH CHINA SEA
PACIFIC OCEAN
KUALA LUMPUR
EQUATOR
JAVA SEA
INDIAN OCEAN
MOZAMBIQUE CHANNEL
TIMOR SEA
6
AUSTRALASIA
ULURU
TROPIC OF CAPRICORN
TASMAN SEA
THE GULF STREAM
SOUTHERN OCEAN
ANTARCTICA

Summer Monsoon

5 India and Southeast Asia

This is a wind that brings heavy rain that may fall continuously for weeks. Asia's vast hot landmass causes great amounts of air above it to rise, drawing in huge clouds of moist sea air. As this rushes in, it releases its moisture as rain. In India the monsoon starts in June in the south and moves north, stopping in September. Up to two thirds of India's annual rainfall occurs in this period.

The Gulf Stream

4 East Coast USA, Eire & UK

The Gulf Stream is a warm water current that travels up the east coast of the USA and on to Eire and the UK. This brings higher air temperatures than you would expect looking at the relative latitudinal position. However, as the warm air originates over the ocean it is also quite moist – hence the frequent wet weather.

Cyclones

6 Tropical Australasia

Like hurricanes, cyclones are low-pressure weather systems – violent storms – that form over tropical oceans. As well as bringing fierce winds, they cause a lot of damage because the combination of low pressure and onshore winds causes a storm surge – a sudden rise in sea level. Cyclones occur in the waters around tropical Australia and the Pacific Islands. (North of these areas they are known as typhoons.) Cyclones are most common during the months of November and April – but only a small percentage actually make landfall.

LONDON
UK, EUROPE

°C	Dec-Feb	Mar-May	Jun-Aug	Sep-Nov
max	7	13	21	14
			13	
min	3	6	13	8
hrs	1 hrs	5 hrs	6 hrs	3 hrs
mm	47 mm	40 mm	54 mm	57 mm

CHICAGO
USA, NORTH AMERICA

°C	Dec-Feb	Mar-May	Jun-Aug	Sep-Nov
max	1	12	26	16
			18	7
min	-6	4		
hrs	4 hrs	7 hrs	9 hrs	6 hrs
mm	51 mm	74 mm	85 mm	69 mm

ANCHORAGE
USA, NORTH AMERICA

°C	Dec-Feb	Mar-May	Jun-Aug	Sep-Nov
max	-6	7	18	6
	-14		8	
min		-4		-2
hrs	2 hrs	8 hrs	8 hrs	3 hrs
mm	20 mm	13 mm	42 mm	49 mm

KATHMANDU
NEPAL, ASIA

°C	Dec-Feb	Mar-May	Jun-Aug	Sep-Nov
max	19	28	29	26
			20	13
min	3	12		
hrs	7 hrs	6 hrs	2 hrs	8 hrs
mm	20 mm	68 mm	321 mm	67 mm

SPITSBERGEN
NORWAY, EUROPE

°C	Dec-Feb	Mar-May	Jun-Aug	Sep-Nov
max	-7	-5	6	0
min	-12	-11	3	-4
hrs	0 hrs	3 hrs	5 hrs	1 hrs
mm	27 mm	20 mm	28 mm	37 mm

Distances Around the World

The tables below show the distances, as the crow flies, between London and the main cities covered in this book. Not all of the destinations will be mentioned below but the nearest major city or airport should be referenced. To get a very rough idea of the time it takes to fly between London and your chosen destination, divide the distance in kilometres or miles by the average cruising speed of a commercial jet – 850 (kph) or 525 (mph) respectively. This will give you an average flying-time in hours, which may be useful when planning your journey. Of course, this calculation doesn't take into account changing planes, stopovers, or indeed jet streams, all of which can have a bearing on flight or travel times.

DISTANCES FROM LONDON TO NORTH AMERICA

City	km	miles	City	km	miles	City	km	miles	City	km	miles
ALBUQUERQUE	8,050	5,000	HONOLULU	11,630	7,228	NASSAU	6,980	4,340	SANTA FE	7,970	4,950
BOSTON	5,280	3,280	HOUSTON	7,821	4,860	NEW ORLEANS	7,770	4,830	SAVANNAH	6,710	4,170
BURLINGTON	5,280	3,280	JACKSON	7,280	4,520	NEW YORK CITY	5,570	3,460	SEATTLE	7,710	4,790
CALGARY	7,030	4,370	JUNEAU	7,130	4,420	ORLANDO	7,000	4,350	TORONTO	5,730	3,560
CANCUN	7,970	4,950	KINGSTON	7,530	4,680	OTTAWA	5,360	3,330	VANCOUVER	7,590	4,720
CHICAGO	6,360	3,950	LAS VEGAS	8,410	5,230	PHILADELPHIA	5,710	3,550	WASHINGTON, D.C.	5,900	3,660
DALLAS	7,660	4,760	LOS ANGELES	8,790	5,460	PHOENIX	8,500	5,280			
DENVER	7,550	4,690	MEMPHIS	7,020	4,370	SALT LAKE CITY	7,840	4,870			
EDMONTON	6,820	4,240	MEXICO CITY	8,940	5,560	SAN DIEGO	8,830	5,490			
GUATEMALA CITY	8,760	5,440	MIAMI	7,120	4,430	SAN FRANCISCO	8,640	5,370			
HALIFAX	4,620	2,870	MONTREAL	5,220	3,240	SAN JOSÉ	8,720	5,420			
HAVANA	7,490	4,650	NASHVILLE	6,750	4,200	SAN JUAN	6,770	4,200			

DISTANCES FROM LONDON TO SOUTH AMERICA

City	km	miles	City	km	miles	City	km	miles	City	km	miles
ASUNCION	10,170	6,320	CAYENNE	7,060	4,390	MONTEVIDEO	11,010	6,840	STANLEY	12,670	7,871
BOGOTA	8,500	5,282	GEORGETOWN	7,270	4,520	QUITO	9,220	5,730	USHUAIA	13,510	8,400
BRASILIA	5,460	8,780	LA PAZ	9,990	6,210	RIO DE JANEIRO	9,270	5,760	VALPARAISO	11,670	7,250
BUENOS AIRES	11,140	6,930	LIMA	10,160	6,320	SANTIAGO	11,660	7,250			
CARACAS	7,500	4,660	MANAUS	8,260	5,130	SAO PAULO	9,480	5,890			

DISTANCES FROM LONDON TO AFRICA

City	km	miles	City	km	miles	City	km	miles	City	km	miles
ACCRA	5,100	3,170	DAR ES SALAAM	7,480	4,650	MARRAKESH	2,310	1,430	TUNIS	1,820	1,130
ADDIS ABABA	5,890	3,660	DURBAN	9,510	5,910	NAIROBI	6,810	4,230	WINDHOEK	8,400	5,220
BAMAKO	4,370	2,710	JOHANNESBURG	9,060	5,630	SHARM EL SHEIKH	3,890	2,420			
CAIRO	3,520	2,190	LIVINGSTONE	8,110	5,040	TIMBUKTU	3,860	2,400			
CAPE TOWN	9,620	5,980	MAPUTO	9,180	5,700	TRIPOLI	2,340	1,454			

DISTANCES FROM LONDON TO EUROPE

City	km	miles	City	km	miles	City	km	miles	City	km	miles
AJACCIO	1,260	780	DIJON	590	370	LJUBLJANA	1,230	760	REYKJAVIK	1,890	1,170
AMSTERDAM	360	220	DUBLIN	460	290	LUXEMBOURG	500	310	ROME	1,430	890
ATHENS	2,390	1,480	DUBROVNIK	1,690	1,050	MADRID	1,260	790	SANTORINI	2,620	1,630
BARCELONA	1,140	710	EDINBURGH	550	340	MALAGA	2,250	1,398	SOFIA	2,420	1,504
BERLIN	930	580	FRANKFURT	800	500	MILAN	1,220	760	STOCKHOLM	1,430	890
BORDEAUX	980	610	FUNCHAL	2,500	1,550	MOSCOW	2,510	1,560	ST PETERSBURG	2,110	1,310
BRUSSELS	320	200	GENEVA	930	580	MUNICH	920	570	STUTTGART	730	450
BUCHAREST	2,110	1,310	GENOA	1,040	644	NICE	1,030	640	TALLINN	2,780	1,730
BUDAPEST	1,450	900	GLASGOW	550	340	OSLO	1,150	720	TROMSØ	2,250	1,400
CALAIS	160	100	HELSINKI	1,820	1,130	PARIS	340	210	VENICE	1,120	700
CARDIFF	210	130	INNSBRUCK	1,240	770	PISA	1,170	730	VIENNA	1,250	780
COPENHAGEN	960	590	LISBON	1,590	990	PRAGUE	1,030	640	WARSAW	1,450	900

DISTANCES FROM LONDON TO AUSTRALASIA

City	km	miles	City	km	miles	City	km	miles	City	km	miles
ALICE SPRINGS	15,050	9,350	CHRISTCHURCH	18,960	11,780	NADI	16,250	10,100	SYDNEY	17,000	10,560
AUCKLAND	18,330	11,390	DARWIN	13,840	8,600	PERTH	14,460	8,990	TAHITI	15,390	9.560
BRISBANE	16,530	10,270	EXMOUTH	13,570	8,440	POHNPEI	13,210	8,210	WELLINGTON	18,900	11,680
CAIRNS	15,150	9,410	HOBART	17,060	10,600	QUEENSTOWN	18,930	11,770			
CANBERRA	16,980	10,550	MELBOURNE	16,900	10,500	RAROTONGA	16,240	10,090			

DISTANCES FROM LONDON TO ASIA

City	km	miles	City	km	miles	City	km	miles	City	km	miles
AMMAN	3,640	2,260	HO CHI MINH CITY	10,220	6,350	KYOTO	9,510	5,910	TAIPEI	9,820	6,100
ANTALYA	2,910	1,810	HONG KONG	9,640	5,990	LHASA	7,580	4,710	TOKYO	9,590	5,960
BALI	12,500	7,770	ISLAMABAD	6,050	3,760	MACAU	9,610	5,970	TRIVANDRUM	8,380	5,210
BANGKOK	9,530	5,920	ISTANBUL	2,500	1,560	MALE	8,290	5,150	ULAN BATOR	6,990	4,340
BANGALORE	7,950	4,940	JAIPUR	6,760	4,200	MANDALAY	8,550	5,310			
BEIJING	8,160	5,070	JAKARTA	11,720	7,280	MANILA	10,730	6,670			
BRUNEI	11,270	7,000	KABUL	5,710	3,550	MUMBAI	7,180	4,460			
CALCUTTA	7,970	4,950	KATHMANDU	7,350	4,570	OSAKA	9,510	5,910			
CHENGDU	8,290	5,150	KARACHI	5,520	3,430	PENANG	10,270	6,380			
CHIANG MAI	9,010	5,600	KOTA KINABALU	11,240	6,990	SEOUL	8,880	5,520			
COLOMBO	8,720	5,420	KUALA LUMPUR	10,550	6,560	SHANGHAI	9,205	5,720			
DELHI	6,730	4,180	KUCHING	11,280	7,010	SINGAPORE	10,850	6,740			
HANOI	9,250	5,750	KUNMING	8,690	5,400	TASHKENT	5,250	3,260			

Index

Page numbers in **bold** indicate main references